THIS PUBLICATION

relates to

the Public General Acts
and General Synod Measures
which received the Royal Assent in 2009
in which year ended the FIFTY-SEVENTH YEAR
and began the FIFTY-EIGHTH YEAR
of the Reign of HER MAJESTY
QUEEN ELIZABETH THE SECOND
and
ended the Fourth Session
of the Fifty-Fourth Parliament
and began the Fifth Session of the Fifty-Fourth Parliament
of the United Kingdom of Great Britain
and Northern Ireland

The Table of Effect of Legislation has been prepared for the Queen's
Printer of Acts of Parliament by Justis Publishing Ltd.

© Crown copyright 2010

First published 2010
Printed in the UK by The Stationery Office Limited under the authority
and superintendence of Carol Tullo, Controller of Her Majesty's
Stationery Office and Queen's Printer of Acts of Parliament.

CONTENTS

TABLE I

Alphabetical List of
the Public General Acts of 2009

TABLE II

Chronological List of
the Public General Acts of 2009

TABLE III

Alphabetical List of
the Local and Personal Acts of 2009

TABLE IV

Chronological List of
the General Synod Measures of 2009

Apprenticeships, Skills, Children and Learning Act 2009

CHAPTER 22

CONTENTS

PART 1

APPRENTICESHIPS, STUDY AND TRAINING

CHAPTER 1

APPRENTICESHIPS

Completing an apprenticeship

Apprenticeship certificates: England

Apprenticeship certificates: Wales

Contents of apprenticeship certificate: England and Wales

CHAPTER 2

STUDY AND TRAINING

PART 2

LEA FUNCTIONS

Education and training for persons over compulsory school age

The core and additional entitlements

Boarding accommodation: persons subject to learning difficulty assessment

Work experience

Persons detained in youth accommodation

Transport in England

Powers in respect of non-maintained schools

CHAPTER 4

GENERAL

PART 5

PARTS 2 TO 4: SUPPLEMENTARY

Information

The Learning and Skills Council for England

PART 6

THE SIXTH FORM COLLEGE SECTOR

PART 7

THE OFFICE OF QUALIFICATIONS AND EXAMINATIONS REGULATION

CHAPTER 1

ESTABLISHMENT, OBJECTIVES AND GENERAL DUTIES

Establishment

Objectives and general duties

Regulated qualifications and regulated assessment arrangements

CHAPTER 2

FUNCTIONS IN RELATION TO QUALIFICATIONS

Recognition of awarding bodies

Accreditation of certain qualifications

Minimum requirements

Guided learning

Surrender

Register

Recognised bodies: monitoring and enforcement

Other

PART 8

THE QUALIFICATIONS AND CURRICULUM DEVELOPMENT AGENCY

CHAPTER 1

THE QCDA, OBJECTIVE AND GENERAL DUTIES

The QCDA

CHAPTER 2

FUNCTIONS IN RELATION TO QUALIFICATIONS

CHAPTER 3

FUNCTIONS IN RELATION TO CURRICULUM, EARLY YEARS FOUNDATION STAGE AND ASSESSMENT

CHAPTER 4

OTHER FUNCTIONS AND SUPPLEMENTARY PROVISION

Other functions

CHAPTER 5

GENERAL

PART 9

CHILDREN'S SERVICES

Co-operation to improve well-being of children

Safeguarding and promoting the welfare of children

Children's centres

Arrangements in respect of early childhood services

Early years provision: budgetary framework

PART 10

SCHOOLS

CHAPTER 1

SCHOOLS CAUSING CONCERN

Schools causing concern: England

Schools causing concern: Wales

CHAPTER 2

COMPLAINTS: ENGLAND

CHAPTER 3

INSPECTIONS

CHAPTER 4

SCHOOL SUPPORT STAFF PAY AND CONDITIONS: ENGLAND

The SSSNB

Consideration of matter by SSSNB

Powers of Secretary of State on submission of SSSNB agreement

Reconsideration by SSSNB

PART 11

LEARNERS

PART 12

MISCELLANEOUS

2172

Apprenticeships, Skills, Children and Learning Act 2009

2009 CHAPTER 22

An Act to make provision about apprenticeships, education, training and children's services; to amend the Employment Rights Act 1996; to establish the Young People's Learning Agency for England, the office of Chief Executive of Skills Funding, the Office of Qualifications and Examinations Regulation and the School Support Staff Negotiating Body and to make provision about those bodies and that office; to make provision about the Qualifications and Curriculum Authority; to make provision about schools and institutions within the further education sector; to make provision about student loans; and for connected purposes.   [12th November 2009]

B E IT ENACTED by the Queen's most Excellent Majesty, by and with the advice and consent of the Lords Spiritual and Temporal, and Commons, in this present Parliament assembled, and by the authority of the same, as follows: —

PART 1

APPRENTICESHIPS, STUDY AND TRAINING

CHAPTER 1

APPRENTICESHIPS

Completing an apprenticeship

1   Meaning of "completing an English apprenticeship"

(1)   This section applies for the purposes of this Chapter.

2174

Apprenticeships, Skills, Children and Learning Act 2009 (c. 22)
Part 1 — Apprenticeships, study and training
Chapter 1 — Apprenticeships

(2) A person completes an English apprenticeship in relation to an apprenticeship framework if —

   (a) the standard English completion conditions are met, or

   (b) the alternative English completion conditions are met.

(3) The standard English completion conditions are —

   (a) that the person has entered into an apprenticeship agreement in connection with the apprenticeship framework,

   (b) that at the date of that agreement the framework was a recognised English framework,

   (c) that the person has completed a course of training for the competencies qualification identified in the framework,

   (d) that, throughout the duration of the course, the person was working under the apprenticeship agreement, and

   (e) that the person meets the requirements specified in the framework for the purpose of the issue of an apprenticeship certificate.

(4) In subsection (3)(d) —

   (a) the reference to the apprenticeship agreement mentioned in subsection (3)(a) includes a reference to any apprenticeship agreement which the person subsequently entered into in connection with the same apprenticeship framework;

   (b) the reference to the course of training for the competencies qualification is to be read, in a case where the person has followed two or more courses of training for the competencies qualification, as a reference to both or all of them.

(5) The alternative English completion conditions are conditions which —

   (a) apply in cases where a person works otherwise than under an apprenticeship agreement, and

   (b) are specified in regulations.

(6) The kinds of working in relation to which provision may be made under subsection (5) include —

   (a) working as a self-employed person;

   (b) working otherwise than for reward.

2 Meaning of "completing a Welsh apprenticeship"

(1) This section applies for the purposes of this Chapter.

(2) A person completes a Welsh apprenticeship in relation to an apprenticeship framework if —

   (a) the standard Welsh completion conditions are met, or

   (b) the alternative Welsh completion conditions are met.

(3) The standard Welsh completion conditions are —

   (a) that the person has entered into an apprenticeship agreement in connection with the apprenticeship framework,

   (b) that at the date of that agreement the framework was a recognised Welsh framework,

   (c) that the person has completed a course of training for the competencies qualification identified in the framework,

Apprenticeships, Skills, Children and Learning Act 2009 (c. 22)
Part 1 — Apprenticeships, study and training
Chapter 1 — Apprenticeships

2175

      (d)   that, throughout the duration of the course, the person was working under the apprenticeship agreement, and

      (e)   that the person meets the requirements specified in the framework for the purpose of the issue of an apprenticeship certificate.

(4)   In subsection (3)(d) —

      (a)   the reference to the apprenticeship agreement mentioned in subsection (3)(a) includes a reference to any apprenticeship agreement which the person subsequently entered into in connection with the same apprenticeship framework;

      (b)   the reference to the course of training for the competencies qualification is to be read, in a case where the person has followed two or more courses of training for the competencies qualification, as a reference to both or all of them.

(5)   The alternative Welsh completion conditions are conditions which —

      (a)   apply in cases where a person works otherwise than under an apprenticeship agreement, and

      (b)   are specified in regulations made by the Welsh Ministers.

(6)   The kinds of working in relation to which provision may be made under subsection (5) include —

      (a)   working as a self-employed person;

      (b)   working otherwise than for reward.

Apprenticeship certificates: England

3   Duty to issue: England

The English certifying authority must issue a certificate relating to an apprenticeship framework to a person who applies to the authority in the prescribed manner if —

      (a)   it appears to the authority that the person has completed an English apprenticeship in relation to the apprenticeship framework,

      (b)   in a case within section 1(2)(a), it appears to the authority that the condition in subsection (3)(e) of that section was met at the date of the person's application, and

      (c)   the person —

            (i)   provides the authority with such information and evidence as the authority requires the person to provide, and

            (ii)   pays any fee charged by the authority for the issue of the certificate (see section 5).

4   Power to issue: England

The English certifying authority may issue a certificate relating to an apprenticeship framework to a person who applies to the authority in the prescribed manner if —

      (a)   it appears to the authority that at the date of the application the person met the requirements specified in the framework for the purpose of the issue of an apprenticeship certificate,

      (b)   the framework is, or has been, a recognised English framework, and

      (c)   the person —

2176

Apprenticeships, Skills, Children and Learning Act 2009 (c. 22)
Part 1 – Apprenticeships, study and training
Chapter 1 – Apprenticeships

      (i)   provides the authority with such information and evidence as the authority requires the person to provide, and

      (ii)   pays any fee charged by the authority for the issue of the certificate (see section 5).

5 Issue by the English certifying authority: supplementary

(1)   The English certifying authority may charge a fee for issuing an apprenticeship certificate only if, and to the extent that, it is authorised to do so by regulations.

(2)   Regulations may make provision about the supply of copies of apprenticeship certificates issued under section 3 or 4.

(3)   Regulations under subsection (2) may include provision authorising the English certifying authority to charge a fee for supplying a copy of an apprenticeship certificate.

6 The English certifying authority

In this Chapter, the "English certifying authority" means the Chief Executive of Skills Funding.

Apprenticeship certificates: Wales

7 Duty to issue: Wales

(1)   The Welsh certifying authority must issue a certificate relating to an apprenticeship framework to a person who applies to the authority in the prescribed manner if —

    (a)   it appears to the authority that the person has completed a Welsh apprenticeship in relation to the apprenticeship framework,

    (b)   in a case within section 2(2)(a), it appears to the authority that the condition in subsection (3)(e) of that section was met at the date of the person's application, and

    (c)   the person—

      (i)   provides the authority with such information and evidence as the authority requires the person to provide, and

      (ii)   pays any fee charged by the authority for the issue of the certificate (see section 9).

(2)   The "prescribed manner" is the manner prescribed by regulations made by the Welsh Ministers.

8 Power to issue: Wales

(1)   The Welsh certifying authority may issue a certificate relating to an apprenticeship framework to a person who applies to the authority in the prescribed manner if—

    (a)   it appears to the authority that at the date of the application the person met the requirements specified in the framework for the purpose of the issue of an apprenticeship certificate,

    (b)   the framework is, or has been, a recognised Welsh framework,

    (c)   the person—

Apprenticeships, Skills, Children and Learning Act 2009 (c. 22)
Part 1 — Apprenticeships, study and training
Chapter 1 — Apprenticeships

2177

      (i)   provides the authority with such information and evidence as the authority requires the person to provide, and

      (ii)   pays any fee charged by the authority for the issue of the certificate (see section 9).

(2)   The "prescribed manner" for the purposes of subsection (1), is the manner prescribed by regulations made by the Welsh Ministers.

9 Issue by the Welsh certifying authority: supplementary

(1)   The Welsh certifying authority may charge a fee for issuing an apprenticeship certificate only if, and to the extent that, it is authorised to do so by regulations made by the Welsh Ministers.

(2)   Regulations made by the Welsh Ministers may make provision about the supply of copies of apprenticeship certificates issued under section 7 or 8.

(3)   Regulations under subsection (2) may include provision authorising a person supplying a copy of an apprenticeship certificate to charge a fee for doing so.

10 The Welsh certifying authority

(1)   In this Chapter, the "Welsh certifying authority", in relation to an apprenticeship certificate of any description, means —

    (a)   the person (if any) designated under this section to issue apprenticeship certificates of that description;

    (b)   if there is no-one within paragraph (a), the person (if any) designated under this section to issue apprenticeship certificates generally;

    (c)   if there is no-one within paragraph (a) or (b), the Welsh Ministers.

(2)   A person designated under this section to issue apprenticeship certificates must, in exercising functions under this Chapter —

    (a)   comply with directions given by the Welsh Ministers, and

    (b)   have regard to guidance given by the Welsh Ministers.

(3)   "Designated" means designated by an order made by the Welsh Ministers.

Contents of apprenticeship certificate: England and Wales

11 Contents of apprenticeship certificate

(1)   An apprenticeship certificate must state —

    (a)   the name of the person to whom it is issued,

    (b)   the apprenticeship framework to which it relates,

    (c)   the level of that framework, and

    (d)   the apprenticeship sector to which that framework relates.

(2)   An apprenticeship certificate must also state such other matters as the appropriate national authority may by regulations require to be stated in a certificate of that description.

(3)   The appropriate national authority, for the purposes of subsection (2), is —

    (a)   in relation to a certificate issued under section 3 or 4, the Secretary of State;

2178   *Apprenticeships, Skills, Children and Learning Act 2009 (c. 22)*
Part 1 – Apprenticeships, study and training
Chapter 1 – Apprenticeships

    (b)   in relation to a certificate issued under section 7 or 8, the Welsh Ministers.

Apprenticeship frameworks: England and Wales

12   Apprenticeship frameworks: interpretation

(1)   In this Chapter, "apprenticeship framework" means a specification of requirements, for the purpose of the issue of apprenticeship certificates, that satisfies subsection (2).

(2)   The requirements specified must—
    (a)   be at a particular level stated in the specification, and
    (b)   relate to a particular skill, trade or occupation included in an apprenticeship sector stated in the specification.

(3)   In this Chapter, "recognised English framework" means an apprenticeship framework issued under section 14(1) from which recognition has not been withdrawn under section 14(2).

(4)   In this Chapter, "recognised Welsh framework" means an apprenticeship framework issued under section 19(1) from which recognition has not been withdrawn under section 19(2).

(5)   For the purposes of this Chapter—
    (a)   an apprenticeship framework is at the level of the requirements stated in it;
    (b)   an apprenticeship framework relates to the apprenticeship sector stated in it.

Apprenticeship frameworks: England

13   English issuing authority

(1)   The Secretary of State may designate a person to issue apprenticeship frameworks relating to a particular apprenticeship sector.

(2)   The power conferred by this section must be exercised so as to secure that, at any time, only one person is designated by the Secretary of State to issue apprenticeship frameworks relating to a particular apprenticeship sector.

(3)   A person designated under this section must, in exercising functions under this Chapter—
    (a)   comply with directions given by the Secretary of State;
    (b)   have regard to guidance given by the Secretary of State.

(4)   A designation under this section may be amended or revoked by the Secretary of State.

(5)   In this Chapter the "English issuing authority", in relation to an apprenticeship framework, means the person designated under this section to issue frameworks of that description.

Apprenticeships, Skills, Children and Learning Act 2009 (c. 22)
Part 1 – *Apprenticeships, study and training*
Chapter 1 – *Apprenticeships*

2179

14 Issue: England

(1) The English issuing authority may issue an apprenticeship framework only if the authority is satisfied that the framework meets the requirements specified, by the specification of apprenticeship standards for England, for recognised English frameworks of that description.

(2) Recognition of a recognised English framework may be withdrawn –
   (a) by the English issuing authority, or
   (b) if there is no English issuing authority in relation to the framework, by the Secretary of State.

15 Recognised English frameworks: notification and publication

(1) On issuing an apprenticeship framework under section 14(1), the English issuing authority must –
   (a) publish the framework;
   (b) notify the Chief Executive of Skills Funding of the issue of the framework.

(2) A notice given under subsection (1)(b) must be accompanied by a copy of the framework.

(3) A person who withdraws recognition of an apprenticeship framework under section 14(2) must –
   (a) publish a notice stating that recognition of the framework has been withdrawn;
   (b) notify the Chief Executive of Skills Funding of the withdrawal.

(4) Where this section imposes a duty on a person to publish a framework or notice, the publication may be in such manner as the person thinks fit.

16 Submission of draft framework for issue: England

(1) This section applies if a person –
   (a) submits a draft of an apprenticeship framework to the English issuing authority, and
   (b) requests that the authority issue a framework in the form of the draft.

(2) The authority may require the person to provide such information and evidence in connection with the draft as the authority thinks appropriate.

(3) If the authority decides not to issue a framework in the form of the draft, it must give the person reasons for its decision.

17 Transitional provision: England

(1) The Secretary of State may by order provide for an existing vocational specification to be treated, for all purposes or for purposes specified in the order, as if it were an apprenticeship framework issued under section 14(1) that specified requirements for the purpose of the issue of apprenticeship certificates.

(2) For the purposes of its application in relation to an existing vocational specification that, by virtue of an order under subsection (1), is treated as an

2180

Apprenticeships, Skills, Children and Learning Act 2009 (c. 22)
Part 1 — Apprenticeships, study and training
Chapter 1 — Apprenticeships

apprenticeship framework issued under section 14(1), this Chapter has effect subject to any modifications specified in the order.

(3) An order under subsection (1) must—

    (a) specify a date on which the deemed framework is to be treated as being issued under section 14(1);

    (b) specify a date on which recognition of the deemed framework is to be treated as having been withdrawn under section 14(2);

    (c) specify a qualification that the deemed framework is to be treated as identifying as the competencies qualification;

    (d) specify the level and apprenticeship sector that are to be treated as being stated in the deemed framework.

(4) The date specified under subsection (3)(b) in an order under subsection (1) must be no later than the day after the day that is the school leaving date for 2013.

(5) In this section—

    "the deemed framework", in relation to an order under subsection (1), means an existing vocational specification that, by virtue of the order, is treated as an apprenticeship framework issued under section 14(1);

    "existing vocational specification" means a specification, prepared before the coming into force of section 14, of training, qualifications and skills appropriate for persons engaging in a particular trade, skill or occupation.

(6) Nothing in this section limits the powers conferred by sections 262 and 265.

Apprenticeship frameworks: Wales

18 Welsh issuing authority

(1) The Welsh Ministers may designate a person to issue apprenticeship frameworks relating to a particular apprenticeship sector.

(2) The power conferred by this section must be exercised so as to secure that, at any time, only one person is designated by the Welsh Ministers to issue apprenticeship frameworks relating to a particular apprenticeship sector.

(3) A person designated under this section must, in exercising functions under this Chapter—

    (a) comply with directions given by the Welsh Ministers;

    (b) have regard to guidance given by the Welsh Ministers.

(4) A designation under this section may be amended or revoked by the Welsh Ministers.

(5) In this Chapter the "Welsh issuing authority", in relation to an apprenticeship framework, means the person designated under this section to issue frameworks of that description.

19 Issue: Wales

(1) The Welsh issuing authority may issue an apprenticeship framework only if the authority is satisfied that the framework meets the requirements specified,

Apprenticeships, Skills, Children and Learning Act 2009 (c. 22)
Part 1 – *Apprenticeships, study and training*
Chapter 1 – *Apprenticeships*

2181

by the specification of apprenticeship standards for Wales, for recognised Welsh frameworks of that description.

(2) Recognition of a recognised Welsh framework may be withdrawn—

    (a) by the Welsh issuing authority, or

    (b) if there is no Welsh issuing authority in relation to the framework, by the Welsh Ministers.

20 Recognised Welsh frameworks: notification and publication

(1) On issuing an apprenticeship framework under section 19(1), the Welsh issuing authority must—

    (a) publish the framework;

    (b) notify the Welsh Ministers of the issue of the framework.

(2) A notice given under subsection (1)(b) must be accompanied by a copy of the framework.

(3) A person who withdraws recognition of an apprenticeship framework under section 19(2) must—

    (a) publish a notice stating that recognition of the framework has been withdrawn;

    (b) in the case of withdrawal otherwise than by the Welsh Ministers, notify the Welsh Ministers of the withdrawal.

(4) Where this section imposes a duty on a person to publish a framework or notice, the publication may be in such manner as the person thinks fit.

21 Submission of draft framework for issue: Wales

(1) This section applies if a person—

    (a) submits a draft of an apprenticeship framework to the Welsh issuing authority, and

    (b) requests that the authority issue a framework in the form of the draft.

(2) The authority may require the person to provide such information and evidence in connection with the draft as the authority thinks appropriate.

(3) If the authority decides not to issue a framework in the form of the draft, it must give the person reasons for its decision.

22 Transitional provision: Wales

(1) The Welsh Ministers may by order provide for an existing vocational specification to be treated, for all purposes or for purposes specified in the order, as if it were an apprenticeship framework issued under section 19(1) that specified requirements for the purpose of the issue of apprenticeship certificates.

(2) For the purposes of its application in relation to an existing vocational specification that, by virtue of an order under subsection (1), is treated as an apprenticeship framework issued under section 19(1), this Chapter has effect subject to any modifications specified in the order.

(3) An order under subsection (1) must—

2182

Apprenticeships, Skills, Children and Learning Act 2009 (c. 22)
Part 1 — Apprenticeships, study and training
Chapter 1 — Apprenticeships

    (a)   specify a date on which the deemed framework is to be treated as being issued under section 19(1);

    (b)   specify a date on which recognition of the deemed framework is to be treated as having been withdrawn under section 19(2);

    (c)   specify a qualification that the deemed framework is to be treated as identifying as the competencies qualification;

    (d)   specify the level and apprenticeship sector that are to be treated as being stated in the deemed framework.

(4)   The date specified under subsection (3)(b) in an order under subsection (1) must be no later than the day after the day that is the school leaving date for 2013.

(5)   In this section—

    "the deemed framework", in relation to an order under subsection (1), means an existing vocational specification that, by virtue of the order, is treated as being an apprenticeship framework issued under section 19(1);

    "existing vocational specification" means a specification, prepared before the coming into force of section 19, of training, qualifications and skills appropriate for persons engaging in a particular trade, skill or occupation.

(6)   Nothing in this section limits the powers conferred by section 262.

Specification of apprenticeship standards: England

23 Duty to prepare and submit draft specification: England

(1)   If the Secretary of State so directs, the Chief Executive of Skills Funding must—

    (a)   prepare a draft specification of apprenticeship standards, and

    (b)   submit it to the Secretary of State.

(2)   In preparing the draft, the Chief Executive must consult—

    (a)   each person designated under section 13,

    (b)   persons who appear to the Chief Executive to represent—

        (i)   employers,

        (ii)   institutions within the further education sector, and

        (iii)   any other providers of training,

    (c)   any other persons or descriptions of persons specified in regulations, and

    (d)   such other persons as the Chief Executive thinks appropriate.

(3)   A direction under subsection (1) may specify the date by which a draft must be submitted to the Secretary of State.

(4)   Subsection (2) does not apply in relation to the first draft specification to be prepared by the Chief Executive after the commencement of this section.

(5)   "Institution within the further education sector" has the same meaning as in the Education Act 1996 (c. 56) (see section 4(3) of that Act).

Apprenticeships, Skills, Children and Learning Act 2009 (c. 22)
Part 1 — Apprenticeships, study and training
Chapter 1 — Apprenticeships

2183

24   Order bringing specification into effect

(1)   Where a draft specification of apprenticeship standards has been submitted under section 23, the Secretary of State may by order provide that a specification of apprenticeship standards ("the specification of apprenticeship standards for England") is to have effect—

   (a)   in the form of the draft, or

   (b)   in that form with such modifications as the Secretary of State thinks appropriate.

(2)   The Secretary of State may not make an order under subsection (1) unless satisfied that the specification of apprenticeship standards given effect to by the order complies with section 27.

(3)   The power conferred by subsection (1) is to be exercised so as to secure that at any time only one specification of apprenticeship standards has effect as the specification of apprenticeship standards for England.

25   Modification: England

(1)   If the Secretary of State so directs, the Chief Executive of Skills Funding must—

   (a)   prepare draft modifications to the specification of apprenticeship standards for England, and

   (b)   submit the modifications to the Secretary of State.

(2)   A direction given under subsection (1) may specify the date by which the draft modifications must be submitted to the Secretary of State.

(3)   Where draft modifications to a specification of apprenticeship standards have been submitted under subsection (1), the Secretary of State may by order provide that the specification of apprenticeship standards for England is to have effect with those modifications.

(4)   The Secretary of State may not make an order under subsection (3) providing that the specification of apprenticeship standards for England is to have effect with modifications unless satisfied that the specification, as so modified, complies with section 27.

26   Replacement or modification: recognised English frameworks

(1)   Subject to subsection (2), a recognised English framework does not cease to be a recognised English framework if, by virtue of an order under section 24 or 25, it ceases to meet the requirements specified for frameworks of its description by the specification of apprenticeship standards for England.

(2)   An order under section 24 may provide for an apprenticeship framework which—

   (a)   immediately before the making of the order is a recognised English framework, but

   (b)   does not meet the requirements specified for frameworks of its description by the specification of apprenticeship standards for England to which the order gives effect,

to cease to have effect as a recognised English framework.

2184

Apprenticeships, Skills, Children and Learning Act 2009 (c. 22)
Part 1 – Apprenticeships, study and training
Chapter 1 – Apprenticeships

27   Contents of specification of apprenticeship standards for England

(1)   The specification of apprenticeship standards for England –

    (a)   must specify requirements to be met by recognised English frameworks,

    (b)   may specify different requirements in relation to recognised English frameworks at different levels, and

    (c)   must, in particular, specify requirements in relation to –

        (i)   recognised English frameworks at level 2, and

        (ii)   recognised English frameworks at level 3.

(2)   The requirements specified by the specification of apprenticeship standards for England must include –

    (a)   requirements as to English certificate requirements, including requirements as to standards of attainment to be required by them,

    (b)   requirements for a recognised English framework to include, as an English certificate requirement, the requirement that an apprenticeship certificate relating to the framework may be issued to a person only if the person has received both on-the-job training and off-the-job training, and

    (c)   requirements for a recognised English framework to –

        (i)   include, as an English certificate requirement, the requirement that one or more qualifications be held,

        (ii)   include, as an English certificate requirement, the requirement that the qualification, or the qualifications taken together, demonstrate the relevant occupational competencies and the relevant technical knowledge, and

        (iii)   identify the qualification that demonstrates the relevant occupational competencies as the competencies qualification in relation to the framework.

(3)   Requirements as to standards of attainment may be specified by reference, in particular, to descriptions of qualifications or training.

(4)   In this section –

    "English certificate requirement" means a requirement specified in a recognised English framework for the purpose of the issue of apprenticeship certificates relating to that framework by the English certifying authority;

    "off-the-job training" in relation to a recognised English framework, is training which –

        (a)   is received for the purposes of the skill, trade or occupation to which the framework relates, and

        (b)   is not on-the-job training;

    "on-the-job training" in relation to a recognised English framework, is training received in the course of carrying on the skill, trade or occupation to which the framework relates;

    "the relevant occupational competencies", in relation to a recognised English framework, means the competencies required to perform the skill, trade or occupation to which the framework relates at the level required in the framework;

    "the relevant technical knowledge", in relation to a recognised English framework, means the technical knowledge required to perform the

Apprenticeships, Skills, Children and Learning Act 2009 (c. 22)
Part 1 – Apprenticeships, study and training
Chapter 1 – Apprenticeships

2185

skill, trade or occupation to which the framework relates at the level required in the framework.

Specification of apprenticeship standards: Wales

28 Specification of apprenticeship standards for Wales

(1) The Welsh Ministers may prepare a draft specification of apprenticeship standards.

(2) In preparing the draft, the Welsh Ministers must consult such persons as they think appropriate.

(3) Having prepared a draft, the Welsh Ministers may by order provide that a specification of apprenticeship standards ("the specification of apprenticeship standards for Wales") is to have effect—

  (a) in the form of the draft, or

  (b) in that form with such modifications as the Welsh Ministers think appropriate.

(4) Subsection (2) does not apply in relation to the first draft specification to be prepared by the Welsh Ministers after the commencement of this section.

(5) The Welsh Ministers may not make an order under subsection (3) unless satisfied that the specification of apprenticeship standards given effect to by the order complies with section 31.

(6) The power conferred by subsection (3) is to be exercised so as to secure that at any time only one specification of apprenticeship standards has effect as the specification of apprenticeship standards for Wales.

29 Modification: Wales

(1) The Welsh Ministers may by order provide that the specification of apprenticeship standards for Wales is to have effect subject to modifications specified in the order.

(2) The Welsh Ministers may not make an order under this section unless satisfied that the specification, as so modified, complies with section 31.

30 Replacement or modification: recognised Welsh frameworks

(1) Subject to subsection (2), a recognised Welsh framework does not cease to be a recognised Welsh framework if, by virtue of an order under section 28 or 29, it ceases to meet the requirements specified for frameworks of its description by the specification of apprenticeship standards for Wales.

(2) An order under section 28 may provide for an apprenticeship framework which—

  (a) immediately before the making of the order is a recognised Welsh framework, but

  (b) does not meet the requirements specified for frameworks of its description by the specification of apprenticeship standards for Wales to which the order gives effect,

to cease to have effect as a recognised Welsh framework.

2186
Apprenticeships, Skills, Children and Learning Act 2009 (c. 22)
Part 1 – Apprenticeships, study and training
Chapter 1 – Apprenticeships

31   Contents of specification of apprenticeship standards for Wales

(1)   The specification of apprenticeship standards for Wales —

    (a)   must specify requirements to be met by recognised Welsh frameworks,

    (b)   may specify different requirements in relation to recognised Welsh frameworks at different levels.

(2)   The requirements specified by the specification of apprenticeship standards for Wales must include —

    (a)   requirements as to Welsh certificate requirements, including requirements as to standards of attainment to be required by them,

    (b)   requirements for a recognised Welsh framework to include, as a Welsh certificate requirement, the requirement that an apprenticeship certificate relating to the framework may be issued to a person only if the person has received both on-the-job training and off-the-job training, and

    (c)   requirements for a recognised Welsh framework to —

        (i)   include, as a Welsh certificate requirement, the requirement that one or more qualifications be held,

        (ii)   include, as a Welsh certificate requirement, the requirement that the qualification, or the qualifications taken together, demonstrate the relevant occupational competencies and the relevant technical knowledge, and

        (iii)   identify the qualification that demonstrates the relevant occupational competencies as the competencies qualification in relation to the framework.

(3)   Requirements as to standards of attainment may be specified by reference, in particular, to descriptions of qualifications or training.

(4)   In this section —

    "off-the-job training" in relation to a recognised Welsh framework, is training which —

        (a)   is received for the purposes of the skill, trade or occupation to which the framework relates, and

        (b)   is not on-the-job training;

    "on-the-job training" in relation to a recognised Welsh framework, is training received in the course of carrying on the skill, trade or occupation to which the framework relates;

    "the relevant occupational competencies", in relation to a recognised Welsh framework, means the competencies required to perform the skill, trade or occupation to which the framework relates at the level required in the framework;

    "the relevant technical knowledge", in relation to a recognised Welsh framework, means the technical knowledge required to perform the skill, trade or occupation to which the framework relates at the level required in the framework;

    "Welsh certificate requirement" means a requirement specified in a recognised Welsh framework for the purpose of the issue of apprenticeship certificates relating to that framework by the Welsh certifying authority.

Apprenticeships, Skills, Children and Learning Act 2009 (c. 22)
Part 1 – *Apprenticeships, study and training*
Chapter 1 – *Apprenticeships*

2187

Apprenticeship agreements: England and Wales

32 Meaning of "apprenticeship agreement"

(1) In this Chapter, "apprenticeship agreement" means an agreement in relation to which each of the conditions in subsection (2) is satisfied.

(2) The conditions are—

    (a) that a person (the "apprentice") undertakes to work for another (the "employer") under the agreement;

    (b) that the agreement is in the prescribed form;

    (c) that the agreement states that it is governed by the law of England and Wales;

    (d) that the agreement states that it is entered into in connection with a qualifying apprenticeship framework.

(3) The power conferred by subsection (2)(b) may be exercised, in particular—

    (a) to specify provisions that must be included in an apprenticeship agreement;

    (b) to specify provisions that must not be included in an apprenticeship agreement;

    (c) to specify all or part of the wording of provisions that must be included in an apprenticeship agreement.

(4) Where an agreement states that it is entered into in connection with an apprenticeship framework ("the relevant framework") that is not a qualifying apprenticeship framework, subsection (2)(d) is to be taken to be satisfied in relation to the agreement if—

    (a) at a time within the period of three years ending with the date of the agreement, the relevant framework was a qualifying apprenticeship framework;

    (b) at the date of the agreement, the apprentice has not completed the whole of a course of training for the competencies qualification identified in the relevant framework,

    (c) before the date of the agreement, the apprentice entered into an apprenticeship agreement ("the earlier agreement") which stated that it was entered into in connection with the relevant framework, and

    (d) at the date of the earlier agreement, the relevant framework was a qualifying apprenticeship framework.

(5) In subsection (4)(b), the reference to a course of training for the competencies qualification is to be read, in a case where the person follows two or more courses of training for the competencies qualification, as a reference to both or all of them.

(6) An apprenticeship framework is a "qualifying apprenticeship framework", for the purposes of this section, if it is—

    (a) a recognised English framework, or

    (b) a recognised Welsh framework.

33 Ineffective provisions

(1) To the extent that provision included in an apprenticeship agreement conflicts with the prescribed apprenticeship provisions, it has no effect.

2188   *Apprenticeships, Skills, Children and Learning Act 2009 (c. 22)*
Part 1 – Apprenticeships, study and training
Chapter 1 – Apprenticeships

(2)   In this section, the "prescribed apprenticeship provisions", in relation to an apprenticeship agreement, means those provisions –

      (a)   that are included in the agreement, and

      (b)   without the inclusion of which the agreement would not satisfy section 32(2)(b).

34   Variation

(1)   If a variation to an apprenticeship agreement is within subsection (2), it has effect only if, before it was made, the employer complied with the requirement in subsection (3).

(2)   A variation to an apprenticeship agreement is within this subsection if its nature is such that, were it to take effect, the agreement would cease to be an apprenticeship agreement.

(3)   The employer must give the apprentice written notice stating that, if the variation takes effect, the agreement will cease to be an apprenticeship agreement.

35   Status

(1)   To the extent that it would otherwise be treated as being a contract of apprenticeship, an apprenticeship agreement is to be treated as not being a contract of apprenticeship.

(2)   To the extent that it would not otherwise be treated as being a contract of service, an apprenticeship agreement is to be treated as being a contract of service.

(3)   This section applies for the purposes of any enactment or rule of law.

36   Crown servants and Parliamentary staff

(1)   Sections 32 to 35 apply in relation to –

      (a)   an agreement under which a person undertakes Crown employment,

      (b)   an agreement under which a person undertakes service as a member of the naval, military or air forces of the Crown, and

      (c)   an agreement under which a person undertakes employment as –

         (i)   a relevant member of the House of Lords staff, or

        (ii)   a relevant member of the House of Commons staff,

as they apply in relation to any other agreement under which a person undertakes to work for another.

(2)   Subsection (1) is subject to subsection (3) and to any modifications which may be prescribed under subsection (5).

(3)   Section 35(2) does not apply in relation to an apprenticeship agreement that is an agreement within paragraph (a), (b) or (c) of subsection (1).

(4)   Without prejudice to section 262(3), the power conferred by section 32(2)(b) may be exercised, in particular, to make provision in relation to an apprenticeship agreement which is an agreement within any of paragraphs (a), (b) and (c) of subsection (1) that differs from provision made in relation to other apprenticeship agreements.

Apprenticeships, Skills, Children and Learning Act 2009 (c. 22)
Part 1 — Apprenticeships, study and training
Chapter 1 — Apprenticeships

2189

(5) Regulations may provide for any provision of this Chapter, or any of sections 91 to 99, to apply with modifications in relation to—

    (a) an agreement within paragraph (a), (b) or (c) of subsection (1), or

    (b) a person working, or proposing to work, under such an agreement.

(6) In subsection (1)—

    "Crown employment" means employment under or for the purposes of a government department or any officer or body exercising on behalf of the Crown functions conferred by a statutory provision (but does not include service as a member of the naval, military or air forces of the Crown);

    "relevant member of the House of Commons staff" has the meaning given by section 195(5) of the Employment Rights Act 1996 (c. 18);

    "relevant member of the House of Lords staff" has the meaning given by section 194(6) of that Act.

Duty to participate in education or training: England

37 Duty to participate in education or training: apprenticeship agreements

(1) Part 1 of the Education and Skills Act 2008 (c. 25) (duty to participate in education or training: England) is amended as follows.

(2) In section 2 (duty to participate), in subsection (1)(b) after "contract of apprenticeship" insert "or an apprenticeship agreement".

(3) In section 66 (interpretation of Part 1), in subsection (1)—

    (a) at the appropriate place insert—

        ""apprenticeship agreement" has the meaning given in section 32 of the Apprenticeships, Skills, Children and Learning Act 2009;";

    (b) in the definition of "contract of employment" after "contract of apprenticeship" insert "or an apprenticeship agreement".

General

38 Apprenticeship sectors

(1) The Secretary of State must by order specify sectors of skill, trade or occupation for the purposes of this Chapter.

(2) The sectors specified under subsection (1) must in the opinion of the Secretary of State encompass the full range of skills, trades and occupations.

39 Interpretation of Chapter

(1) In this Chapter—

    "apprenticeship agreement" has the meaning given by section 32(1);

    "apprenticeship certificate" means a certificate issued under section 3, 4, 7 or 8;

    "apprenticeship framework" has the meaning given by section 12(1);

    "apprenticeship sector" means a sector specified under section 38;

2190   *Apprenticeships, Skills, Children and Learning Act 2009 (c. 22)*
Part 1 — Apprenticeships, study and training
Chapter 1 — Apprenticeships

"the competencies qualification", in relation to an apprenticeship framework, means the qualification identified in the framework as being the competencies qualification;

"English certifying authority" has the meaning given by section 6;

"English issuing authority", in relation to an apprenticeship framework, has the meaning given by section 13(5);

"recognised English framework" has the meaning given by section 12(3);

"recognised Welsh framework" has the meaning given by section 12(4);

"the specification of apprenticeship standards for England" means the specification of apprenticeship standards having effect for the time being by virtue of an order made by the Secretary of State under section 24 or 25;

"the specification of apprenticeship standards for Wales" means the specification of apprenticeship standards having effect for the time being by virtue of an order made by the Welsh Ministers under section 28 or 29;

"Welsh certifying authority", in relation to an apprenticeship certificate of any description, has the meaning given by section 10(1);

"Welsh issuing authority", in relation to an apprenticeship framework, has the meaning given by section 18(5).

(2) References in this Chapter —
    (a) to the level of an apprenticeship framework, or
    (b) to the apprenticeship sector to which an apprenticeship framework relates,
are to be construed in accordance with section 12(5).

(3) References in this Chapter to an employer and an apprentice, in relation to an apprenticeship agreement, are to be construed in accordance with section 32.

CHAPTER 2

STUDY AND TRAINING

40 Employer support for employee study and training

(1) The Employment Rights Act 1996 (c. 18) is amended as follows.

(2) After Part 6 (time off work) insert—

"PART 6A

STUDY AND TRAINING

63D Statutory right to make request in relation to study or training

(1) A qualifying employee may make an application under this section to his or her employer.

(2) An application under this section (a "section 63D application") is an application that meets—
    (a) the conditions in subsections (3) to (5), and
    (b) any further conditions specified by the Secretary of State in regulations.

Apprenticeships, Skills, Children and Learning Act 2009 (c. 22)
Part 1 — Apprenticeships, study and training
Chapter 2 — Study and training

2191

(3) The application must be made for the purpose of enabling the employee to undertake study or training (or both) within subsection (4).

(4) Study or training is within this subsection if its purpose is to improve—
   (a) the employee's effectiveness in the employer's business, and
   (b) the performance of the employer's business.

(5) The application must state that it is an application under this section.

(6) An employee is a qualifying employee for the purposes of this section if the employee—
   (a) satisfies any conditions about duration of employment specified by the Secretary of State in regulations, and
   (b) is not a person within subsection (7).

(7) The following persons are within this subsection—
   (a) a person of compulsory school age (or, in Scotland, school age);
   (b) a person to whom Part 1 of the Education and Skills Act 2008 (duty to participate in education or training for 16 and 17 year olds) applies;
   (c) a person who, by virtue of section 29 of that Act, is treated as a person to whom that Part applies for the purposes specified in that section (extension for person reaching 18);
   (d) a person to whom section 63A of this Act (right to time off for young person for study or training) applies;
   (e) an agency worker;
   (f) a person of a description specified by the Secretary of State in regulations.

(8) Nothing in this Part prevents an employee and an employer from making any other arrangements in relation to study or training.

(9) In this section—
   "agency worker" means a worker supplied by a person (the "agent") to do work for another person (the "principal") under a contract or other arrangement between the agent and principal;
   "compulsory school age" has the meaning given in section 8 of the Education Act 1996;
   "school age" has the meaning given in section 31 of the Education (Scotland) Act 1980.

63E Section 63D application: supplementary

(1) A section 63D application may—
   (a) be made in relation to study or training of any description (subject to section 63D(3) and (4) and regulations under section 63D(2));
   (b) relate to more than one description of study or training.

(2) The study or training may (in particular) be study or training that (if undertaken)—
   (a) would be undertaken on the employer's premises or elsewhere (including at the employee's home);

2192   *Apprenticeships, Skills, Children and Learning Act 2009 (c. 22)*
Part 1 — Apprenticeships, study and training
Chapter 2 — Study and training

(b)   would be undertaken by the employee while performing the duties of the employee's employment or separately;

(c)   would be provided or supervised by the employer or by someone else;

(d)   would be undertaken without supervision;

(e)   would be undertaken within or outside the United Kingdom.

(3)   The study or training need not be intended to lead to the award of a qualification to the employee.

(4)   A section 63D application must—

    (a)   give the following details of the proposed study or training—

        (i)   its subject matter;

        (ii)   where and when it would take place;

        (iii)   who would provide or supervise it;

        (iv)   what qualification (if any) it would lead to;

    (b)   explain how the employee thinks the proposed study or training would improve—

        (i)   the employee's effectiveness in the employer's business, and

        (ii)   the performance of the employer's business;

    (c)   contain information of any other description specified by the Secretary of State in regulations.

(5)   The Secretary of State may make regulations about—

    (a)   the form of a section 63D application;

    (b)   when a section 63D application is to be taken to be received for the purposes of this Part.

63F   Employer's duties in relation to application

(1)   Subsections (4) to (7) apply if—

    (a)   an employer receives a section 63D application (the "current application") from an employee, and

    (b)   during the relevant 12 month period the employer has not received another section 63D application (an "earlier application") from the employee.

(2)   The "relevant 12 month period" is the 12 month period ending with the day on which the employer receives the current application.

(3)   The Secretary of State may make regulations about circumstances in which, at an employee's request, an employer is to be required to ignore an earlier application for the purposes of subsection (1).

(4)   The employer must deal with the application in accordance with regulations made by the Secretary of State.

(5)   The employer may refuse a section 63D application only if the employer thinks that one or more of the permissible grounds for refusal applies in relation to the application.

(6)   The employer may refuse part of a section 63D application only if the employer thinks that one or more of the permissible grounds for refusal applies in relation to that part.

Apprenticeships, Skills, Children and Learning Act 2009 (c. 22)
Part 1 – Apprenticeships, study and training
Chapter 2 – Study and training

2193

(7) The permissible grounds for refusal are—

    (a) that the proposed study or training to which the application, or the part in question, relates would not improve—

        (i) the employee's effectiveness in the employer's business, or

        (ii) the performance of the employer's business;

    (b) the burden of additional costs;

    (c) detrimental effect on ability to meet customer demand;

    (d) inability to re-organise work among existing staff;

    (e) inability to recruit additional staff;

    (f) detrimental impact on quality;

    (g) detrimental impact on performance;

    (h) insufficiency of work during the periods the employee proposes to work;

    (i) planned structural changes;

    (j) any other grounds specified by the Secretary of State in regulations.

63G   Regulations about dealing with applications

(1) Regulations under section 63F(4) may, in particular, include provision—

    (a) for the employee to have a right to be accompanied by a person of a specified description when attending meetings held in relation to a section 63D application in accordance with any such regulations;

    (b) for the postponement of such a meeting if the employee's companion under paragraph (a) is not available to attend it;

    (c) in relation to companions under paragraph (a), corresponding to section 10(6) and (7) of the Employment Relations Act 1999 (right to paid time off to act as companion, etc.);

    (d) in relation to the rights under paragraphs (a) to (c), for rights to complain to an employment tribunal and not to be subjected to a detriment, and about unfair dismissal;

    (e) for section 63D applications to be treated as withdrawn in specified circumstances.

(2) In this section "specified" means specified in the regulations.

63H   Employee's duties in relation to agreed study or training

(1) This section applies if an employer has agreed to a section 63D application, or part of a section 63D application, made by an employee in relation to particular study or training (the "agreed study or training").

(2) The employee must inform the employer if the employee—

    (a) fails to start the agreed study or training;

    (b) fails to complete the agreed study or training;

    (c) undertakes, or proposes to undertake, study or training that differs from the agreed study or training in any respect (including those specified in section 63E(4)(a)).

2194

Apprenticeships, Skills, Children and Learning Act 2009 (c. 22)
Part 1 — Apprenticeships, study and training
Chapter 2 — Study and training

(3) The Secretary of State may make regulations about the way in which the employee is to comply with the duty under subsection (2).

63I   Complaints to employment tribunals

(1) An employee who makes a section 63D application may present a complaint to an employment tribunal that—

    (a) the employer has failed to comply with section 63F(4), (5) or (6), or

    (b) the employer's decision to refuse the application, or part of it, is based on incorrect facts.

This is subject to the following provisions of this section.

(2) No complaint under this section may be made in respect of a section 63D application which has been disposed of by agreement or withdrawn.

(3) In the case of a section 63D application that has not been disposed of by agreement or withdrawn, a complaint under this section may only be made if the employer—

    (a) notifies the employee of a decision to refuse the application (or part of it) on appeal, or

    (b) commits a breach of regulations under section 63F(4), where the breach is of a description specified by the Secretary of State in regulations.

(4) No complaint under this section may be made in respect of failure to comply with provision included in regulations under section 63F(4) because of—

    (a) section 63G(1)(a) or (b), if provision is included in regulations under section 63F(4) by virtue of section 63G(1)(d), or

    (b) section 63G(1)(c).

(5) An employment tribunal may not consider a complaint under this section unless the complaint is presented—

    (a) before the end of the period of three months beginning with the relevant date, or

    (b) within any further period that the tribunal considers reasonable, if the tribunal is satisfied that it was not reasonably practicable for the complaint to be presented before the end of that period of three months.

(6) The relevant date is—

    (a) in the case of a complaint permitted by subsection (3)(a), the date on which the employee is notified of the decision on the appeal;

    (b) in the case of a complaint permitted by subsection (3)(b), the date on which the breach was committed.

63J   Remedies

(1) If an employment tribunal finds a complaint under section 63I well-founded it must make a declaration to that effect and may—

    (a) make an order for reconsideration of the section 63D application;

Apprenticeships, Skills, Children and Learning Act 2009 (c. 22)
Part 1 — Apprenticeships, study and training
Chapter 2 — Study and training

2195

    (b)   make an award of compensation to be paid by the employer to the employee.

(2)   The amount of any compensation must be the amount the tribunal considers just and equitable in all the circumstances, but must not exceed the permitted maximum.

(3)   The permitted maximum is the number of weeks' pay specified by the Secretary of State in regulations.

(4)   If an employment tribunal makes an order under subsection (1)(a), section 63F and regulations under that section apply as if the application had been received on the date of the order (instead of on the date it was actually received).

63K Supplementary

Regulations under this Part may make different provision for different cases."

(3)   After section 47E (protection from suffering detriment in employment: flexible working) insert—

"47F Study and training

(1)   An employee has the right not to be subjected to any detriment by any act, or any deliberate failure to act, by the employee's employer done on the ground that the employee—

    (a)   made (or proposed to make) a section 63D application,

    (b)   exercised (or proposed to exercise) a right conferred on the employee under section 63F,

    (c)   brought proceedings against the employer under section 63I, or

    (d)   alleged the existence of any circumstance which would constitute a ground for bringing such proceedings.

(2)   This section does not apply if the detriment in question amounts to dismissal within the meaning of Part 10."

(4)   After section 104D (unfair dismissal: pension enrolment) insert—

"104E Study and training

An employee who is dismissed is to be regarded for the purposes of this Part as unfairly dismissed if the reason (or, if more than one, the principal reason) for the dismissal is that the employee—

    (a)   made (or proposed to make) a section 63D application,

    (b)   exercised (or proposed to exercise) a right conferred on the employee under section 63F,

    (c)   brought proceedings against the employer under section 63I, or

    (d)   alleged the existence of any circumstance which would constitute a ground for bringing such proceedings."

(5)   Schedule 1 makes amendments to employment legislation relating to the provision made by this section.

PART 2

LEA FUNCTIONS

Education and training for persons over compulsory school age

41   Education and training for persons over compulsory school age: general duty

Before section 15A of the Education Act 1996 (c. 56) insert—

"15ZA Duty in respect of education and training for persons over compulsory school age: England

(1)   A local education authority in England must secure that enough suitable education and training is provided to meet the reasonable needs of—

    (a)   persons in their area who are over compulsory school age but under 19, and

    (b)   persons in their area who are aged 19 or over but under 25 and are subject to learning difficulty assessment.

(2)   A local education authority may comply with subsection (1) by securing the provision of education or training outside as well as within their area.

(3)   In deciding for the purposes of subsection (1) whether education or training is suitable to meet persons' reasonable needs, a local education authority must (in particular) have regard to—

    (a)   the persons' ages, abilities and aptitudes;

    (b)   any learning difficulties the persons may have;

    (c)   the quality of the education or training;

    (d)   the locations and times at which the education or training is provided.

(4)   In performing the duty imposed by subsection (1) a local education authority must—

    (a)   act with a view to encouraging diversity in the education and training available to persons;

    (b)   act with a view to increasing opportunities for persons to exercise choice;

    (c)   act with a view to enabling persons to whom Part 1 of the Education and Skills Act 2008 applies to fulfil the duty imposed by section 2 of that Act;

    (d)   take account of education and training whose provision the authority think might reasonably be secured by other persons.

(5)   A local education authority must, in—

    (a)   making any determination as to the provision of apprenticeship training that should be secured under subsection (1), or

    (b)   securing the provision of any apprenticeship training under that subsection,

co-operate with the Chief Executive of Skills Funding.

(6)   For the purposes of this section a person has a learning difficulty if—

    (a)   the person has a significantly greater difficulty in learning than the majority of persons of the same age, or

    (b)   the person has a disability which either prevents or hinders the person from making use of facilities of a kind generally provided by institutions providing education or training for persons who are over compulsory school age.

(7)   But a person is not to be taken to have a learning difficulty solely because the language (or form of language) in which the person is or will be taught is different from a language (or form of language) which has at any time been spoken in the person's home.

(8)   In this section—

"apprenticeship training" means training provided in connection with—

    (a)   an apprenticeship agreement (within the meaning given in section 32 of the Apprenticeships, Skills, Children and Learning Act 2009),

    (b)   any other contract of employment, or

    (c)   any other kind of working in relation to which alternative English completion conditions apply under section 1(5) of that Act (meaning of "completing an English apprenticeship");

"education" includes full-time and part-time education;

"training" includes—

    (a)   full-time and part-time training;

    (b)   vocational, social, physical and recreational training;

    (c)   apprenticeship training.

(9)   The references in subsection (1) to—

    (a)   persons in a local authority's area who are over compulsory school age but under 19, and

    (b)   persons in a local authority's area who are aged 19 or over but under 25 and are subject to learning difficulty assessment,

do not include persons who are subject to a detention order.

15ZB Co-operation in performance of section 15ZA duty

Local education authorities in England must co-operate with each other in performing their duties under section 15ZA(1)."

42 Encouragement of education and training for persons over compulsory school age

After section 15ZB of the Education Act 1996 (c. 56) (inserted by section 41) insert—

"15ZC Encouragement of education and training for persons over compulsory school age: England

(1)   A local education authority in England must—

    (a)   encourage participation in education and training by persons in their area who are within section 15ZA(1)(a) or (b);

    (b)   encourage employers to participate in the provision of education and training for such persons.

(2)   For the purposes of subsection (1)(b), participating in the provision of training includes participating by entering into—

    (a)   an apprenticeship agreement (within the meaning given in section 32 of the Apprenticeships, Skills, Children and Learning Act 2009), or

    (b)   any other contract of employment in connection with which training is provided.

(3)   In this section "education" and "training" have the same meanings as in section 15ZA."

43   LEA directions: children over compulsory school age

(1)   Chapter 1 of Part 3 of the School Standards and Framework Act 1998 (c. 31) is amended as follows.

(2)   In section 84(6) (admissions code: interpretation) for the definition of "child" substitute—

    ""child" includes a person who has not attained the age of 19, except in sections 96 and 97 in so far as those sections apply in relation to Wales;".

(3)   After section 96(3) (direction to admit child to specified school) insert—

    "(3A)   A direction under this section to admit a child shall not specify a school which has in place admission arrangements that make provision for selection by ability falling within section 99(2)(c) unless the child satisfies the selection criteria."

44   Power to require provision of education by further education institution

(1)   Before section 52 of the Further and Higher Education Act 1992 (c. 13) insert—

"51A   Duty to provide for named individuals: England

    (1)   This section applies to an institution in England within the further education sector which provides education suitable to the requirements of persons over compulsory school age but under the age of 19.

    (2)   A local education authority may by notice given to the governing body of such an institution—

        (a)   require them to provide specified individuals with such education falling within subsection (1) as is appropriate to the individuals' abilities and aptitudes;

        (b)   withdraw such a requirement.

    (3)   A local education authority may specify an individual in a notice under subsection (2) only if the individual—

        (a)   is in the authority's area, and

        (b)   is over compulsory school age but under the age of 19.

    (4)   Before giving a notice under subsection (2) imposing a requirement on a governing body, a local education authority must consult—

        (a)   the governing body, and

        (b)   such other persons as the authority think appropriate.

(5) The governing body of an institution within subsection (1) must secure compliance with a requirement that has been imposed under subsection (2) and has not been withdrawn.

(6) In deciding whether to require a particular institution to provide education to a particular individual under subsection (2) a local education authority in England must have regard to any guidance given from time to time by the Secretary of State."

(2) In section 52 of that Act—
   (a) in subsection (1) after "institution" insert "in Wales";
   (b) in the title, at the end insert ": Wales".

The core and additional entitlements

45 Duties in relation to the core and additional entitlements

After section 17 of the Education Act 1996 (c. 56) insert—

"The core and additional entitlements: England

17A Duties in relation to the core and additional entitlements

(1) A local education authority in England must exercise their functions in such a way as to secure that the core entitlement and the additional entitlement are satisfied in relation to persons in their area who are over compulsory school age but under 19.

(2) A local education authority in England must exercise their functions with a view to securing that courses of study within all the additional entitlement areas are made available to persons in their area who are over compulsory school age but under 19.

(3) Subsection (2) does not apply to the extent that an authority decide that making available a course of study within a particular entitlement area would involve disproportionate expenditure.

(4) An authority may comply with subsection (2) by securing that courses of study are available either within or outside their area.

(5) Subsection (2) does not entitle a person—
   (a) to follow a course of study within a particular additional entitlement area, or
   (b) to follow more than one course of study within different additional entitlement areas.
   (See section 17D for provision conferring entitlement in relation to the additional entitlement areas.)

(6) In exercising their functions as required by this section, a local education authority in England must have regard to any guidance given from time to time by the Secretary of State.

(7) In this section—
   "additional entitlement area" has the meaning given by section 17D(2);

"the additional entitlement" has the meaning given by section 17D;

"the core entitlement" has the meaning given by section 17C.

(8)   In this section and sections 17C and 17D "course of study" means a course of education or training leading to a qualification specified, or a qualification of a description specified, by the Secretary of State by order for the purposes of this subsection.

(9)   The references in subsections (1) and (2) to persons in a local education authority's area who are over compulsory school age but under 19 do not include persons who are subject to a detention order.

17B   Entitlement to education and training for 16 to 18 year olds

A person who is over compulsory school age but under 19 may elect for either or both of —

(a)   the core entitlement (see section 17C), and

(b)   the additional entitlement (see section 17D).

17C   The core entitlement

(1)   The core entitlement is an entitlement to follow a course of study in each of the core subjects chosen by the person electing for the entitlement (the "chosen core subjects").

(2)   The core subjects are —

(a)   mathematics;

(b)   English;

(c)   information and communication technology.

(3)   The core entitlement is satisfied in relation to a person if a course of study in each of the chosen core subjects is made available to the person at a school or institution.

(4)   A person's entitlement to follow a course of study in one of the chosen core subjects ceases if —

(a)   a course of study in the subject is made available to the person, but

(b)   the person does not begin the course of study before reaching the age of 19.

17D   The additional entitlement

(1)   The additional entitlement is an entitlement to follow a course of study in an additional entitlement area.

(2)   An additional entitlement area is an area specified by the Secretary of State by order for the purposes of this subsection.

(3)   The additional entitlement is satisfied in relation to a person if a course of study in one of the additional entitlement areas is made available to the person at a school or institution.

(4)   A person's entitlement to follow a course of study in an additional entitlement area ceases if —

(a)   a course of study in the additional entitlement area is made available to the person, but

(b) the person does not begin the course of study before reaching the age of 19."

Boarding accommodation: persons subject to learning difficulty assessment

46 Boarding accommodation: persons subject to learning difficulty assessment

After section 514 of the Education Act 1996 (c. 56) insert−

"514A Provision of boarding accommodation for persons subject to learning difficulty assessment

(1) A local education authority in England may secure the provision of boarding accommodation in connection with the provision of education or training for a person in their area who is−

    (a) over compulsory school age but under 25, and

    (b) subject to learning difficulty assessment.

(2) A local education authority may secure the provision of boarding accommodation under subsection (1) either within or outside their area.

(3) For the purposes of subsection (1) it is immaterial who provides, or secures the provision of, the education or training.

(4) In this section "education" and "training" have the same meanings as in section 15ZA."

Work experience

47 Work experience for persons over compulsory school age

After section 560 of the Education Act 1996 insert−

"560A Work experience for persons over compulsory school age: England

(1) A local education authority in England may secure the provision of work experience for persons in their area−

    (a) who are over compulsory school age but under 19, or

    (b) who are aged 19 or over but under 25 and are subject to learning difficulty assessment.

(2) A local education authority in England must−

    (a) encourage participation in work experience by persons in their area who are within subsection (1)(a) or (b);

    (b) encourage employers to participate in the provision of work experience for such persons."

Persons detained in youth accommodation

48   Provision of education for persons subject to youth detention

After section 18 of the Education Act 1996 insert—

"18A Provision of education for persons subject to youth detention

(1)   A local education authority must secure that—

    (a)   enough suitable education is provided to meet the reasonable needs of children subject to youth detention in their area;

    (b)   enough suitable education and training is provided to meet the reasonable needs of persons who are—

        (i)   over compulsory school age but under 19, and

        (ii)   subject to youth detention in their area.

(2)   In deciding for the purposes of subsection (1) whether education or training is suitable to meet persons' reasonable needs, a local education authority must (in particular) have regard to—

    (a)   the persons' ages, abilities and aptitudes;

    (b)   any special educational needs or learning difficulties (within the meaning of section 15ZA(6) and (7)) the persons may have;

    (c)   the desirability of enabling persons to complete programmes of study or training which they have begun;

    (d)   any relevant curriculum and the desirability that education received by persons subject to youth detention should be comparable with education which they could be expected to receive if they were attending a school or institution implementing a relevant curriculum;

    (e)   the desirability of the core entitlement and the additional entitlement being satisfied in relation to persons over compulsory school age but under 19 who have elected for them.

(3)   In subsection (2)(d), "relevant curriculum" means—

    (a)   in relation to a local education authority in England, the National Curriculum for England established under section 87 of the Education Act 2002 as subsisting for the time being;

    (b)   in relation to a local education authority in Wales—

        (i)   the National Curriculum for Wales established under section 108 of that Act as subsisting for the time being, or

        (ii)   any local curriculum formed by the authority under section 116A of the Education Act 2002 (formation of local curricula for pupils in Key Stage 4) or for their area under section 33A of the Learning and Skills Act 2000 (formation of local curricula for students aged 16 to 18).

(4)   Sections 17B to 17D apply for the purposes of subsection (2)(e) as they apply for the purposes of section 17A.

(5)   Any arrangements made by a local education authority under subsection (1) for the provision by another person (the "learning provider") of education or training must require the learning provider, in making any determination as to the education or training to be provided for a particular person ("P"), to have regard to any information within subsection (6).

    (6)   The information within this subsection is—

        (a)   information provided under section 562F by a local education authority as to the level of P's literacy and numeracy skills;

        (b)   any other information provided under section 562F by P's home authority (within the meaning of Chapter 5A of Part 10) for the purpose of assisting a determination such as is mentioned in subsection (5).

    (7)   In performing the duty imposed by subsection (1), a local education authority must have regard to any guidance issued—

        (a)   in the case of a local education authority in England, by the Secretary of State;

        (b)   in the case of a local education authority in Wales, by the Welsh Ministers.

    (8)   For the purposes of subsection (1), a person is subject to youth detention in the area of a local education authority if—

        (a)   subject to a detention order, and

        (b)   detained in relevant youth accommodation in the area of the authority."

49 Persons detained in youth accommodation: application of provisions

    (1)   Section 562 of the Education Act 1996 (c. 56) (Act not to apply to persons detained under order of a court) is amended as follows.

    (2)   In subsection (1)—

        (a)   for "detained in pursuance of an order made by a court or of an order of recall made by the Secretary of State" substitute "subject to a detention order and is detained in accommodation that is not relevant youth accommodation", and

        (b)   for "a person who is detained in pursuance of such an order" substitute "such a person".

    (3)   After that subsection insert—

    "(1A)   For the purposes of this Act—

        (a)   a person is subject to a detention order if detained in pursuance of—

            (i)   an order made by a court, or

            (ii)   an order of recall made by the Secretary of State, and

        (b)   relevant youth accommodation is accommodation which—

            (i)   is youth detention accommodation (within the meaning given by section 107(1) of the Powers of Criminal Courts (Sentencing) Act 2000), and

            (ii)   is not in a young offender institution, or part of such an institution, that is used wholly or mainly for the detention of persons aged 18 and over."

    (4)   In subsection (2), for "subsection (1)" substitute "this section".

    (5)   After that subsection add—

    "(3)   A child or young person who is being kept in accommodation provided for the purpose of restricting liberty is not to be regarded for the purposes of this section as detained in pursuance of an order made by a court by reason of the fact that a court has authorised the person to be kept in such accommodation under section 25(4) of the Children Act 1989 (use of accommodation for restricting liberty)."

(6)   In the title, after "apply to" insert "certain".

50   **Persons detained in youth accommodation: further provision**

After section 562 of the Education Act 1996 (c. 56) insert—

"CHAPTER 5A

PERSONS DETAINED IN YOUTH ACCOMMODATION

Provisions applying to detained persons

562A **Application of Act to detained persons**

(1)   In its application in relation to detained persons, this Act has effect subject to modifications prescribed by regulations made by the appropriate national authority.

(2)   The power conferred by subsection (1) may not be exercised to modify the application of a provision of this Act if—

(a)   the provision makes special provision in relation to detained persons, or a description of detained persons,

(b)   the application of the provision in relation to detained persons, or a description of detained persons, is excluded by provision made by this Act, or

(c)   the provision has effect in relation to detained persons, or a description of detained persons, subject to modifications made by this Act.

(3)   References in this Chapter to a detained person are to a child or young person who is—

(a)   subject to a detention order, and

(b)   detained in relevant youth accommodation;

and, in provisions applying on a person's release, also include references to a person who, immediately before release, was a detained person.

562B **Duty to take steps to promote fulfilment of potential**

(1)   Subsection (2) applies in relation to a detained person who is not a looked after child.

(2)   The home authority must—

(a)   during the period of detention in relevant youth accommodation, and

(b)   on the person's release from detention in relevant youth accommodation,

take such steps as they consider appropriate to promote the person's fulfilment of his or her learning potential.

(3) Those steps must include, where it appears to the home authority appropriate for them to do so, making arrangements for the provision, on the person's release from detention —

    (a) of education, or

    (b) in the case of a person who is over compulsory school age, of education or training.

(4) Where the host authority make any determination as to the education or training to be provided for a detained person, the authority must have regard to —

    (a) any information provided under section 562F by a local education authority as to the level of the person's literacy and numeracy skills;

    (b) any other information provided by the home authority under section 562F for the purpose of assisting any such determination.

562C Detained persons with special educational needs

(1) This section applies where, immediately before the beginning of the detention, a local education authority were maintaining a statement under section 324 for a detained person.

(2) The authority must keep the statement while the person is detained in relevant youth accommodation.

(3) The host authority must use best endeavours to secure that appropriate special educational provision is made for the detained person while the person is detained in relevant youth accommodation.

(4) For the purposes of subsection (3), appropriate special educational provision is —

    (a) the special educational provision that, immediately before the beginning of the detention, was specified in the statement,

    (b) educational provision corresponding as closely as practicable to the special educational provision so specified, or

    (c) if it appears to the host authority that the special educational provision so specified is no longer appropriate for the person, such special educational provision as reasonably appears to the host authority to be appropriate for the person.

562D Appropriate special educational provision: arrangements between local education authorities

(1) This section applies where special educational provision is secured for a person in circumstances where section 562C applies.

(2) A local education authority may supply goods and services to —

    (a) the host authority, or

    (b) any other person making the special educational provision in question.

(3) Goods and services may be supplied under subsection (2) only for the purpose of assisting the making or securing of that special educational provision.

562E   **Literacy and numeracy assessments**

(1)   This section applies in relation to a detained person who is detained in particular relevant youth accommodation.

(2)   The host authority must arrange for the level of the detained person's literacy and numeracy skills to be assessed as soon as reasonably practicable after the beginning of the period during which the person is detained in that accommodation.

(3)   Subsection (2) does not apply if the authority are satisfied that they have evidence of the current level of the person's literacy and numeracy skills.

(4)   The "current level" of a detained person's literacy and numeracy skills is the level of those skills at the beginning of the period during which the person is detained in the relevant youth accommodation in question.

Provision of information relating to detained persons

562F   **Provision of information about detained persons**

(1)   Any person who has provided education or training for a detained person (whether before or during the period of detention) may provide information relating to the detained person to —

     (a)   the home authority, or

     (b)   the host authority,

for the purposes of, or in connection with, the provision of education or training for the detained person.

(2)   A local education authority must, on a request under subsection (3), as soon as practicable provide to the person making the request such information that they hold relating to a detained person as is requested.

(3)   A request is made under this subsection if it —

     (a)   is made by a person within subsection (4), and

     (b)   asks only for information which the person requires for the purposes of, or in connection with, the provision of education or training for the detained person (including education or training to be provided after the detained person's release from detention).

(4)   Those persons are —

     (a)   any other local education authority;

     (b)   a youth offending team established under section 39 of the Crime and Disorder Act 1998;

     (c)   the person in charge of any place at which the detained person is detained or is expected to be detained;

     (d)   any person providing or proposing to provide education or training for the detained person.

(5)   The Welsh Ministers must, on a request by the home authority or the host authority, provide a copy of any relevant assessment report for the purposes of the exercise of any function of that authority under section 18A or this Chapter.

(6) In subsection (5), "relevant assessment report" means a report of an assessment of a detained person conducted (whether before or during the period of detention) —

    (a) under section 140 of the Learning and Skills Act 2000, and

    (b) by virtue of arrangements made by the Welsh Ministers.

(7) Subsection (8) applies in relation to a detained person if it appears to the host authority that the person is to be released from detention in relevant youth accommodation.

(8) The host authority must provide to the home authority any information they hold which —

    (a) relates to the detained person, and

    (b) may be relevant for the purposes of, or in connection with, the provision of education or training for the detained person after the release.

(9) The information required to be provided under subsection (8) must be provided at such time as the host authority think reasonable for the purpose of enabling education or training to be provided for the detained person after the release.

(10) Nothing in subsections (7) to (9) requires the host authority to provide to the home authority information which it appears to the host authority that the home authority already have.

(11) In this section any reference to the host authority, in relation to a detained person, includes a reference to any local education authority in whose area the person is expected to be detained.

562G Information to be provided where statement of special educational needs previously maintained

(1) This section applies in relation to a detained person if, immediately before the beginning of the detention, a local education authority were maintaining a statement under section 324 for the person.

(2) Subsections (3) and (4) apply where the home authority become aware (whether by notice under section 39A(2) of the Crime and Disorder Act 1998 (detention of child or young person: local education authorities to be notified) or otherwise) —

    (a) that the person —

        (i) has become subject to a detention order, and

        (ii) is detained in relevant youth accommodation, or

    (b) that the person has been transferred from one place of accommodation to another place of accommodation which is relevant youth accommodation.

(3) If, immediately before the beginning of the detention, the home authority were maintaining the statement, they must send a copy of the statement to the host authority.

(4) If the home authority are or become aware that, immediately before the beginning of the detention, another local education authority were maintaining a statement for the person under section 324, they must notify the host authority —

    (a) of that fact, and

   (b) of the identity of that other local education authority.

(5) The local education authority who, immediately before the beginning of the detention, were maintaining the statement must, on a request by the host authority, send a copy of the statement to the host authority.

(6) Subsections (7) and (8) apply where the person is released from detention in relevant youth accommodation.

(7) The host authority must notify the following of the person's release—
   (a) the home authority, and
   (b) if different, the authority who, immediately before the beginning of the detention, were maintaining the statement under section 324.

(8) If the home authority are not the authority who, immediately before the beginning of the detention, were maintaining the statement, the host authority must also notify the home authority—
   (a) of the fact that immediately before the beginning of the detention a statement was being maintained for the person by a local education authority under section 324, and
   (b) of the identity of that authority.

(9) Nothing in this section requires any local education authority to notify another authority of any matter of which the other authority are already aware, or to send a copy of any statement to another authority who already have a copy of it.

562H Release of detained person appearing to host authority to require assessment

(1) This section applies in relation to the release from detention in relevant youth accommodation of a detained person in relation to whom section 562G does not apply.

(2) Subsection (3) applies where it appears to the host authority that the detained person will, on release, be a child within the meaning of Part 4.

(3) If the host authority are of the opinion that the person has, or may have, special educational needs, they must, on the person's release, notify the home authority of their opinion.

(4) Subsections (5) and (6) apply where, on release, the detained person—
   (a) will be over compulsory school age, or
   (b) will cease to be of compulsory school age within one year.

(5) If—
   (a) the host authority are of the opinion that the person has, or may have, a learning difficulty (within the meaning of section 15ZA (6) and (7)), and
   (b) the home authority are a local education authority in England,
  the host authority must, on the person's release, notify the home authority of their opinion.

(6) If—
   (a) the host authority are of the opinion that the person has, or may have, a learning difficulty (within the meaning of section 41 of

the Learning and Skills Act 2000 (assessments relating to learning difficulties: Wales)) and

(b)   the home authority are a local education authority in Wales,

the host authority must, on the person's release, notify the Welsh Ministers of their opinion.

Supplementary

562I Guidance

In performing their functions under this Chapter a local education authority must have regard to any guidance issued by the appropriate national authority.

562J Interpretation of Chapter

(1)   In this Chapter —

"the appropriate national authority" means —

(a)   in relation to England, the Secretary of State;

(b)   in relation to Wales, the Welsh Ministers;

"beginning of the detention", in relation to a person detained in relevant youth accommodation, means —

(a)   the beginning of the period of detention in such accommodation, or

(b)   where that period is part of a continuous period, comprising periods of detention in relevant youth accommodation and in other accommodation, the beginning of that continuous period;

"detained person" has the meaning given by section 562A(3);

"the home authority" —

(a)   in relation to a child or young person who immediately before the beginning of the detention was, or at any time since then has been, a looked after child, means the local education authority who are the local authority looking after, or who have most recently been looking after, the person;

(b)   in relation to any other child or young person, means the local education authority in whose area the person is ordinarily resident;

"the host authority", in relation to a child or young person detained in relevant youth accommodation, means the local education authority in whose area the child or young person is detained;

"looked after child" means a person who, for the purposes of the Children Act 1989 is a child looked after by a local authority; and references to the local authority looking after the person are to be read accordingly;

"young person" includes a person aged 18.

(2)   For the purposes of the definition of "beginning of the detention" in subsection (1), it is immaterial whether or not a period of detention is pursuant to a single order.

(3)   In determining for the purpose of subsection (1) where a child or young person is ordinarily resident, any period when the person is subject to a detention order is to be disregarded.

(4)   Regulations made by the appropriate national authority may make further provision for determining where a person is ordinarily resident for the purpose of that subsection."

51   Detention of child or young person: local education authorities to be notified

After section 39 of the Crime and Disorder Act 1998 (c. 37) insert —

"39A   Detention of child or young person: local education authorities to be notified

(1)   Subsection (2) applies where a youth offending team becomes aware that —

     (a)   a child or young person has become subject to a detention order and is detained in relevant youth accommodation, or

     (b)   a child or young person who is subject to a detention order has been transferred from one place of accommodation to another which is relevant youth accommodation.

(2)   The youth offending team must as soon as practicable notify —

     (a)   the home local education authority, and

     (b)   the host local education authority,

of the place where the child or young person is detained.

(3)   Subsection (4) applies where a youth offending team becomes aware that a person has been released having immediately before release been —

     (a)   subject to a detention order, and

     (b)   detained in relevant youth accommodation.

(4)   The youth offending team must as soon as practicable notify the following authorities of the release —

     (a)   the home local education authority;

     (b)   the host local education authority;

     (c)   any other local education authority in whose area the youth offending team expects the person to live on release.

(5)   Nothing in this section requires a youth offending team to notify a local education authority of any matter of which the authority is already aware.

(6)   In this section —

     "home local education authority", in relation to a child or young person, means the local education authority which is the home authority in relation to that person within the meaning of Chapter 5A of Part 10 of the Education Act 1996 (persons detained in youth accommodation);

     "host local education authority", in relation to a child or young person who is detained in relevant youth accommodation, means the local education authority for the area in which that person is detained;

"young person" includes a person who is aged 18;

and references in this section to a person subject to a detention order and to relevant youth accommodation have the same meanings as they have in the Education Act 1996 (see section 562(1A) of that Act)."

52 Release from detention of child or young person with special educational needs

(1) The Education Act 1996 (c. 56) is amended as follows.

(2) After section 312 insert—

"312A Children subject to detention

(1) No provision of, or made under, this Part applies in relation to a child who is subject to a detention order and detained in relevant youth accommodation.

(2) The following provisions of this section apply where a child who has been subject to a detention order is released having, immediately before release, been detained in relevant youth accommodation.

(3) Subject to subsection (6), a statement which was maintained for the child by a local education authority under section 324 immediately before the beginning of the detention is, from the child's release, to be treated as being maintained by that authority under section 324.

(4) In subsection (3) "the beginning of the detention" means—
   (a) the beginning of the period of detention in relevant youth accommodation, or
   (b) where that period is part of a continuous period, comprising periods of detention in relevant youth accommodation and in other accommodation, the beginning of that continuous period.

(5) For the purposes of subsection (4), it is immaterial whether or not a period of detention is pursuant to a single order.

(6) Where, on the child's release, a local education authority ("the new authority") other than the authority mentioned in subsection (3) ("the old authority") becomes responsible for the child for the purposes of this Part—
   (a) the old authority must transfer the statement to the new authority, and
   (b) from the child's release, the statement is to be treated as being maintained by the new authority under section 324."

(3) In section 328(5) (reviews of educational needs), at the end of paragraph (a) (but before "and") insert—
   "(aa) where the child concerned—
      (i) has been subject to a detention order, and
      (ii) immediately before release was detained in relevant youth accommodation,
   on the child's release from detention,".

Transport in England

53   Provision of transport etc for persons of sixth form age: duty to have regard to section 15ZA duty

In section 509AB(3) of the Education Act 1996 (c. 56) (provision of transport etc for persons of sixth form age in England: matters to which LEAs must have regard) after paragraph (b) insert—

> "(ba)   what they are required to do under section 15ZA(1) in relation to persons of sixth form age,".

54   Transport policy statements for persons of sixth form age: consultation

In section 509AB(6) of the Education Act 1996 (people to be consulted when preparing transport policy statements for persons of sixth form age in England), in paragraph (c), before "and" insert—

> "(ca)   persons in the local education authority's area who will be of sixth form age when the statement has effect, and their parents,".

55   Transport policy statements for persons of sixth form age: content and publication

(1)   In section 509AB of the Education Act 1996 (provision about transport policy statements for persons of sixth form age in England), after subsection (7) insert—

> "(7A)   In preparing and publishing a statement under section 509AA, a local education authority must have regard (among other things) to the need to—
>
> > (a)   include in the statement sufficient information about the matters that the statement must specify, and
> >
> > (b)   publish the statement in time,
>
> to enable persons who will be of sixth form age when the statement has effect and their parents to take reasonable account of those matters when choosing between different establishments at which education or training is provided."

(2)   In section 509AA(10) of that Act (time by which transport policy statements for persons of sixth form age in England must be published) for "by substituting a different date for 31st May" substitute "to change the time by which the statement must be published".

56   Complaints about transport arrangements etc for persons of sixth form age

(1)   The Education Act 1996 is amended as follows.

(2)   After section 509AD (local education authorities in England: duty to have regard to religion or belief in exercise of travel functions) insert—

> **"509AE   Complaints about transport arrangements etc for persons of sixth form age in England**
>
> > (1)   A local education authority may revise a statement prepared under section 509AA to change the arrangements specified under subsection

(2) or (3) of that section if, as a result of a sixth form transport complaint, they have come to consider the change necessary for the purpose of the arrangements specified under the subsection in question.

(2) A local education authority must revise a statement prepared under section 509AA to change the arrangements specified under subsection (2) or (3) of that section if, as a result of a sixth form transport complaint, the Secretary of State has directed them to do so.

(3) An authority that revise a statement under subsection (1) or (2) must publish the revised statement and a description of the revision as soon as practicable.

(4) The Secretary of State need not consider whether to exercise any power under sections 496 to 497A (powers to prevent unreasonable exercise of functions, etc), section 509AA(9) (power to require LEA to make additional transport arrangements), or subsection (2) of this section in response to a matter that is, or could have been, the subject of a sixth form transport complaint made to him or her unless satisfied that—

    (a) the matter has been brought to the notice of the local education authority concerned, and

    (b) the authority have had a reasonable opportunity to investigate the matter and respond.

(5) In this section "sixth form transport complaint" means a complaint that is—

    (a) about a local education authority's exercise of, or failure to exercise, a function under sections 509AA to 509AD in relation to persons of sixth form age, and

    (b) made by a person who is, or will be, a person of sixth form age when the matter complained of has effect, or by a parent of such a person,

and "sixth form age" is to be construed in accordance with section 509AC(1).

(6) For the purposes of sections 509AA(8) and (9), 509AB(1) to (5), 509AC and 509AD, the revision of a statement under this section is to be treated as the preparation of a statement under section 509AA.

(7) Where a local education authority have published in a single document a statement prepared under section 508G and a statement prepared under 509AA, the requirement to publish a revised statement under subsection (3) is to be treated as a requirement to publish a version of the document that includes the revised statement."

(3) In section 509AA (provision of transport etc for persons of sixth form age), at the end insert—

"(11) Subsection (9) is subject to section 509AE (complaints about transport arrangements etc for persons of sixth form age in England)."

57 Local education authorities in England: provision of transport etc for adult learners

(1) The Education Act 1996 (c. 56) is amended as follows.

(2)   After section 508E (LEAs in England: school travel schemes) insert—

"508F LEAs in England: provision of transport etc for adult learners

(1)   A local education authority in England must make such arrangements for the provision of transport and otherwise as they consider necessary, or as the Secretary of State may direct, for the purposes mentioned in subsections (2) and (3).

(2)   The first purpose is to facilitate the attendance of adults receiving education at institutions—

    (a)   maintained or assisted by the authority and providing further or higher education (or both), or

    (b)   within the further education sector.

(3)   The second purpose is to facilitate the attendance of relevant young adults receiving education or training at institutions outside both the further and higher education sectors, but only in cases where the local education authority have secured for the adults in question—

    (a)   the provision of education or training at the institution in question, and

    (b)   the provision of boarding accommodation under section 514A.

(4)   Any transport provided under subsection (1) must be provided free of charge.

(5)   In considering what arrangements it is necessary to make under subsection (1) in relation to relevant young adults, a local education authority must have regard to what they are required to do under section 15ZA(1) in relation to those persons.

(6)   In considering whether they are required by subsection (1) to make arrangements in relation to a particular adult, a local education authority must have regard (among other things) to the age of the adult and the nature of the route, or alternative routes, which the adult could reasonably be expected to take.

(7)   Arrangements made under subsection (1) by virtue of subsection (3) to facilitate full-time education or training at an institution outside both the further and higher education sectors must be no less favourable than the arrangements made for relevant young adults of the same age for whom the authority secure the provision of education at another institution.

(8)   A local education authority in England may pay all or part of the reasonable travelling expenses of an adult—

    (a)   receiving education or training at an institution mentioned in subsection (2) or (3), and

    (b)   for whose transport no arrangements are made under subsection (1).

(9)   In this section—

    "adult" means a person who is neither a child nor a person of sixth form age,

    "sixth form age" is to be construed in accordance with section 509AC(1), and "relevant young adult" means an adult who is aged under 25 and is subject to learning difficulty assessment.

508G LEAs in England: transport policy statements etc for young adults subject to learning difficulty assessment

(1) A local education authority in England making arrangements, or proposing to pay travelling expenses, under section 508F in relation to relevant young adults must consult—

    (a) any other local education authority that they consider it appropriate to consult,

    (b) governing bodies of institutions within the further education sector in the authority's area,

    (c) persons in the local education authority's area who will be relevant young adults when the arrangements or payments have effect, and their parents,

    (d) the Secretary of State, and

    (e) any other person specified by the Secretary of State.

(2) The authority must prepare for each academic year a transport policy statement complying with the following requirements.

(3) The statement must specify any transport or other arrangements, and any payment of travelling expenses, made or to be made in relation to the year under section 508F in relation to relevant young adults.

(4) The statement must also specify any travel concessions (within the meaning of Part 5 of the Transport Act 1985) which are to be provided under any scheme established under section 93 of that Act to relevant young adults receiving education or training at an institution mentioned in subsection (2) or (3) of section 508F.

(5) The authority must publish the statement by the end of May in the year in which the relevant academic year begins.

(6) In preparing and publishing the statement, the authority must have regard (among other things) to the need to—

    (a) include in the statement sufficient information about the matters that the statement must specify, and

    (b) publish the statement in time,

to enable relevant young adults and their parents to take reasonable account of those matters when choosing between different institutions at which education or training is provided.

(7) The publication of a statement under this section in relation to an academic year does not prevent an authority from—

    (a) making additional arrangements or payments under section 508F in relation to the academic year, or

    (b) providing additional travel concessions in relation to the academic year.

(8) The Secretary of State may amend subsection (5) by order to change the time by which the statement must be published.

(9) In this section—

    "academic year" has the meaning given in section 509AC,

"governing body" has the meaning given in section 509AC, and "relevant young adult" has the meaning given in section 508F.

508H   Guidance: sections 508F and 508G

In making arrangements under section 508F(1) and preparing and publishing a statement under section 508G, a local education authority must have regard to any guidance issued by the Secretary of State under this section.

508I   Complaints about transport arrangements etc for young adults subject to learning difficulty assessment: England

(1) A local education authority may revise a statement prepared under section 508G to change any matter specified under subsection (3) of that section if, as a result of a relevant young adult transport complaint, they have come to consider the change necessary for a purpose mentioned in section 508F(2) or (3).

(2) A local education authority must revise a statement prepared under section 508G to change any matter specified in subsection (3) of that section if, as a result of a relevant young adult transport complaint, the Secretary of State has directed them to do so.

(3) An authority that revise a statement under subsection (1) or (2) must publish the revised statement and a description of the revision as soon as practicable.

(4) The Secretary of State need not consider whether to exercise any power under sections 496 to 497A (powers to prevent unreasonable exercise of functions, etc) or subsection (2) of this section in response to a matter that is, or could have been, the subject of a relevant young adult transport complaint made to him or her unless satisfied that—

    (a) the matter has been brought to the notice of the local education authority concerned, and

    (b) the authority have had a reasonable opportunity to investigate the matter and respond.

(5) In this section "relevant young adult transport complaint" means a complaint that is—

    (a) about a local education authority's exercise of, or failure to exercise, a function under section 508F or 508G in relation to relevant young adults, and

    (b) made by a person who is, or will be, a relevant young adult when the matter complained of has effect, or by a parent of such a person,

and "relevant young adult" has the meaning given in section 508F.

(6) For the purposes of sections 508G(7) and 508H, the revision of a statement under this section is to be treated as the preparation of a statement under section 508G.

(7) Where a local education authority have published in a single document a statement prepared under section 509AA and a statement prepared under 508G, the requirement to publish a revised statement under subsection (3) is to be treated as a requirement to publish a version of the document that includes the revised statement."

(3) In section 509AD(2) (LEAs in England: duty to have regard to religion or belief in exercise of travel functions) for the entry relating to section 508F substitute —

"section 508F (LEAs in England: provision of transport etc for adult learners);".

(4) Section 509 (provision of transport etc) ceases to have effect.

(5) Section 81 of the Education and Inspections Act 2006 (c. 40) (LEAs in England: provision of transport etc for certain adult learners) ceases to have effect.

Powers in respect of non-maintained schools

58 Power of LEAs to arrange provision of education at non-maintained schools

(1) The following provisions cease to have effect —

(a) section 128 of the School Standards and Framework Act 1998 (c. 31), and

(b) paragraph 64 of Schedule 30 to that Act.

(2) Accordingly, sections 16 and 18 of the Education Act 1996 (c. 56) (powers of LEAs to assist, and arrange provision of education at, non-maintained schools) continue to have effect as if the provisions mentioned in subsection (1) had never been enacted.

General

59 Minor and consequential amendments

Schedule 2 contains minor and consequential amendments relating to the provision made by this Part.

PART 3

THE YOUNG PEOPLE'S LEARNING AGENCY FOR ENGLAND

CHAPTER 1

ESTABLISHMENT

60 The Young People's Learning Agency for England

(1) There is to be a body corporate known as the Young People's Learning Agency for England.

(2) In this Part that body is referred to as "the YPLA".

(3) Except as provided for in sections 68 to 70, the YPLA is to perform its functions in relation to England only.

(4) Schedule 3 makes further provision about the YPLA.

2218　　　　　　　　　　*Apprenticeships, Skills, Children and Learning Act 2009 (c. 22)*
Part 3 − The Young People's Learning Agency for England
Chapter 2 − Main functions

CHAPTER 2

MAIN FUNCTIONS

Funding

61　Provision of financial resources

(1)　The YPLA must secure the provision of financial resources to —

　　(a)　persons providing or proposing to provide suitable education or training to persons —

　　　　(i)　who are over compulsory school age but under 19, or

　　　　(ii)　who are aged 19 or over but under 25 and are subject to learning difficulty assessment;

　　(b)　persons providing or proposing to provide suitable education to children subject to youth detention;

　　(c)　local education authorities, for the purposes of their functions in relation to education or training within paragraph (a) or (b).

(2)　The YPLA must also secure the provision of financial resources in accordance with any directions given to it by the Secretary of State.

(3)　The YPLA may secure the provision of financial resources to —

　　(a)　persons providing or proposing to provide education or training to persons who are of or under compulsory school age;

　　(b)　persons providing or proposing to provide education or training to persons aged 19 or over, in respect of education or training begun by them before reaching the age of 19;

　　(c)　local education authorities, for the purposes of their functions in relation to education or training in respect of which the YPLA has power to secure the provision of financial resources under paragraph (a) or (b).

(4)　The YPLA may also secure the provision of financial resources —

　　(a)　to or in respect of persons (of any age) for purposes related to enabling, facilitating or encouraging their participation in education or training;

　　(b)　to persons providing or proposing to provide goods or services in connection with the provision by others of education or training within subsection (1)(a) or (b) or (3)(a) or (b);

　　(c)　to persons undertaking or proposing to undertake research relating to education or training;

　　(d)　to persons providing or proposing to provide work experience for persons receiving education;

　　(e)　to persons carrying out means tests under arrangements made under section 64;

　　(f)　to persons providing or proposing to provide information, advice or guidance about education or training or connected matters (including employment).

(5)　In performing its functions under this section the YPLA must make the best use of its resources.

(6)　The YPLA may secure the provision of financial resources under this section —

　　(a)　by providing the resources;

Apprenticeships, Skills, Children and Learning Act 2009 (c. 22)
Part 3 — The Young People's Learning Agency for England
Chapter 2 — Main functions

2219

    (b)   by making arrangements for the provision of resources by another person;

    (c)   by making arrangements for the provision of resources by persons jointly (whether or not including the YPLA).

(7) The YPLA may under subsection (4)(a) secure the provision of financial resources by reference to —

    (a)   any fees or charges payable by the person receiving or proposing to receive the education or training, or

    (b)   any other matter (such as transport or childcare).

(8) The reference in subsection (1)(a) to persons —

    (a)   who are over compulsory school age but under 19, or

    (b)   who are aged 19 or over but under 25 and are subject to learning difficulty assessment,

does not include persons who are subject to adult detention within the meaning given in section 121(4).

(9) Directions given under subsection (2) may not concern the provision of financial resources to or in respect of a particular person or persons.

62   Financial resources: conditions

(1) Financial resources provided by the YPLA may be provided subject to conditions.

(2) The conditions may include —

    (a)   information conditions;

    (b)   operational conditions;

    (c)   repayment conditions.

(3) Information conditions are conditions which —

    (a)   require the YPLA, or a person designated by the YPLA, to be given access to a person's accounts and documents and to be given rights in relation to a person's computers and associated apparatus and material, or

    (b)   require a person to whom financial resources are provided to give to the YPLA such information as the YPLA may request for the purpose of carrying out its functions.

(4) Operational conditions are conditions which require a person providing or proposing to provide education or training ("the provider") to make arrangements providing for all or any of the matters mentioned in subsection (5).

(5) The matters are the following —

    (a)   the charging of fees by the provider by reference to specified criteria;

    (b)   the making of awards by the provider by reference to specified criteria;

    (c)   the recovery by the provider of amounts from persons receiving education or training or from employers (or from both);

    (d)   the determination of amounts by reference to specified criteria where provision is made under paragraph (c);

    (e)   the operation of specified exemptions where provision is made under paragraph (c);

2220   *Apprenticeships, Skills, Children and Learning Act 2009 (c. 22)*
Part 3 — The Young People's Learning Agency for England
Chapter 2 — Main functions

    (f)   the making by the provider of provision specified in a report of an assessment under section 139A or 140 of the Learning and Skills Act 2000 (c. 21) (assessments relating to learning difficulties).

(6)   Repayment conditions are conditions which—

    (a)   enable the YPLA to require the repayment (in whole or part) of sums paid by the YPLA if any of the conditions subject to which the sums were paid is not complied with;

    (b)   require the payment of interest in respect of any period in which a sum due to the YPLA in accordance with any condition is unpaid.

63   Performance assessments

(1)   The YPLA may adopt or develop schemes for the assessment of the performance of persons in providing education or training funded (directly or indirectly) by the YPLA in the exercise of its functions under section 61.

(2)   The YPLA may take the assessments into account in deciding how to exercise its functions under section 61.

64   Means tests

(1)   The YPLA may—

    (a)   carry out means tests;

    (b)   arrange for other persons to carry out means tests.

(2)   The YPLA may take the results of the tests into account in exercising its functions under section 61(4)(a).

65   Prohibition on charging

(1)   The YPLA must exercise its funding functions so as to secure (so far as practicable) that no charge is made in relation to the provision of relevant education or training funded by it.

(2)   The YPLA's funding functions are its functions under sections 61 and 62.

(3)   "Relevant education or training" means full-time or part-time education or training suitable to the requirements of persons over compulsory school age but under 19, other than education to be provided at a school maintained by a local education authority.

(4)   Education or training is funded by the YPLA for the purposes of this section if the YPLA has secured the provision of financial resources under section 61 in respect of it.

(5)   Regulations may specify charges or descriptions of charges which are, or are not, to be treated as made in relation to the provision of education or training for the purposes of this section.

Securing provision of education and training

66   Securing provision of education and training

(1)   The YPLA may secure the provision of suitable education or training for persons—

Apprenticeships, Skills, Children and Learning Act 2009 (c. 22)
Part 3 – The Young People's Learning Agency for England
Chapter 2 – Main functions

2221

      (a)   who are over compulsory school age but under 19, or

      (b)   who are aged 19 or over but under 25 and are subject to learning difficulty assessment.

(2)   Subsection (1) does not apply to persons who are subject to adult detention within the meaning given in section 121(4).

(3)   The YPLA may secure the provision of suitable education for children subject to youth detention.

(4)   In exercising its powers under subsection (1) in relation to persons who are within section 15ZA(1)(a) or (b) of the Education Act 1996 (c. 56), the YPLA must have regard to things done by local education authorities in the performance of their duties under section 15ZA(1) of that Act.

(5)   In exercising its powers under this section in relation to persons subject to youth detention, the YPLA must have regard to things done by local education authorities in the performance of their duties under section 18A(1) of the Education Act 1996.

67   Intervention for purpose of securing provision of education and training

(1)   This section applies if the YPLA is satisfied that a local education authority is failing, or is likely to fail, to perform –

      (a)   its duty under section 15ZA(1) of the Education Act 1996 (duty to secure provision of enough suitable education and training for persons over compulsory school age), or

      (b)   its duty under section 18A(1) of that Act (duty to secure provision of enough suitable education and training for persons subject to youth detention).

(2)   The YPLA may give directions to the authority for the purpose of securing the provision of education and training to which the duty in question relates.

(3)   A direction given under this section may include provision requiring an authority to permit action of a specified description in relation to any such education or training to be taken by the YPLA or another person.

(4)   The YPLA may give a direction under this section only with the approval of the Secretary of State.

Provision of services and assistance

68   Provision of services

(1)   The YPLA may make arrangements with a permitted recipient for the provision by the YPLA of services that are required by the permitted recipient in connection with the exercise of the recipient's functions relating to education or training.

(2)   The services that may be provided under arrangements made under subsection (1) include –

      (a)   providing accommodation and other facilities to a permitted recipient or managing such facilities on behalf of a permitted recipient;

      (b)   procuring, or assisting in procuring, goods and services for use by a permitted recipient.

2222   *Apprenticeships, Skills, Children and Learning Act 2009 (c. 22)*
Part 3 — The Young People's Learning Agency for England
Chapter 2 — Main functions

(3)   The terms and conditions upon which the arrangements are made may include provision for making payments to the YPLA in respect of expenditure incurred by the YPLA in performing any function under the arrangements.

(4)   In this section "permitted recipient" means —

    (a)   the Secretary of State;

    (b)   the Welsh Ministers;

    (c)   the Scottish Ministers;

    (d)   a Northern Ireland department;

    (e)   the Chief Executive of Skills Funding;

    (f)   any other person, wholly or partly funded from public funds, who has functions relating to education or training;

    (g)   any other person specified, or of a description specified, by order made by the appropriate national authority for the purposes of this section.

(5)   Before making arrangements under which it may provide services to a permitted recipient who falls within any of paragraphs (b) to (g) of subsection (4) in connection with the exercise of the recipient's functions relating to education or training provided in Wales, Scotland or Northern Ireland, the YPLA must obtain the consent of the Secretary of State.

(6)   Before making arrangements under which it may provide services to a permitted recipient who falls within paragraph (a), (e), (f) or (g) of subsection (4) in connection with the exercise of the recipient's functions relating to education or training provided in Wales, Scotland or Northern Ireland, the YPLA must obtain—

    (a)   in relation to education or training provided in Wales, the consent of the Welsh Ministers;

    (b)   in relation to education or training provided in Scotland, the consent of the Scottish Ministers;

    (c)   in relation to education or training provided in Northern Ireland, the consent of the Minister for Employment and Learning in Northern Ireland.

(7)   Consent may be given under subsection (5) or (6) in relation to particular arrangements or arrangements of a particular description.

(8)   "The appropriate national authority" means —

    (a)   in relation to a person exercising functions relating only to education or training provided in Wales, the Welsh Ministers;

    (b)   in relation to a person exercising functions relating only to education or training provided in Scotland, the Scottish Ministers;

    (c)   in relation to a person exercising functions relating only to education or training provided in Northern Ireland, the Department for Employment and Learning in Northern Ireland;

    (d)   in any other case, the Secretary of State.

69   Assistance with respect to employment and training

(1)   The YPLA may take part in arrangements made by the Secretary of State, the Welsh Ministers or the Scottish Ministers under section 2 of the Employment and Training Act 1973 (c. 50) (arrangements for assisting persons to select, train for, obtain and retain employment).

Apprenticeships, Skills, Children and Learning Act 2009 (c. 22)
Part 3 — The Young People's Learning Agency for England
Chapter 2 — Main functions

2223

(2) Before making such arrangements in relation to Wales or Scotland in which the YPLA is to take part, the Secretary of State must obtain the consent of the Welsh Ministers or (as the case may be) the Scottish Ministers to the arrangements.

(3) Before making such arrangements in which the YPLA is to take part, the Welsh Ministers or the Scottish Ministers must obtain the consent of the Secretary of State to the arrangements.

70 Assistance with respect to employment and training: Northern Ireland

(1) The YPLA may take part in any arrangements made by the Department for Employment and Learning in Northern Ireland under section 1 of the Employment and Training Act (Northern Ireland) 1950 (c. 29 (N.I.)) (arrangements for assisting persons to select, train for, obtain and retain employment).

(2) Before making such arrangements in which the YPLA is to take part, the Department must obtain the consent of the Secretary of State to the arrangements.

Miscellaneous

71 Research, information and advice

(1) The YPLA may carry out programmes of research and development connected with any matter relevant to any of its functions.

(2) If requested to do so by the Secretary of State, the YPLA must provide the Secretary of State with information or advice on such matters relating to any of its functions as may be specified in the request.

(3) The YPLA may provide the Secretary of State with other information or advice on any matter in relation to which the YPLA has a function.

(4) The YPLA may provide any person designated by the Secretary of State with information about any matter in relation to which the YPLA has a function.

(5) The YPLA must establish systems for collecting information designed to secure that decisions of the YPLA with regard to education and training are made on a sound basis.

(6) The YPLA may secure the provision of facilities and services for providing information, advice or guidance about education or training or connected matters (including employment).

72 Guidance by YPLA

(1) The YPLA must issue guidance to local education authorities about the performance of their duties under sections 15ZA(1), 15ZB, 15ZC(1)(b) and 18A(1) of the Education Act 1996 (c. 56).

(2) Local education authorities must have regard to any such guidance in performing those duties.

(3) Before issuing guidance under subsection (1) the YPLA must consult—

　　(a) local education authorities in England, and

　　(b) such other persons as it thinks appropriate.

2224

Apprenticeships, Skills, Children and Learning Act 2009 (c. 22)
Part 3 — The Young People's Learning Agency for England
Chapter 2 — Main functions

(4) The YPLA may also issue guidance about any other matter in respect of which it has a function.

73 Intervention powers: policy statement

(1) The YPLA must—

  (a) prepare a statement of its policy with respect to the exercise of its intervention powers,

  (b) keep the statement under review, and

  (c) revise the statement, if it thinks it appropriate in consequence of the review.

(2) When preparing a statement or revised statement of its policy, the YPLA must—

  (a) undertake such consultation as it thinks appropriate, and

  (b) consider any representations made to it about the policy to be set out in the statement.

(3) The YPLA must send a copy of the statement or the revised statement to the Secretary of State for approval.

(4) The YPLA must publish the statement, or revised statement, as soon as practicable after it has been approved by the Secretary of State.

(5) The YPLA must have regard to the statement, or revised statement, most recently published under subsection (4) in exercising, or deciding whether to exercise, any of its intervention powers.

(6) The YPLA's intervention powers are its powers under—

  (a) section 67;

  (b) section 56H of the Further and Higher Education Act 1992 (c. 13);

  (c) section 56I of that Act.

74 Power to confer supplementary functions on YPLA

(1) The Secretary of State may by order confer supplementary functions on the YPLA.

(2) A supplementary function is a function which is—

  (a) exercisable in connection with functions of the Secretary of State, and

  (b) relevant to the provision of education or training within the YPLA's remit.

CHAPTER 3

YPLA'S FUNCTIONS: SUPPLEMENTARY

75 Directions by Secretary of State

(1) The Secretary of State may give directions to the YPLA containing—

  (a) objectives which the YPLA should achieve in carrying out its functions,

  (b) time limits within which the YPLA should achieve the objectives, and

  (c) provision relating to the management of the YPLA.

Apprenticeships, Skills, Children and Learning Act 2009 (c. 22)
Part 3 — The Young People's Learning Agency for England
Chapter 3 — YPLA's functions: supplementary

2225

(2) The Secretary of State may give to the YPLA other directions as to the performance of any of its functions if the Secretary of State is satisfied that the YPLA—

    (a) has failed to discharge a duty imposed by or under any Act, or

    (b) has acted or is proposing to act unreasonably with respect to the performance of any function conferred by or under any Act.

(3) The Secretary of State may give directions under subsection (2) despite any provision made by or under any Act making the performance of a function dependent on the YPLA's opinion.

(4) Directions given under this section with respect to functions conferred on the YPLA by or under section 61 may not concern the provision of financial resources to or in respect of a particular person or persons.

76 Guidance by Secretary of State

(1) The YPLA must, in performing its functions, have regard to any guidance given by the Secretary of State.

(2) Guidance under this section may include in particular guidance about—

    (a) consultation with persons mentioned in subsection (3) in connection with the taking of decisions which affect such persons, and

    (b) taking advice from such persons or descriptions of persons as may be specified in the guidance.

(3) The persons are—

    (a) persons receiving or proposing to receive education or training within the YPLA's remit,

    (b) employers, or

    (c) such other persons or descriptions of persons as may be specified in the guidance.

(4) Guidance under this section about consultation with persons falling within subsection (3)(a) must provide for the views of such persons to be considered in the light of their age and understanding.

CHAPTER 4

ACADEMY ARRANGEMENTS

77 Academy arrangements

(1) The Secretary of State may require the YPLA to enter into Academy arrangements with the Secretary of State.

(2) For the purposes of this Chapter "Academy arrangements" are arrangements under which the YPLA is required to exercise specified Academy functions on the Secretary of State's behalf in accordance with the arrangements.

(3) An "Academy function" is a function of the Secretary of State relating to or exercisable in connection with—

    (a) Academies, city technology colleges or city colleges for the technology of the arts generally, or

2226   *Apprenticeships, Skills, Children and Learning Act 2009 (c. 22)*
Part 3 – The Young People's Learning Agency for England
Chapter 4 – Academy arrangements

        (b)   a particular, or particular description of, Academy, city technology college or city college for the technology of the arts.

(4)   But Academy functions do not include—

        (a)   the function of entering into an agreement under section 482(1) of the Education Act 1996 (c. 56), or

        (b)   functions of making, confirming or approving subordinate legislation.

(5)   Academy arrangements must include provision about the procedure for complaints to be made to the Secretary of State about what the YPLA has done, or failed to do, under the arrangements.

(6)   "Subordinate legislation" has the same meaning as in the Interpretation Act 1978 (c. 30) (see section 21(1) of that Act).

(7)   References in a provision made by or under any Act to the functions of the YPLA do not include any functions conferred or imposed on the YPLA under Academy arrangements.

78   Grants for purposes of Academy arrangements functions

(1)   The Secretary of State may make grants to the YPLA for the purposes of any functions that are or may be conferred or imposed on the YPLA under Academy arrangements.

(2)   Grants to the YPLA under this section are to be made at such times and subject to such conditions (if any) as the Secretary of State thinks appropriate.

(3)   Conditions to which a grant is subject may (in particular)—

        (a)   require the YPLA to use the grant for specified purposes;

        (b)   require the YPLA to comply with specified requirements in respect of persons or persons of a specified description;

        (c)   enable repayment (in whole or part) to be required of sums paid by the Secretary of State if any condition subject to which the grant was made is not complied with;

        (d)   require the payment of interest in respect of any period during which a sum due to the Secretary of State in accordance with any condition remains unpaid.

(4)   Requirements which may be imposed under subsection (3)(b) include in particular requirements that, if the YPLA provides specified financial resources, it is to impose specified conditions.

79   Academy arrangements: information sharing

(1)   This section applies if the Secretary of State and the YPLA enter into Academy arrangements.

(2)   A person within subsection (3) may provide information to any other person within that subsection for the purpose of enabling or facilitating the exercise of any relevant function.

(3)   The persons are—

        (a)   the Secretary of State;

        (b)   the YPLA;

        (c)   a relevant Academy;

Apprenticeships, Skills, Children and Learning Act 2009 (c. 22)
Part 3 — The Young People's Learning Agency for England
Chapter 4 — Academy arrangements

2227

  (d) any other person by or in respect of whom a relevant function is exercisable.

(4) A "relevant function" is —

  (a) a function conferred or imposed on the YPLA under the arrangements;

  (b) a function of the Secretary of State, a relevant Academy, or any other person, which is exercisable in connection with a function conferred or imposed on the YPLA under the arrangements.

(5) A "relevant Academy" is an Academy, city technology college or city college for the technology of the arts in relation to which a function is exercisable by the YPLA under the arrangements.

(6) Nothing in this section —

  (a) affects a power to disclose information that exists apart from this section, or

  (b) authorises the disclosure of any information in contravention of a provision made by or under any Act which prevents disclosure of the information.

CHAPTER 5

GENERAL

80 Interpretation of Part

(1) In this Part a reference to education within the YPLA's remit is a reference to education suitable to the requirements of —

  (a) persons aged under 19, or

  (b) persons aged 19 or over but under 25 who are subject to learning difficulty assessment.

(2) In this Part a reference to training within the YPLA's remit is a reference to training suitable to the requirements of —

  (a) persons aged 14 or over but under 19, or

  (b) persons aged 19 or over but under 25 who are subject to learning difficulty assessment.

(3) For the purposes of this Part a person is subject to youth detention if —

  (a) subject to a detention order, and

  (b) detained in relevant youth accommodation.

(4) In this Part —

  "education" includes full-time and part-time education;

  "training" includes —

    (a) full-time and part-time training;

    (b) vocational, social, physical and recreational training;

    (c) apprenticeship training.

(5) In subsection (4) "apprenticeship training" means training provided in connection with —

  (a) an apprenticeship agreement (within the meaning given in section 32),

  (b) any other contract of employment, or

2228   *Apprenticeships, Skills, Children and Learning Act 2009 (c. 22)*
Part 3 — The Young People's Learning Agency for England
Chapter 5 — General

(c)   any other kind of working in relation to which alternative English completion conditions apply under section 1(5).

(6)   The references in subsections (1) and (2) to persons —

    (a)   aged under 19, or 14 or over but under 19, or

    (b)   aged 19 or over but under 25 who are subject to learning difficulty assessment,

do not include persons who are subject to adult detention within the meaning given in section 121(4).

PART 4

THE CHIEF EXECUTIVE OF SKILLS FUNDING

CHAPTER 1

ESTABLISHMENT AND MAIN DUTIES

The Chief Executive

81   The Chief Executive of Skills Funding

(1)   There is to be a Chief Executive of Skills Funding.

(2)   In this Part that person is referred to as "the Chief Executive".

(3)   The Chief Executive is to be appointed by the Secretary of State.

(4)   Except as provided for in section 107, 108 or 109, the Chief Executive is to perform the functions of the office in relation to England only.

(5)   Schedule 4 makes further provision about the Chief Executive.

Apprenticeship functions

82   Apprenticeship functions

(1)   The Secretary of State may direct the Chief Executive to arrange for apprenticeship functions specified in the direction to be carried out on behalf of the Chief Executive by a person designated by the Chief Executive.

(2)   The Secretary of State may give directions to the Chief Executive —

    (a)   as to the performance of apprenticeship functions;

    (b)   as to the description or identity of the person to be designated under subsection (1);

    (c)   as to the terms of arrangements under that subsection;

    (d)   requiring the Chief Executive to secure that the person designated under subsection (1) reports to the Secretary of State, in such form and at such times as may be specified in the direction, on the performance of apprenticeship functions which are the subject of arrangements under subsection (1).

(3)   A designation of a person under subsection (1) may be made only with the person's consent.

Apprenticeships, Skills, Children and Learning Act 2009 (c. 22)   2229
Part 4 — The Chief Executive of Skills Funding
Chapter 1 — Establishment and main duties

(4)   Arrangements made by virtue of subsection (1) may be made on terms that permit sub-delegation; and the power conferred by subsection (2)(c) includes power to give directions as to—

    (a)   the arrangements for any such sub-delegation;

    (b)   functions which may be sub-delegated;

    (c)   the description or identity of persons to whom functions may be sub-delegated.

(5)   In this section, "apprenticeship functions" means functions of the office which relate to—

    (a)   apprenticeship certificates;

    (b)   recognised English frameworks and the specification of apprenticeship standards for England;

    (c)   apprenticeship training;

    (d)   apprenticeship places (within the meaning of section 93), including functions under section 104 relating to apprenticeship places;

    (e)   the provision of advice and assistance to the Secretary of State under section 106.

(6)   Terms used in subsection (5)(a) and (b) have the same meanings as in Chapter 1 of Part 1.

(7)   Regulations may provide—

    (a)   for any provision relating to a function of the office made by or under any Act—

        (i)   not to apply, or

        (ii)   to apply subject to prescribed modifications,

    in relation to the function where the function is the subject of arrangements under subsection (1);

    (b)   for references to the Chief Executive in any such provisions to be construed in prescribed circumstances as, or as including, references—

        (i)   to a person designated under subsection (1), or

        (ii)   to a person to whom functions are sub-delegated under subsection (4),

    subject to such exceptions or modifications as may be prescribed.

Apprenticeship training for persons aged 16 to 18 and certain young adults

83   Apprenticeship training for persons aged 16 to 18 and certain young adults

(1)   The Chief Executive may secure the provision of facilities for suitable apprenticeship training for persons—

    (a)   who are over compulsory school age but under 19, or

    (b)   who are aged 19 or over but under 25 and are subject to learning difficulty assessment.

(2)   In deciding for the purposes of subsection (1) whether apprenticeship training is suitable for persons for whom facilities are provided, the Chief Executive must have regard (in particular) to—

    (a)   the persons' ages, abilities and aptitudes,

    (b)   any learning difficulties the persons may have,

    (c)   the quality of the training,

2230

Apprenticeships, Skills, Children and Learning Act 2009 (c. 22)
Part 4 — The Chief Executive of Skills Funding
Chapter 1 — Establishment and main duties

      (d)   the locations and times at which the training is provided.

(3)   In exercising the power conferred by subsection (1), the Chief Executive must have regard (in particular) to the desirability of —

      (a)   encouraging diversity of apprenticeship training available to persons;

      (b)   increasing opportunities for persons to exercise choice;

      (c)   enabling persons to whom Part 1 of the Education and Skills Act 2008 (c. 25) applies to fulfil the duty imposed by section 2 of that Act (duty to participate in education or training).

(4)   Subsections (6) and (7) of section 15ZA of the Education Act 1996 (c. 56) (meaning of learning difficulty) apply for the purposes of this section as they apply for the purposes of that section.

(5)   In this Part "apprenticeship training" means training provided in connection with —

      (a)   an apprenticeship agreement,

      (b)   any other contract of employment, or

      (c)   any other kind of working in relation to which alternative English completion conditions apply under section 1(5).

84   Arrangements and co-operation with local education authorities

(1)   The Chief Executive may enter into arrangements with local education authorities in England under which the Chief Executive is to secure the provision of apprenticeship training by virtue of section 83.

(2)   The Chief Executive must co-operate with a local education authority in England where the authority is —

      (a)   making any determination as to the provision of apprenticeship training that should be secured under section 15ZA(1) of the Education Act 1996 (duty in respect of education and training for persons over compulsory school age: England), or

      (b)   securing the provision of any apprenticeship training under that section.

85   Encouragement of training provision etc for persons within section 83

(1)   The Chief Executive must —

      (a)   encourage employers to participate in the provision of training within the Chief Executive's remit for persons who are within section 83(1)(a) or (b);

      (b)   encourage employers to contribute to the costs of training within the Chief Executive's remit for such persons.

(2)   For the purposes of subsection (1)(a), participating in the provision of training includes participating by entering into —

      (a)   an apprenticeship agreement, or

      (b)   any other contract of employment in connection with which training is provided.

Apprenticeships, Skills, Children and Learning Act 2009 (c. 22)
Part 4 — The Chief Executive of Skills Funding
Chapter 1 — Establishment and main duties

2231

Education and training for persons aged 19 or over etc.

86 Education and training for persons aged 19 or over and others subject to adult detention

(1) The Chief Executive must secure the provision of reasonable facilities for —

    (a) education suitable to the requirements of persons who are aged 19 or over, other than persons aged under 25 who are subject to learning difficulty assessment,

    (b) education suitable to the requirements of persons who are subject to adult detention, and

    (c) training suitable to the requirements of persons within paragraphs (a) and (b).

(2) This section does not apply to the provision of facilities to the extent that section 87 applies to the provision of those facilities.

(3) Facilities are reasonable if (taking account of the Chief Executive's resources) their quantity and quality are such that the Chief Executive can reasonably be expected to secure their provision.

(4) In discharging the duty under subsection (1) the Chief Executive must —

    (a) take account of the places where facilities are provided, the character of facilities and the way they are equipped;

    (b) take account of the different abilities and aptitudes of different persons;

    (c) take account of the education and skills required in different sectors of employment for employees and potential employees;

    (d) take account of facilities the provision of which the Chief Executive thinks might reasonably be secured by other persons;

    (e) act with a view to encouraging diversity of education and training available to individuals;

    (f) act with a view to increasing opportunities for individuals to exercise choice;

    (g) have regard to the desirability of enabling persons subject to adult detention to continue programmes of education or training which they have begun;

    (h) have regard to the desirability of the core entitlement and the additional entitlement being satisfied for persons subject to adult detention but aged under 19 who have elected for them;

    (i) make the best use of resources.

(5) For the purposes of this section a reference to the provision of facilities for education or training (except so far as relating to facilities for persons subject to adult detention) includes a reference to the provision of facilities for organised leisure-time occupation in connection with education or (as the case may be) training.

(6) For the purposes of this section —

    "education" includes full-time and part-time education;

    "training" includes —

        (a) full-time and part-time training;

        (b) vocational, social, physical and recreational training;

        (c) apprenticeship training.

2232

Apprenticeships, Skills, Children and Learning Act 2009 (c. 22)
Part 4 − The Chief Executive of Skills Funding
Chapter 1 − Establishment and main duties

(7) In this Part, "organised leisure-time occupation" means leisure-time occupation, in such organised cultural training and recreational activities as are suited to the requirements of persons who fall within subsection (1)(a) or (b), for any such persons who are able and willing to profit by facilities provided for that purpose.

(8) Sections 17B to 17D of the Education Act 1996 (c. 56) (core and additional entitlements: interpretation) apply for the purpose of subsection (4)(h) as they apply for the purpose of section 17A of that Act (duties of local education authorities in relation to the core and additional entitlements).

87 Learning aims for persons aged 19 or over: provision of facilities

(1) The Chief Executive must secure the provision of proper facilities for relevant education or training for persons falling within subsection (3) which is suitable to their requirements.

(2) Relevant education or training is education or vocational training provided by means of a course of study for a qualification to which paragraph 1 of Schedule 5 applies.

(3) The persons falling within this subsection are persons who −
  (a) are aged 19 or over, and are not persons aged under 25 who are subject to learning difficulty assessment,
  (b) do not have the qualification in question or one (including one awarded by a person outside England) which appears to the Chief Executive to be at a comparable or higher level, and
  (c) satisfy such conditions as may be specified in regulations.

(4) Facilities are proper if they are −
  (a) of a quantity sufficient to meet the reasonable needs of individuals, and
  (b) of a quality adequate to meet those needs.

(5) In discharging the duty under subsection (1) the Chief Executive must −
  (a) take account of the places where facilities are provided, the character of facilities and the way they are equipped;
  (b) take account of the different abilities and aptitudes of different persons;
  (c) take account of the education and training required in different sectors of employment for employees and potential employees;
  (d) act with a view to encouraging diversity of education and training available to individuals;
  (e) act with a view to increasing opportunities for individuals to exercise choice;
  (f) make the best use of the Chief Executive's resources.

(6) For the purposes of this section −
  "education" includes full-time and part-time education;
  "training" includes full-time and part-time training.

88 Learning aims for persons aged 19 or over: payment of tuition fees

(1) Functions under this Part must be exercised by the Chief Executive so as to secure that a course of study for a qualification to which paragraph 1 of Schedule 5 applies is free to a person falling within subsection (2) if it is

Apprenticeships, Skills, Children and Learning Act 2009 (c. 22)
Part 4 – *The Chief Executive of Skills Funding*
Chapter 1 – *Establishment and main duties*

2233

provided for the person by virtue of facilities whose provision is secured under section 87.

(2) A person falls within this subsection if, at the time of starting the course in question, the person—

    (a) is aged 19 or over,

    (b) does not have the qualification in question or one (including one awarded by a person outside England) which appears to the Chief Executive to be at a comparable or higher level, and

    (c) satisfies such conditions as may be specified in regulations.

(3) Functions under this Part must be exercised by the Chief Executive so as to secure that a course of study for a qualification to which paragraph 2 of Schedule 5 applies is free to a person falling within subsection (4) if it is provided for the person by virtue of facilities whose provision is secured under section 86.

(4) A person falls within this subsection if, at the time of starting the course in question, the person—

    (a) is aged at least 19 but less than 25,

    (b) does not have the qualification in question or one (including one awarded by a person outside England) which appears to the Chief Executive to be at a comparable or higher level, and

    (c) satisfies such conditions as may be specified in regulations.

(5) The Secretary of State may by order—

    (a) amend subsection (2)(a) by substituting a different age for the age for the time being referred to;

    (b) amend subsection (4)(a) by substituting a different age for either of the ages for the time being referred to.

(6) For the purposes of this section, a course is free to a person if no tuition fees in respect of the provision of the course for the person are payable by a person other than—

    (a) the Chief Executive, or

    (b) a body specified by order by the Secretary of State for the purposes of this section.

(7) In subsection (6) "tuition fees", in relation to a course, means—

    (a) the fees charged in respect of the course by the person providing it, and

    (b) such fees in respect of other matters relating to the course (such as undergoing a preliminary assessment or sitting an examination) as may be specified in regulations.

89 Sections 87 and 88: supplementary

(1) Regulations may make provision as to circumstances in which—

    (a) despite having a specified qualification, a person is to be treated for the purposes of section 87 or 88 as not having that qualification;

    (b) despite not having a specified qualification, a person is to be treated for any of those purposes as having that qualification.

(2) A condition specified in regulations under section 87 or 88 may, in particular, relate to—

    (a) the possession, or lack, of a specified qualification;

2234   *Apprenticeships, Skills, Children and Learning Act 2009 (c. 22)*
                                                    Part 4 — The Chief Executive of Skills Funding
                                                    Chapter 1 — Establishment and main duties

      (b)   the completion of, or failure to complete, a course for a specified qualification.

(3)   A reference in subsection (1) or (2) to a specified qualification is to a qualification specified, or of a description specified, in the regulations.

(4)   Regulations under this section, or under section 87 or 88, may confer a function (which may relate to the administration of an assessment and may include the exercise of a discretion) on a person specified, or of a description specified, in the regulations.

(5)   Nothing in section 87 or 88 applies to the provision of facilities, or to courses of study, for persons subject to adult detention.

(6)   Part 2 of Schedule 5 makes further provision for the purposes of sections 87 and 88.

90   Encouragement of education and training for persons aged 19 or over and others subject to adult detention

(1)   The Chief Executive must—
      (a)   encourage participation by persons within section 86(1)(a) and (b) in education and training within the Chief Executive's remit;
      (b)   encourage employers to participate in the provision of education and training within the Chief Executive's remit for persons within section 86(1)(a);
      (c)   encourage employers to contribute to the costs of education and training within the Chief Executive's remit for such persons.

(2)   For the purposes of subsection (1)(b), participating in the provision of training includes participating by entering into—
      (a)   an apprenticeship agreement, or
      (b)   any other contract of employment in connection with which training is provided.

The apprenticeship offer

91   Duty to secure availability of apprenticeship places

(1)   The Chief Executive must exercise the functions of the office in such a way as to secure that apprenticeship places are available in sufficient number and variety for there to be suitable apprenticeship places available for all persons—
      (a)   who have elected under section 92 for the apprenticeship offer, and
      (b)   for whom places have not already been made available under the apprenticeship offer.

(2)   For the purposes of subsection (1), an apprenticeship place is suitable for a person if it is—
      (a)   in one of the two available sectors chosen by the person under section 92,
      (b)   at the appropriate level, and
      (c)   within the person's reasonable travel area.

Apprenticeships, Skills, Children and Learning Act 2009 (c. 22)
Part 4 — The Chief Executive of Skills Funding
Chapter 1 — Establishment and main duties

2235

(3) Regulations may make provision as to circumstances in which an apprenticeship place is to be treated as having been, or as not having been, made available for a person under the apprenticeship offer.

(4) In securing the provision of facilities for apprenticeship training for the purpose of meeting the requirement imposed by subsection (1) the Chief Executive must make the best use of the Chief Executive's resources.

92 Election for apprenticeship offer

(1) A person who—
   (a) is within subsection (2), (3) or (4), and
   (b) satisfies the apprenticeship offer requirements at level 2 or level 3 (see section 95),
   is entitled to elect for the apprenticeship offer at that level.

(2) A person within this subsection is one who—
   (a) is over compulsory school age, and
   (b) is aged under 19.

(3) A person within this subsection is one who is not within subsection (2) and—
   (a) is a person aged under 21 towards whom a local authority in England has the duties provided for in section 23C of the Children Act 1989 (c. 41) (continuing functions in respect of certain formerly looked after children), or
   (b) is a person to whom section 23CA of that Act applies, in relation to whom a local authority in England is the responsible local authority (within the meaning of that section).

(4) A person within this subsection is one who—
   (a) is not within subsection (2), and
   (b) is of a prescribed description.

(5) If regulations under subsection (4)(b) describe a person by reference to an age or an age range, the age, or the upper age of the age range, must be less than 25.

(6) A person who elects for the apprenticeship offer must choose two available sectors.

(7) A person who elects for the apprenticeship offer and satisfies the apprenticeship offer requirements both at level 2 and at level 3 must choose one of those levels.

(8) The Secretary of State may make arrangements for the making of elections and choices of apprenticeship sectors and levels under this section.

(9) The Secretary of State may delegate the functions conferred by subsection (8) (and may do so on terms which allow sub-delegation).

93 Meaning of "apprenticeship place"

(1) For the purposes of section 91, "apprenticeship place" means a place consisting of arrangements which—
   (a) are arrangements for—
      (i) employment, and
      (ii) training or study,

2236   *Apprenticeships, Skills, Children and Learning Act 2009 (c. 22)*
Part 4 – The Chief Executive of Skills Funding
Chapter 1 – Establishment and main duties

leading to the issue of an apprenticeship certificate under section 3 relating to an apprenticeship framework ("the related framework"), and

(b)   satisfy subsection (2).

(2)   The arrangements must relate to each of the standard English completion conditions specified in section 1(3) in relation to the related framework and must include, in particular —

(a)   arrangements for employment under an apprenticeship agreement in connection with the related framework,

(b)   arrangements for a course, or courses, of training leading to the competencies qualification identified in the related framework, to be provided by —

(i)   a college or other institution, or

(ii)   the employer under the apprenticeship agreement, and

(c)   in relation to each other qualification specified in the related framework, arrangements for study or training, whether provided by means of a course or otherwise.

(3)   A reference to training in subsection (2)(b) or (c) does not include a reference to training provided by an employer to a person while the person is carrying out work for the employer under an apprenticeship agreement.

94   Suitability and availability of apprenticeship places: further provision

(1)   This section has effect for the purposes of section 91.

(2)   An apprenticeship place is in the apprenticeship sector to which the related framework (within the meaning of section 93(1)) relates.

(3)   An apprenticeship place is at the appropriate level —

(a)   in the case of a person who satisfies the apprenticeship offer requirements both at level 2 and at level 3, if the related framework is at the level chosen by the person under section 92,

(b)   in the case of any other person who satisfies the apprenticeship offer requirements at level 2, if the related framework is at level 2, and

(c)   in the case of any other person who satisfies the apprenticeship offer requirements at level 3, if the related framework is at level 3.

(4)   An apprenticeship place is within a person's reasonable travel area if the following are within that area —

(a)   the place, or principal place, at which the person would be required to work under the apprenticeship agreement to which the arrangements mentioned in section 93(2)(a) relate, and

(b)   the place at which tuition or training would be provided under any course of study or training to which the arrangements mentioned in section 93(2)(b) or (c) relate.

(5)   In subsection (4), "reasonable travel area", in relation to a person, means —

(a)   the area specified under subsection (6) in which the person lives, and

(b)   any other area within which it is reasonable for the person's place of work, training or study to be located.

Apprenticeships, Skills, Children and Learning Act 2009 (c. 22)
Part 4 — The Chief Executive of Skills Funding
Chapter 1 — Establishment and main duties

2237

(6) The Secretary of State must specify areas into which England is to be divided for the purposes of subsection (5)(a), and must publish any specification or revised specification under this subsection.

(7) An apprenticeship place is not available to a person if the person is not eligible for appointment to the employment to which the arrangements mentioned in section 93(2)(a) relate because of failure to meet any published criterion.

(8) In subsection (7), "published criterion" includes any requirement for employment of the kind in question—

    (a) which is imposed by the employer, and

    (b) about which information is available to persons proposing to apply for such employment.

95 Apprenticeship offer requirements

(1) In order to satisfy the apprenticeship offer requirements at level 2 a person must—

    (a) hold—

        (i) a specified full level 1 qualification, and

        (ii) specified qualifications, at level 1 or above, in English and mathematics, and

    (b) not hold an apprenticeship certificate at level 2 or above,

and must be available for employment under an apprenticeship agreement.

(2) In order to satisfy the apprenticeship offer requirements at level 3 a person must—

    (a) hold—

        (i) a specified full level 2 qualification, and

        (ii) specified qualifications, at level 2, in English and mathematics, and

    (b) not hold an apprenticeship certificate at level 3 or above,

and must be available for employment under an apprenticeship agreement.

(3) A reference in this section to any specified qualification includes a reference to a qualification (including one awarded by a person outside England) which appears to the Chief Executive to be at a comparable or higher level.

(4) In this section "apprenticeship certificate" means an apprenticeship certificate issued under section 3 or 4; and a reference in this section to an apprenticeship certificate at any level includes a reference to a certificate or other evidence (including a certificate awarded or evidence provided by a person outside England) which appears to the Chief Executive to be evidence of experience and attainment at a comparable or higher level.

(5) Regulations may make provision as to circumstances in which a person who appears to the Chief Executive to have a learning difficulty is to be treated as meeting the requirements set out in subsection (1)(a) or (2)(a).

(6) Subsections (6) and (7) of section 15ZA of the Education Act 1996 (c. 56) (meaning of learning difficulty) apply for the purposes of subsection (5) of this section as they apply for the purposes of that section.

(7) Regulations may make provision as to circumstances in which a person is to be treated as being available, or not being available, for employment under an apprenticeship agreement.

2238

Apprenticeships, Skills, Children and Learning Act 2009 (c. 22)
Part 4 — The Chief Executive of Skills Funding
Chapter 1 — Establishment and main duties

96   Apprenticeship offer requirements: interpretation

(1)   This section has effect for the purposes of section 95.

(2)   A reference to a specified qualification is to a regulated qualification which is specified, or which is of a description specified, in regulations.

(3)   "Full level 1 qualification" means a qualification at the level of attainment (in terms of breadth and depth) which, in the opinion of the Secretary of State, is demonstrated by the General Certificate of Secondary Education in five subjects.

(4)   A reference to a qualification in English or mathematics at level 1 is to a qualification in that subject at the level of attainment (in terms of depth) which, in the opinion of the Secretary of State, is demonstrated by the General Certificate of Secondary Education in that subject.

(5)   "Full level 2 qualification" means a qualification at the level of attainment (in terms of breadth and depth) which, in the opinion of the Secretary of State, is demonstrated by the General Certificate of Secondary Education in five subjects, each at Grade C or above.

(6)   A reference to a qualification in English or mathematics at level 2 is to a qualification in that subject at the level of attainment (in terms of depth) which, in the opinion of the Secretary of State, is demonstrated by the General Certificate of Secondary Education in that subject at Grade C or above.

(7)   In forming an opinion for the purposes of any of subsections (3) to (6), the Secretary of State must consult the Office of Qualifications and Examinations Regulation.

(8)   In subsection (2), "regulated qualification" has the meaning given by section 130.

(9)   The Secretary of State may, by order, amend this section so as to substitute a different qualification for a qualification for the time being referred to in subsection (3), (4), (5) or (6).

(10)   The Secretary of State must consult the Office of Qualifications and Examinations Regulation before exercising the power conferred by subsection (9).

97   Suspension of offer

(1)   The Secretary of State may by order suspend the apprenticeship offer in an area specified in the order, for a period so specified —
    (a)   in relation to a particular apprenticeship sector, or
    (b)   in relation to a particular apprenticeship sector at a particular level.

(2)   The period specified in an order under subsection (1) must not exceed 2 years.

(3)   An apprenticeship sector is an available sector, in relation to a person's election under section 92 for the apprenticeship offer at a particular level, unless the person lives in an area in which the apprenticeship offer is suspended in relation to that sector at that level.

Apprenticeships, Skills, Children and Learning Act 2009 (c. 22)
Part 4 — The Chief Executive of Skills Funding
Chapter 1 — Establishment and main duties

2239

98 Power to amend apprenticeship offer

The Secretary of State may by order amend —
  (a) the age for the time being specified in section 92(2)(b);
  (b) any of the requirements specified in section 95.

99 Apprenticeship offer: interpretation

(1) In sections 91 to 98 —
   "apprenticeship agreement" has the meaning given by section 32(1);
   "apprenticeship framework" has the meaning given by section 12;
   "apprenticeship sector" means a sector specified under section 38;
   "available sector" has the meaning given by section 97.

(2) References in sections 91 to 98 to —
   (a) the level of an apprenticeship framework, or
   (b) the apprenticeship sector to which an apprenticeship framework relates,
   are to be read in accordance with section 12(5).

CHAPTER 2

OTHER FUNCTIONS

Funding

100 Provision of financial resources

(1) The Chief Executive may secure the provision of financial resources to —
   (a) persons providing or proposing to provide education or training within the Chief Executive's remit;
   (b) persons providing or proposing to provide goods or services in connection with the provision by others of such education or training;
   (c) persons receiving or proposing to receive such education or training;
   (d) persons aged 18 receiving or proposing to receive education or training;
   (e) persons making loans to others receiving or proposing to receive education or training;
   (f) persons providing or proposing to provide courses falling within paragraph 1(g) or (h) of Schedule 6 to the Education Reform Act 1988 (c. 40) (courses in preparation for professional examinations at a higher level or providing education at a higher level);
   (g) persons undertaking or proposing to undertake research relating to education or training;
   (h) persons carrying out means tests under arrangements made under section 103;
   (i) persons providing or proposing to provide services relating to finding apprenticeship places under section 104;
   (j) persons providing or proposing to provide information, advice or guidance about education or training or connected matters (including employment).

(2) In performing the functions under this section the Chief Executive must make the best use of the Chief Executive's resources.

(3) The Chief Executive may secure the provision of financial resources under subsection (1) –

    (a) by providing the resources;

    (b) by making arrangements for the provision of resources by another person;

    (c) by making arrangements for the provision of resources by persons jointly (whether or not including the Chief Executive).

(4) The Chief Executive may under subsection (1)(c) secure the provision of financial resources by reference to –

    (a) any fees or charges payable by the person receiving or proposing to receive the education or training, or

    (b) any other matter (such as transport or childcare).

101 Financial resources: conditions

(1) Financial resources provided by the Chief Executive may be provided subject to conditions.

(2) The conditions may include –

    (a) information conditions;

    (b) operational conditions;

    (c) repayment conditions.

(3) Information conditions are conditions which –

    (a) require the Chief Executive, or a person designated by the Chief Executive, to be given access to a person's accounts and documents and to be given rights in relation to a person's computers and associated apparatus and material, or

    (b) require a person to whom financial resources are provided to give to the Chief Executive such information as the Chief Executive may request for the purpose of carrying out the functions of the office.

(4) Operational conditions are conditions which require a person providing or proposing to provide education or training ("the provider") to make arrangements providing for all or any of the matters mentioned in subsection (5).

(5) The matters are the following –

    (a) the charging of fees by the provider by reference to specified criteria;

    (b) the making of awards by the provider by reference to specified criteria;

    (c) the recovery by the provider of amounts from persons receiving education or training or from employers (or from both);

    (d) the determination of amounts by reference to specified criteria where provision is made under paragraph (c);

    (e) the operation of specified exemptions where provision is made under paragraph (c);

    (f) the making by the provider of provision specified in a report of an assessment under section 139A or 140 of the Learning and Skills Act 2000 (c. 21) (assessments relating to learning difficulties).

(6) Repayment conditions are conditions which –

Apprenticeships, Skills, Children and Learning Act 2009 (c. 22)
Part 4 — The Chief Executive of Skills Funding
Chapter 2 — Other functions

2241

    (a)   enable the Chief Executive to require the repayment (in whole or part) of sums paid by the Chief Executive if any of the conditions subject to which the sums were paid is not complied with;

    (b)   require the payment of interest in respect of any period in which a sum due to the Chief Executive in accordance with any condition is unpaid.

102 Performance assessments

(1)   The Chief Executive may adopt or develop schemes for the assessment of the performance of persons in providing education or training within the Chief Executive's remit.

(2)   The Chief Executive may take the assessments into account in deciding how to exercise the powers under section 100.

103 Means tests

(1)   The Chief Executive may —
    (a)   carry out means tests;
    (b)   arrange for other persons to carry out means tests.

(2)   The Chief Executive may take the results of the tests into account in exercising the power under section 100(1)(c), (d) or (e).

Apprenticeships: general

104 Assistance and support in relation to apprenticeship places

(1)   The Chief Executive —
    (a)   must provide or secure the provision of such services as the Chief Executive considers appropriate for assisting persons to find apprenticeship places, and
    (b)   may provide or secure the provision of other services for encouraging, enabling or assisting the effective participation of persons in employment and training provided for by apprenticeship places.

(2)   The services provided by virtue of subsection (1)(a) may, in particular, be or include —
    (a)   services provided by means of the publication, whether electronically or otherwise, of information, advice and guidance;
    (b)   facilities for enabling employers to advertise apprenticeship places.

(3)   In this section, "apprenticeship place" has the meaning given by section 93.

105 Promoting progression from level 2 to level 3 apprenticeships

(1)   The Chief Executive must promote the desirability of persons within subsection (2) undertaking apprenticeship training at level 3.

(2)   The persons are those who —
    (a)   are undertaking apprenticeship training at level 2,
    (b)   have completed an English apprenticeship in relation to an apprenticeship framework at level 2, or
    (c)   hold an apprenticeship certificate at level 2.

(3) For the purposes of this section apprenticeship training is at a particular level if it might reasonably be expected to lead to the issue of an apprenticeship certificate at that level.

(4) The following provisions of Chapter 1 of Part 1 apply for the purposes of this section—

     section 1 (meaning of "completing an English apprenticeship");

     section 12 (meaning of apprenticeship framework and level of an apprenticeship framework).

(5) Section 95(4) (meaning of apprenticeship certificate and level of an apprenticeship certificate) applies for the purposes of this section.

106   Advice and assistance in relation to apprenticeships

The Chief Executive must, on request, provide the Secretary of State with advice and assistance in relation to the exercise of the Secretary of State's functions under Chapter 1 of Part 1.

Provision of services and assistance

107   Provision of services

(1) The Chief Executive may make arrangements with a permitted recipient for the provision by the Chief Executive of services that are required by the permitted recipient in connection with the exercise of the recipient's functions relating to education or training.

(2) The services that may be provided under arrangements made under subsection (1) include—

     (a) providing accommodation and other facilities to a permitted recipient or managing such facilities on behalf of a permitted recipient;

     (b) procuring, or assisting in procuring, goods and services for use by a permitted recipient.

(3) The terms and conditions upon which the arrangements are made may include provision for making payments to the Chief Executive in respect of expenditure incurred by the Chief Executive in performing any function under the arrangements.

(4) In this section "permitted recipient" means—

     (a) the Secretary of State;

     (b) the Welsh Ministers;

     (c) the Scottish Ministers;

     (d) a Northern Ireland department;

     (e) the Young People's Learning Agency for England;

     (f) a person, wholly or partly funded from public funds, who has functions relating to education or training;

     (g) any other person specified, or of a description specified, by order made by the appropriate national authority for the purposes of this section.

(5) Before making arrangements under which it may provide services to a permitted recipient who falls within any of paragraphs (b) to (g) of subsection (4) in connection with the exercise of the recipient's functions relating to

Apprenticeships, Skills, Children and Learning Act 2009 (c. 22)
Part 4 — The Chief Executive of Skills Funding
Chapter 2 — Other functions

2243

education or training provided in Wales, Scotland or Northern Ireland, the Chief Executive must obtain the consent of the Secretary of State.

(6) Before making arrangements under which it may provide services to a permitted recipient who falls within paragraph (a), (e), (f) or (g) of subsection (4) in connection with the exercise of the recipient's functions relating to education or training provided in Wales, Scotland or Northern Ireland, the Chief Executive must obtain —

    (a) in relation to education or training provided in Wales, the consent of the Welsh Ministers;

    (b) in relation to education or training provided in Scotland, the consent of the Scottish Ministers;

    (c) in relation to education or training provided in Northern Ireland, the consent of the Minister for Employment and Learning in Northern Ireland.

(7) Consent may be given under subsection (5) or (6) in relation to particular arrangements or arrangements of a particular description.

(8) "The appropriate national authority" means —

    (a) in relation to a person exercising functions relating only to education or training provided in Wales, the Welsh Ministers;

    (b) in relation to a person exercising functions relating only to education or training provided in Scotland, the Scottish Ministers;

    (c) in relation to a person exercising functions relating only to education or training provided in Northern Ireland, the Department for Employment and Learning in Northern Ireland;

    (d) in any other case, the Secretary of State.

108 Assistance with respect to employment and training

(1) The Chief Executive may take part in arrangements made by the Secretary of State, the Welsh Ministers or the Scottish Ministers under section 2 of the Employment and Training Act 1973 (c. 50) (arrangements for assisting persons to select, train for, obtain and retain employment).

(2) Before making such arrangements in relation to Wales or Scotland in which the Chief Executive is to take part, the Secretary of State must obtain the consent of the Welsh Ministers or (as the case may be) the Scottish Ministers to the arrangements.

(3) Before making such arrangements in which the Chief Executive is to take part, the Welsh Ministers or the Scottish Ministers must obtain the consent of the Secretary of State to the arrangements.

109 Assistance with respect to employment and training: Northern Ireland

(1) The Chief Executive may take part in any arrangements made by the Department for Employment and Learning in Northern Ireland under section 1 of the Employment and Training Act (Northern Ireland) 1950 (c. 29 (N.I.)) (arrangements for assisting persons to select, train for, obtain and retain employment).

(2) Before making such arrangements in which the Chief Executive is to take part, the Department must obtain the consent of the Secretary of State to the arrangements.

Miscellaneous

110   Research, information and advice

(1)   The Chief Executive may carry out programmes of research and development connected with any matter relevant to the functions of the office.

(2)   If requested to do so by the Secretary of State, the Chief Executive must provide the Secretary of State with information or advice on such matters relating to any of the functions of the office as may be specified in the request.

(3)   The Chief Executive may provide the Secretary of State with other information or advice on any matter in relation to which the Chief Executive has a function.

(4)   The Chief Executive may provide any person designated by the Secretary of State with information about any matter in relation to which the Chief Executive has a function.

(5)   The Chief Executive must establish systems for collecting information designed to secure that decisions of the Chief Executive with regard to education and training are made on a sound basis.

(6)   The Chief Executive may secure the provision of facilities and services for providing information, advice or guidance about education or training or connected matters (including employment).

111   Power to confer supplementary functions on Chief Executive

(1)   The Secretary of State may by order confer supplementary functions on the Chief Executive.

(2)   A supplementary function is a function which is —
     (a)   exercisable in connection with functions of the Secretary of State, and
     (b)   relevant to the provision of facilities for education or training within the Chief Executive's remit.

CHAPTER 3

CHIEF EXECUTIVE'S FUNCTIONS: SUPPLEMENTARY

Strategies

112   Strategies for functions of Chief Executive

(1)   The Secretary of State may by order specify an area in England as an area for which a body specified in the order ("a specified body") may formulate and keep under review a strategy setting out how such functions of the Chief Executive as are specified in the order are to be carried out in relation to the area.

(2)   An order under subsection (1) may specify an area comprising the whole of England.

(3)   An order under subsection (1) may not specify an area in England consisting only of Greater London or a part of Greater London.

Apprenticeships, Skills, Children and Learning Act 2009 (c. 22)
Part 4 – The Chief Executive of Skills Funding
Chapter 3 – Chief Executive's functions: supplementary

2245

(4) The Secretary of State may give directions and guidance to a specified body in relation to the formulation and review of its strategy, in particular in relation to —

    (a) the form and content of the strategy;

    (b) the updating of the strategy;

    (c) the steps to be taken when the body is formulating or reviewing the strategy;

    (d) the matters to which the body is to have regard when formulating or reviewing the strategy;

    (e) the consultation to be carried out when the body is formulating or reviewing the strategy.

(5) A specified body must —

    (a) comply with any directions given to it under subsection (4), and

    (b) have regard to any guidance given to it under that subsection.

(6) The Chief Executive may pay to a specified body such sums as appear to the Chief Executive appropriate for enabling the body to meet costs and expenses incurred, or to be incurred, by it in formulating its strategy or keeping it under review.

113 Strategy for functions of Chief Executive: Greater London

(1) Regulations must provide for the establishment of a body ("the London body") for the purposes of this section.

(2) The London body must —

    (a) formulate a strategy setting out how specified functions of the Chief Executive are to be carried out in Greater London, and

    (b) keep it under review.

(3) Specified functions are functions of the Chief Executive specified for the purposes of this section by order of the Secretary of State.

(4) The Secretary of State may give directions and guidance to the London body in relation to the formulation and review of its strategy, in particular in relation to —

    (a) the form and content of the strategy;

    (b) the updating of the strategy;

    (c) the steps to be taken when the body is formulating or reviewing the strategy;

    (d) the matters to which the body is to have regard when formulating or reviewing the strategy;

    (e) the consultation to be carried out when the body is formulating or reviewing the strategy.

(5) The London body must —

    (a) comply with any directions given to it under subsection (4), and

    (b) have regard to any guidance given to it under that subsection.

(6) Where the London body formulates a strategy under this section, or in consequence of a review of the strategy modifies it, the body must publish the strategy or modified strategy in such manner as it thinks fit.

(7) Regulations under this section must include —

2246
Apprenticeships, Skills, Children and Learning Act 2009 (c. 22)
Part 4 — The Chief Executive of Skills Funding
Chapter 3 — Chief Executive's functions: supplementary

(a) provision for the London body to consist of the Mayor of London and such other persons as are appointed by the Mayor in accordance with the regulations;

(b) provision for the Mayor to be the chairman of the body.

(8) The Chief Executive may pay to the London body such sums as appear to the Chief Executive appropriate for enabling the body to meet costs and expenses incurred, or to be incurred, by it in formulating its strategy or keeping it under review.

(9) The Chief Executive may pay to the Greater London Authority such sums as appear to the Chief Executive appropriate for enabling the Authority to meet costs and expenses incurred, or to be incurred, by the Mayor in connection with the exercise of functions conferred on him by regulations under this section or as chairman of the London body.

114 Strategies: duty of Chief Executive

(1) The Chief Executive must carry out any function to which a strategy under section 112 or 113 relates in accordance with that strategy.

(2) Subsection (1) is subject to the following provisions of this section.

(3) The Chief Executive may not carry out a function in accordance with such a strategy if doing so would entail failing to comply with a duty imposed on the Chief Executive by any provision made by or under any Act (other than subsection (1)).

(4) If provision in a strategy under section 112 conflicts with provision in another strategy under section 112 or 113, the Chief Executive may disregard such conflicting provision in one of the strategies or in both of them.

(5) The Chief Executive may disregard a strategy under section 112 or 113 if the body whose strategy it is, in formulating or reviewing the strategy —

(a) failed to comply with directions given under section 112(4) or (as the case may be) section 113(4), or

(b) failed to have regard to guidance given under section 112(4) or (as the case may be) section 113(4).

(6) Nothing in subsection (1) requires the Chief Executive to carry out any functions of the office in a manner that the Chief Executive is satisfied —

(a) would be unreasonable, or

(b) might give rise to disproportionate expenditure.

(7) If the Chief Executive proposes not to carry out, or does not carry out, a function to which a strategy under section 112 or 113 relates in accordance with the strategy —

(a) the Chief Executive must refer the matter to the Secretary of State;

(b) the body whose strategy it is may refer the matter to the Secretary of State.

(8) On a reference under subsection (7) the Secretary of State may give such direction to the Chief Executive as the Secretary of State thinks fit as to the carrying out of the function.

Apprenticeships, Skills, Children and Learning Act 2009 (c. 22)
Part 4 — *The Chief Executive of Skills Funding*
Chapter 3 — *Chief Executive's functions: supplementary*

2247

Other

115 Persons with learning difficulties

(1) The Chief Executive must, in performing the functions of the office, have regard to the needs of persons with learning difficulties to whom this section applies.

(2) This section applies to—
   (a) persons who are aged 19 or over, other than persons aged under 25 who are subject to learning difficulty assessment, and
   (b) persons who are subject to adult detention.

(3) For the purposes of this section, a person has a learning difficulty if—
   (a) the person has a significantly greater difficulty in learning than the majority of persons of the same age, or
   (b) the person has a disability which either prevents or hinders the person from making use of facilities of a kind generally provided by institutions providing education or training falling within section 86(1)(a), (b) or (c).

(4) But a person is not to be taken to have a learning difficulty solely because the language (or form of language) in which the person is or will be taught is different from a language (or form of language) which has at any time been spoken in the person's home.

116 Persons subject to adult detention

The Chief Executive must, in performing the functions of the office, have regard to the needs of persons subject to adult detention.

117 Use of information by Chief Executive

The Chief Executive must, in performing the functions of the office, have regard to information supplied to the Chief Executive by any person designated for the purposes of this section by the Secretary of State.

118 Guidance

(1) The Chief Executive must, in performing the functions of the office, have regard to any guidance given by the Secretary of State.

(2) Guidance under this section may include in particular guidance about—
   (a) consultation with persons mentioned in subsection (3) in connection with the taking of decisions which affect such persons, and
   (b) taking advice from such persons or descriptions of persons as may be specified in the guidance.

(3) The persons are—
   (a) persons receiving or proposing to receive education or training within the Chief Executive's remit,
   (b) employers, or
   (c) such other persons or descriptions of persons as may be specified in the guidance.

2248   *Apprenticeships, Skills, Children and Learning Act 2009 (c. 22)*
Part 4 — The Chief Executive of Skills Funding
Chapter 3 — Chief Executive's functions: supplementary

(4)   Guidance under this section about consultation with persons falling within subsection (3)(a) must provide for the views of such persons to be considered in the light of their age and understanding.

119   Directions: funding of qualifications

(1)   The Secretary of State may direct the Chief Executive that financial resources provided by the Chief Executive to a relevant institution or employer must be provided subject to a condition that the institution or employer does not make an excluded payment which can reasonably be said to consist of or come from financial resources received from the Chief Executive.

(2)   A direction under subsection (1) relating to a qualification may be made after any course of training or education leading to the qualification has begun.

(3)   In this section—

"an excluded payment" is a payment which —

(a)   is in respect of a qualification to which Part 7 applies (see section 130) that is specified or of a description specified in the direction, and

(b)   is made to the person who awards that qualification;

"relevant institution or employer" means an institution or employer who provides or is proposing to provide a course of training or education for persons who are aged 19 or over which leads to a qualification to which Part 7 applies.

120   Other directions relating to functions of the office

(1)   The Secretary of State may give directions to the Chief Executive containing—

(a)   objectives which the Chief Executive should achieve in carrying out the functions of the office, and

(b)   time limits within which the Chief Executive should achieve the objectives.

(2)   The Secretary of State may give to the Chief Executive other directions as to the performance of any of the functions of the office if the Secretary of State is satisfied that the Chief Executive—

(a)   has failed to discharge a duty imposed by or under any Act, or

(b)   has acted or is proposing to act unreasonably with respect to the performance of any function conferred by or under any Act.

(3)   The Secretary of State may give directions under subsection (2) despite any provision made by or under any Act making the performance of a function dependent on the Chief Executive's opinion.

(4)   Directions given under this section with respect to functions conferred on the Chief Executive by or under this Part may not concern the provision of financial resources to a particular person or persons.

Apprenticeships, Skills, Children and Learning Act 2009 (c. 22)
Part 4 – The Chief Executive of Skills Funding
Chapter 4 – General

2249

CHAPTER 4

GENERAL

121   Interpretation of Part

(1)   In this Part—

"apprenticeship agreement" has the meaning given by section 32(1);

"apprenticeship training" has the meaning given by section 83;

"functions of the office" means functions of the Chief Executive conferred by or under any Act;

"organised leisure-time occupation" has the meaning given by section 86.

(2)   In this Part a reference to education within the Chief Executive's remit is a reference to—

(a)   education falling within section 86(1)(a) or (b), and

(b)   organised leisure-time occupation in connection with such education.

(3)   In this Part a reference to training within the Chief Executive's remit is a reference to—

(a)   training falling within section 83(1),

(b)   training falling within section 86(1)(c), and

(c)   organised leisure-time occupation in connection with training falling within section 86(1)(c).

(4)   For the purposes of this Part a person is subject to adult detention if the person is subject to a detention order and—

(a)   aged 19 or over, or

(b)   aged under 19 and detained in—

(i)   a young offender institution, or part of such an institution, that is used wholly or mainly for the detention of persons aged 18 and over, or

(ii)   a prison.

PART 5

PARTS 2 TO 4: SUPPLEMENTARY

Information

122   Sharing of information for education and training purposes

(1)   A person within subsection (3) may provide information to another person within that subsection, or a person within subsection (4), for the purpose of enabling or facilitating the exercise of any relevant function.

(2)   A person within subsection (4) may provide information to a person within subsection (3) for the purpose of enabling or facilitating the exercise of any relevant function.

(3)   The persons within this subsection are—

(a)   the Chief Executive;

(b)   the Young People's Learning Agency for England;

(c)   a designated person;

(d)   a member of the Chief Executive's staff;

(e)   a member of staff of a designated person;

(f)   a person providing services to any person within paragraphs (a) to (c).

(4)   The persons within this subsection are—

     (a)   a local education authority in England;

     (b)   a person providing services to a local education authority in England in its capacity as such.

(5)   In subsections (1) and (2), "relevant function" means—

     (a)   any function of the Chief Executive,

     (b)   any function of the Young People's Learning Agency for England, or

     (c)   any function conferred on a local education authority in England in its capacity as such,

other than a function under this section.

(6)   In this section—

"the Chief Executive" means the Chief Executive of Skills Funding;

"designated person" means a person by whom any function of the Chief Executive is exercisable by virtue of section 82(1);

"member of staff of a designated person" means a person—

     (a)   appointed by a designated person to assist the designated person in connection with the performance of any function exercisable by the designated person by virtue of section 82(1), or

     (b)   exercising any function of the Chief Executive by virtue of section 82(4);

"member of the Chief Executive's staff" means—

     (a)   a member of the Chief Executive's staff appointed by the Chief Executive under paragraph 3 of Schedule 4, or

     (b)   a member of staff provided to the Chief Executive by the Secretary of State under arrangements under paragraph 5 of that Schedule.

(7)   Nothing in this section—

     (a)   affects any power to disclose information that exists apart from this section, or

     (b)   authorises the disclosure of any information in contravention of any provision made by or under any Act which prevents disclosure of the information.

The Learning and Skills Council for England

123   Dissolution of the Learning and Skills Council for England

(1)   The Learning and Skills Council for England ceases to exist on the day on which this section comes into force.

(2)   Schedule 6 contains minor and consequential amendments in relation to the dissolution of the Learning and Skills Council for England.

124 Dissolution of the Learning and Skills Council: transfer schemes

Schedule 7 contains provision about schemes for the transfer of staff, property, rights and liabilities from the Learning and Skills Council for England to other persons.

PART 6

THE SIXTH FORM COLLEGE SECTOR

125 Sixth form college sector

Schedule 8 makes provision about the sixth form college sector.

126 Removal of power to establish sixth form schools

(1) In section 16 of the Education Act 1996 (c. 56) (power to establish etc. primary and secondary schools) after subsection (3) insert—

"(3A) A local education authority in England may not under subsection (1) establish a school which is principally concerned with the provision of full-time education suitable to the requirements of pupils who are over compulsory school age but under 19."

(2) The Education and Inspections Act 2006 (c. 40) is amended as follows.

(3) In section 7 (invitation for proposals for establishment of new schools) after subsection (5) insert—

"(5A) A local education authority may not publish under this section proposals within subsection (5)(b) for the establishment of a school providing education suitable only to the requirements of persons above compulsory school age."

(4) In section 10 (publication of proposals with consent of Secretary of State) in subsection (1)(a) after "school" insert ", other than one providing education suitable only to the requirements of persons above compulsory school age".

(5) In section 11 (publication of proposals to establish maintained schools: special cases) omit subsections (1)(b) and (2)(a).

PART 7

THE OFFICE OF QUALIFICATIONS AND EXAMINATIONS REGULATION

CHAPTER 1

ESTABLISHMENT, OBJECTIVES AND GENERAL DUTIES

Establishment

127 The Office of Qualifications and Examinations Regulation

(1) There is to be a body corporate known as the Office of Qualifications and Examinations Regulation.

(2) In this Part that body is referred to as "Ofqual".

2252   *Apprenticeships, Skills, Children and Learning Act 2009 (c. 22)*
Part 7 – The Office of Qualifications and Examinations Regulation
Chapter 1 – Establishment, objectives and general duties

(3)   Schedule 9 makes further provision about Ofqual.

Objectives and general duties

128   Objectives

(1)   Ofqual's objectives are—
    (a)   the qualifications standards objective,
    (b)   the assessments standards objective,
    (c)   the public confidence objective,
    (d)   the awareness objective, and
    (e)   the efficiency objective.

(2)   The qualifications standards objective is to secure that regulated qualifications—
    (a)   give a reliable indication of knowledge, skills and understanding, and
    (b)   indicate a consistent level of attainment (including over time) between comparable regulated qualifications.

(3)   The assessments standards objective is to promote the development and implementation of regulated assessment arrangements which—
    (a)   give a reliable indication of achievement, and
    (b)   indicate a consistent level of attainment (including over time) between comparable assessments.

(4)   The public confidence objective is to promote public confidence in regulated qualifications and regulated assessment arrangements.

(5)   The awareness objective is to promote awareness and understanding of—
    (a)   the range of regulated qualifications available,
    (b)   the benefits of regulated qualifications to learners, employers and institutions within the higher education sector, and
    (c)   the benefits of recognition under section 132 to bodies awarding or authenticating qualifications to which this Part applies.

(6)   The efficiency objective is to secure that regulated qualifications are provided efficiently and in particular that any relevant sums payable to a body awarding or authenticating a qualification in respect of which the body is recognised under section 132 represent value for money.

(7)   For the purposes of subsection (6) a sum is relevant if it is payable in respect of the award or authentication of the qualification in question.

129   General duties

(1)   So far as reasonably practicable, in performing its functions Ofqual must act in a way—
    (a)   which is compatible with its objectives, and
    (b)   which it considers most appropriate for the purpose of meeting its objectives.

(2)   So far as relevant, in performing its functions Ofqual must have regard to—
    (a)   the need to ensure that the number of regulated qualifications available for award or authentication is appropriate;

Apprenticeships, Skills, Children and Learning Act 2009 (c. 22)
Part 7 – The Office of Qualifications and Examinations Regulation
Chapter 1 – Establishment, objectives and general duties

2253

(b) the other reasonable requirements of relevant learners, including persons with learning difficulties;

(c) the reasonable requirements of pupils and children, including persons with learning difficulties, in relation to regulated assessment arrangements;

(d) the reasonable requirements of industry, commerce, finance, the professions and other employers regarding education and training (including required standards of practical competence);

(e) the reasonable requirements of institutions within the higher education sector;

(f) information provided to Ofqual by a person falling within subsection (4);

(g) the desirability of facilitating innovation in connection with the provision of regulated qualifications;

(h) the specified purposes of regulated assessment arrangements.

(3) For the purposes of subsection (2)(a) the number of regulated qualifications available for award or authentication is appropriate if the number is such that—

(a) there is a reasonable level of choice for learners, in terms of both the number of different regulated qualifications and the number of different forms of such qualifications, but

(b) the number of different regulated qualifications in similar subject areas or serving similar functions is not excessive.

(4) The persons falling within this subsection are—

(a) the Qualifications and Curriculum Development Agency;

(b) Her Majesty's Chief Inspector of Education, Children's Services and Skills;

(c) such other relevant persons, or relevant persons of such a description, as the Secretary of State may direct.

(5) In subsection (4)(c) "relevant person" means a person who appears to the Secretary of State to have knowledge of, or expertise in, requirements of a kind mentioned in subsection (2)(d).

(6) In performing its functions Ofqual must also have regard to such aspects of government policy as the Secretary of State may direct.

(7) The Secretary of State must publish a direction given under subsection (6).

(8) Ofqual must perform its functions efficiently and effectively.

(9) "Persons with learning difficulties" means—

(a) children with special educational needs (as defined in section 312 of the Education Act 1996 (c. 56)), and

(b) other persons who—

(i) have a significantly greater difficulty in learning than the majority of persons of their age, or

(ii) have a disability which either prevents or hinders them from making use of educational facilities of a kind generally provided for persons of their age.

(10) But a person is not to be taken to have a learning difficulty solely because the language (or form of language) in which the person is or will be taught is

2254   *Apprenticeships, Skills, Children and Learning Act 2009 (c. 22)*
Part 7 — The Office of Qualifications and Examinations Regulation
Chapter 1 — Establishment, objectives and general duties

different from a language (or form of language) which has at any time been spoken in the person's home.

(11) "Relevant learner" means a person seeking to obtain, or who may reasonably be expected to seek to obtain, a regulated qualification.

Regulated qualifications and regulated assessment arrangements

130 Meaning of "regulated qualifications" etc.

(1) In this Part a "regulated qualification" means a qualification to which this Part applies which is awarded or authenticated by a body which is recognised under section 132 in respect of the qualification.

(2) This Part applies to any of the following qualifications which is not an excluded qualification—
   (a) an academic or vocational qualification awarded or authenticated in England;
   (b) a vocational qualification awarded or authenticated in Northern Ireland.

(3) An excluded qualification is any of the following—
   (a) a foundation degree;
   (b) a first degree;
   (c) a degree at a higher level.

(4) For the purposes of subsection (2) a qualification is awarded or authenticated in England or Northern Ireland if there are, or may reasonably be expected to be, persons seeking to obtain the qualification who are, will be or may reasonably be expected to be assessed for those purposes wholly or mainly in England or Northern Ireland (as the case may be).

(5) The Secretary of State may by order repeal subsection (2)(b).

(6) An order under subsection (5) may make amendments and repeals to a provision of, or in an instrument made under, this or any other Act (including any Act passed after this Act) in consequence of the repeal of subsection (2)(b).

(7) Before making an order under subsection (5) the Secretary of State must consult the Department for Employment and Learning in Northern Ireland.

131 Meaning of "regulated assessment arrangements" etc.

(1) This section applies for the purposes of this Part.

(2) "Regulated assessment arrangements" means—
   (a) NC assessment arrangements, and
   (b) EYFS assessment arrangements.

(3) "NC assessment arrangements" means arrangements made under or by virtue of an order made under section 87(3)(c) of the Education Act 2002 (c. 32) for assessing pupils in England in respect of each key stage for the specified purposes.

(4) In subsection (3)—
   "assessing" includes testing;

Apprenticeships, Skills, Children and Learning Act 2009 (c. 22)
Part 7 — The Office of Qualifications and Examinations Regulation
Chapter 1 — Establishment, objectives and general duties

2255

"key stage" has the same meaning as in Part 6 of the Education Act 2002 (c. 32) (see section 76 of that Act).

(5) "EYFS assessment arrangements" means arrangements made under or by virtue of an order made under section 39(1)(a) of the Childcare Act 2006 (c. 21) for assessing children in England for the specified purposes.

(6) "The specified purposes" in relation to regulated assessment arrangements —

(a) if the arrangements are NC assessment arrangements, has the same meaning as in section 76(1) of the Education Act 2002;

(b) if the arrangements are EYFS assessment arrangements, has the same meaning as in section 41(2)(c) of the Childcare Act 2006.

CHAPTER 2

FUNCTIONS IN RELATION TO QUALIFICATIONS

Recognition of awarding bodies

132 Recognition

(1) Ofqual must recognise an awarding body in respect of the award or authentication of a specified qualification, or description of qualification, to which this Part applies if—

(a) the awarding body has applied for recognition in the respect in question, and

(b) the body meets the applicable criteria for recognition most recently published under section 133.

(2) Ofqual may not recognise an awarding body if the requirements set out in paragraphs (a) and (b) of subsection (1) are not met by the body.

(3) A recognition—

(a) has effect from such date as Ofqual may specify,

(b) is subject to the general conditions,

(c) if in respect of a qualification subject to the accreditation requirement, is subject to an accreditation condition, and

(d) is subject to such other conditions that Ofqual may impose at the time of recognition or later.

(4) But Ofqual may, at the time of recognition or later, determine that a specified recognition is not to be subject to a specified general condition.

(5) An accreditation condition in respect of a qualification subject to the accreditation requirement is a condition requiring that the recognised body may award or authenticate a particular form of the qualification only if, at the time of the award or authentication, that form of the qualification is accredited under section 139.

(6) Ofqual may not charge an awarding body in respect of recognition.

(7) If Ofqual refuses an application for recognition it must provide the awarding body with a statement setting out the reasons for its decision.

2256   *Apprenticeships, Skills, Children and Learning Act 2009 (c. 22)*
Part 7 – The Office of Qualifications and Examinations Regulation
Chapter 2 – Functions in relation to qualifications

(8) In this section "the general conditions", in respect of a recognition of an awarding body, means the general conditions for the time being in force under section 134 which are applicable to the recognition and the body.

(9) In this Chapter –

"awarding body" means a person who awards or authenticates, or who proposes to award or authenticate, a qualification to which this Part applies;

"recognised body" means an awarding body recognised under this section;

a "recognition" means a recognition under this section.

133 Criteria for recognition

(1) Ofqual must set and publish the criteria for recognition under section 132.

(2) Different criteria may be set for –

    (a) recognition of different descriptions of awarding bodies;

    (b) recognition in respect of different qualifications or different descriptions of qualifications;

    (c) recognition in respect of credits in respect of different components of qualifications or different descriptions of components of qualifications.

(3) Ofqual may revise the criteria.

(4) If Ofqual revises the criteria it must publish them as revised.

(5) Before setting or revising the criteria Ofqual must consult such persons as it considers appropriate.

134 General conditions of recognition

(1) Ofqual must set and publish the general conditions to which a recognition is to be subject.

(2) Different general conditions may be set for –

    (a) recognition of different descriptions of awarding bodies;

    (b) recognition in respect of different qualifications or different descriptions of qualifications;

    (c) recognition in respect of credits in respect of different components of qualifications or different descriptions of components of qualifications.

(3) Ofqual may revise the general conditions.

(4) If Ofqual revises the general conditions it must publish them as revised.

(5) Before setting or revising the general conditions Ofqual must consult such persons as it considers appropriate.

135 Other conditions of recognition

(1) The conditions of recognition that Ofqual may impose under section 132(3)(d) include in particular –

    (a) fee capping conditions;

    (b) entry and inspection conditions.

Apprenticeships, Skills, Children and Learning Act 2009 (c. 22)   **2257**
Part 7 — The Office of Qualifications and Examinations Regulation
Chapter 2 — Functions in relation to qualifications

(2)   Fee capping conditions are conditions limiting the amount of a fee chargeable by a recognised body for —

    (a)   the award or authentication of a qualification in respect of which the body is recognised, or

    (b)   the provision of any other service in relation to such a qualification.

(3)   Entry and inspection conditions are conditions requiring permission to enter premises for the purposes of inspecting and copying documents so far as necessary for Ofqual —

    (a)   to satisfy itself that the appropriate standards are being maintained by a recognised body in relation to the award or authentication of any qualification in respect of which the body is recognised, or

    (b)   to determine whether to impose a fee capping condition and, if so, what that condition should be.

136   Fee capping conditions: supplementary

(1)   Ofqual may impose a fee capping condition limiting the amount of a particular fee only if satisfied that the limit is necessary in order to secure value for money.

(2)   Before imposing a fee capping condition in respect of a recognition Ofqual must give notice to the recognised body of its intention to do so.

(3)   The notice must —

    (a)   set out Ofqual's reasons for proposing to impose the fee capping condition, and

    (b)   specify the period during which, and the way in which, the recognised body may make representations about the proposal.

(4)   Ofqual must have regard to any representations made by the recognised body during the period specified in the notice in deciding whether to impose the fee capping condition.

(5)   Ofqual must establish arrangements (the "review arrangements") for the review, at the request of a recognised body, of a decision to impose a fee capping condition.

(6)   The review arrangements must require the decision on review to be made by a person within subsection (7).

(7)   A person within this subsection is one who —

    (a)   appears to Ofqual to have skills likely to be relevant to decisions to impose fee capping conditions, and

    (b)   is independent of Ofqual.

(8)   A person is independent of Ofqual for the purposes of subsection (7) if the person is —

    (a)   an individual who is not a member of Ofqual or Ofqual's staff, or

    (b)   a body none of whose members is a member of Ofqual or Ofqual's staff.

(9)   A decision to impose a fee capping condition must not take effect before the later of —

    (a)   the expiry of the period during which a review can be requested under the review arrangements, and

    (b)   the completion of any review requested under those arrangements.

2258

Apprenticeships, Skills, Children and Learning Act 2009 (c. 22)
Part 7 – The Office of Qualifications and Examinations Regulation
Chapter 2 – Functions in relation to qualifications

(10) Ofqual must, in performing its functions in relation to fee capping conditions, have regard to any guidance given by the Secretary of State.

(11) The Secretary of State must publish any guidance given under subsection (10).

137 Entry and inspection conditions: supplementary

(1) An entry and inspection condition requires permission to enter premises to be given only if —

   (a) the premises in question are not used as a private dwelling,

   (b) the entry is to be by an authorised person,

   (c) reasonable notice has been given to the recognised body in question, and

   (d) the entry is to be at a reasonable time.

(2) "Authorised person" means a member of Ofqual's staff who is authorised (generally or specifically) for the purpose.

(3) An entry and inspection condition may require an authorised person to be given permission to do anything that a person authorised by a provision of Part 1 of the Education Act 2005 (c. 18) to inspect documents could do by virtue of section 58 of that Act (computer records).

Accreditation of certain qualifications

138 Qualifications subject to the accreditation requirement

(1) Ofqual may determine that a specified qualification, or description of qualification, to which this Part applies is subject to the accreditation requirement.

(2) A determination under subsection (1) may provide that a qualification or description of qualification is subject to the accreditation requirement —

   (a) for all purposes, or

   (b) for the purposes of award or authentication by a specified awarding body.

(3) Ofqual must publish a determination falling within subsection (2)(a).

(4) Ofqual may revise a determination made under subsection (1).

(5) If Ofqual revises a determination falling within subsection (2)(a) it must publish the determination as revised.

(6) Before making or revising a determination under subsection (1) Ofqual must —

   (a) if the determination falls within subsection (2)(a), consult such persons as it considers appropriate, and

   (b) if the determination falls within subsection (2)(b), consult the awarding body in question.

139 Accreditation

(1) Where a qualification is subject to the accreditation requirement Ofqual must accredit a particular form of the qualification if —

Apprenticeships, Skills, Children and Learning Act 2009 (c. 22)
Part 7 − The Office of Qualifications and Examinations Regulation
Chapter 2 − Functions in relation to qualifications

2259

> (a) that form of the qualification has been submitted for accreditation by a recognised body which is recognised in respect of the qualification, and
>
> (b) that form of the qualification meets the applicable criteria for accreditation most recently published under section 140.

(2) Ofqual may not accredit a form of a qualification if the requirements set out in paragraphs (a) and (b) of subsection (1) are not met in respect of that form of the qualification.

(3) An accreditation under this section has effect from such date as Ofqual may specify.

(4) Ofqual may not charge a recognised body in respect of accreditation under this section.

(5) If Ofqual refuses an application for accreditation it must provide the recognised body with a statement setting out the reasons for its decision.

140 Criteria for accreditation

(1) Ofqual must set and publish the criteria for accreditation under section 139.

(2) Different criteria may be set for the accreditation of different qualifications or different descriptions of qualifications.

(3) Ofqual may revise the criteria.

(4) If Ofqual revises the criteria it must publish them as revised.

(5) Before setting or revising the criteria Ofqual must consult such persons as it considers appropriate.

(6) If Ofqual revises the criteria under this section which are applicable to a form of a qualification which is accredited under section 139, the accreditation ceases to have effect on the date specified by Ofqual.

(7) Ofqual may vary the date specified under subsection (6) at any time before the date.

(8) Ofqual may determine that subsection (6) does not apply in relation to a specified revision.

(9) Ofqual must publish a determination made under subsection (8).

(10) Ofqual may make saving or transitional provision in connection with the accreditation of a form of a qualification ceasing to have effect under subsection (6).

Minimum requirements

141 Power to specify minimum requirements

(1) The Secretary of State may by order specify minimum requirements in respect of a specified qualification, or description of qualification, to which this section applies.

(2) But the Secretary of State may make an order under subsection (1) only if satisfied that it is necessary to do so for the purpose of ensuring that the curriculum studied by persons taking a course leading to the qualification, or

2260   *Apprenticeships, Skills, Children and Learning Act 2009 (c. 22)*
Part 7 – The Office of Qualifications and Examinations Regulation
Chapter 2 – Functions in relation to qualifications

a qualification of the description, is appropriate, having regard to the likely ages of those persons.

(3) This section applies to a qualification, or description of qualification, if —

    (a) the qualification, or each qualification of the description, is one to which this Part applies, and

    (b) the condition in subsection (4) is met in relation to the qualification or each qualification of the description.

(4) The condition is that —

    (a) one or more forms of the qualification is (or are) approved under section 98 of the Learning and Skills Act 2000 (c. 21), or

    (b) the Secretary of State reasonably expects approval under that section to be sought for one or more forms of the qualification.

(5) A minimum requirement in respect of a qualification or description of qualification is a requirement which relates to the knowledge, skills or understanding which a person must demonstrate in order to obtain the qualification or a qualification of the description.

142 Consultation before making order specifying minimum requirements

(1) Before making an order under section 141(1) the Secretary of State must consult Ofqual and such other persons as the Secretary of State considers appropriate.

(2) For the purposes of consulting under subsection (1) the Secretary of State must publish a document setting out —

    (a) the grounds on which the Secretary of State is satisfied of the matter specified in section 141(2),

    (b) the proposed minimum requirements, and

    (c) the Secretary of State's reasons for proposing those minimum requirements.

(3) The Secretary of State must provide a copy of the document to Ofqual and any other persons the Secretary of State proposes to consult under subsection (1).

143 Effect of order specifying minimum requirements

(1) This section applies in relation to a qualification or description of qualification in respect of which minimum requirements specified in an order under section 141(1) have effect.

(2) Ofqual must perform its functions under sections 133, 134 and 140 in relation to the qualification or description of qualification in a way which secures that the minimum requirements in respect of the qualification or description of qualification are met.

(3) But Ofqual is not required to comply with the duty imposed by subsection (2) if it appears to Ofqual that complying with that duty would result in the level of attainment (in terms of depth of knowledge, skills or understanding) indicated by the qualification or description of qualification not being consistent with that indicated by comparable regulated qualifications.

144 Revocation and amendment of orders specifying minimum requirements

(1) Subsection (2) applies if —

Apprenticeships, Skills, Children and Learning Act 2009 (c. 22)
Part 7 – The Office of Qualifications and Examinations Regulation
Chapter 2 – Functions in relation to qualifications

2261

    (a)   the Secretary of State has made an order under section 141(1) in respect of a qualification or description of qualification, and

    (b)   the qualification or description of qualification ceases to be one to which section 141 applies.

(2)   The Secretary of State may by order —

    (a)   revoke the order, or

    (b)   amend it for the purpose of removing the qualification or description of qualification from the application of the order.

(3)   Subsections (1) and (2) do not affect the power of the Secretary of State to revoke or amend an order under section 141(1) in other circumstances.

(4)   Sections 141(2) and 142 do not apply to an order —

    (a)   revoking an order under section 141(1), or

    (b)   amending an order under section 141(1) for the purpose only of removing a qualification or description of qualification from the application of the order.

Guided learning

145   Assignment of number of hours of guided learning

(1)   A recognised body may only award or authenticate a particular form of a qualification in respect of which it is recognised if Condition 1 or 2 is met.

(2)   Condition 1 is met if the recognised body determines that the qualification is not relevant for 2008 Act purposes.

(3)   Condition 2 is met if —

    (a)   the recognised body determines that the qualification is relevant for 2008 Act purposes, and

    (b)   the body assigns to the particular form of the qualification a number of hours of guided learning.

(4)   Subsection (1) does not apply in relation to a qualification which is a Northern Ireland-only qualification.

(5)   A recognised body must apply the applicable criteria then in force under section 146 when determining —

    (a)   whether or not a qualification is relevant for 2008 Act purposes, and

    (b)   in respect of a qualification which the body has determined is relevant for those purposes, a number of hours of guided learning to assign to a form of the qualification.

(6)   If revised criteria come into force under section 146, a recognised body must review any determination it has made under this section.

(7)   Ofqual may —

    (a)   review any determination made by a recognised body under this section, and

    (b)   require the recognised body to revise any such determination in such respects as Ofqual may specify.

(8)   If under subsection (7)(b) Ofqual requires a recognised body to revise a determination that a qualification is not relevant for 2008 Act purposes by

2262

Apprenticeships, Skills, Children and Learning Act 2009 (c. 22)
Part 7 — The Office of Qualifications and Examinations Regulation
Chapter 2 — Functions in relation to qualifications

specifying that the determination should provide that the qualification is so relevant—

   (a) Ofqual may assign to a form of the qualification awarded or authenticated by the recognised body a number of hours of guided learning, and

   (b) if it does so, the recognised body is to be treated as having determined to assign that number of hours of guided learning to that form of the qualification.

(9) For the purposes of this Chapter a qualification is relevant for 2008 Act purposes if there are, or may reasonably be expected to be, persons seeking to obtain the qualification for the purposes of discharging the duty under section 2(1)(c) of the Education and Skills Act 2008 (c. 25) (duty to participate in education or training).

(10) In this Chapter a "number of hours of guided learning", in relation to a form of a qualification, means a number of notional hours representing an estimate of the amount of actual guided learning which could reasonably be expected to be required in order for persons to achieve the standard required to obtain that form of the qualification.

(11) In subsection (10) "actual guided learning" means time a person spends—

   (a) being taught or given instruction by a lecturer, tutor, supervisor or other appropriate provider of education or training, or

   (b) otherwise participating in education or training under the immediate guidance or supervision of such a person,

but does not include time spent on unsupervised preparation or study, whether at home or otherwise.

(12) Section 172(2)(a) does not apply for the purposes of this section.

146 Criteria for assignment of number of hours of guided learning

(1) Ofqual must set and publish criteria for determining—

   (a) whether a qualification is relevant for 2008 Act purposes, and

   (b) in respect of a qualification which a recognised body has determined is relevant for those purposes, the number of hours of guided learning that should be assigned to a form of the qualification.

(2) Different criteria may be set for determinations in relation to different qualifications or different descriptions of qualifications.

(3) Ofqual may revise the criteria.

(4) If Ofqual revises the criteria it must publish them as revised.

(5) Before setting or revising the criteria Ofqual must consult such persons as it considers appropriate.

Surrender

147 Surrender of recognition

(1) A recognised body may give notice to Ofqual that it wishes to cease to be recognised in respect of the award or authentication of a specified qualification or description of qualification.

Apprenticeships, Skills, Children and Learning Act 2009 (c. 22)
Part 7 – The Office of Qualifications and Examinations Regulation
Chapter 2 – Functions in relation to qualifications

2263

(2) As soon as reasonably practicable after receipt of a notice under subsection (1) Ofqual must give notice to the recognised body of the date on which the body is to cease to be recognised in the respect in question ("the surrender date").

(3) At any time before the surrender date Ofqual may vary that date by giving further notice to the recognised body.

(4) In deciding or varying the surrender date Ofqual must have regard to the need to avoid prejudicing persons who are seeking, or might reasonably be expected to seek, to obtain the qualification, or a qualification of the description, specified in the notice under subsection (1).

(5) Ofqual may make saving or transitional provision in connection with a recognised body ceasing to be recognised in any respect by virtue of this section.

Register

148 Register

(1) Ofqual must maintain and publish a register containing the following information in relation to each recognised body –
   (a) the qualifications in respect of which it is recognised,
   (b) the forms of those qualifications which are awarded or authenticated by it, and
   (c) if the recognised body has determined under section 145 that any of those qualifications is relevant for 2008 Act purposes, the number of hours of guided learning it has assigned to each form of the qualification awarded or authenticated by it.

(2) The register may include such other information as Ofqual considers appropriate.

Recognised bodies: monitoring and enforcement

149 Review of activities of recognised bodies

(1) Ofqual may keep under review any connected activities of a recognised body.

(2) An activity of a recognised body is a connected activity if Ofqual considers that it is connected or otherwise relevant to –
   (a) the body's recognition (including, in particular, the compliance by the body with the conditions to which the recognition is subject), or
   (b) the award or authentication by the body of any qualification in respect of which it is recognised.

150 Investigation of complaints

(1) Ofqual may investigate, or make arrangements for the investigation of, complaints in relation to the award or authentication of a regulated qualification.

(2) Arrangements made under subsection (1) may in particular include arrangements for the referral of complaints to an independent party.

2264   *Apprenticeships, Skills, Children and Learning Act 2009 (c. 22)*
Part 7 — The Office of Qualifications and Examinations Regulation
Chapter 2 — Functions in relation to qualifications

(3)   "An independent party" means—

    (a)   an individual who is not a member of Ofqual or Ofqual's staff, or

    (b)   a body none of whose members is a member of Ofqual or Ofqual's staff.

151   Power to give directions

(1)   Subsection (2) applies if it appears to Ofqual—

    (a)   that a recognised body has failed or is likely to fail to comply with any condition to which the recognition is subject, and

    (b)   that the failure prejudices or would be likely to prejudice—

        (i)   the proper award or authentication by the body of any qualification in respect of which the body is recognised, or

        (ii)   persons who might reasonably be expected to seek to obtain such a qualification awarded or authenticated by the body.

(2)   Ofqual may direct the recognised body to take or refrain from taking specified steps with a view to securing compliance with the condition.

(3)   Before giving a recognised body a direction under this section Ofqual must give notice to the body of its intention to do so.

(4)   The notice must—

    (a)   set out Ofqual's reasons for proposing to give the direction, and

    (b)   specify the period during which, and the way in which, the recognised body may make representations about the proposal.

(5)   Ofqual must have regard to any representations made by the recognised body during the period specified in the notice in deciding whether to give a direction to the body.

(6)   A recognised body must comply with a direction given to it under this section.

(7)   A direction under this section is enforceable, on the application of Ofqual—

    (a)   in England and Wales, by a mandatory order, or

    (b)   in Northern Ireland, by an order of mandamus.

(8)   A direction given under this section may be amended or revoked by Ofqual; and subsections (3) to (5) apply to the amendment of a direction as they apply to the giving of a direction.

152   Power to withdraw recognition

(1)   Subsection (2) applies if a recognised body has failed to comply with a condition to which the recognition is subject.

(2)   Ofqual may withdraw recognition from the recognised body in respect of the award or authentication of a specified qualification or a specified description of qualification if it appears to Ofqual that the failure mentioned in subsection (1) prejudices or would be likely to prejudice—

    (a)   the proper award or authentication by the body of the qualification or a qualification of the description in question, or

    (b)   persons who might reasonably be expected to seek to obtain the qualification or a qualification of the description in question awarded or authenticated by the body.

Apprenticeships, Skills, Children and Learning Act 2009 (c. 22)
Part 7 – The Office of Qualifications and Examinations Regulation
Chapter 2 – Functions in relation to qualifications

2265

(3) Before withdrawing recognition from a recognised body in any respect Ofqual must give notice to the body of its intention to do so.

(4) The notice must—

    (a) set out Ofqual's reasons for proposing to withdraw recognition from the recognised body in the respect in question, and

    (b) specify the period during which, and the way in which, the recognised body may make representations about the proposal.

(5) Ofqual must have regard to any representations made by the recognised body during the period specified in the notice in deciding whether to withdraw recognition from the body in the respect in question.

(6) If Ofqual decides to withdraw recognition from a recognised body Ofqual—

    (a) must give notice to the body of its decision and of the date on which the withdrawal is to take effect, and

    (b) may make saving or transitional provision.

(7) At any time before a withdrawal takes effect Ofqual may vary the date on which it is to take effect by giving further notice to the recognised body.

(8) Ofqual must establish arrangements for the review, at the request of a recognised body, of a decision to withdraw recognition under this section.

(9) The arrangements established under subsection (8) must require the decision on review to be made by a person who is independent of Ofqual.

(10) A person is independent of Ofqual for the purposes of subsection (9) if the person is—

    (a) an individual who is not a member of Ofqual or Ofqual's staff, or

    (b) a body none of whose members is a member of Ofqual or Ofqual's staff.

153 Qualifications regulatory framework

(1) Ofqual must prepare and publish—

    (a) a statement of how Ofqual intends to perform the monitoring and enforcement functions, and

    (b) guidance to recognised bodies in relation to the award and authentication of qualifications in respect of which they are recognised.

(2) The statement and guidance mentioned in subsection (1) are together referred to in this section as "the qualifications regulatory framework".

(3) Guidance under subsection (1)(b) must include guidance for the purpose of helping to determine whether or not behaviour complies with the general conditions to which a recognition is subject (see section 134).

(4) The guidance may in particular specify—

    (a) descriptions of behaviour which Ofqual considers complies with a general condition;

    (b) descriptions of behaviour which Ofqual considers does not comply with a general condition;

    (c) factors which Ofqual will take into account in determining whether or not a recognised body's behaviour complies with a general condition.

(5) Ofqual—

    (a) may revise the qualifications regulatory framework, and

2266   *Apprenticeships, Skills, Children and Learning Act 2009 (c. 22)*
Part 7 — The Office of Qualifications and Examinations Regulation
Chapter 2 — Functions in relation to qualifications

    (b)   if it does so, must publish the revised version.

(6)   Before publishing the qualifications regulatory framework or a revised version of it, Ofqual must consult such persons as it considers appropriate.

(7)   A recognised body must have regard to guidance under subsection (1)(b) in awarding or authenticating a qualification in respect of which it is recognised.

(8)   In subsection (1) "the monitoring and enforcement functions" means—

    (a)   Ofqual's power under section 132(3)(d) (power to impose other conditions);

    (b)   Ofqual's functions under sections 132(4) and 134 (functions in relation to general conditions);

    (c)   Ofqual's functions under an entry and inspection condition to which a recognition is subject (see section 135);

    (d)   Ofqual's functions under section 138(1) (power to determine that a qualification is subject to the accreditation requirement);

    (e)   Ofqual's functions under sections 149 to 152.

Other

154   Review of qualifications to which Part applies

Ofqual may keep under review all aspects of qualifications to which this Part applies.

155   Review of system for allocating values to qualifications

(1)   Ofqual must keep under review any system used by the Secretary of State for allocating values to qualifications to which this Part applies by reference to the level of attainment indicated by the qualifications.

(2)   The duty in subsection (1) applies only if the values are to be allocated for the purpose of a qualifications-based performance management system.

(3)   A qualifications-based performance management system is a system for measuring the relative performance of schools by reference to the performance of pupils at the schools in qualifications to which this Part applies.

(4)   Ofqual may at any time require the Secretary of State to provide it with any information which Ofqual considers it necessary or expedient to have for the purposes of, or in connection with, the performance by Ofqual of its duty under subsection (1).

156   Co-operation and joint working

(1)   Ofqual may co-operate or work jointly with another public authority where it is appropriate to do so for the efficient and effective performance of any of Ofqual's qualifications functions.

(2)   "Public authority" includes any person who performs functions (whether or not in the United Kingdom) which are of a public nature.

(3)   In this Chapter "qualifications functions" means functions in connection with qualifications to which this Part applies.

Apprenticeships, Skills, Children and Learning Act 2009 (c. 22) 2267
Part 7 – The Office of Qualifications and Examinations Regulation
Chapter 2 – Functions in relation to qualifications

157 Power to provide information to qualifications regulators

(1) Ofqual may provide information to a qualifications regulator for the purpose of enabling or facilitating the performance of a relevant function of the regulator.

(2) For the purposes of this section –
   (a) a qualifications regulator is a person who has functions in any part of the United Kingdom which are similar to Ofqual's qualifications functions, and
   (b) a function of a qualifications regulator is a relevant function if it is similar to any of the qualifications functions of Ofqual.

(3) Nothing in this section –
   (a) affects any power to disclose information that exists apart from this section, or
   (b) authorises the disclosure of information in contravention of any provision made by or under any Act which prevents disclosure of the information.

General

158 Interpretation of Chapter

(1) In this Chapter –
   "awarding body" has the meaning given by section 132;
   "entry and inspection condition" has the meaning given by section 135;
   "fee capping condition" has the meaning given by section 135;
   "Northern Ireland-only qualification" means a qualification in respect of which the persons who are, or who may reasonably be expected to be, seeking to obtain the qualification are, will be or may reasonably be expected to be assessed for those purposes wholly in Northern Ireland;
   "number of hours of guided learning", in relation to a form of a qualification, has the meaning given by section 145;
   "qualifications functions" has the meaning given by section 156;
   "recognised body" has the meaning given by section 132;
   a "recognition" has the meaning given by section 132.

(2) For the purposes of this Chapter a qualification is subject to the accreditation requirement if a determination by Ofqual that the qualification, or a description of qualification which applies to the qualification, is to be subject to that requirement has effect under section 138.

(3) For the purposes of this Chapter a qualification is relevant for 2008 Act purposes if it falls within section 145(9).

2268   *Apprenticeships, Skills, Children and Learning Act 2009 (c. 22)*
Part 7 — The Office of Qualifications and Examinations Regulation
Chapter 3 — Functions in relation to assessment arrangements

CHAPTER 3

FUNCTIONS IN RELATION TO ASSESSMENT ARRANGEMENTS

Development etc. of regulated assessment arrangements

159   NC assessment arrangements: duty to consult Ofqual etc.

(1)   Section 87 of the Education Act 2002 (c. 32) (establishment of the National Curriculum for England by order) is amended as follows.

(2)   Before subsection (7) insert —

"(6A)   Before making an order under subsection   (3)(c) the Secretary of State —

(a)   shall consult the Office of Qualifications and Examinations Regulation, and

(b)   may consult such other persons as the Secretary of State considers appropriate."

(3)   After subsection (8) insert —

"(8A)   An order under subsection (3)(c) which includes provision made by virtue of subsection (8) shall provide that before making or revising the assessment arrangements the person specified in the order —

(a)   shall consult the Office of Qualifications and Examinations Regulation, and

(b)   may consult such other persons as that person considers appropriate."

(4)   After subsection (12) (as inserted by paragraph 35 of Schedule 12) insert —

"(12A)   An order under subsection (3)(c) which authorises a person to make delegated supplementary provisions shall provide that before making, amending or revoking any such provisions the person so authorised —

(a)   shall consult the Office of Qualifications and Examinations Regulation, and

(b)   may consult such other persons as that person considers appropriate."

160   EYFS assessment arrangements: duty to consult Ofqual etc.

(1)   Section 42 of the Childcare Act 2006 (c. 21) (further provisions about assessment arrangements) is amended as follows.

(2)   Before subsection (1) insert —

"(A1)   Before making a learning and development order specifying assessment arrangements the Secretary of State —

(a)   must consult the Office of Qualifications and Examinations Regulation, and

(b)   may consult such other persons as the Secretary of State considers appropriate."

Apprenticeships, Skills, Children and Learning Act 2009 (c. 22)
Part 7 – The Office of Qualifications and Examinations Regulation
Chapter 3 – Functions in relation to assessment arrangements

2269

(3)   After subsection (3) insert—

"(3A)   A learning and development order which includes provision made by virtue of subsection (3) must provide that before making or revising the assessment arrangements the person specified in the order—

    (a)   must consult the Office of Qualifications and Examinations Regulation, and

    (b)   may consult such other persons as that person considers appropriate."

(4)   After subsection (6A) (as inserted by paragraph 40 of Schedule 12) insert—

"(6AA)   A learning and development order which authorises a person to make delegated supplementary provisions must provide that before making, amending or revoking any such provisions the person so authorised—

    (a)   must consult the Office of Qualifications and Examinations Regulation, and

    (b)   may consult such other persons as that person considers appropriate."

Review etc. of regulated assessment arrangements

161   Review of regulated assessment arrangements

(1)   Ofqual must keep under review all aspects of NC assessment arrangements.

(2)   Ofqual must keep under review all aspects of EYFS assessment arrangements.

162   Powers to require information

(1)   Ofqual may at any time require a person falling within subsection (2) to provide it with any information which Ofqual considers it necessary or expedient to have for the purposes of, or in connection with, the performance by Ofqual of its function under section 161(1).

(2)   The persons are—
    (a)   the Secretary of State;
    (b)   an NC responsible body;
    (c)   Her Majesty's Chief Inspector of Education, Children's Services and Skills;
    (d)   any other person specified or of a description specified in regulations.

(3)   Ofqual may at any time require a person falling within subsection (4) to provide it with any information which Ofqual considers it necessary or expedient to have for the purposes of, or in connection with, the performance by Ofqual of its function under section 161(2).

(4)   The persons are—
    (a)   the Secretary of State;
    (b)   an EYFS responsible body;
    (c)   Her Majesty's Chief Inspector of Education, Children's Services and Skills;
    (d)   any other person specified or of a description specified in regulations.

(5)   In this Chapter—

2270   *Apprenticeships, Skills, Children and Learning Act 2009 (c. 22)*
Part 7 – The Office of Qualifications and Examinations Regulation
Chapter 3 – Functions in relation to assessment arrangements

"EYFS responsible body" means a person who under or by virtue of an order made under section 39(1)(a) of the Childcare Act 2006 (c. 21) has functions in relation to the development, implementation or monitoring of EYFS assessment arrangements;

"NC responsible body" means a person who under or by virtue of an order made under section 87(3)(c) of the Education Act 2002 (c. 32) has functions in relation to the development, implementation or monitoring of NC assessment arrangements.

163   Duty to notify significant failings

(1) If it appears to Ofqual that there is or is likely to be a significant failing in NC assessment arrangements Ofqual must notify —

    (a) the Secretary of State, and

    (b) any NC responsible body whose act or omission appears to Ofqual to have contributed to the significant failing.

(2) If it appears to Ofqual that there is or is likely to be a significant failing in EYFS assessment arrangements Ofqual must notify —

    (a) the Secretary of State, and

    (b) any EYFS responsible body whose act or omission appears to Ofqual to have contributed to the significant failing.

(3) There is a significant failing in NC assessment arrangements or (as the case may be) EYFS assessment arrangements if, as a result of the way in which the arrangements are being developed or implemented, they fail in a significant way to achieve one or more of the specified purposes of the arrangements.

Regulatory frameworks

164   NC assessments regulatory framework

(1) Ofqual must prepare and publish a document ("the NC assessments regulatory framework") which —

    (a) contains a description of how Ofqual intends to perform its function under section 161(1), and

    (b) gives guidance to NC responsible bodies about the performance of their functions in relation to NC assessment arrangements.

(2) Ofqual —

    (a) may revise the NC assessments regulatory framework, and

    (b) if it does so, it must publish the revised version.

(3) Before publishing the NC assessments regulatory framework or a revised version of it, Ofqual must consult —

    (a) the Secretary of State, and

    (b) such NC responsible bodies and other persons as it considers appropriate.

(4) An NC responsible body must have regard to the NC assessments regulatory framework in performing its functions in relation to NC assessment arrangements.

Apprenticeships, Skills, Children and Learning Act 2009 (c. 22)
Part 7 — *The Office of Qualifications and Examinations Regulation*
Chapter 3 — Functions in relation to assessment arrangements

2271

165 EYFS assessments regulatory framework

(1) Ofqual must prepare and publish a document ("the EYFS assessments regulatory framework") which—

    (a) contains a description of how Ofqual intends to perform its function under section 161(2), and

    (b) gives guidance to EYFS responsible bodies about the performance of their functions in relation to EYFS assessment arrangements.

(2) Ofqual—

    (a) may revise the EYFS assessments regulatory framework, and

    (b) if it does so, it must publish the revised version.

(3) Before publishing the EYFS assessments regulatory framework or a revised version of it, Ofqual must consult—

    (a) the Secretary of State, and

    (b) such EYFS responsible bodies and other persons as it considers appropriate.

(4) An EYFS responsible body must have regard to the EYFS assessments regulatory framework in performing its functions in relation to EYFS assessment arrangements.

General

166 Interpretation of Chapter

In this Chapter—

    "EYFS assessment arrangements" has the meaning given by section 131;

    "EYFS responsible body" has the meaning given by section 162;

    "NC assessment arrangements" has the meaning given by section 131;

    "NC responsible body" has the meaning given by section 162.

CHAPTER 4

OTHER FUNCTIONS

167 Provision of services

(1) Ofqual may, in connection with any of its functions, provide services to any person (whether or not in the United Kingdom).

(2) Services provided by virtue of this section may be provided on such terms and subject to such conditions (if any) as Ofqual may determine.

(3) Ofqual may charge a fee for, or in connection with, any service provided by virtue of this section.

168 Provision of information or advice

(1) If requested to do so by the Secretary of State, Ofqual must provide the Secretary of State with information or advice on such matters relating to any of its functions as may be specified in the request.

2272   *Apprenticeships, Skills, Children and Learning Act 2009 (c. 22)*
Part 7 – The Office of Qualifications and Examinations Regulation
Chapter 4 – Other functions

(2) If requested to do so by the Department for Employment and Learning in Northern Ireland, Ofqual must provide the Department with information or advice on such matters relating to any of its functions (so far as they relate to Northern Ireland) as may be specified in the request.

169   Research and development

(1) Ofqual may carry out programmes of research and development for purposes connected with—
     (a) qualifications to which this Part applies, or
     (b) regulated assessment arrangements.

(2) Ofqual may commission, co-ordinate or facilitate the carrying out of programmes of research and development for the purposes mentioned in subsection (1).

170   Duty not to impose or maintain unnecessary burdens

(1) Ofqual must keep its regulatory functions under review.

(2) Ofqual must secure that in performing any of its regulatory functions it does not—
     (a) impose burdens which it considers to be unnecessary, or
     (b) maintain burdens which it considers to have become unnecessary.

(3) Subsection (2) does not require the removal of a burden which has become unnecessary where its removal would, having regard to all the circumstances, be impracticable or disproportionate.

(4) Ofqual must publish a statement setting out—
     (a) what it proposes to do pursuant to subsections (1) and (2) in the period to which the statement relates,
     (b) (except in the case of the first statement published under this section) what it has done pursuant to subsections (1) and (2) since the previous statement was published under this section, and
     (c) where a burden which has become unnecessary is maintained pursuant to subsection (3), the reasons why the removal of the burden would, having regard to all the circumstances, be impracticable or disproportionate.

(5) The first statement published under this section—
     (a) must be published as soon as reasonably practicable after the commencement of section 127, and
     (b) is to be a statement for the period of 12 months beginning with the day of its publication.

(6) A subsequent statement published under this section—
     (a) must be published during the period to which the previous statement related or as soon as reasonably practicable after the end of that period, and
     (b) must be a statement for the period of 12 months beginning with the end of the period to which the previous statement related.

(7) Ofqual must, in performing any of its regulatory functions during a period for which a statement is in force under this section, have regard to the statement.

Apprenticeships, Skills, Children and Learning Act 2009 (c. 22)
Part 7 – The Office of Qualifications and Examinations Regulation
Chapter 4 – Other functions

2273

(8)   In this section "regulatory function" has the same meaning as in the Legislative and Regulatory Reform Act 2006 (c. 51) (see section 32 of that Act).

171   Annual and other reports

(1)   As soon as reasonably practicable after the end of each reporting period Ofqual must prepare and publish a report for the period ("the annual report").

(2)   The annual report must include—
    (a)   a statement of what Ofqual has done in performing its functions in the reporting period;
    (b)   an assessment of the extent to which Ofqual has met its objectives in that period;
    (c)   details of any information obtained by Ofqual in that period on the levels of attainment in relevant regulated qualifications.

(3)   "Relevant regulated qualifications" are regulated qualifications that are taken wholly or mainly by pupils at schools in England.

(4)   An assessment under subsection (2)(b) in respect of the qualifications standards objective must in particular explain how, in making the assessment, Ofqual has taken account of any information within subsection (2)(c) obtained in the reporting period or an earlier reporting period.

(5)   If arrangements of the kind mentioned in section 150(2) (arrangements for referral of complaints to an independent party) were in place during the reporting period, the annual report must include a description of the activities of the independent party during the reporting period.

(6)   Ofqual must—
    (a)   lay a copy of each annual report before Parliament;
    (b)   (so far as it relates to Northern Ireland) lay a copy of each annual report before the Northern Ireland Assembly.

(7)   Ofqual may prepare and publish other reports on matters relating to its functions.

(8)   If Ofqual prepares and publishes a report under subsection (7) it may—
    (a)   lay a copy of the report before Parliament;
    (b)   (so far as it relates to Northern Ireland) lay a copy of the report before the Northern Ireland Assembly.

(9)   Ofqual may comply with subsection (1) by preparing and publishing a single document or separate documents in relation to England and to Northern Ireland.

(10)   In this section "reporting period" means—
    (a)   the period (being not longer than 12 months) beginning with the day on which section 127 comes into force and ending on such date as Ofqual decides;
    (b)   each successive period of 12 months.

2274

Apprenticeships, Skills, Children and Learning Act 2009 (c. 22)
Part 7 – The Office of Qualifications and Examinations Regulation
Chapter 5 – General

CHAPTER 5

GENERAL

172 Interpretation of Part

(1) In this Part—

"institution within the higher education sector"—

   (a) in relation to England, has the same meaning as in the Education Act 1996 (c. 56) (see section 4(4) of that Act);

   (b) in relation to Northern Ireland, means a higher education institution within the meaning of Article 30 of the Education and Libraries (Northern Ireland) Order 1993 (S.I. 1993/2810 (N.I. 12));

"Ofqual" means the Office of Qualifications and Examinations Regulation;

"qualification to which this Part applies" has the meaning given by section 130;

"regulated assessment arrangements" has the meaning given by section 131;

"regulated qualification" has the meaning given by section 130;

"the specified purposes", in relation to regulated assessment arrangements, has the meaning given by section 131.

(2) In this Part a reference to the award or authentication of a qualification includes a reference to—

   (a) the award or authentication of credits in respect of components of a qualification, and

   (b) the award or authentication of a qualification by a body either alone or jointly with others.

(3) In this Part a reference to recognition, or being recognised, in respect of a qualification is a reference to recognition, or being recognised, under section 132 in respect of the award or authentication of the qualification or of a description of qualification which applies to the qualification.

173 Transfer schemes

Schedule 10 contains provision for the transfer of staff, property, rights and liabilities from the body to be known as the Qualifications and Curriculum Development Agency to Ofqual.

174 Minor and consequential amendments

Schedule 12 contains minor and consequential amendments relating to the provision made by this Part (and Part 8).

Apprenticeships, Skills, Children and Learning Act 2009 (c. 22)
Part 8 — The Qualifications and Curriculum Development Agency
Chapter 1 — The QCDA, objective and general duties

2275

PART 8

THE QUALIFICATIONS AND CURRICULUM DEVELOPMENT AGENCY

CHAPTER 1

THE QCDA, OBJECTIVE AND GENERAL DUTIES

The QCDA

175 The Qualifications and Curriculum Development Agency

(1) The body corporate originally established under section 21 of the Education Act 1997 (c. 44) as the Qualifications and Curriculum Authority is to continue in existence but is to be known instead as the Qualifications and Curriculum Development Agency.

(2) In this Part the Qualifications and Curriculum Development Agency is referred to as "the QCDA".

(3) Schedule 11 makes further provision about the QCDA.

Objective and general duties

176 Objective

The QCDA's objective is to promote quality and coherence in education and training in England.

177 General duties

(1) So far as reasonably practicable, in performing its functions the QCDA must act in a way —
   (a) which is compatible with its objective, and
   (b) which it considers most appropriate for the purpose of meeting its objective.

(2) So far as relevant, in performing its functions the QCDA must have regard to —
   (a) the reasonable requirements of learners, including persons with learning difficulties;
   (b) the reasonable requirements of industry, commerce, finance, the professions and other employers regarding education and training (including required standards of practical competence);
   (c) the reasonable requirements of institutions within the higher education sector;
   (d) the requirements of section 78 of the Education Act 2002 (c. 32) (general requirements in relation to curriculum);
   (e) information provided to it by a person falling within subsection (3);
   (f) the desirability of facilitating innovation.

(3) The persons falling within this subsection are —
   (a) the Office of Qualifications and Examinations Regulation;

2276   *Apprenticeships, Skills, Children and Learning Act 2009 (c. 22)*
Part 8 — The Qualifications and Curriculum Development Agency
Chapter 1 — The QCDA, objective and general duties

      (b)   Her Majesty's Chief Inspector of Education, Children's Services and Skills;

      (c)   such other persons, or persons of such a description, as the Secretary of State may direct.

(4)   In performing its functions the QCDA must also have regard to such aspects of government policy as the Secretary of State may direct.

(5)   The QCDA must perform its functions efficiently and effectively.

(6)   In this section —

       "learner" means a person who is, or may reasonably be expected to be, in receipt of education or training;

       "persons with learning difficulties" has the same meaning as in section 129.

CHAPTER 2

FUNCTIONS IN RELATION TO QUALIFICATIONS

178   Qualifications within the QCDA's remit

(1)   For the purposes of this Part a qualification is within the QCDA's remit if —

      (a)   it is an academic or vocational qualification awarded or authenticated in England, and

      (b)   it is not an excluded qualification.

(2)   But the Secretary of State may by order provide that a specified qualification, or qualifications of a specified description, despite falling within subsection (1), is or are outside the QCDA's remit for the purposes of this Part.

(3)   For the purposes of subsection (1) a qualification is awarded or authenticated in England if there are, or may reasonably be expected to be, persons seeking to obtain the qualification who are, will be or may reasonably be expected to be assessed for those purposes wholly or mainly in England.

(4)   An excluded qualification is a qualification awarded or authenticated by an institution within the higher education sector —

      (a)   at foundation degree level or any comparable level, or

      (b)   at first degree level, or any comparable or higher level.

179   Qualifications: general functions

(1)   The QCDA must keep under review all aspects of qualifications within its remit.

(2)   The QCDA —

      (a)   may advise the Secretary of State on matters concerning qualifications within its remit, and

      (b)   must advise the Secretary of State on any such matters which are referred to the QCDA by the Secretary of State.

(3)   The QCDA may and, if requested to do so by the Secretary of State, must —

      (a)   carry out programmes of research and development for purposes connected with qualifications within its remit, or

Apprenticeships, Skills, Children and Learning Act 2009 (c. 22)
Part 8 — The Qualifications and Curriculum Development Agency
Chapter 2 — Functions in relation to qualifications

2277

      (b)   commission, co-ordinate or facilitate the carrying out of such programmes.

(4)   The QCDA may publish and disseminate, or facilitate the publication or other dissemination of, information relating to qualifications within its remit.

180 Assistance etc. in relation to qualifications functions of Ofqual

(1)   The QCDA must, if requested to do so by Ofqual, assist Ofqual in setting criteria under section 133 or 140 which relate to a qualification or description of qualification within subsection (2).

(2)   A qualification or description of qualification is within this subsection if Ofqual is required to comply with the duty imposed by section 143(2) in relation to it.

(3)   The QCDA may —
      (a)   assist Ofqual in setting qualifications criteria which do not fall within subsection (1), and
      (b)   provide other assistance, information or advice to Ofqual in connection with the performance by Ofqual of any of its qualifications functions.

(4)   In this section —
      "assistance" does not include financial assistance (and "assist" is to be construed accordingly);
      "Ofqual" means the Office of Qualifications and Examinations Regulation;
      "qualifications criteria" means criteria required to be set by Ofqual under —
          (a)   section 133 (criteria for recognition of awarding bodies),
          (b)   section 140 (criteria for accreditation of qualifications subject to the accreditation requirement), and
          (c)   section 146 (criteria in connection with the assignment of number of hours of guided learning);
      "qualifications functions" means functions in connection with qualifications to which Part 7 applies (see section 130).

CHAPTER 3

FUNCTIONS IN RELATION TO CURRICULUM, EARLY YEARS FOUNDATION STAGE AND ASSESSMENT

181 Curriculum

(1)   The QCDA must keep under review all aspects of the curriculum.

(2)   The QCDA —
      (a)   may advise the Secretary of State on matters concerning the curriculum, and
      (b)   must advise the Secretary of State on any such matters which are referred to the QCDA by the Secretary of State.

(3)   The QCDA may and, if requested to do so by the Secretary of State, must —
      (a)   carry out programmes of research and development for purposes connected with the curriculum, or

2278   Apprenticeships, Skills, Children and Learning Act 2009 (c. 22)
Part 8 – The Qualifications and Curriculum Development Agency
Chapter 3 – Functions in relation to curriculum, Early Years Foundation Stage and assessment

     (b)   commission, co-ordinate or facilitate the carrying out of such programmes.

(4)   The QCDA may publish and disseminate, or facilitate the publication or other dissemination of, information relating to the curriculum.

(5)   In this Part "the curriculum" means the curriculum for –

     (a)   pupils at maintained schools in England who have not ceased to be of compulsory school age, and

     (b)   pupils at maintained nursery schools in England.

182   Early learning goals and educational programmes

(1)   The QCDA must keep under review all aspects of the early learning goals and educational programmes.

(2)   The QCDA –

     (a)   may advise the Secretary of State on matters concerning the early learning goals and educational programmes, and

     (b)   must advise the Secretary of State on any such matters which are referred to the QCDA by the Secretary of State.

(3)   The QCDA may and, if requested to do so by the Secretary of State, must –

     (a)   carry out programmes of research and development for purposes connected with the early learning goals and educational programmes, or

     (b)   commission, co-ordinate or facilitate the carrying out of such programmes.

(4)   The QCDA may publish and disseminate, or facilitate the publication or other dissemination of, information relating to the early learning goals and educational programmes.

(5)   In this Part "the early learning goals and educational programmes" means the requirements specified under section 39(1)(a) of the Childcare Act 2006 (c. 21) by virtue of paragraphs (a) and (b) of section 41(2) of that Act.

183   Assessment arrangements

(1)   The QCDA must keep under review all aspects of assessment arrangements within its remit.

(2)   The QCDA –

     (a)   may advise the Secretary of State on matters concerning assessment arrangements within its remit, and

     (b)   must advise the Secretary of State on any such matters which are referred to the QCDA by the Secretary of State.

(3)   The QCDA may and, if requested to do so by the Secretary of State, must –

     (a)   carry out programmes of research and development for purposes connected with assessment arrangements within its remit, or

     (b)   commission, co-ordinate or facilitate the carrying out of such programmes.

Apprenticeships, Skills, Children and Learning Act 2009 (c. 22)   2279
Part 8 − The Qualifications and Curriculum Development Agency
Chapter 3 − Functions in relation to curriculum, Early Years Foundation Stage and assessment

(4) The QCDA may publish and disseminate, or facilitate the publication or other dissemination of, information relating to assessment arrangements within its remit.

(5) For the purposes of this Part the following are assessment arrangements within the QCDA's remit—

    (a) regulated assessment arrangements;

    (b) arrangements which do not fall within paragraph (a) but which are for tests and other assessments in respect of—

        (i) pupils at maintained schools in England who have not ceased to be of compulsory school age, and

        (ii) pupils at maintained nursery schools in England.

CHAPTER 4

OTHER FUNCTIONS AND SUPPLEMENTARY PROVISION

Other functions

184 Provision of services or other assistance

(1) The QCDA may provide services or other assistance in connection with any of the following—

    (a) qualifications within the QCDA's remit;

    (b) the curriculum;

    (c) the early learning goals and educational programmes;

    (d) assessment arrangements within the QCDA's remit.

(2) The QCDA may, with the consent of the Secretary of State, also provide services or other assistance which—

    (a) do not fall within subsection (1), but

    (b) are otherwise provided in connection with education or training in England.

(3) The QCDA may not lend money.

(4) The power under subsection (1) may only be exercised to provide other forms of financial assistance with the consent of the Secretary of State.

(5) Services or other assistance provided by virtue of this section may be provided on such terms and subject to such conditions (if any) as the QCDA may determine.

(6) The QCDA may, with the consent of the Secretary of State, charge a fee for, or in connection with, any service or other assistance provided under this section.

(7) Any consent of the Secretary of State required under this section may be given—

    (a) unconditionally or subject to conditions, and

    (b) generally or specifically.

(8) Services or other assistance may be provided under this section to any person whether or not in the United Kingdom.

(9) The powers under subsections (1) and (2) must not be exercised—

2280   *Apprenticeships, Skills, Children and Learning Act 2009 (c. 22)*
Part 8 – The Qualifications and Curriculum Development Agency
Chapter 4 – Other functions and supplementary provision

    (a)   to assist Ofqual in setting qualifications criteria, or

    (b)   to provide other assistance, information or advice to Ofqual in connection with the performance by Ofqual of any of its qualifications functions.

(10)   In subsection (9) "Ofqual", "qualifications criteria" and "qualifications functions" have the same meanings as in section 180.

185   Provision of information or advice

(1)   The QCDA must advise the Secretary of State on any additional matters which are referred to it by the Secretary of State.

(2)   An "additional matter" is a matter relating to the provision of education or training in England other than one which may be referred to the QCDA under section 179(2)(b), 181(2)(b), 182(2)(b) or 183(2)(b).

(3)   If requested to do so by the Secretary of State, the QCDA must provide the Secretary of State with information on such matters relating to any of its functions as may be specified in the request.

186   Ancillary activities

(1)   The QCDA must carry out such ancillary activities as the Secretary of State may direct.

(2)   An ancillary activity is an activity which the Secretary of State considers it appropriate for the QCDA to carry out for the purposes of, or in connection with, any of its functions.

187   Co-operation and joint working

(1)   The QCDA may co-operate or work jointly with another public authority where it is appropriate to do so for the efficient and effective performance of any of the QCDA's functions.

(2)   In this section "public authority" includes any person who performs functions (whether or not in the United Kingdom) which are of a public nature.

188   Power to confer supplementary functions on the QCDA

(1)   The Secretary of State may by order confer supplementary functions on the QCDA.

(2)   A supplementary function is a function which is to be performed in connection with any of the following –

    (a)   qualifications within the QCDA's remit;

    (b)   the curriculum;

    (c)   the early learning goals and educational programmes;

    (d)   assessment arrangements within the QCDA's remit.

(3)   The Secretary of State must consult the QCDA before making an order under this section.

Apprenticeships, Skills, Children and Learning Act 2009 (c. 22)
Part 8 — The Qualifications and Curriculum Development Agency
Chapter 4 — Other functions and supplementary provision

2281

Supplementary provision

189 Directions etc. by the Secretary of State

(1) The Secretary of State may give the QCDA directions as to the performance of any of its functions.

(2) The QCDA must, in performing its functions, act in accordance with any plans approved by the Secretary of State.

190 Guidance by the Secretary of State

The QCDA must, in performing its functions, have regard to any guidance given by the Secretary of State.

CHAPTER 5

GENERAL

191 Interpretation of Part

(1) In this Part—

"the curriculum" has the meaning given by section 181;

"the early learning goals and educational programmes" has the meaning given by section 182;

"education" includes the learning by, and development of, young children pursuant to the learning and development requirements within the meaning given by section 39(1)(a) of the Childcare Act 2006 (c. 21);

"maintained school" means—

(a) a community, foundation or voluntary school, and

(b) a community or foundation special school;

"the QCDA" means the Qualifications and Curriculum Development Agency;

"regulated assessment arrangements" has the same meaning as in Part 7 (see section 131);

"young child" has the same meaning as in the Childcare Act 2006 (see section 19 of that Act).

(2) References in this Part to assessment arrangements within the QCDA's remit are to be construed in accordance with section 183.

(3) References in this Part to qualifications within the QCDA's remit are to be construed in accordance with section 178.

192 Minor and consequential amendments

Schedule 12 contains minor and consequential amendments relating to the provision made by this Part (and by Part 7).

PART 9

CHILDREN'S SERVICES

Co-operation to improve well-being of children

193 Arrangements to promote co-operation

(1) Section 10 of the Children Act 2004 (c. 31) (co-operation to improve well-being) is amended as set out in subsections (2) to (5).

(2) In subsection (4)—
    (a) after paragraph (f) insert—
            "(fa) the governing body of a maintained school that is maintained by the authority in their capacity as a local education authority;
            (fb) the proprietor of a school approved by the Secretary of State under section 342 of the Education Act 1996 and situated in the authority's area;
            (fc) the proprietor of a city technology college, city college for the technology of the arts or Academy situated in the authority's area;
            (fd) the governing body of an institution within the further education sector the main site of which is situated in the authority's area;
            (fe) the Secretary of State, in relation to the Secretary of State's functions under section 2 of the Employment and Training Act 1973.";
    (b) omit paragraph (g).

(3) After subsection (5) insert—

    "(5A) For the purposes of arrangements under this section a relevant person or body may—
        (a) provide staff, goods, services, accommodation or other resources to another relevant person or body;
        (b) make contributions to a fund out of which relevant payments may be made."

(4) Omit subsections (6) and (7).

(5) After subsection (9) insert—

    "(10) In deciding for the purposes of subsection (4)(fd) whether the main site of an institution within the further education sector is situated within the area of a children's services authority, the authority and the governing body of the institution must have regard to any guidance given to them by the Secretary of State.

    (11) In this section—
        "governing body", in relation to an institution within the further education sector, has the meaning given by section 90 of the Further and Higher Education Act 1992;
        "institution within the further education sector" has the meaning given by section 4(3) of the Education Act 1996;

"maintained school" has the meaning given by section 39(1) of the Education Act 2002;

"proprietor", in relation to a city technology college, city college for the technology of the arts, Academy or other school, means the person or body of persons responsible for its management;

"relevant payment", in relation to a fund, means a payment in respect of expenditure incurred, by a relevant person or body contributing to the fund, in the exercise of its functions;

"relevant person or body" means—

    (a)   a children's services authority in England;

    (b)   a relevant partner of a children's services authority in England."

194 Children's Trust Boards

(1) Part 2 of the Children Act 2004 (c. 31) (children's services in England) is amended as set out in subsections (2) to (5).

(2) After section 12 insert—

"Children's Trust Boards

12A Establishment of CTBs

(1) Arrangements made by a children's services authority in England under section 10 must include arrangements for the establishment of a Children's Trust Board for their area.

(2) A Children's Trust Board must include a representative of each of the following—

    (a)   the establishing authority;

    (b)   each of the establishing authority's relevant partners (subject to subsection (4)).

(3) A Children's Trust Board may also include any other persons or bodies that the establishing authority, after consulting each of their relevant partners, think appropriate.

(4) A Children's Trust Board need not include any of the establishing authority's relevant partners who are of a description prescribed by regulations made by the Secretary of State.

(5) Subsection (2) does not require a Children's Trust Board to include a separate representative for each of the persons or bodies mentioned in subsection (2)(a) and (b).

(6) Where two or more children's services authorities jointly make arrangements under section 10 for the establishment of a Children's Trust Board, references in sections 12B and 17 to the area of the authority that established the Board are to be read as references to an area consisting of the combined areas of those authorities.

(7) For the purposes of this section and sections 12B and 12C—

    (a)   "the establishing authority", in relation to a Children's Trust Board, is the children's services authority that establishes the Board;

(b) a person or body is a "relevant partner" of a children's services authority if it is a relevant partner of the authority for the purposes of section 10.

12B Functions and procedures of CTBs

(1) The functions of a Children's Trust Board are —

(a) those conferred by or under section 17 or 17A (children and young people's plans);

(b) any further functions conferred by regulations made by the Secretary of State.

(2) Regulations under subsection (1)(b) may confer a function on a Children's Trust Board only if the function relates to improving the well-being of children or relevant young persons in the area of the establishing authority.

(3) In subsection (2) "well-being" means well-being so far as relating to one or more of the matters specified in section 10(2)(a) to (e).

(4) A Children's Trust Board must have regard to any guidance given to it by the Secretary of State in connection with —

(a) the procedures to be followed by it;

(b) the exercise of its functions.

(5) In this section "relevant young persons" means persons, other than children, in relation to whom arrangements under section 10 may be made.

12C Funding of CTBs

(1) The establishing authority and any of their relevant partners represented on a Children's Trust Board may make payments towards expenditure incurred by, or for purposes connected with, the Board —

(a) by making the payments directly; or

(b) by contributing to a fund out of which the payments may be made.

(2) The establishing authority and any of their relevant partners represented on a Children's Trust Board may provide staff, goods, services, accommodation or other resources for purposes connected with the functions of the Board.

(3) Two or more Children's Trust Boards may establish and maintain a pooled fund for the purposes of any of their functions.

(4) A pooled fund is a fund —

(a) which is made up of contributions by the Boards concerned, and

(b) out of which payments may be made towards expenditure incurred in the discharge of functions of any of the Boards.

12D Supply of information to CTBs

(1) A person or body represented on a Children's Trust Board must supply to the Board any information requested by the Board for the purpose of enabling or assisting it to perform its functions.

(2) Information supplied to a Children's Trust Board under this section may be used by the Board only for the purpose of enabling or assisting it to perform its functions.

(3) Information requested under subsection (1) must be information that relates to—

    (a) the person or body to whom the request is made;

    (b) a function of that person or body, or

    (c) a person in respect of whom a function is exercisable by that person or body."

(3) For section 17 substitute—

"17 Children and young people's plans

(1) The Secretary of State may by regulations require a Children's Trust Board established by virtue of arrangements under section 10 from time to time to prepare and publish a children and young people's plan.

(2) A children and young people's plan is a plan setting out the strategy of the persons or bodies represented on the Board for co-operating with each other with a view to improving the well-being of children and relevant young persons in the area of the authority that established the Board.

(3) In subsection (2) "well-being" means well-being so far as relating to the matters specified in section 10(2)(a) to (e).

(4) Regulations under this section may in particular make provision as to—

    (a) the matters to be dealt with in a children and young people's plan;

    (b) the period to which a children and young people's plan is to relate;

    (c) when and how a children and young people's plan must be published;

    (d) keeping a children and young people's plan under review;

    (e) revising a children and young people's plan;

    (f) consultation to be carried out during preparation or revision of a children and young people's plan;

    (g) other steps required or permitted to be taken in connection with the preparation or revision of a children and young people's plan.

(5) In this section "relevant young persons" means persons, other than children, in relation to whom arrangements under section 10 may be made.

17A Children and young people's plans: implementation

(1) This section applies where a Children's Trust Board prepares a children and young people's plan in accordance with regulations under section 17.

(2) The persons and bodies whose strategy for co-operation is set out in the plan must have regard to the plan in exercising their functions.

(3)   The Board must—

    (a)   monitor the extent to which the persons and bodies whose strategy for co-operation is set out in the plan are acting in accordance with the plan;

    (b)   prepare and publish an annual report about the extent to which, during the year to which the report relates, those persons and bodies have acted in accordance with the plan."

(4)   In section 18(2) (functions of children's services authority exercisable by director of children's services) in paragraph (d) for "and 17" substitute ", 12C, 12D and 17A".

(5)   In section 23(3) (sections 20 to 22: meaning of "children's services") in paragraph (b) for "13" substitute "12B".

(6)   In section 50(2) of the Children Act 2004 (c. 31) (intervention: relevant functions) in paragraph (c) for "and 17" substitute ", 12C, 12D and 17A".

(7)   In section 66(3) of that Act (regulations and orders subject to affirmative procedure) after "12" insert ", 12B(1)(b)".

(8)   In section 47A of the School Standards and Framework Act 1998 (schools forums)—

    (a)   after subsection (3) insert—

        "(3A)   In exercising its functions, a schools forum is to have regard to any children and young people's plan prepared by the local Children's Trust Board.";

    (b)   after subsection (9) insert—

        "(10)   In this section—

            (a)   a "children and young people's plan" means a plan published by a Children's Trust Board under section 17 of the Children Act 2004;

            (b)   "the local Children's Trust Board", in relation to a schools forum, is the Children's Trust Board established by arrangements made under section 10 of that Act by the relevant authority in their capacity as a children's services authority within the meaning of that Act."

(9)   In section 21 of the Education Act 2002 (c. 32)—

    (a)   in subsection (9) for paragraph (a) (but not the "and" immediately after it) substitute—

        "(a)   in relation to a school in England, any plan published by the relevant Children's Trust Board under section 17 of the Children Act 2004 (children and young people's plans: England),";

    (b)   after subsection (9) insert—

        "(10)   In subsection (9)(a), "the relevant Children's Trust Board" means the Children's Trust Board established by arrangements made under section 10 of the Children Act 2004 by the local education authority in their capacity as a children's services authority (within the meaning of that Act)."

Safeguarding and promoting the welfare of children

195 Targets for safeguarding and promoting the welfare of children

(1) Before section 10 of the Children Act 2004 (c. 31) insert—

"9A Targets for safeguarding and promoting the welfare of children

(1) The Secretary of State may, in accordance with regulations, set safeguarding targets for a children's services authority in England.

(2) The regulations may, in particular—

   (a) make provision about matters by reference to which safeguarding targets may, or must, be set;

   (b) make provision about periods to which safeguarding targets may, or must, relate;

   (c) make provision about the procedure for setting safeguarding targets;

   (d) specify requirements with which a children's services authority in England must comply in connection with the setting of safeguarding targets.

(3) In exercising their functions, a children's services authority in England must act in the manner best calculated to secure that any safeguarding targets set under this section (so far as relating to the area of the authority) are met.

(4) "Safeguarding targets", in relation to a children's services authority in England, are targets for safeguarding and promoting the welfare of children in the authority's area."

(2) In section 66 of that Act (regulations and orders)—

   (a) in subsection (4) after "containing" insert "the first regulations under section 9A or";

   (b) in subsection (5)(a) for "to which subsection (3) does not apply" substitute "to which neither of subsections (3) and (4) applies".

(3) In Schedule 1 to the Local Authority Social Services Act 1970 (c. 42) (social services functions) in the entry relating to the Children Act 2004—

   (a) in the first column, after "Sections" insert "9A,";

   (b) in the second column, after "to" insert "targets for safeguarding and promoting the welfare of children, and to".

196 Local Safeguarding Children Boards: lay members

(1) Part 2 of the Children Act 2004 is amended as follows.

(2) In section 13 (establishment of LSCBs) after subsection (5) insert—

"(5A) A children's services authority in England must take reasonable steps to ensure that the Local Safeguarding Children Board established by them also includes two persons who appear to the authority to be representative of persons living in the authority's area.

(5B) An authority may pay remuneration, allowances and expenses to persons who are included by virtue of subsection (5A) in a Local Safeguarding Children Board established by them."

(3) In section 14 (functions and procedures of LSCBs) in subsection (1)(a) after "the Board" insert "by virtue of section 13(2), (4) or (5)".

197 Local Safeguarding Children Boards: annual reports

After section 14 of the Children Act 2004 (c. 31) insert—

"14A LSCBs: annual reports

(1) At least once in every 12 month period, a Local Safeguarding Children Board established under section 13 must prepare and publish a report about safeguarding and promoting the welfare of children in its local area.

(2) The Board must submit a copy of the report to the local Children's Trust Board.

(3) For the purposes of this section—
   (a) the local area of a Local Safeguarding Children Board is the area of the children's services authority that established the Board;
   (b) the local Children's Trust Board, in relation to a Local Safeguarding Children Board, is the Children's Trust Board established for the Board's local area."

Children's centres

198 Arrangements for children's centres

In Part 1 of the Childcare Act 2006 (c. 21) (functions of local authorities in England in relation to children) after section 5 insert—

"Children's centres

5A Arrangements for provision of children's centres

(1) Arrangements made by an English local authority under section 3(2) must, so far as is reasonably practicable, include arrangements for sufficient provision of children's centres to meet local need.

(2) "Local need" is the need of parents, prospective parents and young children in the authority's area.

(3) In determining what provision of children's centres is sufficient to meet local need, an authority may have regard to any children's centres—
   (a) that are provided outside the authority's area, or
   (b) that the authority expect to be provided outside their area.

(4) For the purposes of this Part and Part 3A a "children's centre" is a place, or a group of places—
   (a) which is managed by or on behalf of, or under arrangements made with, an English local authority, with a view to securing that early childhood services in their area are made available in an integrated manner,
   (b) through which each of the early childhood services is made available, and

(c) at which activities for young children are provided, whether by way of early years provision or otherwise.

(5) For the purposes of this section, a service is made available —
   (a) by providing the service, or
   (b) by providing advice and assistance to parents and prospective parents on gaining access to the service.

(6) Guidance given under section 3(6) in respect of arrangements made under section 3(2) by virtue of subsection (1) of this section may, in particular, relate to —
   (a) circumstances in which any early childhood services should be made available through children's centres as mentioned in subsection (5)(a);
   (b) circumstances in which any early childhood services should be made available through children's centres as mentioned in subsection (5)(b).

(7) A children's centre provided by virtue of arrangements made by an English local authority under section 3(2) is to be known as a Sure Start Children's Centre.

5B Children's centres: staffing, organisation and operation

(1) Regulations may make provision about the staffing, organisation and operation of children's centres.

(2) The regulations may in particular —
   (a) require English local authorities to secure that children's centres have governing bodies;
   (b) impose obligations and confer powers on any such governing bodies.

5C Children's centres: advisory boards

(1) This section applies where arrangements made by an English local authority under section 3(2) include arrangements for the provision of one or more children's centres.

(2) The authority must make arrangements to secure that each of the children's centres is within the remit of an advisory board.

(3) A children's centre is within the remit of an advisory board if it is specified in relation to the board by the responsible authority.

(4) An advisory board must provide advice and assistance for the purpose of ensuring the effective operation of the children's centres within its remit.

(5) An advisory board must include persons representing the interests of —
   (a) each children's centre within its remit;
   (b) the responsible authority;
   (c) parents or prospective parents in the responsible authority's area.

(6) An advisory board may also include persons representing the interests of any other persons or bodies that the responsible authority think appropriate.

(7)   In exercising their functions under this section, an English local authority must have regard to any guidance given from time to time by the Secretary of State.

(8)   The guidance may in particular relate to—
     (a)   the membership of advisory boards;
     (b)   the organisation and operation of advisory boards.

(9)   The "responsible authority", in relation to an advisory board in respect of which arrangements have been made under subsection (2), is the authority that made the arrangements.

5D   Children's centres: consultation

(1)   An English local authority must secure that such consultation as they think appropriate is carried out—
     (a)   before making arrangements under section 3(2) for the provision of a children's centre;
     (b)   before any significant change is made in the services provided through a relevant children's centre;
     (c)   before anything is done that would result in a relevant children's centre ceasing to be a children's centre.

(2)   In discharging their duty under this section, an English local authority must have regard to any guidance given from time to time by the Secretary of State.

(3)   For the purposes of this section a change in the manner in which, or the location at which, services are provided is to be treated as a change in the services.

(4)   A "relevant children's centre", in relation to an authority, is a children's centre provided by virtue of arrangements made by the authority under section 3(2).

5E   Duty to consider providing services through a children's centre

(1)   This section applies where arrangements made by an English local authority under section 3(2) include arrangements for the provision of one or more children's centres.

(2)   The authority must consider whether each of the early childhood services to be provided by them should be provided through any of those children's centres.

(3)   Each relevant partner of the authority must consider whether each of the early childhood services to be provided by it in the authority's area should be provided through any of those children's centres.

(4)   In discharging their duties under this section, the authority and each relevant partner must take into account whether providing a service through any of the children's centres in question would—
     (a)   facilitate access to it, or
     (b)   maximise its benefit to parents, prospective parents and young children.

(5) In discharging their duties under this section, an English local authority and each of their relevant partners must have regard to any guidance given from time to time by the Secretary of State.

(6) For the purposes of this section, early childhood services are provided by a person or body if they are provided on behalf of, or under arrangements made with, that person or body.

(7) For the avoidance of doubt, nothing in this section is to be taken as preventing an English local authority or any of their relevant partners from providing early childhood services otherwise than through a children's centre.

5F   Children's centres: transitional provision

(1) This section applies if immediately before the commencement date an English local authority has made arrangements for the provision of a children's centre.

(2) To the extent that this would not otherwise be the case, the arrangements are to be treated for the purposes of this Part and Part 3A as made under section 3(2).

(3) "The commencement date" is the day on which section 198 of the Apprenticeships, Skills, Children and Learning Act 2009 comes into force.

5G   Children's centres: interpretation

In sections 5A to 5F —

"children's centre" has the meaning given by section 5A(4);

"early childhood services" has the same meaning as in section 3;

"parent" and "prospective parent" have the same meaning as in section 2;

"relevant partner" has the same meaning as in section 4."

199   Inspection of children's centres

After Part 3 of the Childcare Act 2006 (c. 21) (regulation of provision of childcare in England) insert —

"PART 3A

INSPECTION OF CHILDREN'S CENTRES

98A   Inspections

(1) The Chief Inspector must —
  (a) inspect a children's centre at such intervals as may be prescribed;
  (b) inspect a children's centre at any time when the Secretary of State requires the Chief Inspector to secure its inspection.

(2) The Chief Inspector may inspect a children's centre at any other time when the Chief Inspector considers that it would be appropriate for it to be inspected.

(3)   Regulations may provide that in prescribed circumstances the Chief Inspector is not required to inspect a children's centre at an interval prescribed for the purposes of subsection (1)(a).

(4)   A requirement made by the Secretary of State as mentioned in subsection (1)(b) may be imposed in relation to —

     (a)   children's centres generally;

     (b)   a class of children's centres;

     (c)   a particular children's centre.

(5)   For the purposes of subsection (4)(b) a class of children's centres may be described, in particular, by reference to a geographical area.

(6)   If the Chief Inspector so elects in the case of an inspection falling within subsection (1)(b) or (2), that inspection is to be treated as if it were an inspection falling within subsection (1)(a).

98B   Reports

(1)   After conducting an inspection of a children's centre under section 98A, the Chief Inspector must make a report in writing.

(2)   The report must address the centre's contribution to —

     (a)   facilitating access to early childhood services by parents, prospective parents and young children;

     (b)   maximising the benefit of those services to parents, prospective parents and young children;

     (c)   improving the well-being of young children.

(3)   Regulations may make provision, for the purposes of subsection (2), about —

     (a)   matters required to be dealt with in the report;

     (b)   matters not required to be dealt with in the report.

(4)   The regulations may, in particular, require the matters dealt with in the report to include matters relating to the quality of the leadership and management of the centre, including whether the financial resources made available to it are managed effectively.

(5)   The Chief Inspector —

     (a)   may send a copy of the report to the Secretary of State and must do so without delay if the Secretary of State requests a copy;

     (b)   must ensure that a copy of the report is sent without delay to the relevant local authority;

     (c)   may arrange for the report (or parts of it) to be further published in any manner the Chief Inspector considers appropriate.

(6)   For the purposes of this section and section 98C, the "relevant local authority", in relation to a children's centre, is the English local authority that made the arrangements under section 3(2) by virtue of which the centre is provided.

98C   Action to be taken by local authority on receiving report

(1)   This section applies where a copy of a report relating to a children's centre is sent to the relevant local authority under section 98B(5)(b).

(2)   The authority may —

(a) send a copy of the report (or parts of it) to any person they think appropriate;

(b) otherwise publish the report (or parts of it) in any manner they think appropriate.

(3) The authority must secure that a written statement within subsection (4) is prepared and published.

(4) A statement within this subsection is one setting out —

(a) the action that each relevant person proposes to take in the light of the report, and

(b) the period within which each relevant person proposes to take that action.

(5) For the purposes of this section and section 98D, each of the following is a relevant person in relation to a children's centre —

(a) the relevant local authority;

(b) any person or body, other than the relevant local authority, managing the centre.

(6) In exercising their functions under this section, an English local authority must have regard to any guidance given from time to time by the Secretary of State.

98D Inspections of children's centres: powers of entry

(1) The Chief Inspector may, at any reasonable time, enter any relevant premises in England for the purpose of conducting an inspection of a children's centre under section 98A.

(2) "Relevant premises", for the purposes of subsection (1), are —

(a) premises on which services or activities are being provided through the children's centre;

(b) premises of a relevant person which are used in connection with the staffing, organisation or operation of the children's centre.

(3) But premises used wholly or mainly as a private dwelling are not relevant premises for the purposes of subsection (1).

(4) An authorisation given by the Chief Inspector under paragraph 9(1) of Schedule 12 to the Education and Inspections Act 2006 in relation to functions under subsection (1) —

(a) may be given for a particular occasion or period;

(b) may be given subject to conditions.

(5) Subject to any conditions imposed under subsection (4)(b), subsections (6) to (8) apply where a person ("the inspector") enters premises under this section.

(6) The inspector may —

(a) inspect the premises;

(b) take measurements and photographs or make recordings;

(c) inspect any children for whom activities are provided on the premises, and the arrangements made for their welfare;

(d) interview in private any person working on the premises who consents to be interviewed.

(7) The inspector may inspect, and take copies of, any records or documents relating to —

    (a) the services or activities provided through the children's centre;

    (b) the staffing, organisation or operation of the children's centre.

(8) The inspector may require a person to afford such facilities and assistance, with respect to matters within the person's control, as are necessary to enable the inspector to exercise the powers conferred by this section.

(9) Section 58 of the Education Act 2005 (inspection of computer records) applies for the purposes of this section as it applies for the purposes of Part 1 of that Act.

(10) In this section "documents" and "records" each include information recorded in any form.

98E   Obstruction of power of entry, etc.

(1) A person commits an offence if the person intentionally obstructs another person exercising a power under section 98D.

(2) A person guilty of an offence under subsection (1) is liable on summary conviction to a fine not exceeding level 4 on the standard scale.

98F   Power of constable to assist in exercise of power of entry

(1) The Chief Inspector may apply to a court for a warrant under this section.

(2) Subsection (3) applies if on an application under subsection (1) it appears to the court that the Chief Inspector —

    (a) has attempted to exercise a power conferred by section 98D but has been prevented from doing so, or

    (b) is likely to be prevented from exercising any such power.

(3) The court may issue a warrant authorising any constable to assist the Chief Inspector in the exercise of the power, using reasonable force if necessary.

(4) A warrant under this section must be addressed to, and executed by, a constable.

(5) Schedule 11 to the Children Act 1989 (jurisdiction of courts) applies in relation to proceedings under this section as if they were proceedings under that Act.

(6) Subject to any provision made (by virtue of subsection (5)) by or under Schedule 11 to the Children Act 1989, "court" in this section means —

    (a) the High Court;

    (b) a county court;

    (c) a magistrates' court.

98G   Inspection of children's centres: interpretation

In sections 98A to 98F —

    "the Chief Inspector" means Her Majesty's Chief Inspector of Education, Children's Services and Skills;

    "children's centre" has the meaning given by section 5A(4);

"relevant partner" has the same meaning as in section 4."

200 Children's centres: safeguarding children

In paragraph 3(1) of Schedule 4 to the Safeguarding Vulnerable Groups Act 2006 (c. 47) (regulated activities relating to children: establishments) after paragraph (f) insert—

> "(fa) a children's centre (within the meaning of section 5A(4) of the Childcare Act 2006);".

Arrangements in respect of early childhood services

201 Arrangements in respect of early childhood services

In section 3 of the Childcare Act 2006 (c. 21) (specific duties of local authority in relation to early childhood services) after subsection (4) insert—

> "(4A) In deciding what arrangements to make under this section, an English local authority must in particular have regard to—
>
> (a) the quantity and quality of early childhood services that are provided, or that the authority expect to be provided, in their area, and
>
> (b) where in that area those services are provided or are expected to be provided."

Early years provision: budgetary framework

202 Free of charge early years provision: budgetary framework: England

(1) The School Standards and Framework Act 1998 (c. 31) is amended as follows.

(2) In section 45A (determination of specified budgets of LEA), after subsection (4A) insert—

> "(4B) For the purposes of this Part, the duty imposed on a local authority in England by section 7(1) of the Childcare Act 2006 (duty to secure prescribed early years provision free of charge) is to be treated as imposed on the authority in their capacity as a local education authority."

(3) After section 47 (determination of school's budget share) insert—

> "47ZA Free of charge early years provision outside a maintained school: budgetary framework: England
>
> (1) This section applies where a local education authority in England propose to allocate an amount of relevant financial assistance to a relevant childcare provider for a funding period out of the authority's individual schools budget for the period.
>
> (2) The amount to be allocated is to be determined in accordance with regulations.
>
> (3) Financial assistance provided by a local education authority in England to a childcare provider is "relevant" financial assistance if it is provided—

    (a)   for the purpose of the discharge of the authority's duty under section 7 of the Childcare Act 2006, and

    (b)   in respect of the provision of childcare.

(4)   Regulations under this section may, in particular –

    (a)   specify factors or criteria which an authority are to take into account in determining the amount of any relevant financial assistance to be provided by them to a relevant childcare provider;

    (b)   specify factors or criteria which an authority are to disregard in determining such an amount;

    (c)   specify requirements as to other matters with which an authority are to comply in determining such an amount;

    (d)   make provision about consultation to be carried out by an authority in connection with determining such an amount;

    (e)   authorise an authority, in prescribed circumstances and to a prescribed extent, to determine such an amount in accordance with arrangements approved by the Secretary of State (instead of in accordance with arrangements provided for by the regulations);

    (f)   require an authority to provide relevant childcare providers with prescribed information relating to their determination of such an amount;

    (g)   make provision about the circumstances in which an authority are required to redetermine such an amount;

    (h)   specify a time by which an authority's determination of such an amount is to take place.

(5)   For the purposes of this section –

    (a)   "childcare" has the meaning given in section 18 of the Childcare Act 2006;

    (b)   "relevant childcare provider" means a provider of childcare other than the governing body of a maintained school;

    (c)   a reference to an authority's determination of the amount of any relevant financial assistance includes a reference to the authority's redetermination of such an amount."

PART 10

SCHOOLS

CHAPTER 1

SCHOOLS CAUSING CONCERN

Schools causing concern: England

203   Powers in relation to schools causing concern: England

Schedule 13 makes provision in relation to schools causing concern in England.

Apprenticeships, Skills, Children and Learning Act 2009 (c. 22)
Part 10 — Schools
Chapter 1 — Schools causing concern

2297

204 Power to require LEAs in England to obtain advisory services

(1) Section 62A of the Education Act 2002 (power of Secretary of State to require LEAs in England to obtain advisory services) is amended as follows.

(2) After subsection (1) insert—

"(1A) This section also applies where it appears to the Secretary of State that—

    (a) a local education authority in England maintain a disproportionate number of low-performing schools, and

    (b) the authority—

        (i) have not been effective or are unlikely to be effective in securing an improvement in the standards of performance of pupils at those schools, or

        (ii) are unlikely to be effective in securing an improvement in the standards of performance of pupils at other schools which may in the future be low-performing schools.

(1B) In subsection (1A) "low-performing school" means a school at which the standards of performance of pupils are unacceptably low.

(1C) For the purposes of subsection (1B) the standards of performance of pupils at a school are low if they are low by reference to any one or more of the following—

    (a) the standards that the pupils might in all the circumstances reasonably be expected to attain;

    (b) where relevant, the standards previously attained by them;

    (c) the standards attained by pupils at comparable schools."

(3) In subsection (4) after "section" insert—

""pupil" has the same meaning as in the Education Act 1996 (see sections 3 and 19(5) of that Act);".

Schools causing concern: Wales

205 Powers in relation to schools causing concern: Wales

Schedule 14 makes provision in relation to schools causing concern in Wales.

CHAPTER 2

COMPLAINTS: ENGLAND

206 Complaints to which this Chapter applies

(1) This Chapter applies to a complaint against a school made by—

    (a) a parent of a pupil at a qualifying school in England; or

    (b) a pupil at such a school.

(2) In subsection (1) "a complaint against a school" means (subject to subsection (3)) a complaint that the pupil or a parent of the pupil has sustained injustice in consequence of—

       (a)   an act of the governing body of the school; or

       (b)   an exercise of, or failure to exercise, a prescribed function of the head teacher of the school.

(3)   A "complaint against a school" does not include a complaint that relates to—

       (a)   a decision about admissions to the school;

       (b)   a matter in respect of which the complainant has or had a prescribed right of appeal.

(4)   An act is to be treated as an act of the governing body of a school for the purposes of subsection (2) if it is an act of—

       (a)   a person acting on behalf of the governing body; or

       (b)   a person to whom the governing body has delegated any functions.

(5)   An act is also to be treated as an act of the governing body of a school if—

       (a)   the governing body exercises a function by means of an arrangement with another person; and

       (b)   the act is done by or on behalf of the other person in carrying out the arrangement.

(6)   In this section—

       (a)   "function" includes a power and a duty;

       (b)   "head teacher" has the meaning given by section 579(1) of the Education Act 1996 (c. 56);

       (c)   "qualifying school" means a community, foundation or voluntary school, a community or foundation special school, a maintained nursery school (within the meaning given by section 22(9) of the School Standards and Framework Act 1998 (c. 31)) or a short stay school;

       (d)   references to a pupil at a qualifying school are (subject to section 207(6)) references to a person who is, or was within a prescribed period ending with the date of the complaint, a registered pupil (within the meaning of the Education Act 1996) at the school;

       (e)   "parent", in relation to a pupil, has the meaning given by section 576 of the Education Act 1996 in relation to a child or young person.

(7)   In this Chapter a reference to an act includes an omission.

207   Power of Local Commissioner to investigate complaint

(1)   This section applies where a complaint to which this Chapter applies, and which meets the requirements of section 208—

       (a)   is made by the complainant to a Local Commissioner; or

       (b)   is made by the complainant to a governor, the governing body or the head teacher of the school and referred to a Local Commissioner, with the complainant's consent, by the governing body or the head teacher of the school.

(2)   Where this section applies, a Local Commissioner may under this Chapter investigate the complaint.

(3)   But before investigating a complaint to which this Chapter applies, a Local Commissioner must be satisfied—

       (a)   that the matter was brought to the notice of the governing body by or on behalf of the complainant and that the governing body was given a reasonable opportunity to investigate the matter and respond; or

    (b)   that, in the particular circumstances, it is not reasonable to expect the matter to be brought to the notice of the governing body or for the governing body to be given a reasonable opportunity to investigate the matter and respond.

(4)   Whether to initiate, continue or discontinue an investigation is a matter for the discretion of the Local Commissioner dealing with the complaint.

(5)   A Local Commissioner may in particular decide not to investigate a complaint under this Chapter, or to discontinue an investigation —

    (a)   if satisfied with the action that the governing body has taken or proposes to take; or

    (b)   if satisfied that the complaint is vexatious.

(6)   Regulations prescribing a period for the purposes of section 206(6)(d) may prescribe circumstances in which a Local Commissioner may determine that a person who has not been a registered pupil at the school within the prescribed period is to be treated as a "pupil" for the purposes of that section.

(7)   In this Chapter "Local Commissioner" has the meaning given by section 23 of the Local Government Act 1974 (c. 7).

208   Time-limit etc for making complaint

(1)   The requirements referred to in section 207(1) are that the complaint is made —

    (a)   in writing; and

    (b)   within 12 months beginning with the day the complainant first had notice of the matter complained of;

but this is subject to subsection (2).

(2)   A Local Commissioner may disapply either or both of the requirements in subsection (1) in relation to a particular complainant.

209   Procedure in respect of investigations

(1)   A Local Commissioner who proposes to investigate a complaint to which this Chapter applies must give the following an opportunity to comment on the matter —

    (a)   the respondent;

    (b)   any other person who is alleged in the complaint to have done or authorised the act which would be the subject of the investigation;

    (c)   any person who otherwise appears to the Local Commissioner to have done or authorised the act.

(2)   Every investigation under this Chapter is to be conducted in private.

(3)   Subject to subsection (2), the procedure for conducting an investigation is to be such as the Local Commissioner considers appropriate in the circumstances of the case.

(4)   The Local Commissioner may, in particular —

    (a)   obtain information from such persons and in such manner as the Local Commissioner thinks fit;

    (b)   make such inquiries as the Local Commissioner thinks fit; and

    (c)   determine whether any person may be represented (by counsel, solicitor or otherwise) in the investigation.

(5)   The Local Commissioner may, if the Local Commissioner thinks fit, pay to the complainant, and to any other person who attends or provides information for the purposes of an investigation under this Chapter —

    (a)   sums in respect of the expenses properly incurred by them;

    (b)   allowances by way of compensation for the loss of their time.

(6)   In this Chapter a reference to the "respondent" is a reference to the governing body or head teacher about whose act a complaint to which this Chapter applies was made.

210   Investigations: further provisions

(1)   For the purposes of an investigation under this Chapter a Local Commissioner may require the following persons to provide information or produce documents relevant to the investigation —

    (a)   the respondent;

    (b)   any other person who in the Local Commissioner's opinion is able to provide any such information or produce any such documents.

(2)   For the purposes of an investigation under this Chapter a Local Commissioner has the same powers as the High Court in respect of —

    (a)   the attendance and examination of witnesses; and

    (b)   the production of documents.

(3)   To assist in any investigation, a Local Commissioner may obtain advice from any person who in the Local Commissioner's opinion is qualified to give it.

(4)   A Local Commissioner may pay to a person giving advice such fees or allowances as the Local Commissioner may determine.

(5)   A Local Commissioner may appoint and pay a mediator or other appropriate person to assist in the conduct of an investigation under this Chapter.

(6)   Any person appointed under subsection (5) is deemed to be an officer of the Commission for Local Administration in England in carrying out functions under that appointment.

(7)   No person may be compelled for the purposes of an investigation under this Chapter to give any evidence or produce any document which the person could not be compelled to give or produce in civil proceedings before the High Court.

(8)   If any person, without lawful excuse —

    (a)   obstructs a Local Commissioner in the performance of the Local Commissioner's functions under this Chapter;

    (b)   obstructs a person discharging or assisting in the discharge of those functions; or

    (c)   is guilty of an act in relation to an investigation under this Chapter which, if that investigation were a proceeding in the High Court, would constitute contempt of court,

the Local Commissioner may certify the offence to the High Court.

(9)   Where an offence is certified under subsection (8), the High Court may inquire into the matter and, after hearing any witnesses who may be produced against or on behalf of the person charged ("D"), and after hearing any statement that may be offered in D's defence, deal with D in any manner in which the High

Court could deal with a person who had committed the offence in relation to the High Court.

211 Statements about investigations

(1) A Local Commissioner must prepare a written statement in accordance with subsections (2) to (4) if the Local Commissioner –

    (a) decides not to investigate a matter under this Chapter;

    (b) decides to discontinue an investigation; or

    (c) completes an investigation.

(2) In a case falling within subsection (1)(a) or (b), the statement must set out the Local Commissioner's reasons for the decision.

(3) In a case falling within subsection (1)(c), the statement must –

    (a) set out the Local Commissioner's conclusions on the investigation; and

    (b) include any recommendations the Local Commissioner considers it appropriate to make.

(4) The recommendations the Local Commissioner may make are recommendations with respect to action which, in the Local Commissioner's opinion, the governing body should take –

    (a) to remedy any injustice sustained by the complainant in consequence of the act which was the subject of the investigation; and

    (b) to prevent injustice being caused in the future in consequence of a similar act.

(5) The Local Commissioner must send a copy of a statement prepared under this section to –

    (a) the complainant (or, if the complainant is the pupil and the Local Commissioner thinks it appropriate, a parent of the complainant);

    (b) the respondent; and

    (c) the governing body, if the respondent is the head teacher.

(6) If, on consideration of the statement, it appears to the governing body that a payment should be made to or in respect of a person who has suffered injustice in consequence of the act which was the subject of the investigation, the governing body may make such a payment.

(7) The statement must identify the school concerned.

(8) The statement must not –

    (a) mention the name of any person; or

    (b) contain any particulars which, in the opinion of the Local Commissioner, are likely to identify any person and can be omitted without impairing the effectiveness of the statement.

(9) But, after taking into account the public interest as well as the interests of that person, the complainant and other persons, the Local Commissioner may mention the name of a person, or include in the statement any particulars which are likely to identify the person, if the Local Commissioner considers it necessary to do so.

(10) Nothing in subsection (8) prevents a statement mentioning the name of, or containing particulars which are likely to identify, the head teacher of the school concerned.

212   Adverse findings notices

(1)   This section applies where a governing body receives a statement prepared under section 211 which contains recommendations.

(2)   The governing body must—

    (a)   consider the statement; and

    (b)   notify the Local Commissioner, within the notification period, of the action which the governing body has taken or proposes to take.

(3)   The Local Commissioner may by notice require the governing body to arrange for an adverse findings notice to be published in accordance with subsections (4) and (5) if the Local Commissioner—

    (a)   does not receive the notification mentioned in subsection (2)(b) within the notification period or is satisfied before the end of that period that the governing body has decided to take no action;

    (b)   is not satisfied with the action which the governing body has taken or proposes to take; or

    (c)   does not within the period of one month beginning with the end of the notification period, or such longer period as the Local Commissioner may agree in writing, receive confirmation that the governing body has taken action, as proposed, to the satisfaction of the Commissioner.

(4)   An adverse findings notice is a notice, in such form as the governing body and the Local Commissioner may agree, consisting of—

    (a)   details of any action recommended in the statement which the governing body has not taken;

    (b)   such supporting material as the Local Commissioner may require;

    (c)   if the governing body so requires, an explanation of the reasons for having taken no action, or for not having taken the action recommended in the statement.

(5)   The adverse findings notice must be published by the governing body in such a way as the Local Commissioner may direct.

(6)   If the governing body—

    (a)   fails to arrange for the publication of the adverse findings notice in accordance with subsections (4) and (5); or

    (b)   is unable, within the publication period, to agree with the Local Commissioner the form of the adverse findings notice to be published,

the Local Commissioner must arrange for an adverse findings notice to be published in such a way as the Local Commissioner considers appropriate.

(7)   The governing body must reimburse the Local Commissioner on demand any reasonable expenses incurred by the Local Commissioner in performing the duty under subsection (6).

(8)   In this section—

    "notification period" means—

        (a)   the period of one month beginning with the date on which the governing body received the statement; or

        (b)   such longer period as the Local Commissioner may agree in writing.

    "publication period" means—

    (a) the period of one month beginning with the date on which the governing body received the notice under subsection (3); or

    (b) such longer period as the Local Commissioner may agree in writing.

213 Publication of statements etc. by Local Commissioner

(1) A Local Commissioner may –

    (a) publish all or part of a statement under section 211; or

    (b) publish a summary of a matter which is the subject of a statement under section 211,

if, after taking into account the public interest as well as the interests of the complainant and of other persons, the Local Commissioner considers it appropriate to do so.

(2) A Local Commissioner may –

    (a) supply a copy of all or part of a statement or summary mentioned in subsection (1) to any person who requests it; and

    (b) charge a reasonable fee for doing so.

(3) Where a Local Commissioner publishes all or part of a statement or summary mentioned in subsection (1), the governing body of the school concerned must, on demand, reimburse the Local Commissioner the reasonable expenses of publication.

(4) Subsections (8) to (10) of section 211 apply to a summary of a matter which is published, or a copy of which is supplied, under this section as they apply to a statement prepared under that section.

214 Disclosure of information

(1) Information obtained by a Local Commissioner, or any person discharging or assisting in the discharge of a function of a Local Commissioner, in the course of or for the purposes of an investigation under this Chapter must not be disclosed except –

    (a) for the purpose of the investigation and of any statement, adverse findings notice or summary under section 211, 212 or 213;

    (b) for the purposes of any proceedings for an offence of perjury alleged to have been committed in the course of an investigation under this Chapter;

    (c) for the purposes of proceedings under section 210(9).

(2) A Local Commissioner and a person discharging or assisting in the discharge of a function of a Local Commissioner may not be called upon to give evidence in any proceedings (other than proceedings within paragraph (b) or (c) of subsection (1)) of matters coming to their knowledge in the course of an investigation under this Chapter.

215 Permitted disclosures of information by Local Commissioner

(1) A Local Commissioner may disclose to Her Majesty's Chief Inspector of Education, Children's Services and Skills any information obtained by the Local Commissioner under or for the purposes of this Chapter if the

information appears to the Local Commissioner to relate to a matter in respect of which the Chief Inspector has functions.

(2)   A Local Commissioner may disclose to the Parliamentary Commissioner for Administration any information obtained by the Local Commissioner under or for the purposes of this Chapter if the information appears to the Local Commissioner to relate to a matter in respect of which the Parliamentary Commissioner has functions.

(3)   A Local Commissioner may disclose to the Information Commissioner any information obtained by the Local Commissioner under or for the purposes of this Chapter if the information appears to the Local Commissioner to relate to —

    (a)   a matter in respect of which the Information Commissioner could exercise any power conferred by —

        (i)   Part 5 of the Data Protection Act 1998 (c. 29) (enforcement);

        (ii)   section 48 of the Freedom of Information Act 2000 (c. 36) (practice recommendations); or

        (iii)   Part 4 of that Act (enforcement); or

    (b)   the commission of an offence under —

        (i)   any provision of the Data Protection Act 1998 other than paragraph 12 of Schedule 9 (obstruction of execution of warrant); or

        (ii)   section 77 of the Freedom of Information Act 2000 (offence of altering etc. records with intent to prevent disclosure).

(4)   A Local Commissioner may disclose to a local education authority (within the meaning given by section 12 of the Education Act 1996 (c. 56)) any information obtained by the Local Commissioner under or for the purposes of this Chapter if the information appears to the Local Commissioner to relate to a matter in respect of which the authority has functions.

(5)   A Local Commissioner may disclose to the Secretary of State any information obtained by the Local Commissioner under or for the purposes of this Chapter if the information appears to the Local Commissioner to relate to the Secretary of State's functions under section 220.

(6)   Nothing in section 214(1) applies in relation to the disclosure of information in accordance with this section.

216   Law of defamation

(1)   For the purposes of the law of defamation the following are absolutely privileged —

    (a)   the publication of any matter in communications between a governing body and a Local Commissioner, or any person discharging or assisting in the discharge of a function of a Local Commissioner, for the purposes of this Chapter;

    (b)   the publication of any matter by a Local Commissioner or by any person discharging or assisting in the discharge of a function of a Local Commissioner, in communicating for the purposes of this Chapter with a person mentioned in subsection (2);

    (c)   the publication of any matter in preparing, making and sending a statement in accordance with section 211;

(d)   the publication of any matter by inclusion in an adverse findings notice published in accordance with section 212(3), (4) and (5) or (6);

(e)   the publication of any matter by inclusion in a statement or summary published or supplied under section 213;

(f)   the publication of any matter contained in a report by a Local Commissioner which has been made available to the public, being publication by inclusion in a report made or published under section 219.

(2)   The persons mentioned in subsection (1)(b) are –

(a)   the governing body;

(b)   the complainant (or, if the complainant is the pupil, a parent of the complainant);

(c)   Her Majesty's Chief Inspector of Education, Children's Services and Skills;

(d)   the Parliamentary Commissioner for Administration;

(e)   a local education authority (within the meaning given by section 12 of the Education Act 1996 (c. 56));

(f)   the Secretary of State.

217   Consultation with Parliamentary Commissioner for Administration

(1)   Subsection (2) applies if, at any stage in the course of an investigation under this Chapter, a Local Commissioner forms the opinion that the matters which are the subject of the investigation include a matter which could be the subject of an investigation by the Parliamentary Commissioner for Administration in accordance with the Parliamentary Commissioner Act 1967 (c. 13) ("the 1967 Act").

(2)   The Local Commissioner –

(a)   must consult the Parliamentary Commissioner for Administration about the matter; and

(b)   where a complaint was made about the matter must, if the Local Commissioner considers it necessary, inform the complainant of the steps necessary to initiate a complaint under the 1967 Act.

(3)   Consultation under subsection (2)(a) in relation to a matter under investigation under this Chapter may be about anything relating to the matter, including –

(a)   the conduct of any investigation into the matter; and

(b)   the form, content and publication of any report or statement of the result of such an investigation.

(4)   Subsection (5) applies if, at any stage in the course of conducting an investigation under the 1967 Act, the Parliamentary Commissioner for Administration forms the opinion that the complaint relates partly to a matter which could be the subject of an investigation under this Chapter.

(5)   The Parliamentary Commissioner for Administration –

(a)   must consult the appropriate Local Commissioner about the complaint; and

(b)   where the Parliamentary Commissioner considers it necessary, must inform the person initiating the complaint of the steps necessary to initiate a complaint under this Chapter.

(6) Where a Local Commissioner is consulted about a complaint under the 1967 Act by virtue of subsection (5), subsection (3) applies (with the necessary modifications) as it applies in relation to consultations held by virtue of subsection (2).

(7) Section 11(2) of the 1967 Act (secrecy) does not apply in relation to the disclosure of information in the course of consultations held in accordance with this section.

218 Arrangements etc. to be made by Commission

(1) The Commission for Local Administration in England ("the Commission") must—
  (a) divide the matters which may be investigated under this Chapter into such categories as it considers appropriate; and
  (b) allocate, or make arrangements for allocating, responsibility for each category of matter to one or more of the Local Commissioners.

(2) The Commission—
  (a) must make arrangements for Local Commissioners to deal with matters for which they do not have responsibility pursuant to subsection (1); and
  (b) must publish information about the procedures for making complaints under this Chapter.

(3) The information published under subsection (2)(b) must include details of assistance available to each of the following—
  (a) a pupil at a qualifying school (see section 206(6)(d)) who is, or has been, looked after by a local authority (within the meaning given by section 22(1) of the Children Act 1989 (c. 41));
  (b) a person who has a disability (within the meaning of section 1(1) of the Disability Discrimination Act 1995 (c. 50));
  (c) a person who has special educational needs (within the meaning of section 312 of the Education Act 1996 (c. 56)).

219 Annual reports

(1) Every Local Commissioner must for each financial year—
  (a) prepare a general report on the discharge of the Local Commissioner's functions under this Chapter; and
  (b) submit it to the Commission.

(2) The Commission must, for each financial year, prepare a general report on the discharge of the Local Commissioners' functions under this Chapter (an "annual report").

(3) The annual report must be prepared as soon as practicable after the Commission has received the reports for the year from the Local Commissioners under subsection (1).

(4) The Commission must arrange for the publication of—
  (a) the annual report; and
  (b) the reports which are submitted under subsection (1).

(5) The Commission must lay a copy of the annual report before Parliament.

(6) In this section "financial year" means the period of 12 months ending with 31st March in any year.

220 Secretary of State's power of direction

(1) This section applies where—

    (a) a Local Commissioner has made recommendations under section 211(4); and

    (b) the governing body of the school concerned has not complied with them.

(2) The Secretary of State may direct the governing body to comply with the recommendations within the period specified in the direction.

(3) A direction under subsection (2) is enforceable, on an application made on behalf of the Secretary of State, by a mandatory order.

221 Disapplication of certain powers of Secretary of State

(1) In section 496 of the Education Act 1996 (c. 56) (power of Secretary of State to prevent unreasonable exercise of functions), after subsection (2) insert—

    "(3) The Secretary of State may not make a direction under this section in respect of a matter that—

        (a) has been complained about to a Local Commissioner in accordance with Chapter 2 of Part 10 of the Apprenticeships, Skills, Children and Learning Act 2009 (parental complaints against governing bodies etc.), or

        (b) in the Secretary of State's opinion, could have been so complained about.

    (4) Regulations may disapply subsection (3) in relation to cases where a complaint about the matter has been made to the Secretary of State by—

        (a) a prescribed person, or

        (b) a person of a prescribed description."

(2) In section 497 of that Act (general default powers of Secretary of State), after subsection (3) insert—

    "(4) The Secretary of State may not make an order under this section in respect of a matter that—

        (a) has been complained about to a Local Commissioner in accordance with Chapter 2 of Part 10 of the Apprenticeships, Skills, Children and Learning Act 2009 (parental complaints against governing bodies etc.), or

        (b) in the Secretary of State's opinion, could have been so complained about.

    (5) Regulations may disapply subsection (4) in relation to cases where a complaint about the matter has been made to the Secretary of State by—

        (a) a prescribed person, or

        (b) a person of a prescribed description."

(3) In section 28M of the Disability Discrimination Act 1995 (c. 50) (directions by

Secretary of State and Welsh Ministers) after subsection (7) insert—

"(7A) The Secretary of State may not, unless subsection (7B) applies, give a direction under this section to a responsible body in England in respect of a matter that—

(a) has been complained about to a Local Commissioner in accordance with Chapter 2 of Part 10 of the Apprenticeships, Skills, Children and Learning Act 2009 (parental complaints against governing bodies etc.), or

(b) in the Secretary of State's opinion, could have been so complained about.

(7B) This subsection applies if—

(a) the Local Commissioner has made a recommendation to the responsible body under section 211(4) of the Apprenticeships, Skills, Children and Learning Act 2009 (statement following investigation) in respect of the matter, and

(b) the responsible body has not complied with the recommendation."

222 Power to amend meaning of "qualifying school"

(1) The Secretary of State may by order amend the definition of "qualifying school" in section 206(6)(c).

(2) An order under this section may make consequential amendments of this Chapter.

223 Amendments consequential on Chapter 2

(1) The following provisions of the Education Act 1996 (c. 56) cease to have effect—

(a) section 408(4)(g) (provision of information);

(b) section 409 (complaints and enforcement: maintained schools);

(c) paragraph 6(3) and (4) of Schedule 1 (complaints and enforcement: short stay schools).

(2) In paragraph 1 of Schedule 4 to the Local Government Act 1974 (c. 7) (the Commission), after sub-paragraph (2B) (inserted by the Health Act 2009 (c. 21)) insert—

"(2C) A Local Commissioner may not investigate a complaint against a school under Chapter 2 of Part 10 of the Apprenticeships, Skills, Children and Learning Act 2009 if the Local Commissioner—

(a) is a governor of the school;

(b) is a parent of—

(i) a registered pupil at the school, or

(ii) a person who has been a registered pupil at the school within the five years ending with the making of the complaint; or

(c) works at the school or has worked at the school within those five years.

(2D) In sub-paragraph (2C) "registered pupil" has the same meaning as in the Education Act 1996."

224 Interpretation of Chapter 2

In this Chapter —
    (a)   "act" has the meaning given by section 206(7);
    (b)   "the Commission" has the meaning given by section 218(1);
    (c)   "Local Commissioner" has the meaning given by section 207(7);
    (d)   "respondent" has the meaning given by section 209(6).

CHAPTER 3

INSPECTIONS

225 Interim statements

(1)   The Education Act 2005 (c. 18) is amended as follows.

(2)   After section 10 insert —

"10A Interim statements between inspections

   (1)   The Chief Inspector may make a statement (an "interim statement") about a school in England to which section 5 applies.

   (2)   An interim statement is a statement —
       (a)   that the Chief Inspector is of the opinion that it is not necessary for the school to be inspected under section 5 for at least a year after the date on which the statement is made,
       (b)   setting out the Chief Inspector's reasons for forming that opinion, and
       (c)   containing such other information (if any) as the Chief Inspector considers appropriate.

   (3)   The Chief Inspector may arrange for an interim statement to be published in such manner as the Chief Inspector considers appropriate.

   (4)   Section 151 of the Education and Inspections Act 2006 (publication of inspection reports: privilege and electronic publication) applies in relation to an interim statement as it applies in relation to a report."

(3)   In the italic heading before section 14 after "reports" insert "and interim statements".

(4)   After section 14 insert —

"14A Destination of interim statements: maintained schools

   (1)   The Chief Inspector must ensure that a copy of any interim statement about a maintained school is sent without delay to the appropriate authority for the school.

   (2)   The Chief Inspector must ensure that copies of the statement are sent —
       (a)   to the head teacher of the school,
       (b)   to whichever of the local education authority and the governing body are not the appropriate authority, and
       (c)   in the case of a school having foundation governors, to the person who appoints them and (if different) to the appropriate appointing authority.

(3) If the school provides full-time education suitable to the requirements of pupils over compulsory school age, the Chief Inspector must ensure that a copy of the statement is also sent to the Young People's Learning Agency for England.

(4) The appropriate authority must—

(a) make a copy of any statement sent to the authority under subsection (1) available for inspection by members of the public at such times and at such places as may be reasonable,

(b) provide one copy of the statement free of charge to any person who asks for one, and

(c) take such steps as are reasonably practicable to secure that every registered parent of a registered pupil at the school receives a copy of the statement within such period following receipt of the statement by the authority as may be prescribed."

(5) In the italic heading before section 16 after "reports" insert "and interim statements".

(6) After section 16 insert—

"16A Destination of interim statements: non-maintained schools

(1) The Chief Inspector must ensure that a copy of any interim statement about a school other than a maintained school is sent without delay to the proprietor of the school.

(2) In the case of a special school which is not a community or foundation special school, the proprietor must without delay send a copy of any interim statement sent to the proprietor under subsection (1) to any local education authority that are paying fees in respect of the attendance of a registered pupil at the school.

(3) The proprietor of the school must—

(a) make any statement sent to the proprietor under subsection (1) available for inspection by members of the public at such times and at such place as may be reasonable,

(b) provide one copy of the statement free of charge to any person who asks for one, and

(c) take such steps as are reasonably practicable to secure that every registered parent of a registered pupil at the school receives a copy of the statement within such period following receipt of the statement by the proprietor as may be prescribed."

(7) In section 18 (interpretation of Chapter) after the definition of "the Chief Inspector" insert—

""interim statement" means an interim statement under section 10A;".

226 Powers of persons providing administrative support in connection with inspections

(1) Part 2 of Schedule 12 to the Education and Inspections Act 2006 (c. 40) (inspectors etc acting on behalf of Chief Inspector) is amended as follows.

(2) In paragraph 9(1) (delegation of functions), after paragraph (c) insert "or

(d) any inspection administrator,",

(and omit "or" at the end of paragraph (b)).

(3) In paragraph 9(2)(a) for "and 11(4)" substitute ", 11(4) and 11A(3)".

(4) In paragraph 10(1) (inspectors etc to have necessary qualifications, experience and skills), after paragraph (c) insert "or

      (d) an inspection administrator,",

(and omit "or" at the end of paragraph (b)).

(5) After paragraph 11 insert —

"Inspection administrators

11A (1) The Chief Inspector may enter into arrangements with inspection service providers under which they provide the services of persons to provide administrative support in connection with the carrying out of inspections.

(2) A person providing administrative support in pursuance of arrangements under sub-paragraph (1) is to be known as an inspection administrator.

(3) The Chief Inspector may not authorise an inspection administrator to conduct an inspection."

CHAPTER 4

SCHOOL SUPPORT STAFF PAY AND CONDITIONS: ENGLAND

The SSSNB

227 The School Support Staff Negotiating Body

(1) There is to be an unincorporated body of persons known as the School Support Staff Negotiating Body.

(2) In this Chapter that body is referred to as "the SSSNB".

(3) The SSSNB's functions are those conferred on it by this Chapter.

(4) Schedule 15 makes further provision about the SSSNB.

228 Matters within SSSNB's remit

(1) For the purposes of this Chapter, the matters within the SSSNB's remit are matters relating to —
    (a) the remuneration of school support staff, or
    (b) conditions of employment relating to the duties or working time of school support staff.

(2) The Secretary of State may by order provide that, for the purposes of subsection (1) —
    (a) a payment or entitlement of a specified kind is or is not to be treated as remuneration;
    (b) a specified matter is or is not to be treated as relating to the duties of school support staff;

(c)   a specified matter is or is not to be treated as relating to the working time of school support staff.

Consideration of matter by SSSNB

229   Referral of matter to SSSNB for consideration

(1)   The Secretary of State may refer a matter within the SSSNB's remit to the SSSNB for consideration by it.

(2)   The rest of this section applies if the Secretary of State does so.

(3)   The Secretary of State may specify –
    (a)   factors to which the SSSNB must have regard in considering the matter;
    (b)   a date by which the SSSNB must comply with subsection (5).

(4)   The SSSNB must consider the matter, having regard to any factors specified under subsection (3)(a).

(5)   When it has considered the matter, the SSSNB must –
    (a)   if it has reached an agreement about the matter, submit that agreement to the Secretary of State, and
    (b)   if it has been unable to reach an agreement about the matter, notify the Secretary of State of that.

(6)   If the Secretary of State specifies a date under subsection (3)(b), the SSSNB must comply with subsection (5) no later than that date.

(7)   The Secretary of State may, at any time before the SSSNB have complied with subsection (5) in relation to a matter –
    (a)   withdraw or vary the reference of the matter;
    (b)   if factors have been specified under subsection (3)(a), withdraw or vary those factors, or specify further factors under that paragraph;
    (c)   if a date has been specified under subsection (3)(b), specify a later date under that paragraph.

230   Consideration of other matters by SSSNB

(1)   The SSSNB may consider a matter within its remit, even if the matter has not been referred to it by the Secretary of State under section 229.

(2)   If the SSSNB reaches agreement about the matter, it may submit the agreement to the Secretary of State.

Powers of Secretary of State on submission of SSSNB agreement

231   Agreement submitted by SSSNB under section 229 or 230

(1)   This section applies if the SSSNB submits an agreement to the Secretary of State under section 229(5)(a) or 230(2).

(2)   The Secretary of State may –
    (a)   make an order ratifying the agreement, or

Apprenticeships, Skills, Children and Learning Act 2009 (c. 22)
Part 10 — Schools
Chapter 4 — School Support Staff Pay and Conditions: England

2313

    (b)   if the Secretary of State thinks that it would be inappropriate to make an order ratifying the agreement, refer the agreement back to the SSSNB for reconsideration (see section 232).

Reconsideration by SSSNB

232   Reconsideration of agreement by SSSNB

(1)   This section applies if, under section 231(2)(b) or section 233(2)(b), the Secretary of State refers an agreement back to the SSSNB for reconsideration.

(2)   The Secretary of State may specify —
    (a)   factors to which the SSSNB must have regard in the reconsideration;
    (b)   a date by which the SSSNB must comply with subsection (4).

(3)   The SSSNB must reconsider the agreement, having regard to any factors specified under subsection (2)(a).

(4)   After completing its reconsideration, the SSSNB must —
    (a)   if it has agreed revisions to the agreement, submit to the Secretary of State a new version of the agreement incorporating the revisions;
    (b)   if it has not agreed revisions to the agreement, submit the existing version of the agreement to the Secretary of State.

(5)   If the Secretary of State specifies a date under subsection (2)(b), the SSSNB must comply with subsection (4) no later than that date.

(6)   The Secretary of State may, at any time before the SSSNB has complied with subsection (4) in relation to an agreement referred back to it for reconsideration —
    (a)   withdraw the reference of the agreement;
    (b)   if factors have been specified under subsection (2)(a), withdraw or vary those factors, or specify further factors under that paragraph;
    (c)   if a date has been specified under subsection (2)(b), specify a later date under that paragraph.

233   SSSNB's submission of agreement following reconsideration: powers of Secretary of State

(1)   This section applies if the SSSNB submits an agreement about a matter to the Secretary of State under section 232.

(2)   Subject to subsections (3) and (4), the Secretary of State may —
    (a)   by order ratify the agreement;
    (b)   refer the agreement back to the SSSNB for reconsideration (see section 232);
    (c)   by order require specified persons to have regard to the agreement in exercising specified functions;
    (d)   by order make provision, in relation to a matter to which the agreement relates, otherwise than in the terms of the agreement.

(3)   The Secretary of State may refer an agreement about a matter back to the SSSNB for reconsideration only if it appears to the Secretary of State that the condition in subsection (5) is met.

(4)   The Secretary of State may make an order under subsection (2)(d) in relation to a matter only if it appears to the Secretary of State that—

         (a)   the condition in subsection (5) is met, and

         (b)   there is an urgent need to make provision in relation to the matter.

(5)   The condition is that one or more of the following applies—

         (a)   the agreement does not properly address the matter;

         (b)   it is not practicable to implement the agreement;

         (c)   the SSSNB failed in reconsidering the agreement to have regard to factors specified under section 232(2)(a).

(6)   In this section, "specified", in relation to an order, means specified in the order.

Powers of Secretary of State in absence of SSSNB agreement

234   Powers of Secretary of State in absence of SSSNB agreement

(1)   Subsection (2) applies if—

         (a)   the SSSNB notifies the Secretary of State under section 229(5)(b) that it has been unable to reach agreement on a matter referred to it, or

         (b)   the SSSNB fails to comply with section 229(5) in relation to a matter by any date specified under section 229(3)(b).

(2)   The Secretary of State may—

         (a)   if a date has been specified under section 229(3)(b) in relation to the matter, specify a later date under that paragraph, or

         (b)   if it appears to the Secretary of State that there is an urgent need to do so, by order make provision in relation to the matter.

(3)   Subsection (4) applies if the SSSNB fails to comply with section 232(4) in relation to an agreement by any date specified under section 232(2)(b).

(4)   The Secretary of State may—

         (a)   if a date has been specified under section 232(2)(b) in relation to the SSSNB's reconsideration of the agreement, specify a later date under that paragraph, or

         (b)   if it appears to the Secretary of State that there is an urgent need to do so, by order make provision in relation to a matter to which the agreement relates.

(5)   Before making an order under subsection (2)(b) or (4)(b), the Secretary of State must consult the SSSNB.

Orders

235   Effect of order ratifying SSSNB agreement

(1)   This section applies if the Secretary of State makes an order ratifying an agreement submitted by the SSSNB.

(2)   If the agreement relates to a person's remuneration, the person's remuneration is to be determined and paid in accordance with it.

(3)   A provision of the agreement that relates to any other condition of a person's employment has effect as a term of the person's contract of employment.

Apprenticeships, Skills, Children and Learning Act 2009 (c. 22)
Part 10 – Schools
Chapter 4 – *School Support Staff Pay and Conditions: England*

2315

(4) A term of that contract has no effect to the extent that it makes provision that is prohibited by, or is otherwise inconsistent with, the agreement.

236 Effect of order making provision otherwise than in terms of SSSNB agreement

(1) This section applies if the Secretary of State makes an order under section 233(2)(d) or 234(2)(b) or (4)(b).

(2) The order must either —

    (a) require specified persons, in exercising specified functions, to have regard to the order, or

    (b) provide that it is to have effect for determining the conditions of employment of persons to whom it applies.

(3) If the order makes provision within subsection (2)(b), subsections (4) to (6) apply.

(4) If the order relates to a person's remuneration, the person's remuneration is to be determined and paid in accordance with it.

(5) A provision of the order that relates to any other condition of a person's employment has effect as a term of the person's contract of employment.

(6) A term of that contract has no effect to the extent that it makes provision that is prohibited by, or is otherwise inconsistent with, the order.

(7) In subsection (2)(a), "specified" means specified in the order.

237 Orders: supplementary

(1) An order under this Chapter may make provision that has retrospective effect, subject to subsection (2).

(2) An order under this Chapter may not make provision the effect of which is to —

    (a) reduce remuneration in respect of a period wholly or partly before the date on which the order is made, or

    (b) alter a condition of a person's employment to the person's detriment in respect of such a period.

(3) An order under section 233(2)(d) or 234(2)(b) or (4)(b) may make provision by reference to the exercise of a power under —

    (a) section 35 of the Education Act 2002 (c. 32) (staffing of community schools, etc.), or

    (b) section 36 of that Act (staffing of foundation schools, etc.).

(4) An order under this Chapter may make provision by reference to —

    (a) an agreement submitted to the Secretary of State by the SSSNB, or

    (b) any other document.

(5) If an order under this Chapter does so, it must include provision about the publication of the agreement or other document.

(6) A reference in subsection (3) to an order under section 233(2)(d) or 234(2)(b) or (4)(b), and a reference in section 236(4) to (6) to such an order, or a provision of such an order, includes a reference to a provision of a document referred to by such an order.

2316

Apprenticeships, Skills, Children and Learning Act 2009 (c. 22)
Part 10 – Schools
Chapter 4 – School Support Staff Pay and Conditions: England

(7) In Schedule 2 to the Education Act 2002 (c. 32) (effect on staffing of suspension of delegated budget), after paragraph 10 insert—

> "11 Paragraph 8 has effect subject to—
>
> (a) any provision made by an order under section 231(2)(a) or 233(2)(a) of the Apprenticeships, Skills, Children and Learning Act 2009;
>
> (b) any provision made by an order under section 233(2)(d) or 234(2)(b) or (4)(b) of that Act, where the order provides that it is to have effect for determining the conditions of employment of persons to whom it applies."

Guidance

238 Guidance

(1) The SSSNB may, with the approval of the Secretary of State, issue guidance relating to—

    (a) an agreement to which an order under section 233(2)(c) requires persons to have regard;

    (b) an agreement that has been ratified by an order under this Chapter.

(2) The Secretary of State may issue guidance relating to an order made under section 233(2)(d) or 234(2)(b) or (4)(b).

(3) In exercising functions in respect of school support staff, each of the following is to have regard to guidance issued under this section—

    (a) a local education authority in England;

    (b) the governing body of a school maintained by a local education authority in England.

General

239 Non-statutory School Support Staff Negotiating Body

(1) This section applies for the purposes of this Chapter.

(2) The establishment of the non-statutory School Support Staff Negotiating Body is to be treated as the establishment of the SSSNB.

(3) Arrangements made for the constitution of the non-statutory School Support Staff Negotiating Body are to be treated as if they were arrangements made under paragraph 1(1) of Schedule 15.

(4) Consultation carried out before arrangements are made for the constitution of the non-statutory School Support Staff Negotiating Body is to be treated as carried out under paragraph 1(2) of Schedule 15.

(5) A matter within the SSSNB's remit that has been referred to the non-statutory School Support Staff Negotiating Body by the Secretary of State is to be treated as if it had been referred by the Secretary of State to the SSSNB under section 229.

(6) For the purposes of this section the "non-statutory School Support Staff Negotiating Body" is the body of persons—

Apprenticeships, Skills, Children and Learning Act 2009 (c. 22)
Part 10 — Schools
Chapter 4 — School Support Staff Pay and Conditions: England

2317

    (a)   established by the Secretary of State before the date on which this Chapter comes into force, and

    (b)   known as the School Support Staff Negotiating Body.

240   "School support staff"

(1)   This section has effect for the purposes of this Chapter.

(2)   "School support staff" are persons within subsection (3).

(3)   A person is within this subsection if the person—

    (a)   is employed by a local education authority in England or the governing body of a school maintained by a local education authority in England, under a contract of employment providing for the person to work wholly at a school or schools maintained by a local education authority in England;

    (b)   is not a school teacher, or a person of a prescribed description.

(4)   In this section, "school teacher" means a person who is a school teacher for the purposes of section 122 of the Education Act 2002 (c. 32).

241   General interpretation

For the purposes of this Chapter—

"contract of employment" has the meaning given by section 230(2) of the Employment Rights Act 1996 (c. 18);

"school maintained by a local education authority" means—

    (a)   a community, foundation or voluntary school;

    (b)   a community or foundation special school;

    (c)   a maintained nursery school;

    (d)   a short stay school.

PART 11

LEARNERS

Power to search for prohibited items

242   Power of members of staff to search pupils for prohibited items: England

(1)   After section 550A of the Education Act 1996 (c. 56) insert—

"Powers to search pupils

550ZA Power of members of staff to search pupils for prohibited items: England

(1)   This section applies where a member of staff of a school in England—

    (a)   has reasonable grounds for suspecting that a pupil at the school may have a prohibited item with him or her or in his or her possessions; and

    (b)   falls within section 550ZB(1).

(2)   The member of staff may search the pupil ("P") or P's possessions for that item.

(3)   For the purposes of this section and section 550ZC each of the following is a "prohibited item" —

      (a)   an article to which section 139 of the Criminal Justice Act 1988 applies (knives and blades etc);

      (b)   an offensive weapon, within the meaning of the Prevention of Crime Act 1953;

      (c)   alcohol, within the meaning of section 191 of the Licensing Act 2003;

      (d)   a controlled drug, within the meaning of section 2 of the Misuse of Drugs Act 1971, which section 5(1) of that Act makes it unlawful for P to have in P's possession;

      (e)   a stolen article;

      (f)   an article of a kind specified in regulations.

(4)   In subsection (3)(e) "stolen", in relation to an article, has the same meaning as it has by virtue of section 24 of the Theft Act 1968 in the provisions of that Act relating to goods which have been stolen.

(5)   In this section and section 550ZB —

      "member of staff", in relation to a school, means —

         (a)   any teacher who works at the school; and

         (b)   any other person who, with the authority of the head teacher, has lawful control or charge of pupils for whom education is being provided at the school;

      "possessions", in relation to P, includes any goods over which P has or appears to have control.

(6)   The powers conferred by this section and sections 550ZB and 550ZC are in addition to any powers exercisable by the member of staff in question apart from those sections and are not to be construed as restricting such powers.

550ZB Power of search under section 550ZA: supplementary

(1)   A person may carry out a search under section 550ZA only if that person —

      (a)   is the head teacher of the school; or

      (b)   has been authorised by the head teacher to carry out the search.

(2)   An authorisation for the purposes of subsection (1)(b) may be given in relation to —

      (a)   searches under section 550ZA generally;

      (b)   a particular search under that section;

      (c)   a particular description of searches under that section.

(3)   Nothing in any enactment, instrument or agreement shall be construed as authorising a head teacher of a school in England to require a person other than a member of the security staff of the school to carry out a search under section 550ZA.

(4)   A search under section 550ZA may be carried out only where —

      (a)   the member of staff and P are on the premises of the school; or

     (b)   they are elsewhere and the member of staff has lawful control or charge of P.

(5)   A person exercising the power in section 550ZA may use such force as is reasonable in the circumstances for exercising that power.

(6)   A person carrying out a search of P under section 550ZA –

     (a)   may not require P to remove any clothing other than outer clothing;

     (b)   must be of the same sex as P;

     (c)   may carry out the search only in the presence of another member of staff; and

     (d)   must ensure that the other member of staff is of the same sex as P if it is reasonably practicable to do so.

(7)   P's possessions may not be searched under section 550ZA except in the presence of –

     (a)   P; and

     (b)   another member of staff.

(8)   In this section –

        "member of the security staff", in relation to a school, means a member of staff whose work at the school consists wholly or mainly of security-related activities;

        "outer clothing" means –

     (a)   any item of clothing that is being worn otherwise than wholly next to the skin or immediately over a garment being worn as underwear; or

     (b)   a hat, shoes, boots, gloves or a scarf.

550ZC Power to seize items found during search under section 550ZA

(1)   A person carrying out a search under section 550ZA may seize any of the following found in the course of the search –

     (a)   anything which that person has reasonable grounds for suspecting is a prohibited item;

     (b)   any other thing which that person has reasonable grounds for suspecting is evidence in relation to an offence.

(2)   A person exercising the power in subsection (1) may use such force as is reasonable in the circumstances for exercising that power.

(3)   A person who seizes alcohol under subsection (1) may retain or dispose of the alcohol and its container.

(4)   A person who seizes a controlled drug under subsection (1) –

     (a)   must (subject to paragraph (b)) deliver it to a police constable as soon as reasonably practicable; but

     (b)   may dispose of it if the person thinks that there is a good reason to do so.

(5)   A person who seizes a stolen article under subsection (1) –

     (a)   must (subject to paragraph (b)) deliver it to a police constable as soon as reasonably practicable; but

(b)   may return it to its owner (or, if returning it to its owner is not practicable, may retain it or dispose of it) if the person thinks that there is a good reason to do so.

(6)   In determining, for the purposes of subsections (4) and (5), whether there is a good reason to dispose of a controlled drug or to return a stolen article to its owner, retain it or dispose of it, the person must have regard to any guidance issued by the Secretary of State.

(7)   Regulations may prescribe what must or may be done by a person who, under subsection (1), seizes an article of a kind specified in regulations under section 550ZA(3)(f) (or an article which the person has reasonable grounds for suspecting to be such an article).

(8)   A person who, under subsection (1), seizes —
    (a)   an article to which section 139 of the Criminal Justice Act 1988 applies (knives and blades etc);
    (b)   an offensive weapon; or
    (c)   anything which that person has reasonable grounds for suspecting is evidence in relation to an offence;
must deliver it to a police constable as soon as reasonably practicable.

(9)   Subsection (8)(c) is subject to subsections (3), (4) and (5) and regulations made under subsection (7).

(10)   In subsections (3) to (8), references to alcohol, a controlled drug, a stolen article, an article to which section 139 of the Criminal Justice Act 1988 applies and an offensive weapon include references to anything which the person has reasonable grounds for suspecting is alcohol, a controlled drug, a stolen article, an article to which section 139 of the Criminal Justice Act 1988 applies or an offensive weapon.

550ZD Section 550ZC: supplementary

(1)   The Police (Property) Act 1897 (disposal of property in the possession of the police) applies to property which has come into the possession of a police constable under section 550ZC(4)(a), (5)(a) or (8) as it applies to property which has come into the possession of the police in the circumstances mentioned in that Act.

(2)   Subsection (3) applies where a person —
    (a)   seizes, retains or disposes of alcohol or its container, a controlled drug or a stolen article under section 550ZC; and
    (b)   proves that the seizure, retention or disposal was lawful.

(3)   That person is not liable in any proceedings in respect of —
    (a)   the seizure, retention or disposal; or
    (b)   any damage or loss which arises in consequence of it.

(4)   Subsections (2) and (3) do not prevent any person from relying on any defence on which the person is entitled to rely apart from those subsections.

(5)   Regulations under section 550ZC(7) may make provision corresponding to any provision of this section."

(2)   In section 569 of the Education Act 1996 (c. 56) (regulations) —

    (a)   in subsection (2) after "this Act," insert "other than one falling within subsection (2A),", and

    (b)   after subsection (2) insert—

> "(2A)   A statutory instrument which contains (whether alone or with other provision) regulations under section 550ZA or 550ZC may not be made unless a draft of the instrument has been laid before, and approved by a resolution of, each House of Parliament."

  (3)   In section 94(3) of the Education and Inspections Act 2006 (c. 40) (provision to apply where items confiscated from pupils) before "550AA" insert "550ZC or".

243 Power of members of staff to search pupils for weapons: Wales

  (1)   Section 550AA of the Education Act 1996 (c. 56) (power of members of staff to search pupils for weapons) is amended as follows.

  (2)   At the end of the title insert ": Wales".

  (3)   In each of subsections (1) and (4) after "a school" insert "in Wales".

244 Power of members of staff to search students for prohibited items: England

  (1)   After section 85A of the Further and Higher Education Act 1992 (c. 13) insert—

"85AA Power of members of staff to search students for prohibited items: England

  (1)   This section applies where a member of staff of an institution within the further education sector in England—

    (a)   has reasonable grounds for suspecting that a student at the institution may have a prohibited item with him or her or in his or her possessions; and

    (b)   falls within section 85AB(1).

  (2)   The member of staff may search the student ("S") or S's possessions for that item (but this is subject to subsection (5)).

  (3)   For the purposes of this section and section 85AC each of the following is a "prohibited item"—

    (a)   an article to which section 139 of the Criminal Justice Act 1988 applies (knives and blades etc);

    (b)   an offensive weapon, within the meaning of the Prevention of Crime Act 1953;

    (c)   alcohol, within the meaning of section 191 of the Licensing Act 2003;

    (d)   a controlled drug, within the meaning of section 2 of the Misuse of Drugs Act 1971, which section 5(1) of that Act makes it unlawful for S to have in S's possession;

    (e)   a stolen article;

    (f)   an article of a kind specified in regulations.

  (4)   In subsection (3)(e) "stolen", in relation to an article, has the same meaning as it has by virtue of section 24 of the Theft Act 1968 in the provisions of that Act relating to goods which have been stolen.

(5)   A member of staff may not under this section search S or S's possessions for alcohol if S is aged 18 or over.

(6)   In this section and section 85AB—

"member of staff", in relation to an institution within the further education sector, means any person who works at that institution whether or not as its employee;

"possessions", in relation to S, includes any goods over which S has or appears to have control.

(7)   The powers conferred by this section and sections 85AB and 85AC are in addition to any powers exercisable by the member of staff in question apart from those sections and are not to be construed as restricting such powers.

85AB   Power of search under section 85AA: supplementary

(1)   A person may carry out a search under section 85AA only if that person—

(a)   is the principal of the institution; or

(b)   has been authorised by the principal to carry out the search.

(2)   An authorisation for the purposes of subsection (1)(b) may be given in relation to—

(a)   searches under section 85AA generally;

(b)   a particular search under that section;

(c)   a particular description of searches under that section.

(3)   Nothing in any enactment, instrument or agreement shall be construed as authorising a principal of an institution within the further education sector in England to require a person other than a member of the security staff of the institution to carry out a search under section 85AA.

(4)   A search under section 85AA may be carried out only where—

(a)   the member of staff and S are on the premises of the institution; or

(b)   they are elsewhere and the member of staff has lawful control or charge of S.

(5)   A person exercising the power in section 85AA may use such force as is reasonable in the circumstances for exercising that power.

(6)   A person carrying out a search of S under section 85AA—

(a)   may not require S to remove any clothing other than outer clothing;

(b)   must be of the same sex as S;

(c)   may carry out the search only in the presence of another member of staff; and

(d)   must ensure that the other member of staff is of the same sex as S if it is reasonably practicable to do so.

(7)   S's possessions may not be searched under section 85AA except in the presence of—

(a)   S; and

(b)   another member of staff.

(8) In this section—

"member of the security staff", in relation to an institution, means a member of staff whose work at the institution consists wholly or mainly of security-related activities;

"outer clothing" means—

(a) any item of clothing that is being worn otherwise than wholly next to the skin or immediately over a garment being worn as underwear; or

(b) a hat, shoes, boots, gloves or a scarf.

85AC Power to seize items found during search under section 85AA

(1) A person carrying out a search under section 85AA may seize any of the following found in the course of the search—

(a) anything which that person has reasonable grounds for suspecting is a prohibited item;

(b) any other thing which that person has reasonable grounds for suspecting is evidence in relation to an offence,

but may not seize alcohol from S under this section where S is aged 18 or over.

(2) A person exercising the power in subsection (1) may use such force as is reasonable in the circumstances for exercising that power.

(3) A person who seizes alcohol under subsection (1) may retain or dispose of the alcohol and its container.

(4) A person who seizes a controlled drug under subsection (1)—

(a) must (subject to paragraph (b)) deliver it to a police constable as soon as reasonably practicable; but

(b) may dispose of it if the person thinks that there is a good reason to do so.

(5) A person who seizes a stolen article under subsection (1)—

(a) must (subject to paragraph (b)) deliver it to a police constable as soon as reasonably practicable; but

(b) may return it to its owner (or, if returning it to its owner is not practicable, may retain it or dispose of it) if the person thinks that there is a good reason to do so.

(6) In determining, for the purposes of subsections (4) and (5), whether there is a good reason to dispose of a controlled drug or to return a stolen article to its owner, retain it or dispose of it, the person must have regard to any guidance issued by the Secretary of State.

(7) Regulations may prescribe what must or may be done by a person who, under subsection (1), seizes an article of a kind specified in regulations under section 85AA(3)(f) (or an article which the person has reasonable grounds for suspecting to be such an article).

(8) A person who, under subsection (1), seizes—

(a) an article to which section 139 of the Criminal Justice Act 1988 applies (knives and blades etc);

(b) an offensive weapon; or

(c) anything which that person has reasonable grounds for suspecting is evidence in relation to an offence;

must deliver it to a police constable as soon as reasonably practicable.

(9)   Subsection (8)(c) is subject to subsections (3), (4) and (5) and regulations made under subsection (7).

(10)   In subsections (3) to (8), references to alcohol, a controlled drug, a stolen article, an article to which section 139 of the Criminal Justice Act 1988 applies and an offensive weapon include references to anything which a person has reasonable grounds for suspecting is alcohol, a controlled drug, a stolen article, an article to which section 139 of the Criminal Justice Act 1988 applies or an offensive weapon.

85AD   Section 85AC: supplementary

(1)   The Police (Property) Act 1897 (disposal of property in the possession of the police) applies to property which has come into the possession of a police constable under section 85AC(4)(a), (5)(a) or (8) as it applies to property which has come into the possession of the police in the circumstances mentioned in that Act.

(2)   Subsection (3) applies where a person —
      (a)   seizes, retains or disposes of alcohol or its container, a controlled drug or a stolen article under section 85AC; and
      (b)   proves that the seizure, retention or disposal was lawful.

(3)   That person is not liable in any proceedings in respect of —
      (a)   the seizure, retention or disposal; or
      (b)   any damage or loss which arises in consequence of it.

(4)   Subsections (2) and (3) do not prevent any person from relying on any defence on which the person is entitled to rely apart from those subsections.

(5)   Regulations under section 85AC(7) may make provision corresponding to any provision of this section."

(2)   In section 89 of the Further and Higher Education Act 1992 (c. 13) (regulations etc) —
      (a)   in subsection (3) after "other than" insert "one falling within subsection (3A) or", and
      (b)   after subsection (3) insert —

      "(3A)   A statutory instrument which contains (whether alone or with other provision) regulations under section 85AA or 85AC may not be made unless a draft of the instrument has been laid before, and approved by a resolution of, each House of Parliament."

245   Power of members of staff to search students for weapons: Wales

(1)   Section 85B of the Further and Higher Education Act 1992 (power to search further education students for weapons) is amended as follows.

(2)   At the end of the title insert ": Wales".

(3)   In subsection (1) after "an institution within the further education sector" insert "in Wales".

Recording and reporting use of force

246   Recording and reporting the use of force in schools: England

After section 93 of the Education and Inspections Act 2006 (c. 40) (power of members of staff to use force) insert—

"93A   Recording and reporting the use of force by members of staff: England

(1)   The governing body of a school in England must ensure that a procedure is in place for—

    (a)   recording each significant incident in which a member of the staff uses force on a pupil for whom education is being provided at the school (a "use of force incident"); and

    (b)   reporting each use of force incident (except those where the pupil is aged 20 or over or provision made under subsection (5) applies) to each parent of the pupil as soon as practicable after the incident.

(2)   The governing body must take all reasonable steps to ensure that the procedure is complied with.

(3)   The procedure must require that a record of a use of force incident is made in writing as soon as practicable after the incident.

(4)   In discharging their duty under subsection (1), the governing body must have regard to any guidance issued by the Secretary of State for the purposes of that subsection.

(5)   A procedure under subsection (1) must include provision to the effect—

    (a)   that a person ("R") who would otherwise be required by the procedure to report an incident to a parent must not report it to that parent if it appears to R that doing so would be likely to result in significant harm to the pupil; and

    (b)   that if it appears to R that there is no parent of the pupil to whom R could report the incident without that being likely to result in significant harm to the pupil, R must report the incident to the local authority (within the meaning of the Children Act 1989) within whose area the pupil is ordinarily resident.

(6)   In deciding for the purposes of provision made under subsection (5) whether reporting an incident to a parent would be likely to result in significant harm to the pupil, R must have regard to any guidance issued by the Secretary of State about the meaning of "significant harm" for those purposes.

(7)   In this section—

    "governing body", in relation to a school which is not a maintained school, means the proprietor of the school;

    "maintained school" means—

        (a)   a community, foundation or voluntary school;

        (b)   a community or foundation special school;

        (c)   a maintained nursery school;

"parent", in relation to a pupil, has the meaning given by section 576 of EA 1996 in relation to a child or young person, but includes a local authority which provides accommodation for the pupil under section 20 of the Children Act 1989."

247 Recording and reporting the use of force in FE institutions: England

After section 85C of the Further and Higher Education Act 1992 (power of members of staff to use force) insert—

"85D Recording and reporting the use of force by members of staff: England

(1) The governing body of an institution within the further education sector in England must ensure that a procedure is in place for—

    (a) recording each significant incident in which a member of the staff uses force on a student at the institution (a "use of force incident"); and

    (b) reporting each use of force incident (except those where the student is aged 20 or over or provision made under subsection (5) applies) to each parent of the student as soon as practicable after the incident.

(2) The governing body must take all reasonable steps to ensure that the procedure is complied with.

(3) The procedure must require that a record of a use of force incident is made in writing as soon as practicable after the incident.

(4) In discharging their duty under subsection (1), the governing body must have regard to any guidance issued by the Secretary of State for the purposes of that subsection.

(5) A procedure under subsection (1) must include provision to the effect—

    (a) that a person ("R") who would otherwise be required by the procedure to report an incident to a parent must not report it to that parent if it appears to R that doing so would be likely to result in significant harm to the student; and

    (b) that if it appears to R that there is no parent of the student to whom R could report the incident without that being likely to result in significant harm to the student, R must report the incident to the local authority (within the meaning of the Children Act 1989) within whose area the student is ordinarily resident.

(6) In deciding for the purposes of provision made under subsection (5) whether reporting an incident to a parent would be likely to result in significant harm to the student, R must have regard to any guidance issued by the Secretary of State about the meaning of "significant harm" for those purposes.

(7) In this section, "parent", in relation to a student, has the meaning given by section 576 of EA 1996 in relation to a child or young person, but includes a local authority which provides accommodation for the student under section 20 of the Children Act 1989."

School behaviour and attendance partnerships

248 Co-operation with a view to promoting good behaviour, etc.: England

(1) A "relevant partner" for the purposes of this section is —
  (a) the governing body of a maintained secondary school in England;
  (b) the proprietor of an Academy, city technology college or city college for the technology of the arts in England.

(2) A relevant partner must make arrangements with at least one other relevant partner in their area to co-operate with each other with a view to —
  (a) promoting good behaviour and discipline on the part of pupils;
  (b) reducing persistent absence by pupils.

(3) A relevant partner must secure that, at least once in every 12 month period, a partnership report is prepared and submitted to the local Children's Trust Board in relation to each of the arrangements under subsection (2) to which the relevant partner has been a party at any time during the period to which the report relates.

(4) A partnership report, in relation to arrangements under subsection (2), is a report that —
  (a) gives details of the arrangements and what has been done under them during the period to which the report relates;
  (b) assesses the effectiveness of the arrangements during that period;
  (c) gives details of what is proposed to be done under the arrangements in the future.

(5) In performing their duties under this section, relevant partners must have regard to any guidance given by the Secretary of State.

(6) For the purposes of this section —
  (a) the area of a governing body of a maintained secondary school is the area of the local education authority by which the school is maintained;
  (b) the area of a proprietor of an Academy, city technology college or city college for the technology of the arts is the area of the local education authority in whose area the school is situated;
  (c) the local Children's Trust Board, in relation to a relevant partner, is the Children's Trust Board established for their area by virtue of section 12A of the Children Act 2004 (c. 31).

(7) In this section "maintained secondary school" means —
  (a) a community, foundation or voluntary school that provides secondary education;
  (b) a community or foundation special school that provides secondary education.

Short stay schools

249 Short stay schools: miscellaneous

(1) A school established in England and falling within section 19(2B) of the Education Act 1996 (c. 56) (pupil referral units) is to be known from the day on which this subsection comes into force as a "short stay school".

(2) The Secretary of State may by order make amendments consequential on the change of name effected by subsection (1) to—

    (a) any enactment (including this Act) passed on or before the last day of the Session in which this Act is passed;

    (b) an instrument made under an Act before the passing of this Act.

(3) After paragraph 3 of Schedule 1 to the Education Act 1996 (c. 56) (short stay schools: further provision) insert—

    "3A   Regulations may also—

        (a) require a local education authority in England to obtain the consent of the Secretary of State, in specified circumstances, to the closure of a short stay school;

        (b) confer a power on the Secretary of State to give directions to a local education authority in England about the exercise of—

            (i) their functions under section 19;

            (ii) their functions under any enactment applied to short stay schools (with or without modifications) by regulations under paragraph 3;

            (iii) any other function connected with short stay schools;

        (c) require a local education authority to comply with such directions."

PART 12

MISCELLANEOUS

Careers education

250   Careers education in schools: England

(1) Section 43 of the Education Act 1997 (c. 44) (provision of careers education in schools) is amended as follows.

(2) After subsection (2) insert—

    "(2ZA) Subsection (2ZB) applies to a programme of careers education provided in pursuance of subsection (1) to registered pupils at a school in England that is within subsection (2)(a), (c) or (e).

    (2ZB) The programme must include information on—

        (a) options available in respect of 16-18 education or training, and

        (b) apprenticeships."

(3) In subsection (3) for "subsection (2B)) is" substitute "subsections (2ZB) and (2B)) is (or are)".

(4) In subsection (6), at the appropriate place insert—

        ""apprenticeship" includes employment and training leading to the issue of an apprenticeship certificate under section 3 or 4 of the Apprenticeships, Skills, Children and Learning Act 2009;".

Information about local authority expenditure

251 Information about planned and actual expenditure

(1) The Secretary of State may direct a local authority in England to provide information about its planned and actual expenditure in connection with—

    (a) its education functions;

    (b) its children's social services functions.

(2) The Secretary of State may also direct a local authority in England to provide information about accountable resources held, received or expended by any person in relation to a school maintained by the authority.

(3) Information to which a direction under this section relates must be provided in accordance with the direction.

(4) A direction under this section may (in particular) include provision about—

    (a) the period to which information is to relate;

    (b) the form and manner in which information is to be provided;

    (c) the persons to whom information is to be provided;

    (d) the publication of information.

(5) If a direction under this section requires information to be provided to a person other than the Secretary of State, the direction may also require that person to make the information available for inspection in accordance with the direction.

252 Information about expenditure: supplementary

(1) This section applies for the purposes of section 251.

(2) The education functions of a local authority in England are the functions conferred on or exercisable by the authority in its capacity as a local education authority.

(3) The children's social services functions of a local authority in England are—

    (a) functions conferred on or exercisable by the authority which are social services functions, so far as those functions relate to children;

    (b) functions conferred on the authority under sections 23C to 24D of the Children Act 1989 (c. 41), so far as not within paragraph (a);

    (c) functions conferred on the authority, in its capacity as a children's services authority in England, under sections 10 to 12, 12C, 12D and 17A of the Children Act 2004 (c. 31).

(4) "Accountable resources", in relation to a school maintained by a local authority, means resources that are not provided by the authority in its capacity as a local education authority, but in respect of which an obligation is imposed on the school's governing body by virtue of regulations under section 44 of the Education Act 2002 (c. 32) (accounts of maintained schools).

(5) The Secretary of State may by order amend this section for one or more of the following purposes—

    (a) adding to the functions that are education functions or children's social services functions;

    (b) removing or changing the description of functions that are education functions or children's social services functions.

(6)   In this section—

"children's services authority in England" has the meaning given by section 65(1) of the Children Act 2004 (c. 31);

"social services functions" has the same meaning as in the Local Authority Social Services Act 1970 (c. 42) (see section 1A of that Act).

253   Information about expenditure: consequential amendments

(1)   The School Standards and Framework Act 1998 (c. 31) is amended as follows.

(2)   In section 52 (the title of which becomes "Financial statements: Wales"), in subsections (1) and (2) after "local education authority" insert "in Wales".

(3)   Omit section 53 (certification of statements by Audit Commission).

Support for participation in education and training

254   Provision of social security information for purposes of functions under Education and Skills Act 2008

(1)   The Education and Skills Act 2008 (c. 25) is amended as follows.

(2)   Omit section 15 (supply of social security information for purposes of Part 1).

(3)   Section 17 (sharing and use of information held for purposes of support services or functions under Part 1) is amended as follows.

(4)   In subsection (1), for "provide relevant information to each other" substitute "—

   (a)   provide relevant information to each other;
   (b)   make arrangements for the holding by either of them of information provided, or which could be provided, under paragraph (a)."

(5)   In subsection (7), in the definition of "relevant information", after paragraph (b), insert—

"but does not include information provided under section 72 of the Welfare Reform and Pensions Act 1999;".

(6)   At the end add—

"(9)   Nothing in this section authorises the disclosure of any information in contravention of any provision of, or made under, this or any other Act (whenever passed or made) which prevents disclosure of the information."

(7)   Section 76 (supply of social security information for purposes of support services) is amended as follows.

(8)   Omit subsection (1).

(9)   For subsections (3) and (4) substitute—

"(3)   For the purposes of subsection (2), "personal information" in relation to a young person, means the person's name, address and date of birth.

(3A) The Secretary of State may make arrangements with a person for the supply of social security information for the purposes of the provision of services for young persons in pursuance of section 68 or 70(1)(b).

(3B) Social security information may be supplied to—
   (a) the Secretary of State, or
   (b) a person providing services to the Secretary of State under subsection (3A).

(3C) A person to whom social security information is supplied under subsection (3B) may supply the information to a local education authority or other person involved in the provision of services for young persons or relevant young adults in pursuance of section 68 or 70(1)(b) for the purpose of the provision of those services.

(3D) Information supplied to a person in reliance on subsection (3C) or this subsection may be supplied in accordance with, or with arrangements made under, section 17(1).

(3E) Information supplied to a person in reliance on subsection (3B), (3C) or (3D) may be disclosed—
   (a) for the purpose of the provision of services in pursuance of section 68 or 70(1)(b),
   (b) for the purpose of enabling or assisting the exercise of any function of a local education authority under Part 1,
   (c) in accordance with any provision of, or made under, any other Act,
   (d) in accordance with an order of a court or tribunal,
   (e) for the purpose of actual or contemplated proceedings before a court or tribunal,
   (f) with consent given by or on behalf of the person to whom the information relates, or
   (g) in such a way as to prevent the identification of the person to whom it relates.

(4) It is an offence for a person to disclose restricted information otherwise than in accordance with this section.

(4A) For the purposes of subsection (4), "restricted information", in relation to a person, means information that was disclosed to the person—
   (a) in reliance on subsection (3B), (3C) or (3D), or
   (b) in circumstances that constitute an offence under this section."

255 Provision of other information in connection with support services

(1) The Education and Skills Act 2008 (c. 25) is amended as follows.

(2) In section 69(1) (directions), after paragraph (a) insert—
   "(aa) requiring the authority to secure that any person by whom such services are provided (whether the authority or any other person) provides such relevant information (within the meaning of section 76A) as the Secretary of State may require to—
      (i) the Secretary of State, or

      (ii)   a person providing services to the Secretary of State under section 76A;".

(3)   After section 76 insert—

"76A   Supply of information by Secretary of State or person providing services

(1)   The Secretary of State may make arrangements with any other person for the holding and supply of information in connection with, or for the purposes of, the provision of services in pursuance of section 68 or 70(1)(b).

(2)   In this section "relevant information", in relation to a person by whom services are provided under section 68 or 70(1)(b), means information which—

      (a)   is obtained by a person involved in the provision of those services in, or in connection with, the provision of those services,

      (b)   relates to a person for whom those services are provided;

but does not include information provided under section 72 of the Welfare Reform and Pensions Act 1999.

(3)   Relevant information may be supplied to—

      (a)   the Secretary of State, or

      (b)   a person providing services to the Secretary of State under this section.

(4)   Information supplied under subsection (3) may be supplied to any person involved in the provision of services in pursuance of section 68 or 70(1)(b) for the purposes of the provision of those services.

(5)   Except as provided by subsection (4), information supplied in reliance on subsection (3) must not be disclosed in such a way that the identity of the individual is disclosed to, or capable of being discovered by, the person to whom it is disclosed.

(6)   Nothing in this section authorises the disclosure of any information in contravention of any provision of, or made under, this or any other Act (whenever passed or made) which prevents disclosure of the information."

Further education corporations

256   Further education corporations in England: co-operation and promotion of well-being

(1)   The Further and Higher Education Act 1992 (c. 13) is amended as follows.

(2)   In section 19 (supplementary powers of a further education corporation), after subsection (8) add—

    "(9)   A further education corporation may provide advice or assistance to any other person where it appears to the corporation to be appropriate for them to do so for the purpose of or in connection with the provision of education by the other person."

(3) After that section insert—

"19A Duty in relation to promotion of well-being of local area

(1) This section applies to a further education corporation established in respect of an educational institution in England.

(2) In exercising their functions under sections 18 and 19, the corporation must—

  (a) have regard, amongst other things, to the objective of promoting the economic and social well-being of the local area, and

  (b) in doing so, have regard to any guidance issued by the Secretary of State about co-operation with a view, directly or indirectly, to advancing that objective.

(3) In subsection (2)—

  (a) the reference to the well-being of an area includes a reference to the well-being of people who live or work in the area;

  (b) "co-operation", in relation to a further education corporation, means any form of co-operation, including consulting, seeking advice or assistance from, providing advice or assistance to, or collaborating or otherwise participating in joint working with, other educational institutions, employers or other persons (who may be, or include, persons outside the local area).

(4) In this section, "the local area", in relation to a further education corporation, means the locality of the institution in respect of which they are established.

(5) Nothing in this section is to be taken to affect the operation of section 49A."

Student loans

257 Student loans under the 1998 Act: IVAs

(1) The Teaching and Higher Education Act 1998 (c. 30) is amended as set out in subsections (2) and (3).

(2) In section 22(3) (new arrangements for giving financial support to students), after paragraph (f) insert—

  "(g) with respect to sums which a borrower receives, or is entitled to receive, under such a loan before or after a voluntary arrangement under Part 8 of the Insolvency Act 1986 or Part 8 of the Insolvency (Northern Ireland) Order 1989 (individual voluntary arrangements) takes effect in respect of the borrower;

  (h) excluding or modifying the application of Part 8 of that Act, or Part 8 of that Order, in relation to liability to make repayments in respect of such a loan (whether the repayments relate to sums which the borrower receives, or is entitled to receive, before or after a voluntary arrangement takes effect in respect of the borrower)."

(3) In section 46(8) (provisions extending to Northern Ireland), in the entry relating to section 22, for "(3)(e) or (f)" substitute "(3)(e), (f), (g) or (h)".

(4)   Nothing in this section affects a voluntary arrangement that takes effect before this section comes into force.

258   Student loans under the 1990 Act: IVAs and bankruptcy

(1)   Subsections (2) to (5) have effect in relation to the Education (Student Loans) Act 1990 (c. 6) to the extent that that Act continues in force by virtue of any savings made, in connection with its repeal by the Teaching and Higher Education Act 1998 (c. 30), by an order under section 46(4) of that Act.

(2)   In Schedule 2 (loans for students), in paragraph 5(1) for "or 310" substitute ", 310 or 310A".

(3)   In Schedule 2, after paragraph 5 insert—

      "5A (1) This paragraph applies to a sum by way of public sector student loan or subsidised private sector student loan that a person ("the debtor") receives or is entitled to receive before or after a voluntary arrangement under Part 8 of the Insolvency Act 1986 takes effect in respect of the debtor.

             (2) The sum is to be ignored for the purposes of the voluntary arrangement.

      5B (1) Part 8 of the Insolvency Act 1986 (individual voluntary arrangements) has effect in relation to a student loan debt with the following modifications.

             (2) A student loan debt is to be treated as not included among the debtor's debts.

             (3) A person to whom a student loan debt is owed is to be treated as not being one of the debtor's creditors.

             (4) A "student loan debt" is a debt or liability to which a debtor is or may become subject in respect of a public sector student loan or subsidised private sector student loan."

(4)   In Schedule 2, after paragraph 6 insert—

"Insolvency: Northern Ireland

      7   (1) There shall not be treated as part of a bankrupt's estate or claimed for his estate under article 280 or 283 of the Insolvency (Northern Ireland) Order 1989 any sums to which this paragraph applies that the bankrupt receives or is entitled to receive after the commencement of the bankruptcy.

             (2) No debt or liability to which a bankrupt is or may become subject in respect of a sum to which this paragraph applies shall be included in the bankrupt's bankruptcy debts.

             (3) This paragraph applies to a sum by way of public sector student loan or subsidised private sector student loan payable to the bankrupt pursuant to an agreement entered into by the bankrupt before or after the commencement of the bankruptcy.

      8   (1) This paragraph applies to a sum by way of public sector student loan or subsidised private sector student loan that a person ("the debtor")

receives or is entitled to receive before or after a voluntary arrangement under Part 8 of the Insolvency (Northern Ireland) Order 1989 takes effect in respect of the debtor.

(2) The sum is to be ignored for the purposes of the voluntary arrangement.

9 (1) Part 8 of the Insolvency (Northern Ireland) Order 1989 (individual voluntary arrangements) has effect in relation to a student loan debt with the following modifications.

(2) A student loan debt is to be treated as not included among the debtor's debts.

(3) A person to whom a student loan debt is owed is to be treated as not being one of the debtor's creditors.

(4) A "student loan debt" is a debt or liability to which a debtor is or may become subject in respect of a public sector student loan or subsidised private sector student loan."

(5) In section 4, for subsection (4) (extent) substitute—

"(4) This Act does not extend to Northern Ireland, with the following exceptions—

(a) section 1, so far as necessary for the purpose of defining "public sector student loan" and "subsidised private sector student loan";

(b) section 2;

(c) as respects institutions in Northern Ireland, the power to make regulations under paragraph 2 of Schedule 2;

(d) paragraphs 7 to 9 of Schedule 2."

(6) Nothing in this section affects a voluntary arrangement that takes effect, or a bankruptcy that commences, before this section comes into force.

Foundation degrees: Wales

259 Power to award foundation degrees: Wales

(1) In section 76(1)(b) of the Further and Higher Education Act 1992 (c. 13) (power of Privy Council to specify further education institutions in England that may award foundation degrees) omit "in England".

(2) Within the period of four years beginning with the commencement of subsection (1) of this section, the Welsh Ministers must lay before the National Assembly for Wales a report about its effect.

Complaints: Wales

260 Complaints: Wales

(1) Section 29 of the Education Act 2002 (c. 32) (additional functions of governing body) is amended as follows.

(2) In subsection (1) after "maintained school" insert "in England".

(3)   In subsection (2) for the words from "(in relation to England)" to the end substitute "by the Secretary of State".

(4)   After subsection (2) insert—

     "(2A)   The Welsh Ministers may make regulations establishing procedures in relation to relevant complaints.

       (2B)   For the purposes of subsection (2A), a "relevant complaint" is a complaint which relates to a maintained school in Wales, or to the provision of facilities or services under section 27 by the governing body of such a school, other than a complaint which falls to be dealt with in accordance with any procedures required to be established in relation to the school by virtue of a statutory provision other than this section.

       (2C)   Where the Welsh Ministers establish procedures by regulations under subsection (2A), the governing body of a maintained school in Wales shall—

           (a)   adopt the procedures, and

           (b)   publicise them in the way specified in the regulations.

       (2D)   In adopting or publicising procedures established by virtue of subsection (2A), the governing body shall have regard to any guidance given from time to time by the Welsh Ministers."

Local Government Act 1974

261   Local Government Act 1974: minor amendment

In paragraph 5(2) of Schedule 5 to the Local Government Act 1974 (c. 7) (exclusion of matters relating to teaching etc. in any school maintained by local authority), after "authority" insert ", except so far as relating to special educational needs (within the meaning given by section 312 of the Education Act 1996)".

PART 13

GENERAL

262   Orders and regulations

(1)   A power to make an order or regulations under Chapter 1 of Part 1, or Part 3 or 4—

     (a)   so far as exercisable by the Secretary of State, the Welsh Ministers or the Scottish Ministers, is exercisable by statutory instrument;

     (b)   so far as exercisable by the Department for Employment and Learning in Northern Ireland, is exercisable by statutory rule for the purposes of the Statutory Rules (Northern Ireland) Order 1979 (S.I. 1979/1573 (N.I. 12)).

(2)   Any other power of the Secretary of State to make an order or regulations under this Act is exercisable by statutory instrument.

(3) A power of the Secretary of State or the Welsh Ministers to make an order or regulations under this Act (except a power conferred by section 17, 22 or 269) includes power —

    (a) to make different provision for different purposes (including different areas);

    (b) to make provision generally or in relation to specific cases;

    (c) to make incidental, consequential, supplementary, transitional, transitory or saving provision.

(4) An order under section 98 may amend or repeal any provision of, or in an instrument made under, this or any other Act.

(5) Subject to subsections (6) to (8), a statutory instrument containing an order or regulations made by the Secretary of State under any provision of this Act (other than an order under section 269) is subject to annulment in pursuance of a resolution of either House of Parliament.

(6) A statutory instrument which contains (whether alone or with other provision) any of the following may not be made unless a draft of the instrument has been laid before, and approved by a resolution of, each House of Parliament —

    (aa) regulations under section 1(5);

    (b) an order under section 88 or paragraph 9 of Schedule 5;

    (c) an order under section 96(9) or 98;

    (d) an order under section 130(5);

    (e) an order under section 141(1);

    (f) an order under section 222;

    (g) an order under section 252(5);

    (h) an order under section 265 which amends or repeals any provision of an Act.

(7) Subsections (5) and (6) do not apply to a statutory instrument which contains only —

    (a) an order revoking an order under section 141(1), or

    (b) an order amending an order under section 141(1) for the purpose only of removing a qualification or description of qualification from the application of the order.

(8) A statutory instrument within subsection (7) must be laid before Parliament.

(9) Subject to subsection (10), a statutory instrument containing an order or regulations made by the Welsh Ministers under Chapter 1 of Part 1 (other than an order under section 10) or under section 68 or 107 is subject to annulment in pursuance of a resolution of the National Assembly for Wales.

(10) A statutory instrument which contains (whether alone or with other provision) regulations under section 2(5) may not be made unless a draft of the instrument has been laid before, and approved by a resolution of, the National Assembly for Wales.

(11) A statutory instrument containing an order made by the Scottish Ministers under section 68 or 107 is subject to annulment in pursuance of a resolution of the Scottish Parliament.

(12) A statutory rule containing an order made by the Department for Employment and Learning in Northern Ireland under section 68 or 107 is to be subject to negative resolution within the meaning of section 41(6) of the Interpretation

Act (Northern Ireland) 1954 (c. 33 (N.I.)) as if it were a statutory instrument within the meaning of that Act.

(13) If a draft of an instrument containing an order under paragraph 9 of Schedule 5 would, apart from this subsection, be treated for the purposes of the Standing Orders of either House of Parliament as a hybrid instrument, it is to proceed in that House as if it were not a hybrid instrument.

263   Directions

A direction given under this Act—
- (a) may be amended or revoked by the person or body by whom it is given;
- (b) may make different provision for different purposes.

264   General interpretation of Act

(1) In this Act, unless the context otherwise requires—
"prescribed" means prescribed by regulations;
"regulations" means regulations made by the Secretary of State.

(2) Subject to subsections (4) and (5), the Education Act 1996 (c. 56) and the provisions of this Act specified in subsection (3) are to be construed as if those provisions were contained in that Act.

(3) The provisions are—
- (a) Parts 3, 4 and 5;
- (b) Parts 7 and 8;
- (c) Chapter 4 of Part 10;
- (d) sections 248, 251 and 252.

(4) Section 562 of the Education Act 1996 (Act not to apply to certain persons detained under order of a court) does not apply to functions of the Secretary of State under Part 4.

(5) If—
- (a) an expression is given a meaning for the purposes of a provision within subsection (3) (its "local meaning"), and
- (b) that meaning is different from the meaning given to it for the purposes of the Education Act 1996 (its "1996 Act meaning"),

the expression's local meaning applies instead of its 1996 Act meaning.

(6) Unless the context otherwise requires, a reference in this Act to—
- (a) a community, foundation or voluntary school, or
- (b) a community or foundation special school,

is to such a school within the meaning of the School Standards and Framework Act 1998 (c. 31).

265   Power to make consequential and transitional provision etc.

(1) The Secretary of State may by order make—
- (a) such supplementary, incidental or consequential provision, or
- (b) such transitory, transitional or saving provision,

as the Secretary of State thinks appropriate for the general purposes, or any particular purpose, of this Act or in consequence of, or for giving full effect to, any provision made by this Act.

(2) An order under this section may in particular –

    (a) provide for any provision of this Act which comes into force before another provision made by or under this or any other Act has come into force to have effect, until that other provision has come into force, with specified modifications;

    (b) amend, repeal, revoke or otherwise modify any provision of –

        (i) an Act passed before or in the same Session as this Act, or

        (ii) an instrument made under an Act before the passing of this Act.

(3) Nothing in this section limits the powers conferred by section 262(3)(c) or 269(8)(b).

(4) The amendments that may be made by virtue of subsection (2)(b) are in addition to those that are made by any other provision of this Act.

266 Repeals and revocations

Schedule 16 contains repeals and revocations (including repeals and revocations of spent provisions).

267 Financial provisions

(1) There are to be paid out of money provided by Parliament –

    (a) any expenditure incurred by virtue of this Act by the Secretary of State,

    (b) any expenditure incurred by virtue of this Act by the Office of Qualifications and Examinations Regulation, and

    (c) any increase attributable to this Act in the sums payable by virtue of any other Act out of money provided by Parliament.

(2) Any sums received by the Secretary of State by virtue of Chapter 1 of Part 1, section 78(3)(c), paragraph 18(3)(d) of Schedule 3 or paragraph 6(3)(d) of Schedule 4 are to be paid into the Consolidated Fund.

268 Extent

(1) This Act extends to England and Wales only, subject to subsections (2) to (4).

(2) Sections 40, 68, 69, 107, 108 and this Part also extend to Scotland.

(3) Sections 68, 70, 107, 109, Part 7, sections 257 and 258 and this Part also extend to Northern Ireland.

(4) An amendment, repeal or revocation made by this Act has the same extent as the provision to which it relates.

269 Commencement

(1) This Part (except section 266) comes into force on the day on which this Act is passed.

(2) The following provisions of this Act come into force at the end of two months beginning with the day on which this Act is passed –

        (a)   section 58 (and the associated entries in Schedule 16);

        (b)   sections 198 to 201.

(3)   The following provisions of this Act come into force on such day as the Welsh Ministers may by order appoint —

        (a)   sections 2 and 7 to 10;

        (b)   sections 11 and 12, so far as relating to Wales;

        (c)   sections 18 to 22;

        (d)   sections 28 to 31;

        (e)   section 39, so far as relating to Wales;

        (f)   sections 48 to 52, so far as relating to Wales;

        (g)   paragraphs 54 to 56 of Schedule 6, so far as relating to Wales;

        (h)   paragraphs 11, 13 and 27 of Schedule 12, so far as relating to Wales (and the associated entries in Schedule 16);

        (i)   paragraphs 14 to 19 and 29 of Schedule 12 (and the associated entries in Schedule 16);

        (j)   sections 174 and 192 so far as they relate to the paragraphs of Schedule 12 mentioned in paragraphs (h) and (i);

        (k)   section 205 and Schedule 14;

        (l)   section 259 (and the associated entry in Schedule 16);

        (m)   section 260;

        (n)   section 266, so far as it relates to the entries in Schedule 16 mentioned in paragraphs (h), (i) and (l).

(4)   The other provisions of this Act come into force on such day as the Secretary of State may by order appoint.

(5)   The Secretary of State must exercise the power conferred by subsection (4) so as to secure that, subject to any provision made by virtue of subsection (8), sections 91 to 99 and 104 are in force no later than the day after the day which is the school leaving date for 2013.

(6)   Before making an order under subsection (4) bringing into force any provision of Part 7 which confers functions on the Office of Qualifications and Examinations Regulation in relation to Northern Ireland, the Secretary of State must consult the Department for Employment and Learning in Northern Ireland.

(7)   The powers conferred by this section are exercisable by statutory instrument.

(8)   An order under this section may —

        (a)   appoint different days for different purposes (including different areas);

        (b)   contain transitional, transitory or saving provision in connection with the coming into force of this Act.

270   Short title

(1)   This Act may be cited as the Apprenticeships, Skills, Children and Learning Act 2009.

(2)   This Act is to be included in the list of Education Acts set out in section 578 of the Education Act 1996 (c. 56).

SCHEDULES

SCHEDULE 1 Section 40

EMPLOYEE STUDY AND TRAINING: MINOR AND CONSEQUENTIAL AMENDMENTS

Employment Rights Act 1996 (c. 18)

1   The Employment Rights Act 1996 is amended as follows.

2   In section 48 (right to present complaint of detriment to employment tribunal), in subsection (1) for "or 47E" substitute ", 47E or 47F".

3   In section 105 (unfair dismissal: redundancy), after subsection (7BA) insert—

"(7BB)   This subsection applies if the reason (or, if more than one, the principal reason) for which the employee was selected for dismissal was one of those specified in section 104E."

4   In section 108(3) (exceptions to one year qualifying period of continuous employment for claims for unfair dismissal), after paragraph (gj) insert—
        "(gk)   section 104E applies,".

5   In section 194 (House of Lords staff), in subsection (2)(e) before "VII" insert "6A,".

6   In section 195 (House of Commons staff), in subsection (2)(e) before "VII" insert "6A,".

7   In section 199 (mariners)—
        (a)   in subsection (2), after "47E," insert "47F,";
        (b)   in that subsection, before "VII" insert "6A,";
        (c)   in subsection (8)(d), before "VII" insert "6A,".

8   In section 225 (how to calculate a week's pay in relation to rights during employment) after subsection (4A) insert—

"(4B)   Where the calculation is for the purposes of section 63J, the calculation date is the day on which the section 63D application was made."

9   In section 227(1) (maximum amount of week's pay) before paragraph (za) insert—
        "(zza)   an award of compensation under section 63J(1)(b),".

10   In section 235(1) (other definitions) at the appropriate place insert—
                ""section 63D application" has the meaning given by section 63D(2);".

11   In section 236(3) (orders and regulations subject to affirmative Parliamentary procedure), after "47C," insert "63D, 63F(7),".

Trade Union and Labour Relations (Consolidation) Act 1992 (c. 52)

12   The Trade Union and Labour Relations (Consolidation) Act 1992 is amended as follows.

13   In section 212A (arbitration scheme for unfair dismissal cases etc.), in subsection (1) —

        (a)   before paragraph (za) insert —

            "(zza)   section 63F(4), (5) or (6) or 63I(1)(b) of the Employment Rights Act 1996 (study and training);";

        (b)   in paragraph (za) for "the Employment Rights Act 1996" substitute "that Act".

14   In section 237(1A)(a) (cases where employee may complain of unfair dismissal despite participation in unofficial industrial action) —

        (a)   for "or 104D" substitute ", 104D or 104E";

        (b)   for "and pension scheme membership" substitute ", pension scheme membership, and study and training".

15   In section 238(2A)(a) (cases where employment tribunal to determine whether dismissal of an employee is unfair despite limitation in subsection (2) of that section) —

        (a)   for "or 104D" substitute ", 104D or 104E";

        (b)   for "and pension scheme membership" substitute ", pension scheme membership, and study and training".

Employment Tribunals Act 1996 (c. 17)

16   In section 18 of the Employment Tribunals Act 1996 (conciliation), in subsection (1)(d) after "28," insert "63F(4), (5) or (6), 63I(1)(b),".

SCHEDULE 2   Section 59

LEA FUNCTIONS: MINOR AND CONSEQUENTIAL AMENDMENTS

Education Act 1996 (c. 56)

1   The Education Act 1996 is amended as follows.

2   (1) Section 13 (general responsibility for education) is amended as follows.

    (2) In subsection (1) after "secondary education" insert "and, in the case of a local education authority in England, further education,".

    (3) After subsection (2) insert —

      "(3)   The reference in subsection (1) to further education is to further education for persons —

          (a)   who are over compulsory school age but under 19, or

          (b)   who are aged 19 or over but under 25 and are subject to learning difficulty assessment.

Apprenticeships, Skills, Children and Learning Act 2009 (c. 22)
Schedule 2 — LEA functions: minor and consequential amendments

2343

    (4)   For the purposes of this Act a person is subject to learning difficulty assessment if —

        (a)   a learning difficulty assessment has been conducted in respect of the person, or

        (b)   arrangements for a learning difficulty assessment to be conducted in respect of the person have been made or are required to be made.

    (5)   In subsection (4), a "learning difficulty assessment" means an assessment under section 139A or 140 of the Learning and Skills Act 2000 (assessments relating to learning difficulties).

    (6)   For the purposes of subsection (1), persons who are subject to a detention order are to be regarded as part of the population of the area in which they are detained (and not any other area)."

3   For section 13A substitute —

"13A Duty to promote high standards and fulfilment of potential

    (1)   A local education authority in England must ensure that their relevant education functions and their relevant training functions are (so far as they are capable of being so exercised) exercised by the authority with a view to —

        (a)   promoting high standards,

        (b)   ensuring fair access to opportunity for education and training, and

        (c)   promoting the fulfilment of learning potential by every person to whom this subsection applies.

    (2)   Subsection (1) applies to the following —

        (a)   persons under the age of 20;

        (b)   persons aged 20 or over but under 25 who are subject to learning difficulty assessment.

    (3)   A local education authority in Wales must ensure that their relevant education functions and their relevant training functions are (so far as they are capable of being so exercised) exercised by the authority with a view to —

        (a)   promoting high standards, and

        (b)   promoting the fulfilment of learning potential by every person to whom this subsection applies.

    (4)   Subsection (3) applies to persons under the age of 20.

    (5)   In this section —

        "education" and "training" have the same meanings as in section 15ZA;

        "relevant education function", in relation to a local education authority in England, means a function relating to the provision of education for —

            (a)   persons of compulsory school age (whether at school or otherwise);

            (b)   persons (whether at school or otherwise) who are over compulsory school age and to whom subsection (1) applies;

    (c)   persons who are under compulsory school age and are registered as pupils at schools maintained by the authority;

"relevant education function", in relation to a local education authority in Wales, means a function relating to the provision of education for —

    (a)   persons of compulsory school age (whether at school or otherwise);

    (b)   persons (whether at school or otherwise) who are over compulsory school age but under the age of 20;

    (c)   persons who are under compulsory school age and are registered as pupils at schools maintained by the authority;

"relevant training function" means a function relating to the provision of training."

4   (1) Section 15A (functions in respect of full-time education for 16 to 18 year olds) is amended as follows.

    (2) In subsection (1) after "local education authority" insert "in Wales".

    (3) After subsection (1) insert —

      "(1ZA)   A local education authority in England may secure the provision for their area of full-time or part-time education suitable to the requirements of persons from other areas who are over compulsory school age but have not attained the age of 19."

    (4) In subsection (1A) for "subsection (1)" substitute "subsections (1) and (1ZA)".

    (5) In subsection (3) for "section 13(5) and (6) of the Learning and Skills Act 2000" substitute "section 15ZA(6) and (7)".

    (6) In the title for "Functions in respect of full-time education" substitute "Powers in respect of education and training".

5   In section 15B (functions in respect of education for persons over 19) in subsection (3) for "section 13(5) and (6) of the Learning and Skills Act 2000" substitute "section 15ZA(6) and (7)".

6   (1) Section 312 (meaning of "special educational needs", "learning difficulty" etc) is amended as follows.

    (2) In subsection (2) for the words from "subsection (3)" to "section 507B)" substitute "subsections (3) and (3A)".

    (3) After subsection (3) insert —

      "(3A)   Subsection (2) does not apply —

        (a)   for the purposes of sections 15ZA, 15A, 15B and 507B, or

        (b)   for the purposes of sections 18A and 562H (except for the purpose of determining, for the purposes of those sections, whether a child has special educational needs)."

7   In section 496 (power of Secretary of State to prevent unreasonable exercise of functions) after subsection (4) (as inserted by section 221(1) of this Act)

insert —

> "(5) This section is subject to sections 508I and 509AE (complaints about transport arrangements etc)."

8   In section 497 (general default powers of Secretary of State) after subsection (5) (as inserted by section 221(2) of this Act) insert —

> "(6) This section is subject to sections 508I and 509AE (complaints about transport arrangements etc)."

9   In section 497A (power of Secretary of State to secure proper performance of LEA's functions) at the end insert —

> "(8) This section is subject to sections 508I and 509AE (complaints about transport arrangements etc)."

10 (1) In the title of section 509AA, for "Provision" substitute "LEAs in England: provision".

   (2) For the title of section 509AB substitute "LEAs in England: further provision about transport policy statements for persons of sixth form age".

   (3) In the title of section 509A, for "Travel" substitute "LEAs in England: travel".

11   After section 569 insert —

> **"569A Regulations made by Welsh Ministers under Chapter 5A**
>
> (1) Any power of the Welsh Ministers to make regulations under Chapter 5A shall be exercised by statutory instrument.
>
> (2) A statutory instrument containing any such regulations made by the Welsh Ministers shall be subject to annulment in pursuance of a resolution of the National Assembly for Wales.
>
> (3) Any such regulations may make different provision for different cases, circumstances or areas and may contain such incidental, supplemental, saving or transitional provisions as the Welsh Ministers think fit."

12   In section 579(1) (general interpretation) —

   (a) in the definition of "prescribed", after ""prescribed"" insert "(except in Chapter 5A)";

   (b) in the definition of "regulations", after ""regulations"" insert "(except in Chapter 5A)".

13   In section 580 (index) insert the following entries at the appropriate places —

"relevant young adult (in sections 508F, 508G and 508I)	section 508F(9)";
"relevant youth accommodation	section 562(1A)";
"subject to a detention order	section 562(1A)";
"subject to learning difficulty assessment	section 13(4)".

Education Act 2002 (c. 32)

14   In section 207(2) of the Education Act 2002 (recoupment: adjustment between local education authorities), for "primary education and secondary education)" substitute "—

     (a)   primary education;

     (b)   secondary education;

     (c)   education provided under section 562C of the Education Act 1996 (detention of persons with special educational needs: appropriate special educational provision)."

SCHEDULE 3   Section 60

THE YOUNG PEOPLE'S LEARNING AGENCY FOR ENGLAND

Status

1   (1)   The YPLA is not to be regarded—

     (a)   as a servant or agent of the Crown, or

     (b)   as enjoying any status, immunity or privilege of the Crown.

   (2)   The YPLA's property is not to be regarded—

     (a)   as property of the Crown, or

     (b)   as property held on behalf of the Crown.

Membership

2   (1)   The YPLA is to consist of—

     (a)   between 10 and 16 members appointed by the Secretary of State (the "ordinary members"), and

     (b)   the chief executive of the YPLA.

   (2)   The Secretary of State must appoint one of the ordinary members to chair the YPLA ("the chair").

   (3)   In appointing the ordinary members, the Secretary of State must have regard to the desirability of the ordinary members, taken together, having experience relevant to—

     (a)   the full range of the YPLA's functions, and

     (b)   any functions that may be conferred or imposed on the YPLA under Academy arrangements.

   (4)   "Academy arrangements" has the meaning given by section 77(2).

Tenure

3   (1)   The chair and other ordinary members hold and vacate office in accordance with the terms of their appointments, subject to the following provisions of this Schedule.

   (2)   The chair and other ordinary members may resign from office at any time by giving written notice to the Secretary of State.

Apprenticeships, Skills, Children and Learning Act 2009 (c. 22)
Schedule 3 — The Young People's Learning Agency for England

2347

    (3) The Secretary of State may remove an ordinary member from office on either of the following grounds—

        (a) inability or unfitness to carry out the duties of the office;

        (b) absence from the YPLA's meetings for a continuous period of more than 6 months without the YPLA's permission.

    (4) The previous appointment of a person as the chair or another ordinary member does not affect the person's eligibility for re-appointment.

    (5) If the chair ceases to be an ordinary member, the person also ceases to be the chair.

Remuneration etc. of members

4   (1) The YPLA may, and must if the Secretary of State requires it to do so, pay remuneration, allowances and expenses to any of the ordinary members.

    (2) The YPLA may, and must if the Secretary of State requires it to do so, pay, or make provision for the payment of, a pension, allowances or gratuities to or in respect of a current or former ordinary member.

    (3) If a person ceases to be an ordinary member and the Secretary of State decides that the person should be compensated because of special circumstances, the YPLA must pay compensation to the person.

    (4) The amount of a payment under this paragraph is to be determined by the Secretary of State.

Staff

5   (1) The first chief executive is to be appointed by the Secretary of State, on conditions of service determined by the Secretary of State.

    (2) Later chief executives are to be appointed by the YPLA, on conditions of service determined by the YPLA.

    (3) The appointment and conditions of service of a later chief executive are subject to the approval of the Secretary of State.

    (4) The YPLA may appoint other members of staff.

    (5) The conditions of service of the other members of the YPLA's staff are to be determined by the YPLA with the approval of the Secretary of State.

6   (1) Employment with the YPLA is to be included among the kinds of employment to which a scheme under section 1 of the Superannuation Act 1972 (c. 11) (superannuation schemes as respects civil servants, etc.) can apply.

    (2) The YPLA must pay to the Minister for the Civil Service, at such times as the Minister may direct, such sums as the Minister may determine in respect of increases attributable to this paragraph in the sums payable under the Superannuation Act 1972 out of money provided by Parliament.

    (3) Sub-paragraph (4) applies if a member of staff of the YPLA ("E")—

        (a) is, by reference to employment with the YPLA, a participant in a scheme under section 1 of the Superannuation Act 1972, and

        (b) is also a member of the YPLA.

(4) The Secretary of State may determine that E's service as a member of the YPLA is to be treated for the purposes of the scheme as service as a member of staff of the YPLA (whether or not any benefits are payable to or in respect of E by virtue of paragraph 4(2)).

Committees

7   (1) The YPLA may establish committees, and any committee established by the YPLA may establish sub-committees.

(2) The YPLA may —
    (a) dissolve a sub-committee established under sub-paragraph (1), or
    (b) alter the purposes for which such a sub-committee is established.

(3) In this Schedule a committee or sub-committee established under sub-paragraph (1) is referred to as a "YPLA committee".

(4) A YPLA committee may consist of or include persons who are not members of the YPLA or the YPLA's staff.

(5) The YPLA may arrange for the payment of remuneration, allowances and expenses to any person who —
    (a) is a member of a YPLA committee, but
    (b) is not a member of the YPLA or the YPLA's staff.

(6) The YPLA must keep under review —
    (a) the structure of YPLA committees, and
    (b) the scope of each YPLA committee's activities.

8   (1) The YPLA and any other person may establish a committee jointly.

(2) In this Schedule a committee established under sub-paragraph (1) is referred to as a "joint committee".

(3) A joint committee may establish sub-committees.

(4) In this Schedule a sub-committee established under sub-paragraph (3) is referred to as a "joint sub-committee".

(5) The YPLA may arrange for the payment of remuneration, allowances and expenses to any person who —
    (a) is a member of a joint committee or joint sub-committee, but
    (b) is not a member of the YPLA or the YPLA's staff.

Procedure etc.

9   (1) The YPLA may regulate —
    (a) its own proceedings (including quorum), and
    (b) the procedure (including quorum) of YPLA committees.

(2) A joint committee may regulate —
    (a) its own procedure (including quorum), and
    (b) the procedure (including quorum) of any sub-committee established by it.

(3) The validity of proceedings of the YPLA, or of a YPLA committee, joint committee or joint sub-committee, is not affected by —

Apprenticeships, Skills, Children and Learning Act 2009 (c. 22)
Schedule 3 – The Young People's Learning Agency for England

2349

    (a)   a vacancy;

    (b)   a defective appointment.

10   (1) The following have the right to attend meetings of the YPLA, and of YPLA committees, joint committees and joint sub-committees –

    (a)   the Secretary of State;

    (b)   a representative of the Secretary of State.

   (2) A person attending a meeting of the YPLA, or of a YPLA committee, joint committee or joint sub-committee under sub-paragraph (1) may take part in its deliberations (but not its decisions).

   (3) If a person with a right to attend a meeting of the YPLA, or of a YPLA committee, joint committee or joint sub-committee requests it, the YPLA must provide the person with all information relating to the meeting that –

    (a)   has been distributed to the members of the YPLA, or of the YPLA committee, joint committee or joint sub-committee, and

    (b)   is likely to be needed by the person in order to take part in the meeting.

Delegation

11   (1) The YPLA may delegate any of its functions to –

    (a)   the chair or the chief executive;

    (b)   a committee established by the YPLA;

    (c)   a joint committee.

   (2) If a function is delegated to the chair, the chair may delegate the function to any of the other ordinary members or the chief executive.

   (3) If a function is delegated to the chief executive, the chief executive may delegate the function to a member of the YPLA's staff.

   (4) A function is delegated under this paragraph to the extent and on the terms that the person delegating it determines.

12   (1) A committee established by the YPLA or a joint committee may delegate any of its functions to a sub-committee established by it.

   (2) A function is delegated under this paragraph to the extent and on the terms that the committee determines.

   (3) The power of a committee established by the YPLA to delegate a function under this paragraph, and to determine the extent and terms of the delegation, are subject to the YPLA's powers to direct what a committee established by it may and may not do.

   (4) The power of a joint committee to delegate a function under this paragraph, and to determine the extent and terms of the delegation, are subject to the power of the YPLA and any other person with whom the YPLA established the committee to direct (acting jointly) what the committee may and may not do.

Plans

13   (1) The YPLA must make and publish a plan for each academic year.

2350

Apprenticeships, Skills, Children and Learning Act 2009 (c. 22)
Schedule 3 — The Young People's Learning Agency for England

(2) The YPLA's plan for an academic year must be published before the start of the academic year.

(3) The YPLA's plan for an academic year must include—

(a) the YPLA's proposals as to how it intends to achieve in that year any objectives for the year set out in directions under section 75 or grant conditions;

(b) the YPLA's proposals as to how it proposes to use its grant funding for the year.

(4) In this paragraph—

"academic year" means—

(a) the period beginning on the day on which section 60 comes into force and ending on the following 31 August;

(b) each successive period of 12 months;

"grant conditions" mean conditions to which a grant under paragraph 18 is subject;

"grant funding" means a grant under that paragraph.

Reports

14 (1) As soon as reasonably practicable after the end of each reporting period the YPLA must prepare an annual report for the period.

(2) The annual report must state how the YPLA has performed its functions in the reporting period.

(3) The YPLA must send a copy of each annual report to the Secretary of State.

(4) The Secretary of State must lay before Parliament a copy of each report received under sub-paragraph (3) and arrange for it to be published.

(5) In this paragraph "reporting period" means—

(a) the period specified by the Secretary of State in a direction given to the YPLA;

(b) each successive period of 12 months.

Accounts

15 (1) The YPLA must—

(a) keep proper accounts and proper records in relation to the accounts, and

(b) prepare annual accounts in respect of each financial year.

(2) The annual accounts must comply with any directions given by the Secretary of State as to—

(a) the information to be contained in them,

(b) the manner in which the information contained in them is to be presented, or

(c) the methods and principles according to which the annual accounts are to be prepared.

(3) Before the end of the month of August next following each financial year, the YPLA must send copies of the annual accounts for the year to—

(a) the Secretary of State, and

Apprenticeships, Skills, Children and Learning Act 2009 (c. 22)
Schedule 3 – The Young People's Learning Agency for England

2351

       (b)   the Comptroller and Auditor General.

  (4) The Comptroller and Auditor General must—

       (a)   examine, certify and report on the annual accounts, and

       (b)   give a copy of the report to the Secretary of State.

  (5) The Secretary of State must lay before Parliament—

       (a)   a copy of any annual accounts received under sub-paragraph (3), and

       (b)   a copy of each report received under sub-paragraph (4).

  (6) In this paragraph "financial year" means—

       (a)   the period specified by the Secretary of State in a direction given to the YPLA;

       (b)   each successive period of 12 months.

Documents

16   The application of the YPLA's seal is authenticated by the signatures of—

       (a)   the chair or another person authorised (generally or specifically) for that purpose by the YPLA, and

       (b)   one other member of the YPLA.

17   Any document purporting to be an instrument made or issued by or on behalf of the YPLA, and to be duly executed by a person authorised by the YPLA in that behalf—

       (a)   is to be received in evidence, and

       (b)   is to be taken to be made or issued in that way, unless the contrary is shown.

Funding

18 (1) The Secretary of State may make grants to the YPLA for the purposes of any of its functions.

  (2) Grants to the YPLA under this paragraph are to be made at such times and subject to such conditions (if any) as the Secretary of State thinks appropriate.

  (3) Conditions to which a grant is subject may (in particular)—

       (a)   set the YPLA's budget for any financial year;

       (b)   require the YPLA to use the grant for specified purposes;

       (c)   require the YPLA to comply with specified requirements in respect of persons or persons of a specified description in securing the provision of specified financial resources to such persons;

       (d)   enable repayment (in whole or part) to be required of sums paid by the Secretary of State if any condition subject to which the grant was made is not complied with;

       (e)   require the payment of interest in respect of any period during which a sum due to the Secretary of State in accordance with any condition remains unpaid.

  (4) Requirements which may be imposed under sub-paragraph (3)(c) include in particular requirements that, if the YPLA provides specified financial resources, it is to impose specified conditions.

(5) The Secretary of State may not impose conditions which relate to the YPLA's securing of the provision of financial resources to a particular person or persons.

Supplementary powers

19   (1) The YPLA may do anything that it considers necessary or appropriate for the purposes of, or in connection with, its functions.

     (2) The power in sub-paragraph (1) is subject to any restrictions imposed by or under any provision of any Act.

     (3) The YPLA may not borrow money.

     (4) The YPLA may not do any of the following without the consent of the Secretary of State —
        (a)   lend money;
        (b)   form, participate in forming or invest in a company;
        (c)   form, participate in forming or otherwise become a member of a charitable incorporated organisation (within the meaning of section 69A of the Charities Act 1993 (c. 10)).

     (5) In sub-paragraph (4)(b) the reference to investing in a company includes a reference to —
        (a)   becoming a member of the company, and
        (b)   investing in it by the acquisition of any assets, securities or rights or otherwise.

Parliamentary Commissioner Act 1967 (c. 13)

20   In Schedule 2 to the Parliamentary Commissioner Act 1967 (departments etc. subject to investigation) at the appropriate place insert —
     "The Young People's Learning Agency for England."

House of Commons Disqualification Act 1975 (c. 24)

21   In Part 3 of Schedule 1 to the House of Commons Disqualification Act 1975 (other disqualifying offices) at the appropriate place insert —
     "Any member of the Young People's Learning Agency for England in receipt of remuneration."

Superannuation Act 1972 (c. 11)

22   In Schedule 1 to the Superannuation Act 1972 (kinds of employment, etc, referred to in section 1 of that Act) under the heading "Other bodies" at the appropriate place insert —
     "The Young People's Learning Agency for England".

SCHEDULE 4

THE CHIEF EXECUTIVE OF SKILLS FUNDING

Status

1   (1) The Chief Executive is to perform the functions of the office on behalf of the Crown.

   (2) The person for the time being holding the office of Chief Executive is by the name of that office to be a corporation sole.

Tenure of office and terms of appointment

2   (1) The Secretary of State may remove the Chief Executive from office on the grounds of inability or unfitness to carry out the functions of the office.

   (2) The Chief Executive may resign at any time by giving written notice to the Secretary of State.

   (3) Otherwise, the Chief Executive holds and vacates office in accordance with the terms of appointment to that office (which may include provision for dismissal).

   (4) Service as Chief Executive is to be employment in the civil service of the State.

Staff

3   (1) The Chief Executive may appoint staff.

   (2) Service as a member of the Chief Executive's staff is to be service in the civil service of the State.

   (3) Subject to sub-paragraph (2), the conditions of service of the staff appointed by the Chief Executive are to be determined by the Chief Executive.

Delegation

4   (1) The Chief Executive may delegate any of the functions of the office —
      (a) to a member of the Chief Executive's staff appointed under paragraph 3, or
      (b) to a member of staff provided to the Chief Executive by the Secretary of State under arrangements under paragraph 5.

   (2) Any delegation under sub-paragraph (1) is to be to the extent, and on terms, that the Chief Executive determines.

   (3) This paragraph is subject to section 82.

Arrangements with Secretary of State

5   The Secretary of State and the Chief Executive may enter into arrangements with each other for the provision to the Chief Executive by the Secretary of State, on such terms as may be agreed, of staff, accommodation or services.

Funding

6   (1) The Secretary of State may make grants to the Chief Executive.

     (2) Grants to the Chief Executive are to be made at such times and subject to such conditions (if any) as the Secretary of State thinks appropriate.

     (3) Conditions to which a grant is subject may —
          (a)   set the Chief Executive's budget for any financial year;
          (b)   require the Chief Executive to use the grant for specified purposes;
          (c)   require the Chief Executive to comply with specified requirements in respect of persons or persons of a specified description in securing the provision of specified financial resources to such persons;
          (d)   enable repayment (in whole or part) to be required of sums paid by the Secretary of State if any condition subject to which the grant was made is not complied with;
          (e)   require the payment of interest in respect of any period during which a sum due to the Secretary of State in accordance with any condition remains unpaid.

     (4) Requirements which may be imposed under sub-paragraph (3)(c) include in particular requirements that, if the Chief Executive provides specified financial resources, the Chief Executive is to impose specified conditions.

Reports

7   (1) As soon as reasonably practicable after the end of each financial year the Chief Executive must prepare an annual report for the financial year.

     (2) The annual report must state how the Chief Executive has performed the functions of the office in the financial year.

     (3) The Chief Executive must send a copy of each report prepared under sub-paragraph (1) to the Secretary of State.

     (4) The Secretary of State must lay before Parliament a copy of each report received under sub-paragraph (3) and arrange for it to be published.

     (5) The Chief Executive may —
          (a)   prepare other reports on matters relating to the functions of the office, and
          (b)   must send a copy of each report prepared under paragraph (a) to the Secretary of State.

Accounts

8   (1) The Chief Executive must —
          (a)   keep proper accounts and proper records in relation to the accounts, and
          (b)   prepare annual accounts in respect of each financial year.

     (2) The annual accounts must comply with any directions given by the Secretary of State with the approval of the Treasury as to —
          (a)   the information to be contained in them,
          (b)   the manner in which the information contained in them is to be presented, or

    (c)   the methods and principles according to which the annual accounts are to be prepared.

(3) Before the end of the month of August next following each financial year, the Chief Executive must send copies of the annual accounts for the year to —

    (a)   the Secretary of State, and

    (b)   the Comptroller and Auditor General.

(4) The Comptroller and Auditor General must —

    (a)   examine, certify and report on the annual accounts, and

    (b)   give a copy of the report to the Secretary of State.

(5) The Secretary of State must lay before Parliament —

    (a)   a copy of any annual accounts received under sub-paragraph (3), and

    (b)   a copy of each report received under sub-paragraph (4).

Supplementary powers

9   (1) The Chief Executive may do anything that the Chief Executive considers necessary or appropriate for the purposes of, or in connection with, the functions of the office.

(2) The power in sub-paragraph (1) is subject to any restrictions imposed by or under any provision of any Act.

(3) The Chief Executive may not borrow money.

(4) The Chief Executive may not do any of the following without the consent of the Secretary of State —

    (a)   lend money;

    (b)   form, participate in forming or invest in a company;

    (c)   form, participate in forming or otherwise become a member of a charitable incorporated organisation (within the meaning of section 69A of the Charities Act 1993 (c. 10)).

(5) In sub-paragraph (4)(b) the reference to investing in a company includes a reference to —

    (a)   becoming a member of the company, and

    (b)   investing in it by the acquisition of any assets, securities or rights or otherwise.

Directions about management

10   The Secretary of State may give directions to the Chief Executive about the financial and other management of and administrative arrangements relating to the office comprising the Chief Executive and the staff of the Chief Executive.

Financial year

11   In this Schedule "financial year" means —

    (a)   the period beginning on the day on which section 81 comes into force and ending on the following 31 March;

    (b)   each successive period of 12 months.

2356

Apprenticeships, Skills, Children and Learning Act 2009 (c. 22)
Schedule 5 — Learning aims for persons aged 19 or over
Part 1 — Qualifications to which Schedule applies

SCHEDULE 5

Section 87

LEARNING AIMS FOR PERSONS AGED 19 OR OVER

PART 1

QUALIFICATIONS TO WHICH SCHEDULE APPLIES

1   This paragraph applies to the following qualifications —
    (a)   a specified qualification in literacy;
    (b)   a specified qualification in numeracy;
    (c)   a specified vocational qualification at level 2.

2   This paragraph applies to a specified qualification at level 3.

PART 2

POWER TO SPECIFY

Power to specify

3   (1)   In paragraphs 1 and 2, a reference to a specified qualification is to a regulated qualification which is specified, or which is of a description specified, in regulations.

    (2)   The regulations may specify qualifications, or descriptions of qualifications, by reference to an assessment made by the Chief Executive of the level of attainment demonstrated by a qualification; and for that purpose the regulations may confer functions (which may include the exercise of a discretion) on the Chief Executive.

    (3)   The regulations may make provision which applies subject to exceptions specified in the regulations.

    (4)   In sub-paragraph (1) "regulated qualification" has the meaning given by section 130.

Power to specify qualification in literacy

4   The level of attainment in literacy demonstrated by a specified qualification in literacy must be the level which, in the opinion of the Secretary of State, is the minimum required in that respect by persons aged 19 or over in order to be able to operate effectively in day-to-day life.

Power to specify qualification in numeracy

5   The level of attainment in numeracy demonstrated by a specified qualification in numeracy must be the level which, in the opinion of the Secretary of State, is the minimum required in that respect by persons aged 19 or over in order to be able to operate effectively in day-to-day life.

Level 2

6   Level 2 is the level of attainment (in terms of breadth and depth) which, in the opinion of the Secretary of State, is demonstrated by the General Certificate of Secondary Education in five subjects, each at Grade C or above.

Apprenticeships, Skills, Children and Learning Act 2009 (c. 22)
Schedule 5 – Learning aims for persons aged 19 or over
Part 2 – Power to specify

2357

Level 3

7   Level 3 is the level of attainment (in terms of breadth and depth) which, in the opinion of the Secretary of State, is demonstrated by the General Certificate of Education at the advanced level in two subjects.

Advice and information

8   In forming an opinion for the purposes of this Schedule, the Secretary of State may have regard, in particular, to advice or information relating to qualifications which is provided by —
         (a)   the Chief Executive,
         (b)   the Qualifications and Curriculum Development Agency, or
         (c)   the Office of Qualifications and Examinations Regulation.

Power to amend

9   (1) The Secretary of State may by order amend this Schedule so as to —
         (a)   add a category of qualification to Part 1;
         (b)   remove a category of qualification for the time being referred to in Part 1;
         (c)   substitute a different qualification for a qualification for the time being referred to in Part 2;
         (d)   make consequential amendments.

     (2) The power conferred by sub-paragraph (1)(b) includes power to remove every category of qualification to which a paragraph of Part 1 for the time being applies.

SCHEDULE 6   Section 123

DISSOLUTION OF THE LEARNING AND SKILLS COUNCIL FOR ENGLAND: MINOR AND CONSEQUENTIAL AMENDMENTS

Race Relations Act 1976 (c. 74)

1   In Part 2 of Schedule 1A to the Race Relations Act 1976 (bodies and other persons added after commencement of general statutory duty) for the entry for the Learning and Skills Council for England substitute "The Chief Executive of Skills Funding."

Further and Higher Education Act 1992 (c. 13)

2   The Further and Higher Education Act 1992 is amended as follows.

3   (1) Section 19 (supplementary powers of a further education corporation) is amended as follows.

     (2) In subsection (4AC)(a), for "Learning and Skills Council for England" substitute "Chief Executive of Skills Funding".

     (3) In subsection (4B), for "Learning and Skills Council for England" substitute "Chief Executive of Skills Funding".

     (4) In subsection (4C), for "council" substitute "Chief Executive".

4   In section 29(7A) (government and conduct of designated institutions) —

     (a) for paragraph (a) (but not the "or" following it) substitute —

         "(a) the Chief Executive of Skills Funding under section 56AA,";

     (b) in paragraph (b), for "that Act" substitute "the Learning and Skills Act 2000".

5   In section 31(2A) (designated institutions conducted by companies) —

     (a) for paragraph (a) (but not the "or" following it) substitute —

         "(a) the Chief Executive of Skills Funding under section 56AA,";

     (b) in paragraph (b), for "that Act" substitute "the Learning and Skills Act 2000".

6   In section 54(1) (duty to give information) —

     (a) for "the Learning and Skills Council for England" substitute "the Chief Executive of Skills Funding";

     (b) for "the council", in both places where it occurs, substitute "the Chief Executive".

7   (1) Section 56A (intervention: England) is amended as follows.

     (2) In subsection (1), for "Learning and Skills Council for England" substitute "Chief Executive of Skills Funding (referred to in this section and sections 56AA to 56D as "the Chief Executive")".

     (3) In subsections (3) and (4), for "council", wherever occurring, substitute "Chief Executive".

     (4) In subsection (5) —

     (a) for the words from "If the" to "same time" substitute "At the same time as doing one or more of those things the Chief Executive must";

     (b) in paragraphs (a) to (c) for "council", wherever appearing, substitute "Chief Executive".

     (5) In subsection (6) —

     (a) for "council" substitute "Chief Executive";

     (b) in paragraph (c), for "as it thinks" substitute "as the Chief Executive thinks".

     (6) In subsection (9), for "council" substitute "Chief Executive".

     (7) In subsection (10), for "council, where it considers" substitute "Chief Executive, where the Chief Executive considers".

8   After section 56A insert —

"56AA Appointment by Chief Executive of Skills Funding of members of governing body of further education institutions

     (1) The Chief Executive may appoint a person to be a member of the governing body of an institution which —

     (a) is conducted by a further education corporation, and

     (b) mainly serves the population of England.

    (2)   But no more than two members of the governing body of a given institution may at any given time have been appointed under this section.

    (3)   A member of the governing body of an institution who was appointed before the relevant commencement date by the Learning and Skills Council for England under section 11 of the Learning and Skills Act 2000 is, on and after that date, to be treated for the purposes of subsection (2) of this section as appointed by the Chief Executive under this section.

    (4)   "The relevant commencement date" is the date on which section 123 of the Apprenticeships, Skills, Children and Learning Act 2009 comes into force."

9   (1)   Section 56B (intervention policy: England) is amended as follows.

    (2)   In subsection (1) —

       (a)   for "Learning and Skills Council for England" substitute "Chief Executive";

       (b)   in paragraph (a), for "its policy with respect to the exercise of its powers" substitute "policy with respect to the exercise of the Chief Executive's powers";

       (c)   for paragraph (c) substitute —

           "(c)   if the Chief Executive considers it appropriate in consequence of a review, prepare a revised statement of policy."

    (3)   In subsection (2) —

       (a)   for "council" substitute "Chief Executive";

       (b)   in paragraph (a), for "it thinks" substitute "the Chief Executive thinks";

       (c)   in paragraph (b), for "made to it" substitute "made to the Chief Executive".

    (4)   In subsection (3) —

       (a)   for "council" substitute "Chief Executive";

       (b)   omit "its".

    (5)   In subsection (4), for "council" substitute "Chief Executive".

    (6)   In subsection (5) —

       (a)   for "council" substitute "Chief Executive";

       (b)   for "prepared by it" substitute "prepared under subsection (1)".

    (7)   In subsection (7) —

       (a)   for "council" substitute "Chief Executive";

       (b)   for paragraphs (a) and (b) substitute "any statement or revised statement received under subsection (6)."

    (8)   In subsection (8) —

       (a)   for "council" substitute "Chief Executive";

       (b)   for "its powers" substitute "the Chief Executive's powers".

10   (1)   Section 56C (directions) is amended as follows.

(2) In subsection (1)(b), for "Learning and Skills Council for England" substitute "Chief Executive".

(3) In subsection (2)—

    (a)   for "council" substitute "Chief Executive";

    (b)   for "council's" substitute "Chief Executive's".

(4) In subsection (3), for "council", in both places where it occurs, substitute "Chief Executive".

(5) In subsection (4)—

    (a)   for "council" substitute "Chief Executive";

    (b)   omit "to it".

(6) In subsection (5), for "council", in both places where it occurs, substitute "Chief Executive".

11   After section 56C insert—

"56D Notification by LEA or YPLA of possible grounds for intervention

    (1)   This section applies if a relevant body is of the view that any of the matters listed in section 56A(2) applies in relation to an institution in England within the further education sector, other than a sixth form college.

    (2)   The relevant body must notify the Chief Executive of that view.

    (3)   The Chief Executive must have regard to the relevant body's view in deciding whether to exercise the powers under section 56A.

    (4)   "Relevant body" means a local education authority or the YPLA."

12   In Schedule 4 (instruments and articles of government for further education corporations) in paragraph 1A—

    (a)   for paragraph (a) (but not the "or" following it) substitute—

           "(a)   the Chief Executive of Skills Funding under section 56AA,";

    (b)   in paragraph (b), for "that Act" substitute "the Learning and Skills Act 2000".

Education Act 1996 (c. 56)

13   In section 13(2)(a) (general responsibility for education) for "Learning and Skills Council for England" substitute "Chief Executive of Skills Funding".

Learning and Skills Act 2000 (c. 21)

14   The Learning and Skills Act 2000 is amended as follows.

15   Omit section 1 (the Learning and Skills Council for England).

16   Omit section 2 (duties of Learning and Skills Council: education and training for persons aged 16 to 19).

17   Omit section 3 (duties of Learning and Skills Council: education and training for persons over 19).

18   Omit section 4 (encouragement of education and training).

19   Omit sections 4A to 4C (learning aims for persons aged 19 and over).

20   Omit section 5 (provision of financial resources).

21   Omit section 6 (financial resources: conditions).

22   Omit section 7 (funding of school sixth forms).

23   Omit section 8 (links between education and training and employment).

24   Omit section 9 (assessments and means tests).

25   Omit section 10 (qualifying accounts and arrangements).

26   Omit section 11 (further education: governors).

27   Omit section 11A (support schemes relating to education and training for persons aged 10 to 15).

28   Omit section 12 (research and information).

29   Omit section 13 (persons with learning difficulties).

30   Omit section 14 (equality of opportunity).

31   Omit section 14A (consultation).

32   Omit section 15 (plans).

33   Omit section 16 (strategy).

34   Omit section 17 (use of information by Learning and Skills Council).

35   Omit section 18 (supplementary functions).

36   Omit sections 18A to 18C (regional councils).

37   Omit sections 24A to 24C (strategies for functions of the Learning and Skills Council).

38   Omit section 25 (directions).

39   Omit section 26 (committees).

40   Omit section 27 (grants to Learning and Skills Council).

41   Omit section 28 (annual report).

42   Omit section 29 (Council's financial year).

43   Omit section 97 (external qualifications: persons over 19).

44   (1) Section 98 (approved qualifications: England) is amended as follows.

     (2) In subsection (1), for "sections 96 and 97 in their application" substitute "section 96 in its application".

     (3) Omit subsection (2A).

45   (1) Section 99 (approved qualifications: Wales) is amended as follows.

     (2) In subsection (1), for "sections 96 and 97 in their application" substitute "section 96 in its application".

     (3) Omit subsection (2A).

46 In section 100 (authorised bodies) for "sections 96 and 97 in their application", in both places where the words occur, substitute "section 96 in its application".

47 In section 101 (enforcement: England) in subsection (1) —

 (a) for "sections 96 and 97 in their application" substitute "section 96 in its application";

 (b) after paragraph (a) insert "or";

 (c) omit paragraph (c) (and the word "or" before it).

48 In section 102 (enforcement: Wales) in subsection (1) —

 (a) for "sections 96 and 97 in their application" substitute "section 96 in its application";

 (b) after paragraph (a) insert "or";

 (c) omit paragraph (c) (and the word "or" before it).

49 (1) Section 113A (restructuring of sixth form education) is amended as follows.

 (2) Omit subsections (1), (4)(aa), (5), (7), (8) and (9)(f).

 (3) In subsection (11) —

  (a) in the definition of "regulations" omit paragraph (a) (and the "and" after it);

  (b) in the definition of "relevant authority" omit paragraph (a) (and the "and" after it).

50 Omit Schedule 1 (the Learning and Skills Council for England).

51 Omit Schedule 1A (learning aims for persons aged 19 and over).

52 Omit Schedule 3 (committees (England)).

53 (1) Schedule 7A (implementation of proposals for restructuring sixth form education) is amended as follows.

 (2) In paragraph 1, omit "approved or" and "approval or", wherever occurring.

 (3) In paragraph 3(4), omit paragraph (a).

 (4) Omit paragraphs 5(1), 6(1) and 7(1) and (2).

Education Act 2002 (c. 32)

54 The Education Act 2002 is amended as follows.

55 After section 208 insert —

"208A Recoupment: adjustment between local education authorities and the YPLA

 (1) This section applies in relation to the following cases —

  (a) the YPLA secures the provision of education under section 66 of the Apprenticeships, Skills, Children and Learning Act 2009 in respect of a person who belongs to the area of a local education authority in England or Wales ("the home authority");

  (b) a local education authority in England or Wales ("the providing authority") secures the provision of education within section 66(1) or (3) of that Act in respect of a person who belongs to the area of a local education authority in England.

(2) Regulations made by the appropriate national authority may make provision —

    (a) in relation to cases within subsection (1)(a), requiring or authorising the payment of an amount by the home authority to the YPLA;

    (b) in relation to cases within subsection (1)(b), requiring or authorising the payment of an amount by the YPLA to the providing authority.

(3) The amounts that may be required or authorised to be paid are such sums in respect of amounts described in the regulations as may be —

    (a) agreed between the YPLA and the local education authority in question, or

    (b) failing agreement, determined in accordance with the regulations.

(4) The regulations may provide for the amounts payable —

    (a) to reflect the whole or any part of the average costs incurred by local education authorities in the provision of education (whether in England and Wales as a whole or in any particular area or areas), and

    (b) to be based on figures for average costs determined by such body or bodies representing local education authorities, or on such other figures relating to costs so incurred, as the appropriate national authority thinks appropriate.

(5) Regulations made under this section by the Welsh Ministers may provide that, in cases specified in or determined in accordance with the regulations, the amounts payable are to be determined by the Welsh Ministers with the consent of the Secretary of State.

(6) In a case where the providing authority is a local education authority in Wales, a dispute between the providing authority and the YPLA as to whether the providing authority is entitled to be paid an amount by the YPLA under the regulations is to be determined by the Welsh Ministers with the consent of the Secretary of State.

(7) In this section —

    "the appropriate national authority" means —

        (a) in relation to a case where the providing authority is a local education authority in Wales, the Welsh Ministers;

        (b) in relation to any other case, the Secretary of State;

    "the YPLA" means the Young People's Learning Agency for England."

56   In section 210(6A) (orders and regulations: provisions subject to annulment by National Assembly for Wales) after "section 32(9)" insert "or section 208A".

Education Act 2005 (c. 18)

57   In section 108 of the Education Act 2005 (supply of information: education maintenance allowances), in subsection (3) —

(a)   in paragraph (b) for "Learning and Skills Council for England" substitute "Chief Executive of Skills Funding";

(b)   after paragraph (b) insert —

"(ba)   the Young People's Learning Agency for England;";

(c)   in paragraph (f) for the words from "the Secretary of State" to the end substitute "a person within paragraphs (a) to (e)".

Education and Inspections Act 2006 (c. 40)

58   The Education and Inspections Act 2006 is amended as follows.

59   Section 75 (education and training to satisfy entitlements) ceases to have effect.

Further Education and Training Act 2007 (c. 25)

60   The Further Education and Training Act 2007 is amended as follows.

61   Sections 11 to 13 (provision by Learning and Skills Council for England of services and assistance in respect of employment and training) cease to have effect.

62   Sections 14 to 16 (transfer of functions of Secretary of State in relation to further education corporations to the Learning and Skills Council for England) cease to have effect.

SCHEDULE 7   Section 124

LEARNING AND SKILLS COUNCIL FOR ENGLAND: TRANSFER SCHEMES

Staff transfer schemes

1   The Secretary of State may make a scheme (a "staff transfer scheme") providing for the transfer of designated employees of the LSC —

(a)   to a permitted transferee, or

(b)   so as to become employed in the civil service of the state.

2   (1) This paragraph applies where a staff transfer scheme provides for the transfer of an employee of the LSC to a permitted transferee or so as to become employed in the civil service of the state.

(2) The scheme must provide for the TUPE regulations to apply (to the extent that they would not otherwise apply) as if —

(a)   any transfer of functions (however effected and described) from the LSC to a permitted transferee or the Crown were a transfer of an undertaking;

(b)   the transfer of the undertaking took effect on a designated date;

Apprenticeships, Skills, Children and Learning Act 2009 (c. 22)
Schedule 7 — Learning and Skills Council for England: transfer schemes

2365

        (c)   the transfer of the undertaking were a relevant transfer for the purposes of the regulations;

        (d)   the employee had for those purposes been assigned to an organised grouping of resources or employees that was subject to the relevant transfer.

3   (1)   This paragraph applies where a staff transfer scheme provides for a transfer of an employee of the LSC so as to become employed in the civil service of the state on terms which do not constitute a contract of employment.

    (2)   The scheme must provide for the TUPE regulations to apply with the necessary modifications.

4   A staff transfer scheme may provide for the transfer of an employee of the LSC to a permitted transferee or so as to become employed in the civil service of the state despite any provisions, of whatever nature, which would otherwise prevent the employee from being so transferred.

Property transfer schemes

5   (1)   The Secretary of State may make a scheme (a "property transfer scheme") providing for the transfer from the LSC of designated property, rights or liabilities of the LSC to—

        (a)   a permitted transferee,

        (b)   the Secretary of State, or

        (c)   the Chief Executive of Skills Funding.

    (2)   A property transfer scheme may—

        (a)   create rights, or impose liabilities, in relation to property or rights transferred by virtue of the scheme;

        (b)   provide for anything done by or in relation to the LSC in connection with any property, rights or liabilities transferred by the scheme to be treated as done, or to be continued, by or in relation to the person to whom the property, rights or liabilities in question are transferred;

        (c)   apportion property, rights and liabilities;

        (d)   make provision about the continuation of legal proceedings.

    (3)   The things that may be transferred by a property transfer scheme include—

        (a)   property, rights and liabilities that could not otherwise be transferred;

        (b)   property acquired, and rights and liabilities arising, after the making of the scheme.

Continuity

6   A transfer by virtue of a staff transfer scheme or a property transfer scheme does not affect the validity of anything done by or in relation to the LSC before the transfer takes effect.

Supplementary provision etc.

7   A staff transfer scheme or a property transfer scheme may include supplementary, incidental, transitional and consequential provision.

Interpretation

8   In this Schedule —

"designated", in relation to a staff transfer scheme or a property transfer scheme, means specified in, or determined in accordance with, the scheme;

"the LSC" means the Learning and Skills Council for England;

"permitted transferee" means —

(a)   a local education authority in England;

(b)   the Young People's Learning Agency for England;

(c)   any other person specified in an order made by the Secretary of State;

"the TUPE regulations" means the Transfer of Undertakings (Protection of Employment) Regulations 2006 (S.I. 2006/246).

SCHEDULE 8   Section 125

SIXTH FORM COLLEGE SECTOR

1   The Further and Higher Education Act 1992 (c. 13) is amended as follows.

2   In section 17(1) (meaning of "further education corporation") after "by virtue of section" insert "33D or".

3   After section 33 insert —

"Sixth form college corporations: England

33A   Initial designation of existing bodies corporate as sixth form college corporations

(1)   The Secretary of State may by order designate a body corporate within subsection (2) as a sixth form college corporation, for the purpose of conducting an educational institution specified in the order.

(2)   A body corporate is within this subsection if it is —

(a)   a further education corporation established in respect of an institution in England, or

(b)   a body corporate established by an order under section 143(4) of the Learning and Skills Act 2000 in respect of an institution in England.

(3)   On the date specified in the order —

(a)   a body corporate within subsection (2)(a) ceases to be a further education corporation and becomes a sixth form college corporation;

(b)   a body corporate within subsection (2)(b) ceases to be subject to the order under section 143(4) of the Learning and Skills Act 2000 establishing it and becomes a sixth form college corporation;

      (c)   in the case of a body corporate within subsection (2)(b), a designation under section 28 which has effect in relation to the relevant sixth form college ceases to have effect.

(4)   An order under subsection (1) may –

      (a)   make provision for the continuity of the body corporate, including provision for the continuation of the instrument and articles of government of the body and the relevant sixth form college;

      (b)   make provision as to the initial name of the corporation as a sixth form college corporation.

(5)   The power conferred by subsection (1) –

      (a)   is exercisable only once;

      (b)   is not exercisable after the date specified in an order made by the Secretary of State.

33B Subsequent designation of existing bodies corporate as sixth form college corporations

(1)   The Secretary of State may by order designate a body corporate within subsection (2) as a sixth form college corporation, for the purpose of conducting an educational institution specified in the order.

(2)   A body corporate is within this subsection if it is –

      (a)   a further education corporation established in respect of an institution in England, or

      (b)   a body corporate established by an order under section 143(4) of the Learning and Skills Act 2000 in respect of an institution in England.

(3)   An order under subsection (1) may be made only if –

      (a)   an application for the order has been made by the governing body of the institution mentioned in subsection (2)(a) or (b), and

      (b)   the institution is one within subsection (4).

(4)   An institution is within this subsection if it appears to the Secretary of State that on the date on which the application is made at least 80% of its total enrolment number will be persons over compulsory school age but under 19.

(5)   The total enrolment number of an institution is to be calculated in accordance with paragraph 1(2) of Schedule 3.

(6)   On the date specified in the order –

      (a)   a body corporate within subsection (2)(a) ceases to be a further education corporation and becomes a sixth form college corporation;

      (b)   a body corporate within subsection (2)(b) ceases to be subject to the order under section 143(4) of the Learning and Skills Act 2000 establishing it and becomes a sixth form college corporation;

    (c)   in the case of a body corporate within subsection (2)(b), a designation under section 28 which has effect in relation to the relevant sixth form college ceases to have effect.

(7)   An order under subsection (1) may —

    (a)   make provision for the continuity of the body corporate, including provision for the continuation of the instrument and articles of government of the body and the relevant sixth form college;

    (b)   make provision as to the initial name of the corporation as a sixth form college corporation.

(8)   The power conferred by subsection (1) is exercisable only after the date specified in an order under section 33A(5)(b).

33C   Establishment of new bodies corporate as sixth form college corporations

(1)   The Secretary of State may by order make provision for the establishment of a body corporate as a sixth form college corporation, for the purpose of establishing and conducting an educational institution specified in the order.

(2)   An order under subsection (1) may be made only if —

    (a)   a proposal relating to the order has been made by the responsible local education authority and it appears to the Secretary of State that the requirements in subsection (3) have been met in relation to the proposal, and

    (b)   it appears to the Secretary of State that the institution will when established be one within subsection (4).

(3)   The requirements are that —

    (a)   the authority have published the proposal by the prescribed time and in the prescribed manner;

    (b)   the proposal as published contained prescribed information;

    (c)   the authority have considered any representations about the proposal made to them within the prescribed period.

(4)   An institution is within this subsection if —

    (a)   the institution is in England, and

    (b)   on the date on which it is proposed to be established, at least 80% of its total enrolment number will be persons over compulsory school age but under 19.

(5)   The total enrolment number of an institution is to be calculated in accordance with paragraph 1(2) of Schedule 3.

(6)   An order under subsection (1) —

    (a)   must provide for the institution to be established and conducted by the body corporate as from the date specified in the order;

    (b)   may make provision as to the initial name of the corporation as a sixth form college corporation.

33D Conversion of sixth form college corporations into further education corporations

(1) The Secretary of State may by order convert a sixth form college corporation into a further education corporation.

(2) An order under subsection (1) may be made only if —
    (a) an application for the order has been made by the governing body of the relevant sixth form college, or
    (b) the Secretary of State is satisfied that it is no longer appropriate for the body to be a sixth form college corporation.

(3) An application under subsection (2)(a) may not be made during the period of two years beginning with the date on which the body's designation or establishment as a sixth form college corporation takes effect.

(4) The Secretary of State must consult the governing body of the relevant sixth form college before making an order under subsection (1) in a case within subsection (2)(b).

(5) On the date specified in the order, the body ceases to be a sixth form college corporation and becomes a further education corporation.

(6) An order under subsection (1) may —
    (a) make provision for the continuity of the body corporate, including provision for the continuation of the instrument and articles of government of the body and the relevant sixth form college;
    (b) make provision as to the initial name of the corporation as a further education corporation.

33E Principal powers of a sixth form college corporation

(1) A sixth form college corporation may do any of the following —
    (a) provide further and higher education,
    (b) provide secondary education suitable to the requirements of persons who have attained the age of 14,
    (c) provide education which is secondary education by virtue of section 2(2B) of the Education Act 1996,
    (d) participate in the provision of secondary education at a school,
    (e) supply goods or services in connection with their provision of education.

(2) The powers conferred by subsection (1) are referred to in section 33F as the corporation's principal powers.

(3) A sixth form college corporation may not provide education of a kind specified in subsection (1)(b), (c) or (d) unless they have consulted such local education authorities as they consider appropriate.

(4) For the purposes of subsection (1), goods are supplied in connection with the provision of education by a sixth form college corporation if they result from —

      (a)   their provision of education or anything done by them under this Act for the purpose of or in connection with their provision of education,

      (b)   the use of their facilities or the expertise of persons employed by them in the fields in which they are so employed, or

      (c)   ideas of a person employed by them, or one of their students, arising out of their provision of education.

(5)   For the purposes of subsection (1), services are supplied in connection with the provision of education by a sixth form college corporation if —

      (a)   they result from their provision of education or anything done by them under this Act for the purpose of or in connection with their provision of education,

      (b)   they are provided by making available their facilities or the expertise of persons employed by them in the fields in which they are so employed, or

      (c)   they result from ideas of a person employed by them, or of one of their students, arising out of their provision of education.

33F   Supplementary powers of a sixth form college corporation

(1)   A sixth form college corporation may do anything (including in particular the things referred to in subsections (2) to (6)) which appears to the corporation to be necessary or expedient for the purpose of or in connection with the exercise of any of their principal powers.

(2)   A sixth form college corporation may conduct an educational establishment for the purpose of carrying on activities undertaken in the exercise of their powers to provide further or higher education.

(3)   In particular, a sixth form college corporation may conduct the relevant sixth form college as from the date specified in the order designating or establishing the corporation as a sixth form college corporation.

(4)   A sixth form college corporation may provide facilities of any description appearing to the corporation to be necessary or desirable for the purposes of or in connection with carrying on any activities undertaken in the exercise of their principal powers.

(5)   The facilities include —

      (a)   boarding accommodation and recreational facilities for students and staff, and

      (b)   facilities to meet the needs of students with learning difficulties.

(6)   A sixth form college corporation may —

      (a)   acquire and dispose of land and other property,

      (b)   enter into contracts, including in particular —

            (i)   contracts for the employment of teachers and other staff for the purposes of or in connection with carrying on any activities undertaken in the exercise of their principal powers, and

       (ii)   contracts with respect to the carrying on by the corporation of any such activities,

  (c)   form, participate in forming or invest in a company,

  (d)   form, participate in forming or otherwise become a member of a charitable incorporated organisation (within the meaning of section 69A of the Charities Act 1993),

  (e)   borrow such sums as the corporation think fit for the purposes of —

       (i)   carrying on any activities they have power to carry on, or

       (ii)   meeting any liability transferred to them under sections 23 to 27,

  (f)   in connection with their borrowing, grant any mortgage, charge or other security in respect of any land or other property of the corporation,

  (g)   invest any sums not immediately required for the purpose of carrying on any activities they have power to carry on,

  (h)   accept gifts of money, land or other property and apply it, or hold and administer it on trust for, any of those purposes,

  (i)   do anything incidental to the conduct of an educational institution providing further or higher education, including founding scholarships or exhibitions, making grants and giving prizes.

(7)   The powers conferred by subsection (6) are subject to section 33G.

(8)   For the purposes of this section a person has a learning difficulty if —

  (a)   the person has a significantly greater difficulty in learning than the majority of persons of the same age, or

  (b)   the person has a disability which either prevents or hinders the person from making use of facilities of a kind generally provided by institutions within the further education sector for persons of the same age.

(9)   But a person is not to be taken to have a learning difficulty solely because the language (or form of language) in which the person is or will be taught is different from a language (or form of language) which has at any time been spoken in the person's home.

(10)   A reference in this section or section 33G to investing in a company includes a reference to becoming a member of the company and to investing in it by the acquisition of any assets, securities or rights or otherwise.

(11)   A sixth form college corporation may provide advice or assistance to any other person where it appears to the corporation to be appropriate for them to do so for the purpose of or in connection with the provision of education by the other person.

33G Further provision about supplementary powers

(1)   The power conferred by section 33F(6)(c) may not be exercised for the purpose of —

  (a)   conducting an educational institution, or

2372
Apprenticeships, Skills, Children and Learning Act 2009 (c. 22)
Schedule 8 — Sixth form college sector

(b) investing in a company conducting an educational institution.

(2) The power conferred by section 33F(6)(d) may not be exercised for the purpose of —

(a) conducting an educational institution, or

(b) becoming a member of a charitable incorporated organisation conducting an educational institution.

(3) But a restriction on the exercise of a power imposed by subsection (1) or (2) does not apply to the extent that the responsible local education authority consent to the exercise of the power in a way which does not comply with the restriction.

(4) Neither the power conferred by section 33F(6)(c) nor the power conferred by section 33F(6)(d) may be exercised for the purposes of the provision of education if the provision is secured (wholly or partly) by financial resources provided by a relevant funding body.

(5) But subsection (4) does not apply to the extent that the relevant funding body consents to the exercise of the power in question in a way which does not comply with the restriction in that subsection.

(6) The power conferred on a sixth form college corporation by section 33F(6)(e) to borrow money may not be exercised without the consent of the responsible local education authority.

(7) Consent under subsection (6) may be given for particular borrowing or for borrowing of a particular class.

(8) In this section "relevant funding body" means a local education authority, the YPLA or the Chief Executive of Skills Funding.

33H Duty in relation to promotion of well-being of local area

(1) In exercising their functions under sections 33E and 33F, a sixth form college corporation must have regard, amongst other things, to the objective of promoting the economic and social well-being of the local area.

(2) In subsection (1) —

(a) "the local area", in relation to a sixth form college corporation, means the locality of the relevant sixth form college, and

(b) a reference to the well-being of an area includes a reference to the well-being of people who live or work in that area.

33I Constitution of sixth form college corporation and conduct of sixth form college

(1) For every sixth form college corporation there is to be —

(a) an instrument providing for the constitution of the corporation (to be known as the instrument of government), and

(b) an instrument in accordance with which the corporation, and the relevant sixth form college, are to be conducted (to be known as articles of government).

(2) Instruments of government and articles of government—

   (a) must comply with the requirements of Schedule 4, and

   (b) may make any provision authorised to be made by that Schedule and such other provision as may be necessary or desirable.

(3) Subsection (2) is subject to section 33J.

(4) The validity of any proceedings of a sixth form college corporation, or of any committee of the corporation, is not affected by—

   (a) a vacancy among the members, or

   (b) a defect in the appointment or nomination of a member.

(5) Subsection (6) applies to a document purporting to be an instrument made or issued by or on behalf of a sixth form college corporation and to be—

   (a) duly executed under the seal of the corporation, or

   (b) signed or executed by a person authorised by the corporation to act in that behalf.

(6) The document is to be received in evidence and treated, without further proof, as being made or issued by or on behalf of the corporation unless the contrary is shown.

33J Special provision for certain institutions

(1) Despite anything in section 33I, the instrument of government of a sixth form college corporation to which this section applies must provide—

   (a) for the governing body of the relevant sixth form college to include persons appointed for the purpose of securing so far as practicable that the established character of the sixth form college is preserved and developed and, in particular, that the sixth form college is conducted in accordance with any trust deed relating to it, and

   (b) for the majority of members of the governing body of the relevant sixth form college to be such governors.

(2) This section applies to a sixth form college corporation in respect of which the relevant sixth form college is specified, or falls within a class specified, by the Secretary of State by order.

(3) The reference in subsection (1)(a) to the established character of a sixth form college is, in relation to a sixth form college established shortly before or at the same time as the designation or establishment of the sixth form college corporation in respect of which it is the relevant sixth form college, a reference to the character which the sixth form college is intended to have on its establishment.

33K Instrument and articles of new sixth form college corporations

(1) The first instrument of government and articles of government of a sixth form college corporation established under section 33C are to be made by the YPLA.

(2) Before making an instrument or articles for a sixth form college corporation under this section the YPLA must consult the corporation.

33L   Changes to instruments and articles

(1) The YPLA may—

   (a) if a sixth form college corporation submits a draft of an instrument of government to have effect in place of their existing instrument, by order make a new instrument of government in terms of the draft or in such terms as it thinks fit, and

   (b) if a sixth form college corporation submits draft modifications of an instrument made under paragraph (a), by order modify the instrument in terms of the draft or in such terms as it thinks fit.

(2) The YPLA may not make a new instrument otherwise than in terms of the draft, or modify the instrument otherwise than in terms of the draft, unless it has consulted the corporation.

(3) The YPLA may by order modify, replace or revoke an instrument of government or articles of government of a sixth form college corporation.

(4) An order under subsection (3)—

   (a) may relate to all sixth form college corporations, to a category of sixth form college corporations specified in the order or to a sixth form college corporation specified in the order, but

   (b) may not be made unless the YPLA has consulted each sixth form college corporation to which the order relates.

(5) A sixth form college corporation may, with the consent of the YPLA—

   (a) make new articles of government in place of their existing articles, or

   (b) modify their existing articles.

(6) The YPLA may by a direction under this section require sixth form college corporations, a class of sixth form college corporations specified in the direction or any particular sixth form college corporation specified in the direction—

   (a) to modify, replace or revoke their articles of government in any manner specified in the direction, or

   (b) to secure that any rules or bye-laws made in pursuance of their articles of government are modified, replaced or revoked in any manner specified in the direction.

(7) Before giving a direction under this section the YPLA must consult the sixth form college corporation or (as the case may be) each sixth form college corporation to which the direction applies.

33M   Charitable status of a sixth form college corporation

A sixth form college corporation is a charity within the meaning of the Charities Act 1993.

33N   Dissolution of sixth form college corporations

(1)   Subject to the following provisions of this section, the Secretary of State may by order provide for—

    (a)   the dissolution of a sixth form college corporation, and

    (b)   the transfer to a person mentioned in subsection (4) or (6) of property, rights and liabilities of the corporation.

(2)   An order under subsection (1) may be made only if a proposal relating to the order has been made by the responsible local education authority and it appears to the Secretary of State that the requirements in subsection (3) have been met in relation to the proposal.

(3)   The requirements are that—

    (a)   the authority have published the proposal by the prescribed time and in the prescribed manner;

    (b)   the proposal as published contained prescribed information;

    (c)   the authority have considered any representations about the proposal made to them within the prescribed period.

(4)   Property, rights and liabilities may (subject to subsection (5)) be transferred to—

    (a)   a person appearing to the Secretary of State to be wholly or mainly engaged in the provision of educational facilities or services of any description, or

    (b)   a body corporate established for purposes which include the provision of such facilities or services.

(5)   Property, rights and liabilities may be transferred to a person or body under subsection (4) only with the consent of the person or body.

(6)   Property, rights and liabilities may be transferred to the responsible local education authority.

(7)   Where the recipient of a transfer under an order under this section is not a charity established for charitable purposes which are exclusively educational purposes, any property transferred must be transferred on trust to be used for charitable purposes which are exclusively educational purposes.

(8)   An order under this section may make provision about the transfer of staff (including provision applying section 26 with such modifications as the Secretary of State may consider necessary or desirable).

(9)   Before making an order under this section in respect of a sixth form college corporation the Secretary of State must consult—

    (a)   the corporation, and

    (b)   the YPLA.

(10)   In this section "charity" and "charitable purposes" have the same meanings as in the Charities Act 1993."

4   In section 34(1) (making additional property available for use) after "institution within the further education sector" insert "other than a sixth form college".

5   In section 52A(1) (duty to safeguard pupils receiving secondary education) after "by virtue of section 18(1)(aa) or (ab) of this Act," insert—

           "(aa)   by a sixth form college corporation by virtue of section 33E(1)(b) or (c) of this Act,".

6   In section 56A(1) (intervention: England) after "institution in England within the further education sector" insert "other than a sixth form college".

7   In section 56C(1) (directions as to exercise of section 56A powers) after "institution in England within the further education sector" insert "other than a sixth form college".

8   After section 56D (inserted by Schedule 6) insert—

"56E   Intervention by LEAs: sixth form colleges

(1)   This section applies in relation to a sixth form college if the responsible local education authority are satisfied as to one or more the matters listed in subsection (2) in relation to the sixth form college; and it is immaterial whether or not a complaint is made by any person.

(2)   The matters are—

      (a)   that the sixth form college's affairs have been or are being mismanaged by its governing body;

      (b)   that the sixth form college's governing body have failed to discharge any duty imposed on them by or for the purposes of any Act;

      (c)   that the sixth form college's governing body have acted or are proposing to act unreasonably with respect to the exercise of any power conferred or the performance of any duty imposed by or under any Act;

      (d)   that the sixth form college is performing significantly less well than it might in all the circumstances reasonably be expected to perform, or is failing or likely to fail to give an accepted standard of education or training.

(3)   If this section applies the authority may do one or more of the things listed in subsection (6).

(4)   Before doing one or more of those things, the authority must give the Secretary of State and the YPLA a notice stating—

      (a)   the matter or matters listed in subsection (2) as to which the authority are satisfied;

      (b)   the reasons why the authority are so satisfied;

      (c)   the thing or things that the authority propose to do;

      (d)   the reasons why the authority propose to do that thing or those things.

(5)   If the authority do one or more of those things, the authority must at the same time give the sixth form college's governing body a notice stating—

      (a)   the matter or matters listed in subsection (2) as to which the authority are satisfied;

      (b)   the reasons why the authority have decided to do that thing or those things.

(6) The authority may —

    (a) remove all or any of the members of the sixth form college's governing body;

    (b) appoint new members of that body if there are vacancies (however arising);

    (c) give to that body such directions as the authority think expedient as to the exercise of the body's powers and performance of the body's duties.

(7) The directions that may be given to a governing body under this section include a direction requiring a governing body to make collaboration arrangements (within the meaning of section 166 of the Education and Inspections Act 2006) with such bodies and on such terms as may be specified in the direction.

(8) Directions may be given to a governing body under this section despite any enactment making the exercise of a power or performance of a duty contingent on the body's opinion.

(9) The authority may not direct a governing body under subsection (6)(c) to dismiss a member of staff.

(10) But subsection (9) does not prevent the authority, where the authority consider that it may be appropriate to dismiss a member of staff whom the governing body have power under the governing body's articles of government to dismiss, from giving the governing body such directions under this section as are necessary to secure that the procedures applicable to the consideration of the case for dismissal of that member of staff are given effect to in relation to that member of staff.

(11) A governing body must comply with any directions given to them under this section.

(12) An appointment of a member of a governing body under this section shall have effect as if made in accordance with the governing body's instrument of government and articles of government.

56F Appointment by LEAs of members of sixth form college governing body

(1) The responsible local education authority for a sixth form college may appoint a person to be a member of the governing body of the sixth form college.

(2) But no more than two members of the governing body of a sixth form college may at any given time have been appointed under this section.

(3) Before exercising the power conferred by subsection (1) in relation to a governing body, the responsible local education authority must consult the governing body.

(4) A member of the governing body of a sixth form college who was appointed before the relevant commencement date by the Learning and Skills Council for England under section 11 of the Learning and Skills Act 2000 is, on and after that date, to be treated for the purposes

of subsection (2) of this section as appointed by the responsible local education authority under this section.

(5) "The relevant commencement date" is the date on which section 123 of the Apprenticeships, Skills, Children and Learning Act 2009 comes into force.

56G   Intervention policy: sixth form colleges

(1) The YPLA must—

    (a) prepare a statement of the policy to be followed by local education authorities with respect to the exercise of their powers under section 56E,

    (b) keep the statement under review, and

    (c) if it considers it appropriate in consequence of a review, prepare a revised statement.

(2) When preparing a statement or revised statement, the YPLA must—

    (a) undertake such consultation as it thinks appropriate;

    (b) consider any representations made to it about the policy to be set out in the statement.

(3) Guidance given to the YPLA under section 76 of the Apprenticeships, Skills, Children and Learning Act 2009 in connection with the performance of its functions under this section may, in particular, relate to the form and content of the policy to be set out in a statement or revised statement.

(4) The YPLA must send a copy of the statement or revised statement prepared by it to the Secretary of State.

(5) If the Secretary of State approves it the Secretary of State must lay a copy of it before each House of Parliament.

(6) The YPLA must publish—

    (a) the statement of its policy approved by the Secretary of State;

    (b) where the Secretary of State approves a revised statement of its policy, the revised statement.

(7) A local education authority must have regard to the statement most recently published under subsection (6) in exercising, or deciding whether to exercise, any of their powers under section 56E in relation to a sixth form college.

56H   Intervention by YPLA

(1) This section applies if—

    (a) the YPLA proposes to secure the provision of education or training at a sixth form college in the exercise of the power conferred by section 66 of the Apprenticeships, Skills, Children and Learning Act 2009, and

    (b) the YPLA is satisfied—

        (i) as to one or more of the matters listed in section 56E(2) in relation to the sixth form college, and

        (ii) that the circumstances are such that it would be appropriate for the responsible local education authority to do one or more of the things listed in section 56E(6) in relation to the sixth form college.

(2) If this section applies the YPLA may do one or more of the things listed in subsection (5).

(3) Before doing one or more of those things, the YPLA must give the Secretary of State a notice stating —

    (a) the matter or matters listed in section 56E(2) as to which the YPLA is satisfied;

    (b) the reasons why the YPLA is so satisfied;

    (c) the thing or things that the YPLA proposes to do;

    (d) the reasons why the YPLA proposes to do that thing or those things.

(4) If the YPLA does one or more of those things, it must at the same time give the sixth form college's governing body a notice stating —

    (a) the matter or matters listed in section 56E(2) as to which the YPLA is satisfied;

    (b) the reasons why the YPLA has decided to do that thing or those things.

(5) The YPLA may —

    (a) remove all or any of the members of the sixth form college's governing body;

    (b) appoint new members of that body if there are vacancies (however arising);

    (c) give to that body such directions as the YPLA thinks expedient as to the exercise of the body's powers and performance of the body's duties.

(6) The directions that may be given to a governing body under this section include a direction requiring a governing body to make collaboration arrangements (within the meaning of section 166 of the Education and Inspections Act 2006) with such bodies and on such terms as may be specified in the direction.

(7) Directions may be given to a governing body under this section despite any enactment making the exercise of a power or performance of a duty contingent on the body's opinion.

(8) The YPLA may not direct a governing body under subsection (5)(c) to dismiss a member of staff.

(9) But subsection (8) does not prevent the YPLA, where it considers that it may be appropriate to dismiss a member of staff whom the governing body have power to dismiss under their articles of government, from giving the governing body such directions under this section as are necessary to secure that the procedures applicable to the consideration of the case for dismissal of that member of staff are given effect to in relation to that member of staff.

(10) A governing body must comply with any directions given to them under this section.

(11)   An appointment of a member of a governing body under this section shall have effect as if made in accordance with the governing body's instrument of government and articles of government.

56I   Appointment by YPLA of members of sixth form college governing body

(1)   The YPLA may appoint a person to be a member of the governing body of a sixth form college.

(2)   But no more than two members of the governing body of a sixth form college may at any given time have been appointed under this section.

(3)   Before exercising the power conferred by subsection (1) in relation to a governing body, the YPLA must consult the governing body.

(4)   A member of the governing body of a sixth form college who was appointed before the relevant commencement date by the Learning and Skills Council for England under section 11 of the Learning and Skills Act 2000 is, on and after that date, to be treated for the purposes of subsection (2) of this section as appointed by the YPLA under this section.

(5)   "The relevant commencement date" is the date on which section 123 of the Apprenticeships, Skills, Children and Learning Act 2009 comes into force.

56J   Notification by Chief Executive of Skills Funding of possible grounds for intervention

(1)   This section applies if the Chief Executive of Skills Funding is of the view that any of the matters listed in section 56E(2) applies in relation to a sixth form college.

(2)   The Chief Executive must notify the responsible local education authority and the YPLA of that view.

(3)   The responsible local education authority must have regard to the Chief Executive's view in deciding whether to exercise their powers under section 56E.

(4)   The YPLA must have regard to the Chief Executive's view in deciding whether to exercise its powers under section 56H."

9   In section 88(1) (stamp duty) after "32," insert "33N,".

10   In section 88A(1) (stamp duty land tax) after "32" insert ", 33N".

11   (1) Section 89 (orders, regulations and directions) is amended as follows.

     (2) In subsection (2)—
         (a)   after "30(2)(b)," insert "33A(5)(b),";
         (b)   after "those sections" insert "or section 33L".

     (3) In subsection (4) for "Secretary of State" substitute "person or body making the order or regulations".

(4) For subsection (5) substitute—

"(5) Section 570 of the Education Act 1996 (revocation and variation) applies to directions given by any person or body under this Act as it applies to directions given by the Secretary of State or a local education authority under that Act."

12 (1) Section 90(1) (interpretation) is amended as follows.

(2) In paragraph (a) of the definition of "governing body" after "further education corporation" insert ", a sixth form college corporation".

(3) At the end insert—

""the relevant sixth form college", in relation to a sixth form college corporation, means the educational institution specified in the order under this Act designating the corporation as a sixth form college corporation or establishing it as such,

"the responsible local education authority"—

    (a) in relation to a proposal relating to the establishment of a sixth form college corporation, means the local education authority in whose area the relevant sixth form college, or its main site, is proposed to be situated;

    (b) in relation to a sixth form college corporation, means the local education authority in whose area the relevant sixth form college, or its main site, is situated;

    (c) in relation to a sixth form college, means the local education authority in whose area the sixth form college, or its main site, is situated,

"sixth form college corporation" means a body corporate—

    (a) designated as a sixth form college corporation under section 33A or 33B, or

    (b) established under section 33C,

"the YPLA" means the Young People's Learning Agency for England."

(4) After subsection (2) insert—

"(2ZA) The Secretary of State may give guidance on which of a sixth form college's sites is to be taken to be its main site for the purposes of the definition of "the responsible local education authority" in subsection (1)."

13 (1) Section 91 (interpretation of Education Acts) is amended as follows.

(2) In subsection (3) (institutions within the further education sector) after paragraph (b) insert "and

    (c) sixth form colleges,"

(3) After subsection (3) insert—

"(3A) References to sixth form colleges are to institutions conducted by sixth form college corporations."

14 In section 92 (index) at the appropriate places insert—

"relevant sixth form college	section 90(1)"
"responsible local education authority	section 90(1)"
"sixth form college	section 91(3A)"
"sixth form college corporation	section 90(1)"
"the YPLA	section 90(1)"

15 (1) Schedule 4 (instruments and articles of government for further education corporations) is amended as follows.

(2) For paragraph 1 substitute —

"1   In this Schedule —
"instrument" means an instrument of government or articles of government;
"the institution" means —
(a) in the case of a further education corporation, the institution which the corporation is established to conduct;
(b) in the case of a sixth form college corporation, the relevant sixth form college."

(3) In paragraph 1A, after "appointment of members" insert "of a further education corporation".

(4) After paragraph 1A insert —

"1B   Provision made by an instrument under this Schedule in relation to the appointment of members of a sixth form college corporation must take into account the members who may be appointed by —
(a) the responsible local education authority under section 56F;
(b) the YPLA under section 56I."

(5) In paragraph 2(1) after "further education corporation" insert "or sixth form college corporation".

(6) In the title, after "further education corporations" insert "and sixth form college corporations".

SCHEDULE 9

THE OFFICE OF QUALIFICATIONS AND EXAMINATIONS REGULATION

Status

1   Ofqual is to perform its functions on behalf of the Crown.

Apprenticeships, Skills, Children and Learning Act 2009 (c. 22)
Schedule 9 – The Office of Qualifications and Examinations Regulation

2383

Membership

2 (1) Ofqual is to consist of —

   (a) a member appointed by Her Majesty by Order in Council to chair Ofqual,

   (b) between 7 and 12 members appointed by the Secretary of State (the "ordinary members"), and

   (c) the chief executive of Ofqual.

(2) The person appointed by Her Majesty to chair Ofqual is to be known as the Chief Regulator of Qualifications and Examinations ("the Chief Regulator").

(3) Ofqual may appoint one of the ordinary members as deputy to the Chief Regulator ("the deputy").

(4) Before appointing a person as an ordinary member, the Secretary of State must consult the Chief Regulator or the deputy (subject to sub-paragraph (6)).

(5) The Secretary of State may consult the deputy instead of the Chief Regulator only if satisfied that—

   (a) it is not practicable to consult the Chief Regulator, and

   (b) it is necessary to make the appointment before it would be practicable to do so.

(6) The Secretary of State may appoint a person as an ordinary member without consulting either the Chief Regulator or the deputy if satisfied that—

   (a) it is not practicable to consult either of those persons, and

   (b) it is necessary to make the appointment before it would be practicable to do so.

(7) One of the ordinary members ("the Northern Ireland member") must be a person appointed following consultation with the Department for Employment and Learning in Northern Ireland.

The Chief Regulator

3 (1) The Chief Regulator holds and vacates office in accordance with the terms of the appointment.

(2) Those terms are to be determined by the Secretary of State, subject to the following provisions of this Schedule.

(3) The Chief Regulator must not be appointed for a term of more than 5 years.

(4) The Chief Regulator may resign from office at any time by giving written notice to the Secretary of State.

(5) Her Majesty may remove the Chief Regulator from office on either of the following grounds—

   (a) inability or unfitness to carry out the duties of office;

   (b) absence from Ofqual's meetings for a continuous period of more than 6 months without Ofqual's permission.

(6) The previous appointment of a person as Chief Regulator does not affect the person's eligibility for re-appointment.

The deputy and other ordinary members: tenure

4   (1) The deputy and other ordinary members hold and vacate office in accordance with the terms of their appointments, subject to the following provisions of this Schedule.

     (2) An ordinary member must not be appointed for a term of more than 5 years.

     (3) The deputy may resign from office at any time by giving written notice to Ofqual.

     (4) The ordinary members may resign from office at any time by giving written notice to the Secretary of State

     (5) Ofqual may remove the deputy from office if Ofqual thinks it appropriate to do so.

     (6) The Secretary of State may remove an ordinary member from office on either of the following grounds —
       (a) inability or unfitness to carry out the duties of office;
       (b) absence from Ofqual's meetings for a continuous period of more than 6 months without Ofqual's permission.

     (7) Before removing an ordinary member from office, the Secretary of State must consult the Chief Regulator or the deputy (subject to sub-paragraph (9)).

     (8) The Secretary of State may consult the deputy instead of the Chief Regulator only if —
       (a) the ordinary member to be removed from office is not the deputy, and
       (b) the Secretary of State is satisfied that —
         (i) it is not practicable to consult the Chief Regulator, and
         (ii) it is necessary to remove the ordinary member from office before it would be practicable to do so.

     (9) The Secretary of State may remove an ordinary member from office without consulting either the Chief Regulator or the deputy if satisfied that —
       (a) if the ordinary member to be removed from office is the deputy, sub-paragraph (10) applies;
       (b) in any other case, sub-paragraph (11) applies.

   (10) This sub-paragraph applies if —
       (a) it is not practicable to consult the Chief Regulator, and
       (b) it is necessary to remove the ordinary member from office before it would be practicable to do so.

   (11) This sub-paragraph applies if —
       (a) it is not practicable to consult either the Chief Regulator or the deputy, and
       (b) it is necessary to remove the ordinary member from office before it would be practicable to do so.

   (12) The Secretary of State must consult the Department for Employment and Learning in Northern Ireland before removing the Northern Ireland member from office.

(13) The previous appointment of a person as the deputy or another ordinary member does not affect the person's eligibility for re-appointment.

(14) If the deputy ceases to be an ordinary member, the person also ceases to be the deputy.

Remuneration etc. of Chief Regulator and ordinary members

5 (1) Ofqual must, if the Secretary of State requires it to do so, pay remuneration, allowances and expenses to the Chief Regulator and any of the ordinary members.

(2) Ofqual must, if the Secretary of State requires it to do so, pay, or make provision for the payment of, a pension, allowances or gratuities to or in respect of a current or former Chief Regulator or ordinary member.

(3) If a person ceases to be Chief Regulator or an ordinary member and the Secretary of State decides that the person should be compensated because of special circumstances, Ofqual must pay compensation to the person.

(4) The amount of a payment under this paragraph is to be determined by the Secretary of State.

Chief executive and other staff

6 (1) The first chief executive is to be appointed by the Secretary of State, on conditions of service determined by the Secretary of State.

(2) Later chief executives are to be appointed by Ofqual, on conditions of service determined by Ofqual.

(3) The appointment and conditions of service of a later chief executive are subject to the approval of the Secretary of State.

(4) Ofqual may appoint other members of staff.

(5) The following are to be determined by Ofqual with the approval of the Secretary of State —
   (a) the number of other members of staff of Ofqual;
   (b) their conditions of service.

Committees

7 (1) Ofqual may establish committees, and any committee established by Ofqual may establish sub-committees.

(2) Ofqual may —
   (a) dissolve a sub-committee established under sub-paragraph (1), or
   (b) alter the purposes for which such a sub-committee is established.

(3) In this Schedule a committee or sub-committee established under sub-paragraph (1) is referred to as an "Ofqual committee".

(4) An Ofqual committee must include at least one member of Ofqual or Ofqual's staff.

(5) Ofqual may arrange for the payment of remuneration, allowances and expenses to any person who—

2386
Apprenticeships, Skills, Children and Learning Act 2009 (c. 22)
Schedule 9 — The Office of Qualifications and Examinations Regulation

    (a)   is a member of an Ofqual committee, but

    (b)   is not a member of Ofqual or Ofqual's staff.

(6) Ofqual must at least once in any 5 year period review —

    (a)   the structure of Ofqual committees, and

    (b)   the scope of each Ofqual committee's activities.

(7) The first review under sub-paragraph (6) must be completed not later than the day which is the end of the period of 5 years beginning with the day on which section 127 comes into force.

8   (1) Ofqual and any other person may establish a committee jointly.

(2) In this Schedule a committee established under sub-paragraph (1) is referred to as a "joint committee".

(3) A joint committee may establish sub-committees.

(4) In this Schedule a sub-committee established under sub-paragraph (3) is referred to as a "joint sub-committee".

(5) A joint committee and a joint sub-committee must include at least one member of Ofqual or Ofqual's staff.

(6) Ofqual may arrange for the payment of remuneration, allowances and expenses to any person who —

    (a)   is a member of a joint committee or a joint sub-committee, but

    (b)   is not a member of Ofqual or Ofqual's staff.

Procedure etc.

9   (1) Ofqual may regulate —

    (a)   its own proceedings (including quorum), and

    (b)   the procedure (including quorum) of Ofqual committees.

(2) A joint committee may regulate —

    (a)   its own procedure (including quorum), and

    (b)   the procedure (including quorum) of any sub-committee established by it.

(3) The validity of proceedings of Ofqual, or of an Ofqual committee, a joint committee or joint sub-committee is not affected by —

    (a)   a vacancy;

    (b)   a defective appointment.

Delegation

10   (1) Ofqual may delegate any of its functions to —

    (a)   a member of Ofqual or Ofqual's staff;

    (b)   a committee established by Ofqual;

    (c)   a joint committee.

(2) A function is delegated under this paragraph to the extent and on the terms that Ofqual determines.

11   (1) A committee established by Ofqual or a joint committee may delegate any of its functions to a sub-committee established by it.

Apprenticeships, Skills, Children and Learning Act 2009 (c. 22)
Schedule 9 – The Office of Qualifications and Examinations Regulation

2387

(2) A function is delegated under this paragraph to the extent and on the terms that the committee determines.

(3) The power of a committee established by Ofqual to delegate a function under this paragraph, and to determine the extent and terms of the delegation, are subject to Ofqual's powers to direct what a committee established by it may and may not do.

(4) The power of a joint committee to delegate a function under this paragraph, and to determine the extent and terms of the delegation, are subject to the power of Ofqual and any other person with whom Ofqual established the joint committee to direct (acting jointly) what the committee may and may not do.

Documents

12   The application of Ofqual's seal is authenticated by the signatures of —
    (a)   two members of Ofqual, or
    (b)   one member of Ofqual and another person who has been authorised (generally or specifically) for that purpose by Ofqual.

13   The Documentary Evidence Act 1868 (c. 37) has effect in relation to Ofqual as if —
    (a)   Ofqual were included in the first column of the Schedule to that Act,
    (b)   any member or other person authorised to act on Ofqual's behalf were mentioned in the second column of that Schedule, and
    (c)   the regulations referred to in that Act included any document issued by Ofqual or under its authority.

Supplementary powers

14   (1) Ofqual may do anything that it considers necessary or appropriate for the purposes of, or in connection with, its functions.

(2) The power in sub-paragraph (1) is subject to any restrictions imposed by or under any provision of any Act.

(3) Ofqual may not lend money.

SCHEDULE 10   Section 173

QCA: TRANSFER SCHEMES

Staff transfer schemes

1   (1) The Secretary of State may make a scheme (a "staff transfer scheme") providing —
    (a)   for a designated employee of the QCDA to become a member of Ofqual's staff and, accordingly, to become employed in the civil service of the state;
    (b)   so far as may be consistent with employment in the civil service of the state, for the terms and conditions of the employee's employment to have effect as if they were the conditions of service as a member of Ofqual's staff;

(c) for the transfer to Ofqual of the rights, powers, duties and liabilities of the QCDA under or in connection with the employee's contract of employment;

(d) for anything done (or having effect as if done) before that transfer by or in relation to the QCDA in respect of such a contract or the employee to be treated as having been done by or in relation to Ofqual.

(2) A staff transfer scheme may provide for a period before a person became a member of Ofqual's staff to count as a period during which the person was a member of Ofqual's staff (and for the operation of the scheme not to be treated as having interrupted the continuity of that period).

(3) A staff transfer scheme may provide for an employee of the QCDA who would otherwise become a member of Ofqual's staff not to become such a member of staff if the employee gives notice objecting to the operation of the scheme in relation to the employee.

(4) A staff transfer scheme may provide for any person who would be treated (whether by an enactment or otherwise) as being dismissed by the operation of the scheme not to be so treated.

(5) A staff transfer scheme may provide for an employee of the QCDA to become a member of Ofqual's staff despite any provision, of whatever nature, which would otherwise prevent the person from being employed in the civil service of the state.

Property transfer schemes

2   (1) The Secretary of State may make a scheme (a "property transfer scheme") providing for the transfer from the QCDA to Ofqual of designated property, rights or liabilities.

(2) A property transfer scheme may —
    (a) create rights, or impose liabilities, in relation to property or rights transferred by virtue of the scheme;
    (b) provide for anything done by or in relation to the QCDA in connection with any property, rights or liabilities transferred by the scheme to be treated as done, or to be continued, by or in relation to Ofqual;
    (c) apportion property, rights and liabilities;
    (d) make provision about the continuation of legal proceedings.

(3) The things that may be transferred by a property transfer scheme include —
    (a) property, rights and liabilities that could not otherwise be transferred;
    (b) property acquired, and rights and liabilities arising, after the making of the scheme.

Continuity

3   A transfer by virtue of a staff transfer scheme or a property transfer scheme does not affect the validity of anything done by or in relation to the QCDA before the transfer takes effect.

Supplementary provision etc.

4   A staff transfer scheme or a property transfer scheme may include supplementary, incidental, transitional and consequential provision.

Interpretation

5   In this Schedule —

"designated", in relation to a staff transfer scheme or a property transfer scheme, means specified in, or determined in accordance with, the scheme;

"the QCDA" means the Qualifications and Curriculum Authority, to be known instead as the Qualifications and Curriculum Development Agency by virtue of section 175.

SCHEDULE 11   Section 175

THE QUALIFICATIONS AND CURRICULUM DEVELOPMENT AGENCY

Status

1   (1) The QCDA is not to be regarded —
        (a)   as a servant or agent of the Crown, or
        (b)   as enjoying any status, immunity or privilege of the Crown.

    (2) The QCDA's property is not to be regarded —
        (a)   as property of the Crown, or
        (b)   as property held on behalf of the Crown.

Membership

2   (1) The QCDA is to consist of —
        (a)   between 8 and 13 members appointed by the Secretary of State (the "ordinary members"), and
        (b)   the chief officer of the QCDA.

    (2) The Secretary of State —
        (a)   must appoint one of the ordinary members to chair the QCDA ("the chair"), and
        (b)   may appoint another ordinary member as deputy to the chair ("the deputy").

Chief officer

3   (1) The chief officer is to be appointed by the QCDA, on conditions of service determined by the QCDA.

    (2) The appointment and conditions of service of the chief officer are subject to the approval of the Secretary of State.

Chair and chief officer: division of functions

4   (1) The Secretary of State may confer additional functions in relation to the QCDA on the chair.

     (2) The functions for the time being conferred on the chief officer of the QCDA must not include any function for the time being conferred under sub-paragraph (1) on the chair.

Tenure

5   (1) The chair, the deputy and other ordinary members hold and vacate office in accordance with the terms of their appointments, subject to the following provisions of this Schedule.

     (2) An ordinary member must not be appointed for a term of more than 5 years.

     (3) The chair, the deputy and other ordinary members may resign from office at any time by giving written notice to the Secretary of State.

     (4) The Secretary of State may remove the deputy from office if the Secretary of State thinks it appropriate to do so.

     (5) The Secretary of State may remove an ordinary member from office on either of the following grounds—

        (a) inability or unfitness to carry out the duties of office;

        (b) absence from the QCDA's meetings for a continuous period of more than 6 months without the QCDA's permission.

     (6) The previous appointment of a person as the chair, the deputy or another ordinary member does not affect the person's eligibility for re-appointment.

     (7) If the chair or the deputy ceases to be an ordinary member, the person also ceases to be the chair or the deputy.

Remuneration etc. of ordinary members

6   (1) The QCDA must, if the Secretary of State requires it to do so, pay remuneration, allowances and expenses to any of the ordinary members.

     (2) The QCDA must, if the Secretary of State requires it to do so, pay, or make provision for the payment of, a pension, allowances or gratuities to or in respect of a current or former ordinary member.

     (3) If a person ceases to be an ordinary member and the Secretary of State decides that the person should be compensated because of special circumstances, the QCDA must pay compensation to the person.

     (4) The amount of a payment under this paragraph is to be determined by the Secretary of State.

Staff

7   (1) The QCDA may appoint staff.

     (2) The following are to be determined by the QCDA with the approval of the Secretary of State—

        (a) the number of members of staff of the QCDA;

Apprenticeships, Skills, Children and Learning Act 2009 (c. 22)
Schedule 11 – The Qualifications and Curriculum Development Agency

2391

        (b)   their conditions of service.

8   (1)   Employment with the QCDA is to be included among the kinds of employment to which a scheme under section 1 of the Superannuation Act 1972 (c. 11) (superannuation schemes as respects civil servants, etc.) can apply.

    (2)   The QCDA must pay to the Minister for the Civil Service, at such times as the Minister may direct, such sums as the Minister may determine in respect of increases attributable to this paragraph in the sums payable under the Superannuation Act 1972 out of money provided by Parliament.

    (3)   Sub-paragraph (4) applies if a member of staff of the QCDA ("E") –

        (a)   is, by reference to employment with the QCDA, a participant in a scheme under section 1 of the Superannuation Act 1972, and

        (b)   is also a member of the QCDA.

    (4)   The Secretary of State may determine that E's service as a member of the QCDA is to be treated for the purposes of the scheme as service as a member of staff of the QCDA (whether or not any benefits are payable to or in respect of E by virtue of paragraph 6(2)).

Committees

9   (1)   The QCDA may establish committees, and any committee established under this sub-paragraph may establish sub-committees.

    (2)   If so directed by the Secretary of State, the QCDA must establish a committee for the purpose specified in the direction.

    (3)   A direction under sub-paragraph (2) may specify –

        (a)   the number of members of the committee,

        (b)   the terms and conditions on which members of the committee hold and vacate office,

        (c)   the circumstances in which the committee may establish sub-committees, and

        (d)   the circumstances in which the QCDA can dissolve the committee and any sub-committee established by the committee.

    (4)   The QCDA may –

        (a)   dissolve a sub-committee established under sub-paragraph (1), or

        (b)   alter the purposes for which such a sub-committee is established.

    (5)   In this Schedule a committee or sub-committee established under sub-paragraph (1) or (2) is referred to as a "QCDA committee".

    (6)   A QCDA committee must include at least one member of the QCDA or the QCDA's staff.

    (7)   The QCDA may arrange for the payment of remuneration, allowances and expenses to any person who –

        (a)   is a member of a QCDA committee, but

        (b)   is not a member of the QCDA or the QCDA's staff.

    (8)   The QCDA must at least once in any 5 year period review –

        (a)   the structure of QCDA committees, and

        (b)   the scope of each QCDA committee's activities.

(9) The first review under sub-paragraph (8) must be completed not later than the day which is the end of the period of 5 years beginning with the day on which section 175 comes into force.

10 (1) The QCDA and any other person may establish a committee jointly.

(2) In this Schedule a committee established under sub-paragraph (1) is referred to as a "joint committee".

(3) A joint committee may establish sub-committees.

(4) In this Schedule a sub-committee established under sub-paragraph (3) is referred to as a "joint sub-committee".

(5) A joint committee and a joint sub-committee must include at least one member of the QCDA or the QCDA's staff.

(6) The QCDA may arrange for the payment of remuneration, allowances and expenses to any person who—

    (a)   is a member of a joint committee or a joint sub-committee, but

    (b)   is not a member of the QCDA or the QCDA's staff.

Procedure etc.

11 (1) The QCDA may regulate—

    (a)   its own proceedings (including quorum), and

    (b)   the procedure (including quorum) of QCDA committees.

(2) A joint committee may regulate—

    (a)   its own procedure (including quorum), and

    (b)   the procedure (including quorum) of any sub-committee established by it.

(3) The validity of proceedings of the QCDA, or of a QCDA committee, joint committee or joint sub-committee is not affected by—

    (a)   a vacancy;

    (b)   a defective appointment.

12 (1) The following have the right to attend meetings of the QCDA, and of QCDA committees, joint committees and joint sub-committees—

    (a)   the Secretary of State;

    (b)   a representative of the Secretary of State;

    (c)   Her Majesty's Chief Inspector of Education, Children's Services and Skills;

    (d)   a representative of the Chief Inspector;

    (e)   a representative of such other body as the Secretary of State may direct.

(2) A person attending a meeting of the QCDA, or of a QCDA committee, joint committee or joint sub-committee under sub-paragraph (1) may take part in its deliberations (but not its decisions).

(3) If a person with a right to attend a meeting of the QCDA, or of a QCDA committee, joint committee or joint sub-committee requests it, the QCDA must provide the person with all information relating to the meeting that—

Apprenticeships, Skills, Children and Learning Act 2009 (c. 22)
Schedule 11 — The Qualifications and Curriculum Development Agency

2393

(a) has been distributed to members of the QCDA or of the QCDA committee, joint committee or joint sub-committee, and

(b) is likely to be needed by the person in order to take part in the meeting.

Delegation

13 (1) The QCDA may delegate any of its functions to —

    (a) a member of the QCDA or the QCDA's staff;

    (b) a committee established by the QCDA;

    (c) a joint committee.

  (2) A function is delegated under this paragraph to the extent and on the terms that the QCDA determines.

14 (1) A committee established by the QCDA or a joint committee may delegate any of its functions to a sub-committee established by it.

  (2) A function is delegated under this paragraph to the extent and on the terms that the committee determines.

  (3) The power of a committee established by the QCDA to delegate a function under this paragraph, and to determine the extent and terms of the delegation, are subject to the powers of the QCDA and (in the case of a committee established under paragraph 9(2)) the Secretary of State to direct what the committee may and may not do.

  (4) The power of a joint committee to delegate a function under this paragraph, and to determine the extent and terms of the delegation, are subject to the power of the QCDA and any other person with whom the QCDA established the joint committee to direct (acting jointly) what the committee may and may not do.

15 The Secretary of State may authorise any committee established under paragraph 9(2) to perform such of the QCDA's functions as are specified in the direction given under that provision.

Reports

16 (1) As soon as reasonably practicable after the end of each financial year the QCDA must prepare an annual report for the financial year.

  (2) The annual report must state how the QCDA has performed its functions in the financial year.

  (3) The QCDA must publish each annual report and send a copy to the Secretary of State.

  (4) The Secretary of State must lay before Parliament a copy of each annual report received under sub-paragraph (3).

Accounts

17 (1) The QCDA must —

    (a) keep proper accounts and proper records in relation to the accounts, and

    (b) prepare annual accounts in respect of each financial year.

    (2) The annual accounts must comply with any directions given by the Secretary of State as to—

        (a) the information to be contained in them,

        (b) the manner in which the information contained in them is to be presented, or

        (c) the methods and principles according to which the annual accounts are to be prepared.

    (3) Before the end of the month of August next following each financial year, the QCDA must send copies of the annual accounts for the year to—

        (a) the Secretary of State, and

        (b) the Comptroller and Auditor General.

    (4) The Comptroller and Auditor General must—

        (a) examine, certify and report on the annual accounts, and

        (b) give a copy of the report to the Secretary of State.

    (5) The Secretary of State must lay before Parliament—

        (a) a copy of any annual accounts received under sub-paragraph (3), and

        (b) a copy of each report received under sub-paragraph (4).

Documents

18   The application of the QCDA's seal is authenticated by the signatures of—

        (a) two members of the QCDA, or

        (b) one member of the QCDA and another person who has been authorised (generally or specifically) for that purpose by the QCDA.

19   Any document purporting to be an instrument made or issued by or on behalf of the QCDA, and to be duly executed by a person authorised by the QCDA in that behalf—

        (a) is to be received in evidence, and

        (b) is to be taken to be made or issued in that way, unless the contrary is shown.

Funding

20   (1) The Secretary of State may make grants to the QCDA.

    (2) Grants to the QCDA under this paragraph are to be made at such times and subject to such conditions (if any) as the Secretary of State thinks appropriate.

Supplementary powers

21   (1) The QCDA may do anything that it considers necessary or appropriate for the purposes of, or in connection with, its functions.

    (2) The power in sub-paragraph (1) is subject to any restrictions imposed by or under any provision of any Act.

    (3) The QCDA may not do either of the following without the consent of the Secretary of State—

        (a) form bodies corporate or unincorporate;

        (b) enter into joint ventures with other persons.

Apprenticeships, Skills, Children and Learning Act 2009 (c. 22)
Schedule 12 — Ofqual and the QCDA: minor and consequential amendments

2395

SCHEDULE 12   Sections 174 and 192

OFQUAL AND THE QCDA: MINOR AND CONSEQUENTIAL AMENDMENTS

Public Records Act 1958 (c. 51)

1   In paragraph 3 of Schedule 1 to the Public Records Act 1958, in Part 2 of the
           Table (definition of public records: other establishments and organisations)
           for "Qualifications and Curriculum Authority" substitute "Qualifications
           and Curriculum Development Agency".

Parliamentary Commissioner Act 1967 (c. 13)

2   (1) Schedule 2 to the Parliamentary Commissioner Act 1967 (departments etc.
           subject to investigation) is amended as follows.

       (2) At the appropriate place insert—
               "Office of Qualifications and Examinations Regulation."

       (3) For "Qualifications and Curriculum Authority" substitute "Qualifications
           and Curriculum Development Agency".

Local Authorities (Goods and Services) Act 1970 (c. 39)

3   (1) Subject to sub-paragraph (2), in the Local Authorities (Goods and Services)
           Act 1970 (supply of goods and services by local authorities to public bodies)
           "public body" includes the Qualifications and Curriculum Development
           Agency.

       (2) The provision in sub-paragraph (1) has effect as if made by an order made
           by the Secretary of State under section 1(5) of that Act (power to provide that
           a person is to be a public body for the purposes of the Act) and accordingly
           may be varied or revoked by such an order.

Superannuation Act 1972 (c. 11)

4   In Schedule 1 to the Superannuation Act 1972 (kinds of employment, etc,
           referred to in section 1 of that Act) under the heading "Other bodies" for
           "The Qualifications and Curriculum Authority" substitute "The
           Qualifications and Curriculum Development Agency".

House of Commons Disqualification Act 1975 (c. 24)

5   (1) Part 3 of Schedule 1 to the House of Commons Disqualification Act 1975
           (other disqualifying offices) is amended as follows.

       (2) For the entry relating to members of the Qualifications and Curriculum
           Authority substitute—
               "Any member of the Qualifications and Curriculum Development
               Agency (continued under section 175 of the Apprenticeships, Skills,
               Children and Learning Act 2009) in receipt of remuneration."

       (3) At the appropriate place insert—
               "The Chief Regulator of Qualifications and Examinations and any
               member of the Office of Qualifications and Examinations Regulation in
               receipt of remuneration."

Northern Ireland Assembly Disqualification Act 1975 (c. 25)

6   In Part 3 of Schedule 1 to the Northern Ireland Assembly Disqualification
         Act 1975 (other disqualifying offices) at the appropriate place insert—
                "The Chief Regulator of Qualifications and Examinations and any
                member of the Office of Qualifications and Examinations Regulation in
                receipt of remuneration."

Race Relations Act 1976 (c. 74)

7   In Part 2 of Schedule 1A to the Race Relations Act 1976 (bodies etc. subject to
         general statutory duty which were added after commencement of the duty)
         for "The Qualifications and Curriculum Authority" substitute "The
         Qualifications and Curriculum Development Agency".

Charities Act 1993 (c. 10)

8   In Schedule 2 to the Charities Act 1993 (exempt charities) omit paragraph
         (da).

Education Act 1996 (c. 56)

9   The Education Act 1996 is amended as follows.

10   In section 391(10) (functions of advisory councils) in paragraph (a) for
         "Qualifications and Curriculum Authority" substitute "Qualifications and
         Curriculum Development Agency".

11   (1) Section 408 (provision of information) is amended as follows.

     (2) In subsection (1)(a) after "2002" insert "or the provisions of Parts 7 and 8 of
         the Apprenticeships, Skills, Children and Learning Act 2009".

     (3) In subsection (2)(e)—
         (a)   for "external" substitute "relevant";
         (b)   after "2000)" insert "which are approved under section 98 or 99 of
               that Act".

Education Act 1997 (c. 44)

12   The Education Act 1997 is amended as follows.

13   Sections 21 to 26A (the Qualifications and Curriculum Authority) cease to
         have effect.

14   In section 29 (functions of the Welsh Ministers in relation to curriculum and
         assessment) for subsection (5) substitute—
            "(5)   In this section—
                       "assessment" includes examination and test;
                       "funded nursery education" has the meaning given by section
                         98 of the Education Act 2002;
                       "maintained school" means—
                             (a)   any community, foundation or voluntary school, and
                             (b)   any community or foundation special school.

    (6)   In the definition of "maintained school", the reference to a community, foundation or voluntary school or to a community or foundation special school, is a reference to such a school within the meaning of the School Standards and Framework Act 1998."

15   (1)   Section 30 (functions of the Welsh Ministers in relation to external vocational and academic qualifications) is amended as follows.

    (2)   For subsection (1) substitute—

       "(1)   This section applies for the purposes of the following functions—

          (a)   to keep under review all aspects of relevant qualifications;

          (b)   to provide support and advice to any person providing courses leading to relevant qualifications with a view to establishing and maintaining high standards in the provision of such courses;

          (c)   to publish and disseminate, and assist in the publication and dissemination of, information relating to relevant qualifications;

          (d)   to develop and publish criteria for the recognition of any person who awards or authenticates a relevant qualification;

          (e)   to recognise in respect of the award or authentication of a specified relevant qualification or description of relevant qualification, any person who meets such criteria and applies to be so recognised;

          (f)   to determine that a specified relevant qualification or description of relevant qualification is to be subject to a requirement of accreditation;

          (g)   in respect of relevant qualifications which are subject to that requirement, to develop and publish criteria for the accreditation of particular forms of any such qualifications;

          (h)   where a relevant qualification is subject to that requirement, to accredit a particular form of the qualification which meets such criteria and is submitted for accreditation by a person recognised under paragraph (e) in respect of the qualification;

          (i)   to publish and disseminate, and assist in the publication and dissemination of, information relating to persons recognised under paragraph (e);

          (j)   to make arrangements (whether or not with others) for the development, setting or administration of tests or tasks which fall to be undertaken with a view to obtaining relevant qualifications and which fall within a prescribed description."

    (3)   In subsection (1A)—

       (a)   for "(1)(d)" substitute "(1)(g)";

       (b)   for "(e)" substitute "(h)".

    (4)   For subsection (1B) substitute—

       "(1B)   The functions set out in subsection (1) are exercisable solely by the Welsh Ministers."

    (5)   Omit subsections (1C), (1D) and (2).

(6) For subsection (5) substitute—

"(5) In this Chapter "relevant qualification" means an academic or vocational qualification awarded or authenticated in Wales other than an excluded qualification.

(5A) An excluded qualification is any of the following—
  (a) a foundation degree;
  (b) a first degree;
  (c) a degree at a higher level.

(5B) For the purposes of subsection (5) a qualification is awarded or authenticated in Wales if there are, or may reasonably be expected to be, persons seeking to obtain the qualification who are, will be or may reasonably be expected to be assessed for those purposes wholly or mainly in Wales.

(5C) In this section and sections 32 to 32C a reference to the award or authentication of a qualification includes a reference to—
  (a) the award or authentication of credits in respect of components of a qualification, and
  (b) the award or authentication of a qualification by a person either alone or jointly with others."

(7) Omit subsection (6).

(8) In the title, for "external vocational and academic" substitute "relevant".

16 (1) Section 32 (supplementary provisions relating to discharge by the Welsh Ministers of their functions) is amended as follows.

(2) In subsection (1)(c)—
  (a) in sub-paragraph (ii) before "requirements" insert "reasonable";
  (b) for sub-paragraph (iii) substitute—
      "(iii) the reasonable requirements of persons with learning difficulties."

(3) In subsection (4) for paragraph (a) (but not the "and" after it) substitute—
      "(a) limiting the amount of a fee that can be charged for the award or authentication of, or for the provision of any other service in relation to, the qualification in question;".

(4) Omit subsection (4A).

(5) For subsection (6) substitute—

  "(6) In this section "persons with learning difficulties" means—
    (a) children with special educational needs (as defined in section 312 of the Education Act 1996), and
    (b) other persons who—
        (i) have a significantly greater difficulty in learning than the majority of persons of their age, or
        (ii) have a disability which either prevents or hinders them from making use of educational facilities of a kind generally provided for persons of their age.

(7) But a person is not to be taken to have a learning difficulty solely because the language (or form of language) in which the person is or will be taught is different from a language (or form of language) which has at any time been spoken in the person's home."

17   After section 32 insert—

"32ZA Qualifications functions of Welsh Ministers: co-operation and joint working etc.

(1) The Welsh Ministers may co-operate or work jointly with a relevant authority where it is appropriate to do so in connection with the carrying out of any of their qualifications functions.

(2) The Welsh Ministers may provide information to a relevant authority for the purpose of enabling or facilitating the carrying out of a relevant function of the authority.

(3) Subject to subsection (4), the Welsh Ministers and any other relevant authority may establish a committee jointly, and any committee so established may establish sub-committees.

(4) The Welsh Ministers may only exercise the power in subsection (3) if they consider it appropriate to do so for the purpose of the carrying out of any of their qualifications functions.

(5) In this section a committee established under subsection (3) is referred to as a "joint committee" and a sub-committee established under that subsection is referred to as a "joint sub-committee".

(6) A joint committee and a joint sub-committee must include at least one member of staff of the Welsh Assembly Government.

(7) A joint committee may regulate—
  (a) its own procedure (including quorum), and
  (b) the procedure (including quorum) of any sub-committee established by it.

(8) The validity of proceedings of a joint committee or a joint sub-committee is not affected by—
  (a) a vacancy, or
  (b) a defective appointment.

(9) The Welsh Ministers may delegate any of their qualifications functions to a joint committee to the extent and on the terms that they determine.

(10) A joint committee may delegate any of its functions to a sub-committee established by it to the extent and on the terms that the joint committee determines.

(11) The powers of a joint committee under subsection (10) are subject to the power of the Welsh Ministers and any other person with whom they established the joint committee to direct (acting jointly) what the committee may and may not do.

(12) Nothing in subsection (2)—
  (a) affects any power to disclose information that exists apart from that subsection, or

(b)   authorises the disclosure of information in contravention of any provision made by or under any Act which prevents disclosure of the information.

(13)   In this section—

"qualifications functions" means functions in connection with relevant qualifications;

"relevant authority" means any person who carries out a function (whether or not in the United Kingdom) which is similar to any of the qualifications functions of the Welsh Ministers;

"relevant function" means a function which is similar to any of the qualifications functions of the Welsh Ministers."

18   (1)   Section 32A (power of the Welsh Ministers to give directions) is amended as follows.

(2)   In subsection (1)(b)(i) for "any qualification accredited by them or by the Qualifications and Curriculum Authority" substitute "any qualification in respect of which that person is recognised by them or by the Office of Qualifications and Examinations Regulation".

(3)   In subsection (5) after "this section" insert "and sections 32B and 32C".

(4)   Omit subsection (6).

19   After section 32A insert—

"32B   Power of Welsh Ministers to withdraw recognition

(1)   Subsection (2) applies if a recognised person has failed to comply with any condition subject to which the recognition has effect.

(2)   The Welsh Ministers may withdraw recognition from the recognised person in respect of the award or authentication of a specified qualification or a specified description of qualification if it appears to them that the failure mentioned in subsection (1) prejudices or would be likely to prejudice—

(a)   the proper award or authentication by the person of the qualification or a qualification of the description in question, or

(b)   persons who might reasonably be expected to seek to obtain the qualification or a qualification of the description in question awarded or authenticated by the person.

(3)   Subsection (4) applies if a recognised person who awards or authenticates a qualification accredited by the Welsh Ministers has failed to comply with any condition subject to which the accreditation has effect.

(4)   The Welsh Ministers may withdraw recognition from the recognised person in respect of the qualification if it appears to them that the failure mentioned in subsection (3) prejudices or would be likely to prejudice—

(a)   the proper award or authentication by the person of the qualification, or

(b)   persons who might reasonably be expected to seek to obtain the qualification.

Apprenticeships, Skills, Children and Learning Act 2009 (c. 22)
Schedule 12 – Ofqual and the QCDA: minor and consequential amendments

2401

(5) Before withdrawing recognition from a recognised person in any respect the Welsh Ministers must give notice to the person of their intention to do so.

(6) The notice must—
   (a) set out the Welsh Ministers' reasons for proposing to withdraw recognition from the recognised person in the respect in question, and
   (b) specify the period during which, and the way in which, the recognised person may make representations about the proposal.

(7) The Welsh Ministers must have regard to any representations made by the recognised person during the period specified in the notice in deciding whether to withdraw recognition from the person in the respect in question.

(8) If the Welsh Ministers decide to withdraw recognition from a recognised person they must give notice to the person of their decision and of the date on which the withdrawal is to take effect.

(9) At any time before a withdrawal takes effect the Welsh Ministers may vary the date on which it is to take effect by giving further notice to the recognised person.

(10) The Welsh Ministers must establish arrangements for the review, at the request of a recognised person, of a decision to withdraw recognition under this section.

(11) The arrangements established under subsection (10) may require or permit the decision on review to be made by a person other than the Welsh Ministers.

32C Surrender of recognition

(1) A recognised person may give notice to the Welsh Ministers that the person wishes to cease to be recognised in respect of the award or authentication of a specified qualification or description of qualification.

(2) As soon as reasonably practicable after receipt of a notice under subsection (1) the Welsh Ministers must give notice to the recognised person of the date on which the person is to cease to be recognised in the respect in question ("the surrender date").

(3) At any time before the surrender date the Welsh Ministers may vary that date by giving further notice to the recognised person.

(4) In deciding or varying the surrender date the Welsh Ministers must have regard to the need to avoid prejudicing persons who are seeking, or might reasonably be expected to seek, to obtain the qualification, or a qualification of the description, specified in the notice under subsection (1)."

20   In section 35(1) (transfer of staff) at the end insert ", known instead as the Qualifications and Curriculum Development Agency from the day on which section 175 of the Apprenticeships, Skills, Children and Learning Act 2009 comes into force".

21   Section 36 (levy on bodies awarding qualifications accredited by relevant body) ceases to have effect.

22   In section 54(1) (orders and regulations) omit ", except an order under section 25 or 31,".

23   In section 58(6) (short title, commencement and extent etc) —
    (a)   omit the entries for —
        (i)   sections 21 and 22,
        (ii)   section 24(4), (6) and (7),
        (iii)   sections 26 and 26A, and
        (iv)   Schedule 4;
    (b)   for "34 to 36" substitute "35".

24   Schedule 4 (the Qualifications and Curriculum Authority) ceases to have effect.

25   In Schedule 7 (minor and consequential amendments) omit paragraph 2.

Learning and Skills Act 2000 (c. 21)

26   The Learning and Skills Act 2000 is amended as follows.

27 (1) Section 96 (external qualifications: persons under 19) is amended as follows.

   (2) In subsection (1)(b) for "an external qualification" substitute "a relevant qualification".

   (3) In subsection (2) for "external" substitute "relevant".

   (4) For subsections (5) to (7) substitute —

     "(5)   In this section "a relevant qualification" —
        (a)   in relation to England, means a qualification to which Part 7 of the Apprenticeships, Skills, Children and Learning Act 2009 applies;
        (b)   in relation to Wales, has the same meaning as in section 30 of the Education Act 1997."

28 (1) Section 98 (approved qualifications: England) is amended as follows.

   (2) Before subsection (3) insert —

     "(2B)   A qualification may be approved only if —
        (a)   the conditions mentioned in subsection (2C) are satisfied in relation to the qualification, or
        (b)   the Office of Qualifications and Examinations Regulation is consulted before the approval is given.

     (2C)   The conditions are that —
        (a)   the qualification is a regulated qualification within the meaning of Part 7 of the Apprenticeships, Skills, Children and Learning Act 2009, and
        (b)   if the qualification is subject to the accreditation requirement (within the meaning of Chapter 2 of that Part), it is accredited under section 139 of that Act."

Apprenticeships, Skills, Children and Learning Act 2009 (c. 22)
Schedule 12 – Ofqual and the QCDA: minor and consequential amendments

2403

(3) In subsections (7) and (8) for "Qualifications and Curriculum Authority" substitute "Qualifications and Curriculum Development Agency or the Young People's Learning Agency for England".

29 (1) In section 99 (approved qualifications: Wales) is amended as follows.

(2) In subsection (2) –

    (a) before paragraph (a) insert –

        "(za) the conditions mentioned in subsection (2ZA) are then satisfied in relation to the qualification,";

    (b) in paragraphs (a) and (b) after "then" insert "otherwise".

(3) After subsection (2) insert –

    "(2ZA) The conditions are that –

        (a) the qualification is awarded or authenticated by a person recognised in that respect under section 30(1)(e) of the Education Act 1997, and

        (b) if the qualification is subject to a requirement of accreditation pursuant to a determination made under section 30(1)(f) of that Act, it is accredited under section 30(1)(h) of that Act."

Freedom of Information Act 2000 (c. 36)

30   In Part 6 of Schedule 1 to the Freedom of Information Act 2000 (other public bodies and offices: general) for "The Qualifications Curriculum Authority" substitute "The Qualifications and Curriculum Development Agency".

Education Act 2002 (c. 32)

31   The Education Act 2002 is amended as follows.

32 (1) Section 76 (interpretation of Part 6) is amended as follows.

(2) At the beginning insert "(1)".

(3) In the definition of "assess" omit "examine and".

(4) In the definition of "assessment arrangements" for the words from "for the purpose" to the end substitute "for the specified purposes".

(5) At the end insert –

    "(2) In subsection (1) "the specified purposes", in relation to assessment arrangements for a key stage, means –

        (a) the purpose of ascertaining what pupils have achieved in relation to the attainment targets for that stage, and

        (b) such other purposes as the Secretary of State may by order specify."

33   In section 85(6) (curriculum requirements for the fourth key stage) for "Qualifications and Curriculum Authority" substitute "Qualifications and Curriculum Development Agency".

34   In section 85A(5) (entitlement areas for the fourth key stage) for "Qualifications and Curriculum Authority" substitute "Qualifications and Curriculum Development Agency".

35   (1) Section 87 (establishment of the National Curriculum for England by order) is amended as follows.

    (2) In subsection (5) for "published as specified" substitute "published by a person, and in the manner, specified".

    (3) In subsection (7)—

        (a) omit the "and" at the end of paragraph (a);

        (b) after paragraph (b) insert—

            "(c) the Qualifications and Curriculum Development Agency, and

            (d) any other person with whom the Secretary of State has made arrangements in connection with the development, implementation or monitoring of assessment arrangements,".

    (4) Omit subsection (9).

    (5) In subsection (10) for the words before paragraph (a) substitute "The duties that may be imposed by virtue of subsection (7)(a) or (b) include, in relation to persons exercising any function in connection with the moderation or monitoring of assessment arrangements, the duty to permit them—".

    (6) For subsection (11) substitute—

     "(11) An order under subsection (3)(c) may authorise a person specified in the order to make delegated supplementary provisions in relation to such matters as may be specified in the order.

      (12) In this section "delegated supplementary provisions" means such provisions (other than provisions conferring or imposing functions as mentioned in subsection (7)(a) or (b)) as appear to the authorised person to be expedient for giving full effect to, or otherwise supplementing, the provisions made by the order.

      (13) An order under subsection (3)(c) authorising the making of delegated supplementary provisions may provide that such provisions may be made only with the approval of the Secretary of State.

      (14) Any delegated supplementary provisions shall, on being published as specified in the order under which they are made, have effect for the purposes of this Part as if made by the order."

36   (1) Section 90 (development work and experiments) is amended as follows.

    (2) In subsections (3)(c) and (4) for "Qualifications and Curriculum Authority" substitute "Qualifications and Curriculum Development Agency".

    (3) In subsection (5) for the words from "to the" to the end substitute "on any matters specified by the Secretary of State to—

        (a) the Secretary of State, or

        (b) the reviewing body."

    (4) After subsection (5) insert—

     "(5A) If required by the Secretary of State to do so the reviewing body shall keep under review development work or experiments carried out following a direction given under subsection (1).

Apprenticeships, Skills, Children and Learning Act 2009 (c. 22)
Schedule 12 − Ofqual and the QCDA: minor and consequential amendments

2405

(5B) In this section "the reviewing body" means the Qualifications and Curriculum Development Agency, or any other person, if designated as such by the Secretary of State.

(5C) A designation under subsection (5B) may make different provision for different purposes."

37 (1) Section 96 (procedure for making certain orders and regulations) is amended as follows.

(2) In subsection (2) −

(a) for "Qualifications and Curriculum Authority (in this section referred to as "the Authority")" substitute "Qualifications and Curriculum Development Agency (in this section referred to as "the Agency")";

(b) for "them" substitute "it";

(c) for "they are" substitute "it is".

(3) For subsection (3) substitute −

"(3) The Agency shall give notice of the proposal to such of the following as appear to it to be concerned with the proposal −

(a) associations of local education authorities,

(b) bodies representing the interests of school governing bodies, and

(c) organisations representing school teachers.

(3A) The Agency shall also publish the proposal in such manner as, in its opinion, is likely to bring the proposal to the notice of any other persons who may be concerned with the proposal.

(3B) The Agency shall give the bodies and other persons mentioned in subsections (3) and (3A) a reasonable opportunity of submitting evidence and representations as to the issues arising from the proposal."

(4) In subsection (4) −

(a) for "Authority", wherever appearing, substitute "Agency";

(b) in paragraph (c) for "think" substitute "thinks".

(5) In subsection (5) −

(a) for "Authority" substitute "Agency";

(b) for "their" substitute "its".

(6) In subsection (6) −

(a) for "Authority have" substitute "Agency has";

(b) in paragraph (b) for "Authority" substitute "Agency";

(c) omit the words from "and shall send copies" to the end.

(7) After subsection (6) insert −

"(6A) The Secretary of State shall take such steps as in his opinion are likely to bring the documents mentioned in subsection (6)(a) and (b) to the notice of any person who submitted evidence or representations to the Agency.

(6B)   The Secretary of State shall send copies of those documents to the Agency."

Childcare Act 2006 (c. 21)

38   The Childcare Act 2006 is amended as follows.

39   (1)   Section 41 (the learning and development requirements) is amended as follows.

(2)   In subsection (2)(c) for the words from "for the purpose" to "early learning goals" substitute "for the specified purposes".

(3)   After subsection (4) insert—

"(4A)   In subsection (2)(c) "the specified purposes" means—
  (a)   the purpose of ascertaining what children have achieved in relation to the early learning goals, and
  (b)   such other purposes as the Secretary of State may by order specify."

40   (1)   Section 42 (further provisions about assessment arrangements) is amended as follows.

(2)   In subsection (2)—
  (a)   omit the "and" at the end of paragraph (b);
  (b)   after paragraph (c) insert—
        "(d)   the Qualifications and Curriculum Development Agency, and
        (e)   any other person with whom the Secretary of State has made arrangements in connection with the development, implementation or monitoring of assessment arrangements."

(3)   Omit subsection (4).

(4)   In subsection (5) for the words before paragraph (a) substitute "The duties that may be imposed on a person mentioned in subsection (2)(a) to (c) by virtue of subsection (1) include, in relation to persons exercising any function in connection with the moderation or monitoring of assessment arrangements, the duty to permit them—".

(5)   For subsection (6) substitute—

"(6)   A learning and development order specifying assessment arrangements may authorise a person specified in the order to make delegated supplementary provisions in relation to such matters as may be specified in the order.

(6A)   In this section "delegated supplementary provisions" means such provisions (other than provisions conferring or imposing functions on persons mentioned in subsection (2)(a) to (c)) as appear to the authorised person to be expedient for giving full effect to, or otherwise supplementing, the provisions made by the order.

(6B)   A learning and development order authorising the making of delegated supplementary provisions may provide that such

Apprenticeships, Skills, Children and Learning Act 2009 (c. 22)
Schedule 12 – Ofqual and the QCDA: minor and consequential amendments

2407

provisions may be made only with the approval of the Secretary of State.

(6C) Any delegated supplementary provisions, on being published as specified in the order under which they are made, are to have effect for the purposes of this Chapter as if made by the order."

41 In section 44(1) (instruments specifying learning and development or welfare requirements) for "published as specified" substitute "published by a person, and in the manner, specified".

42 In section 46 (power to enable exemptions from learning and development requirements to be conferred) after subsection (1) insert —

"(1A) Regulations under subsection (1) may make provision about the conditions which may be imposed by the Secretary of State on making a direction.

(1B) If required by the Secretary of State to do so the reviewing body must keep under review the effect of a direction given under regulations made under subsection (1).

(1C) In subsection (1B) "the reviewing body" means the Qualifications and Curriculum Development Agency, or any other person, if designated as such by the Secretary of State.

(1D) A designation under subsection (1C) may make different provision for different purposes."

Safeguarding Vulnerable Groups Act 2006 (c. 47)

43 In section 21(10) of the Safeguarding Vulnerable Groups Act 2006 (controlled activity relating to children) in paragraph (d) for "Qualifications and Curriculum Authority" substitute "Qualifications and Curriculum Development Agency".

SCHEDULE 13   Section 203

POWERS IN RELATION TO SCHOOLS CAUSING CONCERN: ENGLAND

1 Part 4 of the Education and Inspections Act 2006 (c. 40) (schools causing concern: England) is amended as follows.

2 (1) Section 59(2) (meaning of schools being "eligible for intervention") is amended as follows.

(2) For "warning notice by local education authority" substitute "performance standards and safety warning notice".

(3) Before "section 61" insert —
"section 60A (teachers' pay and conditions warning notice),".

3 For the title of section 60 substitute "Performance standards and safety warning notice".

4   After section 60 insert—

     "60A Teachers' pay and conditions warning notice

(1)   A maintained school is by virtue of this section eligible for intervention if—

     (a)   the local education authority have given the governing body a warning notice in accordance with subsection (2),

     (b)   the period beginning with the day on which the warning notice is given and ending with the fifteenth working day following that day ("the initial period") has expired,

     (c)   either the governing body made no representations under subsection (7) to the local education authority against the warning notice during the initial period or the local education authority have confirmed the warning notice under subsection (8),

     (d)   the governing body have failed to comply, or secure compliance, with the notice to the authority's satisfaction by the end of the compliance period (as defined by subsection (10)), and

     (e)   the authority have given reasonable notice in writing to the governing body that they propose to exercise their powers under any one or more of sections 64 to 66.

(2)   A local education authority may give a warning notice to the governing body of a maintained school where the authority are satisfied that—

     (a)   the governing body have failed to comply with a provision of an order under section 122 of EA 2002 (teachers' pay and conditions) that applies to a teacher at the school, or

     (b)   the governing body have failed to secure that the head teacher of the school complies with such a provision.

(3)   In subsection (2) references to an order under section 122 of EA 2002 include a document by reference to which provision is made in such an order.

(4)   For the purposes of this section a "warning notice" is a notice in writing by the local education authority setting out—

     (a)   the matters on which the conclusion mentioned in subsection (2) is based,

     (b)   the action which they require the governing body to take in order to remedy those matters,

     (c)   the initial period applying under subsection (1)(b), and

     (d)   the action which the local education authority are minded to take (under one or more of sections 64 to 66 or otherwise) if the governing body fail to take the required action.

(5)   The warning notice must also inform the governing body of their right to make representations under subsection (7) during the initial period.

(6)   The local education authority must, at the same time as giving the governing body the warning notice, give a copy of the notice to each of the following persons—

Apprenticeships, Skills, Children and Learning Act 2009 (c. 22)
Schedule 13 — Powers in relation to schools causing concern: England

2409

(a) the head teacher of the school,

(b) in the case of a Church of England school or a Roman Catholic Church school, the appropriate diocesan authority, and

(c) in the case of a foundation or voluntary school, the person who appoints the foundation governors.

(7) Before the end of the initial period, the governing body may make representations in writing to the local education authority against the warning notice.

(8) The local education authority must consider any representations made to them under subsection (7) and may, if they think fit, confirm the warning notice.

(9) The local education authority must give notice in writing of their decision whether or not to confirm the warning notice to the governing body and such other persons as the Secretary of State may require.

(10) In this section "the compliance period", in relation to a warning notice, means —

(a) in a case where the governing body does not make representations under subsection (7), the initial period mentioned in subsection (1)(b), and

(b) in a case where the local education authority confirm the warning notice under subsection (8), the period beginning with the day on which they do so and ending with the fifteenth working day following that day."

5 (1) Section 63 (power of LEA to require governing body to enter into arrangements) is amended as follows.

(2) In subsection (1) after "eligible for intervention" insert "other than by virtue of section 60A".

(3) In subsection (3) for "formal warning" substitute "performance standards and safety warning".

6 (1) Section 64 (power of LEA etc to appoint additional governors) is amended as follows.

(2) In subsection (1) for "subsection (2)" substitute "subsections (1A) and (2)".

(3) After subsection (1) insert —

"(1A) Subsection (1) does not apply if the Secretary of State has exercised the power under section 67 (power to appoint additional governors) in connection with —

(a) the same warning notice, where the school is eligible for intervention by virtue of section 60 (school subject to performance standards and safety warning) or 60A (school subject to teachers' pay and conditions warning), or

(b) the same inspection falling within section 61(a) or 62(a), where the school is eligible for intervention by virtue of section 61 (school requiring significant improvement) or 62 (school requiring special measures)."

(4) In subsection (2) —

 (a) for "formal warning)" substitute "performance standards and safety warning) or 60A (school subject to teachers' pay and conditions warning)", and

 (b) after "60(10)" insert "or as the case may be section 60A(10)".

(5) In subsection (4) —

 (a) in paragraph (a) for "formal warning)" substitute "performance standards and safety warning) or 60A (school subject to teachers' pay and conditions warning)",

 (b) after paragraph (b) insert —

> "and
>
> (c) the Secretary of State has not exercised the power under section 67 in connection with the same warning notice,".

7 In section 66(2) (power of LEA to suspend right to delegated budget) —

 (a) for "formal warning)" substitute "performance standards and safety warning) or 60A (school subject to teachers' pay and conditions warning)", and

 (b) after "60(10)" insert "or as the case may be section 60A(10)".

8 In section 67(1) (power of Secretary of State to appoint additional governors) omit the words from "by virtue of" to "special measures)".

9 In section 69(1) (power of Secretary of State to provide for governing body to consist of interim executive members) omit the words from "by virtue of" to "special measures)".

10 After section 69 insert —

"69A Power of Secretary of State to direct LEA to consider giving performance standards and safety warning notice

 (1) This section applies if the Secretary of State thinks that the conditions in subsections (2) and (3) are met.

 (2) The condition is that there are reasonable grounds for a local education authority to give a warning notice to the governing body of a maintained school under section 60 (performance standards and safety warning notice).

 (3) The condition is that one of the following applies —

  (a) the authority have not given a warning notice to the governing body under section 60 on those grounds;

  (b) the authority have done so, but in inadequate terms;

  (c) the authority have given a warning notice to the governing body under section 60 on those grounds, but the Chief Inspector has failed or declined to confirm it;

  (d) the school has become eligible for intervention on those grounds by virtue of section 60, but the period of two months following the end of the compliance period (as defined by section 60(10)) has ended.

Apprenticeships, Skills, Children and Learning Act 2009 (c. 22)
Schedule 13 — Powers in relation to schools causing concern: England

2411

(4) The Secretary of State may direct the local education authority to consider giving a warning notice to the governing body under section 60 in the terms specified in the direction.

(5) A direction under subsection (4) must be in writing.

(6) If the Secretary of State gives a direction under subsection (4) to a local education authority in respect of a governing body, the authority must—

    (a) give the Secretary of State a written response to the direction before the end of the period of 10 working days beginning with the day on which the direction is given, and

    (b) on the same day as they do so, give the Chief Inspector a copy of the response.

(7) The local education authority's response to the direction must do one of the following—

    (a) state that the authority have decided to give a warning notice to the governing body in the specified terms;

    (b) state that the authority have decided not to give a warning notice to the governing body in those terms.

(8) If the response states that the authority have decided to give a warning notice to the governing body in the specified terms, the authority must—

    (a) give the warning notice to the governing body in those terms before the end of the period of 5 working days beginning with the day on which the response is given (and withdraw any previous warning notice given to the governing body under section 60), and

    (b) on the same day as they do so, give the Secretary of State a copy of the notice.

(9) If the response states that the authority have decided not to give a warning notice to the governing body in the specified terms, it must set out the authority's reasons for the decision.

(10) Subsection (8)(b) applies in addition to section 60(6).

69B Power of Secretary of State to direct LEA to give teachers' pay and conditions warning notice

(1) This section applies if the Secretary of State thinks that the conditions in subsections (2) and (3) are met.

(2) The condition is that there are reasonable grounds for a local education authority to give a warning notice to the governing body of a maintained school under section 60A (teachers' pay and conditions warning notice).

(3) The condition is that one of the following applies—

    (a) the authority have not given a warning notice to the governing body under section 60A on those grounds;

    (b) the authority have done so, but in inadequate terms;

    (c) the authority have given a warning notice to the governing body under section 60A on those grounds, but have declined or failed to confirm it;

2412

Apprenticeships, Skills, Children and Learning Act 2009 (c. 22)
Schedule 13 — Powers in relation to schools causing concern: England

      (d)   the school has become eligible for intervention on those grounds by virtue of section 60A, but the period of two months following the end of the compliance period (as defined by section 60A(10)) has ended.

(4)   The Secretary of State may direct the local education authority to consider giving a warning notice to the governing body under section 60A in the terms specified in the direction.

(5)   If the Secretary of State gives a direction under subsection (4) to a local education authority in respect of a governing body, the authority must—

      (a)   give a copy of the direction to the governing body before the end of the period of 2 working days beginning with the day on which the direction is given,

      (b)   when it does so, invite the governing body to give the authority a written response before the end of the period of 7 working days beginning with the day on which the direction is given, and

      (c)   give the Secretary of State the authority's written response, and any response received from the governing body in accordance with paragraph (b), before the end of the period of 10 working days beginning with the day on which the direction is given.

(6)   The local education authority's response to the direction must do one of the following—

      (a)   state that the authority have decided to give a warning notice to the governing body in the specified terms;

      (b)   state that the authority have decided not to give a warning notice to the governing body in those terms.

(7)   If the response states that the authority have decided to give a warning notice to the governing body in the specified terms, the authority must—

      (a)   give the warning notice to the governing body in those terms before the end of the period of 5 working days beginning with the day on which the response is given (and withdraw any previous warning notice given to the governing body under section 60A), and

      (b)   on the same day as they do so, give the Secretary of State a copy of the notice.

(8)   If the response states that the authority have decided not to give a warning notice to the governing body in the specified terms—

      (a)   the response must set out the authority's reasons for the decision, and

      (b)   the Secretary of State may direct the authority to give the warning notice to the governing body in those terms (and to withdraw any previous warning notice given to the governing body under section 60A).

(9)   If the Secretary of State directs the authority under subsection (8)(b) to give a warning notice to the governing body in the specified terms, the authority must—

Apprenticeships, Skills, Children and Learning Act 2009 (c. 22)
Schedule 13 – Powers in relation to schools causing concern: England

2413

      (a)   comply with the direction under subsection (8)(b) before the end of the period of 5 working days beginning with the day on which that direction is given, and

      (b)   on the same day as they do so, give the Secretary of State a copy of the notice.

  (10)   Subsections (7)(b) and (9)(b) apply in addition to section 60A(6).

  (11)   A direction under this section must be in writing."

11   In section 73 (interpretation of Part 4) at the end insert —
           ""working day" has the meaning given by section 60(10)."

SCHEDULE 14

Section 205

POWERS IN RELATION TO SCHOOLS CAUSING CONCERN: WALES

1   Chapter 4 of Part 1 of the School Standards and Framework Act 1998 (c. 31) (measures to raise standards of school education in Wales: intervention powers) is amended as follows.

2   In section 14(4) (intervention powers: interpretation), in paragraph (c) for "that Act" substitute "the Education Act 2005".

3   In section 15 (cases where LEA may exercise powers of intervention), in subsection (2)(a), after "(whether by a breakdown of discipline or otherwise)" insert ", or —

          (iv)   that the governing body have failed to comply with a provision of an order under section 122 of the Education Act 2002 (teachers' pay and conditions) that applies to a teacher at the school, or

          (v)   that the governing body have failed to secure that the head teacher of the school complies with such a provision".

4   In section 18 (power of Welsh Ministers to appoint additional governors), in subsection (1) —

   (a)   in the opening words for "either" substitute "any";

   (b)   before paragraph (a) insert —
          "(za)   subsection (1), in a case within subsection (2)(a)(iv) or (v) (school subject to teachers' pay and conditions warning),".

5   In section 18A (power of Welsh Ministers to provide for governing body to consist of interim executive members), in subsection (1) —

   (a)   in the opening words for "either" substitute "any";

   (b)   before paragraph (a) insert —
          "(za)   subsection (1), in a case within subsection (2)(a)(iv) or (v) (school subject to teachers' pay and conditions warning),".

6   After section 19 insert—

"19ZA Power of Welsh Ministers to direct LEA to give warning notice: teachers' pay and conditions

(1)   This section applies if the Welsh Ministers think that the conditions in subsections (2) and (3) are met.

(2)   The condition is that there are reasonable grounds for a local education authority to give a warning notice to the governing body of a maintained school under section 15(2)(a)(iv) or (v) (teachers' pay and conditions warning notice).

(3)   The condition is that one of the following applies in relation to those grounds—

   (a)   the authority have not given a warning notice to the governing body under section 15 on those grounds, or have not given a copy to the head teacher at the same time;

   (b)   the authority have given a warning notice to the governing body under section 15, but in inadequate terms;

   (c)   section 15 applies to the school on those grounds by virtue of subsection (1) of that section, but the period of two months following the end of the compliance period (as defined by section 15(3)(c)) has ended.

(4)   The Welsh Ministers may direct the local education authority to consider giving a warning notice to the governing body under section 15(2)(a)(iv) or (v) in the terms specified in the direction.

(5)   If the Welsh Ministers give a direction under subsection (4) to a local education authority in respect of a governing body, the authority must—

   (a)   give a copy of the direction to the governing body before the end of the period of 2 working days beginning with the day on which the direction is given,

   (b)   when it does so, invite the governing body to give the authority a written response before the end of the period of 7 working days beginning with the day on which the direction is given, and

   (c)   give the Welsh Ministers the authority's written response, and any response received from the governing body in accordance with paragraph (b), before the end of the period of 10 working days beginning with the day on which the direction is given.

(6)   The local education authority's response to the direction must do one of the following—

   (a)   state that the authority have decided to give a warning notice to the governing body in the specified terms;

   (b)   state that the authority have decided not to give a warning notice to the governing body in those terms.

(7)   If the response states that the authority have decided to give a warning notice to the governing body in the specified terms, the authority must—

> > (a) give the warning notice to the governing body in those terms before the end of the period of 5 working days beginning with the day on which the response is given (and withdraw any previous warning notice given to the governing body under section 15(2)(a)(iv) or (v)), and
> >
> > (b) on the same day as they do so, give the Welsh Ministers a copy of the notice.

> (8) If the response states that the authority have decided not to give a warning notice to the governing body in the specified terms—
> > (a) the response must set out the authority's reasons for the decision, and
> >
> > (b) the Welsh Ministers may direct the authority to give the warning notice to the governing body in those terms (and to withdraw any previous warning notice given to the governing body under section 15(2)(a)(iv) or (v)).

> (9) If the Welsh Ministers direct the authority under subsection (8)(b) to give a warning notice to the governing body in the specified terms, the authority must—
> > (a) comply with the direction under subsection (8)(b) before the end of the period of 5 working days beginning with the day on which that direction is given, and
> >
> > (b) on the same day as they do so, give the Welsh Ministers a copy of the notice.

> (10) Subsections (7)(b) and (9)(b) apply in addition to section 15(1)(a)(ii).

> (11) A direction under this section must be in writing.

> (12) In this section "working day" means a day other than a Saturday, a Sunday, Christmas Day, Good Friday or a day which is a bank holiday under the Banking and Financial Dealings Act 1971 in Wales."

SCHEDULE 15

Section 227

THE SCHOOL SUPPORT STAFF NEGOTIATING BODY

Constitution

1 (1) The SSSNB is to be constituted in accordance with arrangements made by the Secretary of State.

(2) Before making or revising arrangements under sub-paragraph (1), the Secretary of State must consult—
> (a) the prescribed school support staff organisations, and
> (b) the prescribed school support staff employer organisations.

(3) References in this Schedule to the SSSNB's constitutional arrangements are to arrangements made under sub-paragraph (1).

(4) References in this Schedule to the prescribed organisations are to the organisations prescribed under sub-paragraph (2).

2416

Apprenticeships, Skills, Children and Learning Act 2009 (c. 22)
Schedule 15 — The School Support Staff Negotiating Body

Membership

2   (1) The SSSNB's constitutional arrangements must provide for the members of
the SSSNB to include persons representing the interests of —
    (a)   the prescribed organisations;
    (b)   the Secretary of State.

    (2) The arrangements must also provide for the members of the SSSNB to
include a person appointed to chair the SSSNB.

    (3) The arrangements must provide for that person to be a person who, in the
opinion of the Secretary of State, does not represent the interests of —
    (a)   a school support staff organisation,
    (b)   a school support staff employer organisation,
    (c)   the Secretary of State, or
    (d)   any other person or organisation represented on the SSSNB.

    (4) The arrangements may provide for the members of the SSSNB to include
other persons who do not represent the interests of —
    (a)   school support staff organisations, or
    (b)   school support staff employer organisations.

Proceedings

3   (1) The SSSNB's constitutional arrangements must not provide for a member of
the SSSNB to be entitled to vote in respect of its proceedings unless the
member is a person representing the interests of any of the prescribed
organisations.

    (2) Subject to sub-paragraph (1), the arrangements may make provision about
the proceedings of the SSSNB (including provision allowing the SSSNB to
determine its own proceedings).

Administrative support

4   The SSSNB's constitutional arrangements may make provision about the
provision of administrative support to the SSSNB.

Annual reports

5   (1) The SSSNB's constitutional arrangements must provide for the SSSNB to
prepare a report, in respect of each successive period of 12 months beginning
on the day on which it is established, about the performance of its functions
in that period.

    (2) The arrangements may —
    (a)   require the SSSNB to send copies of the report to specified persons;
    (b)   require the SSSNB otherwise to publish the report in a specified
manner.

Fees and expenses

6   The SSSNB's constitutional arrangements may make provision about —
    (a)   the payment of fees to the person appointed to chair the SSSNB;
    (b)   the payment of expenses incurred by the SSSNB.

Apprenticeships, Skills, Children and Learning Act 2009 (c. 22)
Schedule 15 — The School Support Staff Negotiating Body

2417

House of Commons disqualification

7   In the House of Commons Disqualification Act 1975 (c. 24), in Part 3 of Schedule 1 (other disqualifying offices), at the appropriate place insert —

        "Person appointed to chair the School Support Staff Negotiating Body."

Interpretation

8   For the purposes of this Schedule —

    (a) a "school support staff organisation" is an organisation that, in the opinion of the Secretary of State, represents the interests of school support staff;

    (b) a "school support staff employer organisation" is an organisation that, in the opinion of the Secretary of State, represents the interests of employers of school support staff;

    (c) "specified" means specified in the SSSNB's constitutional arrangements.

SCHEDULE 16

Section 266

REPEALS AND REVOCATIONS

PART 1

LEA FUNCTIONS

Title	Extent of repeal
Education Act 1996 (c. 56)	Section 509.
School Standards and Framework Act 1998 (c. 31)	Section 128. In Schedule 30, paragraph 64.
Education and Inspections Act 2006 (c. 40)	Section 81.

PART 2

DISSOLUTION OF THE LSC

Title	Extent of repeal
Further and Higher Education Act 1992 (c. 13)	In section 56B(3), the word "its". In section 56C(4), the words "to it".
Learning and Skills Act 2000 (c. 21)	Part 1. Section 97. Section 98(2A). Section 99(2A). In section 101(1), paragraph (c) (and the word "or" before it). In section 102(1), paragraph (c) (and the word "or" before it).

2418   *Apprenticeships, Skills, Children and Learning Act 2009 (c. 22)*
Schedule 16 — Repeals and revocations
Part 2 — Dissolution of the LSC

Title	Extent of repeal
Learning and Skills Act 2000 (c. 21) — *cont.*	In section 113A — (a) subsections (1), (4)(aa), (5), (7), (8) and (9)(f); (b) in subsection (11), paragraph (a) of the definition of "regulations" (and the word "and" after it) and paragraph (a) of the definition of "relevant authority" (and the word "and" after it). Schedules 1, 1A and 3. In Schedule 7A — (a) in paragraph 1, the words "approved or" and "approval or", wherever occurring; (b) in paragraph 3(4), paragraph (a); (c) paragraphs 5(1), 6(1) and 7(1) and (2).
Education and Inspections Act 2006 (c. 40)	Section 75.
Further Education and Training Act 2007 (c. 25)	Section 1. Section 2. Sections 4 to 10. Sections 11 to 13. Sections 14 to 16.
Education and Skills Act 2008 (c. 25)	Section 159(2). Section 160(2).

PART 3

SIXTH FORM COLLEGE SECTOR

Title	Extent of repeal
Education and Inspections Act 2006	Section 11(1)(b) and (2)(a).

PART 4

OFQUAL AND THE QCDA

Title	Extent of repeal or revocation
Charities Act 1993 (c. 10)	In Schedule 2, paragraph (da).
Education Act 1997 (c. 44)	Sections 21 to 26A. Section 30(1C), (1D), (2) and (6). Section 32(4A). Section 32A(6). Section 36. In section 54(1), the words ", except an order under section 25 or 31,".

Apprenticeships, Skills, Children and Learning Act 2009 (c. 22)   **2419**
Schedule 16 — Repeals and revocations
Part 4 — Ofqual and the QCDA

Title	Extent of repeal or revocation
Education Act 1997 (c. 44) — *cont.*	In section 58(6), the entries for — (a) sections 21 and 22; (b) section 24(4), (6) and (7); (c) sections 26 and 26A; (d) Schedule 4 (and the word "and" before it). Schedule 4. In Schedule 7 — (a) paragraph 1; (b) paragraph 2 (and the italic heading before it); (c) paragraph 3(1)(b) (and the word "and" before it); (d) paragraph 4(3); (e) paragraph 29(a) (and the word "and" after it).
School Standards and Framework Act 1998 (c. 31)	In Schedule 30, paragraph 214.
Learning and Skills Act 2000 (c. 21)	Section 103(2) and (3). In Schedule 9, paragraph 69.
Education Act 2002 (c. 32)	In section 76, in the definition of "assess", the words "examine and". In section 87 — (a) in subsection (7), the word "and" at the end of paragraph (a); (b) subsection (9). In section 96(6), the words from "and shall send copies" to the end. In section 216(2), the words "paragraphs 1 to 4 and 9 of Schedule 17, and section 189 so far as relating to those paragraphs,". In Schedule 17 — (a) paragraphs 1 to 4 and the italic heading before paragraph 1; (b) paragraph 5(6); (c) paragraph 9 and the italic heading before it. In Schedule 21, paragraph 69.
The Qualifications, Curriculum and Assessment Authority for Wales (Transfer of Functions to the National Assembly for Wales and Abolition) Order 2005 (S.I. 2005/3239)	In Schedule 1, paragraphs 7, 22, 23 and 24.
Childcare Act 2006 (c. 21)	In section 42 — (a) in subsection (2), the word "and" at the end of paragraph (b); (b) subsection (4).

2420

Apprenticeships, Skills, Children and Learning Act 2009 (c. 22)
Schedule 16 — Repeals and revocations
Part 4 — Ofqual and the QCDA

Title	*Extent of repeal or revocation*
Childcare Act 2006 (c. 21) — *cont.*	In Schedule 1 — (a) paragraph 2 and the italic heading before it; (b) paragraph 10(9).
Education and Inspections Act 2006 (c. 40)	In Schedule 14, paragraphs 21 and 25.
Education and Skills Act 2008 (c. 25)	Section 9. Section 161. Section 162(2) to (5). Section 163.

PART 5

CO-OPERATION TO IMPROVE WELL-BEING OF CHILDREN

Title	*Extent of repeal*
Children Act 2004 (c. 31)	In section 10 — (a) subsection (4)(g); (b) subsections (6) and (7).

PART 6

SCHOOLS CAUSING CONCERN

Title	*Extent of repeal*
Education and Inspections Act 2006	In section 67(1), the words from "by virtue of" to "special measures)". In section 69(1), the words from "by virtue of" to "special measures)".

PART 7

COMPLAINTS

Title	*Extent of repeal*
Education Act 1996 (c. 56)	Section 408(4)(g). Section 409. In Schedule 1, paragraph 6(3) and (4).

Apprenticeships, Skills, Children and Learning Act 2009 (c. 22)
Schedule 16 – Repeals and revocations
Part 8 – School inspections

2421

PART 8

SCHOOL INSPECTIONS

Title	*Extent of repeal*
Education and Inspections Act 2006 (c. 40)	In Schedule 12 – (a) in paragraph 9(1), the word "or" at the end of paragraph (b); (b) in paragraph 10(1), the word "or" at the end of paragraph (b).

PART 9

INFORMATION ABOUT LOCAL AUTHORITY EXPENDITURE

Title	*Extent of repeal*
School Standards and Framework Act 1998 (c. 31)	Section 53.
Public Audit (Wales) Act 2004 (c. 23)	In Schedule 2, paragraph 40.

PART 10

SUPPORT FOR PARTICIPATION IN EDUCATION AND TRAINING

Title	*Extent of repeal*
Education and Skills Act 2008 (c. 25)	Section 15. Section 76(1).

PART 11

FOUNDATION DEGREES: WALES

Title	*Extent of repeal*
Further and Higher Education Act 1992 (c. 13)	In section 76(1)(b), the words "in England".

2422

Marine and Coastal Access Act 2009

CHAPTER 23

CONTENTS

CHAPTER 3

ENFORCEMENT

Offences

Enforcement notices

Civil sanctions

CHAPTER 4

DELEGATION

CHAPTER 5

SUPPLEMENTARY

Register

Stop notices and emergency safety notices

Other powers

CHAPTER 2

OTHER CONSERVATION SITES

PART 6

MANAGEMENT OF INSHORE FISHERIES

CHAPTER 1

INSHORE FISHERIES AND CONSERVATION AUTHORITIES

Inshore fisheries and conservation districts and authorities

CHAPTER 2

LOCAL FISHERIES COMMITTEES

CHAPTER 3

INSHORE FISHERIES IN WALES

PART 7

FISHERIES

CHAPTER 1

THE SEA FISH (CONSERVATION) ACT 1967

CHAPTER 2

THE SEA FISHERIES (SHELLFISH) ACT 1967

CHAPTER 2

COMMON ENFORCEMENT POWERS

Introductory

CHAPTER 3

LICENSING ENFORCEMENT POWERS

Chapter 4

Fisheries enforcement powers

Inspection and seizure of objects at sea

Seizure for purposes of forfeiture

Forfeiture

Detention of vessels in connection with court proceedings

Production of equipment

Supplementary

Chapter 5

Common enforcement provisions

Introductory

2438

Marine and Coastal Access Act 2009

2009 CHAPTER 23

An Act to make provision in relation to marine functions and activities; to make provision about migratory and freshwater fish; to make provision for and in connection with the establishment of an English coastal walking route and of rights of access to land near the English coast; to enable the making of Assembly Measures in relation to Welsh coastal routes for recreational journeys and rights of access to land near the Welsh coast; to make further provision in relation to Natural England and the Countryside Council for Wales; to make provision in relation to works which are detrimental to navigation; to amend the Harbours Act 1964; and for connected purposes.

[12th November 2009]

B E IT ENACTED by the Queen's most Excellent Majesty, by and with the advice and consent of the Lords Spiritual and Temporal, and Commons, in this present Parliament assembled, and by the authority of the same, as follows: —

PART 1

THE MARINE MANAGEMENT ORGANISATION

CHAPTER 1

ESTABLISHMENT

1   **The Marine Management Organisation**

   (1)   There is to be a body known as the Marine Management Organisation ("the MMO").

   (2)   The MMO is to have the functions conferred on it by or under this Act or any other enactment.

   (3)   Schedule 1 contains further provisions about the MMO.

(4) Schedule 2 contains minor and consequential amendments relating to the MMO.

2 General objective

(1) It is the duty of the MMO to secure that the MMO functions are so exercised that the carrying on of activities by persons in the MMO's area is managed, regulated or controlled —

    (a) with the objective of making a contribution to the achievement of sustainable development (see subsections (2) and (4) to (11)),

    (b) taking account of all relevant facts and matters (see subsection (3)), and

    (c) in a manner which is consistent and co-ordinated (see subsection (12)).

Any reference in this Act to the MMO's "general objective" is a reference to the duty imposed on the MMO by this subsection.

(2) In pursuit of its general objective, the MMO may take any action which it considers necessary or expedient for the purpose of furthering any social, economic or environmental purposes.

(3) For the purposes of subsection (1)(b), the facts and matters that may be taken into account include each of the following —

    (a) scientific evidence, whether available to, or reasonably obtainable by, the MMO;

    (b) other evidence so available or obtainable relating to the social, economic or environmental elements of sustainable development;

    (c) such facts or matters not falling within paragraph (a) or (b) as the MMO may consider appropriate.

See also section 24 (powers of MMO in relation to research).

(4) The Secretary of State is to give the MMO guidance as to the manner in which the MMO is to seek to secure that the contribution to the achievement of sustainable development mentioned in subsection (1)(a) is made (and see also section 38 (guidance)).

(5) In preparing any such guidance the Secretary of State must take into consideration —

    (a) the functions of the MMO, and

    (b) the resources available, or likely to be available, to the MMO.

(6) A draft of any guidance proposed to be given under this section is to be laid before each House of Parliament.

(7) Guidance is not to be given under this section until after the end of the period of 40 days beginning with —

    (a) the day on which a draft of the guidance is so laid, or

    (b) if the draft is laid on different days, the later of the two days.

(8) If, within that period, either House resolves that the guidance, the draft of which was laid before it, should not be given, the Secretary of State must not give that guidance.

(9) In reckoning any period of 40 days for the purposes of subsection (7) or (8), no account is to be taken of any time during which —

    (a) Parliament is dissolved or prorogued, or

    (b) both Houses are adjourned for more than four days.

(10) The Secretary of State must publish, in such manner as the Secretary of State may determine, any guidance given to the MMO under this section.

(11) The MMO must provide any person on request with a copy of the whole or any part of any such guidance.

(12) In this section —

"consistent and co-ordinated" includes taking into account the effect (if any) that decisions in respect of —

    (a) any particular part of the MMO's area, or

    (b) the carrying on of any activity within that area,

will have on any other part of that area or the carrying on of any other activity in that area;

"evidence" includes predictions and other opinions resulting from the consideration of evidence by any person;

"the MMO's area" means those parts of the UK marine area, or of the United Kingdom, where MMO functions are exercisable;

"MMO functions" means functions exercisable by or on behalf of the MMO.

3 Performance

(1) The MMO is to use its best endeavours to meet such objectives as the Secretary of State may from time to time set with regard to the quality and effectiveness of its performance.

(2) Subsection (6) of section 24 of the Legislative and Regulatory Reform Act 2006 (c. 51) (consultation) does not apply in relation to an order under subsection (2) of that section specifying regulatory functions of the MMO as functions to which sections 21 and 22 of that Act (principles and code of practice) apply.

CHAPTER 2

TRANSFER OF FUNCTIONS TO THE MMO

Sea Fish (Conservation) Act 1967

4 Licensing of fishing boats

(1) The Secretary of State's function of granting licences under section 4 of the Sea Fish (Conservation) Act 1967 (c. 84) (licensing of fishing boats) is transferred to the MMO.

(2) In subsection (1)(a) of that section (power by order to prohibit fishing unless authorised by a licence granted by one of the Ministers) the reference to one of the Ministers is to be read as including a reference to the MMO instead of a reference to the Secretary of State.

(3) In the following provisions of that section —

    (a) subsection (6) (conditions of licence),

    (b) subsection (7) (powers to require information),

    (c) subsection (9) (power to vary, revoke or suspend a licence),

    (d) subsection (10) (power to make a refund on variation, revocation or suspension),

2442

Marine and Coastal Access Act 2009 (c. 23)
Part 1 — The Marine Management Organisation
Chapter 2 — Transfer of functions to the MMO

any reference to the Minister granting a licence, or to the Minister who granted a licence, is to be read, in the case of licences granted or treated as granted by the Secretary of State or the MMO, as a reference to the MMO.

(4) In the application of subsection (8) of that section (power to issue limited number of licences) in relation to the licensing powers of the MMO under that section, the reference to the Ministers is to be read as a reference to the MMO.

(5) In any orders made under that section, any reference which includes a reference to the Secretary of State is to be read, as respects any area where the MMO exercises functions under or by virtue of that section, as including instead a reference to the MMO.

(6) After subsection (11) of that section insert—

"(11A) As respects any function under this section, other than a function of making an order,—

    (a) the Marine Management Organisation may make arrangements for the function to be exercised on its behalf by the Scottish Ministers, and

    (b) the Scottish Ministers may make arrangements for the function to be exercised on their behalf by the Marine Management Organisation.

An arrangement under this subsection does not affect a person's responsibility for the exercise of the function.

(11B) A person exercising a function on behalf of another by virtue of subsection (11A) above may charge that other such fees as the person considers reasonable in respect of the cost of doing so.".

(7) The grant, variation, revocation or suspension of a licence under that section by or on behalf of the Secretary of State before the coming into force of this section has effect as from the coming into force of this section as the grant, variation, revocation or suspension of the licence by the MMO.

(8) Where a decision to grant, vary, revoke or suspend a licence under that section—

    (a) has been taken by or on behalf of the Secretary of State before the coming into force of this section, but

    (b) has not been notified in accordance with regulations under section 4B of the Sea Fish (Conservation) Act 1967 (c. 84),

the decision has effect as from the coming into force of this section as a decision taken by the MMO.

(9) Where, before the coming into force of this section, an application for a licence under section 4 of that Act, or for the variation of such a licence,—

    (a) has been made to the Secretary of State or a person acting on behalf of the Secretary of State, but

    (b) has not been determined or withdrawn,

the application is to be treated as from the coming into force of this section as an application made to the MMO.

5 Restrictions on time spent at sea: appeals

In section 4AA(5) of the Sea Fish (Conservation) Act 1967 (duty to vary licence to give effect to determination of tribunal on appeal) the reference to the

Marine and Coastal Access Act 2009 (c. 23)
Part 1 — The Marine Management Organisation
Chapter 2 — Transfer of functions to the MMO

2443

Minister who granted the licence is to be read, in the case of licences granted or treated as granted by the Secretary of State or the MMO, as a reference to the MMO.

6 Trans-shipment licences for vessels

(1) The Secretary of State's function of granting licences under section 4A of the Sea Fish (Conservation) Act 1967 (c. 84) (licences for the receiving by a vessel of fish trans-shipped from another vessel) is transferred to the MMO.

(2) In subsection (1) of that section (power by order to prohibit trans-shipping of fish unless authorised by a licence granted by one of the Ministers) the reference to one of the Ministers is to be read as including a reference to the MMO instead of a reference to the Secretary of State.

(3) In the following provisions of that section —
   (a) subsection (6) (conditions of licence),
   (b) subsection (7) (powers to require information),
   (c) subsection (10) (power to vary, revoke or suspend a licence),
   (d) subsection (11) (power to make a refund on variation, revocation or suspension),
   any reference to the Minister granting a licence, or to the Minister who granted a licence, is to be read, in the case of licences granted or treated as granted by the Secretary of State or the MMO, as a reference to the MMO.

(4) In the application of subsection (9) of that section (power to issue limited number of licences) in relation to the licensing powers of the MMO under that section, the reference to the Ministers is to be read as a reference to the MMO.

(5) In any orders made under that section, any reference which includes a reference to the Secretary of State is to be read, as respects any area where the MMO exercises functions under or by virtue of that section, as including instead a reference to the MMO.

(6) The grant, variation, revocation or suspension of a licence under that section by or on behalf of the Secretary of State before the coming into force of this section has effect as from the coming into force of this section as the grant, variation, revocation or suspension of the licence by the MMO.

(7) Where a decision to grant, vary, revoke or suspend a licence under that section —
   (a) has been taken by or on behalf of the Secretary of State before the coming into force of this section, but
   (b) has not been notified in accordance with regulations under section 4B of the Sea Fish (Conservation) Act 1967,
   the decision has effect as from the coming into force of this section as a decision taken by the MMO.

(8) Where, before the coming into force of this section, an application for a licence under section 4A of that Act, or for the variation of such a licence, —
   (a) has been made to the Secretary of State or a person acting on behalf of the Secretary of State, but
   (b) has not been determined or withdrawn,
   the application is to be treated as from the coming into force of this section as an application made to the MMO.

2444

Marine and Coastal Access Act 2009 (c. 23)
Part 1 – The Marine Management Organisation
Chapter 2 – Transfer of functions to the MMO

(9)   The heading to the section is to be "Licensing of vessels receiving trans-shipped fish".

7   Regulations supplementary to sections 4 and 4A

In any regulations made under section 4B of the Sea Fish (Conservation) Act 1967 (c. 84) any reference to the Secretary of State, or which includes a reference to the Secretary of State, is to be read, in relation to the exercise by the MMO of functions under or by virtue of section 4 or 4A of that Act (licensing of fishing boats and trans-shipment licences for vessels), as a reference to the MMO or, as the case may be, as including instead a reference to the MMO.

8   Exemptions for operations for scientific and other purposes

(1)   The functions of the Secretary of State under subsections (1) to (4) of section 9 of the Sea Fish (Conservation) Act 1967 (exemption of certain things done under the authority of one of the Ministers) are transferred to the MMO.

(2)   In that section, after subsection (6) insert—

"(6A)   The Secretary of State may make regulations with respect to applications to the Marine Management Organisation for authority under this section.

(6B)   The provision that may be made in any such regulations includes provision as to—
    (a)   the manner in which, and time before which, any such application is to be made, and
    (b)   the charging of a reasonable fee by the Marine Management Organisation for dealing with an application.

(6C)   The power to make regulations under this section shall be exercisable by statutory instrument.

(6D)   A statutory instrument containing regulations under this section shall be subject to annulment in pursuance of a resolution of either House of Parliament.".

(3)   Any authority granted or treated as granted by the Secretary of State under that section before the coming into force of this section is to have effect as from the coming into force of this section as an authority granted by the MMO.

Nature conservation

9   Licences to kill or take seals

(1)   The Secretary of State's functions of granting and revoking licences under section 10 of the Conservation of Seals Act 1970 (c. 30) (power to grant licences) are transferred to the MMO.

(2)   Any licences—
    (a)   granted by the Secretary of State under that section before the coming into force of this section, and
    (b)   having effect in relation to the whole or any part of England or the English inshore region,

Marine and Coastal Access Act 2009 (c. 23)   2445
Part 1 – The Marine Management Organisation
Chapter 2 – Transfer of functions to the MMO

are to have effect as from the coming into force of this section as licences granted by the MMO.

(3) Any application for a licence under that section in relation to the whole or any part of England or the English inshore region which was made, but not determined or withdrawn, before the coming into force of this section is to be treated as an application made to the MMO after the coming into force of this section.

10 Wildlife and Countryside Act 1981

(1) Section 16 of the Wildlife and Countryside Act 1981 (c. 69) (power to grant licences) is amended as follows.

(2) After subsection (8) insert—

"(8A) In this section, in the case of a licence under any of subsections (1) to (4), so far as relating to the restricted English inshore region (see subsection (12)), "the appropriate authority" means the Marine Management Organisation.".

(3) In subsection (9) (meaning of "the appropriate authority") at the beginning insert "Except as provided by subsection (8A),".

(4) At the end of the section insert—

"(12) In this section—
(a) "the restricted English inshore region" means so much of the English inshore region as lies to seaward of mean low water mark;
(b) "the English inshore region" has the meaning given by section 322 of the Marine and Coastal Access Act 2009.".

(5) To the extent that an application for a licence under section 16 of the Wildlife and Countryside Act 1981 which was made, but not determined or withdrawn, before the coming into force of this section relates to the restricted English inshore region, the application is to be treated as an application made to the MMO after the coming into force of this section.

11 Sea Fisheries (Wildlife Conservation) Act 1992

In section 1(1) of the Sea Fisheries (Wildlife Conservation) Act 1992 (c. 36) (conservation in the exercise of sea fisheries functions) after "the Minister or Ministers" insert "or the Marine Management Organisation".

Generating and renewable energy installations

12 Certain consents under section 36 of the Electricity Act 1989

(1) The electricity consent functions of the Secretary of State are transferred to the MMO.

(2) The electricity consent functions are functions under any of the following sections of the Electricity Act—
(a) section 36(1), (5) and (7) (giving consent for construction etc of generating stations, and prosecuting breaches of that requirement),

2446

Marine and Coastal Access Act 2009 (c. 23)
Part 1 — The Marine Management Organisation
Chapter 2 — Transfer of functions to the MMO

    (b)   section 36A (making declarations extinguishing etc public rights of navigation), and

    (c)   section 36B (duties in relation to navigation),

so far as relating to any generating station that meets the requirements of subsections (3) and (4).

(3)   The generating station must be in waters which are subject to regulation under section 95 of the Energy Act 2004 (c. 20), other than—

    (a)   any area of Scottish waters, or

    (b)   any area of waters in a Scottish part of a Renewable Energy Zone.

(4)   The generating station must have a capacity such that the construction or extension of the generating station would not be a nationally significant infrastructure project (within the meaning given by sections 14 and 15 of the Planning Act 2008 (c. 29)).

(5)   In accordance with subsection (1), any reference in the following provisions to the Secretary of State is to be read, so far as relating to the exercise of an electricity consent function of the Secretary of State, as a reference to the MMO—

    (a)   Schedule 8 to the Electricity Act (procedure), except paragraphs 1(3), 2(3) and 3(1), and the modifications of paragraph 4 made by paragraph 7A(5)(a)(ii) and (b), of that Schedule;

    (b)   paragraph 1(2) of Schedule 9 to that Act (preservation of amenity);

    (c)   regulations 71 to 74 of the Conservation (Natural Habitats, &c) Regulations 1994 (S.I. 1994/2716) (adaptation of planning and other controls);

    (d)   the Electricity Works (Environmental Impact Assessment) (England and Wales) Regulations 2000 (S.I. 2000/1927).

(6)   Paragraph 1(4) of Schedule 8 to the Electricity Act (payment of sums into Consolidated Fund) does not apply to sums received by the MMO by virtue of this section.

(7)   In consequence of the provision made by this section, insert the subsection set out in subsection (8)—

    (a)   into section 36 of the Electricity Act, after subsection (1B) as subsection (1C), and

    (b)   into each of sections 36A and 36B of that Act, after subsection (1) as subsection (1A).

(8)   The subsection is—

    "( )   This section is subject to section 12 of the Marine and Coastal Access Act 2009 (which transfers certain functions of the Secretary of State to the Marine Management Organisation).".

(9)   In this section "the Electricity Act" means the Electricity Act 1989 (c. 29).

(10)   In this section, the following expressions have the same meaning as in section 95 of the Energy Act 2004—

        "Renewable Energy Zone";

        "Scottish part", in relation to a Renewable Energy Zone;

        "Scottish waters".

Marine and Coastal Access Act 2009 (c. 23)
Part 1 — The Marine Management Organisation
Chapter 2 — Transfer of functions to the MMO

2447

13 Safety zones: functions under section 95 of the Energy Act 2004

(1) The functions of the Secretary of State specified in subsection (2) are transferred to the MMO.

(2) Those functions are any functions of the Secretary of State under section 95 of the Energy Act 2004 (c. 20) (safety zones around renewable energy installations), so far as relating to any renewable energy installation that meets the requirements of subsections (3) and (4).

(3) The renewable energy installation must be in waters subject to regulation under section 95 of the Energy Act 2004, other than—

    (a) any area of Scottish waters, or

    (b) any area of waters in a Scottish part of a Renewable Energy Zone.

(4) The renewable energy installation must have a capacity such that the construction or extension of the installation would not be a nationally significant infrastructure project (within the meaning given by sections 14 and 15 of the Planning Act 2008 (c. 29)).

(5) In accordance with subsection (1), any reference in the following provisions to the Secretary of State is to be read, so far as relating to the exercise of any function falling within subsection (2), as a reference to the MMO—

    (a) section 95 of the Energy Act 2004,

    (b) Schedule 16 to that Act (procedure for declaring safety zones),

but this is subject to the exceptions in subsection (6).

(6) Those exceptions are the following provisions of Schedule 16 to the Energy Act 2004 (which relate to regulations made by the Secretary of State)—

    paragraph 3(2)(b);

    in paragraph 4(1), the words preceding paragraph (a);

    paragraph 4(1)(b);

    paragraph 4(2);

    paragraph 6(2)(b) and (6).

(7) In section 95 of the Energy Act 2004, after subsection (1) insert—

    "(1A) This section is subject to section 13 of the Marine and Coastal Access Act 2009 (which transfers certain functions of the Secretary of State to the Marine Management Organisation).".

(8) In this section, the following expressions have the same meaning as in section 95 of the Energy Act 2004—

    "renewable energy installation";

    "Renewable Energy Zone";

    "Scottish part", in relation to a Renewable Energy Zone;

    "Scottish waters".

2448

Marine and Coastal Access Act 2009 (c. 23)
Part 1 — The Marine Management Organisation
Chapter 3 — Agreements involving the MMO for the exercise of functions

CHAPTER 3

AGREEMENTS INVOLVING THE MMO FOR THE EXERCISE OF FUNCTIONS

Powers to enter into agreements

14   Agreements between the Secretary of State and the MMO

(1)   The Secretary of State may enter into an agreement with the MMO authorising the MMO to perform any marine function of the Secretary of State —

    (a)   either in relation to the UK marine area or in relation to specified parts of that area;

    (b)   subject to paragraph (a), either generally or in specified cases.

    "Specified" means specified in the agreement.

(2)   For the purposes of this Chapter, a "marine function" is any function which relates to, or whose exercise is capable of affecting, the whole or any part of the UK marine area.

(3)   For the purposes of this Chapter, any reference to a marine function of the Secretary of State includes a reference to a marine function exercisable by a person —

    (a)   authorised or appointed by the Secretary of State, or

    (b)   employed in the civil service of the State (but see subsection (4)).

(4)   For the purposes of subsection (3)(b), a person is not to be regarded as employed in the civil service of the State to the extent that the person is any of the following —

    (a)   the holder of an office in the Scottish Administration which is not a ministerial office (within the meaning of section 51 of the Scotland Act 1998 (c. 46));

    (b)   a member of the staff of the Scottish Administration (within the meaning of that section);

    (c)   a member of the staff of the Welsh Assembly Government (within the meaning of section 52 of the Government of Wales Act 2006 (c. 32)).

(5)   An agreement under this section —

    (a)   may be cancelled by the Secretary of State at any time, and

    (b)   does not prevent the Secretary of State from performing a function to which the agreement relates.

(6)   This section is subject to sections 17 and 18 (non-delegable functions and maximum duration of agreement).

15   Agreements between the MMO and eligible bodies

(1)   The MMO may, with the approval of the Secretary of State, enter into an agreement with an eligible body authorising the eligible body to perform any function of the MMO —

    (a)   either in relation to the UK marine area or in relation to specified parts of that area;

    (b)   subject to paragraph (a), either generally or in specified cases.

    "Specified" means specified in the agreement.

Marine and Coastal Access Act 2009 (c. 23)   **2449**
Part 1 — The Marine Management Organisation
Chapter 3 — Agreements involving the MMO for the exercise of functions

(2) For the purposes of this Chapter, any reference to a function of the MMO includes a reference to a function exercisable by a person authorised, appointed or employed by the MMO.

(3) The Secretary of State's approval may be given—
  (a) in relation to a particular agreement or in relation to a description of agreements;
  (b) unconditionally or subject to conditions specified in the approval.

(4) Subject to subsection (6), the Secretary of State—
  (a) must review an agreement under this section no later than the end of the period of 5 years beginning with the date on which the agreement was entered into or was last reviewed by the Secretary of State, and
  (b) if it appears appropriate to do so in the light of the review, may cancel the agreement.

(5) Subject to subsection (6), an agreement under this section may not be varied except—
  (a) by agreement between the MMO and the eligible body, and
  (b) with the approval of the Secretary of State.

(6) An approval given under subsection (1) may provide that subsection (4) or (5) does not apply (or that both of them do not apply).

(7) This section is subject to sections 17 and 18 (non-delegable functions and maximum duration of agreement).

16 Eligible bodies

(1) In this Chapter "eligible body" means any body in the following list—
  (a) the Environment Agency;
  (b) Natural England;
  (c) any inshore fisheries and conservation authority;
  (d) any local fisheries committee constituted by an order made, or having effect as if made, under section 1 of the Sea Fisheries Regulation Act 1966 (c. 38);
  (e) any harbour authority.

(2) The Secretary of State may by order amend subsection (1) so as to—
  (a) add any body or description of body to the list, or
  (b) remove any body or description of body from it.

(3) The Secretary of State may not exercise the power conferred by subsection (2)(a) unless satisfied that at least one of the purposes or functions of the body, or bodies of the description, to be added to the list is, or is related to or connected with, a marine function.

(4) A body to be added to the list need not be a public body.

17 Non-delegable functions

(1) An agreement may not authorise a body to which this section applies to perform a non-delegable function.

(2) The bodies are—

2450

Marine and Coastal Access Act 2009 (c. 23)
Part 1 — The Marine Management Organisation
Chapter 3 — Agreements involving the MMO for the exercise of functions

     (a)   the MMO;

     (b)   an eligible body.

(3)   The non-delegable functions are —

     (a)   any function whose performance by the body would be incompatible with the purposes for which the body was established;

     (b)   any power of a Minister of the Crown to make or terminate appointments, other than appointments of persons for the purpose of enforcing any legislation other than this Act or subordinate legislation made under it;

     (c)   any power of a Minister of the Crown to lay reports or accounts;

     (d)   any power to make subordinate legislation, give directions or guidance or issue codes of practice (or to vary or revoke any of those things);

     (e)   any power to fix fees or charges, other than a power prescribed for the purposes of this section by an order made by the Secretary of State;

     (f)   any function of an accounting officer acting in that capacity;

     (g)   except in relation to an agreement authorising a public body to perform functions —

          (i)   any power to enter, inspect, take samples or seize anything, and

          (ii)   any other power exercisable in connection with suspected offences;

     (h)   any function of the Secretary of State under the Water Industry Act 1991 (c. 56) or under any subordinate legislation made under that Act.

18   Maximum duration of agreement

The maximum period for which an agreement may authorise the MMO or an eligible body to perform a function is 20 years.

Supplementary provisions

19   Particular powers

(1)   The fact that a function is conferred by or under this Act or an Act passed after the passing of this Act does not prevent it from being the subject of an agreement.

(2)   In subsection (3) —

       "A" means the Secretary of State or the MMO;

       "B" means —

     (a)   the MMO, if A is the Secretary of State;

     (b)   an eligible body, if A is the MMO.

(3)   A may, under an agreement, authorise B to perform a function even though, under the enactment or subordinate legislation conferring that function on A, —

     (a)   the function is conferred on A by reference to specified circumstances or cases and the same type of function is conferred on B in different specified circumstances or cases,

     (b)   the function is exercisable by A and B jointly,

     (c)   B is required to be, or may be, consulted about the function (whether generally or in specified circumstances), or

Marine and Coastal Access Act 2009 (c. 23)
Part 1 – The Marine Management Organisation
Chapter 3 – Agreements involving the MMO for the exercise of functions

2451

  (d) B is required to consent to the exercise of the function (whether generally or in specified circumstances).

(4) An agreement may provide—

  (a) for the performance of a function to be subject to the fulfilment of conditions;

  (b) for payments to be made in respect of the performance of the function.

(5) In the following provisions of this section "relevant body" means—

  (a) the MMO;

  (b) any eligible body.

(6) A relevant body which is authorised under an agreement to perform a function—

  (a) is to be treated as having power to do so;

  (b) may, unless (or except to the extent that) the agreement provides for this paragraph not to apply,—

    (i) authorise a committee, sub-committee, member, officer or employee of the body to perform the function on its behalf;

    (ii) form a body corporate and authorise that body to perform the function on its behalf.

(7) Where the eligible body is a harbour authority which is a local authority—

  (a) subsection (6)(a) is subject to section 20(5), and

  (b) section 20 applies in place of subsection (6)(b).

(8) Subject to subsection (6)(b) and section 20, a relevant body which is authorised under an agreement to perform a function may not authorise any other body or person to perform that function.

20 Agreements with certain harbour authorities

(1) This section applies where a harbour authority which is a local authority is authorised under an agreement to perform a function.

(2) Subject to subsections (5) to (7), the function that the local authority is authorised to perform is to be treated as a function of the local authority for the purposes of—

  (a) any power of a local authority to arrange for the discharge of the function jointly with another local authority (but only to the extent that each of the authorities is a harbour authority),

  (b) any power of a local authority to arrange for the discharge of the function by any person mentioned in subsection (3), and

  (c) any power of a person mentioned in subsection (3) to arrange for the discharge of a function by any other person mentioned there.

(3) The persons are any committee, sub-committee, member, officer or employee of the local authority.

(4) In subsection (3)—

  (a) "committee" includes a joint committee of two or more local authorities which are harbour authorities and which include the local authority mentioned in subsection (1);

  (b) "sub-committee" includes a sub-committee of any such joint committee;

2452

Marine and Coastal Access Act 2009 (c. 23)
Part 1 – The Marine Management Organisation
Chapter 3 – Agreements involving the MMO for the exercise of functions

(c)   the reference to a member, officer or employee of the local authority includes a reference to a member, officer or employee of any local authority, or any of the local authorities, with which the local authority may have entered into arrangements for the joint discharge of functions which consist of or include functions which the local authority is authorised under an agreement to perform.

(5)   If the local authority is operating executive arrangements, the function is to be treated as a function of the local authority for the purposes of section 13 of the Local Government Act 2000 (c. 22) (provision for determining which functions of the authority are to be the responsibility of the executive and which are not).

(6)   If, in a case where the local authority is operating executive arrangements, the function is to any extent the responsibility of the executive of the local authority, then to that extent—

(a)   subsection (2) does not apply, but

(b)   the provisions mentioned in subsection (7) have effect.

(7)   The provisions are—

(a)   sections 14 to 16 of the Local Government Act 2000 (discharge of functions in the case of different types of executive arrangements);

(b)   any regulations under section 17 or 18 of that Act (discharge of functions by executive of a type prescribed under section 11(5) of that Act, and discharge of functions by area committees);

(c)   so far as relating to arrangements (including the appointment of joint committees) under section 101(5) of the Local Government Act 1972 (c. 70) which involve another local authority which is a harbour authority, any regulations under section 20 of the Local Government Act 2000 (joint exercise of functions).

(8)   "Executive arrangements" and "executive" have the same meaning as in Part 2 of the Local Government Act 2000.

(9)   An agreement may provide that the provisions of subsection (2) or those mentioned in subsection (7) do not apply (or do not apply to a specified extent).

21   Supplementary provisions with respect to agreements

(1)   An agreement, and any approval given by the Secretary of State under section 15, must be in writing.

(2)   The Secretary of State must arrange for a copy of an agreement to be published in a way that the Secretary of State thinks is suitable for bringing it to the attention of persons likely to be affected by it.

(3)   No power of a Minister of the Crown under any enactment to give directions to a statutory body extends to giving a direction—

(a)   requiring it to enter into an agreement;

(b)   prohibiting it from entering into an agreement;

(c)   requiring it to include, or prohibiting it from including, particular terms in an agreement;

(d)   requiring it to negotiate, or prohibiting it from negotiating, a variation or termination of an agreement.

(4)   Schedule 15 to the Deregulation and Contracting Out Act 1994 (c. 40) (restrictions on disclosure of information) applies in relation to an

Marine and Coastal Access Act 2009 (c. 23)
Part 1 — The Marine Management Organisation
Chapter 3 — Agreements involving the MMO for the exercise of functions

2453

authorisation by the MMO or an eligible body under this Chapter as it applies in relation to an authorisation under section 69 of that Act by an office-holder.

22 Interpretation of this Chapter

(1) In sections 17 to 21 "agreement" means an agreement under section 14 or 15.

(2) In this Chapter —
  "eligible body" has the meaning given by section 16;
  "local authority" means a local authority as defined in section 1(a) of the Local Government Act 2000 (c. 22);
  "marine function" has the meaning given by section 14.

CHAPTER 4

MISCELLANEOUS, GENERAL AND SUPPLEMENTAL PROVISIONS

Applications for development consent

23 MMO's role in relation to applications for development consent

(1) The Planning Act 2008 (c. 29) is amended as set out in subsections (2) to (6).

(2) In section 42 (duty to consult about proposed applications for orders granting development consent) —
  (a) the existing provision is renumbered as subsection (1);
  (b) in that subsection, after paragraph (a) insert —
        "(aa) the Marine Management Organisation, in any case where the proposed development would affect, or would be likely to affect, any of the areas specified in subsection (2),";
  (c) after subsection (1) insert —

    "(2) The areas are —
        (a) waters in or adjacent to England up to the seaward limits of the territorial sea;
        (b) an exclusive economic zone, except any part of an exclusive economic zone in relation to which the Scottish Ministers have functions;
        (c) a Renewable Energy Zone, except any part of a Renewable Energy Zone in relation to which the Scottish Ministers have functions;
        (d) an area designated under section 1(7) of the Continental Shelf Act 1964, except any part of that area which is within a part of an exclusive economic zone or Renewable Energy Zone in relation to which the Scottish Ministers have functions."

(3) In consequence of the amendments made by subsection (2) of this section —
  (a) the heading to section 43 becomes "Local authorities for purposes of section 42(1)(b)", and
  (b) the heading to section 44 becomes "Categories for purposes of section 42(1)(d)".

2454
Marine and Coastal Access Act 2009 (c. 23)
Part 1 — The Marine Management Organisation
Chapter 4 — Miscellaneous, general and supplemental provisions

(4) In section 55 (acceptance of applications), in subsection (5), in the definition of "local authority consultee"—

    (a) for "section 42(b)" substitute "section 42(1)(b)";

    (b) for "section 42(c)" substitute "section 42(1)(c)".

(5) In section 56 (duty to notify persons of accepted applications)—

    (a) in subsection (2), after paragraph (a) insert—

        "(aa) the Marine Management Organisation, in any case where the development for which the application seeks development consent would involve the carrying on of any activity in one or more of the areas specified in subsection (2A),";

    (b) after subsection (2) insert—

        "(2A) The areas are—

        (a) waters in or adjacent to England up to the seaward limits of the territorial sea;

        (b) an exclusive economic zone, except any part of an exclusive economic zone in relation to which the Scottish Ministers have functions;

        (c) a Renewable Energy Zone, except any part of a Renewable Energy Zone in relation to which the Scottish Ministers have functions;

        (d) an area designated under section 1(7) of the Continental Shelf Act 1964, except any part of that area which is within a part of an exclusive economic zone or Renewable Energy Zone in relation to which the Scottish Ministers have functions."

(6) In section 102 (definition of "interested party" etc)—

    (a) in subsection (1), after paragraph (b) insert—

        "(ba) the person is the Marine Management Organisation and the development for which the application seeks development consent would involve the carrying on of any activity in one or more of the areas specified in subsection (1A),";

    (b) after subsection (1) insert—

        "(1A) The areas are—

        (a) waters in or adjacent to England up to the seaward limits of the territorial sea;

        (b) an exclusive economic zone, except any part of an exclusive economic zone in relation to which the Scottish Ministers have functions;

        (c) a Renewable Energy Zone, except any part of a Renewable Energy Zone in relation to which the Scottish Ministers have functions;

        (d) an area designated under section 1(7) of the Continental Shelf Act 1964, except any part of that area which is within a part of an exclusive economic zone or Renewable Energy Zone in relation to which the Scottish Ministers have functions."

(7) The Secretary of State must give guidance to the MMO as to the kind of representations which may be made by the MMO under –

    (a) Chapter 2 of Part 5 of the Planning Act 2008 (c. 29) (pre-application procedure), or

    (b) Part 6 of that Act (deciding applications for orders granting development consent).

General powers and duties

24 Research

(1) The MMO may (whether alone or with other bodies or persons) –

    (a) undertake research into any matter relating to its functions or its general objective, or

    (b) commission or support (by financial means or otherwise) research into any such matter.

(2) The MMO is to make the results of any such research available to any person on request.

(3) Subsection (2) does not require the MMO to make available –

    (a) any information that it could refuse to disclose in response to a request under –

        (i) the Freedom of Information Act 2000 (c. 36), or

        (ii) the Environmental Information Regulations 2004 (S.I. 2004/3391) or any regulations replacing those Regulations;

    (b) any information whose disclosure is prohibited by any enactment.

25 Advice, assistance and training facilities

(1) The MMO must provide the Secretary of State with such advice and assistance as the Secretary of State may request.

(2) The MMO must, at the request of any public body, provide advice to that body on any matter which –

    (a) is within the knowledge or experience of the MMO,

    (b) relates to any of the functions of the MMO or to its general objective, and

    (c) affects the performance by the public body of its functions.

(3) The MMO may provide advice to any person on any matter relating to any of its functions or its general objective –

    (a) at the request of that person, or

    (b) if the MMO considers it appropriate to do so, on its own initiative.

(4) The MMO may provide any person with –

    (a) assistance, or

    (b) the use of training facilities,

as respects any matter of which the MMO has knowledge or experience.

26 Provision of information etc

(1) The MMO may –

2456

Marine and Coastal Access Act 2009 (c. 23)
Part 1 — The Marine Management Organisation
Chapter 4 — Miscellaneous, general and supplemental provisions

    (a)   publish documents or provide information about any matter relating to any of its functions or its general objective, or

    (b)   assist in the publication of such documents or the provision of such information.

(2)   Nothing in any other enactment imposing a duty or conferring a power on the MMO —

    (a)   to publish, or assist in the publication of, documents of a particular kind, or

    (b)   to provide, or assist in the provision of, information of a particular kind,

is to be read as limiting the power conferred by subsection (1).

27 Power to charge for services

(1)   The MMO may charge such fees in respect of the cost of providing its services as appear to it to be reasonable.

(2)   The fees that may be charged under this section include fees in respect of the cost of services provided by the MMO under any arrangements made between the MMO and the Welsh Ministers or a Northern Ireland department under —

    (a)   section 83 of the Government of Wales Act 2006 (c. 32), or

    (b)   section 28 of the Northern Ireland Act 1998 (c. 47).

(3)   For the purposes of this section, "services" includes, in particular, anything done under —

    (a)   section 2(11) (provision of copy of guidance);

    (b)   section 24(2) (making available the results of research);

    (c)   section 25(2), (3)(a) or (4) (advice, assistance and training facilities);

    (d)   section 26 (information).

28 Provision of information by the MMO to the Secretary of State

(1)   The MMO must provide the Secretary of State with all such information as the Secretary of State may reasonably require with respect to any of the following matters —

    (a)   the carrying out, or proposed carrying out, of the MMO's functions;

    (b)   the MMO's responsibilities generally.

(2)   Information required under this section is to be provided in such form and manner, and be accompanied or supplemented by such explanations, as the Secretary of State may require.

(3)   The information which the MMO may be required to provide under this section includes information which, although it is not in the possession of the MMO or would not otherwise come into the possession of the MMO, is information which it is reasonable to require the MMO to obtain.

(4)   A requirement for the purposes of this section —

    (a)   must be made in writing;

    (b)   may describe the information to be provided in such manner as the Secretary of State considers appropriate;

    (c)   may require the information to be provided on a particular occasion, in particular circumstances or from time to time.

Marine and Coastal Access Act 2009 (c. 23)
Part 1 — The Marine Management Organisation
Chapter 4 — Miscellaneous, general and supplemental provisions

2457

29 Power to bring proceedings

(1) The MMO may institute criminal proceedings in England, Wales or Northern Ireland.

(2) The MMO may institute proceedings for the recovery of any monetary penalty imposed under this Act.

(3) Subsection (2) is without prejudice to any other powers the MMO may have to institute proceedings.

(4) The MMO may designate under this subsection any of its employees who would not (apart from subsection (6)) be entitled to carry on, in relation to magistrates' court proceedings, an activity which constitutes —

    (a) the conduct of litigation, or

    (b) the exercise of a right of audience falling within subsection (5).

(5) The rights of audience are —

    (a) a right of audience in trials of summary offences;

    (b) a right of audience in relation to any application for, or relating to, bail in criminal proceedings relating to a summary offence or an offence triable either way, unless (as matters stand at the time when the application is made) the offence is to be tried on indictment;

    (c) a right of audience in relation to interlocutory applications and sentencing in proceedings relating to a summary offence or an offence triable either way;

    (d) a right of audience in proceedings for the recovery of any sum of money.

(6) Subject to any exceptions specified in the designation, a person designated under subsection (4) is entitled to carry on, in relation to magistrates' court proceedings, any activity specified in the designation which constitutes —

    (a) the conduct of litigation, or

    (b) the exercise of a right of audience falling within subsection (5).

(7) For the purposes of subsection (5), a trial —

    (a) begins with the opening of the prosecution case after the entry of a plea of not guilty, and

    (b) ends with the conviction or acquittal of the accused.

(8) In this section —

"bail in criminal proceedings" —

    (a) in relation to England and Wales, has the same meaning as in section 1 of the Bail Act 1976 (c. 63) (see subsection (1) of that section);

    (b) in relation to Northern Ireland, means bail within the meaning of Part 2 of the Criminal Justice (Northern Ireland) Order 2003 (S.I. 2003/1247 (N.I. 13));

"conduct of litigation" has the meaning given by paragraph 4 of Schedule 2 to the Legal Services Act 2007 (c. 29);

"magistrates' court proceedings" means proceedings before a magistrates' court in England, Wales or Northern Ireland;

"right of audience" has the meaning given by paragraph 3 of Schedule 2 to the Legal Services Act 2007.

2458   *Marine and Coastal Access Act 2009 (c. 23)*
Part 1 — The Marine Management Organisation
Chapter 4 — Miscellaneous, general and supplemental provisions

30   Continuation of certain existing prosecutions

(1)   Any prosecution commenced by the Secretary of State before the appropriate
       commencement date—

    (a)   for an offence in relation to any of the functions transferred to the MMO
        by or under Chapter 2 of this Part, or

    (b)   for an offence under the fisheries legislation (see subsections (2) and
        (3)),

    may be continued on or after that day by the MMO.

(2)   In this section "the fisheries legislation" means—

    (a)   any enactments relating to sea fishing, including any enactment
        relating to fishing for shellfish, salmon or migratory trout (but see
        subsection (3));

    (b)   any enforceable EU restrictions and enforceable EU obligations relating
        to sea fishing.

(3)   "The fisheries legislation" does not include—

    (a)   the Salmon and Freshwater Fisheries Act 1975 (c. 51);

    (b)   the Salmon Act 1986 (c. 62);

    (c)   byelaws made by the Environment Agency under Schedule 25 to the
        Water Resources Act 1991 (c. 57);

    (d)   the Scotland Act 1998 (Border Rivers) Order 1999 (S.I. 1999/1746);

    (e)   byelaws made by an inshore fisheries and conservation authority
        under section 155.

(4)   In this section—

    "the appropriate commencement date" means—

        (a)   in relation to an offence falling within paragraph (a) of
            subsection (1), the date on which the function to which the
            offence relates is transferred to the MMO;

        (b)   in relation to an offence falling within paragraph (b) of that
            subsection, the date on which section 1 comes into force;

    "enforceable EU obligation" means an obligation to which section 2(1) of
    the European Communities Act 1972 (c. 68) applies;

    "enforceable EU restriction" means a restriction to which section 2(1) of
    that Act applies.

31   Incidental powers

(1)   The MMO may do anything which appears to it to be incidental or conducive
       to the carrying out of its functions or the achievement of its general objective.

(2)   In particular, the MMO may—

    (a)   enter into agreements;

    (b)   acquire or dispose of land or other property;

    (c)   subject to the restrictions imposed by sections 33 and 34, borrow
        money;

    (d)   subject to the approval of the Secretary of State, form bodies corporate
        or acquire or dispose of interests in bodies corporate;

    (e)   accept gifts;

    (f)   invest money.

Marine and Coastal Access Act 2009 (c. 23)
Part 1 — The Marine Management Organisation
Chapter 4 — Miscellaneous, general and supplemental provisions

2459

Financial provisions

32 Grants

(1) The Secretary of State may make payments by way of grant to the MMO.

(2) Any payments under subsection (1) are to be —
    (a) of such amounts,
    (b) at such times, and
    (c) subject to such conditions (if any),
as the Secretary of State may determine.

33 Borrowing powers

(1) The MMO may borrow money, but only —
    (a) in accordance with the following provisions of this section, and
    (b) subject to section 34 (limit on borrowing).

(2) The MMO may borrow such sums as it may require for meeting its obligations and carrying out its functions.

(3) The MMO may borrow any such sums —
    (a) from the Secretary of State, by way of loan, or
    (b) from persons other than the Secretary of State, by way of overdraft or otherwise.

(4) The MMO may borrow by virtue of subsection (3)(b) only if the Secretary of State consents.

(5) Any consent under subsection (4) may be given subject to conditions.

34 Limit on borrowing

(1) The aggregate amount outstanding in respect of the principal of sums borrowed by the MMO must not at any time exceed £20 million.

(2) The Secretary of State may by order amend subsection (1) so as to substitute for the sum for the time being there specified such sum as may be specified in the order.

(3) The sum specified in an order under subsection (2) must be a sum —
    (a) greater than £20 million, but
    (b) not greater than £80 million.

(4) A statutory instrument containing an order under subsection (2) may not be made unless a draft of the instrument has been laid before, and approved by a resolution of, the House of Commons.

35 Government loans

(1) The Secretary of State may lend money to the MMO.

(2) A loan under this section may be made subject to such conditions as may be determined by, or in accordance with arrangements made by, the Secretary of State.

2460

Marine and Coastal Access Act 2009 (c. 23)
Part 1 – The Marine Management Organisation
Chapter 4 – Miscellaneous, general and supplemental provisions

(3)   The conditions must include provision with respect to –

    (a)   repayment of the loan at such times, and by such methods, as the Secretary of State may from time to time determine, and

    (b)   payment of interest on the loan at such rates, and at such times, as the Secretary of State may from time to time determine.

(4)   The Treasury may issue to the Secretary of State out of money provided by Parliament such sums as are necessary to enable the Secretary of State to make loans under this section.

(5)   The Secretary of State must, in respect of each financial year, –

    (a)   prepare an account of any sums lent or received in pursuance of this section during the year, and

    (b)   send that account to the Comptroller and Auditor General before the end of September in the following financial year.

(6)   The Comptroller and Auditor General must –

    (a)   examine, certify and report on each account sent under subsection (5), and

    (b)   send a copy of the certified account and of the report to the Secretary of State as soon as possible;

and the Secretary of State must lay before each House of Parliament a copy of the certified account and of the report.

36   Government guarantees

(1)   The Secretary of State may guarantee –

    (a)   the repayment of the principal of any sum borrowed by the MMO from a person other than the Secretary of State;

    (b)   the payment of interest on any such sum;

    (c)   the discharge of any other financial obligation in connection with any such sum.

(2)   A guarantee under subsection (1) may be given in such manner, and on such conditions, as the Secretary of State may think fit.

(3)   If a guarantee is given under subsection (1), the Secretary of State must lay a statement of the guarantee before each House of Parliament.

(4)   Where any sum is paid out for fulfilling a guarantee under this section, the Secretary of State must, as soon as reasonably practicable after the end of each financial year in the relevant period, lay before each House of Parliament a statement relating to that sum.

(5)   For the purposes of subsection (4), the relevant period is the period which –

    (a)   begins with the financial year in which the sum is paid out, and

    (b)   ends with the financial year in which all liability in respect of the principal of the sum and in respect of interest on it is finally discharged.

(6)   If any sums are paid out in fulfilment of a guarantee under this section, the MMO must make to the Secretary of State –

    (a)   payments of such amounts as the Secretary of State may from time to time direct in or towards repayment of the sums so paid out, and

    (b)   payments of interest, at such rate as the Secretary of State may so direct, on what is outstanding for the time being in respect of sums so paid out.

Marine and Coastal Access Act 2009 (c. 23)
Part 1 — The Marine Management Organisation
Chapter 4 — Miscellaneous, general and supplemental provisions

2461

(7) Payments under subsection (6) are to be made—

    (a) at such times, and

    (b) in such manner,

as the Secretary of State may from time to time direct.

Directions and guidance

37 Directions by the Secretary of State

(1) The Secretary of State may give the MMO general or specific directions with respect to the exercise of any of the MMO's functions.

(2) The Secretary of State may also give the MMO such general or specific directions as the Secretary of State considers appropriate for the implementation of any obligations of the United Kingdom under—

    (a) the EU Treaties, or

    (b) any international agreement to which the United Kingdom or the European Union is for the time being a party.

(3) Before giving directions under this section, the Secretary of State must consult the MMO.

(4) Consultation under subsection (3) is not required if the Secretary of State considers that there is an emergency.

(5) The MMO must comply with any directions given to it under this section.

(6) The Secretary of State must publish in the London Gazette notice of any directions given under this section.

(7) The giving of any directions under this section must be publicised in such manner as the Secretary of State considers appropriate for the purpose of bringing the matters to which the directions relate to the attention of persons likely to be affected by them.

(8) Copies of any directions given under this section are to be made available by the MMO to members of the public on payment of such reasonable fee as the MMO may determine.

(9) Until the coming into force of Part 2 of the Schedule to the European Union (Amendment) Act 2008 (c. 7) the reference in subsection (2)(a) to the EU Treaties is to be read as a reference to the Community Treaties.

38 Guidance by the Secretary of State

(1) The Secretary of State may give the MMO guidance with respect to the exercise of any of the MMO's functions.

(2) The MMO must have regard to any guidance given to it under this Act by the Secretary of State.

(3) Before giving any such guidance, the Secretary of State must consult—

    (a) the MMO, and

    (b) such other bodies or persons as the Secretary of State considers appropriate.

2462

Marine and Coastal Access Act 2009 (c. 23)
Part 1 – The Marine Management Organisation
Chapter 4 – Miscellaneous, general and supplemental provisions

Transfer schemes etc

39 Transfer schemes

(1) The Secretary of State may, in connection with the establishment of, or the transfer of any functions to, the MMO, make one or more schemes for the transfer to the MMO of designated property, rights or liabilities of any of the following—

    (a) a Minister of the Crown,

    (b) a government department,

    (c) a statutory body.

(2) The Secretary of State may make one or more schemes for the transfer of designated property, rights or liabilities of the MMO to any of the following—

    (a) a Minister of the Crown,

    (b) a government department,

    (c) a statutory body.

(3) In connection with the efficient management for public purposes of any property, rights or liabilities, the Secretary of State may at any time make one or more schemes for the transfer of—

    (a) designated property, rights or liabilities of the Secretary of State to the MMO, or

    (b) designated property, rights or liabilities of the MMO to the Secretary of State.

(4) On the transfer date for any designated property, rights or liabilities, that property and those rights and liabilities are transferred and vest in accordance with the scheme.

(5) In this section and Schedule 3—

    "designated", in relation to a scheme, means specified or described in, or determined in accordance with, the scheme;

    "statutory body" means any body or person established by or under any enactment;

    "transfer date", in relation to any property, rights or liabilities, means a date specified by a scheme as the date on which the scheme is to have effect in relation to that property or those rights or liabilities.

(6) Schedule 3 makes further provision relating to schemes under this section.

40 Interim arrangements

(1) The Secretary of State may by notice require any of the following—

    (a) a Minister of the Crown,

    (b) a government department,

    (c) a statutory body,

to provide to the MMO on a temporary basis such staff, premises or other facilities as may be specified in the notice.

(2) In this section "statutory body" means any body or person established by or under any enactment.

PART 2

EXCLUSIVE ECONOMIC ZONE, UK MARINE AREA AND WELSH ZONE

41   Exclusive economic zone

(1)   The rights to which this section applies have effect as rights belonging to Her Majesty by virtue of this section.

(2)   This section applies to all rights under Part V of the Convention that are exercisable by the United Kingdom in areas outside the territorial sea.

(3)   Her Majesty may by Order in Council designate an area as an area within which the rights to which this section applies are exercisable (an "exclusive economic zone").

(4)   The Secretary of State may by order designate the whole or any part of the exclusive economic zone as an area in relation to which the Scottish Ministers, the Welsh Ministers or any Northern Ireland department are to have functions.

(5)   In any enactment or instrument passed or made after the coming into force of an Order in Council made under this section, any reference to the United Kingdom's exclusive economic zone is to be read as a reference to any area designated in the Order in Council.

(6)   An Order in Council under this section may include incidental, consequential, supplementary or transitional provision or savings.

(7)   In this section "the Convention" means the United Nations Convention on the Law of the Sea (Cmnd 8941) and any modifications of that Convention agreed after the passing of this Act that have entered into force in relation to the United Kingdom.

(8)   Part 1 of Schedule 4 (which contains amendments consequential on this section) has effect.

42   UK marine area

(1)   For the purposes of this Act, the "UK marine area" consists of the following —
   (a)   the area of sea within the seaward limits of the territorial sea adjacent to the United Kingdom,
   (b)   any area of sea within the limits of the exclusive economic zone,
   (c)   the area of sea within the limits of the UK sector of the continental shelf (so far as not falling within the area mentioned in paragraph (b), and see also subsection (2)),
   and includes the bed and subsoil of the sea within those areas.

(2)   The area of sea mentioned in subsection (1)(c) is to be treated as part of the UK marine area for any purpose only to the extent that such treatment for that purpose does not contravene any international obligation binding on the United Kingdom or Her Majesty's government.

(3)   In this section "sea" includes —
   (a)   any area submerged at mean high water spring tide, and
   (b)   the waters of every estuary, river or channel, so far as the tide flows at mean high water spring tide.

(4)   The area of sea referred to in subsection (3)(a) includes waters in any area —

    (a)   which is closed, whether permanently or intermittently, by a lock or other artificial means against the regular action of the tide, but

    (b)   into which seawater is caused or permitted to flow, whether continuously or from time to time, and

    (c)   from which seawater is caused or permitted to flow, whether continuously or from time to time.

(5)   Until the coming into force of the first Order in Council made under section 41 (the exclusive economic zone), the reference in subsection (1)(b) to the exclusive economic zone is to be read as a reference to a renewable energy zone.

43   Welsh zone

(1)   Section 158 of the Government of Wales Act 2006 (c. 32) (interpretation) is amended as follows.

(2)   In subsection (1) after the definition of "Wales" insert ", and

      "Welsh zone" means the sea adjacent to Wales which is —

        (a)   within British fishery limits (that is, the limits set by or under section 1 of the Fishery Limits Act 1976), and

        (b)   specified in an Order in Council under section 58 or an order under subsection (3)."

(3)   For subsection (3) substitute —

    "(3)   The Secretary of State may by order determine, or make provision for determining, for the purposes of the definitions of "Wales" and the "Welsh zone", any boundary between waters which are to be treated as parts of the sea adjacent to Wales, or sea within British fishery limits adjacent to Wales, and those which are not."

(4)   Part 2 of Schedule 4 (which contains amendments consequential on this section) has effect.

(5)   The Secretary of State may by order make such modifications or amendments of —

    (a)   any Act passed before the end of the Session in which this Act is passed, or

    (b)   any instrument made before the end of that Session,

as the Secretary of State considers appropriate in consequence of this section.

PART 3

MARINE PLANNING

CHAPTER 1

MARINE POLICY STATEMENT

44   Marine policy statement

(1)   For the purposes of this Act a "marine policy statement" (an "MPS") is a document—

Marine and Coastal Access Act 2009 (c. 23)
Part 3 – Marine planning
Chapter 1 – Marine policy statement

2465

(a) in which the policy authorities that prepare and adopt it state general policies of theirs (however expressed) for contributing to the achievement of sustainable development in the UK marine area,

(b) which has been prepared and adopted by those authorities in accordance with Schedule 5, and

(c) which states that it has been prepared and adopted for the purposes of this section.

(2) An MPS may also include statements or information relating to policies contained in the MPS.

(3) If to any extent a policy stated in an MPS conflicts with any other statement or information in the MPS, that conflict must be resolved in favour of the policy.

(4) In this Part "policy authority" means any of the following –

(a) the Secretary of State;

(b) the Scottish Ministers;

(c) the Welsh Ministers;

(d) the Department of the Environment in Northern Ireland.

(5) Any reference in this Part to an MPS being adopted by any policy authorities is a reference to the final text of the MPS being adopted by those authorities in accordance with Schedule 5.

45 Preparation and coming into effect of statement

(1) An MPS may only be prepared by –

(a) all the policy authorities, acting jointly,

(b) the Secretary of State and any one or more other policy authorities, acting jointly, or

(c) the Secretary of State.

(2) An MPS must not be prepared by the Secretary of State acting alone under subsection (1)(c) unless the Secretary of State has first invited each of the other policy authorities to participate in the preparation of an MPS.

(3) A later MPS replaces an earlier MPS, whether or not the later MPS is prepared and adopted by the same policy authorities that prepared and adopted the earlier MPS.

(4) An MPS comes into effect when it has been published in accordance with Schedule 5.

46 Review of statement

The policy authorities that prepared and adopted an MPS must review the MPS whenever they consider it appropriate to do so.

47 Amendment of statement

(1) An MPS may be amended from time to time by the policy authorities which prepared and adopted it.

(2) Any amendment of an MPS must be prepared and adopted in accordance with Schedule 5.

2466

Marine and Coastal Access Act 2009 (c. 23)
Part 3 — Marine planning
Chapter 1 — Marine policy statement

(3) Any amendment of an MPS comes into effect when it has been published in accordance with that Schedule.

(4) Any reference in this Part to an amendment of an MPS being adopted by any policy authorities is a reference to the final text of the amendment being adopted by those authorities in accordance with that Schedule.

(5) Any reference in this Act to an MPS includes a reference to an MPS as amended.

48   Withdrawal of, or from, statement

(1) If any of the policy authorities that prepared and adopted an MPS—
   (a)   comes to the conclusion that it desires to withdraw from the MPS, and
   (b)   publishes notice of that conclusion in each of the Gazettes,
   the authority is to be regarded as having withdrawn from the MPS as from the date on which the notice is so published.

(2) Before arranging to publish any such notice, the policy authority must inform each of the other policy authorities that it intends to do so.

(3) If the Secretary of State withdraws from an MPS, the MPS is withdrawn as from the date of the Secretary of State's withdrawal.

(4) If any other policy authority withdraws from an MPS, then, as from the date of the authority's withdrawal, the authority is to be treated for the purposes of this Part as if it were not one of the policy authorities which adopted and published the MPS.

(5) If the Secretary of State withdraws from an MPS, the Secretary of State must take such further steps as the Secretary of State considers appropriate to secure that the withdrawal of the MPS is brought to the attention of interested persons.

(6) If any other policy authority withdraws from an MPS, it must take such further steps as it considers appropriate to secure that its withdrawal from the MPS is brought to the attention of interested persons.

(7) An MPS which is withdrawn by virtue of subsection (3) ceases to have effect as from the date of the withdrawal.

(8) Where a policy authority withdraws from an MPS, or an MPS is withdrawn by virtue of the withdrawal of the Secretary of State, the withdrawal does not affect—
   (a)   the continuing validity or effect of any marine plan for any marine plan area, or
   (b)   until such time as a new MPS governs marine planning for a marine plan area, the construction of any marine plan for that marine plan area.

(9) In this section—
   "the Gazettes" means—
      (a)   the London Gazette,
      (b)   the Edinburgh Gazette, and
      (c)   the Belfast Gazette;
   "interested persons" means—

Marine and Coastal Access Act 2009 (c. 23)   2467
Part 3 — Marine planning
Chapter 1 — Marine policy statement

(a)   any persons appearing to the policy authority to be likely to be interested in, or affected by, the withdrawal of or from the MPS;

(b)   members of the general public.

CHAPTER 2

MARINE PLANS

49   Marine planning regions

(1)   The UK marine area comprises the following marine planning regions—

    (a)   the English inshore region;

    (b)   the English offshore region;

    (c)   the Scottish inshore region;

    (d)   the Scottish offshore region;

    (e)   the Welsh inshore region;

    (f)   the Welsh offshore region;

    (g)   the Northern Ireland inshore region;

    (h)   the Northern Ireland offshore region.

(2)   The definitions of those regions can be found in section 322.

50   Marine plan authorities

(1)   There is to be a marine plan authority for each marine planning region other than—

    (a)   the Scottish inshore region;

    (b)   the Northern Ireland inshore region.

(2)   The marine plan authority for each marine planning region is as follows—

    (a)   for the English inshore region, the Secretary of State;

    (b)   for the English offshore region, the Secretary of State;

    (c)   for the Scottish offshore region, the Scottish Ministers;

    (d)   for the Welsh inshore region, the Welsh Ministers;

    (e)   for the Welsh offshore region, the Welsh Ministers;

    (f)   for the Northern Ireland offshore region, the Department of the Environment in Northern Ireland.

(3)   References to a marine plan authority's region are to be construed accordingly.

51   Marine plans for marine plan areas

(1)   A marine plan authority may prepare a marine plan for an area (a "marine plan area") consisting of the whole or any part of its marine planning region.

(2)   Where an MPS governs marine planning for a marine planning region, the marine plan authority for the region must seek to ensure that every part of the region is within an area for which a marine plan is in effect.

(3)   A "marine plan" is a document which—

    (a)   has been prepared and adopted for a marine plan area by the appropriate marine plan authority in accordance with Schedule 6,

    (b)   states the authority's policies (however expressed) for and in connection with the sustainable development of the area, and

    (c)   states that it is a marine plan prepared and adopted for the purposes of this section.

(4)   For the purposes of this section "the appropriate marine plan authority" in the case of any marine plan area is the marine plan authority in whose region the marine plan area lies.

(5)   A marine plan must identify (by means of a map or otherwise) the marine plan area for which it is a marine plan.

(6)   A marine plan must be in conformity with any MPS which governs marine planning for the marine plan area unless relevant considerations indicate otherwise.

(7)   For the purposes of this Part, an MPS "governs marine planning" for an area if—

    (a)   it has been adopted by the policy authority which is the marine plan authority whose region consists of or includes the area,

    (b)   it has been published in accordance with paragraph 12 of Schedule 5,

    (c)   it has not been replaced or withdrawn, and

    (d)   the policy authority mentioned in paragraph (a) has not withdrawn from it.

As respects paragraphs (c) and (d), see also section 48(8) (effect of withdrawal of, or from, an MPS).

(8)   Unless prepared and adopted by the Secretary of State, a marine plan must state whether it includes provision relating to retained functions (see sections 59 and 60).

(9)   A marine plan may also include statements or information relating to policies contained in the plan.

(10)   If to any extent a policy stated in a marine plan conflicts with any other statement or information in the plan, that conflict must be resolved in favour of the policy.

(11)   A marine plan comes into effect when it has been published by the marine plan authority that prepared and adopted it in accordance with Schedule 6.

52   Amendment of marine plan

(1)   A marine plan may be amended from time to time by the marine plan authority for the marine planning region in which the marine plan area lies.

(2)   The provisions of this Part that relate to the preparation, adoption, publication and coming into effect of a marine plan also apply in relation to amendments of a marine plan.

(3)   Any reference in this Act to a marine plan includes a reference to a marine plan as amended.

53   Withdrawal of marine plan

(1)   A marine plan may be withdrawn at any time, but only in accordance with the following provisions of this section.

(2) In this section —

    (a) subsection (3) has effect where a marine plan authority decides to withdraw a marine plan;

    (b) subsection (4) has effect where the Secretary of State decides to withdraw agreement to a marine plan;

    (c) subsections (5) and (6) make supplementary provision.

(3) If a marine plan authority decides to withdraw a marine plan —

    (a) it is to publish notice of the withdrawal of the plan in each appropriate Gazette, and

    (b) the marine plan is withdrawn as from the date on which the notice is so published.

(4) If at any time the Secretary of State decides to withdraw agreement previously given under paragraph 15 of Schedule 6 to a marine plan —

    (a) the Secretary of State is to give notice of that decision to the marine plan authority,

    (b) within 7 days of receiving that notice, the marine plan authority must publish notice of the withdrawal of the marine plan in each appropriate Gazette, and

    (c) the marine plan is withdrawn as from the date on which the notice is so published.

(5) Where a marine plan is withdrawn under this section, the marine plan authority must take such further steps as it considers appropriate to secure that the withdrawal of the marine plan is brought to the attention of interested persons.

(6) In this section —

    "appropriate Gazette" means —

        (a) the London Gazette, if the marine plan is for a marine plan area in the English inshore region or the Welsh inshore region;

        (b) in any other case, each of the Gazettes;

    "the Gazettes" means —

        (a) the London Gazette;

        (b) the Edinburgh Gazette; and

        (c) the Belfast Gazette;

    "interested persons" means —

        (a) any persons appearing to the marine plan authority to be likely to be interested in, or affected by, the withdrawal of the marine plan, and

        (b) members of the general public.

54   Duty to keep relevant matters under review

(1) A marine plan authority must keep under review the matters which may be expected to affect the exercise of its functions relating to —

    (a) the identification of areas which are to be marine plan areas, and

    (b) the preparation, adoption, review, amendment or withdrawal of marine plans for those areas.

The reference in paragraph (b) to review is a reference to the functions of the marine plan authority under section 61.

(2) The matters include —

    (a) the physical, environmental, social, cultural and economic characteristics of the authority's region and of the living resources which the region supports;

    (b) the purposes for which any part of the region is used;

    (c) the communications, energy and transport systems of the region;

    (d) any other considerations which may be expected to affect those matters.

(3) The matters also include —

    (a) any changes which could reasonably be expected to occur in relation to any such matter;

    (b) the effect that any such changes may have in relation to the sustainable development of the region, its natural resources, or the living resources dependent on the region.

(4) The reference in subsection (2)(a) to the cultural characteristics of the authority's region includes a reference to characteristics of that region which are of a historic or archaeological nature.

CHAPTER 3

DELEGATION OF FUNCTIONS RELATING TO MARINE PLANS

55 Delegation of functions relating to marine plans

(1) A marine plan authority may give directions under this section.

(2) A direction under this section is a direction which —

    (a) designates any of the delegable marine plan functions which would (apart from directions under this section) be exercisable by or in relation to the authority, and

    (b) directs that those functions, instead of being so exercisable, are to be exercisable by or in relation to such public body, acting on behalf of the authority, as is designated in the direction.

(3) An authority which gives a direction under this section may do so only with the consent of the public body.

(4) The public body —

    (a) must comply with the direction, and

    (b) is to be taken to have all the powers necessary to do so.

(5) In this section "delegable marine plan functions" means —

    (a) functions under Chapter 2 of this Part (marine plans), and

    (b) functions under section 61 (monitoring etc of implementation),

other than excepted functions.

(6) The "excepted functions" are the following functions of a marine plan authority —

    (a) deciding under paragraph 15 of Schedule 6 whether to publish a marine plan or any amendment of a marine plan;

    (b) deciding under section 53 whether to withdraw a marine plan.

(7) No direction may be given under this section in respect of any of the following functions of the Secretary of State—

    (a) deciding under paragraph 5 of Schedule 6 whether to give agreement to a statement of public participation;

    (b) deciding under paragraph 7 of that Schedule whether to give agreement to a revised statement of public participation;

    (c) deciding under paragraph 11 of that Schedule whether to give agreement to a consultation draft;

    (d) deciding under paragraph 15 of that Schedule whether to give agreement to a marine plan;

    (e) deciding under section 53 whether to withdraw agreement previously given under that paragraph to a marine plan.

56 Directions under section 55: supplementary provisions

(1) An authority which gives a direction under section 55 must publish the direction in a way calculated to bring the direction to the attention of persons likely to be interested in or affected by it.

(2) For so long as a direction given and published under that section remains in force, the designated functions are exercisable by or in relation to the public body acting on behalf of the authority (and are not exercisable by or in relation to the authority).

(3) Subsection (2) is subject to any provision to the contrary which—

    (a) is made by the direction, or

    (b) is included in a direction under section 57.

(4) A direction under section 55 may include—

    (a) such terms or conditions,

    (b) such obligations or requirements,

    (c) such financial provisions,

as the authority giving the direction may determine.

(5) Directions under section 55 may make different provision for different cases, different areas or different public bodies.

57 Directions to public bodies as regards performance of delegated functions

(1) This section applies where any functions are exercisable by or in relation to a public body by virtue of a direction given under section 55 by an authority.

(2) The authority may from time to time give directions to the public body with respect to the performance of the functions.

(3) Before giving any such directions, the authority must consult the public body.

(4) A public body to which directions are given under this section must comply with the directions.

(5) An authority which gives a direction under this section must publish the direction in a manner likely to bring the direction to the attention of persons likely to be interested in or affected by it.

2472

Marine and Coastal Access Act 2009 (c. 23)
Part 3 – Marine planning
Chapter 4 – Implementation and effect

CHAPTER 4

IMPLEMENTATION AND EFFECT

Decisions affected by an MPS or marine plan

58 Decisions affected by marine policy documents

(1) A public authority must take any authorisation or enforcement decision in accordance with the appropriate marine policy documents, unless relevant considerations indicate otherwise.

(2) If a public authority takes an authorisation or enforcement decision otherwise than in accordance with the appropriate marine policy documents, the public authority must state its reasons.

(3) A public authority must have regard to the appropriate marine policy documents in taking any decision—
   (a) which relates to the exercise of any function capable of affecting the whole or any part of the UK marine area, but
   (b) which is not an authorisation or enforcement decision.

(4) An "authorisation or enforcement decision" is any of the following—
   (a) the determination of any application (whenever made) for authorisation of the doing of any act which affects or might affect the whole or any part of the UK marine area,
   (b) any decision relating to any conditions of such an authorisation,
   (c) any decision about extension, replacement, variation, revocation or withdrawal of any such authorisation or any such conditions (whenever granted or imposed),
   (d) any decision relating to the enforcement of any such authorisation or any such conditions,
   (e) any decision relating to the enforcement of any prohibition or restriction (whenever imposed) on the doing of any act, or of any act of any description, falling within paragraph (a),

but does not include any decision on an application for an order granting development consent under the Planning Act 2008 (c. 29) (in relation to which subsection (3) has effect accordingly).

(5) In section 104(2) of the Planning Act 2008 (matters to which Panel or Council must have regard in deciding application for order granting development consent) after paragraph (a) insert—
   "(aa) the appropriate marine policy documents (if any), determined in accordance with section 59 of the Marine and Coastal Access Act 2009;".

(6) In this section—
   "act" includes omission;
   "appropriate marine policy document" is to be read in accordance with section 59;
   "authorisation" means any approval, confirmation, consent, licence, permission or other authorisation (however described), whether special or general.

Marine and Coastal Access Act 2009 (c. 23)
Part 3 — Marine planning
Chapter 4 — Implementation and effect

2473

59 The appropriate marine policy documents

(1) This section has effect for the purpose of determining what are the appropriate marine policy documents for a public authority taking a decision falling within subsection (1) or (3) of section 58.

(2) For that purpose —

    (a) subsection (3) has effect, subject to subsection (4), for determining whether any marine plan is an appropriate marine policy document, and

    (b) subsection (5) has effect for determining whether an MPS is an appropriate marine policy document.

(3) To the extent that the decision relates to a marine plan area, any marine plan which is in effect for that area is an appropriate marine policy document.

(4) A marine plan for an area in a devolved marine planning region is an appropriate marine policy document in relation to the exercise of retained functions by a public authority only if —

    (a) it contains a statement under section 51(8) that it includes provision relating to retained functions,

    (b) it was adopted with the agreement of the Secretary of State under paragraph 15(2) of Schedule 6, and

    (c) it was prepared and adopted at a time when an MPS was in effect which governed marine planning for the marine planning region.

(5) Any MPS which is in effect is an appropriate marine policy document for each of the following public authorities —

    (a) any Minister of the Crown;

    (b) any government department;

    (c) if a devolved policy authority has adopted the MPS, the devolved policy authority and any primary devolved authority related to it;

    (d) any non-departmental public authority, so far as carrying out functions in relation to the English inshore region or the English offshore region;

    (e) any non-departmental public authority, so far as carrying out retained functions in relation to a devolved marine planning region;

    (f) any non-departmental public authority, so far as carrying out secondary devolved functions in relation to a marine planning region whose marine plan authority is a policy authority which adopted the MPS.

(6) For the purposes of subsection (5)(f) —

    (a) the Scottish Ministers are to be treated as if they were the marine plan authority for the Scottish inshore region, and

    (b) the Department of the Environment in Northern Ireland is to be treated as if it were the marine plan authority for the Northern Ireland inshore region.

(7) In this section —

    "adopted", in relation to an MPS, means adopted and published in accordance with Schedule 5 (but see also section 48(4));

    "Counsel General" means the Counsel General to the Welsh Assembly Government;

    "devolved marine planning region" means any marine planning region other than —

2474

Marine and Coastal Access Act 2009 (c. 23)
Part 3 — Marine planning
Chapter 4 — Implementation and effect

(a)   the English inshore region, and

(b)   the English offshore region;

"devolved policy authority" means—

(a)   the Scottish Ministers;

(b)   the Welsh Ministers;

(c)   the Department of the Environment in Northern Ireland;

"First Minister" has the same meaning as in the Government of Wales Act 2006 (c. 32);

"non-departmental public authority" means any public authority other than—

(a)   a Minister of the Crown or government department;

(b)   the Scottish Ministers;

(c)   the Welsh Ministers, the First Minister or the Counsel General;

(d)   a Northern Ireland Minister or a Northern Ireland department;

"Northern Ireland Minister"—

(a)   has the same meaning as in the Northern Ireland Act 1998 (c. 47), but

(b)   includes a reference to the First Minister and the deputy First Minister, within the meaning of that Act;

"primary devolved authority", in relation to a devolved policy authority, means—

(a)   in the case of the Welsh Ministers, the First Minister or the Counsel General;

(b)   in the case of the Department of the Environment in Northern Ireland, a Northern Ireland Minister or a Northern Ireland department;

"retained functions" is defined for the purposes of this Part in section 60;

"secondary devolved functions" has the same meaning as in section 60.

60   Meaning of "retained functions" etc

(1)   For the purposes of this Part, the functions of a public authority which are "retained functions" as respects any marine planning region are those functions of the public authority which, as respects that region, are not any of the following—

(a)   Scottish Ministerial functions (see subsection (2));

(b)   Welsh Ministerial functions (see subsection (2));

(c)   Northern Ireland government functions (see subsection (2));

(d)   secondary devolved functions (see subsection (3));

(e)   relevant ancillary functions (see subsection (5)).

(2)   In this section—

"Northern Ireland government functions" means—

(a)   any functions exercisable by a Northern Ireland Minister or a Northern Ireland department, other than joint functions and concurrent functions (see subsection (9));

(b)   any concurrent functions, so far as exercised by a Northern Ireland Minister or a Northern Ireland department;

(c)   the function exercised by a Northern Ireland Minister or a Northern Ireland department when exercising a joint function;

Marine and Coastal Access Act 2009 (c. 23)
Part 3 – Marine planning
Chapter 4 – Implementation and effect

2475

"Scottish Ministerial functions" means —

    (a)   any functions exercisable by the Scottish Ministers, other than joint functions and concurrent functions;

    (b)   any concurrent functions, so far as exercised by the Scottish Ministers;

    (c)   the function exercised by the Scottish Ministers when exercising a joint function;

"Welsh Ministerial functions" means —

    (a)   any functions exercisable by the Welsh Ministers, the First Minister or the Counsel General, other than joint functions and concurrent functions;

    (b)   any concurrent functions, so far as exercised by the Welsh Ministers, the First Minister or the Counsel General;

    (c)   the function exercised by the Welsh Ministers, the First Minister or the Counsel General when exercising a joint function.

(3)   "Secondary devolved functions" means —

    (a)   as respects the Scottish inshore region or the Scottish offshore region, any secondary devolved Scottish functions;

    (b)   as respects the Welsh inshore region or the Welsh offshore region, any secondary devolved Welsh functions;

    (c)   as respects the Northern Ireland inshore region or the Northern Ireland offshore region, any secondary devolved Northern Ireland functions.

See subsection (4) for the definition of each of those descriptions of secondary devolved functions.

(4)   In this section —

"secondary devolved Northern Ireland functions" means any of the following —

    (a)   any functions exercisable by a Northern Ireland non-departmental public authority;

    (b)   any functions exercisable by any other non-departmental public authority, so far as relating to transferred or reserved matters (within the meaning of the Northern Ireland Act 1998 (c. 47));

"secondary devolved Scottish functions" means any of the following —

    (a)   any functions exercisable by a Scottish non-departmental public authority;

    (b)   any functions exercisable by any other non-departmental public authority, so far as not relating to reserved matters (within the meaning of the Scotland Act 1998 (c. 46));

"secondary devolved Welsh functions" means any of the following —

    (a)   any functions exercisable by a Welsh non-departmental public authority;

    (b)   any functions conferred or imposed on a non-departmental public authority by or under a Measure or Act of the National Assembly for Wales;

    (c)   any functions exercisable by a non-departmental public authority, so far as relating to matters within the legislative competence of the National Assembly for Wales;

but the definitions in this subsection are subject to subsection (6) (which excludes certain functions in relation to which functions are exercisable by a Minister of the Crown or government department).

2476

Marine and Coastal Access Act 2009 (c. 23)
Part 3 – Marine planning
Chapter 4 – Implementation and effect

(5) "Relevant ancillary functions" means any functions exercisable by a non-departmental public authority in relation to any of the following —

    (a) a Scottish Ministerial function;

    (b) a Welsh Ministerial function;

    (c) a Northern Ireland government function;

    (d) a secondary devolved function;

but this subsection is subject to subsection (6).

(6) Where functions are exercisable by a Minister of the Crown or government department in relation to a function of a non-departmental public authority, the function of the non-departmental public authority is not —

    (a) a secondary devolved Scottish function;

    (b) a secondary devolved Welsh function;

    (c) a secondary devolved Northern Ireland function;

    (d) a relevant ancillary function;

but this subsection is subject to subsection (7).

(7) Functions are not to be regarded as exercisable by a Minister of the Crown or government department in relation to functions of a non-departmental public authority merely because —

    (a) the agreement of a Minister of the Crown or government department is required to the exercise of a function of the non-departmental public authority;

    (b) a Minister of the Crown or government department must be consulted by the non-departmental public authority, or by a primary devolved authority, about the exercise of a function of the non-departmental public authority;

    (c) a Minister of the Crown or government department may exercise functions falling within subsection (8) in relation to functions of the non-departmental public authority.

(8) The functions mentioned in subsection (7)(c) are —

    (a) functions under section 2(2) of the European Communities Act 1972 (c. 68);

    (b) functions by virtue of section 57(1) of the Scotland Act 1998 (c. 46) (Community obligations) or under section 58 of that Act (international obligations);

    (c) functions under section 26 or 27 of the Northern Ireland Act 1998 (c. 47) (international obligations and quotas for international obligations);

    (d) functions by virtue of section 80(3) of, or paragraph 5 of Schedule 3 to, the Government of Wales Act 2006 (c. 32) (Community obligations) or under section 82 of that Act (international obligations etc);

    (e) functions under section 152 of that Act (intervention in case of functions relating to water etc).

(9) In this section —

    "concurrent function" means a function exercisable concurrently with a Minister of the Crown or government department;

    "Counsel General" means the Counsel General to the Welsh Assembly Government;

    "devolved policy authority" means —

        (a) the Scottish Ministers;

        (b) the Welsh Ministers;

Marine and Coastal Access Act 2009 (c. 23)
2477
Part 3 – Marine planning
Chapter 4 – Implementation and effect

(c)   the Department of the Environment in Northern Ireland;

"First Minister" has the same meaning as in the Government of Wales Act 2006 (c. 32);

"joint function" means a function exercisable jointly with a Minister of the Crown or government department;

"non-departmental public authority" has the same meaning as in section 59;

"Northern Ireland Minister" –

   (a)   has the same meaning as in the Northern Ireland Act 1998 (c. 47), but

   (b)   includes a reference to the First Minister and the deputy First Minister, within the meaning of that Act;

"Northern Ireland non-departmental public authority" means any non-departmental public authority so far as exercising functions in relation to which functions are exercisable by a Northern Ireland Minister or a Northern Ireland department;

"primary devolved authority" means any of the following –

   (a)   the Scottish Ministers;

   (b)   the Welsh Ministers, the First Minister or the Counsel General;

   (c)   a Northern Ireland Minister or a Northern Ireland department;

"Scottish non-departmental public authority" means any non-departmental public authority so far as exercising functions in relation to which functions are exercisable by the Scottish Ministers;

"Welsh non-departmental public authority" means any non-departmental public authority so far as exercising functions in relation to which functions are exercisable by the Welsh Ministers, the First Minister or the Counsel General.

Monitoring and reporting

61   Monitoring of, and periodical reporting on, implementation

(1)   This section makes provision for and in connection with imposing the following duties on a marine plan authority –

   (a)   where it has prepared and adopted a marine plan, a duty to keep the matters specified in subsection (3) under review for so long as the marine plan is in effect (see subsections (2) and (3));

   (b)   in any such case, a duty to prepare and publish, and lay a copy of, a report on those matters at intervals of not more than 3 years (see subsections (4) to (9));

   (c)   in any case, a duty to prepare, and lay, at intervals of not more than 6 years ending before 1st January 2030, a report on –

      (i)   any marine plans it has prepared and adopted,

      (ii)   its intentions for their amendment, and

      (iii)   its intentions for the preparation and adoption of any further marine plans,

   (see subsections (10) to (13)).

(2)   For so long as a marine plan is in effect, the marine plan authority must keep under review each of the matters in subsection (3).

(3)   The matters are –

2478

Marine and Coastal Access Act 2009 (c. 23)
Part 3 – Marine planning
Chapter 4 – Implementation and effect

       (a)   the effects of the policies in the marine plan;

       (b)   the effectiveness of those policies in securing that the objectives for which the marine plan was prepared and adopted are met;

       (c)   the progress being made towards securing those objectives;

       (d)   if an MPS governs marine planning for the marine plan authority's region, the progress being made towards securing that the objectives for which the MPS was prepared and adopted are met in that region.

(4)   The marine plan authority must from time to time prepare and publish a report on the matters kept under review pursuant to subsection (2).

(5)   Where the marine plan authority publishes a report under subsection (4), the authority must lay a copy of the report before the appropriate legislature.

(6)   After publishing a report under subsection (4), the marine plan authority must decide whether or not to amend or replace the marine plan.

(7)   The first report under subsection (4) must be published before the expiration of 3 years beginning with the date on which the marine plan was adopted.

(8)   After the publication of the first report under subsection (4), successive reports under that subsection must be published at intervals of no more than 3 years following the date of publication of the previous report.

(9)   Any reference in this section to the replacement of a marine plan is a reference to —

       (a)   preparing and adopting, in accordance with the provisions of this Part, a fresh marine plan (whether or not for the identical marine plan area), and

       (b)   if the marine plan authority has not already done so, withdrawing the marine plan that is to be replaced.

(10)   Each marine plan authority must from time to time prepare and lay before the appropriate legislature a report which —

       (a)   identifies any marine plans which the authority has prepared and adopted;

       (b)   describes any intentions the authority may have for the amendment of any marine plans which it has prepared and adopted;

       (c)   describes any intentions the authority may have for the preparation and adoption of any further marine plans.

(11)   The first report prepared under subsection (10) by each marine plan authority must be laid before the appropriate legislature before the expiration of the period of 6 years beginning with the date of the passing of this Act.

(12)   After a marine plan authority has prepared and laid its first report under subsection (10), it must prepare and lay successive reports under that subsection at intervals of no more than 6 years following the laying of the previous report.

(13)   No report under subsection (10) is required to be laid in a case where the period of 6 years following the laying of the previous report ends on or after 1st January 2030.

(14)   For the purposes of this section, the "appropriate legislature" is —

       (a)   in the case of the Secretary of State, Parliament;

       (b)   in the case of the Scottish Ministers, the Scottish Parliament;

Marine and Coastal Access Act 2009 (c. 23)
Part 3 – Marine planning
Chapter 4 – Implementation and effect

2479

    (c)   in the case of the Welsh Ministers, the National Assembly for Wales;

    (d)   in the case of the Department of the Environment in Northern Ireland, the Northern Ireland Assembly.

CHAPTER 5

MISCELLANEOUS AND GENERAL PROVISIONS

Validity of documents under this Part

62   Validity of marine policy statements and marine plans

(1)   This section applies to—

    (a)   any MPS,

    (b)   any amendment of an MPS,

    (c)   any marine plan,

    (d)   any amendment of a marine plan.

(2)   Anything falling within the paragraphs of subsection (1) is referred to in this section as a "relevant document".

(3)   A relevant document must not be questioned in any legal proceedings, except in so far as is provided by the following provisions of this section.

(4)   A person aggrieved by a relevant document may make an application to the appropriate court on any of the following grounds—

    (a)   that the document is not within the appropriate powers;

    (b)   that a procedural requirement has not been complied with.

(5)   Any such application must be made not later than 6 weeks after the publication of the relevant document.

(6)   In this section—

    "the appropriate court" means—

        (a)   the High Court, if the relevant document is a marine plan, or an amendment of a marine plan, for an area within the English inshore region or the Welsh inshore region;

        (b)   in any other case, any superior court in the United Kingdom;

    "the appropriate powers" means—

        (a)   in the case of an MPS or an amendment of an MPS, the powers conferred by Chapter 1 of this Part;

        (b)   in the case of a marine plan or an amendment of a marine plan, the powers conferred by—

            (i)   Chapter 2 of this Part, or

            (ii)   section 55 (delegation);

    "procedural requirement" means any requirement—

        (a)   under the appropriate powers, or

        (b)   in directions under section 55 or 57,

    which relates to the preparation, adoption or publication of a relevant document;

    "superior court in the United Kingdom" means any of the following—

        (a)   the High Court;

2480

Marine and Coastal Access Act 2009 (c. 23)
Part 3 – Marine planning
Chapter 5 – Miscellaneous and general provisions

(b)   the Court of Session.

63   Powers of the court on an application under section 62

(1)   This section applies in any case where an application under section 62 is made to a court.

(2)   The court may make an interim order suspending the operation of the relevant document—

(a)   wholly or in part,

(b)   generally or as it affects a particular area.

An interim order has effect until the proceedings are finally determined.

(3)   Subsection (4) applies if the court is satisfied as to any of the following—

(a)   that a relevant document is to any extent outside the appropriate powers;

(b)   that the interests of the applicant have been substantially prejudiced by failure to comply with a procedural requirement.

(4)   The court may—

(a)   quash the relevant document;

(b)   remit the relevant document to a body or person with a function relating to its preparation, adoption or publication.

(5)   If the court remits the relevant document under subsection (4)(b), it may give directions as to the action to be taken in relation to the relevant document.

(6)   Directions under subsection (5) may in particular—

(a)   require the relevant document to be treated (generally or for specified purposes) as not having been adopted or published;

(b)   require specified steps in the process that has resulted in the adoption of the relevant document to be treated (generally or for specified purposes) as having been taken or as not having been taken;

(c)   require action to be taken by a body or person with a function relating to the preparation, adoption or publication of the document (whether or not the body or person to whom the document is remitted);

(d)   require action to be taken by one body or person to depend on what action has been taken by another body or person.

(7)   The court's powers under subsections (4) and (5) are exercisable in relation to the whole or any part of the relevant document.

(8)   Expressions used in this section and in section 62 have the same meaning in this section as they have in that section.

Interpretation and Crown application

64   Interpretation and Crown application of this Part

(1)   In this Part—

"adopted" is to be read—

(a)   in the case of an MPS, in accordance with section 44 and paragraph 12 of Schedule 5,

Marine and Coastal Access Act 2009 (c. 23)
Part 3 – Marine planning
Chapter 5 – Miscellaneous and general provisions

2481

(b) in the case of a marine plan, in accordance with section 51 and paragraph 15 of Schedule 6,

and related expressions are to be construed accordingly;

"marine plan" has the meaning given in section 51;

"marine plan area" is to be read in accordance with section 51;

"marine plan authority" is to be read in accordance with section 50;

"marine planning region" is to be read in accordance with section 49;

"policy authority" has the meaning given in section 44;

"retained functions" has the meaning given in section 60.

(2) Any reference in this Part to an MPS governing marine planning for an area is to be construed in accordance with section 51(7).

(3) This Part binds the Crown.

PART 4

MARINE LICENSING

CHAPTER 1

MARINE LICENCES

65 Requirement for licence

(1) No person may –

   (a) carry on a licensable marine activity, or

   (b) cause or permit any other person to carry on such an activity,

   except in accordance with a marine licence granted by the appropriate licensing authority.

(2) Subsection (1) is subject to any provision made by or under sections 74 to 77 (exemptions).

66 Licensable marine activities

(1) For the purposes of this Part, it is a licensable marine activity to do any of the following –

   1. To deposit any substance or object within the UK marine licensing area, either in the sea or on or under the sea bed, from –

      (a) any vehicle, vessel, aircraft or marine structure,

      (b) any container floating in the sea, or

      (c) any structure on land constructed or adapted wholly or mainly for the purpose of depositing solids in the sea.

   2. To deposit any substance or object anywhere in the sea or on or under the sea bed from –

      (a) a British vessel, British aircraft or British marine structure, or

      (b) a container floating in the sea, if the deposit is controlled from a British vessel, British aircraft or British marine structure.

3.   To deposit any substance or object anywhere in the sea or on or under the sea bed from a vehicle, vessel, aircraft, marine structure or floating container which was loaded with the substance or object —

    (a) in any part of the United Kingdom except Scotland, or

    (b) in the UK marine licensing area.

4.   To scuttle any vessel or floating container in the UK marine licensing area.

5.   To scuttle any vessel or floating container anywhere at sea, if the scuttling is controlled from a British vessel, British aircraft or British marine structure.

6.   To scuttle any vessel or floating container anywhere at sea, if the vessel or container has been towed or propelled, for the purpose of that scuttling, —

    (a) from any part of the United Kingdom except Scotland, or

    (b) from the UK marine licensing area, unless the towing or propelling began outside that area.

7.   To construct, alter or improve any works within the UK marine licensing area either —

    (a) in or over the sea, or

    (b) on or under the sea bed.

8.   To use a vehicle, vessel, aircraft, marine structure or floating container to remove any substance or object from the sea bed within the UK marine licensing area.

9.   To carry out any form of dredging within the UK marine licensing area (whether or not involving the removal of any material from the sea or sea bed).

10.   To deposit or use any explosive substance or article within the UK marine licensing area either in the sea or on or under the sea bed.

11.   To incinerate any substance or object on any vehicle, vessel, marine structure or floating container in the UK marine licensing area.

12.   To incinerate any substance or object anywhere at sea on —

    (a) a British vessel or British marine structure, or

    (b) a container floating in the sea, if the incineration is controlled from a British vessel, British aircraft or British marine structure.

13.   To load a vehicle, vessel, aircraft, marine structure or floating container in any part of the United Kingdom except Scotland, or in the UK marine licensing area, with any substance or object for incineration anywhere at sea.

(2) In subsection (1) —

    (a) in item 9, "dredging" includes using any device to move any material (whether or not suspended in water) from one part of the sea or sea bed to another part;

    (b)   in items 12 and 13, "incineration" means the combustion of a substance or object for the purpose of its thermal destruction (and in items 11 and 12 "incinerate" is to be read accordingly).

(3)   The appropriate licensing authority for any area may by order amend subsection (1) so as to add any activity to, or remove any activity from, the list of licensable marine activities as it has effect in that area.

(4)   For the purposes of this Part "the UK marine licensing area" consists of the UK marine area, other than the Scottish inshore region.

67   Applications

(1)   The appropriate licensing authority may require an application for a marine licence—
    (a)   to be made in such form as the authority may determine;
    (b)   to be accompanied by a fee.

(2)   The fee that may be charged under subsection (1)(b) is to be determined by, or in accordance with, regulations made by the appropriate licensing authority.

(3)   A licensing authority may—
    (a)   determine different forms for different descriptions of applications;
    (b)   provide for different fees for different descriptions of applications.

(4)   The appropriate licensing authority may require an applicant—
    (a)   to supply such information,
    (b)   to produce such articles, and
    (c)   to permit such investigations, examinations and tests,
as in the opinion of the authority may be necessary or expedient to enable it to determine the application.

(5)   If the appropriate licensing authority carries out any investigation, examination or test (whether or not by virtue of subsection (4)(c)) which in its opinion is necessary or expedient to enable it to determine an application, the authority may require the applicant to pay a fee towards the reasonable expenses of that investigation, examination or test.

(6)   If an applicant fails to comply with a requirement made by the appropriate licensing authority under this section, the authority may—
    (a)   refuse to proceed with the application, or
    (b)   refuse to proceed with it until the failure is remedied.

68   Notice of applications

(1)   Having received an application for a marine licence, the appropriate licensing authority must—
    (a)   publish notice of the application, or
    (b)   require the applicant to publish notice of it.

(2)   Publication under subsection (1) must be in such manner as the authority thinks is best calculated to bring the application to the attention of any persons likely to be interested in it.

(3)   If the activity in respect of which the application is being made is proposed to be carried on wholly or partly within the area of a local authority in England,

Wales or Northern Ireland, the appropriate licensing authority must give notice of the application, or require the applicant to give notice of the application, to that local authority (whether or not notice has been published under subsection (1)).

(4) The appropriate licensing authority must not proceed with an application unless—

    (a) notice has been published under subsection (1) (but see subsection (7)), and

    (b) notice has been given under subsection (3) to any local authority to which notice of the application is required to be given by virtue of that subsection (but see subsection (8)).

(5) If the appropriate licensing authority —

    (a) publishes notice of an application, in pursuance of subsection (1)(a), or

    (b) gives notice of an application to a local authority, in pursuance of subsection (3),

the licensing authority may require the applicant to pay a fee towards the reasonable expenses of doing so.

(6) If an applicant fails to comply with a requirement made by the authority under subsection (5), the authority may —

    (a) refuse to proceed with the application, or

    (b) refuse to proceed with it until the failure is remedied.

(7) Subsection (1) does not apply in the case of any particular application if —

    (a) the authority considers that notice of the application should not be published, or

    (b) the Secretary of State certifies that in the opinion of the Secretary of State publication of notice of the application would be contrary to the interests of national security.

(8) Subsection (3) does not apply in the case of any particular application and any particular local authority if —

    (a) the appropriate licensing authority considers that notice of the application should not be given to the local authority, or

    (b) the Secretary of State certifies that in the opinion of the Secretary of State it would be contrary to the interests of national security to give notice of the application to the local authority.

(9) In this section "local authority" means—

    (a) in relation to England, a county council, a district council, a London borough council, the Common Council of the City of London or the Council of the Isles of Scilly;

    (b) in relation to Wales, a county council or a county borough council;

    (c) in relation to Northern Ireland, a district council.

69 Determination of applications

(1) In determining an application for a marine licence (including the terms on which it is to be granted and what conditions, if any, are to be attached to it), the appropriate licensing authority must have regard to—

    (a) the need to protect the environment,

    (b) the need to protect human health,

(c) the need to prevent interference with legitimate uses of the sea,

and such other matters as the authority thinks relevant.

(2) In the case of an application for a licence to authorise such activities as are mentioned in item 7 in section 66(1), the appropriate licensing authority must have regard (among other things) to the effects of any use intended to be made of the works in question when constructed, altered or improved.

(3) The appropriate licensing authority must have regard to any representations which it receives from any person having an interest in the outcome of the application.

(4) A licensing authority may –

(a) from time to time consult any person or body it thinks fit as to the general manner in which the licensing authority proposes to exercise its powers in cases involving any matter in which that person or body has particular expertise;

(b) in relation to any particular application, consult any person or body which has particular expertise in any matter arising in relation to that application.

(5) If the appropriate licensing authority consults any person or body under subsection (4)(b), it must give the applicant the opportunity to make representations to the licensing authority about any observations made by the person or body.

(6) A licensing authority may by regulations make further provision as to the procedure to be followed in connection with –

(a) applications to it for marine licences, and

(b) the grant by it of such licences.

(7) The provision that may be made by virtue of subsection (6) includes (in particular) provision as to –

(a) the period within which any function is to be exercised (including when that period is to begin and how it is to be calculated);

(b) notifying the applicant of any licensing determination.

70 Inquiries

(1) The appropriate licensing authority may cause an inquiry to be held in connection with the determination of an application for a marine licence.

(2) Subsection (1) is subject to the following provisions of this section.

(3) Subsections (2) to (5) of section 250 of the Local Government Act 1972 (c. 70) apply to any inquiry which the Secretary of State or the Welsh Ministers may cause to be held under subsection (1) as they apply to inquiries under that section.

(4) Subsections (2) to (8) of section 210 of the Local Government (Scotland) Act 1973 (c. 65) apply to any inquiry which the Scottish Ministers may cause to be held under subsection (1) as they apply to inquiries under that section.

(5) Schedule A1 to the Interpretation Act (Northern Ireland) 1954 (c. 33) applies to any inquiry which the Department of the Environment in Northern Ireland may cause to be held under subsection (1) as it applies to a local inquiry held under an enactment passed or made as mentioned in section 23 of that Act.

(6) Where—

    (a) an inquiry is caused by a licensing authority to be held under subsection (1), and

    (b) in the case of some other matter required or authorised to be the subject of an inquiry ("the other inquiry"), it appears to the relevant authority or authorities that the matters are so far cognate that they should be considered together,

the relevant authority or authorities may direct that the two inquiries be held concurrently or combined as one inquiry.

(7) In subsection (6) "the relevant authority or authorities" means the licensing authority or, where causing the other inquiry to be held is the function of some other person or body, the licensing authority and that other person or body acting jointly.

(8) If, in the case of any particular application, the Secretary of State certifies that it would in the opinion of the Secretary of State be contrary to the interests of national security—

    (a) if an inquiry under subsection (1) were to be held, or

    (b) if any members of the public, or any specified persons, were to be admitted to the inquiry or some specified part of it,

the inquiry is not to be held or, as the case may be, the public is not, or those persons are not, to be admitted to the inquiry or that part of it.

(9) In subsection (8) "specified" means—

    (a) specified in the certificate, or

    (b) of a description specified in the certificate.

71 Licences

(1) The appropriate licensing authority, having considered an application for a marine licence, must—

    (a) grant the licence unconditionally,

    (b) grant the licence subject to such conditions as the authority thinks fit, or

    (c) refuse the application.

(2) The conditions that may be attached to a licence under subsection (1)(b) may relate to—

    (a) the activities authorised by the licence;

    (b) precautions to be taken or works to be carried out (whether before, during or after the carrying out of the authorised activities) in connection with or in consequence of those activities.

(3) Those conditions include, in particular, conditions—

    (a) that no activity authorised by the licence be carried out until the authority or some other specified person has given such further approval of the activity as may be specified;

    (b) as to the provision, maintenance, testing or operation of equipment for measuring or recording specified matters relating to any activity authorised by the licence;

    (c) as to the keeping of records or the making of returns or giving of other information to the authority;

    (d) for the removal, at the end of a specified period, of any object or works to which the licence relates;

(e) for the carrying out, at the end of a specified period, of such works as may be specified for the remediation of the site or of any object or works to which the licence relates;

(f) that any activity authorised by the licence must take place at a specified site, whether or not in the UK marine licensing area.

(4) A licence may provide –

(a) that it is to expire unless the activity which it authorises is begun or completed within a specified period;

(b) that it is to remain in force indefinitely or for a specified period of time (which may be determined by reference to a specified event).

(5) A licence authorising such activities as are mentioned in item 7 in section 66(1) may provide that the conditions attached to it are to bind any other person who for the time being owns, occupies or enjoys any use of the works in question (whether or not the licence is transferred to that other person).

(6) A licensing authority must not grant a licence to carry on any activity which is contrary to international law.

(7) In this section "specified" means specified in the licence in question.

72 Variation, suspension, revocation and transfer

(1) A licensing authority may by notice vary, suspend or revoke a licence granted by it if it appears to the authority that there has been a breach of any of its provisions.

(2) A licensing authority may by notice vary, suspend or revoke a licence granted by it if it appears to the authority that –

(a) in the course of the application for the licence, any person either supplied information to the authority that was false or misleading or failed to supply information, and

(b) if the correct information had been supplied the authority would have, or it is likely that the authority would have, refused the application or granted the licence in different terms.

(3) A licensing authority may by notice vary, suspend or revoke a licence granted by it if it appears to the authority that the licence ought to be varied, suspended or revoked –

(a) because of a change in circumstances relating to the environment or human health;

(b) because of increased scientific knowledge relating to either of those matters;

(c) in the interests of safety of navigation;

(d) for any other reason that appears to the authority to be relevant.

(4) A suspension under subsection (1), (2) or (3) is for such period as the authority specifies in the notice of suspension.

(5) A licensing authority may by further notice extend the period of a suspension.

(6) But a licence may not by virtue of this section be suspended for a period exceeding 18 months.

(7) On an application made by a licensee, the licensing authority which granted the licence –

    (a)   may transfer the licence from the licensee to another person, and

    (b)   if it does so, must vary the licence accordingly.

(8)   A licence may not be transferred except in accordance with subsection (7).

73   Appeals against licensing decisions

(1)   The appropriate licensing authority must by regulations make provision for any person who applies for a marine licence to appeal against a decision under section 71.

(2)   The regulations required by subsection (1) must come into force on the day on which this Part comes into force.

(3)   Regulations under this section may include—

    (a)   provision as to the procedure to be followed with respect to an appeal;

    (b)   provision for or in connection with suspending or varying any condition subject to which the licence was granted, pending determination of the appeal;

    (c)   provision as to the powers of any person to whom the appeal is made;

    (d)   provision as to how any sum payable in pursuance of a decision of that person is to be recoverable.

CHAPTER 2

EXEMPTIONS AND SPECIAL CASES

Exemptions

74   Exemptions specified by order

(1)   The appropriate licensing authority for an area may by order specify, as regards that area, activities—

    (a)   which are not to need a marine licence;

    (b)   which are not to need a marine licence if conditions specified in the order are satisfied.

(2)   The conditions that may be specified in an order under this section include conditions enabling the authority to require a person to obtain the authority's approval before the person does anything for which a licence would be needed but for the order.

(3)   Approval under subsection (2) may be—

    (a)   without conditions;

    (b)   subject to such conditions as the authority considers appropriate.

(4)   In deciding whether to make an order under this section, the appropriate licensing authority must have regard to—

    (a)   the need to protect the environment,

    (b)   the need to protect human health,

    (c)   the need to prevent interference with legitimate uses of the sea,

and such other matters as the authority thinks relevant.

Marine and Coastal Access Act 2009 (c. 23)
Part 4 – Marine licensing
Chapter 2 – Exemptions and special cases

2489

(5) A licensing authority must consult such persons as the authority considers appropriate as to any order the authority contemplates making under this section.

75 Exemptions for certain dredging etc activities

(1) A marine licence is not needed for a dredging or spoil disposal activity if the conditions in subsection (2) are met.

(2) The conditions are—
   (a) that the activity is undertaken by or on behalf of a harbour authority, and
   (b) that the activity is authorised by, and carried out in accordance with, any legislation falling within subsection (3).

(3) The legislation is—
   (a) any local Act,
   (b) any order under section 14 or 16 of the Harbours Act 1964 (c. 40),
   (c) any order under section 1 of the Harbours Act (Northern Ireland) 1970 (c. 1 (N.I.)), or
   (d) section 10(3) of that Act.

(4) In this section—
   "dredging or spoil disposal activity" means—
       (a) any dredging operation, or
       (b) the deposit of any dredged materials that result from an exempt dredging operation;
   "exempt dredging operation" means a dredging operation for which a marine licence is not needed by virtue of this section.

76 Dredging in the Scottish zone

(1) Nothing in this Part applies to anything done, in the exercise of a function falling within subsection (2), in relation to the extraction of minerals by dredging in the Scottish zone.

(2) The functions are—
   (a) any function under Community law (within the meaning given by section 126(9) of the Scotland Act 1998 (c. 46));
   (b) any of Her Majesty's prerogative and other executive functions which is exercisable on behalf of Her Majesty by the Scottish Ministers.

77 Oil and gas activities and carbon dioxide storage

(1) Nothing in this Part applies to any of the following—
   (a) anything done in the course of carrying on an activity for which a licence under section 3 of the Petroleum Act 1998 (c. 17) or section 2 of the Petroleum (Production) Act 1934 (c. 36) (licences to search for and get petroleum) is required;
   (b) anything done for the purpose of constructing or maintaining a pipeline as respects any part of which an authorisation (within the meaning of Part 3 of the Petroleum Act 1998) is in force;

2490

Marine and Coastal Access Act 2009 (c. 23)
Part 4 – Marine licensing
Chapter 2 – Exemptions and special cases

(c)   anything done for the purpose of establishing or maintaining an offshore installation (within the meaning of Part 4 of the Petroleum Act 1998 (c. 17));

(d)   anything done in the course of carrying on an activity for which a licence under section 4 or 18 of the Energy Act 2008 (c. 32) is required (gas unloading, storage and recovery, and carbon dioxide storage).

(2)   For the purposes of subsection (1)(a) or (d), activities are to be regarded as activities for which a licence of the description in question is required if, by virtue of such a licence, they are activities which may be carried on only with the consent of the Secretary of State or another person.

(3)   Subsection (1)(d) does not apply in relation to anything done in the course of carrying on an activity for which a licence under section 4 of the Energy Act 2008 is required in, under or over any area of sea –

(a)   which is within the Welsh inshore region or the Northern Ireland inshore region, or

(b)   which is within both the Scottish offshore region and a Gas Importation and Storage Zone (within the meaning given by section 1 of the Energy Act 2008).

(4)   Subsection (1)(d) does not apply in relation to anything done in, under or over any area of sea within the Welsh inshore region or the Northern Ireland inshore region in the course of carrying on an activity for which a licence under section 18 of the Energy Act 2008 (c. 32) is required.

Special provisions in certain cases

78   Special procedure for applications relating to harbour works

(1)   This section has effect in cases where –

(a)   a person who proposes to carry on an activity must first make an application for a marine licence to carry on that activity (the "marine licence application"), and

(b)   a related application for a harbour order (the "harbour order application") is or has been made by the person, or the harbour order authority has reason to believe that it will be so made.

(2)   A "related application for a harbour order" is an application for an order under section 14 or 16 of the Harbours Act in relation to –

(a)   the activity for which the marine licence is required, or

(b)   other works to be undertaken in connection with that activity.

(3)   In any case where –

(a)   both the marine licence application and the harbour order application have been made,

(b)   the harbour order authority decides (with the agreement of the Welsh Ministers, if they are the marine licence authority and the Secretary of State is the harbour order authority) that the two applications are to be considered together, and

(c)   the harbour order authority has given notice of that decision to the applicant,

the two applications are to be considered together.

(4)   Subsection (5) applies in any case where –

Marine and Coastal Access Act 2009 (c. 23)   2491
Part 4 – Marine licensing
Chapter 2 – Exemptions and special cases

  (a) one of the applications has been received but not the other,

  (b) the harbour order authority decides (with the agreement of the Welsh Ministers, if they are the marine licence authority and the Secretary of State is the harbour order authority) that the two applications are to be considered together, and

  (c) the harbour order authority has given notice of that decision to the applicant.

(5) In any such case —

  (a) the application that has been received is not to be considered until the other application has also been received,

  (b) the two applications are to be considered together, and

  (c) the condition in subsection (3)(b) is to be regarded as satisfied by virtue of subsection (4)(b),

but this is subject to any provision that may be made by virtue of subsection (6)(c) or (d).

(6) The Secretary of State may by order do any of the following —

  (a) make provision falling within subsection (7) for cases where subsection (3) applies;

  (b) make provision falling within subsection (7) for cases where subsection (5) applies;

  (c) make provision falling within subsection (7) or (8) for cases where the harbour order authority (with the agreement of the Welsh Ministers, if they are the marine licence authority and the Secretary of State is the harbour order authority) comes to the conclusion that the marine licence application is not going to be made;

  (d) make provision falling within subsection (7) or (8) for cases where the harbour order authority comes to the conclusion that the harbour order application is not going to be made.

(7) The provision that may be made by virtue of this subsection is —

  (a) provision that such procedural provisions of this Part as are specified in the order are not to apply to the marine licence application;

  (b) provision that such procedural provisions of the Harbours Act as are so specified are to apply to that application instead;

  (c) provision modifying the provisions of the Harbours Act in their application by virtue of paragraph (b).

(8) The provision that may be made by virtue of this subsection is provision modifying —

  (a) such procedural provisions of this Part as are specified in the order, or

  (b) such procedural provisions of the Harbours Act as are specified in the order.

(9) In this section —

  "the harbour order authority" means —

    (a) the Secretary of State, in any case where the harbour order application falls (or would fall) to be determined by the Secretary of State;

    (b) the Welsh Ministers, in any case where the harbour order application falls (or would fall) to be determined by the Welsh Ministers;

  "the Harbours Act" means the Harbours Act 1964 (c. 40);

2492

Marine and Coastal Access Act 2009 (c. 23)
Part 4 – Marine licensing
Chapter 2 – Exemptions and special cases

"the marine licence authority" means—

(a) the Secretary of State, in any case where the marine licence application falls (or would fall) to be made to the Secretary of State;

(b) the Welsh Ministers, in any case where the marine licence application falls (or would fall) to be made to the Welsh Ministers;

"procedural provisions" means any provisions for or in connection with the procedure for determining an application.

79 Special procedure for applications relating to certain electricity works

(1) This section has effect in cases where a person who proposes to carry on an activity must first make both—

(a) an application for a marine licence to carry on that activity (the "marine licence application"), and

(b) a related application for a generating station consent (the "generating station application").

(2) A "related application for a generating station consent" is an application for a consent under section 36 of the Electricity Act (consent for construction etc of generating stations) in relation to—

(a) the activity for which the marine licence is required, or

(b) other works to be undertaken in connection with that activity.

(3) In any case where—

(a) both the marine licence application and the generating station application have been made,

(b) the generating station authority decides (with the agreement of the Welsh Ministers, if they are the marine licence authority and the Secretary of State is the generating station authority) that the two applications are to be considered together, and

(c) the generating station authority has given notice of that decision to the applicant,

the two applications are to be considered together.

(4) Subsection (5) applies in any case where—

(a) one of the applications has been received but not the other,

(b) the generating station authority decides (with the agreement of the Welsh Ministers, if they are the marine licence authority and the Secretary of State is the generating station authority) that the two applications are to be considered together, and

(c) the generating station authority has given notice of that decision to the applicant.

(5) In any such case—

(a) the application that has been received is not to be considered until the other application has also been received,

(b) the two applications are to be considered together, and

(c) the condition in subsection (3)(b) is to be regarded as satisfied by virtue of subsection (4)(b),

but this is subject to any provision that may be made by virtue of subsection (6)(c) or (d).

Marine and Coastal Access Act 2009 (c. 23)
Part 4 — Marine licensing
Chapter 2 — Exemptions and special cases

2493

(6) The Secretary of State may by order do any of the following —

    (a) make provision falling within subsection (7) for cases where subsection (3) applies;

    (b) make provision falling within subsection (7) for cases where subsection (5) applies;

    (c) make provision falling within subsection (7) or (8) for cases where the generating station authority (with the agreement of the Welsh Ministers, if they are the marine licence authority and the Secretary of State is the generating station authority) comes to the conclusion that the marine licence application is not going to be made;

    (d) make provision falling within subsection (7) or (8) for cases where the generating station authority comes to the conclusion that the generating station application is not going to be made.

(7) The provision that may be made by virtue of this subsection is —

    (a) provision that such procedural provisions of this Part as are specified in the order are not to apply to the marine licence application;

    (b) provision that such procedural provisions of the Electricity Act as are so specified are to apply to that application instead;

    (c) provision modifying the provisions of the Electricity Act in their application by virtue of paragraph (b).

(8) The provision that may be made by virtue of this subsection is provision modifying —

    (a) such procedural provisions of this Part as are specified in the order, or

    (b) such procedural provisions of the Electricity Act as are specified in the order.

(9) In this section —

    "the Electricity Act" means the Electricity Act 1989 (c. 29);

    "generating station authority" means —

        (a) the Secretary of State, in any case where the generating station application falls (or would fall) to be determined by the Secretary of State;

        (b) the Scottish Ministers, in any case where the generating station application falls (or would fall) to be determined by the Scottish Ministers;

    "the marine licence authority" means —

        (a) the Secretary of State, in any case where the marine licence application falls (or would fall) to be made to the Secretary of State;

        (b) the Scottish Ministers, in any case where the marine licence application falls (or would fall) to be made to the Scottish Ministers;

        (c) the Welsh Ministers, in any case where the marine licence application falls (or would fall) to be made to the Welsh Ministers;

    "procedural provisions" means any provisions for or in connection with the procedure for determining an application.

2494

Marine and Coastal Access Act 2009 (c. 23)
Part 4 — Marine licensing
Chapter 2 — Exemptions and special cases

80   Electronic communications apparatus

(1)   A licensing authority must not grant a marine licence to carry on any activity which amounts to or involves the exercise of a right conferred by paragraph 11 of the Electronic Communications Code unless it is satisfied that adequate compensation arrangements have been made.

(2)   For the purposes of subsection (1) "adequate compensation arrangements" are adequate arrangements for compensating any persons —
    (a)   who appear to that authority to be owners of interests in the tidal water or lands on, under or over which the right is to be exercised,
    (b)   for any loss or damage sustained by those persons in consequence of the activity being carried on.

(3)   In paragraph 11 of the Electronic Communications Code omit —
    (a)   sub-paragraphs (3) to (10);
    (b)   in sub-paragraph (11), the definition of "remedial works".

(4)   In this section "the Electronic Communications Code" means the code set out in Schedule 2 to the Telecommunications Act 1984 (c. 12).

81   Submarine cables on the continental shelf

(1)   Nothing in this Part applies to anything done in the course of laying or maintaining an offshore stretch of exempt submarine cable.

(2)   Where subsection (1) has effect in relation to part (but not the whole) of an exempt submarine cable —
    (a)   the appropriate licensing authority must grant any application made to it for a marine licence for the carrying on of a licensable marine activity in the course of laying any inshore stretch of the cable, and
    (b)   nothing in this Part applies to anything done in the course of maintaining any inshore stretch of the cable.

(3)   A licensing authority has the same powers to attach conditions to a marine licence required to be granted by virtue of subsection (2) as it has in relation to a marine licence not required to be so granted.

(4)   In the application of this section in relation to any cable —
    "inshore stretch" means any of the cable which is laid, or proposed to be laid, within the seaward limits of the territorial sea;
    "offshore stretch" means any of the cable which is laid, or proposed to be laid, beyond the seaward limits of the territorial sea.

(5)   For the purposes of this section a submarine cable is "exempt" unless it is a cable constructed or used in connection with any of the following —
    (a)   the exploration of the UK sector of the continental shelf;
    (b)   the exploitation of the natural resources of that sector;
    (c)   the operations of artificial islands, installations and structures under the jurisdiction of the United Kingdom;
    (d)   the prevention, reduction or control of pollution from pipelines.

(6)   In this section —
    "natural resources" means —

Marine and Coastal Access Act 2009 (c. 23)
Part 4 – Marine licensing
Chapter 2 – Exemptions and special cases

2495

(a) the mineral and other non-living resources of the sea bed and subsoil,
together with

(b) living organisms belonging to sedentary species;

"living organisms belonging to sedentary species" means organisms which, at the harvestable stage, are either —

(a) immobile on or under the sea bed, or

(b) unable to move except in constant physical contact with the sea bed or the subsoil.

82 Structures in, over or under a main river

(1) Section 109 of the Water Resources Act 1991 (c. 57) (structures in, over or under a main river) is amended as follows.

(2) After subsection (6) insert —

"(7) Subsections (1) to (3) above shall not apply to any work if —

(a) carrying out the work is a licensable marine activity,

(b) the Agency considers that, in view of the terms and conditions that will be included in the marine licence, the provisions of those subsections may be dispensed with, and

(c) the Agency issues a notice to that effect to the applicant for the marine licence.

(8) In subsection (7) above "licensable marine activity" and "marine licence" have the same meaning as in Part 4 of the Marine and Coastal Access Act 2009.".

83 Requirements for Admiralty consent under local legislation

(1) If, in the case of any particular work, —

(a) a marine licence is needed for the carrying out of the work,

(b) Admiralty consent for the carrying out of the work would also be required (apart from this subsection) by virtue of any local legislation, and

(c) the Secretary of State considers that, in view of the need for a marine licence, the requirement for Admiralty consent for the carrying out of the work may be dispensed with, and issues a notice to that effect,

the requirement for Admiralty consent does not apply in relation to that work.

(2) In subsection (1) —

"Admiralty consent" means the consent of the Admiralty, whether alone or jointly with any other government department;

"local legislation" means —

(a) a local Act, or

(b) any such Act and any notice given and published by the Admiralty under section 9 of the Harbours Transfer Act 1862 (c. 69).

2496

Marine and Coastal Access Act 2009 (c. 23)
Part 4 — Marine licensing
Chapter 2 — Exemptions and special cases

84   Byelaws for flood defence and drainage purposes

(1)   Schedule 25 to the Water Resources Act 1991 (c. 57) (byelaw making powers of the Environment Agency) is amended as follows.

(2)   In paragraph 5 (byelaws for flood defence and drainage purposes) after sub-paragraph (3) insert—

      "(3A)   If, in any particular case,—

          (a)   a marine licence is needed for the carrying on of any activity,

          (b)   before that activity may be carried on, the consent of the Agency would also be required (apart from this sub-paragraph) by virtue of any byelaw under this paragraph, and

          (c)   the Agency considers that, in view of the terms and conditions that will be included in the marine licence, the requirement for the consent of the Agency may be dispensed with, and issues a notice to that effect,

      the requirement for the consent of the Agency does not apply in relation to the carrying on of that activity.

      (3B)   In sub-paragraph (3A) "marine licence" has the same meaning as in Part 4 of the Marine and Coastal Access Act 2009.".

CHAPTER 3

ENFORCEMENT

Offences

85   Breach of requirement for, or conditions of, a licence

(1)   A person who—

    (a)   contravenes section 65(1), or

    (b)   fails to comply with any condition of a marine licence,

commits an offence.

(2)   A person who is bound by a condition of a licence by virtue of section 71(5) is not to be taken as having failed to comply with the condition unless the requirements of subsection (3) are satisfied.

(3)   The requirements are that—

    (a)   the appropriate licensing authority has served the person with a notice under this subsection which specifies the condition together with a period (which must be a reasonable period, in all the circumstances of the case) within which the person must comply with the condition, and

    (b)   the person has failed to comply with the condition within that period.

(4)   A person guilty of an offence under subsection (1) is liable—

    (a)   on summary conviction, to a fine not exceeding £50,000;

    (b)   on conviction on indictment, to a fine or to imprisonment for a term not exceeding two years or to both.

86 Action taken in an emergency

(1) It is a defence for a person charged with an offence under section 85(1) in relation to any activity to prove that—

    (a) the activity was carried out for the purpose of securing the safety of a vessel, aircraft or marine structure, or for the purpose of saving life, and

    (b) the person took steps within a reasonable time to inform the appropriate licensing authority of the matters set out in subsection (2).

(2) The matters are—

    (a) the fact that the activity was carried out,

    (b) the locality and circumstances in which it was carried out, and

    (c) any substances or objects concerned.

(3) A person does not have the defence provided by subsection (1) if the court is satisfied that the activity was neither—

    (a) necessary for any purpose mentioned in subsection (1)(a), nor

    (b) a reasonable step to take in the circumstances.

(4) A person does not have the defence provided by subsection (1) if the court is satisfied that—

    (a) the activity was necessary for one of those purposes, but

    (b) the necessity was due to the fault of the person or of some other person acting under the person's direction or control.

87 Electronic communications: emergency works

(1) It is a defence for a person charged with an offence under section 85(1) in relation to any activity to prove that—

    (a) for the purposes of paragraph 23 of the Electronic Communications Code (undertaker's works), the person is the operator or a relevant undertaker, and

    (b) the activity was carried out for the purpose of executing emergency works, within the meaning of that Code.

(2) In this section "the Electronic Communications Code" means the code set out in Schedule 2 to the Telecommunications Act 1984 (c. 12).

88 Activity licensed by another State

(1) It is a defence for a person charged with an offence under section 85(1) in relation to any activity to which subsection (2) applies to prove that subsections (3) and (4) are satisfied in respect of that activity.

(2) This subsection applies to any activity which—

    (a) falls within item 2, 5 or 12 in section 66(1), and

    (b) is carried on outside the UK marine licensing area.

(3) This subsection is satisfied if—

    (a) in the case of an activity falling within item 2 in subsection (1) of section 66, the vessel, aircraft, marine structure or floating container (as the case may be) was loaded in a Convention State, or in the national or territorial waters of a Convention State, with the substances or objects deposited;

      (b)   in the case of an activity falling within item 5 in that subsection, the vessel scuttled was towed or propelled from a Convention State, or from the national or territorial waters of a Convention State, to the place where the scuttling was carried out;

      (c)   in the case of an activity falling within item 12 in that subsection, the vessel or marine structure on which the incineration took place was loaded in a Convention State or the national or territorial waters of a Convention State with the substances or objects incinerated.

(4)   This subsection is satisfied if the activity was carried on —

      (a)   in pursuance of a licence issued by the responsible authority in the Convention State concerned, and

      (b)   in accordance with the provisions of that licence.

(5)   For the purposes of this section —

      "Convention State" means a state which is a party to the London Convention, the London Protocol or the OSPAR Convention;

      "the London Convention" means the Convention on the Prevention of Maritime Pollution by Dumping of Wastes and Other Matter concluded at London in December 1972;

      "the London Protocol" means the Protocol to the London Convention agreed at London in November 1996;

      "the OSPAR Convention" means the Convention for the Protection of the Marine Environment of the North-East Atlantic concluded at Paris in September 1992.

(6)   The references in subsection (5) to the London Convention, the London Protocol and the OSPAR Convention are to them as they have effect from time to time.

(7)   The Secretary of State may by order amend subsections (5) and (6) in such manner as the Secretary of State considers appropriate for the purpose of giving effect to any international agreement which has been ratified by the United Kingdom and which alters the provisions of, or replaces, those Conventions or that Protocol.

89   Information

(1)   A person who, for any of the purposes set out in subsection (2), —

      (a)   makes a statement which is false or misleading in a material particular, knowing the statement to be false or misleading,

      (b)   makes a statement which is false or misleading in a material particular, being reckless as to whether the statement is false or misleading, or

      (c)   intentionally fails to disclose any material particular,

commits an offence.

(2)   The purposes are —

      (a)   the purpose of procuring the issue, variation or transfer of a licence, or

      (b)   the purpose of complying with, or purporting to comply with, any obligation imposed by the provisions of this Part or the provisions of a licence.

(3)   A person guilty of an offence under subsection (1) is liable —

      (a)   on summary conviction, to a fine not exceeding the statutory maximum;

(b) on conviction on indictment, to a fine.

Enforcement notices

90 Compliance notice

(1) If it appears to an enforcement authority that subsections (3) and (4) are satisfied in relation to a person carrying on an activity in its area, it may issue a compliance notice to that person.

(2) A compliance notice is a notice requiring a person to take such steps (falling within subsection (5)(b)) as are specified in it.

(3) This subsection is satisfied if a person holding a marine licence —
    (a) has carried on, or is carrying on, a licensable marine activity under that licence, and
    (b) in carrying on that activity has failed, or is failing, to comply with a condition of the licence.

(4) This subsection is satisfied if the carrying on of the activity has not caused, and is not likely to cause, any of the following —
    (a) serious harm to the environment;
    (b) serious harm to human health;
    (c) serious interference with legitimate uses of the sea.

(5) A compliance notice must —
    (a) state the enforcement authority's grounds for believing that subsections (3) and (4) are satisfied;
    (b) require the person to take such steps as the authority considers appropriate to ensure that the condition in question is complied with;
    (c) state the period before the end of which those steps must be taken.

91 Remediation notice

(1) If it appears to an enforcement authority that each of subsections (3) to (5) is satisfied in relation to a person carrying on an activity in its area, it may issue a remediation notice to that person.

(2) A remediation notice is a notice requiring a person to do either or both of the following —
    (a) to take such steps (falling within subsection (7)(b)) as are specified in it;
    (b) to pay to the enforcement authority such sums (falling within subsection (7)(c)) as are specified in it.

(3) This subsection is satisfied if a person has carried on, or is carrying on, a licensable marine activity.

(4) This subsection is satisfied if the carrying on of the activity has involved, or involves, the commission of an offence under section 85(1).

(5) This subsection is satisfied if the carrying on of the activity has caused, or is causing or is likely to cause, any of the following —
    (a) harm to the environment;
    (b) harm to human health;
    (c) interference with legitimate uses of the sea.

(6) Before issuing a remediation notice, the enforcement authority must consult the person to whom it is proposed to be issued as to the steps or, as the case may be, the sum to be specified in the notice.

(7) A remediation notice —

    (a) must state the enforcement authority's grounds for believing that each of subsections (3) to (5) is satisfied;

    (b) may require the person to take such remedial or compensatory steps as the authority considers appropriate;

    (c) may require the person to pay a sum representing the reasonable expenses of any remedial or compensatory steps taken, or to be taken, by the enforcement authority or the appropriate licensing authority (whether or not under section 106);

    (d) must state the period before the end of which those steps must be taken or, as the case may be, that sum must be paid.

(8) In subsection (7)(b) and (c) "remedial or compensatory steps" means steps taken (or to be taken) for any one or more of the purposes mentioned in subsection (9) (whether or not the steps are to be taken at or near the place where the harm or interference mentioned in subsection (5) has been, is being, or is likely to be, caused or the activity in respect of which the notice is issued is or has been carried on).

(9) The purposes are —

    (a) protecting the environment;

    (b) protecting human health;

    (c) preventing interference with legitimate uses of the sea;

    (d) preventing or minimising, or remedying or mitigating the effects of, the harm or interference mentioned in subsection (5);

    (e) restoring (whether in whole or in part) the condition of any place affected by that harm or interference to the condition, or a condition reasonably similar to the condition, in which the place would have been had the harm or interference not occurred;

    (f) such purposes not falling within the preceding paragraphs as the enforcement authority considers appropriate in all the circumstances of the case.

92 Further provision as to enforcement notices

(1) A compliance notice or remediation notice —

    (a) must be served on any person carrying on, or in control of, the activity to which the notice relates, and

    (b) if a marine licence has been granted in relation to that activity, may also be served on the licensee.

(2) An enforcement authority may by a further notice —

    (a) revoke a compliance notice or remediation notice;

    (b) vary a compliance notice or remediation notice so as to extend the period specified in accordance with section 90(5)(c) or, as the case may be, section 91(7)(d).

(3) A person who fails to comply with —

    (a) a compliance notice, or

    (b) a remediation notice,

commits an offence.

(4) A person guilty of an offence under subsection (3) is liable —

    (a) on summary conviction, to a fine not exceeding £50,000;

    (b) on conviction on indictment, to a fine or to imprisonment for a term not exceeding two years or to both.

(5) A sum specified in a remediation notice by virtue of section 91(7)(c) is recoverable as a civil debt.

Civil sanctions

93 Fixed monetary penalties

(1) The appropriate licensing authority for any area may by order make provision to confer on the appropriate enforcement authority for that area the power by notice to impose on a person in relation to an offence under this Part a fixed monetary penalty.

(2) Provision under this section may only confer such a power in relation to a case where the enforcement authority is satisfied beyond reasonable doubt that the person has committed the offence.

(3) For the purposes of this Part a "fixed monetary penalty" is a requirement to pay to the enforcement authority a penalty of a prescribed amount.

(4) The amount of the fixed monetary penalty that may be imposed in relation to an offence may not exceed the maximum amount of the fine that may be imposed on summary conviction for that offence.

(5) In this section "prescribed" means prescribed in an order made under this section.

94 Fixed monetary penalties: procedure

(1) Provision under section 93 must secure the results in subsection (2).

(2) Those results are that —

    (a) where the enforcement authority proposes to impose a fixed monetary penalty on a person, the authority must serve on that person a notice of what is proposed (a "notice of intent") which complies with subsection (3),

    (b) the notice of intent also offers the person the opportunity to discharge the person's liability for the fixed monetary penalty by payment of a prescribed sum (which must be less than or equal to the amount of the penalty),

    (c) if the person does not so discharge liability —

        (i) the person may make written representations and objections to the enforcement authority in relation to the proposed imposition of the fixed monetary penalty, and

        (ii) the enforcement authority must at the end of the period for making representations and objections decide whether to impose the fixed monetary penalty,

> (d) where the enforcement authority decides to impose the fixed monetary penalty, the notice imposing it ("the final notice") complies with subsection (5), and
>
> (e) the person on whom a fixed monetary penalty is imposed may appeal against the decision to impose it.

(3) To comply with this subsection the notice of intent must include information as to —

> (a) the grounds for the proposal to impose the fixed monetary penalty,
>
> (b) the effect of payment of the sum referred to in subsection (2)(b),
>
> (c) the right to make representations and objections,
>
> (d) the circumstances in which the enforcement authority may not impose the fixed monetary penalty,
>
> (e) the period within which liability to the fixed monetary penalty may be discharged, which must not exceed the period of 28 days beginning with the day on which the notice of intent is received, and
>
> (f) the period within which representations and objections may be made, which must not exceed the period of 28 days beginning with the day on which the notice of intent is received.

(4) Provision pursuant to subsection (2)(c)(ii) —

> (a) must secure that the enforcement authority may not decide to impose a fixed monetary penalty on a person where the authority is satisfied that the person would not, by reason of any defence, be liable to be convicted of the offence in relation to which the penalty is proposed to be imposed, and
>
> (b) may include provision for other circumstances in which the enforcement authority may not decide to impose a fixed monetary penalty.

(5) To comply with this subsection the final notice referred to in subsection (2)(d) must include information as to —

> (a) the grounds for imposing the penalty,
>
> (b) how payment may be made,
>
> (c) the period within which payment must be made,
>
> (d) any early payment discounts or late payment penalties,
>
> (e) rights of appeal, and
>
> (f) the consequences of non-payment.

(6) Provision pursuant to subsection (2)(e) must secure that the grounds on which a person may appeal against a decision of the enforcement authority include the following —

> (a) that the decision was based on an error of fact;
>
> (b) that the decision was wrong in law;
>
> (c) that the decision was unreasonable.

(7) In this section "prescribed" means prescribed in an order made under section 93.

95 Variable monetary penalties

(1) The appropriate licensing authority for any area may by order make provision to confer on the appropriate enforcement authority for that area the power by

notice to impose on a person in relation to an offence under this Part a variable monetary penalty.

(2) Provision under this section may only confer such a power in relation to a case where the enforcement authority is satisfied beyond reasonable doubt that the person has committed the offence.

(3) For the purposes of this Part a "variable monetary penalty" is a penalty of such amount as the enforcement authority may in each case determine.

96 Variable monetary penalties: procedure

(1) Provision under section 95 must secure the results in subsection (2).

(2) Those results are that—
   (a) where the enforcement authority proposes to impose a variable monetary penalty on a person, the enforcement authority must serve on that person a notice (a "notice of intent") which complies with subsection (3),
   (b) that person may make written representations and objections to the enforcement authority in relation to the proposed imposition of the penalty,
   (c) after the end of the period for making such representations and objections, the enforcement authority must decide whether to impose a penalty and, if so, the amount of the penalty,
   (d) where the enforcement authority decides to impose a penalty, the notice imposing it (the "final notice") complies with subsection (6), and
   (e) the person on whom a penalty is imposed may appeal against the decision as to the imposition or amount of the penalty.

(3) To comply with this subsection the notice of intent must include information as to—
   (a) the grounds for the proposal to impose the penalty,
   (b) the right to make representations and objections,
   (c) the circumstances in which the enforcement authority may not impose the penalty, and
   (d) the period within which representations and objections may be made, which may not be less than the period of 28 days beginning with the day on which the notice of intent is received.

(4) Provision pursuant to subsection (2)(c)—
   (a) must secure that the enforcement authority may not decide to impose a penalty on a person where the enforcement authority is satisfied that the person would not, by reason of any defence raised by that person, be liable to be convicted of the offence in relation to which the penalty is proposed to be imposed, and
   (b) may include provision for other circumstances in which the enforcement authority may not decide to impose a penalty.

(5) Provision under subsection (2)(c) must also include provision for—
   (a) the person on whom the notice of intent is served to be able to offer an undertaking as to action to be taken by that person (including the payment of a sum of money) to benefit any person affected by the offence,

(b)   the enforcement authority to be able to accept or reject such an undertaking, and

(c)   the enforcement authority to take any undertaking so accepted into account in its decision.

(6)   To comply with this subsection the final notice referred to in subsection (2)(d) must include information as to—

     (a)   the grounds for imposing the penalty,

     (b)   how payment may be made,

     (c)   the period within which payment must be made,

     (d)   any early payment discounts or late payment penalties,

     (e)   rights of appeal, and

     (f)   the consequences of non-payment.

(7)   Provision pursuant to subsection (2)(e) must secure that the grounds on which a person may appeal against a decision of the enforcement authority include the following—

     (a)   that the decision was based on an error of fact;

     (b)   that the decision was wrong in law;

     (c)   that the amount of the penalty is unreasonable;

     (d)   that the decision was unreasonable for any other reason.

97   Further provision about civil sanctions

Schedule 7 (which makes further provision about civil sanctions) has effect.

CHAPTER 4

DELEGATION

98   Delegation of functions relating to marine licensing

(1)   The appropriate licensing authority for an area may make an order which—

     (a)   designates any of the delegable marine licensing functions which would (apart from any order under this section) be exercisable by or in relation to that authority or an enforcement authority for that area, and

     (b)   provides that those functions, instead of being so exercisable, are to be exercisable by or in relation to such person, acting on behalf of the licensing authority or (as the case may be) the enforcement authority, as is designated in the order.

(2)   The power to make an order under this section includes power to make provision in the order conferring on the person designated ("the delegate"), so far as acting on behalf of an enforcement authority, any power which the appropriate licensing authority may confer on an enforcement authority by an order under section 93 or 95 (fixed or variable monetary penalties).

(3)   An authority which makes an order under this section may do so only with the consent of the delegate.

(4)   The delegate—

     (a)   must comply with the order, and

     (b)   is to be taken to have all the powers necessary to do so.

(5) In this section "delegable marine licensing functions" means —
- (a) functions of a licensing authority under this Part, other than excepted functions;
- (b) functions of an enforcement authority under this Part.

(6) The excepted functions are functions under —
- (a) section 66(3) (altering the list of licensable marine activities);
- (b) section 67(2) (making regulations regarding the fee for an application);
- (c) section 69(6) (making regulations as to the procedure for applications);
- (d) section 73 (making regulations regarding appeals against licensing decisions under section 71);
- (e) section 74(1) and (5) (making orders specifying activities which do not require a marine licence and consulting in relation to such orders);
- (f) sections 93 and 95 (making orders conferring powers to impose civil sanctions);
- (g) this section and section 100;
- (h) section 101(3) (making regulations regarding the register);
- (i) section 108 (making regulations regarding appeals against certain notices).

99 Orders under section 98: supplementary provisions

(1) For so long as an order made under section 98 remains in force, the designated functions are exercisable by or in relation to the delegate acting on behalf of the licensing authority or, as the case may be, the enforcement authority (and are not exercisable by or in relation to the authority).

(2) Subsection (1) is subject to any provision to the contrary which is included in the order.

(3) An order under section 98 may include —
- (a) such terms or conditions,
- (b) such obligations or requirements,
- (c) such financial provisions,

as the authority making the order may determine.

(4) The provision that may be made under subsection (3) includes, in particular, provision (where appropriate) as to —
- (a) the manner in which the delegate is to exercise any of the functions;
- (b) the form and manner in which licence applications must be made to the delegate;
- (c) the persons to whom notice of an application should be published under section 68, and the circumstances in which such notice should not be published;
- (d) matters (in addition to those set out in section 69) to which the delegate must have regard in determining licence applications;
- (e) the circumstances in which the delegate must exercise the power to consult under section 69(4), and the persons who must or may be consulted;
- (f) the form and content of any licence granted;
- (g) appeals from any decision of the delegate (whether to the licensing authority or any other person);

(h) any other provision that may be made by virtue of section 69(6).

(5) An order under section 98 may make different provision for different cases, different areas or different persons.

(6) Where an order has been made under section 98 that a person other than the appropriate licensing authority is to grant licences –

    (a) that other person may (in accordance with subsections (1) to (3) and (7) of section 72) vary, suspend, revoke or transfer a licence granted before the making of the order, and

    (b) any reference in those subsections to a licence granted by a licensing authority includes a reference to a licence granted by that other person.

100 Directions to persons as regards performance of delegated functions

(1) This section applies where any functions are exercisable by or in relation to a person by virtue of an order made under section 98 by a licensing authority.

(2) The authority may from time to time give directions to the person with respect to the performance of the functions.

(3) A person to whom directions are given under this section must comply with the directions.

(4) An authority which gives a direction under this section must publish the direction in a manner likely to bring the direction to the attention of persons likely to be affected by it.

CHAPTER 5

SUPPLEMENTARY

Register

101 Register

(1) Each licensing authority must maintain, as respects activities in relation to which it is the appropriate licensing authority and licences for those activities, a register of licensing information.

(2) The register must contain prescribed particulars of or relating to –

    (a) applications for licences;

    (b) licences granted;

    (c) variations of licences;

    (d) revocations of licences;

    (e) information supplied in connection with any licence in pursuance of any provision of this Part;

    (f) convictions for any offence under this Part;

    (g) any other action taken to enforce any provision of this Part;

    (h) occasions on which any remedial action has been taken;

    (i) such other matters relating to licences or the licensable marine activities as may be prescribed.

(3) The register must be maintained in accordance with regulations made by the appropriate licensing authority.

(4) Each licensing authority must make arrangements—

(a) for its register to be available for inspection at all reasonable times by members of the public free of charge;

(b) for copies of entries in its register to be supplied, on request, to members of the public on payment of a reasonable charge.

(5) Information must not appear in the register if—

(a) the Secretary of State determines that its disclosure in the register would be contrary to the interests of national security, or

(b) the appropriate licensing authority determines that its disclosure in the register would adversely affect the confidentiality of commercial or industrial information where such confidentiality is provided by law to protect a legitimate commercial interest.

(6) The appropriate licensing authority must review a determination to exclude information under subsection (5)(b) every four years.

(7) On a review under subsection (6) the authority must include the information in the register unless, on the application of any person to whom the information relates, the authority determines that it should continue to be excluded.

(8) Where information of any description is excluded from a register by virtue of subsection (5)(b), a statement must be entered in the register indicating the existence of information of that description.

(9) In this section "prescribed" means prescribed in regulations made under this section.

Stop notices and emergency safety notices

102 Notice to stop activity causing serious harm etc

(1) If it appears to an enforcement authority that subsections (3) and (4) are satisfied in relation to a person carrying on an activity in its area, it may issue a stop notice to that person.

(2) A stop notice is a notice prohibiting a person from carrying on an activity specified in the notice.

(3) This subsection is satisfied if a person is carrying on, or is likely to carry on, a licensable marine activity (whether or not in accordance with a marine licence).

(4) This subsection is satisfied if the carrying on of the activity to be specified in the notice—

(a) is causing, or is likely to cause, any of the effects in subsection (5), or

(b) is creating, or is likely to create, an imminent risk of any of those effects.

(5) The effects are—

(a) serious harm to the environment;

(b) serious harm to human health;

(c) serious interference with legitimate uses of the sea.

(6) A stop notice (in addition to specifying the activity to which it relates)—

    (a)   must state the enforcement authority's grounds for believing that subsections (3) and (4) are satisfied;

    (b)   must state the date and time from which the prohibition is to take effect (which may be a time on the date of the notice but must allow a period for compliance which is reasonable in all the circumstances of the case);

    (c)   may require the person to take such steps as the authority considers appropriate to ensure that the cessation of the activity takes place safely.

(7)   Except in a case falling within subsection (9), a stop notice –

    (a)   ceases to have effect at the end of the period of 7 days (or such shorter period as may be specified in the notice) beginning with the date on which the prohibition takes effect, but

    (b)   may be renewed for a period specified in a further notice.

(8)   A stop notice may be renewed more than once under subsection (7)(b), but not so that it has effect for an aggregate period exceeding 35 days.

(9)   If a stop notice relating to a licensable marine activity is issued to a person who does not hold a marine licence authorising that activity, the stop notice may remain in force until such time (if any) as such a licence is granted to that person.

103   Further provision as to stop notices

(1)   Any stop notice issued by an enforcement authority –

    (a)   must be served on any person carrying on, or in control of, the activity to which the notice relates, and

    (b)   if a marine licence has been granted in relation to that activity, may also be served on the licensee.

(2)   An enforcement authority may by a further notice –

    (a)   revoke a stop notice;

    (b)   vary a stop notice so as to substitute a later date for the date specified in accordance with section 102(6)(b).

(3)   A person who fails to comply with a stop notice commits an offence.

(4)   A person guilty of an offence under subsection (3) is liable –

    (a)   on summary conviction, to a fine not exceeding £50,000;

    (b)   on conviction on indictment, to a fine or to imprisonment for a term not exceeding two years or to both.

104   Emergency safety notices

(1)   This section applies if it appears to an enforcement authority that serious interference with legitimate uses of the sea is occurring, or is likely to occur, in its area as a result of –

    (a)   any works for the carrying out of which a marine licence is or was needed, or

    (b)   any substantial and unforeseen change in the state or position of any such works.

(2)   The enforcement authority may issue a notice (an "emergency safety notice") to any person who is in control of the works to which the notice relates.

(3) By issuing an emergency safety notice to a person, the enforcement authority imposes on that person such requirements as are prescribed in the notice with respect to any of the matters specified in subsection (4).

(4) Those matters are —
  (a) the provision of lights, signals or other aids to navigation;
  (b) the stationing of guard ships.

(5) An emergency safety notice (in addition to specifying the requirements which it imposes) —
  (a) must state the enforcement authority's grounds for believing that serious interference with legitimate uses of the sea is occurring or is likely to occur,
  (b) must state the date and time from which the requirements are to take effect (which may be a time on the date of the notice but must allow a period for compliance which is reasonable in all the circumstances of the case), and
  (c) may require the person to take such steps as the authority considers appropriate to ensure that compliance with the requirements takes place safely.

105 Further provision as to emergency safety notices

(1) An emergency safety notice issued by an enforcement authority must be served on each of the following —
  (a) if a marine licence has been granted authorising the carrying out of the works, the licensee,
  (b) if there is in effect a stop notice which relates to the works, any person on whom the stop notice was served.

(2) An enforcement authority may by a further notice —
  (a) revoke an emergency safety notice;
  (b) vary an emergency safety notice so as to substitute a later date for the date specified in accordance with section 104(5)(b).

(3) A person who fails to comply with an emergency safety notice commits an offence.

(4) A person guilty of an offence under subsection (3) is liable —
  (a) on summary conviction, to a fine not exceeding £50,000;
  (b) on conviction on indictment, to a fine or to imprisonment for a term not exceeding two years or to both.

Other powers

106 Power to take remedial action

(1) This section applies if it appears to the appropriate licensing authority for an area that a licensable marine activity has been carried on in its area otherwise than under a licence and in accordance with its conditions.

(2) The authority may carry out any works that appear to it to be necessary or expedient for any one or more of the following purposes —
  (a) protecting the environment;

(b) protecting human health;

(c) preventing interference with legitimate uses of the sea;

(d) preventing or minimising, or remedying or mitigating the effects of, any harm or interference falling within subsection (3);

(e) restoring (whether in whole or in part) the condition of any place affected by any such harm or interference to the condition, or a condition reasonably similar to the condition, in which the place would have been had the harm or interference not occurred.

(3) The harm or interference mentioned in subsection (2)(d) and (e) is any of the following which has been, is being, or is likely to be, caused by the carrying on of the licensable marine activity –

(a) harm to the environment;

(b) harm to human health;

(c) interference with legitimate uses of the sea.

107 Power to test, and charge for testing, certain substances

(1) A licensing authority may, at the request of any person, conduct tests for the purpose of ascertaining the probable effect on the marine environment of using any of the following substances –

(a) any marine chemical treatment substance;

(b) any marine oil treatment substance;

(c) any marine surface fouling cleaner.

(2) In this section –

"marine chemical treatment substance" means any substance used or intended to be used for treating chemicals –

(a) on the surface of the sea or of the sea bed;

(b) in the case of a wash-off substance, on any surface of a marine structure;

"marine oil treatment substance" means any substance used or intended to be used for treating oil on the surface of the sea;

"marine surface fouling cleaner" means any substance used or intended to be used for removing surface fouling matter –

(a) from the surface of the sea or of the sea bed;

(b) in the case of a wash-off substance, from any surface of a marine structure or vessel at times when the structure or vessel is in the sea or on the sea bed;

"surface fouling matter" means any fouling, and includes, in particular, –

(a) any algae;

(b) any surface oil or chemical residue;

"surface oil or chemical residue" means any residual matter on a surface after the removal, or substantial removal, of any oil or chemical (whether by natural processes, or by treatment, or in any other way);

"wash-off substance", in relation to a marine structure or vessel, means any substance which, if used on a surface of the marine structure or vessel, will or might (whether in whole or to a significant extent) –

(a) be removed from that surface, and

(b) be deposited in the sea,

whether by natural processes, or by treatment, or in any other way.

(3) A licensing authority may recover any expenses reasonably incurred in conducting any tests under subsection (1) from any person at whose request those tests were conducted.

Appeals against notices under this Part

108 Appeals against notices

(1) The appropriate licensing authority must by regulations make provision for any person to whom a notice is issued under section 72, 90, 91, 102 or 104 to appeal against that notice.

(2) The regulations required by subsection (1) must come into force on the day on which this Part comes into force.

(3) Regulations under this section may include —
   (a) provision as to the procedure to be followed with respect to an appeal;
   (b) provision suspending the notice pending determination of the appeal;
   (c) provision as to the powers of any person to whom the appeal is made;
   (d) provision as to how any sum payable in pursuance of a decision of that person is to be recoverable.

Offences: supplementary provision

109 General defence of due diligence

(1) In any proceedings for an offence under this Part, it is a defence for the person charged ("the defendant") to prove that the defendant took all reasonable precautions and exercised all due diligence to avoid the commission of the offence.

(2) The defence provided by subsection (1) is to be taken to be established if the defendant —
   (a) acted under an employer's instructions,
   (b) did not know and had no reason to suppose that the acts done constituted a contravention of the provision in question, and
   (c) took all such steps as reasonably could be taken to ensure that no offence would be committed.

(3) The defence provided by subsection (1) is to be taken to be established if the defendant —
   (a) acted in reliance on information supplied by another person,
   (b) did not know and had no reason to suppose that the information was false or misleading, and
   (c) took all such steps as reasonably could be taken to ensure that no offence would be committed.

(4) Subsections (2) and (3) do not affect the generality of subsection (1).

(5) If in any case the defence provided by subsection (1) involves the allegation that the commission of the offence was due to —
   (a) an act or default of another person (other than the giving of instructions to the defendant by an employer), or
   (b) reliance on information supplied by another person,

the defendant is not, without leave of the court, entitled to rely on that defence unless the requirement in subsection (6) is satisfied.

(6)   The requirement is that—

    (a)   at least seven clear days before the hearing, and

    (b)   if the defendant has previously appeared before a court in connection with the alleged offence, within one month of the first such appearance,

the defendant has served on the prosecutor a notice giving such information identifying or assisting in the identification of that other person as was then in the defendant's possession.

110   Offences: jurisdiction

Proceedings for an offence under this Part may be taken, and the offence may for all incidental purposes be treated as having been committed, in any part of the United Kingdom.

Application to the Crown

111   Application to the Crown

(1)   The provisions of this Part bind the Crown.

This is subject to the following provisions of this section.

(2)   No contravention by the Crown of any provision of this Part is to make the Crown criminally liable; but the High Court or, in Scotland, the Court of Session may, on the application of the appropriate licensing authority or any other authority charged with enforcing that provision, declare unlawful any act or omission of the Crown which constitutes such a contravention.

(3)   Despite subsection (2), the provisions of this Part apply to persons in the public service of the Crown as they apply to other persons.

(4)   The Secretary of State may certify that it appears to the Secretary of State that, as respects—

    (a)   any Crown land specified in the certificate, and

    (b)   any powers of entry so specified which are exercisable in relation to that land,

it is necessary or expedient that, in the interests of national security, the powers should not be exercisable in relation to the land.

(5)   If the Secretary of State issues a certificate under subsection (4), the powers specified in the certificate are not exercisable in relation to the land so specified.

(6)   For the purposes of subsection (4) "Crown land" means land held or used by or on behalf of the Crown.

(7)   Nothing in this section is to be taken as in any way affecting Her Majesty in her private capacity or in right of Her Duchy of Lancaster, or the Duke of Cornwall.

Consequential and transitional provision

112   Amendments and transitional provision

(1)   Schedule 8 (which makes minor and consequential amendments) has effect.

(2) Schedule 9 (which makes transitional provision) has effect.

Interpretation

113 The appropriate licensing authority

(1) This section has effect for determining who is the appropriate licensing authority for any area (and any licensable marine activity carried on in that area).

(2) In relation to the Scottish offshore region, the appropriate licensing authority is—

    (a) the Secretary of State, as respects anything done in the course of carrying on an activity falling within subsection (3);

    (b) except as provided by paragraph (a), the Scottish Ministers.

(3) The activities are—

    (a) any activity relating to a matter which is a reserved matter by virtue of Section D2 (oil and gas) of Schedule 5 to the Scotland Act 1998 (c. 46) (but see also section 77 above (this Part not to apply to certain oil and gas etc activities));

    (b) any activity relating to a matter which is a reserved matter by virtue of paragraph 9 in Part 1 of that Schedule (defence);

    (c) any activity falling within the subject matter of Part 6 of the Merchant Shipping Act 1995 (c. 21) (pollution etc).

(4) In relation to Wales and the Welsh inshore region, the appropriate licensing authority is—

    (a) the Secretary of State, as respects anything done in the course of carrying on an activity falling within subsection (5);

    (b) except as provided by paragraph (a), the Welsh Ministers.

(5) The activities are—

    (a) any activity concerning or arising from the exploration for, or production of, petroleum (but see also section 77 (this Part not to apply to certain oil and gas etc activities));

    (b) any defence activity other than an excepted activity.

Subsection (9) supplements this subsection.

(6) In relation to Northern Ireland and the Northern Ireland inshore region, the appropriate licensing authority is—

    (a) the Secretary of State, as respects anything done in the course of carrying on an activity falling within subsection (7);

    (b) except as provided by paragraph (a), the Department of the Environment in Northern Ireland.

(7) The activities are any activities which relate to a matter which is an excepted matter by virtue of paragraph 4 of Schedule 2 to the Northern Ireland Act 1998 (c. 47) (defence of the realm etc).

(8) In relation to any area not mentioned in subsection (2), (4) or (6), the appropriate licensing authority is the Secretary of State.

(9) In subsection (5)—

    "defence activity" means any activity relating to—

(a)   the defence of the realm;

(b)   the naval, military or air forces of the Crown, including reserve forces;

(c)   visiting forces;

(d)   international headquarters and defence organisations;

(e)   trading with the enemy and enemy property;

"excepted activity" means the exercise of civil defence functions by any person otherwise than as a member of—

(a)   any force or organisation referred to in paragraphs (b) to (d) of the definition of "defence activity", or

(b)   any other force or organisation established or maintained for the purposes of, or for purposes connected with, the defence of the realm;

"petroleum" has the same meaning as in Part 3 of the Petroleum Act 1998 (c. 17) (see section 28(1) of that Act).

114   Meaning of "enforcement authority"

(1)   This section has effect for determining who is an enforcement authority for any area.

(2)   For the purposes of sections 90 to 97 and 102 to 105 (and any other provisions of this Part so far as relating to those sections) the appropriate licensing authority for any area is an enforcement authority for that area.

(3)   For the purposes of sections 90, 92 (so far as relating to section 90) and 102 to 105 (and any other provisions of this Part (except sections 91 and 93 to 97) so far as relating to those sections) each of the following persons is also an enforcement authority—

(a)   in relation to the relevant enforcement area (within the meaning of section 236), any marine enforcement officer (as defined in section 235);

(b)   in relation to the relevant enforcement area (within the meaning of section 240), any person appointed under section 240;

(c)   in relation to the relevant enforcement area (within the meaning of section 241), any person appointed under section 241;

(d)   in relation to the Scottish offshore region, any person appointed under section 242.

(4)   A person is an enforcement authority by virtue of subsection (3) (so far as relating to the sections specified in that subsection) only to the extent that the person may exercise powers for the purposes of enforcing this Part.

115   Interpretation of this Part

(1)   In this Part—

"appropriate enforcement authority", in the case of any area and any provision of this Part, means any authority which is an enforcement authority for that area for the purposes of that provision;

"the appropriate licensing authority" has the meaning given by section 113;

"British aircraft" means an aircraft registered in the United Kingdom;

"British marine structure" means a marine structure owned by or leased to an individual residing in, or a body corporate incorporated under the law of, any part of the United Kingdom;

"British vessel" means a vessel —

    (a)   which is registered in the United Kingdom,

    (b)   which falls within section 1(1)(d) of the Merchant Shipping Act 1995 (c. 21) (small ships), or

    (c)   which is exempt from registration under section 294 of that Act;

"compliance notice" means a notice issued under section 90;

"emergency safety notice" means a notice issued under section 104;

"enforcement authority" has the meaning given by section 114;

"fixed monetary penalty" has the meaning given by section 93(3);

"licensable marine activity" is to be read in accordance with section 66;

"licensing authority" means —

    (a)   the Secretary of State;

    (b)   the Welsh Ministers;

    (c)   the Scottish Ministers;

    (d)   the Department of the Environment in Northern Ireland;

"marine licence" means a licence granted under this Part;

"marine structure" means a platform or other artificial structure at sea, other than a pipeline;

"remediation notice" means a notice issued under section 91;

"stop notice" means a notice issued under section 102;

"the UK marine licensing area" has the meaning given by section 66(4);

"variable monetary penalty" has the meaning given by section 95(3);

"vessel" includes —

    (a)   hovercraft, and

    (b)   any other craft capable of travelling on, in or under water, whether or not self-propelled.

(2)   In this Part any reference to the environment includes a reference to any site (including any site comprising, or comprising the remains of, any vessel, aircraft or marine structure) which is of historic or archaeological interest.

PART 5

NATURE CONSERVATION

CHAPTER 1

MARINE CONSERVATION ZONES

Designation of zones

116 Marine conservation zones

(1)   The appropriate authority may by order designate any area falling within subsection (2) as a marine conservation zone (an "MCZ").

Section 117 sets out the grounds on which such an order may be made.

(2)   An area falls within this subsection if —

2516   *Marine and Coastal Access Act 2009 (c.* **23***)*
Part 5 – Nature conservation
Chapter 1 – Marine conservation zones

    (a)   it is an area of the sea within the seaward limits of the territorial sea adjacent to the United Kingdom;

    (b)   it is an area of the sea within the limits of the exclusive economic zone;

    (c)   it is an area of the sea bed or subsoil within the limits of the UK sector of the continental shelf (so far as not falling within an area mentioned in paragraph (b)).

(3)   But an area does not fall within subsection (2) if it is in —

    (a)   the Scottish inshore region, or

    (b)   the Northern Ireland inshore region.

(4)   Section 118 makes further provision as to the areas that may be included in an MCZ.

(5)   For the purposes of this Chapter the appropriate authority is —

    (a)   in relation to an area in Wales, the Welsh Ministers;

    (b)   in relation to an area in the Scottish offshore region, the Scottish Ministers;

    (c)   in any other case, the Secretary of State.

(6)   The Scottish Ministers may not designate any area as an MCZ without the agreement of the Secretary of State.

(7)   An MCZ designated by the Scottish Ministers under this section is to be known as a marine protected area.

Any reference in this Act to an MCZ is, in relation to an MCZ designated by the Scottish Ministers, to be read as a reference to a marine protected area.

(8)   Until the coming into force of the first Order in Council made under section 41 (the exclusive economic zone), the reference in subsection (2)(b) to the exclusive economic zone is to be read as a reference to a renewable energy zone.

117   Grounds for designation of MCZs

(1)   The appropriate authority may make an order under section 116 if it thinks that it is desirable to do so for the purpose of conserving —

    (a)   marine flora or fauna;

    (b)   marine habitats or types of marine habitat;

    (c)   features of geological or geomorphological interest.

(2)   The order must state —

    (a)   the protected feature or features;

    (b)   the conservation objectives for the MCZ.

(3)   Any reference in this Chapter to the conservation objectives stated for an MCZ is a reference to the conservation objectives stated for the MCZ under subsection (2)(b).

(4)   The reference in subsection (1)(a) to conserving marine flora or fauna includes, in particular, a reference to conserving any species that is rare or threatened because of —

    (a)   the limited number of individuals of that species, or

    (b)   the limited number of locations in which that species is present.

Marine and Coastal Access Act 2009 (c. 23)
Part 5 – Nature conservation
Chapter 1 – Marine conservation zones

2517

(5) The references in subsection (1)(a) and (b) to conserving marine flora or fauna or habitat include references to conserving the diversity of such flora, fauna or habitat, whether or not any or all of them are rare or threatened.

(6) Any reference to conserving a thing includes references to –
   (a) assisting in its conservation;
   (b) enabling or facilitating its recovery or increase.

(7) In considering whether it is desirable to designate an area as an MCZ, the appropriate authority may have regard to any economic or social consequences of doing so.

(8) The reference in subsection (7) to any social consequences of designating an area as an MCZ includes a reference to any consequences of doing so for any sites in that area (including any sites comprising, or comprising the remains of, any vessel, aircraft or marine installation) which are of historic or archaeological interest.

118 Further provision as to orders designating MCZs

(1) An order under section 116 must identify the boundaries of the area designated.

(2) The boundary of an MCZ may be determined by, or by reference to, mean high water spring tide.

(3) Any reference in subsection (2)(a) or (b) of section 116 to an area of sea includes a reference to any island in the sea, whether or not any part of it lies above mean high water spring tide.

(4) If an MCZ includes an area falling within subsection (2)(a) of section 116 ("area A"), it may also include an area of the seashore lying above mean high water spring tide ("area B") if –
   (a) area B adjoins area A, and
   (b) any of the conditions in subsection (5) is satisfied.

(5) The conditions are –
   (a) that the protected feature or features leading to the designation of area A is or are also present in area B;
   (b) that area A is designated for the purpose of conserving marine flora or fauna which are dependent (wholly or in part) on anything which takes place in, or is present in, area B;
   (c) that, without the inclusion of area B, the identification of the boundary of the MCZ (either in the order designating the area or on the ground for the purposes of exercising functions in relation to it) would be impossible or impracticable.

(6) An order under section 116 –
   (a) must designate an area of land (whether or not that land is covered by water), and
   (b) in the case of an area falling within subsection (2)(a) or (b) of that section, may designate some or all of the water covering that land.

2518

Marine and Coastal Access Act 2009 (c. 23)
Part 5 – Nature conservation
Chapter 1 – Marine conservation zones

119 Consultation before designation

(1) Before making an order under section 116, the appropriate authority must comply with subsections (2) to (9) of this section.

This is subject to subsection (11).

(2) The appropriate authority must publish notice of its proposal to make the order.

(3) The notice under subsection (2) must—

    (a) be published in such manner as the appropriate authority thinks is most likely to bring the proposal to the attention of any persons who are likely to be affected by the making of the order;

    (b) contain a statement of the terms of the proposed order.

(4) The appropriate authority must consult any persons who the appropriate authority thinks are likely to be interested in, or affected by, the making of the order.

(5) Where the appropriate authority is not the Secretary of State, the authority must consult the Secretary of State.

(6) If the appropriate authority for an area other than Wales considers that—

    (a) the making of the order may affect any activity which is or may be carried on in the Welsh zone, or

    (b) any activity which is or may be carried on in the Welsh zone may affect any part of the proposed MCZ,

the authority must consult the Welsh Ministers.

(7) If the appropriate authority for an area other than the Scottish offshore region considers that—

    (a) the making of the order may affect any activity which is or may be carried on in the Scottish zone, or

    (b) any activity which is or may be carried on in the Scottish zone may affect any part of the proposed MCZ,

the authority must consult the Scottish Ministers.

(8) If the appropriate authority considers that—

    (a) the making of the order may affect any activity which is or may be carried on in the Northern Ireland zone, or

    (b) any activity which is or may be carried on in the Northern Ireland zone may affect any part of the proposed MCZ,

the authority must consult the Department of the Environment in Northern Ireland.

(9) The Secretary of State must consult—

    (a) the Welsh Ministers, if any part of the proposed MCZ lies in the Welsh offshore region;

    (b) the Department of the Environment in Northern Ireland, if any part of the proposed MCZ lies in the Northern Ireland zone.

(10) If the appropriate authority fails to make the order before the end of the period of 12 months beginning with the date on which notice was published under subsection (2), then anything done by the appropriate authority for the purposes of complying with subsections (2) to (9) of this section is, for those purposes, to be treated as not having been done.

Marine and Coastal Access Act 2009 (c. 23)   2519
Part 5 – Nature conservation
Chapter 1 – Marine conservation zones

(11)   In a case where the appropriate authority thinks that there is an urgent need to protect the area proposed to be designated, the authority need not comply with subsections (2) to (4).

(12)   In such a case, the order designating the area as an MCZ remains in force for a period not exceeding two years, unless the appropriate authority makes a further order before the end of that period confirming the designation.

Before making such an order, the appropriate authority must comply with subsections (2) to (9) (and subsection (10) applies accordingly).

120   Publication of orders designating MCZs

(1)   This section applies where an order has been made under section 116.

(2)   The appropriate authority must publish notice of the making of the order.

(3)   The notice under subsection (2) must—
    (a)   be published in such manner as the appropriate authority thinks is most likely to bring the order to the attention of any persons who are likely to be affected by the making of it;
    (b)   give an address at which a copy of the order may be inspected.

(4)   The appropriate authority must—
    (a)   make a copy of the order available for inspection at the address specified under subsection (3)(b) at all reasonable hours without payment;
    (b)   provide a copy of the order to any person who requests one.

(5)   The appropriate authority may charge a fee, not exceeding its costs, for providing a copy under subsection (4)(b).

121   Hearings by appropriate authority

(1)   This section applies where the appropriate authority has the function of deciding whether to make an order under section 116 designating an area as an MCZ.

(2)   The authority may, before making that decision, give to any person the opportunity of—
    (a)   appearing before and being heard by a person appointed for that purpose;
    (b)   providing written representations to such a person.

(3)   The authority may make regulations providing for the procedure to be followed (including decisions as to costs) at hearings held under subsection (2).

(4)   A person appointed under subsection (2) must make a report to the authority of any oral or written representations made under that subsection.

122   Amendment, revocation and review of orders designating MCZs

(1)   An order under section 116 may be amended or revoked by a further order.

(2)   The appropriate authority for an area must review any order it has made under section 116 if the authority receives representations from—
    (a)   the appropriate authority for another area, or

2520

Marine and Coastal Access Act 2009 (c. 23)
Part 5 – Nature conservation
Chapter 1 – Marine conservation zones

   (b)   the Department of the Environment in Northern Ireland,
that the order should be amended or revoked.

Duties relating to network

123   Creation of network of conservation sites

(1)   In order to contribute to the achievement of the objective in subsection (2), the appropriate authority must designate MCZs under section 116.

(2)   The objective is that the MCZs designated by the appropriate authority, taken together with any other MCZs designated under section 116 and any relevant conservation sites in the UK marine area, form a network which satisfies the conditions in subsection (3).

(3)   The conditions are—
   (a)   that the network contributes to the conservation or improvement of the marine environment in the UK marine area;
   (b)   that the features which are protected by the sites comprised in the network represent the range of features present in the UK marine area;
   (c)   that the designation of sites comprised in the network reflects the fact that the conservation of a feature may require the designation of more than one site.

(4)   For the purposes of subsection (2), the following are "relevant conservation sites"—
   (a)   any European marine site;
   (b)   the whole or part of any SSSI;
   (c)   the whole or part of any Ramsar site.

(5)   When complying with the duty imposed by subsection (1), the appropriate authority must have regard to any obligations under EU or international law that relate to the conservation or improvement of the marine environment.

(6)   Before the end of the period of 2 months beginning with the date on which this section comes into force, the appropriate authority must—
   (a)   prepare a statement setting out such principles relating to the achievement of the objective in subsection (2) as the authority intends to follow when complying with the duty imposed by subsection (1), and
   (b)   lay a copy of the statement before the appropriate legislature.

(7)   A statement prepared by the appropriate authority under this section may also set out other matters relating to the achievement of that objective which the authority intends to take into account when complying with the duty imposed by subsection (1).

(8)   The appropriate authority must—
   (a)   keep under review any statement it has prepared under this section, and
   (b)   if it considers it appropriate in consequence of a review, prepare a revised statement of the principles referred to in subsection (6) and lay a copy of it before the appropriate legislature.

(9)   In this section—

Marine and Coastal Access Act 2009 (c. 23)
Part 5 – Nature conservation
Chapter 1 – Marine conservation zones

2521

"the appropriate legislature" means —

    (a)   in relation to the Secretary of State, Parliament;

    (b)   in relation to the Welsh Ministers, the National Assembly for Wales;

    (c)   in relation to the Scottish Ministers, the Scottish Parliament;

"European marine site" means any site which is —

    (a)   a European marine site within the meaning of the Conservation (Natural Habitats, &c) Regulations 1994 (S.I. 1994/2716), or

    (b)   a European offshore marine site within the meaning of the Offshore Marine Conservation (Natural Habitats, &c) Regulations 2007 (S.I. 2007/1842);

"feature" means anything falling within paragraphs (a) to (c) of section 117(1);

"Ramsar site" has the same meaning as in section 37A of the Wildlife and Countryside Act 1981 (c. 69);

"SSSI" means a site of special scientific interest, within the meaning of Part 2 of that Act.

124   Report

(1)   Before the end of every relevant period, the appropriate authority must lay before the appropriate legislature a report setting out —

    (a)   the extent to which, in the opinion of the authority, the objective in section 123(2) has been achieved;

    (b)   any further steps which, in the opinion of the authority, are required to be taken in order to contribute to the achievement of that objective.

(2)   The report must also contain the following information —

    (a)   the number of MCZs which the authority has designated during the relevant period;

    (b)   in relation to each such MCZ —

        (i)   the size of the MCZ, and

        (ii)   the conservation objectives which have been stated for the MCZ;

    (c)   the number of MCZs designated by the authority in which the following activities are prohibited or significantly restricted —

        (i)   any licensable marine activity;

        (ii)   fishing for or taking animals or plants from the sea;

    (d)   information about any amendments which the authority has made to any orders made under section 116;

    (e)   the extent to which, in the opinion of the authority, the conservation objectives stated for each MCZ which it has designated have been achieved;

    (f)   any further steps which, in the opinion of the authority, are required to be taken in relation to any MCZ in order to achieve the conservation objectives stated for it.

(3)   For the purposes of complying with its duty under this section, the appropriate authority for any area may direct the appropriate statutory conservation body for that area to carry out such monitoring of MCZs in that area as is specified in the direction.

2522

Marine and Coastal Access Act 2009 (c. 23)
Part 5 – Nature conservation
Chapter 1 – Marine conservation zones

(4) A body that is given a direction under subsection (3) must comply with it.

(5) In this section—

"the appropriate legislature" means—

    (a) in relation to the Secretary of State, Parliament;

    (b) in relation to the Welsh Ministers, the National Assembly for Wales;

    (c) in relation to the Scottish Ministers, the Scottish Parliament;

"licensable marine activity" has the same meaning as in Part 4;

"relevant period" means—

    (a) the period beginning on the date on which this section comes into force and ending on 31 December 2012;

    (b) each subsequent period of six years.

Duties of public authorities

125 General duties of public authorities in relation to MCZs

(1) This section applies to any public authority having any function the exercise of which is capable of affecting (other than insignificantly)—

    (a) the protected features of an MCZ;

    (b) any ecological or geomorphological process on which the conservation of any protected feature of an MCZ is (wholly or in part) dependent.

(2) Every public authority to which this section applies must (so far as is consistent with their proper exercise)—

    (a) exercise its functions in the manner which the authority considers best furthers the conservation objectives stated for the MCZ;

    (b) where it is not possible to exercise its functions in a manner which furthers those objectives, exercise them in the manner which the authority considers least hinders the achievement of those objectives.

(3) If a public authority considers that any of its functions is such that the exercise of the function would or might significantly hinder the achievement of the conservation objectives for an MCZ, it must inform the appropriate statutory conservation body of that fact.

(4) Subject to subsection (6), subsection (5) applies in any case where a public authority intends to do an act which is capable of affecting (other than insignificantly)—

    (a) the protected features of an MCZ;

    (b) any ecological or geomorphological process on which the conservation of any protected feature of an MCZ is (wholly or in part) dependent.

(5) If the authority believes that there is or may be a significant risk of the act hindering the achievement of the conservation objectives stated for the MCZ, the authority must notify the appropriate statutory conservation body of that fact.

(6) Subsection (5) does not apply where—

    (a) the appropriate statutory conservation body has given the authority advice or guidance under section 127 in relation to acts of a particular description,

Marine and Coastal Access Act 2009 (c. 23)
Part 5 – Nature conservation
Chapter 1 – Marine conservation zones

2523

    (b)   the act which the authority intends to do is an act of that description, and

    (c)   the advice or guidance has not ceased to apply.

(7)   Where the authority has given notification under subsection (5), it must wait until the expiry of the period of 28 days beginning with the date of the notification before deciding whether to do the act.

(8)   Subsection (7) does not apply where –

    (a)   the appropriate statutory conservation body notifies the authority that it need not wait until the end of the period referred to in that subsection, or

    (b)   the authority thinks that there is an urgent need to do the act.

(9)   If a public authority considers that a relevant event has occurred, it must inform –

    (a)   the relevant authority, and

    (b)   the appropriate statutory conservation body,

of that fact.

(10)   A "relevant event" is any act –

    (a)   in relation to which the public authority exercises functions,

    (b)   which the authority believes to be an offence, and

    (c)   which the authority considers will or may significantly hinder the achievement of the conservation objectives for an MCZ.

(11)   For the purposes of subsection (9) "relevant authority" means –

    (a)   in relation to an MCZ in Wales, the Welsh Ministers;

    (b)   in relation to an MCZ in the Scottish offshore region, the Scottish Ministers;

    (c)   in relation to any other MCZ, the MMO.

(12)   In carrying out its duties under this section a public authority must have regard to any advice or guidance given by the appropriate statutory conservation body under section 127.

(13)   In this section –

    "act" includes omission;

    "public authority" does not include a Northern Ireland Minister or Northern Ireland department.

126   Duties of public authorities in relation to certain decisions

(1)   This section applies where –

    (a)   a public authority has the function of determining an application (whenever made) for authorisation of the doing of an act, and

    (b)   the act is capable of affecting (other than insignificantly) –

        (i)   the protected features of an MCZ;

        (ii)   any ecological or geomorphological process on which the conservation of any protected feature of an MCZ is (wholly or in part) dependent.

(2)   If the authority believes that there is or may be a significant risk of the act hindering the achievement of the conservation objectives stated for the MCZ,

2524   *Marine and Coastal Access Act 2009 (c. 23)*
Part 5 – Nature conservation
Chapter 1 – Marine conservation zones

the authority must notify the appropriate statutory conservation body of that fact.

(3)   Where the authority has given notification under subsection (2), it must wait until the expiry of the period of 28 days beginning with the date of the notification before deciding whether to grant authorisation for the doing of the act.

(4)   Subsection (3) does not apply where —

        (a)   the appropriate statutory conservation body notifies the authority that it need not wait until the end of the period referred to in that subsection, or

        (b)   the authority thinks that there is an urgent need to grant authorisation for the doing of the act.

(5)   The authority must not grant authorisation for the doing of the act unless the condition in subsection (6) or the condition in subsection (7) is met.

(6)   The condition in this subsection is that the person seeking the authorisation satisfies the authority that there is no significant risk of the act hindering the achievement of the conservation objectives stated for the MCZ.

(7)   The condition in this subsection is that, although the person seeking the authorisation is not able to satisfy the authority that there is no significant risk of the act hindering the achievement of the conservation objectives stated for the MCZ, that person satisfies the authority that —

        (a)   there is no other means of proceeding with the act which would create a substantially lower risk of hindering the achievement of those objectives,

        (b)   the benefit to the public of proceeding with the act clearly outweighs the risk of damage to the environment that will be created by proceeding with it, and

        (c)   the person seeking the authorisation will undertake, or make arrangements for the undertaking of, measures of equivalent environmental benefit to the damage which the act will or is likely to have in or on the MCZ.

(8)   The reference in subsection (7)(a) to other means of proceeding with an act includes a reference to proceeding with it —

        (a)   in another manner, or

        (b)   at another location.

(9)   In a case falling within subsection (7), the authority must, if it has power to grant the authorisation subject to conditions, exercise that power so as to make it a condition of the authorisation that the measures mentioned in subsection (7)(c) are undertaken.

(10)   In carrying out its duties under this section a public authority must have regard to any advice or guidance given by the appropriate statutory conservation body under section 127.

(11)   In this section —

        "act" includes omission;

        "authorisation" means any approval, confirmation, consent, licence, permission or other authorisation (however described), whether special or general;

Marine and Coastal Access Act 2009 (c. 23)
Part 5 — Nature conservation
Chapter 1 — Marine conservation zones

2525

"damage" includes the prevention of an improvement;

"public authority" does not include a Northern Ireland Minister or Northern Ireland department.

127 Advice and guidance by conservation bodies

(1) The appropriate statutory conservation body may give advice and guidance as to —

    (a) the matters which are capable of damaging or otherwise affecting any protected feature or features;

    (b) the matters which are capable of affecting any ecological or geomorphological process on which the conservation of any protected feature or features is (wholly or in part) dependent;

    (c) how any conservation objectives stated for an MCZ may be furthered, or how the achievement of any such objectives may be hindered;

    (d) how the effect of any activity or activities on an MCZ or MCZs may be mitigated;

    (e) which activities are, or are not, of equivalent environmental benefit (for the purposes of section 126(7)(c)) to any particular damage to the environment (within the meaning of that provision).

(2) Advice or guidance may be given —

    (a) either in relation to a particular MCZ or MCZs or generally;

    (b) either to a particular public authority or authorities or generally.

(3) The appropriate statutory conservation body must give advice to a public authority if the authority requests it.

(4) If the appropriate statutory conservation body for an area proposes to exercise its functions under this section in a manner which may affect an MCZ or MCZs in an area for which another body is the appropriate statutory conservation body, it must consult that other body before doing so.

128 Failure to comply with duties etc

(1) This section applies if, in the opinion of the appropriate statutory conservation body, a public authority has failed —

    (a) to comply with the duty imposed by section 125(2) or the duty imposed by section 126(5);

    (b) to act in accordance with advice or guidance given by the appropriate statutory conservation body under section 127.

(2) Where this section applies —

    (a) the body may request from the authority an explanation for the failure, and

    (b) on such a request, the authority must provide such an explanation in writing.

(3) In this section "public authority" does not include a Northern Ireland Minister or Northern Ireland department.

2526

Marine and Coastal Access Act 2009 (c. 23)
Part 5 — Nature conservation
Chapter 1 — Marine conservation zones

Byelaws for protection of MCZs etc: England

129   Byelaws for protection of MCZs in England

(1)   The MMO may make one or more byelaws for the purpose of furthering the conservation objectives stated for an MCZ in England.

(2)   A byelaw under this section may be made so as to apply to any area in England.

(3)   The provision that may be made by a byelaw under this section includes, in particular, provision —

    (a)   prohibiting or restricting entry into, or any movement or other activity within, the MCZ by persons or animals;

    (b)   prohibiting or restricting entry into, or any movement or other activity within, the MCZ by vessels or (where appropriate) vehicles;

    (c)   restricting the speed at which any vessel may move in the MCZ or in any specified area outside the MCZ where that movement might hinder the conservation objectives stated for the MCZ;

    (d)   prohibiting or restricting the anchoring of any vessel within the MCZ;

    (e)   prohibiting or restricting the killing, taking, destruction, molestation or disturbance of animals or plants of any description in the MCZ;

    (f)   prohibiting or restricting the doing of anything in the MCZ which would interfere with the sea bed or damage or disturb any object in the MCZ.

(4)   The provision that may be made by a byelaw under this section also includes provision prohibiting or restricting entry into, or any movement or other activity on, any part of the seashore that adjoins the MCZ by persons, animals or vehicles.

(5)   A byelaw under this section may provide for the MMO to issue permits authorising anything which would, apart from such a permit, be unlawful under the byelaw.

(6)   The MMO may attach to a permit under subsection (5) any condition which the MMO thinks appropriate to attach to that permit.

(7)   A byelaw under this section may be made subject to specified exceptions.

(8)   A byelaw under this section may make different provision for different cases, including (in particular) —

    (a)   different parts of the MCZ;

    (b)   different times of the year;

    (c)   different means or methods of carrying out any activity.

(9)   In this section "specified" means specified in the byelaw.

130   Byelaws: procedure

(1)   Before making a byelaw under section 129, the MMO must comply with subsections (2) to (7) of this section.

This is subject to subsection (11).

(2)   If the byelaw would or might affect any activity in Wales, the MMO must send a copy of a draft of the byelaw to the Welsh Ministers.

Marine and Coastal Access Act 2009 (c. 23)
Part 5 — Nature conservation
Chapter 1 — Marine conservation zones

2527

(3) The MMO must place a copy of a draft of the byelaw in such place or places as the MMO thinks is or are likely to be most convenient for the purpose of enabling the draft to be inspected by persons likely to be affected by the making of the byelaw.

(4) The MMO must provide a copy of a draft of the byelaw to any person who requests one.

(5) The MMO may charge a fee, not exceeding its costs, for providing a copy under subsection (4).

(6) The MMO must publish notice of its proposal to make the byelaw.

(7) The notice under subsection (6) must —

    (a) be published in such manner as the MMO thinks is most likely to bring the proposal to the attention of any persons who are likely to be affected by the making of the byelaw;

    (b) state where the copy or copies of the draft byelaw have been placed by the MMO in accordance with subsection (3);

    (c) state the time within which representations about the byelaw must be made to the MMO.

(8) A byelaw made under section 129 does not have effect until it is confirmed by the Secretary of State; and a byelaw which is confirmed comes into force —

    (a) on such date as may be determined by the Secretary of State, or

    (b) if no such date is determined, one month after the date on which it is confirmed.

(9) As soon as is reasonably practicable after the confirmation of a byelaw made under section 129, the MMO must publish notice of the making of the byelaw.

(10) The notice under subsection (9) must —

    (a) be published in such manner as the MMO thinks is most likely to bring the byelaw to the attention of any persons who are likely to be affected by the making of it;

    (b) state that a copy of the byelaw may be inspected at the offices of the MMO.

(11) Nothing in this section applies where the MMO thinks that there is an urgent need to protect an MCZ.

131 Emergency byelaws

(1) Where the MMO thinks that there is an urgent need to protect an MCZ, a byelaw made by it for that purpose has effect without being confirmed by the Secretary of State.

(2) A byelaw that has effect by virtue of this section (an "emergency byelaw") —

    (a) comes into force on a date specified in the byelaw, and

    (b) remains in force (unless revoked) for such period, not exceeding 12 months, as is specified in the byelaw.

(3) The MMO must publish notice of the making of an emergency byelaw.

(4) The notice under subsection (3) must —

2528

Marine and Coastal Access Act 2009 (c. 23)
Part 5 — Nature conservation
Chapter 1 — Marine conservation zones

(a) be published in such manner as the MMO thinks is most likely to bring the byelaw to the attention of any persons who are likely to be affected by the making of it;

(b) state that a copy of the byelaw may be inspected at the offices of the MMO;

(c) state that the Secretary of State has power to revoke the byelaw and that any person affected by the making of the byelaw may make representations to the Secretary of State.

(5) The Secretary of State may revoke an emergency byelaw.

(6) The MMO must keep under review the need for an emergency byelaw to remain in force.

(7) The MMO may, by further byelaw, provide that an emergency byelaw is to remain in force for such period beyond that specified under subsection (2)(b) as is specified in the further byelaw.

(8) The MMO may not make a byelaw under subsection (7) unless —

(a) it intends to make a byelaw under section 129 in respect of the MCZ in accordance with section 130 ("the permanent byelaw"), and

(b) it has, in respect of the permanent byelaw, complied with section 130(6).

(9) A period specified under subsection (7) may not exceed 6 months.

132 Interim byelaws

(1) The MMO may make one or more byelaws for the purpose of protecting any feature in an area in England if the MMO thinks —

(a) that there are or may be reasons for the Secretary of State to consider whether to designate the area as an MCZ, and

(b) that there is an urgent need to protect the feature.

(2) In this Chapter "interim byelaw" means a byelaw made under subsection (1).

(3) An interim byelaw must contain a description of the boundaries of the area to which it applies (which must be no greater than is necessary for the purpose of protecting the feature in question).

(4) Subsections (2) to (9) of section 129 apply to an interim byelaw as they apply to a byelaw made under that section, except that any reference to an MCZ is to be read as a reference to the area to which the interim byelaw applies.

(5) An interim byelaw —

(a) comes into force on a date specified in the byelaw, and

(b) remains in force (unless revoked) for such period, not exceeding 12 months, as is specified in the byelaw.

(6) The MMO must publish notice of the making of an interim byelaw.

(7) The notice under subsection (6) must —

(a) be published in such manner as the MMO thinks is most likely to bring the byelaw to the attention of any persons who are likely to be affected by the making of it;

(b) state that a copy of the byelaw may be inspected at the offices of the MMO;

Marine and Coastal Access Act 2009 (c. 23)
Part 5 – Nature conservation
Chapter 1 – Marine conservation zones

2529

      (c)   state that the Secretary of State has power to revoke the byelaw and that any person affected by the making of the byelaw may make representations to the Secretary of State.

(8)   The Secretary of State may revoke an interim byelaw.

(9)   The MMO must keep under review the need for an interim byelaw to remain in force.

(10)   The MMO may by further byelaw extend the period for which an interim byelaw remains in force; but an interim byelaw may not by virtue of this subsection remain in force for an aggregate period exceeding 12 months.

(11)   If, while an interim byelaw is in force, the Secretary of State gives notice of a proposal to make an order under section 116 designating any part of the area in question as an MCZ, the Secretary of State may direct that the interim byelaw is to remain in force —

      (a)   until the Secretary of State has decided whether to make the order under section 116;

      (b)   if the Secretary of State decides to make such an order, until that order comes into effect.

(12)   The Secretary of State must publish a direction under subsection (11) in such manner as the Secretary of State thinks is most likely to bring the direction to the attention of any persons who are likely to be affected by the making of it.

(13)   In this section "feature" means any flora, fauna, habitat or feature which could be a protected feature if the area in question were designated as an MCZ.

133 Further provision as to byelaws

(1)   This section applies to any byelaw made under section 129 or 132.

(2)   A byelaw to which this section applies is to be made under the common seal of the MMO.

(3)   If a byelaw to which this section applies will or may affect any activity in Wales, the MMO must send a copy of the byelaw to the Welsh Ministers.

(4)   The MMO must —

      (a)   make a copy of any byelaw to which this section applies available for inspection at its offices at all reasonable hours without payment;

      (b)   provide a copy of any such byelaw to any person who requests one.

(5)   The MMO may charge a fee, not exceeding its costs, for providing a copy under subsection (4)(b).

(6)   In the case of a byelaw made under section 129 in accordance with section 130, subsections (3) and (4) above apply only after the byelaw has been confirmed under section 130(8).

(7)   A byelaw to which this section applies may be amended or revoked by a further byelaw.

2530   *Marine and Coastal Access Act 2009 (c. 23)*
                                                                              Part 5 — Nature conservation
                                                                     Chapter 1 — Marine conservation zones

Orders for protection of MCZs etc: Wales

134   Orders for protection of MCZs in Wales

(1)   The Welsh Ministers may make one or more orders for the purpose of furthering the conservation objectives stated for an MCZ in Wales.

(2)   An order under this section may be made so as to apply to any area in Wales.

(3)   Subsections (3), (4) and (7) to (9) of section 129 apply in relation to an order under this section as they apply in relation to a byelaw under that section.

(4)   An order under this section may provide for the Welsh Ministers to issue permits authorising anything which would, apart from such a permit, be unlawful under the order.

(5)   The Welsh Ministers may attach to a permit under subsection (4) any condition which the Welsh Ministers think appropriate to attach to that permit.

(6)   An order under this section may be made in respect of more than one MCZ; and in relation to any order so made any reference in this section (or in section 129 as applied by this section) to an MCZ is a reference to any or all of the MCZs in respect of which the order is made.

135   Consultation etc regarding orders under section 134

(1)   Before making an order under section 134, the Welsh Ministers must consult—
    (a)   the Secretary of State, and
    (b)   any other person whom they think fit to consult.

(2)   The Welsh Ministers must publish notice of the making of an order under section 134.

(3)   The notice under subsection (2) must—
    (a)   be published in such manner as the Welsh Ministers think is most likely to bring the order to the attention of any persons who are likely to be affected by the making of it;
    (b)   give an address at which a copy of the order may be inspected.

(4)   Where the Welsh Ministers think that there is an urgent need to make an order under section 134 in order to protect an MCZ—
    (a)   subsection (1) does not apply, and
    (b)   the notice under subsection (2) must also state that any person affected by the making of the order may make representations to the Welsh Ministers.

136   Interim orders

(1)   The Welsh Ministers may make one or more orders for the purpose of protecting any feature in an area in Wales if they think—
    (a)   that there are or may be reasons to consider whether to designate the area as an MCZ, and
    (b)   that there is an urgent need to protect the feature.

(2)   In this Chapter "interim order" means an order under subsection (1).

Marine and Coastal Access Act 2009 (c. 23)
Part 5 – Nature conservation
Chapter 1 – Marine conservation zones

2531

(3) An interim order must contain a description of the boundaries of the area to which it applies (which must be no greater than is necessary for the purpose of protecting the feature in question).

(4) Subsections (2) to (5) of section 134 apply to an interim order as they apply to an order under that section, except that any reference to an MCZ is to be read as a reference to the area to which the interim order applies.

(5) An interim order—
    (a) comes into force on a date specified in the order, and
    (b) remains in force (unless revoked) for such period, not exceeding 12 months, as is specified in the order.

(6) The Welsh Ministers must publish notice of the making of an interim order.

(7) The notice under subsection (6) must—
    (a) be published in such manner as the Welsh Ministers think is most likely to bring the order to the attention of any persons who are likely to be affected by the making of it;
    (b) give an address at which a copy of the order may be inspected;
    (c) state that any person affected by the making of the order may make representations to the Welsh Ministers.

(8) The Welsh Ministers must keep under review the need for an interim order to remain in force.

(9) The Welsh Ministers may by further order extend the period for which an interim order remains in force.

(10) In this section "feature" means any flora, fauna, habitat or feature which could be a protected feature if the area in question were designated as an MCZ.

137 Further provision as to orders made under section 134 or 136

(1) This section applies to any order made under section 134 or 136.

(2) The Welsh Ministers must send a copy of any order to which this section applies to the Secretary of State.

(3) The Welsh Ministers must—
    (a) make a copy of any order to which this section applies available for inspection at such place as they think fit for that purpose at all reasonable hours without payment;
    (b) provide a copy of any such order to any person who requests one.

(4) Subject to subsection (5), an order to which this section applies may make such provision amending, modifying or excluding any statutory provision of local application which has effect in the area to which the order relates as the Welsh Ministers think is necessary or expedient in consequence of the order.

(5) An order to which this section applies may not amend, modify or exclude any statutory provision of local application which was made by the Secretary of State unless the Secretary of State consents.

(6) An order to which this section applies may be amended or revoked by a further order.

(7) In this section "statutory provision" means—

2532

Marine and Coastal Access Act 2009 (c. 23)
Part 5 — Nature conservation
Chapter 1 — Marine conservation zones

(a) provision of an Act of Parliament, or

(b) provision of an instrument made under an Act of Parliament.

Hearings

138 Hearings by Secretary of State or Welsh Ministers

(1) This section applies where the Secretary of State has the function of—

    (a) deciding (under section 130(8)) whether to confirm a byelaw made under section 129;

    (b) deciding (under section 131(5)) whether to revoke an emergency byelaw;

    (c) deciding (under section 132(8)) whether to revoke an interim byelaw.

(2) This section also applies where the Welsh Ministers have the function of—

    (a) deciding whether to make an order under section 134;

    (b) deciding whether to make an interim order under section 136(1).

(3) The Secretary of State or (as the case may be) the Welsh Ministers may, before making that decision, give to any person the opportunity of—

    (a) appearing before and being heard by a person appointed for that purpose;

    (b) providing written representations to such a person.

(4) The Secretary of State or (as the case may be) the Welsh Ministers may make regulations providing for the procedure to be followed (including decisions as to costs) at hearings held under subsection (3).

(5) A person appointed under subsection (3) must make a report to the Secretary of State or (as the case may be) the Welsh Ministers of any oral or written representations made under that subsection.

Offences

139 Offence of contravening byelaws or orders

(1) It is an offence for a person to contravene—

    (a) any byelaw made under section 129 or 132(1);

    (b) any order made under section 134 or 136(1).

(2) A person who is guilty of an offence under this section is liable on summary conviction to a fine not exceeding level 5 on the standard scale.

(3) In this section "contravene" includes fail to comply.

(4) Proceedings for an offence under this section may be taken, and the offence may for all incidental purposes be treated as having been committed, in any part of England and Wales.

140 Offence of damaging etc protected features of MCZs

(1) A person is guilty of an offence under this section if—

    (a) the person without lawful excuse does a prohibited act,

Marine and Coastal Access Act 2009 (c. 23)   2533
Part 5 – Nature conservation
Chapter 1 – Marine conservation zones

    (b)   at the time of doing that act, the person knows, or ought to have known, that the feature to which the act relates is in, or forms part of, an MCZ, and

    (c)   the act has significantly hindered, or may significantly hinder, the achievement of the conservation objectives stated for the MCZ.

(2)   For the purposes of subsection (1), a person does a prohibited act if the person —

    (a)   intentionally or recklessly kills or injures any animal in an MCZ which is a protected feature of that MCZ,

    (b)   intentionally picks or collects, or intentionally or recklessly cuts, uproots or destroys, any plant in an MCZ which is a protected feature of that MCZ,

    (c)   intentionally or recklessly takes anything from an MCZ which is, or forms part of, a protected feature of that MCZ, or

    (d)   intentionally or recklessly destroys or damages any habitat or feature which is a protected feature of an MCZ.

(3)   For the purposes of determining whether anything done by a person in relation to a protected feature is a prohibited act for the purposes of subsection (1), it is immaterial whether the person knew, or ought to have known, that the feature was a protected feature.

(4)   A person who is guilty of an offence under this section is liable —

    (a)   on summary conviction, to a fine not exceeding £50,000;

    (b)   on conviction on indictment, to a fine.

(5)   In determining the amount of any fine to be imposed on a person convicted of an offence under this section, the court must in particular have regard to any financial benefit which has accrued or appears likely to accrue to the person in consequence of the offence.

(6)   Proceedings for an offence under this section may be taken, and the offence may for all incidental purposes be treated as having been committed, in any part of the United Kingdom.

141   Exceptions to offences under section 139 or 140

(1)   A person is not guilty of an offence under section 139 or 140 if the act which is alleged to constitute the offence —

    (a)   was done in accordance with section 125(2) by a public authority;

    (b)   was expressly authorised by an authorisation granted in accordance with section 126, or was necessarily incidental to such an act;

    (c)   was done in accordance with —

        (i)   a permit issued under section 129(5) or 134(4), or

        (ii)   a permit issued by the appropriate authority;

    (d)   was necessary in the interests of national security or the prevention or detection of crime, or was necessary for securing public health;

    (e)   was necessary for the purpose of securing the safety of any vessel, aircraft or marine installation;

    (f)   was done for the purpose of saving life.

(2)   Subsection (1)(e) does not apply where the necessity was due to the fault of the person or of some other person acting under the person's direction or control.

2534

Marine and Coastal Access Act 2009 (c. 23)
Part 5 – Nature conservation
Chapter 1 – Marine conservation zones

(3) A person is not guilty of an offence under section 139 by reason of doing anything that is an offence under section 140.

(4) It is a defence for a person who is charged with an offence under section 140 to show that—

    (a) the act which is alleged to constitute the offence was—

        (i) an act done for the purpose of, and in the course of, sea fishing, or

        (ii) an act done in connection with such an act,

    and

    (b) the effect of the act on the protected feature in question could not reasonably have been avoided.

(5) The Secretary of State may by order amend this section so as to remove, or restrict the application of, the defence provided by subsection (4).

(6) Until the coming into force of the first Order in Council made under section 41 (the exclusive economic zone), nothing in section 140 applies to anything done in relation to an MCZ lying beyond the seaward limits of the territorial sea by a person on a third country vessel.

(7) In this section—

    "act" includes omission;

    "third country vessel" means a vessel which—

    (a) is flying the flag of, or is registered in, any State or territory (other than Gibraltar) which is not a member State, and

    (b) is not registered in a member State.

Fixed monetary penalties

142 Fixed monetary penalties

(1) The appropriate authority for any area (other than the Scottish offshore region) may by order make provision to confer on any enforcement authority for that area the power by notice to impose a fixed monetary penalty on a person in relation to an offence under section 139.

(2) Provision under this section may only confer such a power in relation to a case where the enforcement authority is satisfied beyond reasonable doubt that the person has committed the offence.

(3) For the purposes of this Chapter a "fixed monetary penalty" is a requirement to pay to the enforcement authority a penalty of a prescribed amount.

(4) The amount of the fixed monetary penalty that may be imposed in relation to an offence may not exceed level 1 on the standard scale.

(5) In this section "prescribed" means prescribed in an order made under this section.

143 Fixed monetary penalties: procedure

(1) Provision under section 142 must secure the results in subsection (2).

(2) Those results are that—

Marine and Coastal Access Act 2009 (c. 23)
Part 5 — *Nature conservation*
Chapter 1 — *Marine conservation zones*

2535

    (a)   where the enforcement authority proposes to impose a fixed monetary penalty on a person, the authority must serve on that person a notice of what is proposed (a "notice of intent") which complies with subsection (3),

    (b)   the notice of intent also offers the person the opportunity to discharge the person's liability for the fixed monetary penalty by payment of a prescribed sum (which must be less than or equal to the amount of the penalty),

    (c)   if the person does not so discharge liability —

        (i)   the person may make written representations and objections to the enforcement authority in relation to the proposed imposition of the fixed monetary penalty, and

        (ii)   the enforcement authority must at the end of the period for making representations and objections decide whether to impose the fixed monetary penalty,

    (d)   where the enforcement authority decides to impose the fixed monetary penalty, the notice imposing it ("the final notice") complies with subsection (5), and

    (e)   the person on whom a fixed monetary penalty is imposed may appeal against the decision to impose it.

(3)   To comply with this subsection the notice of intent must include information as to —

    (a)   the grounds for the proposal to impose the fixed monetary penalty,

    (b)   the effect of payment of the sum referred to in subsection (2)(b),

    (c)   the right to make representations and objections,

    (d)   the circumstances in which the enforcement authority may not impose the fixed monetary penalty,

    (e)   the period within which liability to the fixed monetary penalty may be discharged, which must not exceed the period of 28 days beginning with the day on which the notice of intent is received, and

    (f)   the period within which representations and objections may be made, which must not exceed the period of 28 days beginning with the day on which the notice of intent is received.

(4)   Provision pursuant to subsection (2)(c)(ii) —

    (a)   must secure that the enforcement authority may not decide to impose a fixed monetary penalty on a person where the authority is satisfied that the person would not, by reason of any defence, be liable to be convicted of the offence in relation to which the penalty is proposed to be imposed, and

    (b)   may include provision for other circumstances in which the enforcement authority may not decide to impose a fixed monetary penalty.

(5)   To comply with this subsection the final notice referred to in subsection (2)(d) must include information as to —

    (a)   the grounds for imposing the penalty,

    (b)   how payment may be made,

    (c)   the period within which payment must be made,

    (d)   any early payment discounts or late payment penalties,

    (e)   rights of appeal, and

    (f)   the consequences of non-payment.

2536

Marine and Coastal Access Act 2009 (c. 23)
Part 5 — Nature conservation
Chapter 1 — Marine conservation zones

(6)   Provision pursuant to subsection (2)(e) must secure that the grounds on which a person may appeal against a decision of the enforcement authority include the following —

    (a)   that the decision was based on an error of fact;

    (b)   that the decision was wrong in law;

    (c)   that the decision was unreasonable.

(7)   In this section "prescribed" means prescribed in an order made under section 142.

144   Further provision about fixed monetary penalties

Schedule 10 (which makes further provision about fixed monetary penalties) has effect.

Miscellaneous and supplemental

145   Application to the Crown

(1)   This Chapter is binding on the Crown and applies in relation to any Crown land as it applies in relation to any other land.

This is subject to subsection (2).

(2)   No contravention by the Crown of any provision of this Chapter is to make the Crown criminally liable; but the High Court or, in Scotland, the Court of Session may, on the application of the appropriate authority or any other authority charged with enforcing that provision, declare unlawful any act or omission of the Crown which constitutes such a contravention.

(3)   Despite subsection (2), the provisions of this Chapter apply to persons in the public service of the Crown as they apply to other persons.

(4)   For the purposes of this section "Crown land" means land an interest in which —

    (a)   belongs to Her Majesty in right of the Crown or in right of Her private estates,

    (b)   belongs to Her Majesty in right of the Duchy of Lancaster,

    (c)   belongs to the Duchy of Cornwall, or

    (d)   belongs to a government department or is held in trust for Her Majesty for the purposes of a government department.

(5)   In this section references to Her Majesty's private estates are to be construed in accordance with section 1 of the Crown Private Estates Act 1862 (c. 37).

146   Consequential and transitional provision

(1)   Schedule 11 (which makes consequential amendments) has effect.

(2)   Schedule 12 (which makes transitional provision) has effect.

147   Interpretation of this Chapter

(1)   In this Chapter —

Marine and Coastal Access Act 2009 (c. 23)
Part 5 – Nature conservation
Chapter 1 – Marine conservation zones

2537

"animal" includes any egg, larva, pupa, or other immature stage of an animal;

"appropriate authority" has the meaning given by section 116(5);

"the appropriate statutory conservation body" means —

(a) in respect of an area in England, Natural England,

(b) in respect of an area in Wales, the Countryside Council for Wales,

(c) in respect of an area outside the seaward limits of the territorial sea, the Joint Nature Conservation Committee;

"emergency byelaw" has the meaning given by section 131;

"enforcement authority" means, in relation to any area, any authority which has a function (whether or not statutory) of taking any action with a view to or in connection with the imposition of any sanction, criminal or otherwise, in a case where an offence under this Chapter is committed in that area;

"England" includes the English inshore region;

"interim byelaw" means a byelaw made under section 132(1);

"interim order" means an order made under section 136(1);

"marine installation" means any artificial island, installation or structure;

"MCZ" means a marine conservation zone designated by an order under section 116;

"protected feature", in relation to an MCZ or proposed MCZ, means any flora, fauna, habitat or feature which is sought to be conserved by the making of the order designating the zone;

"sea" has the meaning given by section 322(1), except that it does not include any waters upstream of the fresh-water limit of estuarial waters;

"seashore" means —

(a) the foreshore, that is to say, land which is covered and uncovered by the ordinary movement of the tide, and

(b) any land, whether or not covered intermittently by water, which is in apparent continuity (determined by reference to the physical characteristics of that land) with the foreshore, as far landward as any natural or artificial break in that continuity;

"vehicles" includes —

(a) bicycles and other non-motorised forms of transport, and

(b) hovercraft;

"vessels" includes —

(a) hovercraft,

(b) aircraft capable of landing on water, and

(c) any other craft capable of travelling on, in or under water, whether or not capable of carrying any person;

"Wales" includes the Welsh inshore region.

(2) In the definition of "sea" in subsection (1) "estuarial waters" means any waters within the limits of transitional waters, within the meaning of the Water Framework Directive (that is to say, Directive 2000/60/EC of the European Parliament and of the Council of 23 October 2000 establishing a framework for Community action in the field of water policy).

2538

Marine and Coastal Access Act 2009 (c. 23)
Part 5 — Nature conservation
Chapter 2 — Other conservation sites

CHAPTER 2

OTHER CONSERVATION SITES

148 Marine boundaries of SSSIs and national nature reserves

Schedule 13 (which amends the Wildlife and Countryside Act 1981 (c. 69) in relation to sites of special scientific interest and national nature reserves) has effect.

PART 6

MANAGEMENT OF INSHORE FISHERIES

CHAPTER 1

INSHORE FISHERIES AND CONSERVATION AUTHORITIES

Inshore fisheries and conservation districts and authorities

149 Establishment of inshore fisheries and conservation districts

(1) The Secretary of State may by order establish inshore fisheries and conservation districts.

(2) An inshore fisheries and conservation district (an "IFC district") is an area that consists of —

    (a) one or more local authority areas in England that include part of the seashore, and

    (b) such part of the English inshore region lying seawards from that part of the seashore as is specified in the order establishing the district.

(3) Before making an order establishing an IFC district the Secretary of State must consult —

    (a) the council for every local authority area that would, if the order were made, fall within the IFC district established by the order,

    (b) the Environment Agency,

    (c) Natural England,

    (d) the MMO,

    (e) the authority for any existing IFC district that would, if the order were made, adjoin the IFC district established by the order,

    (f) the Welsh Ministers, in a case where, if the order were made, the IFC district established by the order would adjoin the Welsh inshore region,

and any other person likely to be affected by the making of the order.

150 Inshore fisheries and conservation authorities

(1) There is to be an inshore fisheries and conservation authority (an "IFC authority") for every IFC district established under section 149.

(2) Any reference in this Chapter to the authority for an IFC district is a reference to the IFC authority for that district.

(3) An authority for an IFC district is —

Marine and Coastal Access Act 2009 (c. 23)
Part 6 – Management of inshore fisheries
Chapter 1 – Inshore fisheries and conservation authorities

2539

    (a)   a committee of the council for the local authority area falling within the district;

    (b)   where there is more than one local authority area falling within the district, a joint committee of the councils for those local authority areas.

151   Membership and proceedings of IFC authorities

(1)   An order under section 149 establishing an IFC district must provide for the IFC authority for the district to consist of –

    (a)   persons who are members of a relevant council,

    (b)   persons appointed by the MMO, and

    (c)   other persons.

(2)   The persons appointed as members of the authority for the district by virtue of subsection (1)(b) must comprise –

    (a)   persons acquainted with the needs and opinions of the fishing community of the district, and

    (b)   persons with knowledge of, or expertise in, marine environmental matters.

(3)   The Secretary of State may by order amend subsection (2) so as to –

    (a)   add descriptions of persons who may be appointed by virtue of subsection (1)(b) as members of an IFC authority;

    (b)   vary or remove any descriptions added by virtue of paragraph (a).

An order under this subsection may make such other amendments of this section as appear to the Secretary of State to be necessary in consequence of the order.

(4)   An order under section 149 establishing an IFC district must specify the number of members of the authority for the district.

(5)   The order must also specify –

    (a)   the number of members falling within paragraph (a), and the number of members falling within paragraph (b), of subsection (1);

    (b)   in a case where there is more than one relevant council for the IFC district established by the order, the number of members to be appointed from each council (which may, in the case of any particular council, be none);

    (c)   the number of members falling within paragraph (c) of subsection (1) and the person or persons by whom they are to be appointed.

(6)   An order under section 149 establishing an IFC district may also include provision about –

    (a)   how a member of the authority for the district is to be appointed;

    (b)   qualification and disqualification for membership of the authority;

    (c)   the conduct of members of the authority;

    (d)   the appointment of a member of the authority as the chair of the authority;

    (e)   the holding and vacation of office as a member, or as chair, of the authority (including the circumstances in which a person ceases to hold office or may be removed or suspended from office);

    (f)   re-appointment as a member, or as chair, of the authority;

2540

Marine and Coastal Access Act 2009 (c. 23)
Part 6 – Management of inshore fisheries
Chapter 1 – Inshore fisheries and conservation authorities

(g) the validity of acts and proceedings of a person appointed as a member of the authority in the event of disqualification or lack of qualification;

(h) the validity of proceedings of the authority in the event of a vacancy in membership or of a defect in the appointment of a member;

(i) procedure to be followed by the authority;

(j) the delegation by the authority of any of its functions to a sub-committee, member or employee of the authority;

(k) the payment by the authority of allowances to a member and the reimbursement by it of a member's expenses.

(7) The following provisions (which make provision about proceedings of local authority committees and joint committees) have effect in relation to the authority for an IFC district subject to provision made by the order establishing the district—

(a) sections 100A to 100D, 104 and 106 of, and paragraphs 39 to 43 of Schedule 12 to, the Local Government Act 1972 (c. 70);

(b) section 13 of the Local Government and Housing Act 1989 (c. 42);

(c) Chapter 1 of Part 3 of the Local Government Act 2000 (c. 22).

(8) In this section—

"the fishing community" means all persons with any sort of interest in the exploitation of sea fisheries resources or in fisheries for such resources;

"marine environmental matters" means—

(a) the conservation or enhancement of the natural beauty or amenity of marine or coastal areas (including their geological or physiographical features) or of any features of archaeological or historic interest in such areas, or

(b) the conservation of flora or fauna which are dependent on, or associated with, a marine or coastal environment.

(9) Until the date of the coming into force of section 1, the reference in subsection (1)(b) to the MMO is to be read as a reference to the Secretary of State.

Any person appointed by the Secretary of State as a member of an IFC authority is, on and after that date, to be treated as if appointed by the MMO.

152 Amendment or revocation of orders under section 149

(1) The Secretary of State may amend or revoke an order made under section 149.

(2) Before amending or revoking an order made under section 149 the Secretary of State must consult—

(a) the authority for the IFC district established by the order,

(b) the council for every local authority area that falls within the IFC district established by the order,

(c) the Environment Agency,

(d) Natural England,

(e) the MMO,

(f) the authority for any IFC district that adjoins the IFC district established by the order,

(g) the Welsh Ministers, in a case where the IFC district established by the order adjoins the Welsh inshore region,

and any other person likely to be affected by the amendment or revocation of the order.

Marine and Coastal Access Act 2009 (c. 23)
Part 6 – Management of inshore fisheries
Chapter 1 – Inshore fisheries and conservation authorities

2541

Main duties

153 Management of inshore fisheries

(1) The authority for an IFC district must manage the exploitation of sea fisheries resources in that district.

(2) In performing its duty under subsection (1), the authority for an IFC district must—

    (a) seek to ensure that the exploitation of sea fisheries resources is carried out in a sustainable way,

    (b) seek to balance the social and economic benefits of exploiting the sea fisheries resources of the district with the need to protect the marine environment from, or promote its recovery from, the effects of such exploitation,

    (c) take any other steps which in the authority's opinion are necessary or expedient for the purpose of making a contribution to the achievement of sustainable development, and

    (d) seek to balance the different needs of persons engaged in the exploitation of sea fisheries resources in the district.

(3) The Secretary of State may give guidance to the authority for an IFC district with respect to the performance of its duty under subsection (1).

(4) The Secretary of State must give every IFC authority guidance as to how the authority is to perform its duty under subsection (1) so as to make a contribution to the achievement of sustainable development.

(5) In performing its duty under subsection (1), the authority for an IFC district must have regard to any guidance given to it by the Secretary of State.

(6) Before giving any such guidance the Secretary of State must consult—

    (a) every IFC authority to which the Secretary of State is proposing to give guidance, and

    (b) such other bodies or persons as the Secretary of State considers appropriate.

(7) In preparing any such guidance the Secretary of State must take into consideration—

    (a) the functions of IFC authorities,

    (b) functions which are exercisable in IFC districts by other bodies and persons, and

    (c) the resources available, or likely to be available, to each IFC authority to which the Secretary of State is proposing to give guidance.

(8) The Secretary of State must publish, in such manner as the Secretary of State may determine, any guidance given to IFC authorities by virtue of subsection (4).

(9) An IFC authority that has been given any such guidance must provide any person on request with a copy of the whole or any part of any such guidance.

(10) In this Chapter "sea fisheries resources" means any animals or plants, other than fish falling within subsection (11), that habitually live in the sea, including those that are cultivated in the sea.

(11) The fish referred to in subsection (10) are—

2542   *Marine and Coastal Access Act 2009 (c. 23)*
Part 6 − Management of inshore fisheries
Chapter 1 − Inshore fisheries and conservation authorities

    (a)   salmon, trout, eels, lampreys, smelt and shad;

    (b)   any other fish of a kind which migrates from fresh to salt water, or from salt to fresh water, in order to spawn;

    (c)   any freshwater fish.

In this subsection "eels", "freshwater fish", "salmon", "smelt" and "trout" have the same meanings as in the Salmon and Freshwater Fisheries Act 1975 (c. 51) (see section 41 of that Act).

(12)   Any reference in this Chapter to the "exploitation" of sea fisheries resources is a reference to any activity relating to the exploitation of such resources, whether carried out for commercial purposes or otherwise, including—

    (a)   fishing for, taking, retaining on board, trans-shipping, landing, transporting or storing such resources,

    (b)   selling, displaying, exposing or offering for sale or possessing such resources, and

    (c)   introducing such resources to the sea or cultivating such resources.

154   Protection of marine conservation zones

(1)   The authority for an IFC district must seek to ensure that the conservation objectives of any MCZ in the district are furthered.

(2)   Nothing in section 153(2) is to affect the performance of the duty imposed by this section.

(3)   In this section—

    (a)   "MCZ" means a marine conservation zone designated by an order under section 116;

    (b)   the reference to the conservation objectives of an MCZ is a reference to the conservation objectives stated for the MCZ under section 117(2)(b).

Byelaws

155   Power to make byelaws

(1)   For the purposes of performing the duty imposed by section 153 or the duty imposed by section 154, the authority for an IFC district may make byelaws for that district.

(2)   Byelaws made under this section must be observed within the district for which they are made.

(3)   A byelaw made under this section does not have effect until it is confirmed by the Secretary of State.

This is subject to section 157 (emergency byelaws).

(4)   The Secretary of State may confirm a byelaw without modification or with such modifications as are agreed to by the IFC authority that made the byelaw.

(5)   Before confirming a byelaw, the Secretary of State may cause a local inquiry to be held.

Marine and Coastal Access Act 2009 (c. 23)
Part 6 — Management of inshore fisheries
Chapter 1 — Inshore fisheries and conservation authorities

2543

156 Provision that may be made by byelaw

(1) The provision that may be made by a byelaw under section 155 includes provision falling within any one or more of the Heads set out in—

    (a) subsection (3) (prohibition or restriction of exploitation of sea fisheries resources),

    (b) subsection (4) (permits),

    (c) subsection (5) (vessels, methods and gear),

    (d) subsection (6) (protection of fisheries for shellfish),

    (e) subsection (7) (monitoring of exploitation of resources);

    (f) subsection (8) (information).

(2) In the following provisions of this section "specified" means specified in the byelaw.

(3) Head 1 is provision prohibiting or restricting the exploitation of sea fisheries resources, including—

    (a) provision prohibiting or restricting such exploitation in specified areas or during specified periods;

    (b) provision limiting the amount of sea fisheries resources a person or vessel may take in a specified period;

    (c) provision limiting the amount of time a person or vessel may spend fishing for or taking sea fisheries resources in a specified period.

(4) Head 2 is provision prohibiting or restricting the exploitation of sea fisheries resources without a permit issued by an IFC authority, including—

    (a) provision for the charging of fees for permits;

    (b) provision enabling conditions to be attached to a permit;

    (c) provision enabling an IFC authority to limit the number of permits issued by it.

(5) Head 3 is—

    (a) provision prohibiting or restricting the use of vessels of specified descriptions;

    (b) provision prohibiting or restricting any method of exploiting sea fisheries resources;

    (c) provision prohibiting or restricting the possession, use, retention on board, storage or transportation of specified items, or items of a specified description, that are used in the exploitation of sea fisheries resources;

    (d) provision for determining whether such items are items of a specified description.

(6) Head 4 is provision for and in connection with the protection of fisheries for shellfish, including—

    (a) provision requiring shellfish the removal or possession of which is prohibited by or in pursuance of any Act to be re-deposited in specified localities;

    (b) provision for the protection of culch and other material for the reception of the spat or young of shellfish;

    (c) provision requiring such material to be re-deposited in specified localities;

    (d) provision constituting, within an IFC district, a district of oyster cultivation for the purposes of subsection (2)(c) of section 16 of the Sea

2544

Marine and Coastal Access Act 2009 (c. 23)
Part 6 – Management of inshore fisheries
Chapter 1 – Inshore fisheries and conservation authorities

Fisheries (Shellfish) Act 1967 (c. 83) (which prohibits the sale of oysters between certain dates);

    (e)   provision directing that section 17(2) of that Act (which affords a defence to a person charged with an offence under that section) does not apply.

(7)   Head 5 is provision for and in connection with the monitoring of exploitation of sea fisheries resources, including—

    (a)   provision requiring vessels to be fitted with specified equipment;

    (b)   provision requiring vessels to carry on board specified persons, or persons of a specified description, for the purpose of observing activities carried out on those vessels;

    (c)   provision requiring specified items, or items of a specified description, that are used in the exploitation of sea fisheries resources to be marked in such manner as may be specified.

(8)   Head 6 is provision requiring persons involved in the exploitation of sea fisheries resources in an IFC district to provide the authority for the district with specified information.

157   Emergency byelaws

(1)   A byelaw that is made by an IFC authority in the circumstances described in subsection (2) has effect without being confirmed by the Secretary of State.

(2)   The circumstances are that—

    (a)   the IFC authority considers that there is an urgent need for the byelaw, and

    (b)   the need to make the byelaw could not reasonably have been foreseen.

(3)   A byelaw that has effect by virtue of this section (an "emergency byelaw")—

    (a)   comes into force on a date specified in the byelaw, and

    (b)   remains in force (unless revoked or extended) for such period, not exceeding 12 months, as is specified in the byelaw.

(4)   An IFC authority may, with the written approval of the Secretary of State, extend the period for which an emergency byelaw is to remain in force.

(5)   An IFC authority—

    (a)   may extend that period only once;

    (b)   may not extend that period by more than 6 months.

(6)   The Secretary of State may not give the approval referred to in subsection (4) unless satisfied that—

    (a)   during the period for which the emergency byelaw has been in force, the IFC authority has used its best endeavours to make a byelaw that will make the emergency byelaw unnecessary, and

    (b)   there would be a significant and adverse effect on the marine environment if the approval was not given.

(7)   An IFC authority must within 24 hours of making an emergency byelaw notify the Secretary of State of it.

Marine and Coastal Access Act 2009 (c. 23)   2545
Part 6 – Management of inshore fisheries
Chapter 1 – Inshore fisheries and conservation authorities

158   Byelaws: supplementary provision

(1)   The power to make byelaws under section 155 includes power to make different provision for different cases or different circumstances, including (in particular) —

    (a)   different parts of an IFC district;

    (b)   different times of the year;

    (c)   different descriptions of sea fisheries resources.

(2)   The power to make byelaws under section 155 also includes —

    (a)   power to provide for exceptions or conditions;

    (b)   power to provide for a byelaw to cease to have effect after a specified period.

(3)   Subject to subsection (5), the provision that may be made by a byelaw under section 155 includes provision that prohibits, restricts or otherwise interferes with the exercise of a right to which subsection (4) applies.

(4)   This subsection applies to —

    (a)   any right of several fishery;

    (b)   any right on, to or over any portion of the seashore that is enjoyed by a person under a local or special Act, a Royal charter, letters patent, or by prescription or immemorial usage.

(5)   An IFC authority may make a byelaw that prohibits, or significantly restricts or interferes with, the exercise of a right to which subsection (4) applies only if the person who enjoys the right consents.

(6)   Subsection (5) does not apply in relation to the exercise of such a right in relation to any of the following sites —

    (a)   a site of special scientific interest, within the meaning of Part 2 of the Wildlife and Countryside Act 1981 (c. 69);

    (b)   a national nature reserve declared in accordance with section 35 of that Act;

    (c)   a Ramsar site, within the meaning of section 37A of that Act;

    (d)   a European marine site, within the meaning of the Conservation (Natural Habitats, &c) Regulations 1994 (S.I. 1994/2716);

    (e)   a marine conservation zone designated by an order under section 116.

(7)   In this section "specified" means specified in the byelaw.

159   Power of Secretary of State to amend or revoke byelaws

(1)   If the Secretary of State is satisfied that any provision made by a byelaw under section 155 is unnecessary, inadequate or disproportionate, the Secretary of State may by order —

    (a)   revoke the byelaw, or

    (b)   amend the byelaw so as to restrict its application.

(2)   Before amending or revoking a byelaw under this section, the Secretary of State must —

    (a)   notify the IFC authority that made the byelaw, and

    (b)   consider any objection made by it.

2546

Marine and Coastal Access Act 2009 (c. 23)
Part 6 — Management of inshore fisheries
Chapter 1 — Inshore fisheries and conservation authorities

(3) Before amending or revoking a byelaw under this section, the Secretary of State may cause a local inquiry to be held.

(4) An order made under this section must be published in such manner as the Secretary of State may by regulations provide.

(5) Nothing in this section affects the power of an IFC authority by virtue of section 14 of the Interpretation Act 1978 (c. 30) to amend or revoke any byelaw that it has made.

160 Byelaws: procedure

(1) The Secretary of State may make regulations about the procedure to be followed by an IFC authority in relation to byelaws.

(2) The provision that may be made in regulations under this section includes —
   (a) provision about steps to be taken, including consultation with persons or bodies specified, or of a description specified, in the regulations, before a byelaw may be made or revoked;
   (b) provision about obtaining confirmation of a byelaw;
   (c) provision about any procedure for making or revoking emergency byelaws;
   (d) provision treating a byelaw that extends the period for which an emergency byelaw is to remain in force as if it were an emergency byelaw;
   (e) provision for and in connection with the publication of byelaws;
   (f) provision requiring any byelaws made for an IFC district to be displayed in that district in such manner as the regulations may specify;
   (g) provision for copies of byelaws to be supplied to persons on request;
   (h) provision for and in connection with keeping byelaws under review, including provision for and in connection with the consideration of any representations made in relation to byelaws;
   (i) provision about steps to be taken by an IFC authority where a byelaw is amended or revoked by the Secretary of State.

(3) Regulations under this section may make different provision for cases where an IFC authority has entered into an agreement under section 167 authorising a body to perform any of the authority's functions relating to byelaws.

161 Inquiries

(1) Subsections (2) to (5) of section 250 of the Local Government Act 1972 (c. 70) (local inquiries: evidence and costs) apply, with the modifications described in subsection (2) of this section, to any inquiry under section 155(5) or section 159(3) as they apply to inquiries under section 250 of that Act.

(2) The modifications are —
   (a) references in section 250 of the Local Government Act 1972 to the person appointed to hold the inquiry are to be read as references to the Secretary of State;
   (b) references in that section to the Minister causing an inquiry to be held are to be read as references to the Secretary of State;

Marine and Coastal Access Act 2009 (c. 23)
Part 6 – Management of inshore fisheries
Chapter 1 – Inshore fisheries and conservation authorities

2547

  (c) subsection (3) of that section applies as if for the words from "a fine" to the end there were substituted "a fine not exceeding level 1 on the standard scale";

  (d) references in subsection (4) of that section to a local authority or a party to the inquiry are to be read as references to the IFC authority that made the byelaw to which the inquiry relates.

162 Evidence of byelaws

(1) The production of a signed copy of any byelaw made under section 155 is conclusive evidence of the byelaw and of the fact that it has been made and has effect in accordance with provision made by or under this Chapter.

(2) In subsection (1) "signed" means —

  (a) in the case of an emergency byelaw, signed by a person who —

   (i) is a member or officer of the IFC authority that made the byelaw, and

   (ii) is authorised by the authority for that purpose;

  (b) in the case of any other byelaw, signed by or on behalf of the Secretary of State.

(3) A copy of a byelaw purporting to be signed as mentioned in subsection (2) is to be treated as having been properly signed unless the contrary is shown.

Offences

163 Offences

(1) A person who contravenes any byelaw made under section 155 is guilty of an offence under this section.

(2) Where any vessel is used in contravention of any byelaw made under section 155, the master, the owner and the charterer (if any) are each guilty of an offence under this section.

(3) A person who is guilty of an offence under this section is liable on summary conviction to a fine not exceeding £50,000.

(4) Proceedings for an offence under this section may be taken, and the offence may for all incidental purposes be treated as having been committed, in any part of England and Wales.

(5) In this section "contravention" includes failure to comply; and "contravene" is to be read accordingly.

164 Powers of court following conviction

(1) This section applies where a person is convicted of an offence under section 163.

(2) The court by which the person is convicted may order the forfeiture of —

  (a) any fishing gear used in the commission of the offence;

  (b) any sea fisheries resources in respect of which the offence was committed.

2548

Marine and Coastal Access Act 2009 (c. 23)
Part 6 – Management of inshore fisheries
Chapter 1 – Inshore fisheries and conservation authorities

(3)   The power conferred by subsection (2) to order the forfeiture of any sea fisheries resources includes power to order the forfeiture of any container in which the resources are being kept.

(4)   The court may, instead of ordering the forfeiture of any fishing gear or any sea fisheries resources, order the person to pay a sum of money representing the value of the fishing gear or resources.

(5)   In a case where the offence involved the breach of a condition of an IFC authority permit, the court may –

    (a)   suspend the permit, or

    (b)   disqualify the person from holding or obtaining any IFC authority permit relating to any activity to which that permit related,

for such period as the court thinks fit.

(6)   In subsection (5) "IFC authority permit" means a permit granted by an IFC authority.

Enforcement

165   Inshore fisheries and conservation officers

(1)   An IFC authority may appoint persons to be inshore fisheries and conservation officers ("IFC officers").

(2)   The carrying out of any functions of an IFC officer by a person appointed by an IFC authority under this section is subject to any limitations specified by the authority in relation to that person.

(3)   In this Chapter any reference to the IFC district for which an officer has been appointed is a reference to the district of the IFC authority that appointed the officer.

166   Powers of IFC officers

(1)   An IFC officer appointed for an IFC district has the powers referred to in subsection (3) for the purposes of enforcing –

    (a)   any byelaws made under section 155 for the district (or having effect as if so made);

    (b)   sections 1 to 3, 5 and 6 of the Sea Fish (Conservation) Act 1967 (c. 84) and any orders made under any of those sections;

    (c)   any provision made by or under an order under section 1 of the Sea Fisheries (Shellfish) Act 1967 (c. 83) conferring a right of regulating a fishery;

    (d)   any provision of, or any rights conferred by, section 7 of that Act;

    (e)   any byelaws made under section 129 or 132 of this Act;

    (f)   section 140 of this Act.

(2)   The Secretary of State may by order amend subsection (1).

(3)   The powers are –

    (a)   the common enforcement powers conferred by this Act;

    (b)   the powers conferred by sections 264, 268, 269 and 284.

(4) Subject to subsection (9), the powers which an IFC officer has for the purposes referred to in subsection (1) may be exercised—

    (a) in the IFC district for which the officer has been appointed;

    (b) in any IFC district adjoining that district;

    (c) in any other place in England and Wales, in relation to an offence which the officer reasonably believes has been committed within the IFC district for which the officer has been appointed;

    (d) in relation to any vessel in waters within British fishery limits, excluding the Scottish zone and the Northern Ireland zone, which the officer reasonably believes has been involved in the commission of an offence within the IFC district for which the officer has been appointed;

    (e) in relation to any vessel or vehicle in Scotland or the Scottish zone which has been pursued there in accordance with subsection (5).

(5) A vessel or vehicle is pursued in accordance with this subsection if—

    (a) immediately before the pursuit of the vessel or vehicle commences—

        (i) the vessel or vehicle is in the IFC district for which the officer has been appointed, or

        (ii) in the case of a vessel operating together with one or more other vessels to carry out a single activity, any of those vessels is in that district,

    (b) before the pursuit of the vessel or vehicle commences, a signal is given for it to stop, and

    (c) the pursuit of the vessel or vehicle is not interrupted.

(6) The signal referred to in subsection (5)(b) must be given in such a way as to be audible or visible from the vessel or vehicle in question.

(7) For the purposes of subsection (5)(c), pursuit is not interrupted by reason only of the fact that—

    (a) the method of carrying out the pursuit, or

    (b) the identity of the vessel, vehicle or aircraft carrying out the pursuit,

changes during the course of the pursuit.

(8) Nothing in this section affects any right of hot pursuit which an IFC officer may have under international law.

(9) The powers which an IFC officer has for the purposes referred to in subsection (1) may not be exercised in relation to any warship belonging to Her Majesty and forming part of Her Majesty's armed forces.

Power to delegate functions

167 Power to enter into agreements with eligible bodies

(1) The authority for an IFC district may, with the approval of the Secretary of State, enter into an agreement with an eligible body authorising the eligible body to perform any function of the IFC authority—

    (a) either in relation to the district or in relation to specified parts of that district;

    (b) subject to paragraph (a), either generally or in specified cases.

"Specified" means specified in the agreement.

(2) For the purposes of this section and sections 168 to 171—

2550

Marine and Coastal Access Act 2009 (c. 23)
Part 6 — Management of inshore fisheries
Chapter 1 — Inshore fisheries and conservation authorities

       (a)   any reference to a function of an IFC authority includes a reference to a function exercisable by a person authorised, appointed or employed by the IFC authority;

       (b)   any reference to an agreement is to an agreement under this section.

(3)   The Secretary of State's approval may be given —

       (a)   in relation to a particular agreement or in relation to a description of agreements;

       (b)   unconditionally or subject to conditions specified in the approval.

(4)   An agreement under this section may not authorise an eligible body to perform any of the following functions —

       (a)   any function whose performance by the body would be incompatible with the purposes for which the body was established;

       (b)   functions under section 176 (accounts).

(5)   An agreement under this section does not prevent the IFC authority from performing a function to which the agreement relates.

(6)   The maximum period for which an agreement under this section may authorise an eligible body to perform a function is 20 years.

168   Eligible bodies

(1)   In this Chapter "eligible body", in relation to an agreement entered into by the authority for an IFC district, means any body in the following list —

       (a)   the authority for any IFC district that adjoins the district;

       (b)   the Environment Agency.

(2)   The Secretary of State may by order amend subsection (1) so as to —

       (a)   add any body or description of body to the list, or

       (b)   remove any body or description of body from it.

(3)   The Secretary of State may not exercise the power conferred by subsection (2)(a) unless —

       (a)   the body, or every body of the description, to be added to the list is a public body, and

       (b)   the Secretary of State is satisfied that at least one of the purposes or functions of the body, or bodies of the description, to be added to the list is, or is related to or connected with, an inshore marine function.

(4)   In this section "inshore marine function" means any function which relates to, or whose exercise is capable of affecting, the whole or any part of the English inshore region.

169   Variation, review and cancellation of agreements under section 167

(1)   Subject to subsection (3), the Secretary of State —

       (a)   must review an agreement no later than the end of the period of 5 years beginning with the date on which the agreement was entered into or was last reviewed by the Secretary of State, and

       (b)   if it appears appropriate to do so in the light of the review, may cancel the agreement.

(2)   Subject to subsection (3), an agreement may not be varied except —

Marine and Coastal Access Act 2009 (c. 23)
Part 6 – Management of inshore fisheries
Chapter 1 – Inshore fisheries and conservation authorities

2551

     (a)   by agreement between the IFC authority and the eligible body, and

     (b)   with the approval of the Secretary of State.

(3)   An approval given under section 167(1) may provide that subsection (1) or (2) of this section does not apply (or that both of them do not apply).

170 Agreements under section 167: particular powers

(1)   The fact that a function is conferred by or under this Act or an Act passed after the passing of this Act does not prevent it from being the subject of an agreement.

(2)   An IFC authority may, under an agreement, authorise an eligible body to perform a function even though, under the enactment or subordinate legislation conferring that function on the IFC authority, –

     (a)   the function is conferred on the IFC authority by reference to specified circumstances or cases and the same type of function is conferred on the eligible body in different specified circumstances or cases,

     (b)   the function is exercisable by the IFC authority and the eligible body jointly,

     (c)   the eligible body is required to be, or may be, consulted about the function (whether generally or in specified circumstances), or

     (d)   the eligible body is required to consent to the exercise of the function (whether generally or in specified circumstances).

(3)   An agreement may provide –

     (a)   for the performance of a function to be subject to the fulfilment of conditions;

     (b)   for payments to be made in respect of the performance of the function.

(4)   Any eligible body which is authorised under an agreement to perform a function –

     (a)   is to be treated as having power to do so;

     (b)   may, unless (or except to the extent that) the agreement provides for this paragraph not to apply, authorise a committee, sub-committee, member, officer or employee of the body to perform the function on its behalf.

(5)   Subject to subsection (4)(b), an eligible body which is authorised under an agreement to perform a function may not authorise any other body or person to perform that function.

(6)   Section 182 (exemption from liability) applies in relation to any function which an eligible body is authorised under an agreement to perform as if the reference to an IFC authority were a reference to the eligible body.

171 Supplementary provisions with respect to agreements under section 167

(1)   An agreement under section 167, and any approval given by the Secretary of State under that section, must be in writing.

(2)   An IFC authority which has entered into an agreement with an eligible body must arrange for a copy of the agreement to be published in a way that the IFC authority thinks is suitable for bringing it to the attention of persons likely to be affected by it.

2552   *Marine and Coastal Access Act 2009 (c. 23)*
Part 6 – Management of inshore fisheries
Chapter 1 – Inshore fisheries and conservation authorities

(3)   No power of a Minister of the Crown under any enactment to give directions to a statutory body extends to giving a direction—

      (a)   requiring it to enter into an agreement under section 167;

      (b)   prohibiting it from entering into such an agreement;

      (c)   requiring it to include, or prohibiting it from including, particular terms in such an agreement;

      (d)   requiring it to negotiate, or prohibiting it from negotiating, a variation or termination of such an agreement.

(4)   Schedule 15 to the Deregulation and Contracting Out Act 1994 (c. 40) (restrictions on disclosure of information) applies in relation to an authorisation by an IFC authority or an eligible body under section 167 or 170 of this Act as it applies in relation to an authorisation under section 69 of that Act by an office-holder.

Other powers and duties of IFC authorities

172   Development, etc of fisheries

(1)   An IFC authority may take such steps as it considers necessary or expedient for or in connection with the development of any fishery for any sea fisheries resources.

(2)   Subject to any provision made by or under any Act, the power conferred by subsection (1) includes power to stock or restock a public fishery for any sea fisheries resources.

(3)   Nothing in this Chapter is to be taken as preventing an IFC authority from making an application for, or being the grantee of, an order under section 1 of the Sea Fisheries (Shellfish) Act 1967 (c. 83) (orders as to fisheries for shellfish).

173   Provision of services by IFC authorities

(1)   An IFC authority may enter into arrangements with another person or body for the provision by the authority of services that are required by the person or body in connection with the exercise of the person's or body's functions.

(2)   The power conferred by subsection (1) includes—

      (a)   power to enter into arrangements with any person who is entitled to a right of regulating a fishery conferred by an order under section 1 of the Sea Fisheries (Shellfish) Act 1967 for the provision of services that are required by the person in connection with the enforcement of any provision made by or under the order;

      (b)   power to enter into arrangements with—

          (i)   any person who is entitled to a right of several fishery conferred by an order under that section, or

          (ii)   any person who owns a private shellfish bed (within the meaning of that Act),

      for the provision of services that are required by the person in connection with the enforcement of any provision of, or any rights conferred by, section 7 of that Act.

Marine and Coastal Access Act 2009 (c. 23)
Part 6 – Management of inshore fisheries
Chapter 1 – Inshore fisheries and conservation authorities

2553

(3) The terms and conditions upon which arrangements under subsection (1) are made may include provision for the making of payments to the authority by the person or body to whom the services are provided.

174 Duty of co-operation

The authority for an IFC district must take such steps as it considers appropriate to co-operate with—

(a) the authority for every IFC district adjoining that district,

(b) the Welsh Ministers, in a case where that district adjoins the Welsh inshore region, and

(c) any other public authority that exercises functions relating to—

    (i) the regulation of activities carried on in any part of the sea lying within that district, or

    (ii) enforcement in that part of the sea.

175 Information

(1) Every IFC authority must collect such statistics relating to the exploitation of sea fisheries resources within its district as it considers necessary for the purposes of performing its duty under section 153.

(2) Every IFC authority must provide the Secretary of State with such information as the Secretary of State may reasonably require about—

(a) proceedings of the IFC authority;

(b) sea fisheries within the authority's district;

(c) the effect of the exploitation of sea fisheries resources in that district on the marine environment.

176 Accounts

(1) An IFC authority must keep proper accounts and proper records in relation to the accounts.

(2) The accounts of an IFC authority that by virtue of section 150(3) is a joint committee of councils must be made up yearly to 31st March.

177 Annual plan

(1) Before the beginning of each financial year every IFC authority must make and publish a plan setting out the authority's main objectives and priorities for the year.

(2) The IFC authority must send a copy of its plan to the Secretary of State.

178 Annual report

(1) As soon as is reasonably practicable after the end of each financial year, every IFC authority must prepare a report on its activities in that year.

(2) A report under this section must be in such form and contain such information as the Secretary of State may require.

(3) A report under this section must be published in such manner as the Secretary of State may require.

2554   *Marine and Coastal Access Act 2009 (c. 23)*
                                       Part 6 – Management of inshore fisheries
                            Chapter 1 – Inshore fisheries and conservation authorities

(4)   The IFC authority must send a copy of the report to the Secretary of State.

179   Supplementary powers

(1)   An IFC authority may do anything which appears to it to be necessary or expedient for the purpose of or in connection with the exercise of any of its other functions.

(2)   In particular it may —
   (a)   acquire or dispose of land or other property;
   (b)   enter into arrangements with other IFC authorities for the establishment of a body to co-ordinate the activities of those authorities which are party to the arrangements.

(3)   But an IFC authority has no power to borrow money.

Miscellaneous and supplemental

180   Expenses of IFC authorities

(1)   The expenses incurred by the authority for an IFC district are to be defrayed by the relevant council or councils.

(2)   Where there is more than one relevant council for an IFC district, each council must pay such portion of the expenses incurred by the authority for the district as is specified in, or determined in accordance with, the order establishing the district.

   The order may provide for the portion of the expenses payable by a relevant council to be calculated by reference to any circumstances whatsoever.

(3)   Accordingly, section 103 of the Local Government Act 1972 (c. 70) (expenses of joint committees) does not apply in relation to an IFC authority.

(4)   The total amount of an IFC authority's expenses to be defrayed under subsection (1) for any particular financial year may be vetoed by a vote of those members of the IFC authority who are members of a relevant council.

181   IFC authority as party to proceedings

An IFC authority is capable (despite being an unincorporated body) of —
   (a)   making contracts;
   (b)   bringing proceedings under this Act in its own name;
   (c)   bringing or defending any other proceedings in its own name.

182   Exemption from liability

(1)   No person who is a member or employee of an IFC authority is to be liable for anything done (or omitted to be done) in, or in connection with, the discharge or purported discharge of the authority's functions.

(2)   Subsection (1) does not apply if the act or omission is shown to have been in bad faith.

(3)   The reference in subsection (1) to an employee of an IFC authority does not include any IFC officer acting as such an officer.

Marine and Coastal Access Act 2009 (c. 23)
Part 6 – Management of inshore fisheries
Chapter 1 – Inshore fisheries and conservation authorities

2555

(For provision exempting such officers from liability, see section 291.)

183 Report by Secretary of State

(1) As soon as is reasonably practicable after the end of every relevant four-year period, the Secretary of State must lay before Parliament a report about the conduct and operation of the authorities for any IFC districts in existence during the whole or part of that period.

(2) In this section "relevant four-year period" means—
  (a) the period of four years beginning with the day on which the Secretary of State first made an order under section 149;
  (b) each subsequent period of four years.

184 Minor and consequential amendments

Schedule 14 (which contains minor and consequential amendments relating to IFC authorities) has effect.

185 Application to the Crown

(1) This Chapter is binding on the Crown and applies in relation to any Crown land as it applies in relation to any other land.
This is subject to subsection (2).

(2) No contravention by the Crown of any provision of this Chapter is to make the Crown criminally liable; but the High Court may declare unlawful any act or omission of the Crown which constitutes such a contravention.

(3) Despite subsection (2), the provisions of this Chapter apply to persons in the public service of the Crown as they apply to other persons.

(4) For the purposes of this section "Crown land" means land an interest in which—
  (a) belongs to Her Majesty in right of the Crown or in right of Her private estates,
  (b) belongs to Her Majesty in right of the Duchy of Lancaster,
  (c) belongs to the Duchy of Cornwall, or
  (d) belongs to a government department or is held in trust for Her Majesty for the purposes of a government department.

(5) In this section references to Her Majesty's private estates are to be construed in accordance with section 1 of the Crown Private Estates Act 1862 (c. 37).

186 Interpretation of this Chapter

(1) In this Chapter—
    "authority for an IFC district" is to be read in accordance with section 150(2);
    "eligible body" has the meaning given by section 168;
    "IFC authority" means an inshore fisheries and conservation authority (see section 150);
    "IFC district" means an inshore fisheries and conservation district (see section 149);

2556

Marine and Coastal Access Act 2009 (c. 23)
Part 6 – Management of inshore fisheries
Chapter 1 – Inshore fisheries and conservation authorities

"IFC officer" means an inshore fisheries and conservation officer (see section 165);

"local authority area" means—

    (a)   a county, a London borough or a metropolitan district,

    (b)   a non-metropolitan district comprised in an area for which there is no county council,

    (c)   the City of London, or

    (d)   the Isles of Scilly;

"the marine environment" includes—

    (a)   geological or physiographical features of marine or coastal areas;

    (b)   features of archaeological or historic interest in such areas;

    (c)   flora and fauna which are dependent on, or associated with, a marine or coastal environment;

"master" includes, in relation to any vessel, the person for the time being in command or charge of the vessel;

"relevant council", in relation to an IFC district, means the council for a local authority area falling within the district;

"sea fisheries resources" has the meaning given by section 153;

"seashore" means the shore and bed of the sea;

"shellfish" includes crustaceans and molluscs of any kind;

"vessel" includes any ship or boat or any other description of vessel used in navigation.

(2)   Any reference in this Chapter to the exploitation of sea fisheries resources is to be read in accordance with section 153(12).

CHAPTER 2

LOCAL FISHERIES COMMITTEES

187 Abolition of local fisheries committees

The Sea Fisheries Regulation Act 1966 (c. 38), which provides for the establishment of sea fisheries districts and local fisheries committees, is repealed.

188 Power to make consequential or transitional provision, etc

(1)   The appropriate national authority may by order make such incidental, consequential, supplemental or transitional provision or savings as appear to the authority to be necessary or expedient in consequence of the repeal of the Sea Fisheries Regulation Act 1966 ("the 1966 Act").

(2)   The provision that may be made by an order under this section includes—

    (a)   provision for and in connection with the transfer of any staff, property, rights or liabilities of a local fisheries committee to such bodies or persons (including the authority making the order) as may be specified;

    (b)   provision about byelaws made by a local fisheries committee or a body having the powers of such a committee, including—

        (i)   in so far as any provision of any such byelaw in force at the time of the making of the order could have been made under some

Marine and Coastal Access Act 2009 (c. 23)
Part 6 – Management of inshore fisheries
Chapter 2 – Local fisheries committees

2557

other enactment, provision for that provision to have effect as if comprised in subordinate legislation made by a specified body or person under that enactment;

    (ii)   provision as to the area to which any provision having effect by virtue of sub-paragraph (i) applies;

  (c)   provision about the local fisheries committee for any sea fisheries district lying partly in England and partly in Wales, including—

    (i)   provision for that part of the district lying in England or (as the case may be) Wales to be treated as if it were a sea fisheries district created under section 1 of the 1966 Act, and

    (ii)   provision for the committee to continue in being as a local fisheries committee for the district established by virtue of sub-paragraph (i), with such changes to its constitution as appear to the authority making the order to be necessary or expedient;

  (d)   provision amending, repealing or revoking any provision of this Act or any other enactment passed or made before, or in the same Session as, this Act.

(3)   The provision that may be made by virtue of subsection (2)(a) includes—

  (a)   provision for the transfer of any property, rights or liabilities to have effect subject to exceptions or reservations specified in, or determined in accordance with, the order;

  (b)   provision for the transfer of any property, rights or liabilities, whether or not otherwise capable of being transferred or assigned, including any rights conferred by an order made under section 1 of the Sea Fisheries (Shellfish) Act 1967 (c. 83);

  (c)   provision for an order under this section providing for the transfer of property, rights or liabilities to have effect in spite of any provision (of whatever nature) which would prevent or restrict the transfer of the property, rights or liabilities otherwise than by the order.

(4)   The reference in subsection (2)(a) to property of a local fisheries committee includes a reference to—

  (a)   any property held on behalf of such a committee;

  (b)   any property of a relevant local authority held for the purposes of such a committee.

(5)   In subsection (2)(d) "enactment" includes an enactment comprised in subordinate legislation.

(6)   In this section—

    "appropriate national authority" means—

      (a)   in relation to sea fisheries districts in England, or any part of a sea fisheries district lying in England, the Secretary of State;

      (b)   in relation to sea fisheries districts in Wales, or any part of a sea fisheries district lying in Wales, the Welsh Ministers;

    "England" includes the English inshore region;

    "local fisheries committee" means a local fisheries committee constituted by an order made, or having effect as if made, under section 1 of the 1966 Act;

    "relevant local authority" means—

      (a)   in the case of a local fisheries committee that is a committee of a county, county borough or metropolitan district council, that council;

2558

Marine and Coastal Access Act 2009 (c. 23)
Part 6 — Management of inshore fisheries
Chapter 2 — Local fisheries committees

  (b) in the case of a local fisheries committee that is a joint committee of two or more such councils, any of those councils;

"specified" means specified in the order;

"Wales" includes the Welsh inshore region.

CHAPTER 3

INSHORE FISHERIES IN WALES

189 Power of Welsh Ministers in relation to fisheries in Wales

(1) Subject to subsection (2), the Welsh Ministers may by order make any provision in relation to Wales which the authority for an IFC district may make for that district by a byelaw made under section 155.

(2) To the extent that the Welsh Ministers have power, apart from this section, to make provision of the kind referred to in subsection (1) (whether by order or otherwise), subsection (1) does not apply.

(3) In this section—

  "authority for an IFC district" has the same meaning as in Chapter 1 of this Part;

  "Wales" has the same meaning as in the Government of Wales Act 2006 (c. 32).

190 Offences

(1) A person who contravenes any provision of an order made under section 189 is guilty of an offence under this section.

(2) Where any vessel is used in contravention of any provision of an order made under section 189, the master, the owner and the charterer (if any) are each guilty of an offence under this section.

(3) A person who is guilty of an offence under this section is liable on summary conviction to a fine not exceeding £50,000.

(4) Proceedings for an offence under this section may be taken, and the offence may for all incidental purposes be treated as having been committed, in any part of England and Wales.

(5) No contravention by the Crown of this section is to make the Crown criminally liable; but the High Court may declare unlawful any act or omission of the Crown which constitutes such a contravention.

(6) Despite subsection (5), this section applies to persons in the public service of the Crown as it applies to other persons.

(7) In this section "contravention" includes failure to comply; and "contravene" is to be read accordingly.

191 Powers of court following conviction

(1) This section applies where a person is convicted of an offence under section 190.

Marine and Coastal Access Act 2009 (c. 23)
Part 6 – Management of inshore fisheries
Chapter 3 – Inshore fisheries in Wales

2559

(2) The court by which the person is convicted may order the forfeiture of —

    (a) any fishing gear used in the commission of the offence;

    (b) any sea fisheries resources in respect of which the offence was committed.

(3) The power conferred by subsection (2) to order the forfeiture of any sea fisheries resources includes power to order the forfeiture of any container in which the resources are being kept.

(4) The court may, instead of ordering the forfeiture of any fishing gear or any sea fisheries resources, order the person to pay a sum of money representing the value of the fishing gear or resources.

(5) In a case where the offence involved the breach of a condition of a permit granted by the Welsh Ministers, the court may —

    (a) suspend the permit, or

    (b) disqualify the person from holding or obtaining any such permit relating to any activity to which that permit related,

for such period as the court thinks fit.

(6) In this section "sea fisheries resources" has the same meaning as in Chapter 1 of this Part (see section 153).

192 Power to provide services for purposes of enforcement

(1) The Welsh Ministers may —

    (a) enter into arrangements with any person who is entitled to a right of regulating a fishery conferred by an order under section 1 of the Sea Fisheries (Shellfish) Act 1967 (c. 83) for the provision of services that are required by the person in connection with the enforcement of any provision made by or under the order;

    (b) enter into arrangements with —

        (i) any person who is entitled to a right of several fishery conferred by an order under that section, or

        (ii) any person who owns a private shellfish bed (within the meaning of that Act),

    for the provision of services that are required by the person in connection with the enforcement of any provision of, or any rights conferred by, section 7 of that Act.

(2) The terms and conditions upon which arrangements under subsection (1) are made may include provision for the making of payments to the Welsh Ministers by the person or body to whom the services are provided.

193 Miscellaneous amendments

(1) Section 2 of the Coast Protection Act 1949 (c. 74) (constitution of coast protection boards) is amended as set out in subsections (2) and (3).

(2) In subsection (2), after paragraph (b) insert —

        "(ba) the Welsh Ministers, in relation to any powers or duties they have in relation to fishing and fisheries in any part of the area;".

(3) In subsection (8)(a), after "Sea Fish Industry Act 1951," insert "or the Welsh Ministers,".

2560   *Marine and Coastal Access Act 2009 (c. 23)*
Part 6 – Management of inshore fisheries
Chapter 3 – Inshore fisheries in Wales

(4) In section 27(1) of the Wildlife and Countryside Act 1981 (c. 69) (interpretation of Part 1), in paragraph (c) of the definition of "authorised person", for "by any" substitute "by –

> (i) the Welsh Ministers, in relation to things done for purposes relating to fishing or fisheries in the Welsh inshore region (within the meaning of the Marine and Coastal Access Act 2009);
>
> (ii) any".

PART 7

FISHERIES

CHAPTER 1

THE SEA FISH (CONSERVATION) ACT 1967

194   Size limits for sea fish

(1) Section 1 of the Sea Fish (Conservation) Act 1967 (c. 84) (size limits, etc for fish) is amended as follows.

(2) In subsection (1), for the words from ", being a fish" to "prescribed" substitute "which does not meet such requirements as to size as may be prescribed".

(3) In subsection (2), for the words from ", being a fish" to "prescribed" substitute "which does not meet such requirements as to size as may be prescribed".

(4) For subsection (3) substitute –

> "(3) Sea fish of any description which do not meet the requirements as to size prescribed in relation to sea fish of that description by an order of the appropriate national authority shall not be carried, whether within or outside relevant British fishery limits, on a relevant British vessel; and an order under this subsection may prohibit the carrying by a Scottish or Northern Ireland fishing boat or a foreign vessel in waters to which subsection (3A) applies of sea fish of any description prescribed by the order which do not meet the requirements as to size so prescribed in relation to sea fish of that description.
>
> (3A) This subsection applies to the sea within British fishery limits, other than the Scottish zone and the Northern Ireland zone.
> "Northern Ireland zone" has the meaning given by the Northern Ireland Act 1998 (see section 98 of that Act)."

(5) For subsection (9) substitute –

> "(9) In this section –
>> "the appropriate national authority" means –
>>> (a) in relation to Wales (within the meaning of the Government of Wales Act 2006), the Welsh Ministers;
>>> (b) in any other case, the Secretary of State;
>> "foreign vessel" means any vessel other than a relevant British vessel, a Scottish fishing boat or a Northern Ireland fishing boat;
>> "Northern Ireland fishing boat" means a fishing boat which is registered in the United Kingdom under Part 2 of the Merchant

Shipping Act 1995 and whose entry in the register specifies a port in Northern Ireland as the port to which the boat is to be treated as belonging;

"relevant British vessel" means a vessel, other than a Scottish fishing boat or a Northern Ireland fishing boat, which—

(a) is registered in the United Kingdom under Part 2 of the Merchant Shipping Act 1995, or

(b) is owned wholly by persons qualified to own British ships for the purposes of that Part of that Act."

195 Regulation of nets and other fishing gear

(1) Section 3 of the Sea Fish (Conservation) Act 1967 (c. 84) (regulation of nets and other fishing gear) is amended as follows.

(2) After subsection (2) insert—

"(2A) An order under this section may be made by the appropriate national authority so as to extend to nets or other fishing gear used by any person, otherwise than from a fishing boat, for fishing for or taking sea fish in the sea within the seaward limits of the territorial sea adjacent to England and Wales.

(2B) In subsection (2A) above "the appropriate national authority" means—
(a) in relation to England, the Secretary of State;
(b) in relation to Wales, the Welsh Ministers."

(3) After subsection (5) insert—

"(5A) A person who contravenes an order made under this section by virtue of subsection (2A) above shall be guilty of an offence under this section."

196 Charging for commercial fishing licences

(1) In section 4 of the Sea Fish (Conservation) Act 1967 (licensing of fishing boats) after subsection (4) (power to authorise charges for licences) insert—

"(4A) The provision that may be made in an order by virtue of subsection (4) above includes—
(a) provision for the amount of any charge to be specified in, or determined in accordance with provision made by, the order;
(b) different provision in relation to different classes of licence;
(c) provision for no charge to be payable in such circumstances as may be specified in the order."

(2) In section 22 of that Act (interpretation) after subsection (3) insert—

"(3A) Any reference in this Act to a class is a reference to a class defined or described by reference to any circumstances whatsoever (whether or not relating to fishing or vessels)."

197 Grant of licences subject to conditions imposed for environmental purposes

In section 4 of the Sea Fish (Conservation) Act 1967 (licensing of fishing boats) after subsection (6) (power to grant licences subject to conditions) insert—

"(6ZA)   The conditions subject to which a licence may be granted under this section include conditions imposed for the purposes of—

     (a)   conserving or enhancing the natural beauty or amenity of marine or coastal areas (including their geological or physiographical features) or of any features of archaeological or historic interest in such areas; or

     (b)   conserving flora or fauna which are dependent on, or associated with, a marine or coastal environment."

198   Power to restrict fishing for sea fish

(1)   Section 5 of the Sea Fish (Conservation) Act 1967 (c. 84) (power to restrict fishing for sea fish) is amended as follows.

(2)   For subsection (1) substitute—

"(1)   Subject to the provisions of this section, the appropriate national authority may make an order—

     (a)   prohibiting, in any area specified in the order and either for a period so specified or without limitation of time—

        (i)   all fishing for sea fish;

        (ii)   fishing for any description of sea fish specified in the order;

        (iii)   fishing for sea fish, or for any description of sea fish specified in the order, by any method so specified;

     (b)   restricting, in any area specified in the order and either for a period so specified or without limitation of time, the amount of sea fish, or sea fish of a description specified in the order, that may, in any period so specified, be taken by—

        (i)   any person;

        (ii)   any fishing boat.

A person who contravenes any prohibition or restriction imposed by an order under this section shall be guilty of an offence under this subsection.

(1A)   Where any fishing boat is used in contravention of any prohibition or restriction imposed by an order under this section, the master, the owner and the charterer (if any) shall each be guilty of an offence under subsection (1) above.

(1B)   An order under this section which prohibits in any area—

     (a)   fishing for sea fish, or for any description of sea fish specified in the order, or

     (b)   fishing for sea fish, or for any description of sea fish specified in the order, by any method so specified,

may provide that any fishing gear, or any fishing gear of a description specified in the order, of any fishing boat in that area must be stowed in accordance with provision made by the order.

(1C)   An order under this section restricting the amount of sea fish of any description that may be caught in a period specified in the order may provide that, for the purposes of paragraph (b) of subsection (1) above, any sea fish of that description that, after being caught in that period, is returned to the sea as soon as that amount is exceeded is not to be treated as having been caught in contravention of the restriction imposed by the order."

(3) For subsection (8) substitute —

"(8) The only provision that may be made by an order under this section in relation to an area outside British fishery limits, or an area within the Scottish zone or the Northern Ireland zone, is provision applying to —

(a) a British fishing boat, other than a Scottish fishing boat or a Northern Ireland fishing boat, that is registered in the United Kingdom; or

(b) in so far as the order relates to fishing for salmon or migratory trout, a fishing boat which is British-owned but not registered under the Merchant Shipping Act 1995.

(9) In this section —

"the appropriate national authority" means —

(a) in relation to Wales (within the meaning of the Government of Wales Act 2006), the Welsh Ministers;

(b) in any other case, the Secretary of State;

"Northern Ireland fishing boat" means a fishing boat which is registered in the United Kingdom under Part 2 of the Merchant Shipping Act 1995 and whose entry in the register specifies a port in Northern Ireland as the port to which the boat is to be treated as belonging;

"Northern Ireland zone" has the meaning given by the Northern Ireland Act 1998 (see section 98 of that Act)."

199 Penalties for offences

(1) The Sea Fish (Conservation) Act 1967 (c. 84) is amended as follows.

(2) In section 11 (penalties for offences), in subsection (1)(a) —

(a) for "section 4(3) or (6)" substitute "section 1, 2, 3, 4(3), (6) or (9A)";

(b) for "5(1) or 6(5A)(a)" substitute "5(1) or (6) or 6(5) or (5A)".

(3) In section 15 (powers of British sea-fishery officers for enforcement of that Act) —

(a) in subsection (2C) (penalties for certain offences) omit paragraph (b) and the "or" preceding it;

(b) after that subsection insert —

"(2D) Any person who assaults an officer who is exercising any of the powers conferred on him by subsection (2A) or (2B) above shall be guilty of an offence and liable on summary conviction to a fine not exceeding £50,000.

(2E) Any person who wilfully obstructs an officer in the exercise of any of the powers conferred on him by subsection (2A) or (2B) above shall be guilty of an offence and liable on summary conviction to a fine not exceeding £20,000."

(4) In section 16 (enforcement of orders under sections 1 and 2 of that Act), for

subsection (1A) (penalties for certain offences) substitute —

"(1A) Any person who assaults an officer who is exercising any of the powers conferred on him by subsection (1) above shall be guilty of an offence and liable on summary conviction to a fine not exceeding £50,000.

(1B) Any person who wilfully obstructs an officer in the exercise of any of the powers conferred on him by subsection (1) above shall be guilty of an offence and liable on summary conviction to a fine not exceeding £20,000."

200 Offences by directors, partners, etc

In the Sea Fish (Conservation) Act 1967 (c. 84), for section 12 (offences committed by bodies corporate) substitute —

"12 Offences by directors, partners, etc

(1) Where a relevant offence has been committed by a body corporate and it is proved that the offence —
  (a) has been committed with the consent or connivance of a person falling within subsection (2), or
  (b) is attributable to any neglect on the part of such a person,
that person (as well as the body corporate) is guilty of that offence and liable to be proceeded against and punished accordingly.

(2) The persons are —
  (a) a director, manager, secretary or similar officer of the body corporate;
  (b) any person who was purporting to act in such a capacity.

(3) Where the affairs of a body corporate are managed by its members, subsection (1) applies in relation to the acts and defaults of a member, in connection with that management, as if the member were a director of the body corporate.

(4) Where a relevant offence has been committed by a Scottish firm and it is proved that the offence —
  (a) has been committed with the consent or connivance of a partner of the firm or a person purporting to act as such a partner, or
  (b) is attributable to any neglect on the part of such a person,
that person (as well as the firm) is guilty of that offence and liable to be proceeded against and punished accordingly.

(5) In this section "relevant offence" means an offence under any provision of sections 1 to 6 of this Act."

201 Minor and consequential amendments

Schedule 15 contains minor and consequential amendments relating to this Chapter.

CHAPTER 2

THE SEA FISHERIES (SHELLFISH) ACT 1967

202 Power to make orders as to fisheries for shellfish

(1) Section 1 of the Sea Fisheries (Shellfish) Act 1967 (c. 83) (power to make orders as to fisheries for shellfish) is amended as set out in subsections (2) and (3).

(2) In subsection (1), for the words from "shellfish" to "Minister" substitute "shellfish of any kind specified in the order".

(3) Omit subsection (4) (certain consents required for orders made in relation to land belonging to Crown etc).

(4) In Schedule 1 to that Act (provisions with respect to making of orders under section 1), in paragraph 6 –
   (a) the existing provision is renumbered as sub-paragraph (1), and
   (b) after that sub-paragraph insert –

   "(2) Where the proposed order relates to any portion of the sea shore belonging to Her Majesty in right of the Crown, the appropriate Minister shall also have regard to the powers and duties of the Crown Estate Commissioners under the Crown Estate Act 1961."

(5) In section 15 of the Sea Fisheries Act 1968 (c. 77) (which amended section 1 of the Sea Fisheries (Shellfish) Act 1967) –
   (a) omit subsection (2);
   (b) in subsection (3), for "that section" substitute "section 1 of that Act".

203 Variation etc of orders as a result of development

In section 1 of the Sea Fisheries (Shellfish) Act 1967 (power to make orders as to fisheries for shellfish), for subsection (6) substitute –

"(6) Any order made under this section may be varied or revoked by a subsequent order made under this section.

(7) Subject to subsection (8) below, subsections (1) to (5) above shall apply in relation to any such subsequent order and to an application for such an order as they apply in relation to an original order made under this section and to an application for such an order.

(8) Subsection (7) above does not apply in the case of any order made by virtue of subsection (10) below.

(9) Subsection (10) below applies in any case where it appears to the appropriate Minister that –
   (a) permission has been granted for the carrying out of any development in, on or over any portion of the sea shore to which an order made under this section relates (the "affected area"), and
   (b) as a result of the development, it will be impossible or impracticable to exercise any right of several fishery or of regulating a fishery conferred by the order in the affected area.

(10) In any such case, the appropriate Minister may –

    (a) vary the order so that the area to which the order relates no longer includes the affected area, or

    (b) if the affected area comprises the whole or the greater part of the area to which the order relates, revoke the order.

(11) The provision that may be made by an order made by virtue of subsection (10) above includes –

    (a) provision requiring the owners of the affected area to pay compensation to any persons who, at the time of the making of the order, are entitled to a right of several fishery in any part of the affected area by virtue of an order under this section;

    (b) provision for the amount of any such compensation to be specified in, or determined in accordance with provision made by, the order (including provision for or in connection with the appointment of a person to make any such determination).

(12) Before making an order by virtue of subsection (10) above, the appropriate Minister must consult –

    (a) any persons who are entitled to a right of several fishery or a right of regulating a fishery in any part of the affected area by virtue of an order under this section, and

    (b) the owners or reputed owners, lessees or reputed lessees and occupiers, if any, of the affected area.

(13) The appropriate Minister may require the owners of the affected area to provide him with such information relating to the development as he may reasonably require for the purpose of deciding whether to make an order by virtue of subsection (10) above.

(14) In this section "development" has the same meaning as in the Town and Country Planning Act 1990."

204 Purposes for which tolls etc may be applied

(1) Section 3 of the Sea Fisheries (Shellfish) Act 1967 (c. 83) (effect of grant of right of regulating a fishery) is amended as follows.

(2) In subsection (1)(c), for "improving and cultivating" substitute "regulating".

(3) In subsection (2) –

    (a) before "any such tolls" insert ", subject to subsection (2A) of this section,";

    (b) for "in the improvement and cultivation of" substitute "for purposes relating to the regulation of".

(4) After that subsection insert –

"(2A) An order under section 1 of this Act which –

    (a) confers on the grantees a right of regulating a fishery, and

    (b) imposes tolls or royalties upon persons dredging, fishing for and taking shellfish within the limits of the fishery, or of that part of the fishery within which the right is exercisable,

may provide that the grantees may, for the purposes of recouping any costs incurred by the grantees in connection with applying for the order, retain such portion of those tolls and royalties as may be specified in the order."

(5) In subsection (4), for "for the improvement and cultivation of" substitute "for purposes relating to the regulation of".

205 Increase in penalties for certain offences relating to fisheries for shellfish

(1) The Sea Fisheries (Shellfish) Act 1967 (c. 83) is amended as follows.

(2) In section 3(3) (offence of dredging, fishing for or taking shellfish in contravention of any restriction or regulation, etc.), for "level 5 on the standard scale" substitute "£50,000".

(3) In section 7(4) (offences in relation to certain fisheries), for "level 5 on the standard scale" substitute "£50,000".

206 Liability of master, etc where vessel used in commission of offence

(1) In section 3 of the Sea Fisheries (Shellfish) Act 1967 (effect of grant of right of regulating a fishery), after subsection (4) insert—

"(5) Where any sea fishing boat is used in the commission of an offence under subsection (3) of this section, the master, the owner and the charterer (if any) shall each be guilty of an offence and liable on summary conviction to a fine not exceeding £50,000."

(2) In section 22(2) of that Act (interpretation), after the definition of "land" insert—

""master" includes, in relation to any sea fishing boat, the person for the time being in command or charge of the boat;".

207 Restrictions imposed by grantees, etc

In section 3 of the Sea Fisheries (Shellfish) Act 1967 (effect of grant of right of regulating a fishery), after subsection (5) (inserted by section 206) insert—

"(6) Subsection (1) of this section applies where an order under section 1 of this Act—
(a) confers on the grantees a right of regulating a fishery, and
(b) by virtue of section 15(3) of the Sea Fisheries Act 1968, enables the grantees to impose restrictions on, or make regulations respecting, the dredging, fishing for and taking of shellfish within the limits of the regulated fishery or part,

as it applies where an order under section 1 of this Act confers such a right and imposes such restrictions or makes such regulations.

(7) Accordingly, any reference in this section to restrictions or regulations is to be read as including a reference to any restrictions imposed by, or any regulations made by, the grantees."

208 Cancellation of licence after single relevant conviction

In section 4(7) of the Sea Fisheries (Shellfish) Act 1967 (which enables a licence granted in respect of a regulated fishery to be cancelled if the holder is convicted of two relevant offences) —

(a) for ", having been convicted" substitute "is convicted";

(b) omit ", is subsequently convicted of another such offence".

209 Register of licences

After section 4 of the Sea Fisheries (Shellfish) Act 1967 (c. 83) (licensing powers in case of regulated fishery) insert—

"4ZA Register of licences

(1) This section applies where the grantees of an order to which section 4 of this Act applies issue one or more licences in pursuance of the order.

(2) The grantees shall establish and maintain a register containing the names and addresses of all persons who for the time being hold licences issued by the grantees.

(3) The register shall be available for inspection free of charge by any person at such place or places, and during such hours, as are determined by the grantees.

(4) The grantees shall make arrangements for the provision of a copy of an entry in the register to any person on request.

(5) The arrangements that may be made under subsection (4) of this section include arrangements for the payment of a reasonable fee by the person making the request."

210 Protection of private shellfish beds

(1) Section 7 of the Sea Fisheries (Shellfish) Act 1967 (protection of fisheries) is amended as follows.

(2) In subsection (1)(b), for "private oyster bed" substitute "private shellfish bed".

(3) In subsections (2) and (3)—
    (a) for "oysters" substitute "relevant shellfish";
    (b) for "private oyster bed" substitute "private shellfish bed".

(4) In subsections (4) and (5)(b), for "private oyster bed" substitute "private shellfish bed".

(5) For subsection (6) substitute—

    "(6) In this section—
        "the grantees" means the persons for the time being entitled to the right of several fishery conferred by the order under section 1 of this Act;
        "relevant shellfish", in relation to a private shellfish bed, means the shellfish in respect of which the owner of the bed has private rights independently of this Act."

211 Use of implements of fishing

(1) Section 7 of the Sea Fisheries (Shellfish) Act 1967 (protection of fisheries) is amended as follows.

(2) In subsection (4), at the end of paragraph (a)(ii) insert "or

    (iii) in the case of several fishery, an implement of a type specified by or under the order and so used as not to disturb or injure in any manner shellfish of the description in question or any bed for such shellfish or the fishery for such shellfish;".

(3) After subsection (4) insert—

"(4A) The power to specify a type of implement for the purposes of subsection (4)(a)(iii) of this section includes power to specify—

    (a) periods during which implements of that type may or may not be used;

    (b) parts of the area of the fishery with respect to which the right of several fishery is conferred in which implements of that type may or may not be used.

The exception in subsection (4)(a)(iii) of this section does not apply in a case of a person who uses an implement otherwise than in accordance with provision made by virtue of this subsection."

212 Taking of crabs and lobsters for scientific purposes

(1) Section 17 of the Sea Fisheries (Shellfish) Act 1967 (c. 83) (taking and sale of certain crabs and lobsters prohibited) is amended as follows.

(2) In subsection (1), for "subsection (2)" substitute "subsections (2) and (2A)".

(3) After subsection (2) insert—

"(2A) Any person who takes or has in his possession any edible crab falling within paragraph (a) or (b) of subsection (1) of this section shall not be guilty of an offence under that subsection if—

    (a) the crabs were taken from that part of the sea that is within British fishery limits and does not include the Scottish zone or the Northern Ireland zone,

    (b) the person has been granted authority by the appropriate body to take such crabs for the purpose of scientific investigation, and

    (c) the crabs were taken for that purpose and in accordance with such authority."

(4) In subsection (3), for "and any person" substitute "and, subject to subsection (3B) of this section, any person".

(5) Before subsection (4) insert—

"(3B) Any person who lands any lobster falling within subsection (3) of this section shall not be guilty of an offence under that subsection if—

    (a) the lobsters were taken from that part of the sea that is within British fishery limits and does not include the Scottish zone or the Northern Ireland zone,

    (b) the person has been granted authority by the appropriate body to take such lobsters for the purpose of scientific investigation, and

    (c) the lobsters were taken for that purpose and in accordance with such authority."

(6)   After subsection (5) insert —

"(6)   In this section —

"the appropriate body" means —

(a)   the Marine Management Organisation, in the case of crabs and lobsters taken from that part of the sea that is within British fishery limits and does not include —

(i)   the Scottish zone,

(ii)   the Northern Ireland zone, or

(iii)   the Welsh zone;

(b)   the Welsh Ministers, in the case of crabs and lobsters taken from the Welsh zone;

"British fishery limits" has the meaning given by section 1 of the Fishery Limits Act 1976;

"Northern Ireland zone" has the same meaning as in the Northern Ireland Act 1998;

"Welsh zone" has the same meaning as in the Government of Wales Act 2006."

213   Orders prohibiting the taking and sale of certain lobsters

(1)   Section 17 of the Sea Fisheries (Shellfish) Act 1967 (c. 83) (taking and sale of certain crabs and lobsters prohibited) is amended as set out in subsections (2) and (3) below.

(2)   In subsection (3) (orders prohibiting the taking and sale of certain lobsters), for the words from "If the Minister" to "England and Wales," substitute "If the appropriate national authority by order so directs, no person shall, in the part of the United Kingdom to which the order relates,".

(3)   For subsection (3A) substitute —

"(3ZA)   In subsection (3) of this section "the appropriate national authority" means —

(a)   in relation to England, the Secretary of State;

(b)   in relation to Wales, the Welsh Ministers;

(c)   in relation to Scotland, the Scottish Ministers."

(4)   In section 20(3) of that Act (procedure for orders made under section 17(3)), for the words from "shall be laid before Parliament" to the end substitute "shall —

(a)   in the case of an order in relation to England, be laid before Parliament;

(b)   in the case of an order in relation to Wales, be laid before the National Assembly for Wales;

(c)   in the case of an order in relation to Scotland, be laid before the Scottish Parliament."

214   Power to appoint inspector before making orders as to fisheries for shellfish

(1)   Schedule 1 to the Sea Fisheries (Shellfish) Act 1967 (provisions with respect to making of orders under section 1) is amended as follows.

(2)   In paragraph 4 (appointment of inspector) —

(a)   omit sub-paragraph (1);

(b) in sub-paragraph (2), for "The appropriate Minister shall" substitute "Where he considers it appropriate to do so, the appropriate Minister may".

(3) Omit paragraph 5.

(4) In paragraph 6, after "in paragraph 3 above or" insert ", in a case where an inspector has been appointed under paragraph 4 above,".

(5) The amendments made by this section do not apply in relation to any application made for an order under section 1 of that Act before the coming into force of this section.

CHAPTER 3

MIGRATORY AND FRESHWATER FISH

Taking fish etc

215 Prohibited implements

(1) In the Salmon and Freshwater Fisheries Act 1975 (c. 51), section 1 (prohibited implements) is amended as follows.

(2) In subsection (1), in paragraph (a) –
    (a) in sub-paragraph (iv) after "gaff," insert "tailer,";
    (b) for "salmon, trout or freshwater fish" substitute "salmon, trout, eels, lampreys, smelt, shad, freshwater fish and any specified fish in any waters".

(3) In that subsection, in paragraph (b), for "salmon, trout or freshwater fish" substitute "any such fish in any waters".

(4) In that subsection, in paragraph (c), for "any salmon, trout or freshwater fish" substitute "any such fish in any waters".

(5) After that subsection insert –

"(1A) In this section "specified fish" means fish of such description as may be specified for the purposes of this section by order under section 40A below.

(1B) The appropriate national authority may by order amend subsection (1)(a) above so as to –
    (a) add any instrument to it; or
    (b) remove any instrument for the time being specified in it."

(6) After subsection (3) insert –

"(3A) References in this section to any waters include waters adjoining the coast of England and Wales to a distance of six nautical miles measured from the baselines from which the breadth of the territorial sea is measured."

(7) The following are omitted –
    (a) in subsection (1), the words "Subject to subsection (4) below,";
    (b) subsection (4).

2572

Marine and Coastal Access Act 2009 (c. 23)
Part 7 — Fisheries
Chapter 3 — Migratory and freshwater fish

216 Roe etc

(1) Section 2 of the Salmon and Freshwater Fisheries Act 1975 (c. 51) (roe, spawning and unclean fish, etc) is amended as follows.

(2) In subsection (1) —

    (a) for "salmon, trout or freshwater fish" substitute "salmon, trout, eels, lampreys, smelt, shad, freshwater fish or any specified fish in any waters";

    (b) in paragraph (b), for "any roe of salmon or trout" substitute "any fish roe".

(3) In subsection (2) —

    (a) after "subsections (3)" insert ", (3A)";

    (b) in paragraph (a), for "salmon, trout or freshwater fish" substitute "salmon, trout, lamprey, smelt, shad, freshwater fish or specified fish in any waters";

    (c) in paragraph (b), for "any salmon, trout or freshwater fish" substitute "any such fish".

(4) After subsection (3) insert —

    "(3A) Subsection (2) above does not apply where a person takes an immature freshwater fish in circumstances prescribed by byelaws."

(5) In subsection (5), for "salmon, trout or freshwater fish" substitute "fish of any description".

(6) After that subsection insert —

    "(6) In this section "specified fish" means fish of such description as may be specified for the purposes of this section by order under section 40A below.

    (7) Subsection (3A) of section 1 above applies for the purposes of this section."

217 Licences to fish

(1) In section 25 of the Salmon and Freshwater Fisheries Act 1975 (licences to fish), for subsection (1) substitute —

    "(1) The Agency shall by means of a system of licensing regulate fishing by licensable means of fishing for —

        (a) salmon, trout, eels, lampreys, smelt and freshwater fish; and

        (b) fish of such other description as may be specified for the purposes of this section by order under section 40A below.

    (1A) In this Act "licensable means of fishing" means any of the following —

        (a) rod and line;

        (b) an historic installation;

        (c) such other means of fishing as the appropriate national authority may by order specify.

    (1B) In this Act "historic installation" means any of the following —

        (a) a fixed engine certified in pursuance of the Salmon Fishery Act 1865 to be a privileged fixed engine;

Marine and Coastal Access Act 2009 (c. 23)
Part 7 — Fisheries
Chapter 3 — Migratory and freshwater fish

2573

(b)   a fixed engine which was in use for taking salmon or migratory trout during the open season of 1861, in pursuance of an ancient right or mode of fishing as lawfully exercised during that open season, by virtue of any grant or charter or immemorial usage;

(c)   a fishing weir or fishing mill dam which was lawfully in use on 6th August 1861 by virtue of a grant or charter or immemorial usage."

(2)   In that section, in subsection (2), after "area or areas" insert "(or in waters of such description or descriptions)".

(3)   In that section, in subsection (4), the words from "gaff" to "tailer or" are omitted.

(4)   In that section, subsections (5) and (6) are omitted.

(5)   In that section, at the end insert —

"(10)   For the purposes of this Part, the Agency may permit a person to take fish of any description in circumstances where he would for those purposes otherwise require a fishing licence.

(11)   Permission under subsection (10) above —
(a)   must be in writing;
(b)   may be given generally or specifically;
(c)   may be given subject to conditions."

(6)   In Schedule 2 to that Act (licences) —
(a)   in paragraph 11, the words from "together" to the end are omitted;
(b)   paragraph 12 is omitted.

(7)   In that Schedule, after paragraph 14 insert —

"Historic installations

14A (1)   Where a fishing licence is granted in respect of an historic installation, the Agency may at any time, subject to this paragraph, impose conditions on its use pursuant to the licence.

(2)   Conditions under sub-paragraph (1) above are to be imposed by notice in writing to the person holding the licence.

(3)   A notice under sub-paragraph (1) above may be varied or revoked by a further such notice.

(4)   The Agency may only impose conditions under sub-paragraph (1) above where it considers that it is necessary to do so for the protection of any fishery."

218   Limitation of licences

(1)   Section 26 of the Salmon and Freshwater Fisheries Act 1975 (c. 51) (limitation of fishing licences) is amended as follows.

(2)   In subsection (1) —
(a)   at the beginning insert "Subject to this section";

2574
Marine and Coastal Access Act 2009 (c. 23)
Part 7 – Fisheries
Chapter 3 – Migratory and freshwater fish

(b) in paragraph (a), for the words from "to be issued" to "rod and line" substitute "of any description to be issued pursuant to section 25 above in any year in relation to that area or those areas".

(3) After that subsection insert—

"(1A) The Agency may only make an order under subsection (1) above in relation to licences for fishing for fish of any description if it is satisfied that it is necessary to do so for the purposes of—

(a) maintaining, improving or developing fisheries of any fish referred to in section 25(1) above; or

(b) protecting the marine or aquatic environment from significant harm.

(1B) The Agency may not make an order under subsection (1) above in relation to licences for fishing for fish by—

(a) rod and line; or

(b) an historic installation."

(4) In subsection (3), for "shall cause" substitute "may cause".

(5) For subsections (4) and (5) substitute—

"(4) If it appears to the Agency that an order under this section would prevent a person from fishing in circumstances where that person is wholly dependent on the fishing for his livelihood, the Agency may pay that person such amount by way of compensation as it considers appropriate."

219 Authorisation to fish

(1) In the Salmon and Freshwater Fisheries Act 1975 (c. 51), in the heading to Part 4, after "Fishing licences" insert "and authorisations".

(2) After section 27 of that Act insert—

"27A Authorisation of fishing otherwise than by licensable means

(1) The Agency may authorise a person to use any means, other than a licensable means of fishing, to fish for—

(a) salmon, trout, eels, lampreys, smelt and freshwater fish; and

(b) fish of such other description as may be specified for the purposes of this section by order under section 40A below.

(2) An application for an authorisation under this section must be in such form as the Agency may specify.

(3) An authorisation under this section must be in writing, but subject to that may be in such form as the Agency may determine.

(4) An authorisation under this section—

(a) must be granted for a specified period of time;

(b) may be granted to more than one person;

(c) may be limited as to the waters in respect of which it is granted;

(d) may be subject to conditions.

(5) The Agency may at any time, on application or on its own initiative—

Marine and Coastal Access Act 2009 (c. 23)
Part 7 — *Fisheries*
Chapter 3 — *Migratory and freshwater fish*

2575

> (a) amend an authorisation under this section;
>
> (b) revoke an authorisation under this section.

(6) In determining whether to grant, amend or revoke an authorisation the Agency must consider the effect of doing so on—

> (a) fisheries in the area to which the authorisation relates; and
>
> (b) the aquatic or marine environment in that area.

(7) An authorisation under this section granted to a body corporate—

> (a) may, if the authorisation so specifies, apply in relation to any individual acting on behalf of that body (as well as to the body corporate); or
>
> (b) may, if the authorisation so specifies, apply only in relation to individuals named in the authorisation when acting on behalf of the body (as well as to the body corporate).

(8) The Agency may charge a fee for the grant of an authorisation under this section.

(9) Where the Agency determines standard fees for the grant of authorisations of particular descriptions, it must publish them.

(10) Where—

> (a) the Agency has determined a standard fee for the grant of an authorisation of a particular description, but
>
> (b) the Agency considers, in any case, that special circumstances apply to the grant of an authorisation of that description,

it may charge a fee of another amount.

27B Unauthorised fishing etc

(1) A person is guilty of an offence if, by any means other than a licensable means of fishing, he fishes for or takes any fish in circumstances where—

> (a) the fishing or taking may be authorised under section 27A above, but
>
> (b) he is not authorised to fish for or take the fish under that section (or is so authorised but the fishing or taking is in breach of any condition of his authorisation).

(2) A person is guilty of an offence if he has an instrument in his possession, other than an instrument which is a licensable means of fishing, with intent to use it to fish for or take fish in circumstances where—

> (a) the fishing or taking may be authorised under section 27A above, but
>
> (b) he is not authorised to fish for or take the fish under that section (or is so authorised but the fishing or taking would be in breach of any condition of an authorisation under that section)."

(3) In Schedule 4 to that Act (offences), in the table in paragraph 1(2), at the end

2576

Marine and Coastal Access Act 2009 (c. 23)
Part 7 – Fisheries
Chapter 3 – Migratory and freshwater fish

insert—

| "Section 27B | Unauthorised fishing etc | (a) Summarily | A fine not exceeding £50,000. |
| | | (b) On indictment | A fine." |

220 Enforcement

(1) Part 5 of the Salmon and Freshwater Fisheries Act 1975 (c. 51) (administration and enforcement) is amended as follows.

(2) In section 31 (powers of search), in subsection (1) —
   (a) in paragraph (b), the words "in contravention of this Act" are omitted;
   (b) in paragraph (c)(i), the words "which has been caught in contravention of this Act" are omitted;
   (c) in paragraph (d) after "fish" insert "(or a sample of any fish)";
   (d) after paragraph (d) insert—
      "(e) may disable or destroy any dam, fishing weir, fishing mill dam or fixed engine which he has reasonable cause to suspect of having operated or been used, or of being likely to be used, in contravention of this Act."

(3) In section 32 (power to enter lands), subsection (1)(ii) and the preceding "or" are omitted.

(4) In section 33 (orders and warrants to enter suspected premises), in subsection (2), for the words from "seize" to the end substitute —
      "(a) seize any illegal net or other instrument, or any net or other instrument suspected to have been illegally used, that may be found on the premises;
      (b) seize any fish suspected to have been illegally taken or sold that may be found on the premises; or
      (c) disable or destroy any dam, fishing weir, fishing mill dam or fixed engine suspected to have operated or been used illegally that may be found on the premises."

(5) In that section, in subsection (3), for "one week" substitute "three months".

(6) In section 34 (power to apprehend persons fishing illegally etc) —
   (a) in the heading, the words "at night" are omitted;
   (b) the words from "between the end" to "following morning" are omitted.

(7) In section 35 (power to require production of fishing licences), in subsection (1) —
   (a) for "being about to" substitute "intending to";
   (b) for "to have within the preceding half hour" substitute "of having recently";
   (c) after "in any area," insert "in circumstances where the fishing would require a licence or authorisation under this Act or a licence under section 16 of the Wildlife and Countryside Act 1981,".

Marine and Coastal Access Act 2009 (c. 23)
Part 7 — Fisheries
Chapter 3 — Migratory and freshwater fish

2577

(8) In that section, subsection (2) is omitted.

(9) In Schedule 4 (offences), in paragraph 1(2), in the fourth column of the table, in the entry relating to section 5(1), for "The prescribed sum" substitute "£50,000".

221 Power to specify fish

(1) After section 40 of the Salmon and Freshwater Fisheries Act 1975 (c. 51) insert —

"40A Power to specify fish

The appropriate national authority may by order specify fish of any description for the purposes of any or all of the following —
  (a) section 1, 2, 25 or 27A above;
  (b) section 32 of the Salmon Act 1986;
  (c) paragraph 6 of Schedule 25 to the Water Resources Act 1991;
  (d) section 6(6) of the Environment Act 1995."

(2) In section 41 of that Act (interpretation), in subsection (1), after the definition of "the Agency" insert —

""the appropriate national authority" means —
  (a) the Secretary of State, except in relation to Wales (within the meaning of the Government of Wales Act 2006);
  (b) in relation to Wales (within that meaning), the Welsh Ministers;".

222 Order-making powers: supplementary

After section 40A of the Salmon and Freshwater Fisheries Act 1975 (as inserted by section 221 above) insert —

"40B Orders: supplementary

(1) An order under section 1, 25 or 40A above may make different provision for different purposes (and, in particular, different provision in relation to different areas or waters).

(2) Such an order is to be made by statutory instrument.

(3) A statutory instrument containing such an order is subject to annulment in pursuance of a resolution of —
  (a) either House of Parliament, in the case of an order made by the Secretary of State;
  (b) the National Assembly for Wales, in the case of an order made by the Welsh Ministers."

223 Definitions relating to fish

(1) In section 41 of the Salmon and Freshwater Fisheries Act 1975 (interpretation), subsection (1) is amended as follows.

(2) For the definition of "eels" substitute —

""eels" means any fish of the species *Anguilla anguilla*, and includes elvers and the fry of eels;".

2578

Marine and Coastal Access Act 2009 (c. 23)
Part 7 – Fisheries
Chapter 3 – Migratory and freshwater fish

(3)   After that definition insert —

""fish" includes crustaceans and molluscs;".

(4)   After the definition of "foreshore" insert —

""freshwater crayfish" means any freshwater decapod crustacean of the Families Astacidae, Cambaridae or Parastacidae;".

(5)   For the definition of "freshwater fish" substitute —

""freshwater fish" means any fish habitually living in fresh water, exclusive of —
  (a)   salmon, trout, eels, lampreys, smelt and any other fish of a kind which migrates from fresh to salt water, or from salt to fresh water, in order to spawn;
  (b)   any kind of crustacean other than freshwater crayfish and Chinese mitten crabs (*Eriocheir sinensis*); and
  (c)   any kind of mollusc;".

(6)   After the definition of "screen" insert —

""smelt" means any fish of the species *Osmerus eperlanus*;".

Byelaws

224   Power to make byelaws

(1)   In Schedule 25 to the Water Resources Act 1991 (c. 57) (byelaw-making powers of the Agency), paragraph 6 (byelaws for purposes of fisheries functions) is amended as follows.

(2)   In sub-paragraph (1), in paragraph (b), for the words from "salmon fisheries" to the end substitute "fisheries of fish to which this paragraph applies."

(3)   After that sub-paragraph insert —

"(1A) This paragraph applies to —
  (a)   salmon, trout, eels, lampreys, smelt, shad and freshwater fish; and
  (b)   fish of such other description as may be specified for the purposes of this paragraph by order under section 40A of the Salmon and Freshwater Fisheries Act 1975."

(4)   In sub-paragraph (2), after paragraph (a) insert —

"(aa)   specifying close seasons or times for the taking of any fish to which this paragraph applies by such means as may be prescribed by the byelaws;".

(5)   In that sub-paragraph, in paragraph (b)(i), after "size" insert "greater or".

(6)   In that sub-paragraph, in paragraph (e) at the end insert "(including requiring fixed engines during close seasons or times to be removed or made incapable of taking or obstructing the passage of fish)".

(7)   Sub-paragraph (3) is omitted.

(8)   Sub-paragraph (4) is omitted.

Marine and Coastal Access Act 2009 (c. 23)
Part 7 – Fisheries
Chapter 3 – Migratory and freshwater fish

2579

(9) After sub-paragraph (5) insert—

"(5A) A byelaw under this paragraph does not apply to a person (including an employee or agent of the Agency) to the extent that he is acting—

    (a) with the written authority of the Agency; and

    (b) in accordance with any conditions imposed by the Agency in relation to that authority.

(5B) For the avoidance of doubt, a byelaw under this paragraph may apply to an historic installation as to any other fixed engine."

(10) Any byelaw made by the Environment Agency under paragraph 6(3) of that Schedule and in force immediately before the coming into force of subsection (7) above shall in relation to any period after the coming into force of that subsection be regarded as having been made under paragraph 6(2) of that Schedule, as amended by this section.

225 Byelaws: emergency procedures

(1) In the Water Resources Act 1991 (c. 57), in section 210 (byelaw-making powers of the Agency) at the end insert—

"(3) Schedule 27 to this Act (emergency fisheries byelaws) shall have effect."

(2) In that Act, after Schedule 26 insert—

"SCHEDULE 27   Section 210(3)

EMERGENCY FISHERIES BYELAWS

Emergency fisheries byelaws

1   (1) In this Schedule, "emergency fisheries byelaw" means a byelaw made under paragraph 6 of Schedule 25 to this Act (fisheries) in the circumstances in sub-paragraph (2) below.

    (2) The circumstances are that—

      (a) the Agency considers that, because of any event or likely event, harm is occurring or is likely to occur to—

        (i) any fish to which paragraph 6 of Schedule 25 to this Act applies or to the spawn, gametes or food of any such fish, or

        (ii) the marine or coastal, or aquatic or waterside, environment,

      (b) the Agency considers that the byelaw would prevent or limit that harm, or would be reasonably likely to do so,

      (c) the Agency considers that for that purpose there is a need for the byelaw to come into force as a matter of urgency, and

      (d) the event or the likelihood of the event could not reasonably have been foreseen.

    (3) Schedule 26 to this Act (procedure relating to byelaws made by the Agency) does not apply in relation to an emergency fisheries byelaw.

    (4) In sub-paragraph (2)(a), the reference to harm to the marine or coastal, or aquatic or waterside, environment is to—

2580

Marine and Coastal Access Act 2009 (c. 23)
Part 7 – Fisheries
Chapter 3 – Migratory and freshwater fish

(a) harm to the natural beauty or amenity of marine or coastal, or aquatic or waterside, areas (including their geological or physiographical features) or to any features of archaeological or historic interest in such areas, or

(b) harm to flora or fauna which are dependent on or associated with the marine or coastal, or aquatic or waterside, environment.

Commencement

2   An emergency fisheries byelaw comes into force –
    (a)   on the date specified in the byelaw, or
    (b)   if no date is so specified, on the day after that on which it is made.

Notification of the appropriate national authority

3   The Agency must, within 24 hours of making an emergency fisheries byelaw –
    (a)   send a copy of the byelaw to the appropriate national authority, and
    (b)   explain to the appropriate national authority why the byelaw is being made as an emergency fisheries byelaw.

Publication

4   The Agency must publish notice of the making of an emergency fisheries byelaw (including a copy of the byelaw) –
    (a)   in the London Gazette;
    (b)   where the byelaw has effect in Wales, in the Welsh language in such manner as the Agency thinks appropriate;
    (c)   in such other manner as it thinks appropriate for the purpose of bringing the byelaw to the attention of persons likely to be affected by it.

Amendment and revocation

5   (1) If at any time the appropriate national authority is satisfied that an emergency fisheries byelaw would better serve to prevent or limit the harm referred to in paragraph 1(2)(a) above if it were amended, the authority must amend it accordingly.

    (2) If at any time the appropriate national authority is satisfied that an emergency fisheries byelaw is no longer needed in order to prevent or limit the harm referred to in paragraph 1(2)(a) above, the authority must revoke it.

    (3) The Agency must publish notice of an amendment or revocation under this paragraph as specified in paragraph 4(a) to (c) above.

Expiry and extension

6   (1) Subject to paragraph 7 below, an emergency fisheries byelaw expires (unless earlier revoked) –

Marine and Coastal Access Act 2009 (c. 23)
Part 7 — Fisheries
Chapter 3 — Migratory and freshwater fish

2581

        (a)   in accordance with provision made by the byelaw, or

        (b)   if the byelaw does not contain provision for its expiry, at the end of the period of twelve months beginning with the day on which it comes into force.

    (2)   A byelaw may not under sub-paragraph (1)(a) above remain in force for longer than the period of twelve months beginning with the day on which it comes into force.

7   (1)   The Agency may, at any time before an emergency fisheries byelaw expires, apply to the appropriate national authority for it to be extended.

    (2)   On such an application, the appropriate national authority may extend the byelaw at any time before its expiry, provided the authority is satisfied that—

        (a)   the byelaw is still needed to prevent or limit the harm referred to in paragraph 1(2)(a) above, and

        (b)   the need for the extension could not reasonably have been avoided by the Agency.

    (3)   A byelaw may be extended under sub-paragraph (2) above for such period not exceeding six months as the appropriate national authority may specify.

    (4)   A byelaw may not be extended under sub-paragraph (2) above on more than one occasion.

Availability

8   (1)   Every emergency fisheries byelaw shall be printed and deposited at one or more of the offices of the Agency, including (if there is one) at an office in the area to which the byelaw applies; and copies of the byelaw shall be available at those offices, at all reasonable times, for inspection by the public free of charge.

    (2)   Every person shall be entitled, on application to the Agency and on payment of such reasonable sum as the Agency may determine, to be furnished with a copy of any emergency fisheries byelaw so deposited by the Agency.

Proof

9   The production of a printed copy of an emergency fisheries byelaw purporting to be made by the Agency upon which is indorsed a certificate, purporting to be signed on its behalf, stating—

        (a)   that the byelaw was made by the Agency, and

        (b)   that the copy is a true copy of the byelaw,

shall be prima facie evidence of the facts stated in the certificate, and without proof of the handwriting or official position of any person purporting to sign the certificate.

"Appropriate national authority"

10   In this Schedule "appropriate national authority" has the same meaning as in the Salmon and Freshwater Fisheries Act 1975."

2582

Marine and Coastal Access Act 2009 (c. 23)
Part 7 — Fisheries
Chapter 3 — Migratory and freshwater fish

226 Byelaws: enforcement

In section 211 of the Water Resources Act 1991 (c. 57) (enforcement of byelaws), in subsection (3), for the words from "to a fine" to the end substitute—

"(a) in the case of byelaws made by virtue of paragraph 4, to a fine not exceeding level 4 on the standard scale or such smaller sum as may be specified in the byelaws;

(b) in the case of byelaws made by virtue of paragraph 6, to a fine not exceeding £50,000."

227 Byelaws: compensation

(1) Section 212 of the Water Resources Act 1991 (compensation in respect of certain fisheries byelaws) is amended as follows.

(2) In subsection (1), for the words from "the claim" to the end substitute "the Agency may pay that person such amount by way of compensation as it considers appropriate."

(3) Subsection (3) is omitted.

Supplementary

228 Theft of fish from private fisheries etc

(1) In the Theft Act 1968 (c. 60), in Schedule 1 (offences of taking or destroying fish), paragraph 2 is amended as follows.

(2) For sub-paragraph (1) substitute—

"(1) A person who unlawfully takes or destroys, or attempts to take or destroy, any fish in water which is private property or in which there is any private right of fishery shall on summary conviction be liable to a fine not exceeding level 5 on the standard scale."

(3) Sub-paragraph (2) is omitted.

(4) In sub-paragraph (3), for "this paragraph" substitute "sub-paragraph (1) above".

229 Handling fish

(1) Section 32 of the Salmon Act 1986 (c. 62) (handling salmon in suspicious circumstances) is amended as follows.

(2) In the heading, for "salmon" substitute "fish".

(3) In subsection (1)—
   (a) for "any salmon" substitute "any fish to which this section applies";
   (b) for "the salmon" substitute "that fish";
   (c) the words "by or for the benefit of another person" are omitted.

(4) After that subsection insert—

"(1A) This section applies to—
   (a) salmon, trout, eels, lampreys, smelt and freshwater fish; and

Marine and Coastal Access Act 2009 (c. 23)
Part 7 — Fisheries
Chapter 3 — Migratory and freshwater fish

2583

(b) fish of such other description as may be specified for the purposes of this section by order under section 40A of the Salmon and Freshwater Fisheries Act 1975."

(5) In subsection (2) —

   (a) for "a salmon" substitute "a fish to which this section applies";

   (b) in paragraph (a) —

      (i) after "or landing" insert ", or selling,";

      (ii) for "that salmon" substitute "that fish";

   (c) in paragraph (b) —

      (i) for "that salmon" substitute "that fish";

      (ii) after "or landed," insert "or sold,".

(6) In subsection (3), for "salmon" substitute "fish".

(7) In subsection (4), for "salmon" substitute "fish to which this section applies".

(8) In subsection (5) —

   (a) in paragraph (a), for the words from "to imprisonment" to the end substitute "to a fine not exceeding the statutory maximum";

   (b) in paragraph (b), for the words from "to imprisonment" to the end substitute "to a fine".

(9) In subsection (7) —

   (a) after "or landing" insert ", or selling,"

   (b) for "a salmon" substitute "a fish to which this section applies";

   (c) for "the salmon" substitute "the fish";

   (d) at the end insert "or sold".

(10) At the end insert —

   "(8) In this section "salmon", "trout", "eels", "smelt", "fish" and "freshwater fish" have the same meanings as in the Salmon and Freshwater Fisheries Act 1975."

230 Duties of the Environment Agency

(1) Section 6 of the Environment Act 1995 (c. 25) (general duties of the Agency) is amended as follows.

(2) In subsection (6), for the words from "salmon" to the end substitute "fisheries of —

   (a) salmon, trout, eels, lampreys, smelt and freshwater fish, and

   (b) fish of such other description as may be specified for the purposes of this subsection by order under section 40A of the Salmon and Freshwater Fisheries Act 1975".

(3) In subsection (8), at the end insert —

   ""salmon", "trout", "eels", "smelt", "fish" and "freshwater fish" have the same meanings as in the Salmon and Freshwater Fisheries Act 1975".

2584

Marine and Coastal Access Act 2009 (c. 23)
Part 7 – Fisheries
Chapter 3 – Migratory and freshwater fish

231 Tweed and Esk fisheries

(1) Section 111 of the Scotland Act 1998 (c. 46) (regulation of Tweed and Esk fisheries) is amended as follows.

(2) In subsection (1), for "salmon, trout, eels and freshwater fish" substitute "salmon, trout, eels, lampreys, smelt, shad and freshwater fish".

(3) In subsection (4), in the definition of "conservation", for "salmon, trout, eels and freshwater fish," substitute "salmon, trout, eels, lampreys, smelt, shad and freshwater fish,".

(4) In subsection (4), in the definition of "eels", "freshwater fish", "salmon" and "trout" —

   (a) after ""eels"," insert ""fish",";

   (b) after ""salmon"" insert ", "smelt"";

   (c) after "Salmon and Freshwater Fisheries Act 1975" insert "(as amended by the Marine and Coastal Access Act 2009)".

(5) At the end insert —

   "(6) An Order under subsection (1) may amend that subsection so as to —

      (a) add any description of fish to it, or

      (b) remove any description of fish from it."

232 Keeping, introduction and removal of fish

(1) The appropriate national authority may by regulations make provision for the purpose of prohibiting persons, in such cases as may be specified in the regulations, from carrying on any of the activities specified in subsection (2) otherwise than under and in accordance with a permit issued by the Environment Agency.

(2) The activities referred to in subsection (1) are —

   (a) keeping any fish in the area to which this section applies;

   (b) introducing any fish into any inland waters in that area;

   (c) removing any fish from any inland waters in that area.

(3) The area to which this section applies is the area consisting of —

   (a) England,

   (b) Wales, and

   (c) so much of the catchment area of the River Esk as is in Scotland.

(4) The references in subsection (2)(b) and (c) to inland waters do not include the River Tweed.

(5) Regulations made under this section may in particular —

   (a) make provision as to the descriptions of permits to be issued;

   (b) specify the manner and form of an application for a permit from the Environment Agency to carry out any activity specified in subsection (2) and the sum, or maximum sum, to be paid on the making of such an application;

   (c) specify the circumstances in which such an application is to be granted or refused and any considerations which the Environment Agency may or must take into account when determining whether or not to issue such a permit;

Marine and Coastal Access Act 2009 (c. 23)
Part 7 — Fisheries
Chapter 3 — Migratory and freshwater fish

2585

   (d)   specify the conditions that may be incorporated into such a permit;

   (e)   make provision for the amendment, suspension or revocation of such a permit;

   (f)   make provision authorising the Environment Agency to exempt persons from any requirement under the regulations to obtain such a permit;

   (g)   make provision as to the effect of a prohibition under regulations made under this section on fishing pursuant to any licence, authorisation, permission, or right to fish;

   (h)   make provision enabling the Environment Agency to require a person in breach of any requirement under regulations made under this section, or in breach of any condition of a permit under such regulations—

      (i)   to take steps to ensure that the position is, so far as possible, restored to what it would have been had there been no such breach;

      (ii)   to allow the Environment Agency to take such steps;

      (iii)   to pay to the Environment Agency a sum representing reasonable expenses of any such steps taken or to be taken by the Agency;

   (i)   make provision creating criminal offences for the purpose of securing compliance with regulations made under this section or of any requirements under paragraph (h);

   (j)   make other provision for the enforcement of requirements under the regulations, including provision conferring the following powers on the Agency—

      (i)   powers of entry;

      (ii)   powers of search and seizure;

      (iii)   powers to destroy or release any fish seized.

(6)   Provision under subsection (5)(a) may specify that a permit may be issued—

   (a)   in respect of one or more of the activities specified in subsection (2);

   (b)   in relation to the carrying on of any one or more of those activities on one occasion or more than one occasion;

   (c)   for periods of limited or unlimited duration.

(7)   Provision under subsection (5)(i) must provide that where a person is guilty of an offence created under that subsection, the person is liable—

   (a)   on summary conviction, to a fine not exceeding £50,000;

   (b)   on conviction on indictment, to a fine.

(8)   In this section—

"appropriate national authority" means—

   (a)   the Secretary of State, otherwise than in relation to Wales;

   (b)   the Welsh Ministers, in relation to Wales;

references to "fish" include the spawn of fish;

"inland waters" has the same meaning as in the Water Resources Act 1991 (c. 57);

"River Tweed" means "the river" within the meaning of the Tweed Fisheries Amendment Act 1859 (c. lxx), as amended by byelaws.

2586

Marine and Coastal Access Act 2009 (c. 23)
Part 7 — Fisheries
Chapter 3 — Migratory and freshwater fish

233 Consequential and supplementary amendments

(1) Schedule 16 (which contains consequential and supplementary amendments relating to this Chapter) has effect.

(2) The following provisions of the Salmon and Freshwater Fisheries Act 1975 (c. 51) (which are obsolete or no longer of practical utility) are omitted —

    (a) in section 4 (poisonous matter etc), subsection (2);

    (b) section 23 (export of salmon and trout);

    (c) section 24 (consignment of salmon and trout).

CHAPTER 4

OBSOLETE FISHERIES ENACTMENTS

234 Repeal of spent or obsolete enactments

The following enactments are repealed —

    (a) the White Herring Fisheries Act 1771 (c. 31);

    (b) the Seal Fishery Act 1875 (c. 18);

    (c) section 13 of the Fisheries Act 1891 (c. 37) (proceedings for enforcement of Acts relating to salmon and freshwater fisheries);

    (d) the North Sea Fisheries Act 1893 (c. 17);

    (e) the Behring Sea Award Act 1894 (c. 2);

    (f) the Seal Fisheries (North Pacific) Act 1895 (c. 21);

    (g) the Seal Fisheries (North Pacific) Act 1912 (c. 10);

    (h) sections 86, 87 and 163 of the Port of London Act 1968 (c. xxxii) (powers of Port of London Authority in relation to fisheries).

PART 8

ENFORCEMENT

CHAPTER 1

ENFORCEMENT OFFICERS

Marine enforcement officers

235 Marine enforcement officers

(1) In this Chapter "marine enforcement officer" means —

    (a) any person appointed as such an officer by the MMO;

    (b) any person appointed as such an officer by the Welsh Ministers;

    (c) any person who is a commissioned officer of any of Her Majesty's ships;

    (d) any person in command or charge of any aircraft or hovercraft of the Royal Navy, the Army or the Royal Air Force.

(2) The carrying out of any functions of a marine enforcement officer by a person appointed under this section by the MMO or the Welsh Ministers (a "civilian

marine enforcement officer") is subject to any limitations specified by the MMO or (as the case may be) the Welsh Ministers in relation to that person.

(3) Until the coming into force of section 1, any power conferred on the MMO by this section is exercisable by the Secretary of State.

Any reference in this Chapter to a marine enforcement officer includes a reference to any person appointed by the Secretary of State as a marine enforcement officer by virtue of this subsection.

236 Enforcement of marine licensing regime

(1) For the purposes of enforcing Part 4 of this Act, a marine enforcement officer has—

    (a) the common enforcement powers conferred by this Act;

    (b) the power conferred by section 263.

This is subject to subsection (2).

(2) A marine enforcement officer does not have the powers referred to in subsection (1) for the purposes of enforcing Part 4 of this Act so far as relating to—

    (a) any activity in Wales or the Welsh inshore region concerning or arising from the exploration for, or production of, petroleum;

    (b) anything done in the course of taking installation abandonment measures in any other part of the relevant enforcement area.

(3) Subject to subsection (8), the powers which a marine enforcement officer has for the purposes of enforcing Part 4 of this Act may be exercised—

    (a) in the relevant enforcement area (and in relation to any vessel, aircraft or marine structure in that area);

    (b) in relation to any vessel or marine structure outside the UK marine area which was loaded within the relevant enforcement area;

    (c) in relation to any British vessel, British aircraft or British marine structure outside the UK marine area;

    (d) in Scotland or the Scottish inshore region, in relation to an offence which the officer reasonably believes has been committed—

        (i) within the relevant enforcement area, or

        (ii) outside the UK marine area and in circumstances where a vessel, aircraft or marine structure referred to in paragraph (b) or (c) was involved in the commission of the offence;

    (e) in relation to any vessel, aircraft or marine structure in the Scottish offshore region which has been pursued there in accordance with subsection (4).

(4) A vessel, aircraft or marine structure is pursued in accordance with this subsection if—

    (a) immediately before the pursuit of the vessel, aircraft or structure commences, the vessel, aircraft or structure is in the relevant enforcement area,

    (b) before the pursuit of the vessel, aircraft or structure commences, a signal is given for it to stop, and

    (c) the pursuit of the vessel, aircraft or structure is not interrupted.

(5) The signal referred to in subsection (4)(b) must be given in such a way as to be audible or visible from the vessel, aircraft or structure in question.

(6) For the purposes of subsection (4)(c), pursuit is not interrupted by reason only of the fact that —

    (a) the method of carrying out the pursuit, or

    (b) the identity of the vessel or aircraft carrying out the pursuit,

changes during the course of the pursuit.

(7) Nothing in this section affects any right of hot pursuit which a marine enforcement officer may have under international law.

(8) The powers which a civilian marine enforcement officer has for the purposes of enforcing Part 4 of this Act may not be exercised in relation to any British warship.

(9) In this section —

"installation abandonment measures" means any measures taken in connection with the abandonment of —

    (a) an offshore installation or submarine pipeline, within the meaning of Part 4 of the Petroleum Act 1998 (c. 17), or

    (b) a carbon storage installation, within the meaning of section 30 of the Energy Act 2008 (c. 32),

whether or not the measures are taken in pursuance of an abandonment programme;

"abandonment programme" means —

    (a) an abandonment programme under Part 4 of the Petroleum Act 1998;

    (b) an abandonment programme under that Part, as it applies by virtue of section 30 of the Energy Act 2008;

"the relevant enforcement area" means the area that consists of —

    (a) England and Wales and Northern Ireland, and

    (b) the UK marine licensing area, excluding the Scottish offshore region.

(10) Any term used in this section and in Part 4 of this Act has the same meaning in this section as it has in that Part.

237 Enforcement of nature conservation legislation

(1) For the purposes of enforcing the nature conservation legislation, a marine enforcement officer has the common enforcement powers conferred by this Act.

(2) In this section "the nature conservation legislation" means —

    (a) sections 1 and 2 of the Conservation of Seals Act 1970 (c. 30), and any orders made under section 3 of that Act;

    (b) sections 1, 5 to 7, 9, 11, 13, 14 and 14ZA of the Wildlife and Countryside Act 1981 (c. 69);

    (c) regulations 37C, 39, 41 and 43 of the Conservation (Natural Habitats, &c) Regulations 1994 (S.I. 1994/2716);

    (d) any byelaws or orders made by virtue of regulation 28 or 36 of those Regulations;

    (e) the Offshore Marine Conservation (Natural Habitats, &c) Regulations 2007 (S.I. 2007/1842);

    (f) any byelaws made under section 129 or 132 of this Act;

(g)   any orders made under section 134 or 136 of this Act;

(h)   section 140 of this Act.

(3)   Subject to subsections (8) and (9), the powers which a marine enforcement officer has for the purposes of enforcing the nature conservation legislation may be exercised—

(a)   in the relevant enforcement area (and in relation to any vessel, aircraft or marine installation in that area);

(b)   in relation to any British vessel or British marine installation outside the UK marine area;

(c)   in Scotland or Northern Ireland, or the Scottish or Northern Ireland inshore region, in relation to an offence which the officer reasonably believes has been committed—

(i)   within the relevant enforcement area, or

(ii)   outside the UK marine area and in circumstances where a British vessel or British marine installation was involved in the commission of the offence;

(d)   in relation to any vessel, aircraft or marine installation in the Scottish offshore region which has been pursued there in accordance with subsection (4).

(4)   A vessel, aircraft or marine installation is pursued in accordance with this subsection if—

(a)   immediately before the pursuit of the vessel, aircraft or installation commences, the vessel, aircraft or installation is in the relevant enforcement area,

(b)   before the pursuit of the vessel, aircraft or installation commences, a signal is given for it to stop, and

(c)   the pursuit of the vessel, aircraft or installation is not interrupted.

(5)   The signal referred to in subsection (4)(b) must be given in such a way as to be audible or visible from the vessel, aircraft or installation in question.

(6)   For the purposes of subsection (4)(c), pursuit is not interrupted by reason only of the fact that—

(a)   the method of carrying out the pursuit, or

(b)   the identity of the vessel or aircraft carrying out the pursuit,

changes during the course of the pursuit.

(7)   Nothing in this section affects any right of hot pursuit which a marine enforcement officer may have under international law.

(8)   The powers which a civilian marine enforcement officer has for the purposes of enforcing the nature conservation legislation may not be exercised in relation to any British warship.

(9)   The powers which a marine enforcement officer has for the purposes of enforcing the nature conservation legislation may not be exercised in relation to any vessel within subsection (10) unless—

(a)   in the case of a third country vessel, other than a vessel falling within paragraph (b) or (c) of that subsection, the United Kingdom is entitled under international law to exercise those powers without the consent of the flag state, or

(b)   the Commissioners have given authority to exercise those powers.

(10) The vessels are—

    (a) a third country vessel;

    (b) a warship that is being used by the government of a State other than the United Kingdom;

    (c) any other vessel that is being used by such a government for any non-commercial purpose.

(11) The Commissioners may give authority under subsection (9)(b) only if the flag state has consented to the United Kingdom exercising those powers (whether generally or in relation to the vessel in question).

(12) In giving such authority, the Commissioners must impose such conditions or limitations on the exercise of the powers as are necessary to give effect to any conditions or limitations imposed by the flag state.

(13) In this section—

    "British vessel" means any vessel which—

        (a) is registered in the United Kingdom under Part 2 of the Merchant Shipping Act 1995 (c. 21),

        (b) is, as a Government ship, registered in the United Kingdom in pursuance of an Order in Council under section 308 of that Act,

        (c) falls within section 1(1)(d) of that Act (small ships),

        (d) is exempt from registration under section 294 of that Act (general power to dispense),

        (e) is a British warship, or

        (f) is registered under the law of Gibraltar;

    "Government ship" has the same meaning as in the Merchant Shipping Act 1995;

    "the relevant enforcement area" means the area that consists of—

        (a) England and Wales, and

        (b) the UK marine area, excluding—

            (i) the Scottish inshore region,

            (ii) the Scottish offshore region, and

            (iii) the Northern Ireland inshore region.

238 Enforcement of fisheries legislation

(1) For the purposes of enforcing the fisheries legislation, a marine enforcement officer has—

    (a) the common enforcement powers conferred by this Act;

    (b) the powers conferred by sections 264, 268, 269, 279 and 284.

(2) In this section "the fisheries legislation" means—

    (a) any enactments relating to sea fishing, including any enactment relating to fishing for shellfish, salmon or migratory trout (but see subsection (3));

    (b) any enforceable EU restrictions and enforceable EU obligations relating to sea fishing.

(3) "The fisheries legislation" does not include—

    (a) the Salmon and Freshwater Fisheries Act 1975 (c. 51);

    (b) the Salmon Act 1986 (c. 62);

  (c) byelaws made by the Environment Agency under Schedule 25 to the Water Resources Act 1991 (c. 57);

  (d) the Scotland Act 1998 (Border Rivers) Order 1999 (S.I. 1999/1746);

  (e) byelaws made by an inshore fisheries and conservation authority under section 155.

(4) Subject to subsection (9), the powers which a marine enforcement officer has for the purposes of enforcing the fisheries legislation may be exercised −

  (a) in the relevant enforcement area (and in relation to any vessel, aircraft or marine installation in that area);

  (b) in relation to any vessel, vehicle, aircraft or marine installation in any other area within the United Kingdom or the UK marine area which has been pursued there in accordance with subsection (5);

  (c) in relation to any relevant British fishing boat in the Scottish zone or the Northern Ireland zone;

  (d) in relation to any British vessel or British marine installation outside British fishery limits, other than a Scottish or Northern Ireland fishing boat.

(5) A vessel, vehicle, aircraft or marine installation is pursued in accordance with this subsection if −

  (a) immediately before the pursuit of the vessel, vehicle, aircraft or installation commences −

   (i) the vessel, vehicle, aircraft or installation is in the relevant enforcement area, or

   (ii) in the case of a vessel, aircraft or marine installation operating together with one or more other vessels, aircraft or marine installations to carry out a single activity, any of those vessels, aircraft or installations is in that area,

  (b) before the pursuit of the vessel, vehicle, aircraft or installation commences, a signal is given for it to stop, and

  (c) the pursuit of the vessel, vehicle, aircraft or installation is not interrupted.

(6) The signal referred to in subsection (5)(b) must be given in such a way as to be audible or visible from the vessel, vehicle, aircraft or installation in question.

(7) For the purposes of subsection (5)(c), pursuit is not interrupted by reason only of the fact that −

  (a) the method of carrying out the pursuit, or

  (b) the identity of the vessel, vehicle or aircraft carrying out the pursuit,

changes during the course of the pursuit.

(8) Nothing in this section affects any right of hot pursuit which a marine enforcement officer may have under international law.

(9) The powers which a civilian marine enforcement officer has for the purposes of enforcing the fisheries legislation may not be exercised in relation to any British warship.

(10) In this section −

  "British vessel" means any vessel which −

   (a) is registered in the United Kingdom under Part 2 of the Merchant Shipping Act 1995 (c. 21),

    (b)   is wholly owned by persons qualified to own British ships for the purposes of that Part,

    (c)   is, as a Government ship, registered in the United Kingdom in pursuance of an Order in Council under section 308 of that Act, or

    (d)   is a British warship;

"enforceable EU obligation" means an obligation to which section 2(1) of the European Communities Act 1972 (c. 68) applies;

"enforceable EU restriction" means a restriction to which section 2(1) of that Act applies;

"Government ship" has the same meaning as in the Merchant Shipping Act 1995 (c. 21);

"relevant British fishing boat" means a fishing boat, other than a Scottish or Northern Ireland fishing boat, which—

    (a)   is registered in the United Kingdom under Part 2 of the Merchant Shipping Act 1995, or

    (b)   is wholly owned by persons qualified to own British ships for the purposes of that Part;

"the relevant enforcement area" means the area that consists of—

    (a)   England and Wales, and

    (b)   the sea within British fishery limits, excluding the Scottish zone and the Northern Ireland zone.

239 Marine enforcement officers as British sea-fishery officers

(1)   Section 7 of the Sea Fisheries Act 1968 (c. 77) (sea-fishery officers) is amended as follows.

(2)   In subsection (1)—

    (a)   after paragraph (c) insert—

        "(ca)   persons appointed as marine enforcement officers under section 235 of the Marine and Coastal Access Act 2009;";

    (b)   in paragraph (d), omit "of the Secretary of State or".

(3)   After subsection (1) insert—

    "(1A)   A person falling within paragraph (b), (c) or (ca) of subsection (1) above may not exercise the powers or perform the duties of a British sea-fishery officer in any case where the person may, in the person's capacity as a marine enforcement officer, exercise the common enforcement powers conferred by the Marine and Coastal Access Act 2009 (see Chapter 1 of Part 8 of that Act)."

(4)   In subsection (5) (definition of "the appropriate Minister"), omit paragraph (a).

Other enforcement officers

240 Marine licensing: oil and gas and other reserved matters

(1)   The Secretary of State may appoint persons for the purposes of enforcing Part 4 of this Act, so far as relating to—

(a) any activity in the Scottish offshore region falling within section 113(3) (activities relating to certain reserved matters);

(b) any activity in Wales or the Welsh inshore region concerning or arising from the exploration for, or production of, petroleum;

(c) anything done in the course of taking installation abandonment measures in any other part of the relevant enforcement area.

(2) For the purposes referred to in subsection (1), a person appointed under this section has —

(a) the common enforcement powers conferred by this Act;

(b) the power conferred by section 263.

(3) Subject to subsection (4), the powers which a person appointed under this section has for the purposes referred to in subsection (1) may be exercised —

(a) in the relevant enforcement area (and in relation to any vessel, aircraft or marine structure in that area);

(b) in relation to any vessel or marine structure outside the UK marine area which was loaded within the relevant enforcement area;

(c) in relation to any British vessel, British aircraft or British marine structure outside the UK marine area;

(d) in Scotland or Northern Ireland, or the Scottish or Northern Ireland inshore region, in relation to an offence which the person reasonably believes has been committed —

(i) within the relevant enforcement area, or

(ii) outside the UK marine area and in circumstances where a vessel, aircraft or marine structure referred to in paragraph (b) or (c) was involved in the commission of the offence.

(4) The powers which a person appointed under this section has for the purposes referred to in subsection (1) may not be exercised in relation to any British warship.

(5) Nothing in this section affects any right of hot pursuit which a person appointed under this section may have under international law.

(6) In this section —

"installation abandonment measures" means any measures taken in connection with the abandonment of —

(a) an offshore installation or submarine pipeline, within the meaning of Part 4 of the Petroleum Act 1998 (c. 17), or

(b) a carbon storage installation, within the meaning of section 30 of the Energy Act 2008 (c. 32),

whether or not the measures are taken in pursuance of an abandonment programme;

"abandonment programme" means —

(a) an abandonment programme under Part 4 of the Petroleum Act 1998;

(b) an abandonment programme under that Part, as it applies by virtue of section 30 of the Energy Act 2008;

"the relevant enforcement area" means the area that consists of —

(a) England and Wales, and

(b) the UK marine licensing area, excluding the Northern Ireland inshore region.

(7) Any term used in this section and in Part 4 of this Act has the same meaning in this section as it has in that Part.

241 Marine licensing: Northern Ireland

(1) The Department of the Environment in Northern Ireland may appoint persons for the purposes of enforcing Part 4 of this Act.

(2) For the purposes of enforcing Part 4 of this Act, a person appointed under this section has —

    (a) the common enforcement powers conferred by this Act;

    (b) the power conferred by section 263.

This is subject to subsection (3).

(3) A person appointed under this section does not have the powers referred to in subsection (2) for the purposes of enforcing Part 4 of this Act so far as relating to —

    (a) any activity in Wales or the Welsh inshore region concerning or arising from the exploration for, or production of, petroleum;

    (b) anything done in the course of taking installation abandonment measures in any other part of the relevant enforcement area, other than Northern Ireland and the Northern Ireland inshore region.

(4) Subject to subsection (9), the powers which a person appointed under this section has for the purposes of enforcing Part 4 of this Act may be exercised —

    (a) in the relevant enforcement area (and in relation to any vessel, aircraft or marine structure in that area);

    (b) in Scotland or the Scottish inshore region, in relation to an offence which the person reasonably believes has been committed within the relevant enforcement area;

    (c) in relation to any vessel, aircraft or marine structure in the Scottish offshore region which has been pursued there in accordance with subsection (5).

(5) A vessel, aircraft or marine structure is pursued in accordance with this subsection if —

    (a) immediately before the pursuit of the vessel, aircraft or structure commences, the vessel, aircraft or structure is in the relevant enforcement area,

    (b) before the pursuit of the vessel, aircraft or structure commences, a signal is given for it to stop, and

    (c) the pursuit of the vessel, aircraft or structure is not interrupted.

(6) The signal referred to in subsection (5)(b) must be given in such a way as to be audible or visible from the vessel, aircraft or structure in question.

(7) For the purposes of subsection (5)(c), pursuit is not interrupted by reason only of the fact that —

    (a) the method of carrying out the pursuit, or

    (b) the identity of the vessel or aircraft carrying out the pursuit,

changes during the course of the pursuit.

(8) Nothing in this section affects any right of hot pursuit which a person appointed under this section may have under international law.

(9) The powers which a person appointed under this section has for the purposes of enforcing Part 4 of this Act may not be exercised in relation to any British warship.

(10) In this section—

"installation abandonment measures" means any measures taken in connection with the abandonment of—

(a) an offshore installation or submarine pipeline, within the meaning of Part 4 of the Petroleum Act 1998 (c. 17), or

(b) a carbon storage installation, within the meaning of section 30 of the Energy Act 2008 (c. 32),

whether or not the measures are taken in pursuance of an abandonment programme;

"abandonment programme" means—

(a) an abandonment programme under Part 4 of the Petroleum Act 1998;

(b) an abandonment programme under that Part, as it applies by virtue of section 30 of the Energy Act 2008;

"the relevant enforcement area" means the area that consists of—

(a) England and Wales and Northern Ireland, and

(b) the UK marine licensing area, excluding the Scottish offshore region.

(11) Any term used in this section and in Part 4 of this Act has the same meaning in this section as it has in that Part.

242 Marine licensing: enforcement in Scottish offshore region

(1) The Scottish Ministers may appoint persons for the purposes of enforcing Part 4 of this Act, except so far as relating to any activity falling within section 113(3) (activities relating to certain reserved matters).

(2) For the purposes referred to in subsection (1), a person appointed under this section has—

(a) the common enforcement powers conferred by this Act;

(b) the power conferred by section 263.

(3) Subject to subsection (8), the powers which a person appointed under this section has for the purposes referred to in subsection (1) may be exercised—

(a) in the Scottish offshore region (and in relation to any vessel, aircraft or marine structure in that region);

(b) in any area within the United Kingdom or the UK inshore region, in relation to an offence which the person reasonably believes has been committed within the Scottish offshore region;

(c) in relation to any vessel, aircraft or marine structure in any other area within the UK marine area which has been pursued there in accordance with subsection (4).

(4) A vessel, aircraft or marine structure is pursued in accordance with this subsection if—

(a) immediately before the pursuit of the vessel, aircraft or structure commences, the vessel, aircraft or structure is in the Scottish offshore region,

    (b)   before the pursuit of the vessel, aircraft or structure commences, a signal is given for it to stop, and

    (c)   the pursuit of the vessel, aircraft or structure is not interrupted.

(5)   The signal referred to in subsection (4)(b) must be given in such a way as to be audible or visible from the vessel, aircraft or structure in question.

(6)   For the purposes of subsection (4)(c), pursuit is not interrupted by reason only of the fact that—

    (a)   the method of carrying out the pursuit, or

    (b)   the identity of the vessel or aircraft carrying out the pursuit,

changes during the course of the pursuit.

(7)   Nothing in this section affects any right of hot pursuit which a person appointed under this section may have under international law.

(8)   The powers which a person appointed under this section has for the purposes referred to in subsection (1) may not be exercised in relation to any British warship.

(9)   In this section "UK inshore region" means the area of sea within the seaward limits of the territorial sea adjacent to the United Kingdom.

(10)   Any term used in this section and in Part 4 of this Act has the same meaning in this section as it has in that Part.

243   Enforcement of MCZs in Scottish offshore region

(1)   The Scottish Ministers may appoint persons for the purposes of enforcing section 140 of this Act.

(2)   For the purposes of enforcing section 140 of this Act, a person appointed under this section has the common enforcement powers conferred by this Act.

(3)   Subject to subsections (8) and (9), the powers which a person appointed under this section has for the purposes of enforcing section 140 of this Act may be exercised—

    (a)   in the Scottish offshore region (and in relation to any vessel, aircraft or marine installation in that region);

    (b)   in any area within the United Kingdom or the UK inshore region, in relation to an offence which the person reasonably believes has been committed within the Scottish offshore region;

    (c)   in relation to any vessel, aircraft or marine installation in any other area within the UK marine area which has been pursued there in accordance with subsection (4).

(4)   A vessel, aircraft or marine installation is pursued in accordance with this subsection if—

    (a)   immediately before the pursuit of the vessel, aircraft or installation commences, the vessel, aircraft or installation is in the Scottish offshore region,

    (b)   before the pursuit of the vessel, aircraft or installation commences, a signal is given for it to stop, and

    (c)   the pursuit of the vessel, aircraft or installation is not interrupted.

(5)   The signal referred to in subsection (4)(b) must be given in such a way as to be audible or visible from the vessel, aircraft or installation in question.

(6)   For the purposes of subsection (4)(c), pursuit is not interrupted by reason only of the fact that—

    (a)   the method of carrying out the pursuit, or

    (b)   the identity of the vessel or aircraft carrying out the pursuit,

changes during the course of the pursuit.

(7)   Nothing in this section affects any right of hot pursuit which a person appointed under this section may have under international law.

(8)   The powers which a person appointed under this section has for the purposes of enforcing section 140 of this Act may not be exercised in relation to any British warship.

(9)   The powers which a person appointed under this section has for the purposes of enforcing section 140 of this Act may not be exercised in relation to any vessel within subsection (10) unless—

    (a)   in the case of a third country vessel, other than a vessel falling within paragraph (b) or (c) of that subsection, the United Kingdom is entitled under international law to exercise those powers without the consent of the flag state, or

    (b)   the Commissioners have given authority to exercise those powers.

(10)   The vessels are—

    (a)   a third country vessel;

    (b)   a warship that is being used by the government of a State other than the United Kingdom;

    (c)   any other vessel that is being used by such a government for any non-commercial purpose.

(11)   The Commissioners may give authority under subsection (9)(b) only if the flag state has consented to the United Kingdom exercising those powers (whether generally or in relation to the vessel in question).

(12)   In giving such authority, the Commissioners must impose such conditions or limitations on the exercise of the powers as are necessary to give effect to any conditions or limitations imposed by the flag state.

(13)   In this section "UK inshore region" means the area of sea within the seaward limits of the territorial sea adjacent to the United Kingdom.

Interpretation

244   Interpretation of this Chapter

(1)   In this Chapter—

    "British marine installation" means a marine installation owned by or leased to an individual residing in, or a body corporate incorporated under the law of, any part of the United Kingdom;

    "British warship" means a ship belonging to Her Majesty and forming part of Her Majesty's armed forces;

    "civilian marine enforcement officer" means a person appointed as a marine enforcement officer by the MMO or the Welsh Ministers;

    "the Commissioners" means the Commissioners for Her Majesty's Revenue and Customs;

"fishing boat" means any vessel that is being used for fishing or for any activity relating to fishing;

"flag state", in relation to a vessel, means the State whose flag the vessel is flying or is entitled to fly;

"marine installation" means any artificial island, installation or structure (other than a vessel);

"Northern Ireland fishing boat" means a fishing boat which is registered in the United Kingdom under Part 2 of the Merchant Shipping Act 1995 (c. 21) and whose entry in the register specifies a port in Northern Ireland as the port to which the boat is to be treated as belonging;

"petroleum" has the same meaning as in Part 3 of the Petroleum Act 1998 (c. 17) (see section 28(1) of that Act);

"Scottish fishing boat" means a fishing boat which is registered in the United Kingdom under Part 2 of the Merchant Shipping Act 1995 and whose entry in the register specifies a port in Scotland as the port to which the boat is to be treated as belonging;

"third country vessel" means a vessel which—

    (a) is flying the flag of, or is registered in, any State or territory (other than Gibraltar) which is not a member State, and

    (b) is not registered in a member State.

(2) In this Chapter, except where otherwise provided, any reference to a vessel includes a reference to—

    (a) any ship or boat or any other description of vessel used in navigation, and

    (b) any hovercraft, submersible craft or other floating craft,

but does not include a reference to anything that permanently rests on, or is permanently attached to, the sea bed.

CHAPTER 2

COMMON ENFORCEMENT POWERS

Introductory

245 Common enforcement powers

(1) This Chapter sets out the powers that may be exercised by a person who has the common enforcement powers conferred by this Act.

(2) In this Chapter—

"enforcement officer" means any person who has the common enforcement powers conferred by this Act;

"relevant activity", in relation to an enforcement officer, means any activity in respect of which the officer has functions;

"relevant function", in relation to an enforcement officer, means any function of that officer;

"relevant offence", in relation to an enforcement officer, means any offence in respect of which the officer has functions.

Marine and Coastal Access Act 2009 (c. 23)
Part 8 — Enforcement
Chapter 2 — Common enforcement powers

2599

(3)   The powers conferred on an enforcement officer by any section in this Chapter are without prejudice to any powers exercisable by the officer apart from that section.

Entry, search and seizure

246   Power to board and inspect vessels and marine installations

(1)   For the purposes of carrying out any relevant functions, an enforcement officer may at any time board and inspect a vessel or marine installation.
This is subject to section 249 (which provides that a warrant is necessary to enter a dwelling).

(2)   For the purposes of exercising the power conferred by subsection (1), the officer may require a vessel or marine installation—

    (a)   to stop, or

    (b)   to do anything else that will facilitate the boarding of that or any other vessel or marine installation.

(3)   An enforcement officer who has boarded a vessel or marine installation may, for the purposes of disembarking from the vessel or installation, require that or any other vessel or marine installation—

    (a)   to stop, or

    (b)   to do anything else that will enable the officer, and any person accompanying the officer, to disembark from the vessel or installation.

(4)   An enforcement officer may require any person on board a vessel or marine installation to afford such facilities and assistance with respect to matters under that person's control as the officer considers would facilitate the exercise of any power conferred by this section.

247   Power to enter and inspect premises

(1)   For the purposes of carrying out any relevant functions, an enforcement officer may enter and inspect any premises.
This is subject to section 249 (which provides that a warrant is necessary to enter a dwelling).

(2)   The officer may only exercise the power conferred by this section at a reasonable time, unless it appears to the officer that there are grounds for suspecting that the purpose of entering the premises may be frustrated if the officer seeks to enter at a reasonable time.

(3)   An enforcement officer may require any person in or on the premises to afford such facilities and assistance with respect to matters under that person's control as the officer considers would facilitate the exercise of the power conferred by this section.

(4)   In this section "premises" includes land, but does not include any vehicle, vessel or marine installation.

248   Power to enter and inspect vehicles

(1)   For the purposes of carrying out any relevant functions, an enforcement officer may at any time—

2600

Marine and Coastal Access Act 2009 (c. 23)
Part 8 – Enforcement
Chapter 2 – Common enforcement powers

   (a)   enter and inspect any vehicle;

   (b)   stop and detain any vehicle for the purposes of entering and inspecting it.

   This is subject to section 249 (which provides that a warrant is necessary to enter a dwelling).

(2) Where—

   (a)   an enforcement officer has stopped a vehicle under this section, and

   (b)   the officer considers that it would be impracticable to inspect the vehicle in the place where it has stopped,

   the officer may require the vehicle to be taken to such place as the officer directs to enable the vehicle to be inspected.

(3) An enforcement officer may require—

   (a)   any person travelling in a vehicle, or

   (b)   the registered keeper of a vehicle,

   to afford such facilities and assistance with respect to matters under that person's control as the officer considers would facilitate the exercise of any power conferred by this section.

(4) The powers conferred by this section may be exercised in any place (whether or not it is a place to which the public has access).

(5) In this section "vehicle" does not include any vessel.

249   Dwellings

(1) An enforcement officer may not by virtue of section 246, 247 or 248 enter any dwelling unless a justice has issued a warrant authorising the officer to enter the dwelling.

(2) A justice may only issue such a warrant if, on an application by the officer, the justice is satisfied—

   (a)   that the officer has reasonable grounds for believing that there is material in the dwelling which for the purposes of carrying out any relevant functions the officer wishes to inspect, examine or seize, and

   (b)   that any of the conditions in subsection (3) is satisfied.

(3) The conditions are—

   (a)   that it is not practicable to communicate with any person entitled to grant entry to the dwelling;

   (b)   that it is not practicable to communicate with any person entitled to grant access to that material;

   (c)   that entry to the dwelling is unlikely to be granted unless a warrant is produced;

   (d)   that the purpose of entry may be frustrated or seriously prejudiced unless an enforcement officer arriving at the dwelling can secure immediate entry to it.

(4) Schedule 17 contains further provision about warrants issued under this section.

(5) In this Chapter "justice" means—

   (a)   in relation to England and Wales, a justice of the peace;

   (b)   in relation to Northern Ireland, a lay magistrate;

Marine and Coastal Access Act 2009 (c. 23)
Part 8 – Enforcement
Chapter 2 – Common enforcement powers

2601

(c)   in relation to Scotland, a sheriff, stipendiary magistrate or justice of the peace.

250   Powers of search, examination, etc

(1)   Where an enforcement officer is exercising a power of inspection conferred by section 246, 247 or 248, the officer may –

  (a)   search the relevant premises for any item;

  (b)   examine anything that is in or on the relevant premises.

(2)   Where an enforcement officer reasonably believes that a person is or has been carrying on a relevant activity, the officer may –

  (a)   search or examine anything which appears to be in the person's possession or control;

  (b)   stop and detain the person for the purposes of such a search or examination.

(3)   An enforcement officer may carry out any measurement or test of anything which the officer has power under this section to examine.

(4)   The power conferred by subsection (3) includes power to take a sample from any live animal or plant.

(5)   For the purpose of exercising any power conferred by this section, an enforcement officer may, so far as is reasonably necessary for that purpose, break open any container or other locked thing.

(6)   Where an enforcement officer is exercising a power of inspection conferred by section 246, 247 or 248, the officer may require any person in or on the relevant premises to afford such facilities and assistance with respect to matters under that person's control as the officer considers would facilitate the exercise of any power conferred by this section.

(7)   Where an enforcement officer reasonably believes that a person is or has been carrying on a relevant activity, the officer may require that person to afford such facilities and assistance with respect to matters under that person's control as the officer considers would facilitate the exercise in relation to that person of any power conferred by this section.

(8)   Nothing in this section confers any power to search a person.

(9)   The reference in subsection (1) to anything that is in or on the relevant premises includes a reference to –

  (a)   anything that is attached to or otherwise forms part of the relevant premises, and

  (b)   anything that is controlled from the relevant premises.

(10)   In this section –

  "animal" includes any egg, larva, pupa, or other immature stage of an animal;

  "item" includes –

   (a)   any document or record (in whatever form it is held);

   (b)   any animal or plant;

  "sample" means a sample of blood, tissue or other biological material.

2602

Marine and Coastal Access Act 2009 (c. 23)
Part 8 — Enforcement
Chapter 2 — Common enforcement powers

251 Power to require production of documents, etc

(1) This section applies where an enforcement officer is exercising a power of inspection conferred by section 246, 247 or 248.

(2) The officer may require any person in or on the relevant premises to produce any document or record that is in the person's possession or control.

(3) A reference in this section to the production of a document includes a reference to the production of —

    (a) a hard copy of information recorded otherwise than in hard copy form, or

    (b) information in a form from which a hard copy can be readily obtained.

(4) For the purposes of this section —

    (a) information is recorded in hard copy form if it is recorded in a paper copy or similar form capable of being read (and references to hard copy have a corresponding meaning);

    (b) information can be read only if —

        (i) it can be read with the naked eye, or

        (ii) to the extent that it consists of images (for example photographs, pictures, maps, plans or drawings), it can be seen with the naked eye.

252 Powers of seizure, etc

(1) An enforcement officer who is exercising a power of inspection conferred by section 246, 247 or 248 may —

    (a) seize and detain or remove any item found on the relevant premises;

    (b) take copies of or extracts from any document or record found on the relevant premises.

(2) Where an enforcement officer reasonably believes that a person is or has been carrying on a relevant activity, the officer may seize and detain or remove any item which appears to be in the person's possession or control.

(3) An enforcement officer to whom any document or record has been produced in accordance with a requirement imposed under section 251 may —

    (a) seize and detain or remove that document or record;

    (b) take copies of or extracts from that document or record.

In this subsection "document" includes anything falling within paragraph (a) or (b) of section 251(3).

(4) The powers conferred by this section may only be exercised —

    (a) for the purposes of determining whether a relevant offence has been committed, or

    (b) in relation to an item which an enforcement officer reasonably believes to be evidence of the commission of a relevant offence.

(5) Subject to subsection (6), an enforcement officer who is exercising a power of inspection conferred by section 246, 247 or 248 may not remove from the relevant premises any item which is required by law to be kept on the relevant premises.

(6) An enforcement officer may remove such an item from a vessel while it is being detained in a port.

Marine and Coastal Access Act 2009 (c. 23)
Part 8 – Enforcement
Chapter 2 – Common enforcement powers

2603

(7)   Nothing in this section confers power on an enforcement officer to seize an item which the officer has reasonable grounds for believing to be —

    (a)   an item subject to legal privilege (within the meaning of the Police and Criminal Evidence Act 1984 (c. 60)), or

    (b)   an item in respect of which a claim to confidentiality of communications could be maintained in legal proceedings in Scotland.

253   Further provision about seizure

(1)   Where —

    (a)   any items which an enforcement officer wishes to seize and remove are in a container, and

    (b)   the officer reasonably considers that it would facilitate the seizure and removal of the items if they remained in the container for that purpose,

any power to seize and remove the items conferred by section 252 includes power to seize and remove the container.

(2)   Where —

    (a)   any items which an enforcement officer wishes to seize and remove are not in a container, and

    (b)   the officer reasonably considers that it would facilitate the seizure and removal of the items if they were placed in a container suitable for that purpose,

the officer may require the items to be placed into such a container.

(3)   If, in the opinion of an enforcement officer, it is not for the time being practicable for the officer to seize and remove any item, the officer may require —

    (a)   the person from whom the item is being seized, or

    (b)   where the officer is exercising a power of inspection conferred by section 246, 247 or 248, any person in or on the relevant premises,

to secure that the item is not removed or otherwise interfered with until such time as the officer may seize and remove it.

(4)   Where an enforcement officer is exercising a power of inspection conferred by section 246, 247 or 248, the officer may require any person in or on the relevant premises to afford such facilities and assistance with respect to matters under that person's control as the officer considers would facilitate the exercise of any power conferred by section 252 or this section.

(5)   Where an enforcement officer reasonably believes that a person is or has been carrying on a relevant activity, the officer may require that person to afford such facilities and assistance with respect to matters under that person's control as the officer considers would facilitate the exercise in relation to that person of any power conferred by section 252 or this section.

(6)   In section 66 of the Criminal Justice and Police Act 2001 (c. 16) (general interpretation of Part 2) in subsection (1) —

    (a)   before the definition of "premises" insert —

              ""marine installation" has the meaning given by section 262 of the Marine and Coastal Access Act 2009;";

    (b)   in the definition of "premises", after "offshore installation" insert "or other marine installation".

(7)   In Part 1 of Schedule 1 to that Act (powers of seizure to which section 50

2604

Marine and Coastal Access Act 2009 (c. 23)
Part 8 — Enforcement
Chapter 2 — Common enforcement powers

applies), after paragraph 73K insert—

"*Marine and Coastal Access Act 2009 (c. 23)*

   73L   Each of the powers of seizure conferred by section 252(1) and (3) of the Marine and Coastal Access Act 2009."

254   Retention of seized items

(1)   This section applies to any item seized in the exercise of a power conferred by section 252.

(2)   The item may be retained so long as is necessary in all the circumstances and in particular—

    (a)   for use as evidence at a trial for a relevant offence, or

    (b)   for forensic examination or for investigation in connection with a relevant offence.

(3)   No item may be retained for either of the purposes mentioned in subsection (2) if a photograph or a copy would be sufficient for that purpose.

Miscellaneous and ancillary powers

255   Power to record evidence of offences

(1)   An enforcement officer may use any device for the purpose of taking visual images of anything which the officer believes is evidence of the commission of a relevant offence.

(2)   The power conferred by this section is exercisable in relation to—

    (a)   anything that is in or on,

    (b)   anything that is attached to or otherwise forms part of, or

    (c)   anything that is controlled from,

any vessel, marine installation, premises or vehicle.

(3)   The officer may require any person in or on the vessel, marine installation, premises or vehicle to afford such facilities and assistance with respect to matters under that person's control as the officer considers would facilitate the exercise of the power conferred by this section.

256   Power to require name and address

Where an enforcement officer reasonably believes that a person has committed a relevant offence, the officer may require the person to provide the person's name and address.

257   Power to require production of licence, etc

(1)   Where an enforcement officer reasonably believes—

    (a)   that a person is or has been carrying on a relevant activity, and

    (b)   that the person requires a licence or other authority to carry on that activity,

the officer may require the person to produce that licence or other authority.

Marine and Coastal Access Act 2009 (c. 23)
Part 8 — *Enforcement*
Chapter 2 — *Common enforcement powers*

2605

(2) If the person is unable to produce the licence or other authority when required to do so, the person must produce it at such place, and within such period of time, as the officer may specify.

258 Power to require attendance of certain persons

(1) This section applies where an enforcement officer has —
   (a) boarded a vessel or marine installation, or
   (b) entered any premises.

(2) For the purposes of carrying out any relevant functions, the officer may require the attendance of —
   (a) the person who is for the time being in charge of the vessel or marine installation;
   (b) any other person who is on board the vessel or marine installation;
   (c) the owner or occupier of the premises;
   (d) any person who is on the premises.

259 Power to direct vessel or marine installation to port

(1) This section applies where —
   (a) an enforcement officer considers that it would not be reasonably practicable for the officer to exercise a power which the officer wishes to exercise in relation to a vessel or marine installation without detaining the vessel or marine installation in a port, or
   (b) an enforcement officer reasonably believes that —
      (i) a vessel or marine installation is itself evidence of the commission of a relevant offence, and
      (ii) the only reasonably practicable way to preserve that evidence is to detain the vessel or marine installation in a port.

(2) The officer may —
   (a) take, or arrange for another person to take, the vessel or marine installation and its crew to the port which appears to the officer to be the nearest convenient port, or
   (b) require the person who is for the time being in charge of the vessel or marine installation to take it and its crew to that port.

(3) When the vessel or marine installation has been taken to a port, the officer may —
   (a) detain it there, or
   (b) require the person for the time being in charge of it to do so.

(4) An enforcement officer who detains any vessel or marine installation under this section must serve a notice on the person who is for the time being in charge of it.

(5) The notice must state that the vessel or marine installation is to be detained until the notice is withdrawn.

(6) A notice served under subsection (4) may be withdrawn by service of a further notice signed by an appropriate enforcement officer.

(7) In subsection (6) the reference to an appropriate enforcement officer is a reference to any enforcement officer acting on behalf of the same relevant

2606

Marine and Coastal Access Act 2009 (c. 23)
Part 8 — Enforcement
Chapter 2 — Common enforcement powers

authority as the enforcement officer who served the notice under subsection (4), and includes a reference to that officer.

"Relevant authority" means the person or body on whose behalf the officer who detained the vessel or marine installation was acting.

260 Assistance etc

(1) To assist in carrying out any relevant functions, an enforcement officer may bring —

    (a)   any other person;

    (b)   any equipment or materials.

(2) A person who is brought by an enforcement officer to provide assistance may exercise any powers conferred by this Act which the officer may exercise, but only under the supervision or direction of the officer.

261 Power to use reasonable force

(1) An enforcement officer may use reasonable force, if necessary, in the exercise of any power conferred by this Act.

(2) A person assisting an enforcement officer under section 260 may use reasonable force, if necessary, in the exercise of any power conferred by this Act.

Interpretation

262 Interpretation of this Chapter

(1) In this Chapter —

    "common enforcement power" means any power conferred by sections 246 to 261;

    "enforcement officer" has the meaning given by section 245;

    "item" has the meaning given by section 250(10);

    "justice" has the meaning given by section 249(5);

    "marine installation" means any artificial island, installation or structure (other than a vessel);

    "premises" has the meaning given by section 247(4);

    "relevant activity", "relevant function" and "relevant offence" have the meaning given by section 245;

    "the relevant premises", in relation to an enforcement officer exercising a power of inspection conferred by section 246, 247 or 248, means the vessel, marine installation, premises or vehicle in relation to which the power is being exercised.

(2) In this Chapter any reference to a vessel includes a reference to —

    (a)   any ship or boat or any other description of vessel used in navigation,

    (b)   any hovercraft, submersible craft or other floating craft, and

    (c)   any aircraft,

but does not include a reference to anything that permanently rests on, or is permanently attached to, the sea bed.

Marine and Coastal Access Act 2009 (c. 23)
Part 8 — Enforcement
Chapter 3 — Licensing enforcement powers

2607

CHAPTER 3

LICENSING ENFORCEMENT POWERS

263   Power to require information relating to certain substances and objects

(1)   A person who has the power conferred by this section may require any person—

    (a)   to give details of any substances or objects on board a vehicle, vessel, aircraft or marine structure;

    (b)   to give information concerning any substances or objects lost from a vehicle, vessel, aircraft or marine structure.

(2)   A statement made by a person in response to a requirement made under this section may not be used against the person in criminal proceedings in which the person is charged with an offence to which this subsection applies.

(3)   Subsection (2) applies to any offence other than an offence under one of the following provisions (which concern false statements made otherwise than on oath)—

    (a)   section 5 of the Perjury Act 1911 (c. 6);

    (b)   section 44(2) of the Criminal Law (Consolidation) (Scotland) Act 1995 (c. 39);

    (c)   Article 10 of the Perjury (Northern Ireland) Order 1979 (S.I. 1979/1714 (N.I. 19)).

(4)   In this section "marine structure" and "vessel" have the meaning given by section 115.

CHAPTER 4

FISHERIES ENFORCEMENT POWERS

Inspection and seizure of objects at sea

264   Power to inspect and seize objects at sea

(1)   For the purposes of carrying out any relevant functions, an enforcement officer who has the power conferred by this section may inspect any object in the sea which the officer believes has been or is being used for or in connection with fishing.

The officer may lift an object out of the sea for the purposes of inspecting it under this section.

(2)   An enforcement officer who has inspected an object under this section may seize the object.

(3)   The power conferred by subsection (2) may only be exercised—

    (a)   for the purposes of determining whether a relevant offence has been committed, or

    (b)   in relation to an object which an enforcement officer reasonably believes to be evidence of the commission of a relevant offence.

2608

Marine and Coastal Access Act 2009 (c. 23)
Part 8 — Enforcement
Chapter 4 — Fisheries enforcement powers

(4) If, having inspected an object under this section, the officer decides not to seize it under subsection (2), the officer must, if it is reasonably practicable to do so, replace the object in the location where it was found.

(5) If it is not reasonably practicable to replace the object in accordance with subsection (4), the officer may seize the object until such time as it may be collected by its owner.

(6) Any power conferred by this section to seize an object includes power to seize —

  (a) anything that is attached to the object;

  (b) anything that is contained within the object.

(7) Any reference in this section to replacing an object includes, in the case of fishing gear, a reference to re-setting the gear in the same way in which it was placed in the sea.

(8) The powers conferred on an enforcement officer by this section are without prejudice to any powers exercisable by the officer apart from this section.

265 Reports of inspections under section 264

(1) This section applies where an enforcement officer inspects any object under section 264.

(2) The officer must prepare a report in relation to the inspection.

(3) The report must state —

  (a) the date and time of the inspection;

  (b) the identity of the officer who carried out the inspection;

  (c) how the officer may be contacted.

(4) In the case of an object seized under section 264(2) or (5), the report must also state —

  (a) what has been seized;

  (b) the reasons for its seizure;

  (c) any further action that it is proposed will be taken in relation to the object.

(5) Where the object has not been seized under section 264(2) or (5), the officer must, if it is reasonably practicable to do so, attach a copy of the report to the object.

  If it is not reasonably practicable to attach a copy of the report to the object, the officer must serve a copy of the report on every person who appears to the officer to be the owner, or one of the owners, of the object.

(6) In a case where the officer, after taking reasonable steps to do so, is unable to identify any person as owning the object, the officer must take such steps as the officer thinks fit to bring the contents of the report to the attention of persons likely to be interested in it.

(7) Where —

  (a) the object has been seized under section 264(2), and

  (b) either of the conditions in subsection (8) is satisfied,

Marine and Coastal Access Act 2009 (c. 23)   2609
Part 8 – Enforcement
Chapter 4 – Fisheries enforcement powers

the relevant authority must, if it has not already done so, serve a copy of the report on every person who appears to the authority to be the owner, or one of the owners, of the object.

(8)   The conditions are —

(a)   that the relevant authority has decided not to take proceedings in respect of any offence in relation to which the object was seized;

(b)   that any proceedings taken in respect of such an offence have concluded.

(9)   Where the object has been seized under section 264(5), the relevant authority must serve a copy of the report on every person who appears to the authority to be the owner, or one of the owners, of the object at the same time as it serves a notice of collection on that person under section 267.

(10)   In a case where the relevant authority, after taking reasonable steps to do so, is unable to identify any person as owning the object —

(a)   any reference in this section to a requirement for the authority to serve a copy of a report on such a person is to be read as a reference to a requirement to take such steps as the authority thinks fit to bring the contents of the report to the attention of persons likely to be interested in it, and

(b)   the reference in subsection (9) to serving a notice of collection under section 267 is to be read as a reference to taking the steps referred to in subsection (5) of that section.

266   Retention of objects seized under section 264(2)

(1)   Any object seized by an enforcement officer under section 264(2) may be retained by the relevant authority.

(2)   If either of the grounds of release in subsection (3) applies, the relevant authority must, as soon as is reasonably practicable, make the object available for collection.

(3)   The grounds of release referred to in subsection (2) are —

(a)   that the relevant authority has decided not to take proceedings in respect of any offence in relation to which the object was seized;

(b)   that any proceedings taken in respect of such an offence have concluded without any order for forfeiture having been made.

(4)   But subsection (2) does not apply if the object is liable to forfeiture under section 275 or 276.

(5)   Any reference in this section to an object seized under subsection (2) of section 264 includes a reference to anything seized by virtue of subsection (6) of that section.

267   Disposal of objects seized under section 264

(1)   This section applies to —

(a)   any object seized under section 264(2) which the relevant authority —

(i)   no longer wishes to retain for any purpose, or

(ii)   is required to make available for collection by virtue of section 266;

2610

Marine and Coastal Access Act 2009 (c. 23)
Part 8 – Enforcement
Chapter 4 – Fisheries enforcement powers

(b)   any object seized under section 264(5).

(2)   In this section a "notice of collection" is a notice stating that—

(a)   the object specified in the notice is available to be collected from the location so specified, and

(b)   if the object is not collected before the end of the period of three months beginning with the date specified in the notice, the relevant authority will dispose of the object.

(3)   The relevant authority must serve a notice of collection on every person who appears to the authority to be the owner, or one of the owners, of the object.

(4)   The relevant authority may take any other steps it thinks fit to notify every such person that the object is available to be collected.

(5)   If the relevant authority, after taking reasonable steps to do so, is unable to identify any person as owning the object in order to serve a notice of collection, the relevant authority must take such steps as it thinks fit to bring the information contained in the notice of collection to the attention of persons likely to be interested in it.

(6)   If the relevant authority complies with subsection (3) or subsection (5), as the case may be, the relevant authority may, at the end of the period mentioned in subsection (2)(b), dispose of the object in whatever way it thinks fit.

(7)   Any reference in this section to an object seized under subsection (2) or (5) of section 264 includes a reference to anything seized by virtue of subsection (6) of that section.

Seizure for purposes of forfeiture

268   Power to seize fish for purposes of forfeiture

(1)   An enforcement officer who has the power conferred by this section may seize and detain or remove any fish in respect of which the officer reasonably believes a relevant offence has been committed.

(2)   The power conferred by this section may only be exercised for the purposes of securing that, in the event of a conviction for a relevant offence, the court may exercise any relevant power of forfeiture in relation to fish in respect of which the offence was committed.

(3)   Where—

(a)   any fish which an enforcement officer wishes to seize and remove are in a container, and

(b)   the officer reasonably considers that it would facilitate the seizure and removal of the fish if they remained in the container for that purpose,

any power to seize and remove the fish includes power to seize and remove the container.

(4)   Where—

(a)   any fish which an enforcement officer wishes to seize and remove are not in a container, and

(b)   the officer reasonably considers that it would facilitate the seizure and removal of the fish if they were placed in a container suitable for that purpose,

Marine and Coastal Access Act 2009 (c. 23)
Part 8 — Enforcement
Chapter 4 — Fisheries enforcement powers

2611

the officer may require the fish to be placed into such a container.

(5) If, in the opinion of an enforcement officer, it is not for the time being practicable for the officer to seize and remove any fish, the officer may require—

(a) the person from whom the fish are being seized, or

(b) where the officer is exercising a power of inspection conferred by section 246, 247 or 248, any person in or on the relevant premises,

to secure that the fish are not removed or otherwise interfered with until such time as the officer may seize and remove them.

(6) Where an enforcement officer is exercising a power of inspection conferred by section 246, 247 or 248, the officer may require any person in or on the relevant premises to afford such facilities and assistance with respect to matters under that person's control as the officer considers would facilitate the exercise of any power conferred by this section.

(7) Where an enforcement officer reasonably believes that a person is or has been carrying on a relevant activity, the officer may require that person to afford such facilities and assistance with respect to matters under that person's control as the officer considers would facilitate the exercise in relation to that person of any power conferred by this section.

(8) In this section—

"relevant activity", in relation to an enforcement officer, means any activity in respect of which the officer has functions;

"relevant power of forfeiture" means any power of a court to order the forfeiture of any fish in respect of which an offence has been committed;

"the relevant premises", in relation to an enforcement officer exercising a power of inspection conferred by section 246, 247 or 248, means the vessel, marine installation, premises or vehicle in relation to which the power is being exercised.

269 Power to seize fishing gear for purposes of forfeiture

(1) An enforcement officer who has the power conferred by this section may seize and detain or remove any fishing gear which the officer reasonably believes has been used in the commission of a relevant offence.

(2) The power conferred by this section may only be exercised for the purposes of securing that, in the event of a conviction for a relevant offence, the court may exercise any relevant power of forfeiture in relation to fishing gear used in the commission of the offence.

(3) If, in the opinion of an enforcement officer, it is not for the time being practicable for the officer to seize and remove any fishing gear, the officer may require—

(a) the person from whom the fishing gear is being seized, or

(b) where the officer is exercising a power of inspection conferred by section 246, 247 or 248, any person in or on the relevant premises,

to secure that the fishing gear is not removed or otherwise interfered with until such time as the officer may seize and remove it.

(4) Where an enforcement officer is exercising a power of inspection conferred by section 246, 247 or 248, the officer may require any person in or on the relevant premises to afford such facilities and assistance with respect to matters under

2612

Marine and Coastal Access Act 2009 (c. 23)
Part 8 — Enforcement
Chapter 4 — Fisheries enforcement powers

that person's control as the officer considers would facilitate the exercise of any power conferred by this section.

(5) Where an enforcement officer reasonably believes that a person is or has been carrying on a relevant activity, the officer may require that person to afford such facilities and assistance with respect to matters under that person's control as the officer considers would facilitate the exercise in relation to that person of any power conferred by this section.

(6) In this section—

"relevant activity", in relation to an enforcement officer, means any activity in respect of which the officer has functions;

"relevant power of forfeiture" means any power of a court to order the forfeiture of any fishing gear used in the commission of an offence;

"the relevant premises", in relation to an enforcement officer exercising a power of inspection conferred by section 246, 247 or 248, means the vessel, marine installation, premises or vehicle in relation to which the power is being exercised.

270 Procedure in relation to seizure under section 268 or 269

(1) An enforcement officer who seizes any property under section 268 or 269 must, if it is reasonably practicable to do so, serve a notice on each of the following persons—

(a) every person who appears to the officer to have been the owner, or one of the owners, of the property at the time of its seizure;

(b) in the case of property seized from a vessel, the master, owner and charterer (if any) of the vessel at that time;

(c) in the case of property seized from premises, every person who appears to the officer to have been an occupier of the premises at that time;

(d) in any other case, the person (if any) from whom the property was seized.

(2) The notice must state—

(a) what has been seized;

(b) the reason for its seizure;

(c) the offence which the officer believes has been committed;

(d) any further action that it is proposed will be taken;

(e) that, unless the property is liable to forfeiture under section 275 or 276, it is to be detained until such time as it is released or its forfeiture is ordered by the court.

(3) Subsections (4) and (5) apply in a case where the property was seized following an inspection carried out in exercise of the power conferred by section 264.

(4) The officer must serve a copy of the report referred to in section 265 on every person falling within paragraph (a) of subsection (1) above at the same time as the officer serves a notice on that person under this section.

(5) In a case where the officer, after taking reasonable steps to do so, is unable to identify any person as owning the property—

(a) any reference in this section to a requirement to serve a notice on that person is to be read as a reference to a requirement to take such steps as the officer thinks fit to bring the contents of the notice to the attention of persons likely to be interested in it, and

Marine and Coastal Access Act 2009 (c. 23)
Part 8 – Enforcement
Chapter 4 – Fisheries enforcement powers

2613

       (b)   the reference in subsection (4) to serving a copy of the report referred to in section 265 is to be read as a reference to taking the steps referred to in subsection (10)(a) of that section.

271 Retention of property seized under section 268 or 269

(1)   Any property seized by an enforcement officer under section 268 or 269 may be retained by the relevant authority.

(2)   If either of the grounds for release in subsection (3) applies, the relevant authority must, as soon as is reasonably practicable, make the property available for collection.

(3)   The grounds for release referred to in subsection (2) are—
    (a)   that the relevant authority has decided not to take proceedings in respect of any offence in relation to which the property was seized;
    (b)   that any proceedings taken in respect of such an offence have concluded without any order for forfeiture having been made.

(4)   But subsection (2) does not apply if the property is liable to forfeiture under section 275 or 276.

272 Bonds for release of seized fish or gear

(1)   This section applies to any property which is being retained by the relevant authority under section 271.

(2)   The relevant authority may enter into an agreement with any person falling within subsection (3) for security for the property to be given to the relevant authority by way of bond in return for the release of the property.

(3)   The persons referred to in subsection (2) are—
    (a)   the owner, or any of the owners, of the property;
    (b)   in the case of property seized from a vessel, the owner or charterer, or any of the owners or charterers, of the vessel.

(4)   Any bond given under this section is to be—
    (a)   for such amount as may be agreed, or
    (b)   in the event of a failure to agree an amount, for such amount as may be determined by the court.
    "The court" means a magistrates' court in England and Wales.

(5)   A person who gives a bond under this section must comply with such conditions as to the giving of the bond as the relevant authority may determine.

(6)   If either of the grounds for release mentioned in subsection (7) applies, then any bond given under this section must be returned as soon as possible.

(7)   The grounds for release referred to in subsection (6) are—
    (a)   that the relevant authority has decided not to take proceedings in respect of any offence in relation to which the property was seized;
    (b)   that any proceedings taken in respect of such an offence have concluded without any order for forfeiture having been made.

2614

Marine and Coastal Access Act 2009 (c. 23)
Part 8 – Enforcement
Chapter 4 – Fisheries enforcement powers

(8)   Any power which a court has to order the forfeiture of any fish or any fishing gear may instead be exercised in relation to any bond given under this section as security for that fish or fishing gear.

273   Power of relevant authority to sell seized fish in its possession

(1)   Any fish which are being retained by the relevant authority under section 271 may be sold by the authority.

(2)   Any power which a court has to order the forfeiture of any fish may instead be exercised in relation to the proceeds of any sale of the fish under this section.

(3)   Subject to subsection (6), the proceeds of any sale under this section may be retained by the relevant authority until such time as —
         (a)   a court exercises any power it has to order the forfeiture of the proceeds, or
         (b)   either of the grounds for release mentioned in subsection (4) applies.

(4)   The grounds for release referred to in subsection (3) are —
         (a)   that the relevant authority has decided not to take proceedings in respect of any offence in relation to which the fish were seized;
         (b)   that any proceedings taken in respect of such an offence have concluded without any order for forfeiture having been made.

(5)   If either of the grounds for release mentioned in subsection (4) applies, the relevant authority must, as soon as is reasonably practicable, release the proceeds of sale to any person who appears to the authority to have been the owner, or one of the owners, of the fish at the time of the seizure of the fish.

(6)   If the proceeds of sale are still in the relevant authority's possession after the end of the period of six months beginning with the date on which the fish were sold, the relevant authority may retain the proceeds and apply them in any manner it thinks fit.

         The relevant authority may exercise its power under this subsection to retain and apply the proceeds of sale only if it is not practicable at the time when the power is exercised to dispose of the proceeds by releasing them immediately to the person to whom they are required to be released.

(7)   Subject to subsection (9), any fish sold under this section must be sold at auction.

(8)   Before selling the fish, the relevant authority must give the owner of the fish a reasonable opportunity to make representations as to the manner in which the fish are sold.

(9)   If —
         (a)   the owner of the fish requests that the fish be sold —
                 (i)   at a particular auction, or
                 (ii)   by a method of sale other than auction,
                 and
         (b)   the relevant authority does not consider that it would be unreasonable to comply with that request,
         the relevant authority must comply with the request when selling the fish.

(10)   The relevant authority may deduct any reasonable expenses it has incurred in selling any fish under this section from the proceeds of the sale.

Marine and Coastal Access Act 2009 (c. 23)
Part 8 – Enforcement
Chapter 4 – Fisheries enforcement powers

2615

(11) In a case where there is more than one owner of the fish, subsection (9) applies only if the request is made by or on behalf of all of them.

274 Disposal of property seized under section 268 or 269

(1) This section applies to any property seized under section 268 or 269 which the relevant authority –

(a) no longer wishes to retain for any purpose, or

(b) is required to make available for collection by virtue of section 271.

(2) In this section a "notice of collection" is a notice stating that –

(a) the property specified in the notice is available to be collected from the location so specified, and

(b) if the property is not collected before the end of the period of three months beginning with the date specified in the notice, the relevant authority will dispose of the property.

(3) The relevant authority must serve a notice of collection on every person who appears to the authority to be the owner, or one of the owners, of the property.

(4) The relevant authority may take any other steps it considers appropriate to notify every such person that the property is available to be collected.

(5) If the relevant authority, after taking reasonable steps to do so, is unable to identify any person as owning the property, the relevant authority must –

(a) if it is reasonably practicable to do so, serve a notice of collection on every person who is an appropriate person for the purposes of this subsection, and

(b) take such steps as it thinks fit to bring the information contained in the notice of collection to the attention of persons likely to be interested in it.

(6) For the purposes of subsection (5), the following persons are "appropriate persons" –

(a) in the case of property seized from a vessel, the master, owner and charterer (if any) of the vessel at the time of the seizure of the property;

(b) in the case of property seized from premises, every person who appears to the relevant authority to have been an occupier of the premises at that time;

(c) in any other case, the person (if any) from whom the property was seized.

(7) If the relevant authority complies with subsection (3) or subsection (5), as the case may be, the relevant authority may, at the end of the period mentioned in subsection (2)(b), dispose of the property in whatever way it thinks fit.

Forfeiture

275 Forfeiture etc of prohibited items

(1) Any item to which this section applies is liable to forfeiture under this section if the use of that item for sea fishing would in any circumstances constitute an offence under the law of England and Wales.

2616

Marine and Coastal Access Act 2009 (c. 23)
Part 8 – Enforcement
Chapter 4 – Fisheries enforcement powers

(2) This section applies to any item seized on board a vessel or from the sea by an enforcement officer in the exercise of any power conferred by this Act.

(3) Any item forfeited under this section is to be forfeited to the relevant authority and may be disposed of by that authority in any manner it thinks fit.

276 Forfeiture etc of fish failing to meet size requirements

(1) Any fish to which this section applies are liable to forfeiture under this section if, by virtue of the fish failing to meet requirements as to size, an offence under the law of England and Wales has been committed in respect of the fish.

(2) This section applies to fish seized by an enforcement officer in the exercise of any power conferred by this Act.

(3) Any fish forfeited under this section are to be forfeited to the relevant authority and may be disposed of by that authority in any manner it thinks fit.

277 Further provision about forfeiture under section 275 or 276

Schedule 18 (which makes provision in relation to the forfeiture of property liable to forfeiture under section 275 or 276) has effect.

278 Forfeiture by court following conviction

(1) This section applies where a court by or before which a person is convicted of an offence under the fisheries legislation orders the forfeiture of any fish or any fishing gear in respect of that offence.

(2) The court must order that the property to be forfeited is to be taken into the possession of the person or body by whom proceedings for the offence were brought.

(3) The property may be disposed of as that person or body thinks fit.

(4) Any proceeds arising from the disposal of the property may be retained by the person or body.

(5) The court may order any person convicted of the offence to pay any costs reasonably incurred by any person or body in storing the property that is to be forfeited.

(6) In this section —

"the fisheries legislation" means —

(a) any enactments relating to sea fishing (including any enactment relating to fishing for shellfish, salmon or migratory trout);

(b) any enforceable EU restrictions and enforceable EU obligations relating to sea fishing;

"enforceable EU obligation" means an obligation to which section 2(1) of the European Communities Act 1972 (c. 68) applies;

"enforceable EU restriction" means a restriction to which section 2(1) of that Act applies.

Marine and Coastal Access Act 2009 (c. 23)   2617
Part 8 — Enforcement
Chapter 4 — Fisheries enforcement powers

Detention of vessels in connection with court proceedings

279   Power to detain vessels in connection with court proceedings

(1)   This section applies where—

    (a)   an enforcement officer has reasonable grounds for suspecting that a relevant offence has been committed by the master, owner or charterer of a vessel, and

    (b)   the officer reasonably believes that—

        (i)   if proceedings are taken against the person for the offence, there is a real risk that the person will not attend court unless the vessel is detained under this section, or

        (ii)   if the person is convicted of the offence and the court by or before which the person is convicted imposes a fine on that person, it is likely that the court will order the vessel to be detained.

(2)   Where this section applies, an enforcement officer who has the power conferred by this section may—

    (a)   take, or arrange for another person to take, the vessel and its crew to the port which appears to the officer to be the nearest convenient port, or

    (b)   require any person who is for the time being in charge of the vessel to take it and its crew to that port.

(3)   When a vessel has been taken to a port in pursuance of this section, the officer may—

    (a)   detain it there, or

    (b)   require the person for the time being in charge of it to do so.

(4)   An enforcement officer who detains any vessel under this section must, if it is reasonably practicable to do so, serve a notice on—

    (a)   the owner of the vessel,

    (b)   the charterer (if any) of the vessel, and

    (c)   the person who is for the time being in charge of the vessel.

(5)   The notice must state—

    (a)   the reasons for detaining the vessel;

    (b)   the circumstances in which the vessel may be released.

280   Release of vessels detained under section 279

(1)   This section applies where a vessel is being detained under section 279.

(2)   The vessel ceases to be detained under that section if one of the following things occurs—

    (a)   the notice of detention is withdrawn;

    (b)   the court orders the release of the vessel under section 281;

    (c)   any proceedings taken against the master, owner or charterer of the vessel have concluded;

    (d)   the court referred to in section 279(1)(b)(ii) exercises any power it has to order the vessel to be detained.

(3)   A notice of detention may be withdrawn by service of a further notice signed by an appropriate enforcement officer.

2618

Marine and Coastal Access Act 2009 (c. 23)
Part 8 – Enforcement
Chapter 4 – Fisheries enforcement powers

(4) In subsection (3) the reference to an appropriate enforcement officer is a reference to any enforcement officer acting on behalf of the same relevant authority as the enforcement officer who served the notice of detention, and includes a reference to that officer.

(5) If any of the grounds for release mentioned in subsection (6) applies, then any notice of detention must be withdrawn as soon as possible.

(6) The grounds for release referred to in subsection (5) are—
   (a) that the relevant authority has decided not to take proceedings against the master, owner or charterer of the vessel;
   (b) that there are no grounds for believing that any person referred to in paragraph (a) against whom proceedings have been, or may be, taken will fail to attend court;
   (c) that there are no grounds for believing that the court referred to in section 279(1)(b)(ii) will order the vessel to be detained.

(7) In this section "notice of detention" means a notice served under section 279(4).

281 Power of court to order release of vessels

(1) This section applies where a vessel is being detained under section 279.

(2) If, on an application made to a magistrates' court in England and Wales by the owner or charterer, or any of the owners or charterers, of the vessel, the court is satisfied that—
   (a) the continued detention of the vessel under section 279 is not necessary to secure that the master, owner or charterer of the vessel will attend court, or
   (b) there are no grounds for believing that the court referred to in section 279(1)(b)(ii) will order the vessel to be detained,
   the court may order that the vessel be released.

282 Bonds for release of vessels

(1) Where a vessel is being detained under section 279, the relevant authority may enter into an agreement with the owner or charterer, or any of the owners or charterers, of the vessel for security for the vessel to be given to the relevant authority by way of bond in return for the withdrawal of the notice of detention.

(2) Any bond given under this section is to be—
   (a) for such amount as may be agreed, or
   (b) in the event of a failure to agree an amount, for such amount as may be determined by the court.
   "The court" means a magistrates' court in England and Wales.

(3) A person who gives a bond under this section must comply with such conditions as to the giving of the bond as the relevant authority may determine.

(4) If any of the grounds for release mentioned in subsection (5) applies, then any bond given under this section must be returned as soon as possible.

(5) The grounds for release referred to in subsection (4) are—

Marine and Coastal Access Act 2009 (c. 23)
Part 8 — Enforcement
Chapter 4 — Fisheries enforcement powers

2619

    (a)   that the relevant authority has decided not to take proceedings against the master, owner or charterer of the vessel;

    (b)   that there are no grounds for believing that any person referred to in paragraph (a) against whom proceedings have been, or may be, taken will fail to attend court;

    (c)   that there are no grounds for believing that the court referred to in section 279(1)(b)(ii) would, in the absence of the bond, have ordered the vessel to be detained;

    (d)   that any proceedings taken against the master, owner or charterer of the vessel have concluded without any fine having been imposed.

(6)   Where a court imposes a fine on the master, owner or charterer of the vessel, the court may order any sum of money given as a bond under this section to be used towards the payment of the fine.

    If the fine is less than the amount of the bond, any sum not required to be used in payment of the fine must be returned to the person who gave the bond as soon as possible.

(7)   In this section "notice of detention" means a notice served under section 279(4).

283 Power of court to order repayment of bonds

(1)   This section applies where a notice of detention served under section 279(4) in respect of a vessel has been withdrawn in return for a bond given as security for the vessel under section 282.

(2)   If, on an application to a magistrates' court in England and Wales by the person who gave the bond, the court is satisfied that—

    (a)   the continued detention of the bond under section 282 is not necessary to secure that the master, owner or charterer of the vessel will attend court, or

    (b)   there are no grounds for believing that the court referred to in section 279(1)(b)(ii) would, in the absence of the bond, have ordered the vessel to be detained,

    the court may order that the bond be returned to the person who gave it.

Production of equipment

284 Power to require production of certain equipment

(1)   An enforcement officer who has the power conferred by this section may require any person on board a vessel to produce any equipment falling within subsection (2).

(2)   The equipment referred to in subsection (1) is—

    (a)   any automatic recording equipment or transmitting equipment used in accordance with a condition included in a licence by virtue of section 4(6) or 4A(6) of the Sea Fish (Conservation) Act 1967 (c. 84);

    (b)   any equipment which is required to be carried on board a vessel by virtue of a byelaw made by an inshore fisheries and conservation authority under section 155;

    (c)   any equipment which is required to be carried on board a vessel by virtue of an order made by the Welsh Ministers under section 189.

2620

Marine and Coastal Access Act 2009 (c. 23)
Part 8 – Enforcement
Chapter 4 – Fisheries enforcement powers

Supplementary

285 Service of notices, etc

(1) Any notice or other thing that is required to be served on or given to a person under any provision of this Chapter may be served on or given to the person only by one of the following methods –

    (a) personal delivery;

    (b) addressing it to the person and leaving it at the appropriate address;

    (c) addressing it to the person and sending it to that address by post.

(2) "The appropriate address", in relation to the owner of a vessel that is registered in any country or territory, means the address given by that register as the address of the owner of the vessel.

(3) In relation to any other person "the appropriate address" means –

    (a) in the case of a body corporate, its registered or principal office in the United Kingdom;

    (b) in the case of a firm, the principal office of the partnership;

    (c) in the case of an unincorporated body or association, the principal office of the body or association;

    (d) in any other case, the person's usual or last known place of residence in the United Kingdom or last known place of business in the United Kingdom.

(4) In the case of –

    (a) a company registered outside the United Kingdom,

    (b) a firm carrying on business outside the United Kingdom, or

    (c) an unincorporated body or association with offices outside the United Kingdom,

the references in subsection (3) to its principal office include references to its principal office within the United Kingdom (if any).

286 Conclusion of proceedings

(1) This section applies for determining when any proceedings have concluded for the purposes of this Chapter.

(2) Where proceedings are terminated by an appealable decision, they are not to be regarded as concluded –

    (a) until the end of the ordinary time for appeal against the decision, if no appeal in respect of the decision is brought within that time, or

    (b) if an appeal in respect of the decision is brought within that time, until the conclusion of the appeal.

(3) Subsection (2) applies for determining, for the purposes of paragraph (b) of that subsection, when proceedings on an appeal are concluded as it applies for determining when the original proceedings are concluded.

(4) Any reference in subsection (2) to a decision which terminates proceedings includes a reference to a verdict, sentence, finding or order that puts an end to the proceedings.

Marine and Coastal Access Act 2009 (c. 23)
Part 8 – *Enforcement*
Chapter 4 – *Fisheries enforcement powers*

2621

(5) An appealable decision is a decision of a description against which an appeal will lie, whether by way of case stated or otherwise and whether with or without permission.

(6) Any reference in this section to an appeal includes a reference to an application for permission to appeal.

287 Interpretation of this Chapter

In this Chapter —
"fish" includes shellfish;
"relevant authority" means —
    (a) in relation to the seizure of any object or property by an enforcement officer, the person or body on whose behalf the officer who seized it was acting;
    (b) in relation to the detention of a vessel by an enforcement officer, the person or body on whose behalf the officer who detained the vessel was acting;
"relevant function", in relation to an enforcement officer, means any function of that officer;
"relevant offence", in relation to an enforcement officer, means any offence in respect of which the officer has functions;
"shellfish" includes crustaceans and molluscs of any kind;
"vessel" includes any ship or boat or any description of vessel used in navigation.

CHAPTER 5

COMMON ENFORCEMENT PROVISIONS

Introductory

288 Meaning of "enforcement officer"

In this Chapter "enforcement officer" means a person who has any powers conferred by this Part, other than a person who has such powers only by virtue of section 260(2) (persons assisting enforcement officers).

Duties of enforcement officers

289 Duty to provide evidence of authority

(1) Before exercising any power conferred by this Part, an enforcement officer must, if requested to do so, produce evidence that the officer is authorised to exercise that power.

(2) An enforcement officer may exercise a power conferred by this Part only if the officer complies with the duty imposed by subsection (1).

(3) If, at the time the request is made, the officer does not consider it practicable to produce the evidence referred to in subsection (1), that subsection does not apply until such time as the officer considers it practicable to comply with the request.

2622   *Marine and Coastal Access Act 2009 (c. 23)*
Part 8 — Enforcement
Chapter 5 — Common enforcement provisions

(4)   Nothing in this section applies to a person falling within paragraph (c) or (d) of section 235(1).

290   Duty to state name and purpose, etc

(1)   Before exercising any power conferred by this Part, an enforcement officer must, if requested to do so, give the information in subsection (3).

(2)   Before exercising any power conferred by this Part, any person assisting an enforcement officer by virtue of section 260 must, if requested to do so, give the information in paragraphs (b) and (c) of subsection (3).

(3)   The information is —
     (a)   the person's name;
     (b)   the power the person is proposing to exercise;
     (c)   the grounds for proposing to do so.

(4)   A person may exercise a power conferred by this Part only if the person complies with the duty imposed by subsection (1) or the duty imposed by subsection (2) (as the case may be).

(5)   If, at the time the request is made, the person does not consider it practicable to give the information referred to in subsection (1) or the information referred to in subsection (2) (as the case may be), that subsection does not apply until such time as the person considers it practicable to comply with the request.

Liability of enforcement officers

291   Liability of enforcement officers etc

(1)   A person within subsection (2) is not to be liable in any civil or criminal proceedings for anything done (or omitted to be done) in, or in connection with, the discharge or purported discharge of the person's functions under this Act.

(2)   The persons are —
     (a)   any enforcement officer;
     (b)   any person assisting an enforcement officer by virtue of section 260.

(3)   Subsection (1) does not apply —
     (a)   if the act or omission is shown to have been in bad faith,
     (b)   if there were no reasonable grounds for the act or omission, or
     (c)   so as to prevent an award of damages in respect of the act or omission on the ground that it was unlawful as a result of section 6(1) of the Human Rights Act 1998 (c. 42) (acts of public authorities incompatible with Convention rights).

Offences in relation to enforcement officers

292   Offences in relation to enforcement officers

(1)   A person is guilty of an offence if —
     (a)   the person fails without reasonable excuse to comply with a requirement reasonably made, or a direction reasonably given, by an

Marine and Coastal Access Act 2009 (c. 23)
Part 8 — Enforcement
Chapter 5 — Common enforcement provisions

2623

enforcement officer in the exercise of any power conferred by this Part, or

   (b)   the person prevents any other person from complying with any such requirement or direction.

(2)   A person is not guilty of an offence by reason of a failure to comply with a requirement made under subsection (1) of section 257 if the person complies with subsection (2) of that section.

(3)   A person who provides information in pursuance of a requirement reasonably made by an enforcement officer in the exercise of the power conferred by section 263 is guilty of an offence if —

   (a)   the information is false in a material particular, and the person knows that it is or is reckless as to whether it is, or

   (b)   the person intentionally fails to disclose any material particular.

(4)   A person who intentionally obstructs an enforcement officer in the performance of any of the officer's functions under this Act is guilty of an offence.

(5)   A person who assaults an enforcement officer in the performance of any of the officer's functions under this Act is guilty of an offence.

(6)   A person who, with intent to deceive, falsely pretends to be an enforcement officer is guilty of an offence.

(7)   A person who is guilty of an offence under subsection (1), (3) or (6) is liable —

   (a)   on summary conviction, to a fine not exceeding the statutory maximum;

   (b)   on conviction on indictment, to a fine.

(8)   A person who is guilty of an offence under subsection (4) is liable on summary conviction to a fine not exceeding £20,000.

(9)   A person who is guilty of an offence under subsection (5) is liable on summary conviction to a fine not exceeding £50,000.

(10)   Proceedings for an offence under this section may be taken, and the offence may for all incidental purposes be treated as having been committed, in any part of the United Kingdom.

(11)   In this section any reference to an enforcement officer includes a reference to a person assisting an enforcement officer by virtue of section 260.

CHAPTER 6

MISCELLANEOUS AND SUPPLEMENTARY

Enforcement of Community rules

293   Enforcement of Community rules

(1)   Section 30 of the Fisheries Act 1981 (c. 29) (enforcement of Community rules) is amended as follows.

(2)   In subsection (1) —

2624

Marine and Coastal Access Act 2009 (c. 23)
Part 8 – Enforcement
Chapter 6 – Miscellaneous and supplementary

    (a)   after "enforceable Community restrictions" insert ", and enforceable Community obligations,";

    (b)   for paragraph (a) substitute —

        "(a)   if any fishing boat within British fishery limits —

            (i)   fishes in contravention of any such restriction, or

            (ii)   fails to comply with any such obligation,

        the master, the owner and the charterer (if any) are each guilty of an offence;";

    (c)   after paragraph (a) insert —

        "(aa)   if any English or Welsh fishing boat outside British fishery limits —

            (i)   fishes in contravention of any such restriction, or

            (ii)   fails to comply with any such obligation,

        the master, the owner and the charterer (if any) are each guilty of an offence;

        (ab)   if any person in England or Wales —

            (i)   fishes in contravention of any such restriction, or

            (ii)   fails to comply with any such obligation,

        that person is guilty of an offence;";

    (d)   in paragraph (b), for "such offences" substitute "offences under paragraph (a), (aa) or (ab) of this subsection";

    (e)   in paragraph (c), after "restrictions" insert "and obligations".

(3)   After subsection (2) insert —

    "(2ZA)   The provision that may be made by an order made under subsection (2) by the Secretary of State includes —

        (a)   provision applying to English or Welsh fishing boats outside British fishery limits;

        (b)   provision applying to persons of a specified description on board any fishing boat, other than a Scottish or Northern Ireland fishing boat, outside British fishery limits.

    In this subsection "specified" means specified in the order."

(4)   After subsection (2A) insert —

    "(2B)   Her Majesty may by Order in Council provide for subsection (1) or (2) above to apply, with or without modifications, to any fishing boat within subsection (2C) below that is outside British fishery limits as it applies to any English or Welsh fishing boat outside those limits.

    (2C)   A fishing boat is within this subsection if —

        (a)   it is registered under the law of the Isle of Man or any of the Channel Islands; or

        (b)   it is wholly owned by persons qualified for the purposes of the law relating to the registration of vessels in the Isle of Man or any of the Channel Islands to own fishing vessels which are entitled to be registered as such under that law."

(5)   In subsection (3), insert at the appropriate places the following definitions —

    ""English fishing boat" means —

        (a)   a fishing boat which is registered in the United Kingdom under Part 2 of the Merchant Shipping Act

Marine and Coastal Access Act 2009 (c. 23)   2625
Part 8 – Enforcement
Chapter 6 – Miscellaneous and supplementary

1995 and whose entry in the register specifies a port in England as the port to which the boat is to be treated as belonging; or

(b)   a fishing boat which is wholly owned by persons qualified to own British ships for the purposes of that Part, other than—

    (i)   a Welsh, Scottish or Northern Ireland fishing boat,

    (ii)   a fishing boat within subsection (2C) above, or

    (iii)   a fishing boat registered in any country or territory other than the United Kingdom, the Isle of Man or any of the Channel Islands;";

""Northern Ireland fishing boat" means a fishing boat which is registered in the United Kingdom under Part 2 of the Merchant Shipping Act 1995 and whose entry in the register specifies a port in Northern Ireland as the port to which the boat is to be treated as belonging;";

""Scottish fishing boat" means a fishing boat which is registered in the United Kingdom under Part 2 of that Act and whose entry in the register specifies a port in Scotland as the port to which the boat is to be treated as belonging;";

""Welsh fishing boat" means a fishing boat which is registered in the United Kingdom under Part 2 of that Act and whose entry in the register specifies a port in Wales as the port to which the boat is to be treated as belonging."

Administrative penalty schemes

294   Administrative penalty schemes

(1)   The appropriate national authority for any area may by order make provision to confer on any enforcement authority for that area the power to issue penalty notices for offences within subsection (2).

(2)   The offences referred to in subsection (1) are offences relating to sea fishing, other than—

(a)   an offence under section 30 of the Fisheries Act 1981 (c. 29) or any order made under that section;

(b)   an offence under regulations made under section 2(2) of the European Communities Act 1972 (c. 68).

(3)   A penalty notice is a notice offering the opportunity, by payment of a specified sum of money, to discharge any liability to be convicted of the offence to which the notice relates.

(4)   The provision that may be made by an order under subsection (1) includes—

(a)   provision prescribing the offences in relation to which penalty notices may be issued;

(b)   provision as to circumstances in which penalty notices may be issued;

(c)   provision as to the content and form of penalty notices;

(d)   provision as to how the amount of any penalty that may be specified in a penalty notice is to be determined;

2626   *Marine and Coastal Access Act 2009 (c. 23)*
Part 8 – Enforcement
Chapter 6 – Miscellaneous and supplementary

       (e)   provision for the issuing of guidance by the appropriate national authority as to matters to be taken into account when making such a determination;

       (f)   provision prescribing the minimum or maximum amount of any penalty;

       (g)   provision about the payment of penalties, including provision as to the period within which any penalty must be paid;

       (h)   provision for and in connection with the withdrawal of penalty notices;

       (i)   provision as to circumstances in which proceedings for an offence may be commenced after the payment of a penalty in relation to that offence.

(5)   An order under subsection (1) may apply in relation to —

       (a)   England;

       (b)   Wales;

       (c)   any vessels in waters within British fishery limits, other than —

           (i)   the Scottish zone,

           (ii)   the Northern Ireland zone, and

           (iii)   the territorial sea adjacent to the Isle of Man, Jersey and Guernsey;

       (d)   any English or Welsh fishing boats, wherever they may be.

(6)   Her Majesty may by Order in Council provide for this section to apply, with or without modifications, to any fishing boat within subsection (7) that is outside British fishery limits as it applies to any English or Welsh fishing boat outside those limits.

(7)   A fishing boat is within this subsection if —

       (a)   it is registered under the law of the Isle of Man or any of the Channel Islands, or

       (b)   it is wholly owned by persons qualified for the purposes of the law relating to the registration of vessels in the Isle of Man or any of the Channel Islands to own fishing vessels which are entitled to be registered as such under that law.

(8)   In this section —

       "appropriate national authority" means —

           (a)   in relation to Wales or vessels within the Welsh zone, the Welsh Ministers;

           (b)   in relation to England or vessels outside the Welsh zone, the Secretary of State;

       "enforcement authority" means, in relation to any area, any authority which has a function (whether or not statutory) of taking any action with a view to or in connection with the imposition of any sanction, criminal or otherwise, in a case where an offence within subsection (2) is committed in that area;

       "England" includes the English inshore region;

       "English fishing boat" means —

           (a)   a fishing boat which is registered in the United Kingdom under Part 2 of the Merchant Shipping Act 1995 (c. 21) and whose entry in the register specifies a port in England as the port to which the boat is to be treated as belonging, or

           (b)   a fishing boat which is wholly owned by persons qualified to own British ships for the purposes of that Part, other than —

Marine and Coastal Access Act 2009 (c. 23)
Part 8 – Enforcement
Chapter 6 – Miscellaneous and supplementary

2627

     (i)   a Welsh, Scottish or Northern Ireland fishing boat,

    (ii)   a fishing boat within subsection (7) above, or

   (iii)   a fishing boat registered in any country or territory other than the United Kingdom, the Isle of Man or any of the Channel Islands;

"fishing boat" means any vessel that is being used for fishing or for any activity relating to fishing;

"Northern Ireland fishing boat" means a fishing boat which is registered in the United Kingdom under Part 2 of the Merchant Shipping Act 1995 (c. 21) and whose entry in the register specifies a port in Northern Ireland as the port to which the boat is to be treated as belonging;

"Scottish fishing boat" means a fishing boat which is registered in the United Kingdom under Part 2 of the Merchant Shipping Act 1995 and whose entry in the register specifies a port in Scotland as the port to which the boat is to be treated as belonging;

"sea fishing" includes fishing for or taking shellfish;

"shellfish" includes crustaceans and molluscs of any kind;

"vessel" includes any ship or boat or any description of vessel used in navigation;

"Wales" includes the Welsh inshore region;

"Welsh fishing boat" means a fishing boat which is registered in the United Kingdom under Part 2 of the Merchant Shipping Act 1995 and whose entry in the register specifies a port in Wales as the port to which the boat is to be treated as belonging.

Crown application

295   Application to the Crown

(1)   The provisions of Chapters 1 to 5 of this Part are binding on the Crown.
This is subject to subsection (2).

(2)   No contravention by the Crown of any provision of Chapter 5 is to make the Crown criminally liable; but the High Court or, in Scotland, the Court of Session may declare unlawful any act or omission of the Crown which constitutes such a contravention.

(3)   Despite subsection (2), the provisions of Chapters 1 to 5 of this Part apply to persons in the public service of the Crown as they apply to other persons.

PART 9

COASTAL ACCESS

The coastal access duty

296   The coastal access duty

(1)   Natural England and the Secretary of State must exercise the relevant functions in order to secure the following objectives.

(2)   The first objective is that there is a route for the whole of the English coast which—

    (a)   consists of one or more long-distance routes along which the public are enabled to make recreational journeys on foot or by ferry, and

    (b)   (except to the extent that it is completed by ferry) passes over land which is accessible to the public.

(3)   The second objective is that, in association with that route ("the English coastal route"), a margin of land along the length of the English coast is accessible to the public for the purposes of its enjoyment by them in conjunction with that route or otherwise, except to the extent that the margin of land is relevant excepted land.

(4)   The duty imposed on Natural England and the Secretary of State by subsection (1) —

    (a)   is referred to in this Part as the coastal access duty, and

    (b)   is to be discharged by them in such stages and within such period as appear to them to be appropriate.

(5)   For the purposes of this section, land is accessible to the public if it is —

    (a)   land which is available to the public for the purposes of open-air recreation, by virtue of provision made under section 3A of the CROW Act and subject to any exclusions or restrictions imposed by or under Part 1 of that Act (access to the countryside),

    (b)   land in England which, for the purposes of section 1(1) of that Act, is treated by section 15(1) of that Act as being accessible to the public apart from that Act, or

    (c)   excepted land in England which is accessible to the public by virtue of any enactment or rule of law (other than a military lands byelaw).

(6)   Nothing in this section requires Natural England or the Secretary of State, in discharging the coastal access duty so far as it relates to the objective in subsection (3), to exercise functions so as to secure that any land becomes land within subsection (5)(b) or (c).

(7)   For the purposes of the coastal access duty, a person is to be regarded as enabled to make a journey by ferry even if that journey can be made at certain times, or during certain periods, only.

(8)   In this section —

    "the 1949 Act" means the National Parks and Access to the Countryside Act 1949 (c. 97);

    "the CROW Act" means the Countryside and Rights of Way Act 2000 (c. 37);

    "excepted land" has the same meaning as in Part 1 of the CROW Act;

    "military lands byelaw" means a byelaw under section 14 of the Military Lands Act 1892 (c. 43) or section 2 of the Military Lands Act 1900 (c. 56);

    "relevant excepted land" means excepted land other than land within subsection (5)(c);

    "the relevant functions" means —

        (a)   in relation to Natural England —

            (i)   its functions under this Part, Part 4 of the 1949 Act (long-distance routes) and Part 1 of the CROW Act (access to the countryside), and

            (ii)   such of its other functions as it considers it appropriate to exercise for the purpose of securing the objectives in subsections (2) and (3), and

(b) in relation to the Secretary of State –

(i) the Secretary of State's functions under this Part, Part 4 of the 1949 Act and Part 1 of the CROW Act, and

(ii) such of the Secretary of State's other functions as the Secretary of State considers it appropriate to exercise for the purpose of securing the objectives in subsections (2) and (3).

297 General provision about the coastal access duty

(1) In discharging the coastal access duty, Natural England and the Secretary of State must comply with the requirements of this section.

(2) They must have regard to –

(a) the safety and convenience of those using the English coastal route,

(b) the desirability of that route adhering to the periphery of the coast and providing views of the sea, and

(c) the desirability of ensuring that so far as reasonably practicable interruptions to that route are kept to a minimum.

(3) They must aim to strike a fair balance between the interests of the public in having rights of access over land and the interests of any person with a relevant interest in the land.

(4) For this purpose a person has a relevant interest in land if the person –

(a) holds an estate in fee simple absolute in possession in the land,

(b) holds a term of years absolute in the land, or

(c) is in lawful occupation of the land.

298 The coastal access scheme

(1) Natural England must –

(a) prepare a scheme setting out the approach it will take when discharging the coastal access duty, and

(b) submit the scheme to the Secretary of State.

(2) The Secretary of State may –

(a) approve the scheme, with or without modifications, or

(b) reject the scheme and give Natural England a notice requiring it to prepare and submit a new scheme under subsection (1).

(3) The scheme must be submitted to the Secretary of State within the period of 12 months beginning with the day on which this section comes into force or, in a case within subsection (2)(b), within the period specified in the notice.

(4) Natural England may, with the approval of the Secretary of State, revise a scheme approved under this section.

(5) A scheme approved under this section (and any revised scheme) must set out the approach Natural England will take when deciding, for the purposes of section 55A(4) of the 1949 Act, whether it would be appropriate for an access authority to carry out any preliminary activity (within the meaning of section 55A(3) of that Act).

(6) The Secretary of State must lay before Parliament a copy of the scheme approved under this section and, where that scheme is revised, a copy of the revised scheme.

(7) Before preparing or revising a scheme under this section, Natural England must consult such persons as it considers appropriate.

(8) Natural England must, as soon as reasonably practicable, publish in such manner as it considers appropriate—

    (a) the scheme approved by the Secretary of State, and

    (b) where that scheme is revised, the revised scheme.

(9) In discharging the coastal access duty, Natural England must act in accordance with the scheme approved under this section (or, where that scheme has been revised, the revised scheme).

(10) Until such time as there is an approved scheme under this section, Natural England may not prepare or submit a report under section 51 or 55 of the 1949 Act (report containing proposals for long-distance routes) pursuant to the coastal access duty.

(11) Nothing in subsection (10) prevents Natural England from surveying any land in connection with the preparation of such a report.

299 Review of the coastal access scheme

(1) Where a scheme has been approved under section 298, Natural England may, from time to time, review the scheme (as revised from time to time under that section).

(2) At least one review must be completed within the period of 3 years beginning with the day on which a scheme is first approved under section 298(2).

(3) Natural England must publish a report of each review under this section as soon as reasonably practicable after the review is completed.

300 The English coast

(1) In this Part "the English coast" means the coast of England adjacent to the sea, including the coast of any island (in the sea) comprised in England (other than an excluded island).

(2) An island is "excluded" if it is neither—

    (a) an accessible island, nor

    (b) an island specified by the Secretary of State by order for the purposes of this paragraph.

(3) An island is "accessible" if it is possible to walk to the island from the mainland of England, or from another island within subsection (2)(a) or (b), across the foreshore or by means of a bridge, tunnel or causeway.

(4) For the purposes of subsection (3), it is possible to walk to an island even if it is possible to do so at certain times, or during certain periods, only.

(5) An island may be specified by an order under subsection (2)(b) only if the Secretary of State is satisfied that the coast of the island is of sufficient length to enable the establishment of one or more long-distance routes along its length capable of affording the public an extensive journey on foot.

(6)   For the purposes of the objective in section 296(2) (the English coastal route), the means of access to an accessible island is (to the extent that it would not otherwise be the case) to be regarded as part of the English coast.

(7)   This section is subject to section 307 (Isles of Scilly).

301   River estuaries

(1)   This section applies in a case where the continuity of any part of the English coast is interrupted by a river.

(2)   Natural England may exercise its functions as if the references in the coastal access provisions to the sea included the relevant upstream waters of the river.

(3)   For this purpose "the relevant upstream waters", in relation to a river, means—
   (a)   the waters from the seaward limit of the estuarial waters of the river upstream to the first public foot crossing, or
   (b)   if Natural England so decides, the waters from the seaward limit of the estuarial waters of the river upstream to such limit, downstream of the first public foot crossing, as may be specified by it.

(4)   When exercising any power conferred by subsection (2) or (3), Natural England must have regard to the following matters (in addition to the matters mentioned in section 297(2))—
   (a)   the nature of the land which would, for the purposes of this Part, become part of the coast of England if Natural England exercised the power in subsection (2) in respect of the relevant upstream waters for the limit under consideration;
   (b)   the topography of the shoreline adjacent to those waters;
   (c)   the width of the river upstream to that limit;
   (d)   the recreational benefit to the public of the coastal access duty being extended to apply in relation to the coast adjacent to those waters;
   (e)   the extent to which the land bordering those waters would, if it were coastal margin, be excepted land;
   (f)   whether it is desirable to continue the English coastal route to a particular physical feature (whether of the landscape or otherwise) or viewpoint;
   (g)   the existence of a ferry by which the public may cross the river.

(5)   Anything done pursuant to subsection (2) (including any decision under subsection (3)(b)) is to be regarded as done pursuant to, and for the purpose of discharging, the coastal access duty.

(6)   Subsections (1) to (5) apply in relation to the Secretary of State as they apply in relation to Natural England.

(7)   A decision by Natural England to exercise a power conferred by subsection (2) or (3) in relation to a river—
   (a)   is without prejudice to any decision by the Secretary of State (by virtue of subsection (6)) as to whether or not to exercise such a power in relation to the river, and
   (b)   does not affect the requirements of subsection (4) (as they apply by virtue of subsection (6)) or of section 297(2) and (3), in relation to such a decision by the Secretary of State.

(8)   In this section—

"coastal access provisions" means—

    (a)   this Part (other than this section), and

    (b)   sections 55A to 55J of the 1949 Act;

"excepted land" has the same meaning as in Part 1 of the CROW Act;

"public foot crossing", in relation to a river, means a bridge over which, or tunnel through which, there is a public right of way, or a public right of access, by virtue of which the public are able to cross the river on foot.

Implementation of the coastal access duty

302   Long-distance routes

(1)   After section 55 of the 1949 Act insert—

"55A Proposals relating to the English coastal route

(1)   Pursuant to the coastal access duty, Natural England may prepare and submit a report under section 51 containing proposals for a route (whether or not the requirements of section 51(1) are satisfied).

(2)   For the purposes of subsection (1) it is immaterial whether the route or any part of it is already a route in approved proposals relating to a long-distance route.

(3)   In subsections (4) and (5) "preliminary activity" means activity which Natural England considers would facilitate the preparation by it of a report under section 51 pursuant to the coastal access duty.

(4)   Where Natural England considers it necessary or expedient for preliminary activity to be carried out as respects any land, it must—

    (a)   consider whether it would be appropriate for the access authority in relation to that land to carry out any of the preliminary activity, and

    (b)   if it concludes that it would be so appropriate, take all reasonable steps to enter into an agreement with the access authority for that purpose.

(5)   An access authority may, as respects any land in its area, enter into an agreement with Natural England under which the access authority undertakes to carry out preliminary activity.

(6)   In this section "the coastal access duty" means the duty imposed on Natural England and the Secretary of State by section 296(1) of the Marine and Coastal Access Act 2009.

55B Route subject to erosion etc

(1)   This section applies in relation to a report under section 51 prepared pursuant to the coastal access duty.

(2)   Where Natural England considers that the area through which the route passes is an area to which subsection (3) applies, the report may set out proposals for the route, or any part of it, to be determined at any time in accordance with provision made in the proposals (rather than as shown on a map).

(3)   This subsection applies to an area if it is or may be—

      (a)   subject to significant coastal erosion or encroachment by the sea, or

      (b)   subject to significant physical change due to other geomorphological processes.

(4)   The provision made by virtue of subsection (2) may, in particular, provide for the route to be determined by reference to the edge of a cliff or boundary of a field (as it exists from time to time).

(5)   Where the report contains proposals under subsection (2), the map included in the report in accordance with section 51(2) must show the route as determined, at the time the report is prepared, in accordance with those proposals.

(6)   Natural England must consult the Environment Agency before exercising its powers under subsection (2) in respect of an area which is or may be —

      (a)   subject to significant coastal erosion or encroachment by the sea, or

      (b)   subject to significant physical change due to other geomorphological processes in relation to which the Agency has functions.

55C   Alternative routes

(1)   This section applies in relation to a report under section 51 prepared pursuant to the coastal access duty.

(2)   The report may include, in relation to the route ("the ordinary route") or any part of it, a proposal under subsection (3) or (4).

(3)   A proposal under this subsection is a proposal for an alternative route which is to operate as a diversion from the ordinary route, or part, during one or both of the following —

      (a)   any specified period (or periods), and

      (b)   any period during which access to the ordinary route or part is excluded by reason of a direction under Chapter 2 of Part 1 of the CROW Act (exclusion or restriction of access).

(4)   A proposal under this subsection is a proposal for an alternative route which is to operate as an optional alternative to the ordinary route, or part, during any period for which the ordinary route, or part, might reasonably be regarded as unsuitable for use by reason of —

      (a)   flooding,

      (b)   the action of the tide,

      (c)   coastal erosion or encroachment by the sea, or

      (d)   the effect of any other geomorphological process.

(5)   In subsection (3)(a) "specified" means —

      (a)   specified in, or determined in accordance with, the proposal, or

      (b)   determined in accordance with the proposal by —

         (i)   a person specified in the proposal, or

        (ii)   a person determined in accordance with the proposal, details of whom are notified to Natural England in accordance with the proposal.

(6)   Sections 51(2) and 55B apply in relation to an alternative route as they apply in relation to the ordinary route.

55D   Coastal margin

(1)   This section applies in relation to a report prepared under section 51 pursuant to the coastal access duty.

(2)   The proposals set out in the report may include—

    (a)   a proposal for any part of the landward boundary of the relevant coastal margin to coincide with a physical feature identified in the proposal,

    (b)   where those proposals include an alternative route, a proposal for any part of the landward or seaward boundary of the alternative route strip to coincide with a physical feature so identified, or

    (c)   a proposal for the landward or seaward boundary of any area excluded from any description of excepted land to coincide with a physical feature so identified.

(3)   The report must contain—

    (a)   a map showing the landward boundary of the relevant coastal margin, or

    (b)   a description of that boundary which is sufficient to identify the relevant coastal margin.

(4)   Where a map is contained in a report pursuant to subsection (3)(a), Natural England must provide a person with a relevant interest in affected land, on request, with a copy of that map.

(5)   The report must set out such proposals (if any) as Natural England considers appropriate as to the directions to be made by it under Chapter 2 of Part 1 of the CROW Act for the exclusion or restriction of the right of access that would arise under section 2(1) of that Act in relation to any land if the proposals in the report were to be approved.

(6)   Before preparing the report, Natural England must (in addition to complying with section 51(4))—

    (a)   take reasonable steps to consult persons with a relevant interest in affected land,

    (b)   consult any body of a kind mentioned in section 51(4) in whose Park or area affected land is situated (but which is not required to be consulted under section 51(4)),

    (c)   consult each London borough council for an area in which affected land is situated,

    (d)   consult each local access forum for an area in which affected land is situated,

    (e)   consult the Secretary of State in relation to any interests of defence or national security which may be affected by the proposals which Natural England is minded to include in the report,

    (f)   consult the Historic Buildings and Monuments Commission for England in relation to any interests in the preservation of any monument, structure or other thing, mentioned in section 26(3)(b) of the CROW Act which may be affected by those proposals, and

(g)   consult the Environment Agency in relation to any interests in flood defence, or in the management of the effects of coastal erosion or encroachment by the sea, which may be affected by those proposals.

(7)   A body within subsection (6)(b), (c) or (d) must provide Natural England with such information as it may reasonably require for the purposes of the report.

(8)   Where the Secretary of State is consulted under subsection (6)(e), the Secretary of State must—

    (a)   provide Natural England with such information as it may reasonably require as to any exclusion or restriction of the right of access to affected land under section 2(1) of the CROW Act which the Secretary of State proposes to make provision for under section 28 of that Act (defence and national security), and

    (b)   notify Natural England if the Secretary of State is of the opinion that this information, or any part of it, ought not to be disclosed by it on the grounds of the public interest in defence and national security.

(9)   Subject to subsection (10), the report must contain such of the information provided under subsection (8)(a) as Natural England considers relevant for the purposes of the report.

(10)   The report may not contain information which Natural England has been notified under subsection (8)(b) ought not to be disclosed by it.

55E   Consideration of reports made pursuant to the coastal access duty

Schedule 1A contains—

    (a)   provision about the procedure to be followed when a report is submitted under section 51 pursuant to the coastal access duty;

    (b)   provision which, in relation to such reports, supplements the provision made by section 52.

55F   Directions under Part 1 of the CROW Act

(1)   This section applies where approved proposals relating to a long-distance route contain proposals as regards a direction to be made by Natural England under Chapter 2 of Part 1 of the CROW Act for the exclusion or restriction of the right of access that would otherwise arise under section 2(1) of that Act.

(2)   Natural England must make the direction in accordance with those proposals.

(3)   Subsection (2) is without prejudice to any power Natural England may have to revoke or vary the direction after it is made.

55G   Ferries for the purposes of the English coastal route

(1)   This section applies where—

    (a)   pursuant to the coastal access duty, approved proposals relating to a long-distance route include proposals for the provision and operation of a ferry, and

    (b)   an approach route to the ferry is not a highway.

(2)   The reference in section 53(1) to the highway authority for either or both of the highways to be connected by the ferry is to be read as including the highway authority in whose area the approach route is situated.

(3)   In this section "approach route", in relation to a ferry, means a part of the English coastal route to be connected to another part of that route by the ferry.

55H   Variation pursuant to the coastal access duty

(1)   In the case of a report made by Natural England under section 55(1) pursuant to the coastal access duty −

        (a)   the procedural requirements apply with the necessary modifications, and

        (b)   section 55(3) does not apply.

(2)   The Secretary of State may by regulations provide −

        (a)   that, in relation to a direction under section 55(2) pursuant to the coastal access duty, the procedural requirements apply with the modifications specified in the regulations, and

        (b)   that section 55(3) does not apply in relation to such a direction.

(3)   The Secretary of State may not make a direction under section 55(2) pursuant to the coastal access duty at a time when there are no regulations under subsection (2) in force.

(4)   For the purposes of this section −

        "modify" includes amend, add to or repeal, and "modification" is to be construed accordingly;

        "the procedural requirements" means sections 51(4) and (5), 52(1) and (2), 55D(6) to (10) and 55E, Schedule 1A and regulations under that Schedule.

55I   Temporary diversions

(1)   This section applies where Natural England or the Secretary of State gives a direction by virtue of Chapter 2 of Part 1 of the CROW Act which excludes the right of access under section 2(1) of that Act, for any period ("the exclusion period"), in relation to any land over which (or any part of which) the English coastal route or any official alternative route passes.

(2)   This section does not apply if the direction by virtue of that Chapter is expressed to have effect indefinitely.

(3)   Natural England may give a direction under this section specifying a route ("the temporary route") which is to apply for the duration of the exclusion period or such part of it as is specified in the direction.

(4)   The temporary route specified by Natural England may pass only −

        (a)   over land which is access land for the purposes of Part 1 of the CROW Act,

        (b)   over land which, for the purposes of section 1(1) of that Act, is treated by section 15(1) of that Act as being accessible to the public apart from that Act,

        (c)   along a highway, or

    (d)   over any other land the owner of which has agreed to the temporary route (so far as it passes over that land).

(5)   Natural England must consult the Environment Agency before giving a direction where the temporary route specified passes over land of a type described in subsection (4)(d).

(6)   A direction under this section—

    (a)   must be in writing, and

    (b)   may be revoked or varied by a subsequent direction under this section.

55J   Interpretation of sections 55A to 55J

(1)   In sections 55A to 55I, Schedule 1A and this section—

"access authority" has the same meaning as in Part 1 of the CROW Act;

"affected land" means—

    (a)   land over which the route, or any alternative route, to which the proposals relate passes, and

    (b)   any other land which—

        (i)   is relevant coastal margin, or an alternative route strip in relation to such an alternative route, and

        (ii)   is not excepted land;

"alternative route" is to be construed in accordance with section 55C;

"alternative route strip", in relation to an alternative route, means—

    (a)   in a case where the proposal for the alternative route has not yet been approved under section 52, the land which would become coastal margin during the operation of that route if the proposals in the report were to be so approved (without modifications), and

    (b)   in the case of an official alternative route, the land which would become coastal margin during the operation of that route;

"the coastal access duty" has the meaning given by section 55A;

"coastal margin" has the same meaning as in Part 1 of the CROW Act;

"the CROW Act" means the Countryside and Rights of Way Act 2000 (c. 37);

"the English coastal route" means the route secured pursuant to the coastal access duty;

"excepted land" has the same meaning as in Part 1 of the CROW Act;

"local access forum" means a local access forum established under section 94 of the CROW Act;

"official alternative route" means an alternative route which is contained in approved proposals relating to a long-distance route;

"owner", in relation to land, means the person who holds an estate in fee simple absolute in possession in the land;

"relevant coastal margin", in relation to proposals, means—

    (a) in a case where the proposals have not yet been approved under section 52, land which would become coastal margin if the proposals were to be approved (without modifications) under that section (disregarding the alternative route strip in relation to any alternative route), and

    (b) in a case where the proposals have been so approved (with or without modifications), land which becomes coastal margin as a result of the proposals having been so approved (disregarding the alternative route strip in relation to any official alternative route).

(2) For the purposes of sections 55A to 55I and Schedule 1A, a person has a relevant interest in land if the person—

    (a) is the owner of the land,

    (b) holds a term of years absolute in the land, or

    (c) is in lawful occupation of the land.

(3) Any power conferred by sections 55A to 55I or Schedule 1A to make regulations includes—

    (a) power to make different provision for different cases, and

    (b) power to make incidental, consequential, supplemental or transitional provision or savings."

(2) After Schedule 1 to the 1949 Act insert the Schedule set out in Schedule 19 to this Act.

303   Access to the coastal margin

(1) Part 1 of the CROW Act (access to the countryside) is amended as follows.

(2) In section 1—

    (a) in subsection (1) (definition of "access land") omit "or" at the end of paragraph (d) and after that paragraph insert—

        "(da)   is coastal margin, or",

    (b) in subsection (2), after the definition of "the appropriate countryside body" insert—

        ""coastal margin" means land which is of a description specified by an order under section 3A;",

    (c) in that subsection, in the definition of "open country", in paragraph (b) after "land" insert "or coastal margin", and

    (d) in subsection (3), after "2006" insert "(but is not coastal margin)".

(3) In section 2 (rights of public in relation to access land)—

    (a) in subsection (3), for "prohibition" to the end substitute "relevant statutory prohibition", and

    (b) after that subsection insert—

        "(3A)   In subsection (3) "relevant statutory prohibition" means—

            (a) in the case of land which is coastal margin, a prohibition contained in or having effect under any enactment, and

            (b) in any other case, a prohibition contained in or having effect under any enactment other than an enactment contained in a local or private Act."

(4) In section 3 (power to extend to coastal land)—

    (a) at the end of the heading insert ": Wales",

    (b) in subsection (1) for "Secretary" to "Wales)" substitute "Welsh Ministers", and

    (c) in that subsection after "include" insert "as respects Wales".

(5) After that section insert—

"3A Power to extend to coastal land etc: England

(1) The Secretary of State may by order specify the descriptions of land in England which are coastal margin for the purposes of this Part.

(2) An order under subsection (1) may, in particular—

    (a) describe land by reference to it being—

        (i) land over which the line taken by the English coastal route passes,

        (ii) land which is adjacent to and within a specified distance of that line, or

        (iii) land which is adjacent to land within sub-paragraph (ii),

    if the land described under paragraphs (i) to (iii), taken as a whole, is coastal land;

    (b) in relation to cases where a proposal of the kind mentioned in section 55B of the 1949 Act (power to determine the route in accordance with provision made in the report) is contained in relevant approved proposals, describe land by reference to the line taken by the English coastal route as it has effect from time to time in accordance with that proposal;

    (c) in relation to cases where a proposal of the kind mentioned in section 55C of that Act (alternative routes) is contained in relevant approved proposals, describe land by reference to it being—

        (i) land over which the line taken by an official alternative route which is for the time being in operation passes, or

        (ii) land which is adjacent to and within a specified distance of that line,

    whether or not it is coastal land;

    (d) in relation to cases where a proposal of the kind mentioned in section 55D(2)(a) or (b) of that Act (proposal that boundary should coincide with a physical feature) is contained in relevant approved proposals, provide that the boundary of an area of coastal margin is to coincide with a physical feature as provided for in that proposal (and for this purpose it is immaterial if the effect is to include other land as coastal margin or to exclude part of an area of coastal land);

    (e) in relation to cases where a direction under subsection (3) of section 55I of that Act (temporary diversions) specifies a route which (or any part of which) passes over land within subsection (4)(d) of that section, describe land by reference to it being—

        (i) land over which the line taken by that route (so far as it passes over land within subsection (4)(d) of that section) passes, or

        (ii) land which is adjacent to and within a specified distance of that line (so far as it so passes), whether or not it is coastal land.

(3) For the purposes of subsection (2) it is immaterial whether the English coastal route is in existence at the time the order is made.

(4) An order under subsection (1) may modify the provisions of this Part in their application to land which is coastal margin.

(5) Provision made by virtue of subsection (4) may, in particular —

    (a) confer functions on the Secretary of State or Natural England;

    (b) if providing for any description of land which is coastal margin to be excluded from any description of excepted land —

        (i) describe that land as mentioned in subsection (2)(a)(i) to (iii), (b) or (c), or

        (ii) in relation to cases where a proposal of the kind mentioned in section 55D(2)(c) of the 1949 Act (proposal that boundary should coincide with a physical feature) is contained in relevant approved proposals, provide that the boundary of that land (or any part of it) is to coincide with a physical feature as provided for in that proposal.

(6) Where, as a result of proposals becoming approved proposals relating to a long-distance route, land becomes coastal margin by virtue of an order under subsection (1) —

    (a) section 2(1) does not apply in relation to the land by reason of it being coastal margin until the end of the access preparation period in relation to the land,

    (b) any direction given under Chapter 2 in relation to the land may be expressed to take effect immediately after the end of that period, and

    (c) until the end of that period, the land is not to be regarded as coastal margin —

        (i) for the purpose of determining whether it is open country or registered common land, or

        (ii) for the purposes of section 1(6AA) of the Occupiers' Liability Act 1984 (duty of occupier of coastal margin to persons other than the occupier's visitors).

(7) Where, as a result of proposals becoming approved proposals relating to a long-distance route, land becomes coastal margin by virtue of an order under subsection (1), any exclusion or restriction under Chapter 2 of access to the land by virtue of section 2(1) ceases to have effect at the end of the access preparation period.

(8) Subsection (7) does not apply to any exclusion or restriction resulting from a direction under Chapter 2 which takes effect after the end of the access preparation period.

(9) Subsections (6) and (7) do not apply to land if, at the time it becomes coastal margin by virtue of an order under subsection (1), it is already dedicated as coastal margin under section 16.

(10) In this section —

    "the 1949 Act" means the National Parks and Access to the Countryside Act 1949;

"access preparation period", in relation to any land, means the period which−

    (a)   begins when the land becomes coastal margin, and

    (b)   ends with the day appointed by the Secretary of State by order under this subsection in relation to that land;

"approved proposals relating to a long-distance route" is to be construed in accordance with sections 52(3) and 55(4) of the 1949 Act;

"coastal land" has the same meaning as in section 3;

"the English coastal route" means the route secured (or to be secured) pursuant to the coastal access duty (within the meaning of section 296 of the Marine and Coastal Access Act 2009);

"modify" includes amend, add to or repeal;

"official alternative route" has the meaning given by section 55J of the 1949 Act;

"relevant approved proposals" means approved proposals relating to a long-distance route which is or forms part of the English coastal route;

"specified" means specified in an order under subsection (1);

and references to the exclusion or restriction under Chapter 2 of access to any land by virtue of section 2(1) are to be interpreted in accordance with section 21(2) and (3)."

(6)   In section 16 (dedication of land as access land)−

    (a)   after subsection (2) insert−

        "(2A)   Where a person makes a dedication under this section in respect of land within subsection (2B), that dedication may also dedicate the land as coastal margin.

        (2B)   The land within this subsection is−

            (a)   land which is coastal margin, and

            (b)   any other land in England which is adjacent to land which is coastal margin.

        (2C)   Where land is dedicated as coastal margin−

            (a)   in the case of land within subsection (2B)(b), it is to be treated as coastal margin for the purposes of any provision made by or by virtue of this Part (other than section 1), and

            (b)   if−

                (i)   disregarding this paragraph, it would be excepted land, and

                (ii)   it is not land which is accessible to the public by virtue of any enactment or rule of law (other than this Act),

            it is to be treated for the purposes of any provision made by or by virtue of this Part as if it were not excepted land.",

    (b)   in subsection (6), omit "and" at the end of paragraph (c) and after that paragraph insert—

> "(ca) in the case of land within subsection (2B), enable a dedication previously made under this section in respect of the land (otherwise than by virtue of subsection (2A)) to be amended, by the persons by whom a dedication could be made, so as to provide that the land is dedicated as coastal margin for the purposes of subsection (2C),
>
> (cb) provide for any exclusion or restriction under Chapter 2 of access by virtue of section 2(1) which has effect in relation to land which is within subsection (2B)(b) immediately before it is dedicated as coastal margin to cease to have effect at the time the dedication takes effect, and", and

  (c) after subsection (6) insert—

> "(6A) In subsection (6)(cb) the reference to the exclusion or restriction under Chapter 2 of access to any land by virtue of section 2(1) is to be interpreted in accordance with section 21(2) and (3)."

(7) In section 20 (codes of conduct and other information)—

  (a) in subsection (1), omit "and" at the end of paragraph (a) and after paragraph (b) insert ", and

> (c) that, in relation to access land which is coastal margin, the public are informed that the right conferred by section 2(1) does not affect any other right of access that may exist in relation to that land.", and

  (b) after that subsection insert—

> "(1A) The duty imposed by subsection (1) to issue and revise a code of conduct may be discharged, in relation to access land which is coastal margin, by (or in part by) issuing and revising a separate code relating to such access land only."

(8) In section 44 (orders and regulations under Part 1), in subsection (3) after "section 3" insert "or 3A(1)".

(9) In section 45 (interpretation of Part 1), after the definition of "the appropriate countryside body" insert—

> ""coastal margin" has the meaning given by section 1(2);".

304 Establishment and maintenance of the English coastal route etc

Schedule 20 (establishment and maintenance of the English coastal route etc) has effect.

Liabilities

305 Restricting liabilities of Natural England and the Secretary of State

(1) No duty of care is owed by Natural England to any person under the law of negligence—

  (a) when preparing or submitting proposals under section 51 or 55 of the 1949 Act (long-distance routes and variations of such routes) pursuant to the coastal access duty,

(b) in connection with any failure by it to erect, under paragraph 6 of Schedule 20, a notice or sign of the kind mentioned in sub-paragraph (2)(b) of that paragraph (notices or signs warning of obstacles or hazards), or

(c) in connection with any failure by it to exclude or restrict access under Chapter 2 of Part 1 of the CROW Act to any land which is coastal margin, other than a failure within subsection (2).

(2) A failure is within this subsection if it arises as a result of Natural England —

(a) deciding not to act in accordance with an application under section 24 or 25 of that Act, or

(b) deciding not to act in accordance with representations made by a person on being consulted under section 27(5) of that Act (consultation of original applicant etc before revoking or varying a direction).

(3) In subsections (1) and (2) the references to Natural England include any person acting on its behalf.

(4) No duty of care is owed by the Secretary of State to any person under the law of negligence when —

(a) approving proposals (with or without modifications) under section 52 or 55 of the 1949 Act pursuant to the coastal access duty, or

(b) giving a direction under section 55 of that Act, pursuant to that duty.

306 Occupiers' liability

In section 1 of the Occupiers' Liability Act 1984 (c. 3) (duty of occupier to persons other than the occupier's visitors), after subsection (6A) insert —

"(6AA) Where the land is coastal margin for the purposes of Part 1 of that Act (including any land treated as coastal margin by virtue of section 16 of that Act), subsection (6A) has effect as if for paragraphs (a) and (b) of that subsection there were substituted "a risk resulting from the existence of any physical feature (whether of the landscape or otherwise).""

General

307 Isles of Scilly

(1) Subject to the provisions of an order under subsection (2), sections 296 to 301, 304, 305, 308 and 309 and Schedule 20 do not apply in relation to the Isles of Scilly.

(2) The Secretary of State may by order provide for the application of any of those provisions in relation to the Isles of Scilly, subject to such modifications as may be specified in the order.

(3) Before making an order under subsection (2), the Secretary of State must consult the Council of the Isles of Scilly.

(4) The power exercisable under section 111 of the 1949 Act (application to Isles of Scilly as if a separate county) in relation to the provisions of Part 4 of that Act is exercisable in relation to that Part as amended by section 302.

(5)   The powers exercisable under section 100(1), (2) and (4) of the CROW Act (application to Isles of Scilly) in relation to provisions of Part 1 of that Act are exercisable in relation to that Part as amended by section 303.

308   The Crown

(1)   This Part is binding on the Crown and applies in relation to any Crown land as it applies in relation to any other land.

(2)   For this purpose "Crown land" means land an interest in which—

    (a)   belongs to Her Majesty in right of the Crown or in right of Her private estates,

    (b)   belongs to Her Majesty in right of the Duchy of Lancaster,

    (c)   belongs to the Duchy of Cornwall, or

    (d)   belongs to a government department or is held in trust for Her Majesty for the purposes of a government department.

(3)   The appropriate authority may enter into—

    (a)   an agreement under section 35 of the CROW Act (means of access) entered into by Natural England or an access authority by virtue of paragraph 1 of Schedule 20, or

    (b)   an agreement under paragraph 2 of that Schedule (establishment and maintenance of the English coastal route),

as respects an interest in Crown land held by or on behalf of the Crown.

(4)   An agreement described in subsection (3)(a) or (b) as respects any other interest in Crown land is of no effect unless approved by the appropriate authority.

(5)   The "appropriate authority" means—

    (a)   in the case of land which belongs to Her Majesty in right of the Crown, the Crown Estate Commissioners or other government department having management of the land in question;

    (b)   in the case of land which belongs to Her Majesty in right of Her private estates, a person appointed by Her Majesty in writing under the Royal Sign Manual, or if no such appointment is made, the Secretary of State;

    (c)   in the case of land which belongs to Her Majesty in right of the Duchy of Lancaster, the Chancellor of the Duchy;

    (d)   in the case of land which belongs to the Duchy of Cornwall, such person as the Duke of Cornwall, or the possessor for the time being of the Duchy of Cornwall, appoints;

    (e)   in the case of land which belongs to a government department or is held in trust for Her Majesty for the purposes of a government department, that department.

(6)   If any question arises under this section as to what authority is the appropriate authority in relation to any land, that question is to be referred to the Treasury, whose decision is final.

(7)   In this section references to Her Majesty's private estates are to be construed in accordance with section 1 of the Crown Private Estates Act 1862 (c. 37).

309   Interpretation of this Part

In this Part—

    "the 1949 Act" has the meaning given by section 296(8);

"access authority", in relation to any land, has the same meaning as in Part 1 of the CROW Act;

"the coastal access duty" has the meaning given by section 296(4);

"coastal margin" means land which is coastal margin for the purposes of Part 1 of the CROW Act (including any land treated as coastal margin by virtue of section 16 of that Act);

"the CROW Act" has the meaning given by section 296(8);

"the English coast" has the meaning given by section 300;

"the English coastal route" has the meaning given by section 296(3);

"estuarial waters" means any waters within the limits of transitional waters, within the meaning of the Water Framework Directive (that is to say, Directive 2000/60/EC of the European Parliament and of the Council of 23 October 2000 establishing a framework for Community action in the field of water policy);

"functions" includes powers and duties;

"long-distance route" means a route provided for in approved proposals relating to a long-distance route within the meaning of section 52(3) of the 1949 Act (as read with section 55(4) of that Act);

"the sea", subject to section 301, does not include any part of a river which is upstream of the seaward limit of the river's estuarial waters.

Wales

310 Powers of National Assembly for Wales

In Part 1 of Schedule 5 to the Government of Wales Act 2006 (c. 32) (Assembly measures), in field 16 (sport and recreation), after matter 16.1 insert—

"Matter 16.2

The establishment and maintenance of a route (or a number of routes) for the coast to enable the public to make recreational journeys.

This matter does not include—

(a) enabling the public to make journeys by mechanically propelled vehicles (except permitted journeys by qualifying invalid carriages);

(b) the creation of new highways (whether under the Highways Act 1980 or otherwise).

Matter 16.3

Securing public access to relevant land for the purposes of open-air recreation.

Land is relevant land if it—

(a) is at the coast,

(b) can be used for the purposes of open-air recreation in association with land within paragraph (a), or

(c) can be used for the purposes of open-air recreation in association with a route within matter 16.2.

In this matter the reference to land at the coast is not limited to coastal land within the meaning of section 3 of the Countryside and Rights of Way Act 2000.

Interpretation of this field

In this field —

"coast" means the coast of Wales adjacent to the sea, including the coast of any island (in the sea) comprised in Wales;

"estuarial waters" means any waters within the limits of transitional waters within the meaning of the Water Framework Directive (that is to say, Directive 2000/60/EC of the European Parliament and of the Council of 23 October 2000 establishing a framework for Community action in the field of water policy);

"highway" has the same meaning as in the Highways Act 1980;

"public foot crossing", in relation to a river, means a bridge over which, or tunnel through which, there is a public right of way, or a public right of access, by virtue of which the public are able to cross the river on foot;

"qualifying invalid carriage" means an invalid carriage within the meaning of section 20 of the Chronically Sick and Disabled Persons Act 1970 (use of invalid carriages on highways) which complies with the prescribed requirements within the meaning of that section;

"relevant upstream waters", in relation to a river, means the waters from the seaward limit of the estuarial waters of the river upstream to the first public foot crossing;

"sea" includes the relevant upstream waters of a river;

and a journey by a qualifying invalid carriage is a permitted journey if the carriage is being used in accordance with the prescribed conditions within the meaning of section 20 of the Chronically Sick and Disabled Persons Act 1970."

PART 10

MISCELLANEOUS

Natural England

311   Area in which functions of Natural England exercisable

(1)   Section 1 of the Natural Environment and Rural Communities Act 2006 (c. 16) (constitution of Natural England) is amended as follows.

(2)   In subsection (3) (area in which functions exercisable) after "in relation to England" insert "(including, where the context requires, the territorial sea adjacent to England)".

(3)   After subsection (3) insert —

"(3A)   An order or Order in Council made —

(a)   under section 158(3) of the Government of Wales Act 2006 for the purposes of determining which waters are treated as being adjacent to Wales, or

(b)   under section 126(2) of the Scotland Act 1998 for the purposes of determining which waters are treated as being adjacent to Scotland, applies for the purposes of this section as it applies for the purposes of the Act under which it is made.".

312   Natural England not to be responder for Civil Contingencies Act 2004

In Schedule 1 to the Civil Contingencies Act 2004 (c. 36) (category 1 and 2 responders) omit paragraph 11A (Natural England).

Countryside Council for Wales

313   Area in which functions of Countryside Council for Wales exercisable

(1)   The Environmental Protection Act 1990 (c. 43) is amended as follows.

(2)   In section 128 (Countryside Council for Wales) after subsection (1) insert—

"(1A)   Except where otherwise expressly provided, the functions of the Countryside Council for Wales are exercisable in relation to Wales only.
In this Part "Wales" has the same meaning as in the Government of Wales Act 2006."

(3)   In section 132 (general functions of the Council) after subsection (2) insert—

"(2A)   The following functions are exercisable in relation to Wales and the Welsh zone—
  (a)   the functions conferred by paragraphs (c) to (e) of subsection (1);
  (b)   the functions conferred by subsection (2).
In this subsection "Welsh zone" has the same meaning as in the Government of Wales Act 2006."

(4)   In section 134 (grants and loans by the Council) after subsection (4) insert—

"(5)   The functions conferred by this section are exercisable in relation to Wales and the Welsh zone.
In this subsection "Welsh zone" has the same meaning as in the Government of Wales Act 2006."

Works detrimental to navigation

314   Works detrimental to navigation

(1)   In the Energy Act 2008 (c. 32), after Part 4 (decommissioning of energy

installations) insert—

"PART 4A

WORKS DETRIMENTAL TO NAVIGATION

Consent required for carrying out of certain operations

82A Restriction of works detrimental to navigation

(1) A person must not, without the written consent of the Secretary of State, carry out in the regulated zone (see section 82Q) any operation to which this subsection applies (see subsections (2) and (3)).

(2) Subsection (1) does not apply to an operation if a marine licence under Part 4 of the Marine and Coastal Access Act 2009 is needed to carry out the operation.

(3) Subject to that, subsection (1) applies to an operation if—
    (a) it causes, or is likely to result in, obstruction or danger to navigation (whether while the operation is being carried out or subsequently),
    (b) it is of a description falling within subsection (4), and
    (c) it may be carried out only with a permission falling within subsection (5).

(4) The descriptions of operations are—
    (a) the construction, alteration, improvement, dismantlement or abandonment of any works;
    (b) the deposit of any object or materials;
    (c) the removal of any object or materials.

(5) The permissions are—
    (a) a licence under section 3 of the Petroleum Act 1998 or section 2 of the Petroleum (Production) Act 1934,
    (b) a licence under section 4 or 18 of this Act (gas storage and gas unloading, and carbon capture and storage licences),
    (c) a works authorisation under Part 3 of the Petroleum Act 1998 (construction etc of submarine pipelines),
and see also subsection (6).

(6) For the purposes of this Part, the operations which may be carried out only with a permission falling within subsection (5) include operations which, by virtue of a permission falling within paragraph (a) or (b) of that subsection, may be carried out only with the consent of the Secretary of State or another person.

(7) In the case of an authorised exploration or exploitation operation (see subsection (8))—
    (a) the reference in subsection (3) to an operation being likely to result in obstruction or danger to navigation,
        includes
    (b) a reference to the operation being likely to result in obstruction or danger to navigation by reason of any use intended to be made of the works in question when constructed, altered or improved.

(8) In this Part "authorised exploration or exploitation operation" means any operation—

    (a) which is of a description falling within subsection (4)(a), and

    (b) which may be carried out only with a permission falling within subsection (5).

82B   Applications for consent under section 82A

(1) The Secretary of State may, as a condition of considering an application for consent under section 82A, require to be furnished with such plans and particulars of the proposed operation as the Secretary of State may consider necessary.

(2) On receipt of any such application, the Secretary of State may cause to be published notice of—

    (a) the application, and

    (b) the time within which, and the manner in which, objections to the application may be made.

(3) Any such notice is to be published in such a manner as to be likely to come to the attention of those likely to be interested in, or affected by, the application.

(4) The Secretary of State may cause an inquiry to be held in connection with the determination of an application for consent.

82C   Determination of applications for consent under section 82A

(1) If the Secretary of State is of the opinion that any operation in respect of which an application is made for consent under section 82A will cause, or is likely to result in, obstruction or danger to navigation, subsection (2) applies.

(2) In any such case, the Secretary of State must either—

    (a) refuse to give consent, or

    (b) give consent subject to such conditions as the Secretary of State considers appropriate.

(3) In exercising functions under subsection (2), the Secretary of State must have regard to the nature and extent of the obstruction or danger which it appears to the Secretary of State would otherwise be caused or be likely to result.

(4) In the case of an authorised exploration or exploitation operation—

    (a) any reference in subsection (1) or (3) to an operation being likely to result in obstruction or danger to navigation,
        includes

    (b) a reference to the operation being likely to result in obstruction or danger to navigation by reason of any use intended to be made of the works in question when constructed, altered or improved.

(5) A consent of the Secretary of State under section 82A may be given so as to continue in force, unless renewed, only if the operation for which the consent is given is begun or completed within such period as may be specified in the consent.

(6)   Subsection (5) applies in relation to the renewal of a consent as it applies in relation to the giving of consent.

82D   Authorised exploration or exploitation operations: consent conditions

(1)   This section applies where the Secretary of State has given consent for an authorised exploration or exploitation operation, but subject to a condition (a "consent condition").

(2)   A consent condition shall either —
> (a)   remain in force for a specified period, or
> (b)   remain in force without limit of time,

but this is subject to subsection (5).

(3)   A consent condition, in addition to binding the person to whom the consent is given, also binds, so far as is appropriate, any other person who for the time being owns, occupies, or enjoys any use of, the works in question.

(4)   Where —
> (a)   a consent condition relates to the taking of navigational precautions, and
> (b)   the Secretary of State considers it appropriate to vary the condition in the interests of the safety of navigation (whether or not the operation has been completed),

the Secretary of State may vary the condition for the purpose of enhancing the effectiveness of the aids to navigation which are to be provided or the other measures which are to be taken.

(5)   The Secretary of State may revoke any consent condition.

(6)   In this section "taking of navigational precautions" means any of the following —
> (a)   the provision of any lights, signals or other aids to navigation;
> (b)   the stationing of guard ships in the vicinity of the works in question;
> (c)   the taking of any other measures for the purpose of, or in connection with, controlling the movements of ships in the vicinity of those works.

Directions by the Secretary of State

82E   Secretary of State's power of direction

(1)   This section applies if —
> (a)   the person to whom a consent under section 82A is given fails to comply with any provision of the consent, or
> (b)   a person who, by virtue of section 82D(3), is bound by a consent condition fails to comply with the condition.

(2)   The Secretary of State may direct that person (the "defaulter") to take steps which the Secretary of State considers necessary or appropriate to comply with the provision or condition within a period specified in the direction.

(3)   The Secretary of State must consult the defaulter before giving a direction under subsection (2).

(4)   If the defaulter fails to comply with a direction under subsection (2), the Secretary of State may—

      (a)   comply with the direction on behalf of the defaulter, or

      (b)   make arrangements for another person to do so.

(5)   A person taking action by virtue of subsection (4) may—

      (a)   do anything which the defaulter could have done, and

      (b)   recover from the defaulter any reasonable costs incurred in taking the action.

(6)   A person ("P") liable to pay any sum by virtue of subsection (5)(b) must also pay interest on that sum for the period beginning with the day on which the person taking action by virtue of subsection (4) notified P of the sum payable and ending with the date of payment.

(7)   The rate of interest payable in accordance with subsection (6) is a rate determined by the Secretary of State as comparable with commercial rates.

(8)   The defaulter must provide a person taking action by virtue of subsection (4) with such assistance as the Secretary of State may direct.

(9)   The power to give a direction under this section is without prejudice to any provision made—

      (a)   in the consent, with regard to the enforcement of any of its provisions, or

      (b)   in the condition, with regard to the enforcement of the condition.

Emergency safety requirements

82F   Damage to, or changes in, the works: emergency safety notices

(1)   This section applies in any case where—

      (a)   the Secretary of State has given consent ("the relevant consent") for an authorised exploration or exploitation operation, and

      (b)   at any time after the giving of that consent, the condition in subsection (2) is met.

(2)   The condition is that it appears to the Secretary of State that any danger to navigation has arisen by reason of—

      (a)   any substantial damage to any works to which the relevant consent relates, or

      (b)   any other substantial and unforeseen change in the state or position of any such works.

(3)   If it appears to the Secretary of State necessary to do so in the interests of the safety of navigation, the Secretary of State may serve a notice (an "emergency safety notice") on the consent holder.

(4)   By serving an emergency safety notice on the consent holder, the Secretary of State imposes on the consent holder such requirements as are prescribed in the notice with respect to any of the matters specified in subsection (5).

(5)   Those matters are—

>   (a)   the provision on, or in the vicinity of, the works in question of any lights, signals or other aids to navigation, and
>
>   (b)   the stationing of guard ships in the vicinity of those works.

(6)   An emergency safety notice may be served by the Secretary of State whether or not—

>   (a)   the operation in question has been completed, or
>
>   (b)   any condition was imposed by the Secretary of State, on giving the relevant consent, with respect to any of the matters referred to in subsection (5).

82G   Emergency safety notices: supplementary provisions

(1)   If the consent holder fails to comply with an emergency safety notice within the time allowed, the Secretary of State may—

>   (a)   comply with the notice on behalf of the consent holder, or
>
>   (b)   make arrangements for another person to do so.

(2)   For the purposes of subsection (1) "the time allowed" is the period of 24 hours beginning with the time when the emergency safety notice is served on the consent holder or as soon after the end of that period as is reasonably practicable.

(3)   A person taking action by virtue of subsection (1) may—

>   (a)   do anything which the consent holder could have done, and
>
>   (b)   recover any reasonable costs incurred in taking the action from such one or more persons falling within subsection (4) as the Secretary of State considers appropriate.

(4)   The persons are—

>   (a)   the consent holder;
>
>   (b)   any other person or persons bound by a consent condition by virtue of section 82D(3).

(5)   A person ("P") liable to pay any sum by virtue of subsection (3)(b) must also pay interest on that sum for the period beginning with the day on which the person taking action by virtue of subsection (1) notified P of the sum payable and ending with the date of payment.

(6)   The rate of interest payable in accordance with subsection (5) is a rate determined by the Secretary of State as comparable with commercial rates.

(7)   Once an emergency safety notice has been complied with (whether by the consent holder or otherwise)—

>   (a)   the requirements of the notice are, subject to subsection (8), to be treated for the purposes of this Part as conditions subject to which the consent was given, but
>
>   (b)   section 82D(2) and (5) are not to apply in the case of those requirements.

(8)   If it appears to the Secretary of State (whether on the application of any person or otherwise) that the circumstances giving rise to the urgent necessity for the imposition of the requirements no longer exist, the Secretary of State must revoke the requirements by notice served on the consent holder.

(9) Where the Secretary of State has served an emergency safety notice in respect of any particular circumstances, subsection (7) does not preclude the Secretary of State from serving a further such notice in respect of those circumstances.

82H Failure to comply with condition: immediate action notice

(1) This section applies where —

    (a) a consent under section 82A(1) has been given subject to conditions,

    (b) a person falling within subsection (2) fails to comply with a condition, and

    (c) it appears to the Secretary of State that any danger to navigation has arisen by reason of the failure to comply with the condition.

(2) The persons are —

    (a) the consent holder;

    (b) any person bound by the condition by virtue of section 82D(3).

(3) If it appears to the Secretary of State necessary to do so in the interests of the safety of navigation, the Secretary of State may serve a notice (an "immediate action notice") on the person, imposing on the person one or more specified requirements falling within subsection (4).

(4) The requirements are —

    (a) a requirement to comply with the condition;

    (b) a requirement to take any specified action or actions to remedy the failure to comply with the condition.

(5) Subsections (1) to (6) of section 82G apply in relation to a person and an immediate action notice as they apply in relation to the consent holder and an emergency safety notice.

(6) In this section "specified" means specified in the immediate action notice.

Enforcement

82I Carrying out operation without consent etc

(1) It is an offence for a person —

    (a) to carry out an operation to which subsection (1) of section 82A applies without the written consent of the Secretary of State under that subsection, or

    (b) to fail to comply with a condition of such a consent.

(2) A person guilty of an offence under this section is liable —

    (a) on summary conviction, to a fine not exceeding £50,000, or

    (b) on conviction on indictment, to imprisonment for a term not exceeding 2 years or to a fine, or both.

82J Offences relating to consents

(1) It is an offence for a person to make a statement which the person knows to be false, or recklessly to make a statement which is false, in order to obtain the consent of the Secretary of State under section 82A(1).

(2)   It is an offence for a person to fail to disclose information which the person knows, or ought to know, to be relevant to an application for the consent of the Secretary of State under section 82A(1).

(3)   A person guilty of an offence under this section is liable —

       (a)   on summary conviction, to a fine not exceeding the statutory maximum, or

       (b)   on conviction on indictment, to a fine.

82K   Failure to comply with direction under section 82E

(1)   It is an offence for a person to fail to comply with a direction under section 82E, unless the person proves that due diligence was exercised in order to avoid the failure.

(2)   A person guilty of an offence under this section is liable —

       (a)   on summary conviction, to a fine not exceeding £50,000, or

       (b)   on conviction on indictment, to imprisonment for a term not exceeding 2 years or to a fine, or both.

82L   Failure to comply with notice under section 82F or 82H

(1)   It is an offence for a person to fail to comply with —

       (a)   an emergency safety notice, or

       (b)   an immediate action notice,

within the time allowed (within the meaning of section 82G(1)).

(2)   A person guilty of an offence under this section is liable —

       (a)   on summary conviction, to a fine not exceeding £50,000, or

       (b)   on conviction on indictment, to imprisonment for a term not exceeding 2 years or to a fine, or both.

82M   Injunctions restraining breaches of section 82A(1)

(1)   Where the Secretary of State considers it necessary or expedient to restrain any actual or apprehended breach of section 82A(1), the Secretary of State may apply to the court for an injunction or, in Scotland, an interdict.

(2)   An application may be made whether or not the Secretary of State has exercised, or is proposing to exercise, any of the other powers under this Part.

(3)   On an application under subsection (1), the court may grant such an injunction or interdict as the court considers appropriate for the purpose of restraining the breach.

(4)   Rules of court may provide for an injunction or interdict to be issued against a person whose identity is unknown.

(5)   In this section "the court" means —

       (a)   the High Court, or

       (b)   in Scotland, the Court of Session.

82N   Inspectors

(1)   The Secretary of State may appoint persons to act as inspectors to assist in carrying out the functions of the Secretary of State under this Part.

(2) The Secretary of State may make payments, by way of remuneration or otherwise, to inspectors appointed under this section.

(3) The Secretary of State may make regulations about—

    (a) the powers and duties of inspectors appointed under this section;

    (b) the powers and duties of any other person acting on the directions of the Secretary of State in connection with a function under this Part;

    (c) the facilities and assistance to be accorded to persons mentioned in paragraph (a) or (b).

(4) The powers conferred by virtue of subsection (3) may include powers of a kind specified in section 108(4) of the Environment Act 1995 (powers of entry, investigation, etc).

(5) Any regulations under this section may provide for the creation of offences which are punishable—

    (a) on summary conviction, by a fine not exceeding the statutory maximum or such lesser amount as is specified in the regulations, and

    (b) on conviction on indictment, by a fine.

82O Criminal proceedings

(1) Proceedings for a relevant offence may be taken, and the offence may for all incidental purposes be treated as having been committed, in any place in the United Kingdom.

(2) Section 3 of the Territorial Waters Jurisdiction Act 1878 (restriction on prosecutions) does not apply to any proceedings for a relevant offence.

(3) In this section "relevant offence" means—

    (a) an offence under this Part, or

    (b) an offence created by regulations under section 82N.

Supplementary provisions

82P Power to extend the application of this Part

(1) The Secretary of State may by order provide that specified provisions of this Part are to apply, subject to any specified modifications, in relation to the carrying out of specified operations, or operations of a specified description, in the Scottish inshore region.

(2) The operations must be operations—

    (a) which either fall within section 82A(4) or are carried on in the course of taking installation abandonment measures (or both),

    (b) which cause, or are likely to result in, obstruction or danger to navigation (whether while the operation is being carried out or subsequently), and

    (c) which the Scottish Ministers do not have power to control or regulate for the purpose of preventing such obstruction or danger.

(3) The reference in subsection (1) to "the Scottish inshore region" includes a reference to—

      (a)   the shore adjoining that region, and

      (b)   any land in Scotland adjoining or adjacent to that shore.

(4)   If an order under this section makes provision in relation to the carrying out of an operation in the course of taking installation abandonment measures —

      (a)   section 82A(3)(c) does not apply in relation to the operation, but

      (b)   paragraph (a) is subject to any different modification or other provision to the contrary made by an order under this section.

(5)   For the purposes of this section "installation abandonment measures" are any measures taken in connection with the abandonment of —

      (a)   an offshore installation or submarine pipeline, within the meaning of Part 4 of the Petroleum Act 1998, or

      (b)   a carbon storage installation, within the meaning of section 30 of this Act,

whether or not the measures are taken in pursuance of an abandonment programme.

(6)   In subsection (5) "abandonment programme" means —

      (a)   an abandonment programme under Part 4 of the Petroleum Act 1998;

      (b)   an abandonment programme under that Part, as it applies by virtue of section 30 of this Act.

(7)   In this section "specified" means specified in the order.

82Q   Interpretation of this Part

In this Part —

"authorised exploration or exploitation operation" has the meaning given by section 82A(8);

"consent holder" means the person to whom a consent under section 82A is given;

"emergency safety notice" is to be read in accordance with section 82F(3);

"immediate action notice" is to be read in accordance with section 82H(3);

"regulated zone" means the area that consists of —

      (a)   the area of sea within the seaward limits of the territorial sea, other than the Scottish inshore region, and

      (b)   the area of sea within the limits of the UK sector of the continental shelf,

and includes the bed and subsoil of the sea within those areas, the shore adjoining, and any land adjoining or adjacent to that shore, but does not include any land in Scotland;

"Scottish inshore region" has the same meaning as in the Marine and Coastal Access Act 2009 (see section 322 of that Act);

"sea" includes —

      (a)   any tidal waters; and

      (b)   any land covered with water at mean high water spring tide;

"UK sector of the continental shelf" means the areas for the time being designated by an Order in Council under section 1(7) of the Continental Shelf Act 1964.".

(2) In section 105(2)(a) of the Energy Act 2008 (c. 32) (instruments requiring draft affirmative procedure) after sub-paragraph (v) insert—

"(va) section 82N (power to make regulations in relation to persons appointed as inspectors etc),

(vb) section 82P (power to extend application of Part 4A),".

Harbours Act 1964

315 Amendments of the Harbours Act 1964

Schedule 21 (which contains amendments of the Harbours Act 1964 (c. 40)) has effect.

PART 11

SUPPLEMENTARY PROVISIONS

316 Regulations and orders

(1) Any power conferred by this Act on the Secretary of State, the Scottish Ministers, the Welsh Ministers or a Northern Ireland department to make regulations or an order includes—

(a) power to make different provision for different cases, and

(b) power to make incidental, consequential, supplemental or transitional provision or savings.

(2) The power conferred by subsection (1)(b) includes power, for the purpose of making any such provision or savings, to amend any primary or secondary legislation passed or made before, or in the same Session as, this Act.

(3) Any power conferred by this Act on the Secretary of State, the Scottish Ministers or the Welsh Ministers to make regulations or an order is exercisable by statutory instrument.

(4) Subsections (2) and (3) do not apply to—

(a) an order made under any of sections 116 to 137 (orders made for the purpose of designating, or furthering the objectives of, MCZs);

(b) an order made under section 159 (orders amending or revoking byelaws made by IFC authorities).

(5) Any regulations or order made under this Act by a Northern Ireland department are to be a statutory rule for the purposes of the Statutory Rules (Northern Ireland) Order 1979 (S.I. 1979/1513 (N.I. 12)).

(6) A statutory instrument or statutory rule which contains (whether alone or with other provisions)—

(a) any regulation or order which by virtue of subsection (2) or section 188(2)(d) makes provision amending primary legislation, or

(b) any regulation or order under any of the provisions specified in subsection (7),

is subject to draft affirmative procedure.

(7)   The provisions are—

        (a)   section 43(5)(a);

        (b)   section 66(3);

        (c)   section 73;

        (d)   section 93 or 95;

        (e)   section 98(1) by virtue of section 98(2);

        (f)   section 108;

        (g)   section 141(5);

        (h)   section 142;

        (i)   section 232;

        (j)   paragraph 6 of Schedule 1.

(8)   A statutory instrument or statutory rule made under this Act which is not subject to—

        (a)   draft affirmative procedure, or

        (b)   Commons draft affirmative procedure,

is subject to negative resolution procedure.

(9)   Subsection (8) does not apply to a statutory instrument containing only orders under section 324 (commencement orders).

(10)   In this Act—

        "draft affirmative procedure" means—

           (a)   in relation to any Order in Council, or any statutory instrument made by the Secretary of State, a requirement that a draft of the instrument be laid before, and approved by a resolution of, each House of Parliament;

           (b)   in relation to any statutory instrument made by the Scottish Ministers, a requirement that a draft of the instrument be laid before, and approved by a resolution of, the Scottish Parliament;

           (c)   in relation to any statutory instrument made by the Welsh Ministers, a requirement that a draft of the instrument be laid before, and approved by a resolution of, the National Assembly for Wales;

           (d)   in relation to any statutory rule made by a Northern Ireland department, a requirement that a draft of the rule be laid before, and approved by a resolution of, the Northern Ireland Assembly;

        "negative resolution procedure" means—

           (a)   in relation to any Order in Council, or any statutory instrument made by the Secretary of State, annulment in pursuance of a resolution of either House of Parliament;

           (b)   in relation to any statutory instrument made by the Scottish Ministers, annulment in pursuance of a resolution of the Scottish Parliament;

           (c)   in relation to any statutory instrument made by the Welsh Ministers, annulment in pursuance of a resolution of the National Assembly for Wales;

           (d)   in relation to any statutory rule made by a Northern Ireland department, negative resolution within the meaning of section

41(6) of the Interpretation Act (Northern Ireland) 1954 (c. 33 N.I.).

(11) In this section—

"Commons draft affirmative procedure" means, in relation to any statutory instrument, a requirement that a draft of the instrument be laid before, and approved by a resolution of, the House of Commons;

"primary legislation" means—

    (a) an Act of Parliament;

    (b) an Act of the Scottish Parliament;

    (c) a Measure of the National Assembly for Wales;

    (d) Northern Ireland legislation;

"secondary legislation" means subordinate legislation or any other instrument made under primary legislation.

317 Directions

(1) Any directions given under this Act must be in writing.

(2) Any power conferred by this Act to give a direction includes power, exercisable in the same manner and subject to the same conditions or limitations, to vary or revoke the direction.

318 Offences by directors, partners, etc

(1) Where an offence under this Act has been committed by a body corporate and it is proved that the offence—

    (a) has been committed with the consent or connivance of a person falling within subsection (2), or

    (b) is attributable to any neglect on the part of such a person,

that person (as well as the body corporate) is guilty of that offence and liable to be proceeded against and punished accordingly.

(2) The persons are—

    (a) a director, manager, secretary or similar officer of the body corporate;

    (b) any person who was purporting to act in such a capacity.

(3) Where the affairs of a body corporate are managed by its members, subsection (1) applies in relation to the acts and defaults of a member, in connection with that management, as if the member were a director of the body corporate.

(4) Where an offence under this Act has been committed by a Scottish firm and it is proved that the offence—

    (a) has been committed with the consent or connivance of a partner of the firm or a person purporting to act as such a partner, or

    (b) is attributable to any neglect on the part of such a person,

that person (as well as the firm) is guilty of that offence and liable to be proceeded against and punished accordingly.

319 Disapplication of requirement for consent to certain prosecutions

Section 3 of the Territorial Waters Jurisdiction Act 1878 (c. 73) (consents to prosecutions of offences committed on the open sea by persons who are not

British citizens) does not apply to any proceedings for an offence under this Act.

320 Power to make transitional provisions and savings

(1) The Secretary of State may by order make such transitional provision or savings as the Secretary of State considers necessary or expedient in consequence of any provisions of this Act.

(2) The power conferred by subsection (1) includes power to make provision in addition to, or different from, that made by this Act.

321 Repeals

Schedule 22 contains repeals.

322 Interpretation

(1) In this Act—

"baseline" means the baseline from which the breadth of the territorial sea is measured;

"British fishery limits" has the meaning given by section 1 of the Fishery Limits Act 1976 (c. 86);

"draft affirmative procedure" has the meaning given in section 316;

"English inshore region" means the area of sea within the seaward limits of the territorial sea adjacent to England;

"English offshore region" means so much of the UK marine area as is beyond the seaward limits of the territorial sea but is not within any of the following—

    (a) the Scottish offshore region;

    (b) the Welsh offshore region;

    (c) the Northern Ireland offshore region;

"exclusive economic zone" means any area for the time being designated by an Order in Council under section 41(3);

"financial year" means any period of twelve months ending with 31st March (except where the context otherwise requires);

"general objective", in relation to the MMO, is to be read in accordance with section 2(1);

"marine policy statement" is to be construed in accordance with sections 44 and 47;

"Minister of the Crown" has the same meaning as in the Ministers of the Crown Act 1975 (c. 26);

"the MMO" means the Marine Management Organisation;

"MPS" means a marine policy statement;

"nautical mile" means an international nautical mile of 1,852 metres;

"negative resolution procedure" has the meaning given in section 316;

"Northern Ireland inshore region" means the area of sea within the seaward limits of the territorial sea adjacent to Northern Ireland;

"Northern Ireland offshore region" means so much of the Northern Ireland zone as lies beyond the seaward limits of the territorial sea;

"Northern Ireland zone" has the same meaning as in the Northern Ireland Act 1998 (c. 47) (see section 98(1) and (8) of that Act);

"notice" means notice in writing;

"public authority" means any of the following –

    (a)   a Minister of the Crown;

    (b)   a public body;

    (c)   a public office holder;

"public body" includes –

    (a)   a government department;

    (b)   a Northern Ireland department;

    (c)   a local authority (see subsection (2));

    (d)   a local planning authority;

    (e)   a statutory undertaker (see subsection (2));

"public office holder" means a person holding any of the following offices –

    (a)   an office under the Crown;

    (b)   an office created or continued in existence by a public general Act or by devolved legislation (see subsection (3));

    (c)   an office the remuneration in respect of which is paid out of money provided by Parliament or a devolved legislature (see subsection (3));

"renewable energy zone" means any area for the time being designated by an Order in Council under section 84(4) of the Energy Act 2004 (c. 20);

"Scottish inshore region" means the area of sea within the seaward limits of the territorial sea adjacent to Scotland;

"Scottish offshore region" means so much of the UK marine area as lies outside the Scottish inshore region and consists of –

    (a)   areas of sea which lie within the Scottish zone, and

    (b)   areas of sea which lie outside the Scottish zone but which are nearer to any point on the baselines from which the breadth of the territorial sea adjacent to Scotland is measured than to any point on the baselines in any other part of the United Kingdom;

"Scottish zone" has the same meaning as in the Scotland Act 1998 (c. 46) (see section 126(1) and (2) of that Act);

"sea", except in Part 9 (coastal access), is to be read in accordance with section 42(3) and (4);

"subordinate legislation" has the same meaning as in the Interpretation Act 1978 (c. 30) (see section 21 of that Act);

"territorial sea" means the territorial sea of the United Kingdom;

"UK marine area" has the meaning given by section 42;

"UK sector of the continental shelf" means the areas for the time being designated by an Order in Council under section 1(7) of the Continental Shelf Act 1964 (c. 29);

"Welsh inshore region" means the area of sea within the seaward limits of the territorial sea adjacent to Wales;

"Welsh offshore region" means so much of the Welsh zone as lies beyond the seaward limits of the territorial sea;

"Welsh zone" has the same meaning as in the Government of Wales Act 2006 (c. 32) (see section 158(1) and (3) of that Act).

(2)   In the definition of "public body" in subsection (1) –

    "local authority" means –

(a)   in relation to England, a county council, a district council, a parish council, a London borough council, the Common Council of the City of London or the Council of the Isles of Scilly;

(b)   in relation to Scotland, a council for any local government area constituted under section 2(1) of the Local Government etc. (Scotland) Act 1994 (c. 39);

(c)   in relation to Wales, a county council, a county borough council or a community council;

(d)   in relation to Northern Ireland, a district council;

"statutory undertaker" means a person who is, or is deemed to be, a statutory undertaker for the purposes of any provision of any of the following—

(a)   Part 11 of the Town and Country Planning Act 1990 (c. 8);

(b)   Part 10 of the Town and Country Planning (Scotland) Act 1997 (c. 8);

(c)   the Planning (Northern Ireland) Order 1991 (S.I. 1991/1220 (N.I. 11)).

(3)   For the purposes of the definition of "public office holder" in subsection (1)—

"devolved legislation" means legislation passed by a devolved legislature;

"devolved legislature" means—

(a)   the Scottish Parliament;

(b)   the National Assembly for Wales;

(c)   the Northern Ireland Assembly.

(4)   Subsection (5) applies to the question of which waters, or parts of the sea, of any particular description—

(a)   are adjacent to Northern Ireland (and, in consequence, are not adjacent to England, Wales or Scotland), or

(b)   are not adjacent to Northern Ireland (and, in consequence, are not precluded from being adjacent to England, Wales or Scotland).

(5)   The question is to be determined by reference to an Order in Council under section 98(8) of the Northern Ireland Act 1998 (c. 47) if, or to the extent that, the Order in Council is expressed to apply—

(a)   by virtue of this subsection, for the purposes of this Act, or

(b)   if no provision has been made by virtue of paragraph (a), for the general or residual purposes of that Act.

(6)   Subsection (7) applies to the question of which waters, or parts of the sea, of any particular description—

(a)   are adjacent to Wales (and, in consequence, are not adjacent to England), or

(b)   are not adjacent to Wales (and, in consequence, (but subject to subsections (4) and (5)) are adjacent to England).

(7)   The question is to be determined by reference to an order or Order in Council made under or by virtue of section 158(3) or (4) of the Government of Wales Act 2006 (c. 32) (apportionment of sea areas) if, or to the extent that, the order or Order in Council is expressed to apply—

(a)   by virtue of this subsection, for the purposes of this Act, or

    (b)   if no provision has been made by virtue of paragraph (a), for the general or residual purposes of that Act.

(8) Subsection (9) applies to the question of which waters, or parts of the sea, of any particular description—

    (a)   are adjacent to Scotland (and, in consequence, are not adjacent to England), or

    (b)   are not adjacent to Scotland (and, in consequence, (but subject to subsections (4) and (5)) are adjacent to England).

(9) The question is to be determined by reference to an Order in Council made under section 126(2) of the Scotland Act 1998 (c. 46) if, or to the extent that, the Order in Council is expressed to apply—

    (a)   by virtue of this subsection, for the purposes of this Act, or

    (b)   if no provision has been made by virtue of paragraph (a), for the general or residual purposes of that Act.

323 Extent

(1) Subject to the following provisions of this section, this Act extends to England and Wales only.

(2) The amendment or repeal of any enactment (including an enactment comprised in subordinate legislation) by, or in consequence of, the following provisions of this Act has the same extent as the enactment amended or repealed—

    (a)   Part 1 (the MMO);

    (b)   Part 2 (exclusive economic zone, UK marine area and Welsh zone), other than paragraph 2 of Schedule 4;

    (c)   Chapter 3 of Part 7 (migratory and freshwater fish);

    (d)   Chapter 4 of Part 7 (obsolete fisheries enactments);

    (e)   Part 9 (coastal access);

    (f)   in Part 10—

        (i)   sections 311 and 312 (Natural England);

        (ii)   section 313 (Countryside Council for Wales);

        (iii)   section 314 (which inserts Part 4A into the Energy Act 2008 (c. 32));

    (g)   Schedule 14 (minor and consequential amendments relating to IFC authorities).

(3) Subject to subsection (2)—

    (a)   any repeal in Schedule 22 (and section 321 so far as relating to the repeal) has the same extent as the provisions of this Act to which the repeal relates, but

    (b)   paragraph (a) is subject to any provision in the notes in that Schedule.

(4) Subject to subsection (2), the following provisions also extend to Scotland—

    (a)   Part 1 (the MMO);

    (b)   Part 2 (exclusive economic zone, UK marine area and Welsh zone);

    (c)   Part 3 (marine planning);

    (d)   Part 4 (marine licensing), other than paragraph 1 of Schedule 8;

    (e)   Chapter 1 of Part 5 (MCZs), other than section 146 and Schedules 11 and 12;

      (f)   in Chapter 1 of Part 6, sections 165, 166 and 186 (powers of IFC officers etc);

      (g)   in Part 7 (fisheries) —

          (i)   sections 212 and 213 (crabs and lobsters);

          (ii)   section 232 (keeping, introduction and removal of fish);

      (h)   in Part 8 (enforcement), Chapters 1 to 5 and section 295;

      (i)   this Part (other than section 321 and Schedule 22, except as provided by subsection (2) or (3)).

(5)   Subject to subsection (2), the following provisions also extend to Northern Ireland —

      (a)   Part 1 (the MMO);

      (b)   Part 2 (exclusive economic zone, UK marine area and Welsh zone);

      (c)   Part 3 (marine planning);

      (d)   Part 4 (marine licensing), other than paragraph 1 of Schedule 8;

      (e)   Chapter 1 of Part 5 (MCZs), other than section 146 and Schedules 11 and 12;

      (f)   in Part 8 (enforcement), Chapters 1 to 5 and section 295;

      (g)   this Part (other than section 321 and Schedule 22, except as provided by subsection (2) or (3)).

(6)   The amendments and repeals made by this Act to provisions of the Food and Environment Protection Act 1985 (c. 48) do not extend to any of the Channel Islands or any British overseas territory.

(7)   Her Majesty may by Order in Council —

      (a)   provide for any of the provisions of Part 4 (marine licensing) or this Part, so far as relating to Part 4, to extend, with or without modifications, to any of the territories specified in subsection (8), and

      (b)   where any such provision is made in relation to any of those territories, repeal any provisions of Part 2 or 4 of the Food and Environment Protection Act 1985 (deposits in the sea etc) as they have effect as part of the law of that territory.

(8)   The territories mentioned in subsection (7) are —

      (a)   the Bailiwick of Jersey;

      (b)   the Falkland Islands;

      (c)   South Georgia and the Sandwich Islands;

      (d)   St Helena and Dependencies.

(9)   In section 24 of the Sea Fish (Conservation) Act 1967 (c. 84) (power to extend provisions of that Act to Isle of Man or Channel Islands), as it applies in relation to the Bailiwick of Guernsey, any reference to a provision of that Act includes a reference to that provision as amended by any provision of Chapter 1 of Part 7 of this Act.

(10)   The amendments made by —

      (a)   paragraph 2 of Schedule 4 (amendments to the Fishery Limits Act 1976 (c. 86)),

      (b)   section 212 (taking of crabs and lobsters for scientific purposes), and

      (c)   section 213 (orders prohibiting the taking and sale of certain lobsters),

do not extend to the Isle of Man or the Channel Islands.

324 Commencement

(1) The following provisions of this Act come into force on the day on which this Act is passed—

    (a) in Part 3 (marine planning)—

        (i) paragraphs 4(1) to (4), 5 and 6 of Schedule 5 (statement of public participation relating to MPS) and, so far as relating to those paragraphs, paragraphs 1 and 2 of that Schedule;

        (ii) sections 44(1)(b) and (5) and 45(4), so far as relating to those paragraphs;

    (b) this Part, other than section 321 and Schedule 22;

    (c) any power of a Minister of the Crown, the Scottish Ministers, the Welsh Ministers or a Northern Ireland department to make regulations or an order under or by virtue of this Act;

    (d) any power to make an Order in Council under the Government of Wales Act 2006 (c. 32) by virtue of the amendments made by section 43 and paragraph 6 of Schedule 4 (Welsh zone).

(2) So far as not already brought into force by virtue of subsection (1), the following provisions of this Act come into force at the end of the period of 2 months beginning with the day on which this Act is passed—

    (a) Part 3 (marine planning);

    (b) in Part 5—

        (i) Chapter 1 (MCZs), so far as not relating to MCZs in Wales;

        (ii) Chapter 2 (other conservation sites), so far as not relating to Wales;

    (c) sections 190 to 193 (inshore fisheries in Wales);

    (d) Part 9 (coastal access).

(3) Subject to subsection (4), the other provisions of this Act come into force on an appointed day.

(4) Any repeal in Schedule 22 (and section 321 so far as relating to the repeal) comes into force in the same way as the provisions of this Act to which the repeal relates.

(5) In this section "appointed day" means such day or days as the Secretary of State may by order appoint.

(6) The power conferred by subsection (5) is exercisable by the Welsh Ministers (and not the Secretary of State) in relation to the following provisions—

    (a) so far as relating to MCZs in Wales—

        (i) Chapter 1 of Part 5 (MCZs);

        (ii) the repeals in Schedule 22 relating to that Chapter;

        (iii) section 321 so far as relating to those repeals;

    (b) Chapter 2 of Part 5 (other conservation sites), so far as relating to Wales;

    (c) so far as relating to sea fisheries districts in Wales, or any part of a sea fisheries district lying in Wales—

        (i) in Part 6, section 187 (repeal of the Sea Fisheries Regulation Act 1966 (c. 38));

        (ii) the repeals in Schedule 22 relating to that section;

        (iii) section 321 so far as relating to that section and those repeals.

(7) An order under subsection (5) may appoint different days for different purposes.

(8) In this section "Wales" includes the Welsh inshore region.

325 Short title

This Act may be cited as the Marine and Coastal Access Act 2009.

SCHEDULES

SCHEDULE 1

THE MARINE MANAGEMENT ORGANISATION

Status of the MMO

1   (1) The MMO is a body corporate.

      (2) The MMO is not to be regarded —
          (a) as a servant or agent of the Crown,
          (b) as enjoying any status, privilege or immunity of the Crown, or
          (c) as exempt, by virtue of any connection with the Crown, from any tax, duty, rate, levy or other charge whatsoever, whether general or local,

      and the property of the MMO is not to be regarded as property of, or held on behalf of, the Crown.

      (3) Accordingly, employees of the MMO are not to be regarded as —
          (a) servants or agents of the Crown, or
          (b) enjoying any status, immunity or privilege of the Crown.

The chair of the MMO

2   A person (the "chair of the MMO") is to be appointed by the Secretary of State to chair the MMO.

Membership

3   (1) The members of the MMO are to be —
          (a) the person who is for the time being the chair of the MMO, and
          (b) not fewer than 5, nor more than 8, other members ("ordinary members") who are to be appointed by the Secretary of State.

      (2) The Secretary of State must consult the chair of the MMO before appointing any of the ordinary members.

      (3) If a person who is an ordinary member is to become the chair of the MMO, the appointment as ordinary member ceases immediately before the person becomes the chair of the MMO.

The deputy chair of the MMO

4   The Secretary of State may appoint one of the ordinary members to be the deputy chair of the MMO ("the deputy chair").

Considerations in making appointments

5   In appointing any person to be the chair of the MMO or an ordinary member, the Secretary of State must have regard to the desirability —

    (a)   of appointing a person who has experience of, and has shown some capacity in, some matter relevant to the exercise of the MMO's functions, and

    (b)   of securing that a variety of skills and experience is available among the members.

Power to amend the numbers of members specified in paragraph 3(1)

6   (1) The Secretary of State may by order amend paragraph 3(1) so as to substitute a different number for any of the numbers for the time being specified there.

    (2) An order under sub-paragraph (1) must not amend paragraph 3(1)(b) so that it provides that there may be fewer than 5 ordinary members.

Terms of appointment

7   (1) A person appointed as —

    (a)   the chair of the MMO, or

    (b)   an ordinary member,

    holds and vacates office in accordance with the terms of the appointment.

    (2) A person appointed as the deputy chair holds and vacates that office in accordance with any particular terms of appointment there may be in the case of that appointment in addition to the terms of the person's appointment as an ordinary member.

    (3) Sub-paragraphs (1) and (2) are subject to paragraphs 3(3) and 8 to 10.

    (4) The terms of appointment to any office in any particular case are to be such as the Secretary of State may determine.

    (5) No appointment is to be for longer than 5 years.

    (6) No person may be a member for a total period of more than 10 years (whether or not continuous).

Resignation from office

8   A person may, by giving notice to the Secretary of State, resign from office as —

    (a)   the chair of the MMO,

    (b)   the deputy chair, or

    (c)   an ordinary member.

Suspension from, or termination of, office

9   (1) The Secretary of State may suspend or terminate the appointment of any person as the chair of the MMO, the deputy chair, or an ordinary member, if —

    (a)   the person has become bankrupt or made an arrangement with creditors,

(b)   the person's estate has been sequestrated in Scotland or the person has entered into a debt arrangement programme under Part 1 of the Debt Arrangement and Attachment (Scotland) Act 2002 (asp 17) as the debtor or has, under Scots law, granted a trust deed for creditors,

(c)   the person has been absent from meetings of the MMO for a period of more than 6 months without the permission of the MMO,

(d)   the person is disqualified from acting as a company director,

(e)   the person has been convicted (whether before or after appointment) of a criminal offence, the conviction not being spent for the purposes of the Rehabilitation of Offenders Act 1974 (c. 53),

or if the person is, in the opinion of the Secretary of State, unable or unfit to discharge the functions of the appointment for any other reason.

(2)   A person whose appointment as the chair of the MMO is suspended is accordingly also suspended as a member.

(3)   If a person's appointment as an ordinary member is suspended, any appointment of that person as the deputy chair is also suspended.

Eligibility for re-appointment

10   A person who ceases to hold any of the following offices —
(a)   chair of the MMO,
(b)   deputy chair,
(c)   ordinary member,
is not by reason of that cessation prevented from subsequently being re-appointed to that office (or, in the case of paragraph (a) or (c), from subsequently becoming a member again).

Members' remuneration and allowances

11   The MMO may pay to its members such remuneration and allowances as the Secretary of State may determine.

Pensions, allowances and gratuities

12   If required to do so by the Secretary of State, the MMO must —
(a)   pay such pensions, allowances or gratuities as the Secretary of State may determine to or in respect of any person who is or has been a member;
(b)   pay such sums as the Secretary of State may determine towards provision for the payment of pensions, allowances or gratuities to or in respect of any such person.

Compensation for loss of office

13   If —
(a)   a person ceases to be a member, and
(b)   it appears to the Secretary of State that there are special circumstances which make it appropriate for the person to receive compensation,
the Secretary of State may require the MMO to make such payments to the person as the Secretary of State may determine.

Chief executive

14 (1) The MMO must appoint a person to be its chief executive.

 (2) The person appointed must have been approved by the Secretary of State.

 (3) The chief executive is an employee of the MMO.

 (4) The Secretary of State may appoint the first chief executive.

Chief scientific adviser

15 (1) The MMO must appoint a person to be its chief scientific adviser.

 (2) The chief scientific adviser is an employee of the MMO.

 (3) The MMO may only make an appointment under sub-paragraph (1) with the approval of the Secretary of State as to any terms and conditions of employment not falling within paragraph 17 or 18.

Other staff

16 (1) The MMO may appoint other employees.

 (2) The MMO may only make an appointment under sub-paragraph (1) with the approval of the Secretary of State as to any terms and conditions of employment not falling within paragraph 17 or 18.

Staff remuneration and allowances

17 (1) The MMO may pay such remuneration and allowances as it may determine to any of its employees.

 (2) The MMO may only make a determination under sub-paragraph (1) with the approval of the Secretary of State.

Staff pensions etc

18 (1) The MMO may —
    (a) pay such pensions, allowances or gratuities as it may determine to or in respect of any person who is or has been an employee of the MMO;
    (b) pay such sums as it may determine towards provision for the payment of pensions, allowances or gratuities to or in respect of any such person.

 (2) The MMO may only make a determination under sub-paragraph (1) with the approval of the Secretary of State.

Staff superannuation

19 (1) Employment with the MMO is to be included among the kinds of employment to which a scheme under section 1 of the Superannuation Act 1972 (c. 11) can apply.

 (2) Accordingly, in Schedule 1 to that Act (kinds of employment to which the Act applies) insert at the appropriate place —
    "Marine Management Organisation."

(3) The MMO must pay to the Minister for the Civil Service, at such times as that Minister may direct, such sums as that Minister may determine in respect of any increase attributable to this paragraph in the sums payable out of money provided by Parliament under that Act.

Procedure

20   Subject to the following provisions of this Schedule, the MMO may regulate —
    (a)   its own procedure (including quorum), and
    (b)   the procedure of any of its committees or sub-committees (including quorum).

Delegation of functions

21   (1) The MMO may authorise a committee, sub-committee, member or employee of the MMO to exercise any of the MMO's functions.

    (2) The MMO must keep a record of any authorisations under sub-paragraph (1).

    (3) Sub-paragraph (1) does not —
        (a)   prevent the MMO from exercising the function itself, or
        (b)   affect the power of the MMO to authorise an employee of the MMO to carry out functions of the MMO.

Membership of committees and sub-committees

22   (1) A committee or sub-committee may include persons who are not members of the MMO.

    (2) The MMO may pay such remuneration and allowances as it may determine to any person who —
        (a)   is a member of a committee or sub-committee, but
        (b)   is not a member of the MMO.

    (3) The MMO may only make a determination under sub-paragraph (2) with the approval of the Secretary of State.

Validity of proceedings

23   The validity of anything done by the MMO, or by any committee or sub-committee of the MMO, is not affected by any of the following —
    (a)   any vacancy in the office of chair of the MMO or chair of the committee or sub-committee,
    (b)   any deficiency in the number of ordinary members or in the number of members of the committee or sub-committee,
    (c)   any defect in, or suspension of, any person's appointment as the chair or other member of the MMO or of the committee or sub-committee.

Application of seal and proof of documents

24   (1) The application of the MMO's seal must be authenticated by the signature of —

     (a)   a member who is authorised (generally or specially) for that purpose, or

     (b)   an employee of the MMO who is so authorised.

  (2) A document purporting to be duly executed under the seal of the MMO is to be received in evidence and taken to be so executed, unless the contrary is shown.

Documents served etc by the MMO

25 (1) Any document which the MMO is authorised or required by or under any enactment to serve, make or issue may be signed on behalf of the MMO by any member or employee of the MMO who has been authorised for the purpose, whether generally or specially, by the MMO.

  (2) Every document purporting—

     (a)   to be an instrument made or issued by or on behalf of the MMO, and

     (b)   to be signed by a person authorised by the MMO for the purpose,

is to be received in evidence and taken to be so made or issued, unless the contrary is shown.

Annual report

26 (1) For each financial year, the MMO must prepare an annual report on how it has discharged its functions during the year.

  (2) The MMO must send the report to the Secretary of State as soon as possible after the end of the year to which it relates.

  (3) The Secretary of State must lay a copy of the report before each House of Parliament.

  (4) In this paragraph "financial year" means—

     (a)   the period that—

        (i)   begins with the day on which the MMO is established, and

       (ii)   ends with the next 31st March,

     (b)   each subsequent period of 12 months ending with 31st March.

Accounts and records

27 (1) The MMO must keep proper accounts and proper records in relation to the accounts.

  (2) For each financial year, the MMO must prepare a statement of accounts in respect of that financial year.

  (3) The statement must be in such form as the Secretary of State may direct.

  (4) Within such period as the Secretary of State may direct, the MMO must send a copy of the statement to—

     (a)   the Secretary of State, and

     (b)   the Comptroller and Auditor General.

  (5) In this paragraph "financial year" has the same meaning as in paragraph 26.

Audit

28   (1)   This paragraph applies where, in pursuance of paragraph 27, the MMO has sent a copy of a statement of accounts to the Comptroller and Auditor General.

       (2)   The Comptroller and Auditor General must—
          (a)   examine, certify and report on the statement, and
          (b)   send a copy of the certified statement and of the report to the Secretary of State as soon as possible.

       (3)   The Secretary of State must lay before each House of Parliament a copy of the certified statement and of the report.

Duty to provide information to the Secretary of State

29   (1)   The MMO must provide the Secretary of State with—
          (a)   copies of such returns or accounts, or
          (b)   such information,
       as the Secretary of State may require.

       (2)   Sub-paragraph (1) applies only in relation to accounts, returns or information relating to—
          (a)   the MMO's property, or
          (b)   the discharge, or proposed discharge, of the MMO's functions.

       (3)   The MMO must also—
          (a)   permit any person authorised by the Secretary of State to inspect and make copies of any accounts or other documents of the MMO, and
          (b)   provide such explanation of them as the Secretary of State or that person may require.

SCHEDULE 2   Section 1

MINOR AND CONSEQUENTIAL AMENDMENTS RELATING TO THE MMO

Public Records Act 1958 (c. 51)

1   In Schedule 1 to the Public Records Act 1958 (definition of public records) in Part 2 of the Table at the end of paragraph 3 insert at the appropriate place—
             "The Marine Management Organisation."

Parliamentary Commissioner Act 1967 (c. 13)

2   In Schedule 2 to the Parliamentary Commissioner Act 1967 (departments and authorities subject to investigation) insert at the appropriate place—
             "The Marine Management Organisation."

House of Commons Disqualification Act 1975 (c. 24)

3   In Part 2 of Schedule 1 to the House of Commons Disqualification Act 1975 (bodies of which all members are disqualified) insert at the appropriate

place —

"The Marine Management Organisation."

Race Relations Act 1976 (c. 74)

4   In Part 2 of Schedule 1A to the Race Relations Act 1976 (bodies and other persons subject to general statutory duty) insert at the appropriate place under the heading "Other Bodies, Etc." —

"The Marine Management Organisation."

Inheritance Tax Act 1984 (c. 51)

5   In Schedule 3 to the Inheritance Tax Act 1984 (gifts for national purposes etc) after the entry for the Countryside Council for Wales insert —

"The Marine Management Organisation."

Freedom of Information Act 2000 (c. 36)

6   In Part 6 of Schedule 1 to the Freedom of Information Act 2000 (other public bodies and offices which are public authorities) insert at the appropriate place —

"The Marine Management Organisation."

SCHEDULE 3   Section 39

TRANSFER SCHEMES

Introductory

1   In this Schedule —

"transferor" means the person from whom any property, rights or liabilities are transferred;

"transferee" means the person to whom any property, rights or liabilities are transferred.

The property, rights and liabilities that may be transferred

2   (1) A scheme may provide for the transfer of any property, rights or liabilities, whether or not otherwise capable of being transferred or assigned.

    (2) A scheme may provide for the transfer of any property, rights or liabilities to take effect regardless of any such —

       (a) contravention,

       (b) liability, or

       (c) interference with an interest or right,

    as there would be (apart from this sub-paragraph) by reason of an inhibiting provision.

    (3) For the purposes of sub-paragraph (2) an "inhibiting provision" is a provision having effect (whether under an enactment or an agreement or in any other way) in relation to the terms on which the transferor is entitled to

the property or right, or is subject to the liability, that is the subject of the transfer.

Creation and apportionment of property, rights or liabilities

3   (1) A scheme may —
      (a) create for the transferor interests in or rights over property transferred by virtue of the scheme;
      (b) create for the transferee interests in or rights over property retained by the transferor;
      (c) create rights or liabilities between the transferor and the transferee.

    (2) In this Schedule, any reference —
      (a) to the transfer of interests, rights or liabilities by virtue of a scheme, or
      (b) to any interests, rights or liabilities transferred by virtue of a scheme,
    includes a reference to the creation of interests, rights or liabilities, or to interests, rights or liabilities created, by virtue of sub-paragraph (1).

    (3) A scheme may make incidental provision as to the interests, rights and liabilities of persons other than the transferor and the transferee with respect to the subject matter of the scheme.

Vesting certificates

4   A certificate by the Secretary of State that anything specified in the certificate has vested in any person by virtue of a scheme is conclusive evidence of that fact for all purposes.

Employment contracts

5   (1) This paragraph applies if rights and liabilities under a contract of employment are transferred by virtue of a scheme.

    (2) The contract of employment —
      (a) is not terminated by the transfer, and
      (b) has effect from the transfer date as if made between the employee and the transferee.

    (3) The rights, powers, duties and liabilities of the transferor under or in connection with the contract are transferred to the transferee on the transfer date.

    (4) Anything done before the transfer date by or in relation to the transferor in respect of the contract or the employee is to be treated from that date as having been done by or in relation to the transferee.

    (5) This paragraph is subject to paragraph 6.

Employee expressing objection to transfer of contract of employment

6   (1) Rights and liabilities under a contract of employment are not transferred under this Schedule if the employee objects to the transfer and informs the transferor or transferee of that objection.

(2) If the employee informs the transferor or transferee of an objection under sub-paragraph (1) —

    (a) the employee's contract of employment is terminated immediately before the transfer date, but

    (b) the employee is not to be treated, for any purpose, as having been dismissed by the transferor.

Right to terminate contract of employment for substantial detrimental change in conditions

7   Nothing in this Schedule affects any right a person has to terminate a contract of employment if (apart from the change of employer) a substantial detrimental change is made in the person's working conditions.

Civil servants

8   (1) This Schedule applies with the following modifications in relation to employment in the civil service of the State on terms which do not constitute a contract of employment.

    (2) In the case of an individual who holds employment in the civil service of the State immediately before the transfer date —

        (a) the individual is to be treated as employed by virtue of a contract of employment,

        (b) the terms of that employment are to be regarded as constituting the terms of that contract, and

        (c) the reference in paragraph 6 to dismissal by the transferor is to be read as a reference to termination of that employment.

    (3) In the case of an individual who is to hold employment in the civil service of the State on and after the transfer date, the terms and conditions of the individual's contract of employment immediately before that date have effect on and after that date as if they were terms and conditions of the individual's employment in the civil service of the State.

Compensation

9   A scheme may contain provision for the payment of compensation by the Secretary of State to any person whose interests are adversely affected by the scheme.

Validity

10   A transfer under this Schedule does not affect the validity of anything done by or in relation to the transferor before the transfer takes effect.

Continuity

11   (1) Anything which —

        (a) is done by the transferor for the purposes of, or otherwise in connection with, anything transferred by virtue of a scheme, and

        (b) is in effect immediately before the transfer date,

    is to be treated as done by the transferee.

    (2) There may be continued by or in relation to the transferee anything (including legal proceedings) —

      (a)   which relates to anything transferred by virtue of a scheme, and

      (b)   which is in the process of being done by or in relation to the transferor immediately before the transfer date.

Documents

12   In any document which—

      (a)   relates to anything transferred by virtue of a scheme, and

      (b)   is in effect immediately before the transfer date,

any reference to the transferor is to be read as a reference to the transferee.

Remedies

13   As from the date on which a transfer takes effect—

      (a)   the transferee, and

      (b)   any other persons,

are to have the same rights, powers and remedies with regard to any right or liability transferred as if the right or liability had at all times been a right or liability of the transferee.

Interim arrangements

14   (1)   A scheme may include provision requiring a transferor to make available to a transferee during any interim period any of the following—

      (a)   any designated premises or facilities occupied or used by the transferor;

      (b)   any designated officers or employees of the transferor.

   (2)   In this paragraph "interim period", in the case of any transfer by virtue of a scheme, means a period—

      (a)   beginning with the day following the making of the scheme, and

      (b)   ending with the date on which the transfer takes effect.

Retrospective modification of schemes

15   (1)   If, at any time after a scheme has come into force, the Secretary of State considers it appropriate to do so, the Secretary of State may direct that the scheme shall be taken to have come into force with such modifications as may be specified in the direction.

   (2)   A direction under this paragraph—

      (a)   may make, with effect from the coming into force of the scheme, such provision as could have been made by the scheme, and

      (b)   in connection with giving effect to that provision from that time, may contain such incidental, consequential, supplemental or transitional provision or savings as the Secretary of State thinks fit.

Incidental, consequential, supplemental or transitional provision or savings

16   A scheme may include such incidental, consequential, supplemental or transitional provision or savings as the Secretary of State thinks fit.

2678   *Marine and Coastal Access Act 2009 (c. **23**)*
Schedule 4 — Exclusive economic zone and Welsh zone: consequential amendments
Part 1 — Exclusive economic zone

SCHEDULE 4   Sections 41 and 43

EXCLUSIVE ECONOMIC ZONE AND WELSH ZONE: CONSEQUENTIAL AMENDMENTS

PART 1

EXCLUSIVE ECONOMIC ZONE

Continental Shelf Act 1964

1   (1) Section 8 of the Continental Shelf Act 1964 (c. 29) (application of the Submarine Telegraph Act 1885 (c. 49) to pipe-lines and submarine cables) is amended as follows.

     (2) In subsection (1A) (submarine cables and pipe-lines under waters in an area designated under section 1(7) of the 1964 Act) for "section 1(7) of this Act" substitute "section 41(3) of the Marine and Coastal Access Act 2009 (exclusive economic zone).".

Fishery Limits Act 1976

2   (1) Section 1 of the Fishery Limits Act 1976 (c. 86) (British fishery limits) is amended as follows.

     (2) For subsection (1) substitute —

         "(1) Subject to the following provisions of this section, British fishery limits extend to the seaward limits of any area for the time being designated by Order in Council under section 41(3) of the Marine and Coastal Access Act 2009 (exclusive economic zone).".

     (3) In consequence of the amendment made by sub-paragraph (2), subsections (3) and (4) of that section cease to have effect.

     (4) Her Majesty may by Order in Council repeal, substitute or amend section 1 of the Fishery Limits Act 1976 (British fishery limits), in so far as it extends to the Channel Islands or the Isle of Man, to make appropriate provision in consequence of the creation of the exclusive economic zone.

     (5) An Order in Council under sub-paragraph (4) may —
         (a) make incidental, consequential, supplementary or transitional provision or savings;
         (b) make different provision for different cases.

Merchant Shipping (Prevention of Pollution) (Law of the Sea Convention) Order 1996

3   (1) Article 2 of the Merchant Shipping (Prevention of Pollution) (Law of the Sea Convention) Order 1996 (S.I. 1996/282) (provision that may be made by regulations) is amended as follows.

     (2) In paragraph (2)(g) (power to specify areas of sea in which jurisdiction and rights of the United Kingdom are exercisable) for "above any of the areas for the time being designated under section 1(7) of the Continental Shelf Act 1964" substitute "within any area for the time being designated under section 41(3) of the Marine and Coastal Access Act 2009 (exclusive economic zone)".

Marine and Coastal Access Act 2009 (c. 23)
Schedule 4 — Exclusive economic zone and Welsh zone: consequential amendments
Part 1 — Exclusive economic zone

2679

(3) After paragraph (2)(g), insert—

> "(h) varying the area within which areas may for the time being be specified under paragraph (g) to such area as may be specified or described in the regulations.".

(4) The amendment by this paragraph of a provision contained in subordinate legislation is without prejudice to any power to amend that provision by subordinate legislation.

Energy Act 2004

4 (1) Section 84 of the Energy Act 2004 (c. 20) (exploitation of areas outside the territorial sea for energy production) is amended as follows.

(2) For subsection (4) substitute—

> "(4) The area within which the rights to which this section applies are exercisable (the "Renewable Energy Zone")—
>
> (a) is any area for the time being designated under section 41(3) of the Marine and Coastal Access Act 2009 (exclusive economic zone), but
>
> (b) if Her Majesty by Order in Council declares that the Renewable Energy Zone extends to such other area as may be specified in the Order, is the area resulting from the Order.".

Energy Act 2008

5 (1) The Energy Act 2008 (c. 32) is amended as follows.

(2) In section 1 (exploitation of areas outside the territorial sea for gas importation and storage), for subsection (5) substitute—

> "(5) The area within which the rights to which this section applies are exercisable (the "Gas Importation and Storage Zone")—
>
> (a) is any area for the time being designated under section 41(3) of the Marine and Coastal Access Act 2009 (exclusive economic zone), but
>
> (b) if Her Majesty by Order in Council declares that the Gas Importation and Storage Zone extends to such other area as may be specified in the Order, is the area resulting from the Order.".

(3) In section 35 (interpretation of Chapter 3), in subsection (1), for the definition of "Gas Importation and Storage Zone" substitute—

> ""Gas Importation and Storage Zone" is to be read in accordance with section 1(5);".

PART 2

WELSH ZONE

Government of Wales Act 2006

6 (1) The Government of Wales Act 2006 (c. 32) is amended as follows.

2680   *Marine and Coastal Access Act 2009 (c. 23)*
Schedule 4 — Exclusive economic zone and Welsh zone: consequential amendments
Part 2 — Welsh zone

(2) In section 37(2) (power of Assembly to call for witnesses and documents) after "Wales" insert "or the Welsh zone".

(3) In section 58 (transfer of Ministerial functions) —

    (a)   in subsection (1)(a), after "Wales" insert "or the Welsh zone",

    (b)   in subsection (1)(c), after "Wales" insert "or the Welsh zone", and

    (c)   after subsection (1) insert —

       "(1A)   An Order in Council under this section may not make provision about a function of a Minister of the Crown exercisable in relation to the area of the Welsh zone beyond the seaward limit of the territorial sea unless the function is connected with fishing, fisheries or fish health.

       (1B)   Subsection (1A) does not have effect in relation to an Order in Council to the extent that it contains provision made by virtue of paragraph 4 of Schedule 3 (functions exercisable beyond the territorial sea)."

(4) In section 59 (implementation of Community law) —

    (a)   in subsection (4)(c) for "Wales or a part of Wales" substitute "Wales, the Welsh zone or a part of Wales or the Welsh zone", and

    (b)   in subsection (7)(c) for "Wales or a part of Wales" substitute "Wales, the Welsh zone or a part of Wales or the Welsh zone".

(5) In section 80(2)(b) (Community law) for "the whole or part of Wales" substitute "the whole or part of Wales or of the Welsh zone".

(6) In section 82(5)(b) (international obligations) for "the whole or part of Wales" substitute "the whole or part of Wales or of the Welsh zone".

(7) In section 155(1)(b) (functions exercisable in relation to Wales) after "Wales" insert "or the Welsh zone".

(8) In section 159 (index of defined expressions), insert at the appropriate place —

    ""Welsh zone"   section 158(1), (3) and (4)".

SCHEDULE 5   Sections 44 and 47

PREPARATION OF AN MPS OR OF AMENDMENTS OF AN MPS

Introductory

1   Before any policy authorities publish a relevant document, they must comply with the requirements imposed by the following provisions of this Schedule.

Interpretation

2   (1) In this Schedule —

       "consultation draft" is to be read in accordance with paragraph 8;

"the final text" means that draft of the relevant document which is adopted by the relevant authorities and published by them under paragraph 12 as the relevant document;

"the relevant authorities" means the policy authorities that publish the relevant document;

"relevant document" means —

    (a)   an MPS, or

    (b)   amendments of an MPS;

"SPP" means a statement of public participation under paragraph 4.

(2) In this Schedule —

    (a)   any reference to each, some or any of the relevant authorities is a reference to those authorities separately,

    (b)   any other reference to the relevant authorities is a reference to those authorities acting jointly.

Consultation in Northern Ireland

3   (1) If one of the relevant authorities is the Department of the Environment in Northern Ireland, that Department must consult the other relevant Northern Ireland departments —

    (a)   during the preparation of the consultation draft, and

    (b)   during the settling of the final text.

(2) For the purposes of this paragraph, the relevant Northern Ireland departments are those Northern Ireland departments which have functions in relation to the whole or any part of the UK marine area.

Statement of public participation

4   (1) The relevant authorities must prepare and publish a statement of public participation (an "SPP").

(2) An SPP is a statement of the policies settled by the relevant authorities for or in connection with the involvement of interested persons in the preparation of the relevant document.

(3) The relevant authorities must publish the SPP in a way calculated to bring it to the attention of interested persons.

(4) In this paragraph "interested persons" means —

    (a)   any persons appearing to the relevant authorities to be likely to be interested in, or affected by, policies proposed to be included in the relevant document, and

    (b)   members of the general public.

(5) Each of the relevant authorities must take all reasonable steps to comply with the SPP.

Further provision about the content of an SPP

5   (1) An SPP must include a proposed timetable.

(2) The proposed timetable must include such provision as the relevant authorities consider reasonable for each of the following —

    (a)   the preparation and publication of a consultation draft under paragraph 8 (including the carrying out of the sustainability appraisal under paragraph 7);

    (b)   the making of representations about the consultation draft;

    (c)   the consideration of representations under paragraph 9 and the settling of the final text;

    (d)   the adoption and publication of the relevant document.

(3) An SPP may include provision for or in connection with the holding of public meetings about the consultation draft.

(4) An SPP must include provision about the making of representations under paragraph 9 about the consultation draft, including provision about —

    (a)   the manner in which representations may be made;

    (b)   the time within which representations must be made.

(5) An SPP must state the period which it is proposed will be allocated for legislative scrutiny of the consultation draft under paragraph 10 (resolution or recommendations by appropriate legislative body or committee).

Review and revision of an SPP

6   (1) The relevant authorities must keep the SPP under review.

    (2) If at any time the relevant authorities consider it necessary or expedient to revise the SPP, they must do so.

    (3) Where the relevant authorities revise the SPP, they must publish it as revised.

    (4) Any reference in this Schedule to an SPP includes a reference to an SPP as revised.

Sustainability appraisal

7   (1) The relevant authorities must carry out an appraisal of the sustainability of their proposals for inclusion in the relevant document.

    (2) The relevant authorities may proceed with those proposals only if they consider that the results of the appraisal indicate that it is appropriate to do so.

    (3) The relevant authorities must publish a report of the results of the appraisal.

    (4) The report is to be published when the relevant authorities publish the consultation draft under paragraph 8.

Preparation and publication of a consultation draft

8   (1) The relevant authorities must prepare and publish a draft of the proposed relevant document (the "consultation draft").

    (2) The relevant authorities must publish the consultation draft in such manner as they consider appropriate.

    (3) They must also take such steps as they consider appropriate to secure that the proposals contained in the consultation draft are brought to the attention of interested persons.

    (4) In sub-paragraph (3) "interested persons" means —

        (a) any persons appearing to the relevant authorities to be likely to be interested in, or affected by, policies proposed to be included in the relevant document, and

        (b) members of the general public.

Representations about the consultation draft

9   (1) Any person may make representations about the consultation draft.

    (2) Any such representations are to be made in accordance with the SPP.

    (3) If any representations are made about the consultation draft, the relevant authorities must consider them in the course of settling the final text.

The appropriate legislative procedure

10   (1) A policy authority must not adopt the final text unless it has complied with the requirements of this paragraph.

    (2) The policy authority must lay a copy of the consultation draft before the appropriate legislature.

    (3) The appropriate legislature is —

        (a) in the case of the Secretary of State, Parliament;

        (b) in the case of the Scottish Ministers, the Scottish Parliament;

        (c) in the case of the Welsh Ministers, the National Assembly for Wales;

        (d) in the case of the Department of the Environment in Northern Ireland, the Northern Ireland Assembly.

    (4) If during the period allocated to it for legislative scrutiny of the consultation draft —

        (a) an appropriate legislative body makes a resolution with regard to the consultation draft, or

        (b) an appropriate legislative committee makes recommendations with regard to the consultation draft,

    sub-paragraph (5) applies.

    (5) The policy authority must lay before the appropriate legislature a statement setting out the policy authority's response to the resolution or recommendations.

    (6) The period allocated to an appropriate legislative body or appropriate legislative committee for legislative scrutiny of the consultation draft is such period as the policy authority may specify.

    (7) The policy authority must specify the period allocated for legislative scrutiny of the consultation draft on or before the day on which a copy of that draft is laid before the appropriate legislature under sub-paragraph (2).

    (8) In this paragraph —

      "appropriate legislative body" means —

        (a) in the case of the Secretary of State, either House of Parliament;

        (b) in the case of any other policy authority, the appropriate legislature;

"appropriate legislative committee" means —

    (a)   in the case of the Secretary of State, a committee of either House of Parliament;

    (b)   in the case of any other policy authority, a committee of the appropriate legislature.

Differences between the consultation draft and the final text

11   (1)   This paragraph applies if there are any differences between —

    (a)   the proposed policies, statements and information contained in the consultation draft, and

    (b)   the policies, statements and information contained in the final text.

    (2)   When the relevant authorities publish the relevant document, they must also publish —

    (a)   a summary of the differences, and

    (b)   a statement of the reasons for them.

Adoption and publication of the relevant document

12   (1)   A policy authority adopts the final text by —

    (a)   deciding that the final text is to be published as the relevant document, and

    (b)   giving notice of that decision to each of the other policy authorities.

    (2)   The relevant document is to be published by the relevant authorities, acting jointly, as soon as reasonably practicable after the final text has been adopted by each of them.

    (3)   If the final text has been adopted by one or more, but not all, of the policy authorities, the authorities that have not adopted the final text must be allowed a reasonable period in which to do so before the relevant document is published.

Validity of document where policy authority participates in preparation but does not adopt

13   (1)   If any policy authority —

    (a)   participates to any extent in the preparation of a relevant document, but

    (b)   does not adopt the final text,

sub-paragraph (2) applies.

    (2)   The participation of the policy authority in the preparation of the relevant document does not affect the validity of —

    (a)   the relevant document, or

    (b)   the adoption of that document by any of the other policy authorities.

SCHEDULE 6   Section 51

MARINE PLANS: PREPARATION AND ADOPTION

Marine plan authority to notify related planning authorities of decision to prepare plan

1   (1) A marine plan authority which decides to prepare a marine plan for a marine plan area must, before beginning to prepare the plan, give notice of its intention to do so to each of the related planning authorities.

      (2) The "related planning authorities" are—

          (a) the Secretary of State (unless the Secretary of State is the marine plan authority);

          (b) any marine plan authority whose marine planning region adjoins or is adjacent to the marine plan area;

          (c) if the Scottish inshore region adjoins or is adjacent to the marine plan area, the Scottish Ministers;

          (d) any local planning authority whose area adjoins or is adjacent to the marine plan area;

          (e) any responsible regional authorities whose region adjoins or is adjacent to the marine plan area.

      (3) In this paragraph—

         "local planning authority" means an authority which is—

          (a) a local planning authority for the purposes of Part 2 of the Planning and Compulsory Purchase Act 2004 (c. 5) (see section 37 of that Act), or

          (b) a planning authority for the purposes of the Town and Country Planning (Scotland) Act 1997 (c. 8) (see section 1 of that Act);

         "responsible regional authorities" has the same meaning as in Part 5 of the Local Democracy, Economic Development and Construction Act 2009 (regional strategy).

Secretary of State to be kept informed of authority's intentions as to certain matters

2   (1) This paragraph applies in any case where a marine plan authority gives notice to the Secretary of State under paragraph 1(2)(a).

      (2) The notice must state whether the marine plan authority proposes to include in the plan provision relating to retained functions (see sections 59 and 60).

      (3) The notice must state whether the marine plan authority proposes so to prepare the marine plan that it will not be in conformity with any MPS which governs marine planning for the marine plan area.

      (4) The marine plan authority must keep the Secretary of State informed (by giving further notices) of any changes that may from time to time occur in its intentions with respect to any of the matters mentioned in sub-paragraph (2) or (3).

Marine plans to be compatible with certain other marine plans and Planning Act plans

3   (1) In preparing or amending a marine plan for a marine plan area in its region, a marine plan authority must take all reasonable steps to secure that the plan

is compatible with the marine plan for any marine plan area (whether or not within its marine planning region) which is related to that area.

(2) The marine plan authority for —

    (a)   the English inshore region, or

    (b)   the Welsh inshore region,

must also take all reasonable steps to secure that any marine plan for a marine plan area in its marine planning region is compatible with the relevant Planning Act plan for any area in England, Wales or Scotland which is related to the marine plan area.

(3) For the purposes of this paragraph, one area is "related to" another if one or more of the following conditions is met—

    (a)   the one area adjoins or is adjacent to the other;

    (b)   the one area lies wholly or partly within the other;

    (c)   the whole or any part of the one area affects or is affected by the whole or any part of the other.

(4) In the case of an area in England or Scotland, the "relevant Planning Act plan" is the development plan.

(5) In the case of an area in Wales, each of the following is a "relevant Planning Act plan" —

    (a)   the development plan;

    (b)   the Wales Spatial Plan.

(6) In this paragraph —

    "development plan"—

        (a)   in the case of an area in England or Wales, is to be read in accordance with section 38(2) to (4) of the Planning and Compulsory Purchase Act 2004 (c. 5);

        (b)   in the case of an area in Scotland, is to be read in accordance with section 24 of the Town and Country Planning (Scotland) Act 1997 (c. 8);

    "the Wales Spatial Plan" means the Wales Spatial Plan under section 60 of the Planning and Compulsory Purchase Act 2004.

Consultation in Northern Ireland

4   (1) In the case of a marine plan for a marine plan area in the Northern Ireland offshore region, the marine plan authority must consult the relevant Northern Ireland departments—

    (a)   during the preparation of the consultation draft under paragraph 11, and

    (b)   during the settling of the text of the plan for adoption and publication under paragraph 15.

(2) For the purposes of this paragraph the relevant Northern Ireland departments are those Northern Ireland departments which have functions in relation to the whole or any part of the UK marine area.

Statement of public participation

5   (1) Before preparing a marine plan for any marine plan area, a marine plan authority must prepare and publish a statement of public participation (an "SPP").

     (2) An SPP is a statement of the policies settled by the marine plan authority for or in connection with the involvement of interested persons in the preparation of the proposed marine plan.

     (3) An SPP must identify (by means of a map or otherwise) the area for which the marine plan is being prepared.

     (4) If the marine plan authority proposes to include provision relating to retained functions, the SPP —
        (a) must state that that is the case, and
        (b) may be published only with the agreement of the Secretary of State.

     (5) An SPP must invite the making of representations in accordance with the SPP as to matters to be included in the proposed marine plan.

     (6) The marine plan authority must publish the SPP in a way calculated to bring it to the attention of interested persons.

     (7) The marine plan authority must take all reasonable steps to comply with the SPP.

     (8) In this paragraph "interested persons" means —
        (a) any persons appearing to the marine plan authority to be likely to be interested in, or affected by, policies proposed to be included in the marine plan, and
        (b) members of the general public.

Further provision about the content of an SPP

6   (1) An SPP must include a proposed timetable.

     (2) The proposed timetable must include such provision as the marine plan authority considers reasonable for each of the following —
        (a) the preparation and publication of the consultation draft under paragraph 11 (including the carrying out of the sustainability appraisal under paragraph 10);
        (b) the making of representations about the consultation draft;
        (c) the consideration of representations under paragraph 12 and the settling of the text of the marine plan for adoption and publication under paragraph 15;
        (d) the adoption and publication of the marine plan under that paragraph.

     (3) An SPP may include provision for or in connection with the holding of public meetings about the consultation draft.

     (4) An SPP must include provision about the making of —
        (a) representations, in response to the invitation issued under paragraph 5(5), about the matters to be included in the proposed marine plan, and
        (b) representations under paragraph 12 about the consultation draft.

(5) The provision to be made under sub-paragraph (4) includes provision about—

    (a)   the manner in which representations may be made, and

    (b)   the time within which representations must be made.

Review and revision of the SPP

7   (1)   The marine plan authority must keep the SPP under review.

    (2)   If at any time the marine plan authority considers it necessary or expedient to revise the SPP, it must do so.

    (3)   The marine plan authority must revise the SPP if—

       (a)   it proposes to include in the marine plan provision relating to retained functions, and

       (b)   the SPP does not already include a statement that that is the case.

    (4)   Where the marine plan authority revises the SPP, it must publish the SPP as revised.

    (5)   In any case where the SPP is required to be revised by virtue of sub-paragraph (3), the revised SPP may be published only with the agreement of the Secretary of State.

    (6)   Any reference in this Schedule to an SPP includes a reference to an SPP as revised.

Advice and assistance

8   (1)   In connection with the preparation of a marine plan, or of any proposals for a marine plan, the marine plan authority may seek advice or assistance from any body or person in relation to any matter in which that body or person has particular expertise.

    (2)   The steps that a marine plan authority may take for the purpose of facilitating the involvement of interested persons in—

       (a)   the development of proposals for inclusion in a proposed marine plan, or

       (b)   consultation in connection with such proposals,

include the convening of groups of persons for such purposes, and in such manner, as the marine plan authority considers appropriate.

    (3)   In this paragraph "interested persons" has the same meaning as in paragraph 5.

Matters to which a marine plan authority is to have regard in preparing a marine plan

9   (1)   The matters to which a marine plan authority is to have regard in preparing a marine plan include each of the matters in sub-paragraph (2).

    (2)   Those matters are—

       (a)   the requirement under section 51(6) for a marine plan to be in conformity with any MPS which governs marine planning for the marine plan area, unless relevant considerations indicate otherwise,

    (b)   the duties imposed by paragraph 3(1) and (2) with respect to securing compatibility with marine plans or Planning Act plans for areas which are related to the marine plan area,

    (c)   the effect which any proposal for inclusion in the plan is likely to have on any area which is related to the marine plan area;

    (d)   the results of the review required by section 54,

    (e)   the SPP,

    (f)   any representations made in response to the invitation issued pursuant to sub-paragraph (5) of paragraph 5,

    (g)   any advice received under paragraph 8(1),

    (h)   any plan (not falling within paragraph 3(1) or (2)) prepared by a public or local authority in connection with the management or use of the sea or the coast, or of marine or coastal resources, in the marine plan area or in any adjoining or adjacent area in England or Wales, Scotland or Northern Ireland,

    (i)   the powers and duties of the Crown Estate Commissioners under the Crown Estate Act 1961 (c. 55),

and such other matters as the marine plan authority considers relevant.

(3)   For the purposes of this paragraph, one area is related to another if one or more of the following conditions is met—

    (a)   the one area adjoins or is adjacent to the other;

    (b)   the one area lies wholly or partly within the other;

    (c)   the whole or any part of the one area affects or is affected by the whole or any part of the other.

Sustainability appraisal

10   (1)   A marine plan authority preparing a marine plan must carry out an appraisal of the sustainability of its proposals for inclusion in the plan.

(2)   The authority may proceed with those proposals only if it considers that the results of the appraisal indicate that it is appropriate to do so.

(3)   The marine plan authority must publish a report of the results of the appraisal.

(4)   The report is to be published when the marine plan authority publishes the consultation draft under paragraph 11.

Preparation and publication of a consultation draft

11   (1)   A marine plan authority preparing a marine plan must publish a draft containing its proposals for inclusion in the plan (the "consultation draft").

(2)   If the draft includes provision relating to retained functions, it may be published only with the agreement of the Secretary of State.

(3)   The marine plan authority must publish the consultation draft in such manner as it considers appropriate.

(4)   The marine plan authority must also take such steps as it considers appropriate to secure that the proposals contained in the consultation draft are brought to the attention of interested persons.

(5) In this paragraph "interested persons" has the same meaning as in paragraph 5.

Representations about the consultation draft

12   (1) Any person may make representations about the consultation draft.

     (2) Any such representations are to be made in accordance with the SPP.

     (3) If any representations are made about the consultation draft, the marine plan authority must consider them in the course of settling the text of the marine plan for adoption and publication under paragraph 15.

Independent investigation

13   (1) A marine plan authority which has published a consultation draft in accordance with paragraph 11 must consider appointing an independent person to investigate the proposals contained in that draft and to report on them.

     (2) In deciding whether to appoint such a person, the marine plan authority must have regard to —
        (a) any representations received about the matters to be included in the proposed marine plan, in response to the invitation issued pursuant to paragraph 5(5),
        (b) any representations received about the proposals published in the consultation draft,
        (c) the extent to which matters raised by representations falling within paragraph (b) have not been resolved,
     and such other matters as the marine plan authority considers relevant.

     (3) Any person so appointed must —
        (a) make recommendations, and
        (b) give reasons for the recommendations.

     (4) The marine plan authority must publish the recommendations and the reasons given for them.

Matters to which marine plan authority to have regard in settling text for adoption etc

14   A marine plan authority settling the text of a marine plan for adoption and publication under paragraph 15 must have regard to —
        (a) any recommendations made by any person appointed under paragraph 13,
        (b) the reasons given by any such person for any such recommendations,
     and any other matters that the marine plan authority considers relevant.

Adoption and publication of a marine plan

15   (1) A marine plan is "adopted" by a marine plan authority when the authority has decided to publish the plan (and "adopt" and related expressions are to be read accordingly).

     (2) A marine plan may be so adopted only by, or with the agreement of, the Secretary of State.

(3) Sub-paragraph (2) does not apply in the case of a marine plan for the Welsh inshore region if the plan does not include provision relating to retained functions.

(4) The conferral on a devolved authority by this Part of functions whose exercise is subject to the agreement of the Secretary of State under sub-paragraph (2) does not affect any functions, or the exercise of any functions, of the devolved authority apart from this Part (whenever conferred or imposed).

(5) In sub-paragraph (4) "devolved authority" means —
   (a) the Scottish Ministers;
   (b) the Welsh Ministers;
   (c) the Department of the Environment in Northern Ireland.

(6) The marine plan which a marine plan authority decides to publish may be —
   (a) the same as the proposals published in the consultation draft, or
   (b) those proposals with such modifications as the marine plan authority thinks fit.

(7) A marine plan authority which adopts a marine plan must publish the plan as soon as reasonably practicable after its adoption, together with statements of each of the following —
   (a) any modifications that have been made to the proposals published in the consultation draft,
   (b) the reasons for those modifications,
   (c) if any recommendations made by any independent person appointed under paragraph 13 have not been implemented in the marine plan, the reasons why those recommendations have not been implemented.

SCHEDULE 7
Section 97

FURTHER PROVISION ABOUT CIVIL SANCTIONS UNDER PART 4

Interpretation

1   In this Schedule "civil sanction" means a fixed monetary penalty or a variable monetary penalty.

Fixed monetary penalties: other sanctions

2 (1) Provision under section 93 must secure that, in a case where a notice of intent referred to in section 94(2)(a) is served on a person —
   (a) no criminal proceedings for the offence to which the notice relates may be instituted against the person in respect of the act or omission to which the notice relates before the end of the period in which the person may discharge liability to the fixed monetary penalty pursuant to section 94(2)(b), and
   (b) if the person so discharges liability, the person may not at any time be convicted of the offence to which the notice relates in relation to that act or omission.

(2) Provision under section 93 must also secure that, in a case where a fixed monetary penalty is imposed on a person—

    (a) that person may not at any time be convicted of the offence in relation to which the penalty is imposed in respect of the act or omission giving rise to the penalty;

    (b) the enforcement authority may not issue a compliance notice or a remediation notice to that person in respect of the act or omission giving rise to the penalty.

Variable monetary penalties: other sanctions

3   Provision under section 95 must secure that, in a case where a variable monetary penalty is imposed on a person—

    (a) that person may not at any time be convicted of the offence in relation to which the penalty is imposed in respect of the act or omission giving rise to the penalty;

    (b) the enforcement authority may not issue a compliance notice to that person in respect of the act or omission giving rise to the penalty.

Combination of sanctions

4   (1) Provision may not be made under section 93 and section 95 conferring powers on an enforcement authority in relation to the same offence unless it secures that—

    (a) the authority may not serve a notice of intent referred to in section 94(2)(a) on a person in relation to any act or omission where a variable monetary penalty has been imposed on that person in relation to that act or omission, and

    (b) the authority may not serve a notice of intent referred to in section 96(2)(a) on a person in relation to any act or omission where—

        (i) a fixed monetary penalty has been imposed on that person in relation to that act or omission, or

        (ii) the person has discharged liability to a fixed monetary penalty in relation to that act or omission pursuant to section 94(2)(b).

(2) Provision under section 93 which results in an enforcement authority having power to impose a fixed monetary penalty or to issue a stop notice in relation to the same offence must secure that—

    (a) the authority may not serve a notice of intent referred to in section 94(2)(a) on a person in relation to any act or omission where a stop notice has been served on that person in relation to that act or omission, and

    (b) the authority may not serve a stop notice on a person in relation to any act or omission where—

        (i) a fixed monetary penalty has been imposed on that person in relation to that act or omission, or

        (ii) the person has discharged liability to a fixed monetary penalty in relation to that act or omission pursuant to section 94(2)(b).

Monetary penalties

5   (1) An order under section 93 or 95 which confers power on an enforcement authority to require a person to pay a fixed monetary penalty or a variable monetary penalty may include provision—

(a) for early payment discounts;

(b) for the payment of interest or other financial penalties for late payment of the penalty, such interest or other financial penalties not in total to exceed the amount of that penalty;

(c) for enforcement of the penalty.

(2) Provision under sub-paragraph (1)(c) may include—

(a) provision for the enforcement authority to recover the penalty, and any interest or other financial penalty for late payment, as a civil debt;

(b) provision for the penalty, and any interest or other financial penalty for late payment, to be recoverable, on the order of a court, as if payable under a court order.

Costs recovery

6   (1) Provision under section 95 may include provision for an enforcement authority, by notice, to require a person on whom a variable monetary penalty is imposed to pay the costs incurred by the enforcement authority in relation to the imposition of the penalty up to the time of its imposition.

(2) In sub-paragraph (1) the references to costs include in particular—

(a) investigation costs;

(b) administration costs;

(c) costs of obtaining expert advice (including legal advice).

(3) Provision under this paragraph must secure that, in any case where a notice requiring payment of costs is served—

(a) the notice specifies the amount required to be paid;

(b) the enforcement authority may be required to provide a detailed breakdown of that amount;

(c) the person required to pay costs is not liable to pay any costs shown by the person to have been unnecessarily incurred;

(d) the person required to pay costs may appeal against—

(i) the decision of the enforcement authority to impose the requirement to pay costs;

(ii) the decision of the enforcement authority as to the amount of those costs.

(4) Provision under this paragraph may include the provision referred to in sub-paragraphs (1)(b) and (c) and (2) of paragraph 5.

(5) Provision under this paragraph must secure that an enforcement authority is required to publish guidance about how it will exercise the power conferred by the provision.

Appeals

7   (1) An order under section 93 or 95 may not provide for the making of an appeal other than to—

(a)   the First-Tier Tribunal, or

(b)   another tribunal created under an enactment.

This sub-paragraph does not apply in the case of an order made by the Scottish Ministers.

(2) In sub-paragraph (1)(b)—

"enactment" includes an enactment contained in, or in an instrument made under, Northern Ireland legislation;

"tribunal" does not include an ordinary court of law.

(3) An order under section 93 or 95 which makes provision for an appeal in relation to the imposition of any requirement or service of any notice may include—

(a)   provision suspending the requirement or notice pending determination of the appeal;

(b)   provision as to the powers of any person to whom the appeal is made;

(c)   provision as to how any sum payable in pursuance of a decision of that person is to be recoverable.

(4) The provision referred to in sub-paragraph (3)(b) includes provision conferring on the person to whom the appeal is made power—

(a)   to withdraw the requirement or notice;

(b)   to confirm the requirement or notice;

(c)   to take such steps as the enforcement authority could take in relation to the act or omission giving rise to the requirement or notice;

(d)   to remit the decision whether to confirm the requirement or notice, or any matter relating to that decision, to the enforcement authority;

(e)   to award costs.

Consultation

8   (1) Before making an order under section 93 or 95, the appropriate licensing authority must consult the following (in addition to any persons who must be consulted under paragraph 9)—

(a)   the enforcement authority to which the order relates,

(b)   such organisations as appear to the licensing authority to be representative of persons substantially affected by the proposals, and

(c)   such other persons as the licensing authority considers appropriate.

(2) If, as a result of any consultation required by sub-paragraph (1), it appears to the licensing authority that it is appropriate substantially to change the whole or any part of the proposals, the licensing authority must undertake such further consultation with respect to the changes as it considers appropriate.

(3) If, before the day on which this Schedule comes into force, any consultation was undertaken which, had it been undertaken after that day, would to any

extent have satisfied the requirements of this paragraph, those requirements may to that extent be taken to have been satisfied.

Guidance as to use of civil sanctions

9   (1) Where power is conferred on an enforcement authority under section 93 or 95 to impose a civil sanction in relation to an offence the provision conferring the power must secure the results in sub-paragraph (2).

   (2) Those results are that—
       (a) the enforcement authority must publish guidance about its use of the sanction,
       (b) in the case of guidance relating to a fixed monetary penalty or a variable monetary penalty, the guidance must contain the relevant information,
       (c) the enforcement authority must revise the guidance where appropriate,
       (d) the enforcement authority must consult such persons as the provision may specify before publishing any guidance or revised guidance, and
       (e) the enforcement authority must have regard to the guidance or revised guidance in exercising its functions.

   (3) In the case of guidance relating to a fixed monetary penalty, the relevant information referred to in sub-paragraph (2)(b) is information as to—
       (a) the circumstances in which the penalty is likely to be imposed,
       (b) the circumstances in which it may not be imposed,
       (c) the amount of the penalty,
       (d) how liability for the penalty may be discharged and the effect of discharge, and
       (e) rights to make representations and objections and rights of appeal.

   (4) In the case of guidance relating to a variable monetary penalty, the relevant information referred to in sub-paragraph (2)(b) is information as to—
       (a) the circumstances in which the penalty is likely to be imposed,
       (b) the circumstances in which it may not be imposed,
       (c) the matters likely to be taken into account by the enforcement authority in determining the amount of the penalty (including, where relevant, any discounts for voluntary reporting of non-compliance), and
       (d) rights to make representations and objections and rights of appeal.

Guidance as to enforcement of offences

10   (1) Where power is conferred on an enforcement authority under section 93 or 95 to impose a civil sanction in relation to an offence the enforcement authority must prepare and publish guidance about how the offence is enforced.

   (2) The guidance must include guidance as to—
       (a) the sanctions (including criminal sanctions) to which a person who commits the offence may be liable,
       (b) the action which the enforcement authority may take to enforce the offence, whether by virtue of section 93 or 95 or otherwise, and

     (c)   the circumstances in which the enforcement authority is likely to take any such action.

(3)   An enforcement authority may from time to time revise guidance published by it under this paragraph and publish the revised guidance.

(4)   The enforcement authority must consult such persons as it considers appropriate before publishing any guidance or revised guidance under this paragraph.

Publication of enforcement action

11   (1)   Where power is conferred on an enforcement authority under section 93 or 95 to impose a civil sanction in relation to an offence, the provision conferring the power must, subject to this paragraph, secure the result in sub-paragraph (2).

(2)   That result is that the enforcement authority must from time to time publish reports specifying—

    (a)   the cases in which the civil sanction has been imposed,

    (b)   where the civil sanction is a fixed monetary penalty, the cases in which liability to the penalty has been discharged pursuant to section 94(2)(b), and

    (c)   where the civil sanction is a variable monetary penalty, the cases in which an undertaking referred to in section 96(5) is accepted from such a person.

(3)   In sub-paragraph (2)(a), the reference to cases in which the civil sanction has been imposed does not include cases where the sanction has been imposed but overturned on appeal.

(4)   The provision conferring the power need not secure the result in sub-paragraph (2) in cases where the appropriate licensing authority considers that it would be inappropriate to do so.

Payment of penalties into Consolidated Fund etc

12   (1)   Where pursuant to any provision made under section 93 or 95 an enforcement authority receives—

    (a)   a fixed monetary penalty or a variable monetary penalty, or

    (b)   any interest or other financial penalty for late payment of such a penalty,

the authority must pay it into the relevant Fund.

(2)   In sub-paragraph (1) "the relevant Fund" means—

    (a)   in a case where the authority has functions only in relation to Wales, the Welsh Consolidated Fund;

    (b)   in a case where the authority has functions only in relation to Scotland, the Scottish Consolidated Fund;

    (c)   in a case where the authority has functions only in relation to Northern Ireland, the Consolidated Fund of Northern Ireland;

    (d)   in any other case, the Consolidated Fund.

Disclosure of information

13 (1) Information held by or on behalf of a person mentioned in sub-paragraph (2) may be disclosed to an enforcement authority on whom powers are conferred under section 93 or 95 where—

  (a) the person has an enforcement function in relation to an offence, and

  (b) the information is disclosed for the purpose of the exercise by the enforcement authority of any powers conferred on it under any of those sections in relation to that offence.

  (2) The persons are—

  (a) the Crown Prosecution Service,

  (b) a member of a police force in England or Wales,

  (c) a Procurator Fiscal,

  (d) a constable of a police force in Scotland,

  (e) the Public Prosecution Service for Northern Ireland, or

  (f) a member of the Police Service of Northern Ireland.

  (3) It is immaterial for the purposes of sub-paragraph (1) whether the information was obtained before or after the coming into force of this paragraph.

  (4) A disclosure under this paragraph is not to be taken to breach any restriction on the disclosure of information (however imposed).

  (5) Nothing in this paragraph authorises the making of a disclosure in contravention of—

  (a) the Data Protection Act 1998 (c. 29), or

  (b) Part 1 of the Regulation of Investigatory Powers Act 2000 (c. 23).

  (6) This paragraph does not affect a power to disclose which exists apart from this paragraph.

SCHEDULE 8   Section 112(1)

LICENSING: MINOR AND CONSEQUENTIAL AMENDMENTS

PART 1

CONSEQUENTIAL AMENDMENTS

The Coast Protection Act 1949

1 (1) The Coast Protection Act 1949 (c. 74) is amended as follows.

  (2) Omit Part 2 (provisions for safety of navigation).

  (3) In section 49(1) (interpretation), in the definitions of "sea" and "seashore", for "subsections (2) and (2A)" substitute "subsection (2)".

The Food and Environment Protection Act 1985

2 (1) The Food and Environment Protection Act 1985 (c. 48) is amended as

2698

Marine and Coastal Access Act 2009 (c. 23)
Schedule 8 — Licensing: minor and consequential amendments
Part 1 — Consequential amendments

follows.

(2) In section 5 (requirement for licences) —

    (a)   in paragraph (a), for "United Kingdom waters or United Kingdom controlled waters" substitute "the Scottish inshore region";

    (b)   omit paragraph (b);

    (c)   in paragraph (e)(i), for "United Kingdom waters or United Kingdom controlled waters" substitute "the Scottish inshore region";

    (d)   omit paragraph (e)(ii) and the preceding "or";

    (e)   in paragraph (f), for "the United Kingdom or United Kingdom waters" substitute "Scotland or the Scottish inshore region";

    (f)   in paragraph (g), for "the United Kingdom" substitute "Scotland";

    (g)   in paragraph (h), for "the United Kingdom or United Kingdom waters" substitute "Scotland or the Scottish inshore region".

(3) In section 6(1) (requirements for licences for incineration at sea etc) —

    (a)   in paragraph (a)(i), for "United Kingdom waters or United Kingdom controlled waters" substitute "the Scottish inshore region";

    (b)   omit paragraph (a)(ii) and the preceding "or";

    (c)   in paragraph (b), for "the United Kingdom or United Kingdom waters" substitute "Scotland or the Scottish inshore region".

(4) In section 7A (exclusion of Part 2 for certain purposes) —

    (a)   in subsection (4), for paragraphs (a) and (b) substitute "the Scottish inshore region.";

    (b)   omit subsection (5).

(5) In section 8 (licences) —

    (a)   in subsection (4)(b), for "United Kingdom waters" substitute "the Scottish inshore region";

    (b)   in subsection (6), omit "evidence, and in Scotland".

(6) In section 9 (licensing offences) —

    (a)   in subsection (1) (which is expressed to be subject to subsections (3) to (7)) for "to (7)" substitute ", (4)";

    (b)   omit subsections (5) to (7).

(7) In section 11 (enforcement powers) —

    (a)   in subsection (2) —

        (i)   in paragraph (a), for "the United Kingdom" substitute "Scotland";

        (ii)   for paragraphs (b) and (c) substitute —

        "(b)   vessels, aircraft, hovercraft and marine structures in Scotland or within the Scottish inshore region,";

    (b)   in subsection (3), for paragraphs (a) and (b) substitute "any vessel within the Scottish inshore region".

(8) In section 21 (offences) omit subsection (8).

(9) In section 24(1) (interpretation) —

    (a)   omit the definition of "adjacent to Scotland";

    (b)   omit the definition of "Gas Importation and Storage Zone";

    (c)   in the definition of "licensing authority" —

        (i)   omit paragraph (a);

(ii) in paragraph (b)(i), for "United Kingdom waters, or United Kingdom controlled waters, adjacent to Scotland" substitute "waters within the Scottish inshore region";

(iii) in paragraph (b)(ii) and (iii), for "United Kingdom waters, or United Kingdom controlled waters, adjacent to Scotland" in each place where it appears substitute "the Scottish inshore region";

(iv) in paragraph (b)(iii), omit "and the functions of that authority under this sub-paragraph shall be treated as exercisable in or as regards Scotland and may be exercised separately";

(d) after the definition of "plants" insert—

""Scottish inshore region" has the same meaning as in the Marine and Coastal Access Act 2009 (see section 322 of that Act);";

(e) omit the definitions of "United Kingdom waters" and "United Kingdom controlled waters".

The Government of Wales Act 2006

3 (1) In Schedule 3 to the Government of Wales Act 2006 (c. 32) (transfer etc of functions: further provisions) paragraph 4 (power to direct that certain functions exercisable by a Minister of the Crown are exercisable in relation to Welsh controlled waters only after consultation with the Welsh Ministers) is amended as follows.

(2) In sub-paragraph (1) (which extends the power conferred by section 58(1)(c) of that Act and specifies the enactments to which it applies)—

(a) omit paragraph (a) (Part 2 of the Food and Environment Protection Act 1985 (c. 48)), and

(b) after paragraph (b) insert—

"(c) the provisions of Parts 4 and 8 of the Marine and Coastal Access Act 2009 (marine licensing and enforcement) specified in sub-paragraph (1A), or

(d) regulations under section 73 of that Act (appeals),".

(3) After sub-paragraph (1) insert—

"(1A) The provisions of the Marine and Coastal Access Act 2009 mentioned in sub-paragraph (1)(c) are—

(a) sections 67(1) to (5), 69(1), (3) and (4), 71(1) to (3) and 72(1) to (3) (marine licences), so far as relating to items 1 to 6 and 11 to 13 in section 66(1) of that Act (licensable marine activities);

(b) section 101 (registers);

(c) sections 106 and 91(7)(c) (power to take remedial action, and power to require payment of sum representing reasonable expenses of taking such action);

(d) section 107 (power to test, and charge for testing, certain substances);

(e) sections 235(3) and 240(1)(c) (enforcement officers).".

The Planning Act 2008

4 (1) The Planning Act 2008 (c. 29) is amended as follows.

2700

Marine and Coastal Access Act 2009 (c. 23)
Schedule 8 – Licensing: minor and consequential amendments
Part 1 – Consequential amendments

(2) After section 149 insert—

"149A Deemed consent under a marine licence

(1)　An order granting development consent may include provision deeming a marine licence to have been issued under Part 4 of the Marine and Coastal Access Act 2009 (marine licensing) for any activity only if the activity is to be carried out wholly in one or more of the areas specified in subsection (2).

(2)　The areas are—

   (a)　England,

   (b)　waters adjacent to England up to the seaward limits of the territorial sea,

   (c)　an exclusive economic zone, except any part of an exclusive economic zone in relation to which the Scottish Ministers have functions,

   (d)　a Renewable Energy Zone, except any part of a Renewable Energy Zone in relation to which the Scottish Ministers have functions,

   (e)　an area designated under section 1(7) of the Continental Shelf Act 1964, except any part of that area which is within a part of an exclusive economic zone or Renewable Energy Zone in relation to which the Scottish Ministers have functions.

(3)　Subsections (4) and (5) apply if an order granting development consent includes provision—

   (a)　deeming a marine licence to have been granted under Part 4 of the Marine and Coastal Access Act 2009 subject to specified conditions, and

   (b)　deeming those conditions to have been attached to the marine licence by the Secretary of State under that Part.

(4)　A person who fails to comply with such a condition does not commit an offence under section 161 of this Act.

(5)　Sections 68 (notice of applications) and 69(3) and (5) (representations) of the Marine and Coastal Access Act 2009 do not apply in relation to the deemed marine licence.".

(3) In section 161 (breach of terms of order granting development consent), in subsection (2), for "sections 148(4) and 149(4)" substitute "section 149A(4)".

(4) In Schedule 4, in paragraph 1(11) (power to correct certain errors or omissions in development consent decisions) for the words from "any of paragraphs" to the end of the sub-paragraph substitute "paragraph 30A or 30B of Schedule 5 (deemed marine licence under Marine and Coastal Access Act 2009).".

(5) In Schedule 5 (provision relating to, or to matters ancillary to, development) after paragraph 30 insert—

   "30A　Deeming a marine licence under Part 4 of the Marine and Coastal Access Act 2009 to have been given by the Secretary of State for activities specified in the order and subject to such conditions as may be specified in the order.

      30B   Deeming any such conditions to have been attached to the marine licence by the Secretary of State under that Part.".

(6)   In Schedule 6 (changes to, and revocation of, orders granting development consent) in—

    (a)   paragraph 2(13) (power to make non-material changes to development consent order not to apply in relation to deemed consents and licences), and

    (b)   paragraph 5(6) (power to change or revoke development consent order not to apply in relation to deemed consents and licences),

for the words from "any of paragraphs" to the end of the sub-paragraph substitute "paragraph 30A or 30B of Schedule 5 (deemed marine licence under Marine and Coastal Access Act 2009).".

(7)   The following provisions cease to have effect—

    (a)   section 148 (deemed consent under section 34 of the Coast Protection Act 1949 (c. 74)),

    (b)   section 149 (deemed consent under Part 2 of the Food and Environment Protection Act 1985 (c. 48)),

    (c)   in Schedule 5, paragraphs 27 to 30 (which relate to deemed consents).

PART 2

OTHER AMENDMENTS

The Food and Environment Protection Act 1985

Electronic communications apparatus: operations in tidal waters etc

5   In the Food and Environment Protection Act 1985 after section 8 (licences) insert—

"8A   Electronic communications apparatus: operations in tidal waters etc

(1)   The Scottish Ministers must not issue a licence to carry out any operation which amounts to, or involves the exercise of, a right conferred by paragraph 11 of the electronic communications code set out in Schedule 2 to the Telecommunications Act 1984 unless they are satisfied that adequate compensation arrangements have been made.

(2)   For the purposes of subsection (1) "adequate compensation arrangements" are adequate arrangements for compensating any persons—

    (a)   who appear to the Scottish Ministers to be owners of interests in the tidal water or lands on, under or over which the right is to be exercised,

    (b)   for any loss or damage sustained by those persons in consequence of the operation being carried out.".

Electronic communications: emergency works

6   (1)   Section 9 of the Food and Environment Protection Act 1985 (offences relating to the licensing system) is amended as follows.

2702

Marine and Coastal Access Act 2009 (c. 23)
Schedule 8 — Licensing: minor and consequential amendments
Part 2 — Other amendments

(2) In subsection (1) (which is expressed to be subject to certain later subsections) in the words preceding paragraph (a), before "below" insert "and (8)".

(3) After subsection (7) insert—

"(8) It shall be a defence for a person charged with an offence under subsection (1) in relation to any operation to prove that—

    (a) for the purposes of paragraph 23 of the electronic communications code (undertaker's works), the person is the operator or a relevant undertaker, and

    (b) the activity was carried out for the purpose of executing emergency works, within the meaning of that code.

In this subsection "the electronic communications code" means the code set out in Schedule 2 to the Telecommunications Act 1984.".

The Petroleum Act 1998

Application of Part 3 in relation to submarine pipelines

7 (1) Section 24 of the Petroleum Act 1998 (c. 17) (application of Part 3) is amended as follows.

(2) After subsection (2) insert—

"(2A) If a pipeline—

    (a) is specified in an order made by the Secretary of State under this subsection, or

    (b) is of a description so specified,

the pipeline shall be disregarded for the purposes of this Part of this Act (other than this subsection) or shall be so disregarded while any specified condition is satisfied.".

(3) After subsection (3) insert—

"(3A) The Secretary of State may by order provide that specified provisions of this Part of this Act shall apply, subject to such modifications (if any) as are specified, in relation to a controlled pipeline—

    (a) which is specified or of a specified description, and

    (b) which meets the conditions in subsection (3B).

(3B) The conditions are—

    (a) that the pipeline is used in connection with exploration for, or exploitation of, petroleum, or the importation of petroleum into the United Kingdom;

    (b) that, by virtue of the date when construction of the pipeline was begun, section 14(1)(b) would not apply in relation to use of the pipeline but for an order under this subsection.".

(4) In subsection (5) (negative resolution procedure) after "an order under subsection (2)" insert ", (2A) or (3A)".

(5) Any authorisation issued under section 14(1)(b) of the Petroleum Act 1998 (use of certain pipelines) continues to have effect notwithstanding the provisions of any order under section 24(2A) of that Act.

Marine and Coastal Access Act 2009 (c. 23)
Schedule 8 — Licensing: minor and consequential amendments
Part 2 — Other amendments

2703

(6) Where an order under subsection (3A) of section 24 of the Petroleum Act 1998 (c. 17) comes into force in relation to a pipeline, the Secretary of State must grant an authorisation under section 14(1)(b) of that Act in respect of the conveyance, on and after the day on which the order comes into force, of any substances for which the pipeline was normally used before the coming into force of the order.

(7) Sub-paragraph (6) is without prejudice to the provision that may be included in the authorisation with respect to information to be provided by the owner of the pipeline.

Exception of certain pipelines from being "submarine pipelines" for the purposes of Part 4

8 (1) Section 45 of the Petroleum Act 1998 (interpretation of Part 4) is amended as follows.

(2) In the definition of "submarine pipeline", after the paragraphs, insert—
"but does not include any such pipeline which, by virtue of an order under subsection (2A) of section 24, is to be disregarded for the purposes of Part 3 of this Act (other than that subsection).".

SCHEDULE 9   Section 112(2)

LICENSING: TRANSITIONAL PROVISION RELATING TO PART 4

PART 1

INTERPRETATION

1   In this Schedule—
"the commencement date" means the date on which section 65 comes into force;
"the CPA" means the Coast Protection Act 1949 (c. 74);
"FEPA" means the Food and Environment Protection Act 1985 (c. 48).

PART 2

COAST PROTECTION ACT 1949

Consents previously given and outstanding applications

2 (1) Any consent given under subsection (1) of section 34 of the CPA which—
   (a)   is in effect immediately before the commencement date, and
   (b)   relates to an operation which—
        (i)   falls within that subsection, and
        (ii) is a licensable marine activity,
has effect on and after that date as if it were a marine licence granted by the appropriate licensing authority in relation to that activity (a "deemed licence").

(2) In accordance with sub-paragraph (1)—

2704

Marine and Coastal Access Act 2009 (c. 23)
Schedule 9 — Licensing: transitional provision relating to Part 4
Part 2 — Coast Protection Act 1949

    (a)   a consent given for a specified period remains in force (subject to the provisions of this Part of this Act) for so much of that period as falls after the commencement date;

    (b)   any condition subject to which a consent under subsection (1) of section 34 of the CPA has been given has effect as if it were a condition attached to the deemed licence;

    (c)   any provision made under subsection (4) of that section in respect of a consent has effect as if it were provision made under section 71(4)(a) of this Act in respect of the deemed licence;

    (d)   any condition having effect under section 34(4A)(b) of the CPA has effect as if it were such a condition as is mentioned in section 71(5) of this Act.

(3)   Any reference in sub-paragraph (1) or (2) to a consent given under section 34(1) of the CPA, or to a condition subject to which such a consent is given, includes a reference to a consent deemed to have been given, or a condition deemed to have been imposed, by virtue of provision included in an order granting development consent (see paragraphs 27 and 28 of Schedule 5 to the Planning Act 2008 (c. 29)).

(4)   Any application for consent under subsection (1) of section 34 of the CPA which—

    (a)   is made before the commencement date, and

    (b)   relates to an operation which—

        (i)   falls within that subsection, and

        (ii)   is a licensable marine activity,

has effect on and after that date as if it were an application for a marine licence made to the appropriate licensing authority in relation to that activity.

Safety requirements

3   The repeal of section 36A of the CPA does not affect the operation of that provision in relation to anything occurring before the date on which that repeal takes effect.

PART 3

FOOD AND ENVIRONMENT PROTECTION ACT 1985

Licences previously issued and outstanding applications

4   (1)   Any licence having effect under Part 2 of FEPA (a "FEPA licence") which—

    (a)   is in effect immediately before the commencement date, and

    (b)   relates to the doing of anything which—

        (i)   falls within section 5 or 6 of that Act, and

        (ii)   is an activity which, on or after that date, must not be carried on except in accordance with a marine licence granted by the appropriate licensing authority,

has effect on and after that date as if it were a marine licence granted by the appropriate licensing authority in relation to that activity (a "deemed licence").

(2)   In accordance with sub-paragraph (1)—

Marine and Coastal Access Act 2009 (c. 23)
Schedule 9 – Licensing: transitional provision relating to Part 4
Part 3 – Food and Environment Protection Act 1985

2705

> (a) a licence issued for a specified period remains in force (subject to the provisions of this Part of this Act) for so much of that period as falls after the commencement date;
>
> (b) any provision included in a FEPA licence by virtue of section 8(3) or (4) of that Act has effect as if it were a condition attached to the deemed licence.

(3) Any reference in sub-paragraph (1) or (2) to a FEPA licence, or to a provision included in such a licence, includes a reference to a licence deemed to have been issued, or a provision deemed to have been included, by virtue of provision included in a order granting development consent (see paragraphs 29 and 30 of Schedule 5 to the Planning Act 2008 (c. 29)).

(4) Any application for a FEPA licence which—

> (a) was made before the commencement date, and
>
> (b) relates to an activity which—
>
> > (i) falls within section 5 or 6 of FEPA, and
> >
> > (ii) on or after that date, must not be carried on except in accordance with a marine licence granted by the appropriate licensing authority,

has effect on and after that date as if it were an application for a marine licence made to the appropriate licensing authority in relation to that activity.

(5) An applicant who has paid a fee under section 8(7) or (8) of FEPA must not be charged a fee under section 67(1)(b) of this Act in respect of the deemed licence.

5 (1) Despite the amendments made by paragraph 2 of Schedule 8, paragraphs 5 to 17 of Schedule 3 to FEPA continue to apply in any case where a person—

> (a) makes written representations (in accordance with paragraph 5 of that Schedule) before the commencement date, or
>
> (b) within the period of 28 days ending with that date, is issued with a FEPA licence or receives notice under paragraph 1, 3 or 4 of that Schedule.

(2) Sub-paragraph (1) has effect in place of any provision made under section 73 of this Act for appeals against any decision of an appropriate licensing authority on an application for a licence.

Remedial action

6 The amendments made by paragraph 2 of Schedule 8 do not affect the operation of section 10 of FEPA in relation to anything carried out otherwise than under and in accordance with a FEPA licence before the commencement date.

Register

7 (1) This paragraph applies in any case where—

> (a) immediately before the commencement date, an authority was required to maintain under section 14 of FEPA a register (the "FEPA register") containing information of any particular description in respect of any particular area,

2706
Marine and Coastal Access Act 2009 (c. 23)
Schedule 9 – Licensing: transitional provision relating to Part 4
Part 3 – Food and Environment Protection Act 1985

  (b) on that date the authority ceased to be required to maintain a register under that section containing information of that description in respect of that area, and

  (c) as from that date the authority is required to maintain a register under section 101 of this Act (the "new register") containing information in respect of that area.

(2) In any such case, the authority must include in the new register any information falling within sub-paragraph (1)(a) that was contained (or was required to have been contained) in the FEPA register immediately before the commencement date.

(3) For the purpose of giving effect to this paragraph —

  (a) references in section 101 to marine licences are to be read as including references to FEPA licences, and

  (b) references in that section to this Part of this Act or to any provision of this Part are to be read as including references to Part 2 of FEPA or to the corresponding provision of that Part.

Channel Islands and British overseas territories

8   (1) In this paragraph "relevant territory" means any of the following —

  (a) any of the Channel Islands;

  (b) any British overseas territory.

(2) An Order in Council under section 26 of FEPA which is in force immediately before the commencement date remains in force, and may be revoked, amended or re-enacted, as if that section had not been repealed.

(3) If it appears to Her Majesty —

  (a) that provision with respect to the licensing of marine activities has been made in the law of any relevant territory, and

  (b) that that provision was made otherwise than by virtue of an Order in Council under section 323 extending provisions of this Act,

Her Majesty may by Order in Council repeal any provisions of Part 2 or 4 of FEPA as they have effect as part of the law of that territory.

PART 4

MISCELLANEOUS

Dredging

9   (1) During the relevant transitional period, section 65 does not apply in respect of the carrying on by a person of a dredging operation —

  (a) which falls within item 9 in section 66(1) of this Act, but

  (b) which meets the conditions in sub-paragraph (2).

(2) The conditions are that the dredging operation —

  (a) does not fall within section 34 of the CPA,

  (b) is not an activity for which a licence is required under Part 2 of FEPA, and

  (c) is not excluded from this paragraph by virtue of an order under section 320.

Marine and Coastal Access Act 2009 (c. 23)   2707
Schedule 9 — Licensing: transitional provision relating to Part 4
Part 4 — Miscellaneous

(3) The references in sub-paragraph (2) to section 34 of the CPA and Part 2 of FEPA are references to those provisions as they would apply but for this Act.

(4) The "relevant transitional period", in the case of any person and any dredging operation, —

    (a) is the period of one year beginning with the commencement date, but

    (b) if a marine licence which authorises the carrying on of the dredging operation by the person comes into force (or has come into force) at any time before the end of that period, the transitional period ends with the coming into force of that licence.

Water Resources Act 1991

10   The amendment made by section 82 of this Act applies to any application for consent under section 109 of the Water Resources Act 1991 (c. 57) which is submitted, but not determined or withdrawn, before the date on which that section comes into force (as well as to any application submitted after that date).

Electronic Communications Code: England and Wales

11 (1) In this paragraph—

    (a) "the Code" means the Electronic Communications Code set out in Schedule 2 to the Telecommunications Act 1984 (c. 12);

    (b) "communications approval" means an approval under paragraph 11 of the Code;

    (c) "transitional date" means the date on which the repeals made in paragraph 11 of the Code by this Act take effect in relation to England and Wales.

(2) Subsections (3) to (5) apply to any communications approval (a "qualifying approval") —

    (a) which is in effect immediately before the transitional date, and

    (b) which relates to any works, falling within sub-paragraph (3) or (4) of paragraph 11 of the Code, the execution of which on or after that date is a licensable marine activity.

(3) A qualifying approval has effect on and after the transitional date as if it were a marine licence granted by the appropriate licensing authority in relation to the licensable marine activity (a "deemed marine licence").

(4) If the qualifying approval was given for a specified period, the deemed marine licence is to remain in force (subject to the provisions of this Part of this Act) for so much of that period as falls after the transitional date.

(5) If, by virtue of paragraph 11(5) of the Code, the qualifying approval was given subject to a condition, the deemed marine licence has effect as if the condition were a condition attached to the deemed marine licence.

(6) Any application for a communications approval—

    (a) which was submitted before the transitional date, and

    (b) which relates to an activity which, on or after that date, is a licensable marine activity,

2708

Marine and Coastal Access Act 2009 (c. 23)
Schedule 9 — Licensing: transitional provision relating to Part 4
Part 4 — Miscellaneous

has effect on and after that date as if it were an application for a marine licence made to the appropriate licensing authority in relation to that activity.

Electronic Communications Code: Scotland

12 (1) In this paragraph—

    (a) "the Code" means the Electronic Communications Code set out in Schedule 2 to the Telecommunications Act 1984 (c. 12);

    (b) "communications approval" means an approval under paragraph 11 of the Code;

    (c) "Scottish transitional date" means the date on which the repeals made in paragraph 11 of the Code by this Act take effect in relation to Scotland.

(2) Sub-paragraphs (3) to (5) apply to any communications approval (a "qualifying Scottish approval")—

    (a) which is in effect immediately before the Scottish transitional date, and

    (b) which relates to any works, falling within sub-paragraph (3) or (4) of paragraph 11 of the Code, the execution of which on or after that date needs a licence under section 5 or 6 of FEPA.

(3) A qualifying Scottish approval has effect on and after the Scottish transitional date as if it were a licence granted under section 5 or 6 (as the case may be) of FEPA by the licensing authority in relation to the activity (a "deemed FEPA licence").

(4) If the qualifying Scottish approval was given for a specified period, the deemed FEPA licence is to remain in force (subject to the provisions of FEPA) for so much of that period as falls after the Scottish transitional date.

(5) If, by virtue of paragraph 11(5) of the Code, the qualifying Scottish approval was given subject to a condition, the deemed FEPA licence has effect as if the condition were a condition attached to the deemed FEPA licence.

(6) Any application for a communications approval—

    (a) which was submitted before the transitional date, and

    (b) which relates to an activity which, on or after that date, needs a licence under section 5 or 6 of FEPA,

has effect on and after that date as if it were an application for a licence under the section in question made to the licensing authority in relation to that activity.

Direction under section 58(1)(c) of the Government of Wales Act 2006

13 (1) To the extent that they relate to the abandonment of an offshore installation, any functions exercisable under the provisions of this Part of this Act specified in sub-paragraph (2) are exercisable in relation to Welsh controlled waters by a Minister of the Crown only after consultation with the Welsh Ministers.

(2) The provisions are—

    (a) sections 67(1) to (5), 69(1), (3) and (4), 71(1) to (3) and 72(1) to (3) (marine licences), so far as relating to items 1 to 6 and 11 to 13 in section 66(1) (licensable marine activities);

Marine and Coastal Access Act 2009 (c. 23)
Schedule 9 — Licensing: transitional provision relating to Part 4
Part 4 — Miscellaneous

2709

        (b)   section 106 (power to take remedial action).

    (3) In this paragraph —

        "offshore installation" has the meaning given by section 44 of the Petroleum Act 1998 (c. 17);

        "Welsh controlled waters" has the same meaning as in paragraph 4 of Schedule 3 to the Government of Wales Act 2006 (c. 32).

    (4) The provision made by the preceding provisions of this paragraph has effect as if it were a direction made by Order in Council under section 58(1)(c) of the Government of Wales Act 2006 made by virtue of paragraph 4(1)(c) of Schedule 3 to that Act and may accordingly be amended, modified or repealed by any such Order in Council.

SCHEDULE 10   Section 144

FURTHER PROVISION ABOUT FIXED MONETARY PENALTIES UNDER SECTION 142

Fixed monetary penalties: other sanctions

1   (1) Provision under section 142 must secure that, in a case where a notice of intent referred to in section 143(2)(a) is served on a person —

        (a)   no criminal proceedings for the offence to which the notice relates may be instituted against the person in respect of the act or omission to which the notice relates before the end of the period in which the person may discharge liability to the fixed monetary penalty pursuant to section 143(2)(b), and

        (b)   if the person so discharges liability, the person may not at any time be convicted of the offence to which the notice relates in relation to that act or omission.

    (2) Provision under section 142 must also secure that, in a case where a fixed monetary penalty is imposed on a person, that person may not at any time be convicted of the offence in relation to which the penalty is imposed in respect of the act or omission giving rise to the penalty.

Monetary penalties

2   (1) An order under section 142 which confers power on an enforcement authority to require a person to pay a fixed monetary penalty may include provision —

        (a)   for early payment discounts;

        (b)   for the payment of interest or other financial penalties for late payment of the penalty, such interest or other financial penalties not in total to exceed the amount of that penalty;

        (c)   for enforcement of the penalty.

    (2) Provision under sub-paragraph (1)(c) may include —

        (a)   provision for the enforcement authority to recover the penalty, and any interest or other financial penalty for late payment, as a civil debt;

2710

Marine and Coastal Access Act 2009 (c. 23)
Schedule 10 — Further provision about fixed monetary penalties under section 142

(b)   provision for the penalty, and any interest or other financial penalty for late payment, to be recoverable, on the order of a court, as if payable under a court order.

Appeals

3   (1)   An order under section 142 may not provide for the making of an appeal other than to—

(a)   the First-tier Tribunal, or

(b)   another tribunal created under an enactment.

(2)   In sub-paragraph (1)(b) "tribunal" does not include an ordinary court of law.

(3)   An order under section 142 which makes provision for an appeal in relation to the imposition of any requirement or service of any notice may include—

(a)   provision suspending the requirement or notice pending determination of the appeal;

(b)   provision as to the powers of the tribunal to which the appeal is made;

(c)   provision as to how any sum payable in pursuance of a decision of that person is to be recoverable.

(4)   The provision referred to in sub-paragraph (3)(b) includes provision conferring on the tribunal to which the appeal is made power—

(a)   to withdraw the requirement or notice;

(b)   to confirm the requirement or notice;

(c)   to take such steps as the enforcement authority could take in relation to the act or omission giving rise to the requirement or notice;

(d)   to remit the decision whether to confirm the requirement or notice, or any matter relating to that decision, to the enforcement authority;

(e)   to award costs.

Consultation

4   (1)   Before making an order under section 142, the appropriate authority must consult the following—

(a)   the enforcement authority to which the order relates,

(b)   such organisations as appear to the appropriate authority to be representative of persons substantially affected by the proposals, and

(c)   such other persons as the appropriate authority considers appropriate.

(2)   If, as a result of any consultation required by sub-paragraph (1), it appears to the authority that it is appropriate substantially to change the whole or any part of the proposals, the authority must undertake such further consultation with respect to the changes as it considers appropriate.

(3)   If, before the day on which this Schedule comes into force, any consultation was undertaken which, had it been undertaken after that day, would to any extent have satisfied the requirements of this paragraph, those requirements may to that extent be taken to have been satisfied.

Guidance as to use of fixed monetary penalties

5   (1) Where power is conferred on an enforcement authority under section 142 to impose a fixed monetary penalty in relation to an offence, the provision conferring the power must secure the results in sub-paragraph (2).

      (2) Those results are that—
           (a) the enforcement authority must publish guidance about its use of the penalty,
           (b) the guidance must contain the relevant information,
           (c) the enforcement authority must revise the guidance where appropriate,
           (d) the enforcement authority must consult such persons as the provision may specify before publishing any guidance or revised guidance, and
           (e) the enforcement authority must have regard to the guidance or revised guidance in exercising its functions.

      (3) The relevant information referred to in sub-paragraph (2)(b) is information as to—
           (a) the circumstances in which the penalty is likely to be imposed,
           (b) the circumstances in which it may not be imposed,
           (c) the amount of the penalty,
           (d) how liability for the penalty may be discharged and the effect of discharge, and
           (e) rights to make representations and objections and rights of appeal.

Guidance as to enforcement of offences

6   (1) Where power is conferred on an enforcement authority under section 142 to impose a fixed monetary penalty in relation to an offence, the enforcement authority must prepare and publish guidance about how the offence is enforced.

      (2) The guidance must include guidance as to—
           (a) the sanctions (including criminal sanctions) to which a person who commits the offence may be liable,
           (b) the action which the enforcement authority may take to enforce the offence, whether by virtue of section 142 or otherwise, and
           (c) the circumstances in which the enforcement authority is likely to take any such action.

      (3) The enforcement authority may from time to time revise guidance published by it under this paragraph and publish the revised guidance.

      (4) The enforcement authority must consult such persons as it considers appropriate before publishing any guidance or revised guidance under this paragraph.

Publication of enforcement action

7   (1) Where power is conferred on an enforcement authority under section 142 to impose a fixed monetary penalty in relation to an offence, the provision conferring the power must, subject to this paragraph, secure the result in sub-paragraph (2).

2712

Marine and Coastal Access Act 2009 (c. 23)
Schedule 10 — Further provision about fixed monetary penalties under section 142

(2) That result is that the enforcement authority must from time to time publish reports specifying —

    (a) the cases in which a fixed monetary penalty has been imposed, and

    (b) the cases in which liability to the penalty has been discharged pursuant to section 143(2)(b).

(3) In sub-paragraph (2)(a), the reference to cases in which a fixed monetary penalty has been imposed does not include cases where a penalty has been imposed but overturned on appeal.

(4) The provision conferring the power need not secure the result in sub-paragraph (2) in cases where the appropriate authority considers that it would be inappropriate to do so.

Payment of penalties into Consolidated Fund etc

8   (1) Where pursuant to any provision made under section 142 an enforcement authority receives —

    (a) a fixed monetary penalty, or

    (b) any interest or other financial penalty for late payment of such a penalty,

the authority must pay it into the relevant Fund.

(2) In sub-paragraph (1) "the relevant Fund" means —

    (a) in a case where the authority has functions only in relation to Wales, the Welsh Consolidated Fund;

    (b) in any other case, the Consolidated Fund.

Disclosure of information

9   (1) Information held by or on behalf of a person mentioned in sub-paragraph (2) may be disclosed to an enforcement authority on whom powers are conferred under section 142 where —

    (a) the person has an enforcement function in relation to an offence, and

    (b) the information is disclosed for the purpose of the exercise by the enforcement authority of any powers conferred on it under that section in relation to that offence.

(2) The persons are —

    (a) the Crown Prosecution Service,

    (b) a member of a police force in England or Wales,

    (c) a Procurator Fiscal,

    (d) a constable of a police force in Scotland,

    (e) the Public Prosecution Service for Northern Ireland, or

    (f) a member of the Police Service of Northern Ireland.

(3) It is immaterial for the purposes of sub-paragraph (1) whether the information was obtained before or after the coming into force of this paragraph.

(4) A disclosure under this paragraph is not to be taken to breach any restriction on the disclosure of information (however imposed).

(5) Nothing in this paragraph authorises the making of a disclosure in contravention of —

     (a)   the Data Protection Act 1998 (c. 29), or

     (b)   Part 1 of the Regulation of Investigatory Powers Act 2000 (c. 23).

  (6) This paragraph does not affect a power to disclose which exists apart from this paragraph.

SCHEDULE 11

Section 146

CONSEQUENTIAL AMENDMENTS RELATING TO MCZS

Conservation of Seals Act 1970 (c. 30)

1   In section 10 of the Conservation of Seals Act 1970 (power to grant licences) in subsection (4)(d) for "a marine nature reserve under section 36 of that Act" substitute "a marine conservation zone under section 116 of the Marine and Coastal Access Act 2009".

Wildlife and Countryside Act 1981 (c. 69)

2   (1) The Wildlife and Countryside Act 1981 is amended as follows.

  (2) The following provisions are omitted—
     (a)   sections 36 and 37;
     (b)   Schedule 12.

  (3) In consequence of sub-paragraph (2), in the italic cross-heading preceding section 34A, the words "marine nature reserves" are omitted.

Water Resources Act 1991 (c. 57)

3   In paragraph 5 of Schedule 25 to the Water Resources Act 1991 (powers of the Environment Agency to make byelaws for flood defence and drainage purposes) in sub-paragraph (4) for the words from "the operation of" to the end of that sub-paragraph substitute "the operation of—
     (a)   any byelaw made by a navigation authority, harbour authority or conservancy authority;
     (b)   any byelaw made under section 129 or 132 of the Marine and Coastal Access Act 2009 (byelaws for protecting marine conservation zones in England);
     (c)   any order made under section 134 or 136 of that Act (orders for protecting marine conservation zones in Wales)."

Conservation (Natural Habitats, &c) Regulations 1994 (S.I. 1994/2716)

4   (1) For regulation 36 of the Conservation (Natural Habitats, &c) Regulations 1994 (S.I. 1994/2716) (byelaws for protection of European marine sites) substitute—

"36   Protection of European marine sites

  (1) The MMO may make byelaws for the protection of a European marine site in England under section 129 of the Marine and Coastal Access Act 2009 (byelaws for protection of marine conservation zones).

(2) The Welsh Ministers may make orders for the protection of a European marine site in Wales under section 134 of that Act (orders for protection of marine conservation zones).

(3) The provisions of Chapter 1 of Part 5 of that Act relating to byelaws under section 129 or orders under section 134 apply, with the modifications described in paragraph (4) of this regulation, in relation to byelaws made by virtue of paragraph (1) of this regulation or (as the case may be) orders made by virtue of paragraph (2) of this regulation.

(4) The modifications are—

   (a) any reference to an MCZ is to be read as a reference to a European marine site;

   (b) in sections 129(1) and 134(1), the reference to furthering the conservation objectives of an MCZ is to be read as a reference to protecting a European marine site;

   (c) the reference in section 129(3)(c) to hindering the conservation objectives stated for an MCZ is to be read as a reference to damaging a European marine site.

(5) Nothing in byelaws or orders made by virtue of this regulation shall interfere with the exercise of any functions of a relevant authority, any functions conferred by or under an enactment (whenever passed) or any right of any person (whenever vested)."

(2) The amendment by this paragraph of a provision contained in subordinate legislation is without prejudice to any power to amend that provision by subordinate legislation.

SCHEDULE 12

Section 146

TRANSITIONAL PROVISION RELATING TO MCZs

1   In this Schedule—

   "the 1981 Act" means the Wildlife and Countryside Act 1981 (c. 69);

   "the commencement date", in relation to an area, means the date on which paragraph 2 of Schedule 11 comes into force in relation to that area.

2 (1) Any area which, immediately before the commencement date, is designated by an order under section 36 of the 1981 Act as a marine nature reserve is to be treated, on and after that date, as if it were a marine conservation zone designated by an order under section 116.

   (2) The designation having effect by virtue of sub-paragraph (1) includes (in accordance with section 118(6)(b)) the area of land designated by the order under section 36, together with all of the water covering that land.

3   Any byelaw which, immediately before the commencement date, is in force under section 37 of the 1981 Act for the protection of any area designated as a marine nature reserve has effect, on and after that date, as if it were—

   (a) in the case of an area in England, a byelaw made under section 129;

   (b) in the case of an area in Wales, an order made under section 134.

4   Any provision of this Chapter which—
       (a)   confers any function on the MMO, and
       (b)   comes into force before the date on which section 1 of this Act comes into force,
has effect until that date as if it conferred that function on the Secretary of State.

SCHEDULE 13   Section 148

MARINE BOUNDARIES OF SSSIS AND NATIONAL NATURE RESERVES

PART 1

INTRODUCTORY

1   In this Schedule "the 1981 Act" means the Wildlife and Countryside Act 1981 (c. 69).

PART 2

SITES OF SPECIAL SCIENTIFIC INTEREST

Marine boundaries of sites of special scientific interest

2   (1)   Section 28 of the 1981 Act (sites of special scientific interest) is amended as follows.

     (2)   In subsection (1)(a) after "the local planning authority" insert "(if any)".

     (3)   After subsection (1) insert—

       "(1A)   The reference in subsection (1) to land includes—
           (a)   any land lying above mean low water mark;
           (b)   any land covered by estuarial waters.

       (1B)   Where the area of land to which a notification under subsection (1) relates includes land falling within subsection (1A)(a) or (b) ("area A"), it may also include land not falling within subsection (1A)(a) or (b) ("area B") if—
           (a)   area B adjoins area A, and
           (b)   any of the conditions in subsection (1C) is satisfied.

       (1C)   The conditions are—
           (a)   that the flora, fauna or features leading to the notification of area A is or are also present in area B;
           (b)   that the notification of area A is by reason of any flora or fauna which are dependent (wholly or in part) on anything which takes place in, or is present in, area B;
           (c)   that, without the inclusion of area B, the identification of the boundary of the land notified (either in the notification or on the ground for the purposes of exercising functions in relation to it) would be impossible or impracticable."

(4) In subsection (2) for "that fact" substitute "the fact mentioned in subsection (1)".

(5) In subsection (5) (confirmation of notification of SSSIs) after paragraph (b) insert—

> "In the case of a notification given in relation to land lying below mean low water mark by virtue of subsection (1B), this subsection is subject to section 28CB(4) and (6)."

(6) After subsection (6) (when notification ceases to have effect) insert—

> "(6A)   Subsection (6)(b) does not apply in a case where notice has been given to Natural England under section 28CB(3)."

(7) After subsection (9) insert—

> "(9A)   For the purposes of this Part "estuarial waters" means any waters within the limits of transitional waters, within the meaning of the Water Framework Directive (that is to say, Directive 2000/60/EC of the European Parliament and of the Council of 23 October 2000 establishing a framework for Community action in the field of water policy)."

(8) No notification under subsection (1) of that section made before the coming into force of this paragraph may be questioned in legal proceedings on the ground that the area of land to which the notification relates includes land lying below mean low water mark.

3   In section 28A of the 1981 Act (variation of notification under section 28), in subsection (3)(a) after "the local planning authority" insert "(if any)".

4   In section 52(1) of the 1981 Act (interpretation of Part 2), after the definition of "agricultural land" insert—

> ""estuarial waters" has the meaning given by section 28(9A);".

Notification of additional land that is subtidal

5   (1) Section 28B of the 1981 Act (notification of additional land) is amended as follows.

(2) In subsection (2)(a) after "the local planning authority" insert "(if any)".

(3) After subsection (2) insert—

> "(2A)   The reference in subsection (1) to land includes—
>
>   (a)   any land lying above mean low water mark;
>
>   (b)   any land covered by estuarial waters.
>
> (2B)   If any of the conditions in subsection (2C) is satisfied, the extra land may consist of or include an area of land not falling within subsection (2A)(a) or (b).
>
> (2C)   The conditions are—
>
>   (a)   that the flora, fauna or features that led to the notification of the SSSI is or are also present in the area of the extra land not falling within subsection (2A)(a) or (b);

Marine and Coastal Access Act 2009 (c. 23)
Schedule 13 — Marine boundaries of SSSIs and national nature reserves
Part 2 — Sites of special scientific interest

2717

      (b)   that the notification of the SSSI is by reason of any flora or fauna which are dependent (wholly or in part) on anything which takes place in, or is present in, that area;

      (c)   that, without the inclusion of that area, the identification of the boundary of the SSSI (either in the notification or on the ground for the purposes of exercising functions in relation to it) would be impossible or impracticable."

(4) In subsection (3) for "such notification" substitute "notification under subsection (2)".

(5) In subsection (7) (application of section 28(5) to (7) in relation to notifications under section 28B)—

      (a)   after ""subsection (1)"" insert "and "subsection (1B)"";

      (b)   for "of this section" (in the second place where it occurs) substitute "and subsection (2B) of this section respectively".

(6) No notification under subsection (2) of that section made before the coming into force of this paragraph may be questioned in legal proceedings on the ground that the area of land to which the notification relates consists of or includes land lying below mean low water mark.

Enlargement of SSSI to include subtidal land

6   (1) Section 28C of the 1981 Act (enlargement of SSSI) is amended as follows.

    (2) In subsection (2)(a) after "the local planning authority" insert "(if any)".

    (3) After subsection (2) insert—

"(2A) The reference in subsection (1) to land includes—

      (a)   any land lying above mean low water mark;

      (b)   any land covered by estuarial waters.

(2B) If any of the conditions in subsection (2C) is satisfied, the area of land to which a notification under subsection (2) relates may include an area of land not falling within subsection (2A)(a) or (b).

(2C) The conditions are—

      (a)   that the flora, fauna or features that led to the notification of the SSSI is or are also present in the area of land not falling within subsection (2A)(a) or (b);

      (b)   that the notification of the SSSI is by reason of any flora or fauna which are dependent (wholly or in part) on anything which takes place in, or is present in, that area;

      (c)   that, without the inclusion of that area, the identification of the boundary of the SSSI (either in the notification or on the ground for the purposes of exercising functions in relation to it) would be impossible or impracticable."

(4) In subsection (3) (application of section 28(2) to (8) in relation to notifications under section 28C)—

      (a)   for "and "subsection (1)(b)"" substitute ", "subsection (1)(b)" and "subsection (1B)"";

      (b)   for "and subsection (2)(b)" substitute ", subsection (2)(b) and subsection (2B)".

2718

Marine and Coastal Access Act 2009 (c. 23)
Schedule 13 — Marine boundaries of SSSIs and national nature reserves
Part 2 — Sites of special scientific interest

(5) No notification under subsection (2) of that section made before the coming into force of this paragraph may be questioned in legal proceedings on the ground that the area of land to which the notification relates includes land lying below mean low water mark.

Guidance in relation to subtidal notifications of SSSIs

7   After section 28C of the 1981 Act insert—

"28CA Guidance in relation to subtidal notifications of SSSIs

(1) The ministerial authority may issue guidance to Natural England about the exercise of the power conferred by section 28(1B), 28B(2B) or 28C(2B) to give a notification under section 28(1), 28B(2) or 28C(2) (as the case may be) in relation to land lying below mean low water mark.

(2) In this section and section 28CB "the ministerial authority" means—
   (a) in relation to England, the Secretary of State;
   (b) in relation to Wales, the Welsh Ministers."

Power to call in subtidal notifications of SSSIs

8   After section 28CA of the 1981 Act (inserted by paragraph 7) insert—

"28CB Power to call in subtidal notifications

(1) This section applies where a notification under section 28(1), 28B(2) or 28C(2) has been given in relation to land lying below mean low water mark ("the subtidal land") by virtue of section 28(1B), 28B(2B) or 28C(2B) (as the case may be).

(2) Natural England may not give notice under section 28(5)(b) confirming the notification unless, at least 21 days before doing so, they have given notice of their intention to the ministerial authority. (For the meaning of "the ministerial authority", see section 28CA.)

(3) At any time before the notification is confirmed the ministerial authority may give notice to Natural England that the ministerial authority is considering whether to give a direction under subsection (5) regarding the subtidal land.

(4) If the ministerial authority gives notice under subsection (3), Natural England may not give notice under section 28(5) until the ministerial authority has given a direction under subsection (5).

(5) The ministerial authority may direct—
   (a) that the notification (if confirmed) must include all of the subtidal land;
   (b) that the notification (if confirmed) must not include any of the subtidal land;
   (c) that the notification (if confirmed) must, or must not, include such part of that land as is specified in the direction;
   (d) that the decision whether the notification (if confirmed) should include the subtidal land is to be taken by Natural England.

Marine and Coastal Access Act 2009 (c. 23)
2719
Schedule 13 – Marine boundaries of SSSIs and national nature reserves
Part 2 – Sites of special scientific interest

(6) If the ministerial authority gives a direction under subsection (5), Natural England must give notice under section 28(5)(a) or (b), in accordance with that direction, within the period of three months beginning with the date on which the direction is received by them.

(7) The ministerial authority may, before deciding whether to give a direction under subsection (5), give to any person the opportunity of –

(a) appearing before and being heard by a person appointed by the ministerial authority for that purpose;

(b) providing written representations to such a person.

(8) A person appointed under subsection (7) must make a report to the ministerial authority of any oral or written representations made under that subsection.

(9) The ministerial authority may make regulations providing for the procedure to be followed (including decisions as to costs) at hearings held under subsection (7).

(10) The power to make regulations under subsection (9) is exercisable by statutory instrument.

(11) A statutory instrument containing regulations made under subsection (9) by the Secretary of State shall be subject to annulment in pursuance of a resolution of either House of Parliament.

(12) A statutory instrument containing regulations made under subsection (9) by the Welsh Ministers shall be subject to annulment in pursuance of a resolution of the National Assembly for Wales."

Denotification of SSSI on designation of area as MCZ

9   (1) Section 28D of the 1981 Act (denotification) is amended as follows.

(2) In subsection (1) before "is not of special interest" insert "(a)" and after "mentioned in section 28(1)," insert "or

(b) should no longer be the subject of a notification under section 28(1) because that land has been designated as (or as part of) a marine conservation zone under section 116 of the Marine and Coastal Access Act 2009,".

(3) In subsection (2)(a) –

(a) after "the local planning authority" insert "(if any)";

(b) for "the land which Natural England no longer consider to be of special interest" substitute "the land mentioned in subsection (1)".

(4) In subsection (3) for "that fact" substitute "the fact mentioned in subsection (1)(a) or (b)".

PART 3

NATIONAL NATURE RESERVES

Marine boundaries of national nature reserves

10   (1) In section 35 of the 1981 Act (national nature reserves) after subsection (1)

2720

Marine and Coastal Access Act 2009 (c. 23)
Schedule 13 — Marine boundaries of SSSIs and national nature reserves
Part 3 — National nature reserves

insert—

"(1A) The land which may be declared to be a national nature reserve in England or Wales includes—

    (a) any land lying above mean low water mark;

    (b) any land covered by estuarial waters.

(1B) Where the area of land to which a declaration under subsection (1) relates includes land falling within subsection (1A)(a) or (b) ("area A"), it may also include land not falling within subsection (1A)(a) or (b) ("area B") if—

    (a) area B adjoins area A, and

    (b) any of the conditions in subsection (1C) is satisfied.

(1C) The conditions are—

    (a) that the flora, fauna or features leading to the management of area A as a nature reserve is or are also present in area B;

    (b) that the management of area A as a nature reserve is by reason of any flora or fauna which are dependent (wholly or in part) on anything which takes place in, or is present in, area B;

    (c) that, without the inclusion of area B, the identification of the boundary of the land declared to be a national nature reserve (either in the declaration or on the ground for the purposes of exercising functions in relation to it) would be impossible or impracticable.

(1D) The ministerial authority may issue guidance to the appropriate conservation body about the exercise of the power conferred by subsection (1B) to make a declaration in relation to land lying below mean low water mark.

"The ministerial authority" has the meaning given by section 35A(12)."

(2) No declaration under subsection (1) of that section made before the coming into force of this paragraph may be questioned in legal proceedings on the ground that the area of land to which the declaration relates includes land lying below mean low water mark.

Power to call in subtidal declarations of national nature reserves

11   After section 35 of the 1981 Act insert—

"35A Power to call in subtidal declarations

(1) This section applies where—

    (a) the appropriate conservation body propose to declare land to be a national nature reserve under section 35(1), and

    (b) the land to which the proposed declaration relates includes, by virtue of section 35(1B), land lying below mean low water mark ("the subtidal land").

(2) The appropriate conservation body may not declare the reserve unless, at least 21 days before doing so, they have given notice of their intention to the ministerial authority.

(3) At any time before the reserve is declared the ministerial authority may give notice to the appropriate conservation body that the ministerial authority is considering whether to give a direction under subsection (5) regarding the subtidal land.

(4) If the ministerial authority gives notice under subsection (3), the appropriate conservation body may not declare the reserve until the ministerial authority has given a direction under subsection (5).

(5) The ministerial authority may direct —
   (a) that the reserve (if declared) must include all of the subtidal land;
   (b) that the reserve (if declared) must not include any of the subtidal land;
   (c) that the reserve (if declared) must, or must not, include such part of that land as is specified in the direction;
   (d) that the decision whether the reserve (if declared) should include the subtidal land is to be taken by the appropriate conservation body.

(6) The ministerial authority may, before deciding whether to give a direction under subsection (5), give to any person the opportunity of —
   (a) appearing before and being heard by a person appointed by the ministerial authority for that purpose;
   (b) providing written representations to such a person.

(7) A person appointed under subsection (6) must make a report to the ministerial authority of any oral or written representations made under that subsection.

(8) The ministerial authority may make regulations providing for the procedure to be followed (including decisions as to costs) at hearings held under subsection (6).

(9) The power to make regulations under subsection (8) is exercisable by statutory instrument.

(10) A statutory instrument containing regulations made under subsection (8) by the Secretary of State shall be subject to annulment in pursuance of a resolution of either House of Parliament.

(11) A statutory instrument containing regulations made under subsection (8) by the Welsh Ministers shall be subject to annulment in pursuance of a resolution of the National Assembly for Wales.

(12) In this section "the ministerial authority" means —
   (a) in relation to England, the Secretary of State;
   (b) in relation to Wales, the Welsh Ministers."

SCHEDULE 14   Section 184

INSHORE FISHERIES AND CONSERVATION AUTHORITIES: AMENDMENTS

Coast Protection Act 1949 (c. 74)

1   The Coast Protection Act 1949 is amended as follows.

2   In section 2 (constitution of coast protection boards) —
         (a)   in subsection (2)(b), after "fishery board," insert "inshore fisheries
                and conservation authority,";
         (b)   in subsection (8)(a), after "(other than the Tweed Commissioners)"
                insert ", inshore fisheries and conservation authority".

3   In section 45 (service of notices and other documents), in subsection (1)(b),
         after "fishery board," insert "inshore fisheries and conservation authority,".

4   In section 49(1) (interpretation) after the definition of "functions" insert —
                ""inshore fisheries and conservation authority" means the
                authority for an inshore fisheries and conservation district
                established under section 149 of the Marine and Coastal
                Access Act 2009;".

5   In Part 1 of the First Schedule (general provisions concerning procedure for
         making orders, etc), in paragraph 1(b), after "fishery board," insert "inshore
         fisheries and conservation authority,".

Nuclear Installations Act 1965 (c. 57)

6   In section 3 of the Nuclear Installations Act 1965 (grant and variation of
         nuclear site licences), in subsection (3), after paragraph (b) insert —
                "(ba)   any inshore fisheries and conservation authority;".

Sea Fish (Conservation) Act 1967 (c. 84)

7   In section 3 of the Sea Fish (Conservation) Act 1967 (regulation of nets and
         other fishing gear), in subsection (7), before "or in any regulation made"
         insert "or in any byelaw made under section 155 of the Marine and Coastal
         Access Act 2009,".

Prevention of Oil Pollution Act 1971 (c. 60)

8   In section 19 of the Prevention of Oil Pollution Act 1971 (prosecutions) after
         subsection (5) insert —

         "(5A)   If an inshore fisheries and conservation authority for a district
                  established under section 149 of the Marine and Coastal Access Act
                  2009, or any inshore fisheries and conservation officer appointed by
                  the authority under section 165 of that Act, is authorised in that
                  behalf under subsection (1) of this section, the authority may
                  institute proceedings for any offence under this Act committed
                  within the district."

Local Government Act 1974 (c. 7)

9   In section 31A of the Local Government Act 1974 (consideration of adverse reports), in subsection (3) –
         (a)   after paragraph (a) insert –
                      "(aa)   an inshore fisheries and conservation authority for a district established under section 149 of the Marine and Coastal Access Act 2009,";
         (b)   after "that committee" insert ", authority".

Fisheries Act 1981 (c. 29)

10   In Part 1 of Schedule 4 to the Fisheries Act 1981 (exemptions for fish farming: offences to which section 33(1) applies), after paragraph 17A (inserted by the Inshore Fishing (Scotland) Act 1984 (c. 26)) insert –

         "17B.   Any offence under section 163 of the Marine and Coastal Access Act 2009 (contravention of byelaws made by inshore fisheries and conservation authorities)."

Wildlife and Countryside Act 1981 (c. 69)

11   In section 27(1) of the Wildlife and Countryside Act 1981 (interpretation of Part 1) –
         (a)   in paragraph (c) of the definition of "authorised person", after "the Salmon Fisheries (Scotland) Act 1862" insert "or an inshore fisheries and conservation authority";
         (b)   after the definition of "inland waters" insert –
                      ""inshore fisheries and conservation authority" means the authority for an inshore fisheries and conservation district established under section 149 of the Marine and Coastal Access Act 2009;".

Local Government and Housing Act 1989 (c. 42)

12   The Local Government and Housing Act 1989 is amended as follows.

13   (1) Section 5 (designation and reports of monitoring officer) is amended as follows.

     (2) After subsection (3) insert –

         "(3A)   The references in subsection (2) above, in relation to a relevant authority in England, to a committee or sub-committee of the authority and to a joint committee on which they are represented shall be taken to include references to –
                 (a)   any inshore fisheries and conservation authority ("IFC authority") the members of which include persons who are members of the relevant authority, and
                 (b)   any sub-committee appointed by such an authority;
                 but in relation to any such IFC authority or sub-committee the reference in subsection (3)(b) above to each member of the authority shall have effect as a reference to each member of the IFC authority or, as the case may be, of the IFC authority which appointed the sub-committee."

(3) In subsection (5), after "a relevant authority" insert "and of any IFC authority falling within paragraph (a) of subsection (3A) above".

(4) In subsection (8), after the definition of "chief finance officer" insert—

""inshore fisheries and conservation authority" means the authority for an inshore fisheries and conservation district established under section 149 of the Marine and Coastal Access Act 2009;".

14   In section 13 (voting rights of members of certain committees), in subsection (4), after paragraph (f) insert—

"(fa)   an inshore fisheries and conservation authority for a district established under section 149 of the Marine and Coastal Access Act 2009;".

15   In paragraph 2(1) of Schedule 1 (political balance on local authority committees etc) after paragraph (bb) insert—

"(bc)   an inshore fisheries and conservation authority for a district established under section 149 of the Marine and Coastal Access Act 2009;".

Radioactive Substances Act 1993 (c. 12)

16   The Radioactive Substances Act 1993 is amended as follows.

17   In section 47(1) (general interpretation provisions), in the definition of "relevant water body", after "sewerage undertaker" insert "or an inshore fisheries and conservation authority".

18   In Schedule 3 (enactments to which section 40 applies), after paragraph 10 insert—

"10A   Section 155 of the Marine and Coastal Access Act 2009."

Freedom of Information Act 2000 (c. 36)

19   In Part 2 of Schedule 1 to the Freedom of Information Act 2000 (local government bodies which are public authorities), after paragraph 35A insert—

"35B   An inshore fisheries and conservation authority for a district established under section 149 of the Marine and Coastal Access Act 2009."

Natural Environment and Rural Communities Act 2006 (c. 16)

20   In Schedule 7 to the Natural Environment and Rural Communities Act 2006 (designated bodies), after paragraph 1 insert—

"1A   An inshore fisheries and conservation authority for a district established under section 149 of the Marine and Coastal Access Act 2009."

SCHEDULE 15   Section 201

SEA FISH (CONSERVATION) ACT 1967: MINOR AND CONSEQUENTIAL AMENDMENTS

Sea Fish (Conservation) Act 1967 (c. 84)

1   (1) Section 1 (size limits, etc for fish) is amended as follows.

     (2) In subsection (4) —
          (a)   for "Different sizes" substitute "Different requirements as to size";
          (b)   for "different sizes" substitute "different requirements as to size".

     (3) In subsection (5) —
          (a)   for "a size" substitute "requirements as to size";
          (b)   for the words from "if the part" to the end substitute "if the part does not meet the requirements as to size so prescribed."

     (4) In subsection (8) —
          (a)   for "a relevant British fishing boat or a Scottish fishing boat" substitute "a relevant British vessel, a Scottish fishing boat or a Northern Ireland fishing boat";
          (b)   for "foreign fishing boat" substitute "foreign vessel".

2   (1) Section 3 (regulation of nets and other fishing gear) is amended as follows.

     (2) In subsection (3)(c), after "classes of fishing boats," insert "or particular persons or persons of a particular description,".

     (3) In subsection (7), after "carrying" (in each place where it occurs) insert "or use".

3   (1) Section 5 (power to restrict fishing for sea fish) is amended as follows.

     (2) In subsection (2), for the words after "different provision" substitute "for different cases".

     (3) In subsection (5), after "prohibition" insert "or restriction".

     (4) In subsection (6) —
          (a)   after "is made" insert "by virtue of paragraph (a) of subsection (1) above";
          (b)   for "any fishing operations conducted" substitute "fishing";
          (c)   for the words from "are taken" to "applies" substitute "are caught by a person, or taken on board a fishing boat, in contravention of the prohibition".

     (5) After subsection (6) insert —

          "(6A)   A person who does not comply with subsection (6) above shall be guilty of an offence under that subsection."

4   In section 11 (penalties for offences), in subsection (3), for "subsection (5)" substitute "subsection (4)".

Fisheries Act 1981 (c. 29)

5   (1) Schedule 4 (exemptions for fish farming) is amended as follows.

(2) In Part 1 (offences to which section 33(1) applies) —

    (a)   in paragraph 12, for "smaller than prescribed size" substitute "which do not meet prescribed size requirements";

    (b)   in paragraph 13, after "section 3(5)" insert "or (5A)";

    (c)   in paragraph 16, after "prohibiting" insert "or restricting".

(3) In Part 2 (offences to which section 33(5) applies), in paragraph 33 —

    (a)   for "the Sea Fisheries (Conservation) Act 1967" substitute "the Sea Fish (Conservation) Act 1967";

    (b)   for "smaller than the prescribed size" substitute "which do not meet prescribed size requirements".

SCHEDULE 16

Section 233(1)

MIGRATORY AND FRESHWATER FISH: CONSEQUENTIAL AND SUPPLEMENTARY
AMENDMENTS

Salmon and Freshwater Fisheries Act 1975 (c. 51)

1   The Salmon and Freshwater Fisheries Act 1975 has effect subject to the amendments in paragraphs 2 to 17.

2   Section 3 (nets) is omitted.

3   (1) Section 5 (prohibition of use of explosives etc) is amended as follows.

    (2) In subsection (1), for "subsection (2)" substitute "subsections (2) and (2A)".

    (3) In subsection (2)(b), at the end insert ", for which the Agency may charge a fee".

    (4) After subsection (2) insert —

        "(2A)   Subsection (1) above shall not apply to anything done pursuant to an authorisation granted by the Agency under section 27A below."

4   Sections 6 to 8 (fixed engines, fishing weirs and fishing mill dams) are omitted.

5   Section 16 (boxes and cribs in weirs and dams) is omitted.

6   Section 17 (restrictions on taking salmon or trout above or below an obstruction or in mill races) is omitted.

7   In section 18 (supplementary provisions), in subsection (4), for ", 15 or 17" substitute "or 15".

8   Sections 19 to 22 (close seasons etc) are omitted.

9   (1) Section 25 (licences to fish) is amended as follows.

    (2) In subsection (2), for "an instrument" substitute "the means of fishing".

    (3) In subsection (3) —

        (a)   for "an instrument" substitute "any means of fishing";

        (b)   for "the instrument" substitute "that means of fishing".

10   (1)   Section 26 (limitation of fishing licences) is amended as follows.

      (2)   In subsection (1), for "the Minister" substitute "the appropriate national authority".

      (3)   In subsection (2) —
- (a)   for "the Minister" substitute "the appropriate national authority";
- (b)   for "he" (in both places) substitute "that authority";
- (c)   for "his" substitute "that authority's";
- (d)   for "him" substitute "that authority".

      (4)   In subsection (3) —
- (a)   for "The Minister" substitute "The appropriate national authority";
- (b)   for "him" substitute "that authority";
- (c)   for "he" substitute "that authority".

      (5)   In subsection (6) —
- (a)   for "The Minister" substitute "The appropriate national authority";
- (b)   for "him" substitute "that authority";
- (c)   for "he" substitute "that authority".

      (6)   In subsection (7) —
- (a)   for "the Minister", in the first place, substitute "the appropriate national authority";
- (b)   for "the Minister", in the second place, substitute "that authority".

11   (1)   Section 27 (unlicensed fishing) is amended as follows.

      (2)   The existing provision is renumbered as subsection (1).

      (3)   In that subsection, after "of any description" insert "by any licensable means of fishing".

      (4)   In that subsection, for paragraphs (a) and (b) substitute —

> "(a)   fishes for or takes fish of that description by that means and —
> - (i)   is not entitled to use that means for that purpose by virtue of a fishing licence, or
> - (ii)   is acting in breach of any condition of such a licence, or
>
> (b)   where that licensable means of fishing is an instrument, has that instrument in his possession with intent to use it for that purpose and is not entitled to use it for that purpose by virtue of a fishing licence."

      (5)   After that subsection insert —

> "(2)   Subsection (1) above does not apply to a person where —
> - (a)   he has permission under section 25(10) above to take fish of that description in that place by that means, and
> - (b)   he is not acting in breach of any condition of that permission."

12   In section 33 (orders and warrants to enter suspected premises), in subsection (2), for "or any salmon, trout, freshwater fish or eels to have been illegally taken" substitute "or an offence against this Act to have been committed in the taking of any fish".

2728

Marine and Coastal Access Act 2009 (c. 23)
Schedule 16 — Migratory and freshwater fish: consequential and supplementary amendments

13 In section 34 (power to apprehend persons fishing illegally), for the words from "illegally takes or kills" to "by this Act" substitute "takes or kills any fish where the taking or killing constitutes an offence under this Act, or is found on or near any waters with intent to take or kill any fish where the taking or killing would constitute an offence under this Act, or having an instrument prohibited by this Act in his possession for the capture of any fish, where the capture would constitute an offence under this Act".

14 (1) In section 41 (interpretation), subsection (1) is amended as follows.

 (2) In the definition of "fixed engine", in paragraph (d), for "salmon or trout" substitute "fish".

 (3) After the definition of "general licence" insert—

   ""historic installation" has the meaning given by section 25 above;".

 (4) After the definition of "inland water" insert—

   ""licensable means of fishing" has the meaning given by section 25 above;".

15 Schedule 1 (close seasons and close times) is omitted.

16 (1) Schedule 2 (licences) is amended as follows.

 (2) In paragraph 1(2), for "in special cases" substitute "in such cases as it considers appropriate".

 (3) In paragraph 2, for the words from "different instruments" to "different descriptions of fish" substitute "different descriptions of licence".

 (4) In paragraph 3, for "any instrument" substitute "any licensable means of fishing".

 (5) In paragraph 4—
  (a) for "the Minister", in the first place, substitute "the appropriate national authority";
  (b) for "the Minister", in the second place, substitute "that authority".

 (6) In paragraph 5—
  (a) for "The Minister" substitute "The appropriate national authority";
  (b) for "his" substitute "that authority's";
  (c) for "the Minister" substitute "that authority".

 (7) In paragraph 7—
  (a) for "an instrument" substitute "any licensable means of fishing";
  (b) for "that instrument" substitute "that means".

 (8) In paragraph 9—
  (a) in sub-paragraph (1)—
   (i) for "an instrument of any description" substitute "any licensable means of fishing";
   (ii) for "with instruments of that description" substitute "by that means";
   (iii) for "an instrument of that description", in the first place, substitute "that means of fishing";

Marine and Coastal Access Act 2009 (c. 23)
Schedule 16 — Migratory and freshwater fish: consequential and supplementary amendments

2729

    (iv) for "the instrument", in the first place, substitute "that means of fishing";

    (v) in paragraph (b), for "an instrument of that description", substitute "that means of fishing";

    (vi) in paragraph (c), for "the instrument" substitute "that means of fishing";

   (b) in sub-paragraph (2) —

    (i) for "an instrument of any description" substitute "any licensable means of fishing";

    (ii) for "an instrument of that description" substitute "that means of fishing";

    (iii) for "the instrument", in the first place, substitute "that means of fishing";

    (iv) in paragraph (c), for "the instrument" substitute "that means of fishing".

 (9) In paragraph 10, after "entered on" insert "or removed from".

 (10) In paragraph 13, for "the instrument", in both places, substitute "the means of fishing".

 (11) In paragraph 15, for "the instrument" substitute "the means of fishing".

 (12) In paragraph 17, for "instrument" substitute "other thing".

17 (1) Schedule 4 (offences) is amended as follows.

 (2) In the table in paragraph 1(2), the entries relating to section 19(2), section 19(4), section 19(6), section 19(7) and section 21 are omitted.

 (3) In that table, in the entry relating to section 27 —

   (a) in the second column —

    (i) after "fishing for fish" insert "by licensable means of fishing";

    (ii) after "unlicensed" insert "licensable";

   (b) in the third column, in paragraph (a), for the words from "instrument" to "rod and line" substitute "offence is one alleged to be committed by use or possession of rod and line (only)".

 (4) In paragraph 1(3), for the words from "both" to the end substitute —

   "(a) both are engaged in committing —

    (i) an offence under section 1 above, other than one committed without any instrument, or

    (ii) an offence under section 27 above, other than one committed by means of a rod and line (only), or

   (b) one is aiding, abetting, counselling or procuring the commission of such an offence by the other."

 (5) In paragraph 7, for "salmon, trout or freshwater fish" substitute "fish".

 (6) In paragraph 9 —

   (a) after "any fishing or general licence" insert "or authorisation under section 27A above";

   (b) after "a fishing or general licence" (in both places) insert "or authorisation under section 27A above".

 (7) In paragraph 10 —

        (a)   after "a fishing or general licence" insert "or authorisation under section 27A above";

        (b)   after "the licence" (in every place) insert "or authorisation under section 27A above".

(8)   In paragraph 11 –

        (a)   after "a fishing or general licence" insert "or authorisation under section 27A above";

        (b)   after "a licence" insert "or authorisation";

        (c)   after "the licence" insert "or authorisation".

Fisheries Act 1981 (c. 29)

18   (1)   In the Fisheries Act 1981, in Part 1 of Schedule 4 (offences to which section 33(1) of that Act applies), paragraph 6 is amended as follows.

    (2)   In paragraph (a), after "any fish" insert "to which paragraph 6 of that Schedule applies".

    (3)   After paragraph (a) insert—

                "(aa)   specifying close seasons or times for the taking of any fish to which that paragraph applies by such means as may be prescribed by the byelaws;".

    (4)   In paragraph (b), for "trout or any freshwater fish of a size" substitute "any fish to which that paragraph applies of a size greater or".

    (5)   In paragraph (c) –

        (a)   for "salmon, trout, or freshwater fish" substitute "fish to which that paragraph applies";

        (b)   the words "(not being a fixed engine)" are omitted.

    (6)   In paragraph (d) –

        (a)   the words "(not being fixed engines)" are omitted;

        (b)   for "salmon, trout, freshwater fish and eels" substitute "fish to which that paragraph applies".

    (7)   In paragraph (f) –

        (a)   for "salmon or trout" substitute "fish to which that paragraph applies";

        (b)   for "which is not licensed" substitute "which may not lawfully be used".

    (8)   In paragraph (g), for "the annual close season for salmon of a net capable of taking salmon" substitute "any close season or time for any description of fish to which that paragraph applies of a net capable of taking fish of that description".

Salmon Act 1986 (c. 62)

19   In section 32 of the Salmon Act 1986 (handling salmon in suspicious circumstances), subsection (6)(a) is omitted.

Water Resources Act 1991 (c. 57)

20   The Water Resources Act 1991 has effect subject to the amendments in paragraphs 21 to 25.

21   In section 115 (fisheries orders), in subsection (1) —
    (a)   in paragraph (a), after "Salmon and Freshwater Fisheries Act 1975" insert "(as amended by the Marine and Coastal Access Act 2009)";
    (b)   in paragraph (b), after "this Act" insert "(as so amended)".

22   In section 116 (power to give effect to international obligations) —
    (a)   the existing provision is renumbered as subsection (1);
    (b)   after that subsection insert —

        "(2)   In subsection (1), the reference to functions includes any functions conferred on the Agency by virtue of the Marine and Coastal Access Act 2009."

23 (1) Section 212 (compensation in respect of certain fisheries byelaws) is amended as follows.

  (2) In subsection (2) —
    (a)   in paragraph (a) —
      (i)   for "salmon, trout, or freshwater fish" substitute "any fish to which paragraph 6 of that Schedule applies";
      (ii)   the words "(not being a fixed engine)" are omitted;
    (b)   in paragraph (b) —
      (i)   the words "(not being fixed engines)" are omitted;
      (ii)   for "salmon, trout, freshwater fish and eels" substitute "any such fish".

24 (1) In Schedule 25 (byelaw-making powers of the Agency), paragraph 6 (byelaws for purposes of fisheries functions) is amended as follows.

  (2) In sub-paragraph (2) —
    (a)   the words "Subject to paragraph 7(1) below" are omitted;
    (b)   in paragraph (a), after "any fish" insert "to which this paragraph applies";
    (c)   in paragraph (b) —
      (i)   in sub-paragraph (i), for "trout or any freshwater fish" substitute "any fish to which this paragraph applies";
      (ii)   in sub-paragraph (ii), after "fish" insert "to which this paragraph applies";
    (d)   in paragraph (c) —
      (i)   for "salmon, trout, or freshwater fish" substitute "fish to which this paragraph applies";
      (ii)   the words "(not being a fixed engine)" are omitted;
    (e)   in paragraph (d) —
      (i)   the words "(not being fixed engines)" are omitted;
      (ii)   for "salmon, trout, freshwater fish and eels" substitute "fish to which this paragraph applies";
    (f)   in paragraph (g), the word "licensed" is omitted;
    (g)   in paragraph (h) —

2732

Marine and Coastal Access Act 2009 (c. 23)
Schedule 16 — Migratory and freshwater fish: consequential and supplementary amendments

> > > (i)   for "salmon or trout" substitute "fish to which this paragraph applies";
> > >
> > > (ii)   for "which is not licensed" substitute "which may not lawfully be used";
> >
> > (h)   in paragraph (i), for "the annual close season for salmon of a net capable of taking salmon" substitute "any close season or time for any description of fish to which this paragraph applies of a net capable of taking fish of that description".
>
> (3)   In sub-paragraph (5) for "salmon, trout, freshwater fish or eels" substitute "fish to which this paragraph applies".

25   In that Schedule, paragraph 7 is omitted.

Environment Act 1995 (c. 25)

26   In section 13 of the Environment Act 1995 (regional and local fisheries advisory committees), in subsection (1)(a), for the words from "salmon fisheries" to "eel fisheries" substitute "fisheries referred to in section 6(6) above".

SCHEDULE 17

Section 249

WARRANTS ISSUED UNDER SECTION 249

Introductory

1   (1)   This Schedule has effect in relation to the issue to enforcement officers of warrants under section 249.

> (2)   An entry into a dwelling under such a warrant is unlawful unless it complies with the provisions of this Schedule.

Applications for warrants

2   (1)   Where an enforcement officer applies for a warrant, the officer must—

> > (a)   state the ground on which the application is made,
> >
> > (b)   state the enactment under which the warrant would be issued,
> >
> > (c)   specify the dwelling which it is desired to enter and inspect, and
> >
> > (d)   identify, so far as is practicable, the purpose for which entry is desired.
>
> (2)   An application for a warrant must be made without notice and must be supported by an information in writing or, in Scotland, evidence on oath.
>
> (3)   The officer must answer on oath any question that the justice hearing the application asks the officer.

Safeguards in connection with power of entry conferred by warrant

3   A warrant authorises an entry on one occasion only.

4   (1)   A warrant must specify—

> > (a)   the name of the person who applies for it,

        (b)   the date on which it is issued,

        (c)   the enactment under which it is issued, and

        (d)   the dwelling to be entered.

    (2)   A warrant must identify, so far as is practicable, the purpose for which entry is desired.

5   (1)   Two copies are to be made of a warrant.

    (2)   The copies must be clearly certified as copies.

Execution of warrants

6   (1)   A warrant may be executed by any appropriate enforcement officer.

    (2)   In sub-paragraph (1) the reference to an appropriate enforcement officer is a reference to any enforcement officer acting on behalf of the same relevant authority as the enforcement officer who applied for the warrant, and includes a reference to that officer.

    (3)   In sub-paragraph (2) "relevant authority" means the person or body on whose behalf the officer who applied for the warrant was acting.

7   (1)   A warrant may authorise persons to accompany any enforcement officer who is executing it.

    (2)   A person authorised under this paragraph has the same powers as the officer whom the person is accompanying in respect of the execution of the warrant, but may exercise those powers only in the company of, and under the supervision of, an enforcement officer.

8   (1)   Execution of a warrant must be within three months from the date of its issue.

    (2)   Execution of a warrant must be at a reasonable time, unless it appears to the officer executing it that there are grounds for suspecting that the purpose of entering the dwelling may be frustrated if the officer seeks to enter at a reasonable time.

9   (1)   Where the occupier of a dwelling that is to be entered under a warrant is present at the time when an enforcement officer seeks to execute the warrant, the following requirements must be satisfied —

        (a)   the occupier must be told the officer's name;

        (b)   the officer must produce to the occupier documentary evidence of the fact that the officer is an enforcement officer;

        (c)   the officer must produce the warrant to the occupier;

        (d)   the officer must supply the occupier with a certified copy of it.

    (2)   Where —

        (a)   the occupier of a dwelling that is to be entered under a warrant is not present when an enforcement officer seeks to execute it, but

        (b)   some other person who appears to the officer to be in charge of the dwelling is present,

    sub-paragraph (1) has effect as if any reference to the occupier were a reference to that other person.

(3) If there is no person present who appears to the enforcement officer to be in charge of the dwelling, the officer must leave a certified copy of the warrant in a prominent place in the dwelling.

Return of warrants

10 (1) A warrant which —

(a) has been executed, or

(b) has not been executed within the time authorised for its execution,

must be returned to the appropriate person.

(2) In sub-paragraph (1) the appropriate person is —

(a) in the case of a warrant issued by a justice of the peace in England and Wales, the designated officer for the local justice area in which the justice was acting when the warrant was issued;

(b) in the case of a warrant issued by a lay magistrate in Northern Ireland, the clerk of petty sessions for the petty sessions district in which the dwelling is situated;

(c) in the case of a warrant issued by a sheriff, the sheriff clerk;

(d) in the case of a warrant issued by a justice of the peace or stipendiary magistrate in Scotland, the clerk of the justice of the peace court.

(3) A warrant that is returned under this paragraph must be retained by the person to whom it is returned for a period of 12 months.

(4) If during that period the occupier of the dwelling to which the warrant relates asks to inspect it, the occupier must be allowed to do so.

SCHEDULE 18

Section 277

FORFEITURE OF PROPERTY UNDER SECTION 275 OR 276

Application of Schedule

1 (1) This Schedule applies where —

(a) property seized by an enforcement officer in the exercise of any power conferred by this Act is in the possession of the relevant authority,

(b) the relevant authority is satisfied that there are reasonable grounds for believing that the property is forfeitable property, and

(c) either —

(i) no proceedings are being taken against any person in respect of the property, or

(ii) any such proceedings have concluded without any order for forfeiture having been made in respect of the property.

(2) The following property is "forfeitable property" —

(a) any item the use of which for sea fishing would in any circumstances constitute an offence under the law of England and Wales;

(b) any fish in respect of which, by virtue of the fish failing to meet requirements as to size, an offence under the law of England and Wales has been committed.

Notice of intended forfeiture

2   (1)   The relevant authority must give notice of the intended forfeiture of the property ("notice of intended forfeiture") to each of the following persons —

    (a)   every person who appears to the authority to have been the owner of the property, or one of its owners, at the time of the seizure of the property;

    (b)   in the case of property seized from a vessel, the master, owner and charterer (if any) of the vessel at that time;

    (c)   in the case of property seized from premises, every person who appears to the authority to have been an occupier of the premises at that time;

    (d)   in any other case, the person (if any) from whom the property was seized.

    (2)   The notice of intended forfeiture must set out —

    (a)   a description of the property,

    (b)   the grounds of the intended forfeiture, and

    (c)   how a person may give a notice of claim under this Schedule and the period within which such a notice must be given.

    (3)   In a case where —

    (a)   the property was seized following an inspection carried out in exercise of the power conferred by section 264, and

    (b)   the relevant authority, after taking reasonable steps to do so, is unable to identify any person as owning the property,

the reference in sub-paragraph (1) to a requirement to give notice of intended forfeiture to such a person is to be read as a reference to a requirement to take such steps as the authority thinks fit to bring the contents of the notice to the attention of persons likely to be interested in it.

    (4)   Property may be treated or condemned as forfeited under this Schedule only if —

    (a)   the requirements of this paragraph have been complied with in the case of the property, or

    (b)   it was not reasonably practicable for them to be complied with.

Notice of claim

3   A person claiming that the property is not liable to forfeiture must give written notice of the claim to the relevant authority.

4   (1)   A notice of claim must be given —

    (a)   within one month of the day of the giving of the notice of intended forfeiture, or

    (b)   if no such notice has been given, within one month of the date of the seizure of the property.

    (2)   A notice of claim must specify —

    (a)   the name and address of the claimant, and

    (b)   in the case of a claimant who is outside the United Kingdom, the name and address of a solicitor in the United Kingdom who is authorised to accept service of process and to act on behalf of the claimant.

(3) Service of process upon a solicitor so specified is to be taken to be proper service upon the claimant.

(4) In a case in which notice of intended forfeiture was given to different persons on different days, the reference in this paragraph to the day on which that notice was given is a reference—

   (a)   in relation to a person to whom notice of intended forfeiture was given, to the day on which that notice was given to that person, and

   (b)   in relation to any other person, to the day on which notice of intended forfeiture was given to the last person to be given such a notice.

Automatic forfeiture in a case where no claim is made

5   The property is to be taken to have been duly condemned as forfeited if—

   (a)   by the end of the period for the giving of a notice of claim in respect of the property, no notice of claim has been given to the relevant authority, or

   (b)   a notice of claim has been given which does not comply with the requirements of paragraphs 3 and 4.

Decision whether to take court proceedings to condemn property as forfeited

6   (1) Where a notice of claim in respect of the property is duly given in accordance with paragraphs 3 and 4, the relevant authority must decide whether to take proceedings to ask the court to condemn the property as forfeited.

   (2) The decision whether to take such proceedings must be taken as soon as reasonably practicable after the receipt of the notice of claim.

Return of property if no forfeiture proceedings

7   (1) If, in a case in which a notice of claim has been given, the relevant authority decides not to take proceedings for condemnation of the property, it must return the property to the person appearing to it to be the owner of the property, or, if there is more than one such person, to one of those persons.

   (2) Any property required to be returned in accordance with sub-paragraph (1) must be returned as soon as reasonably practicable after the decision not to take proceedings for condemnation.

Forfeiture proceedings

8   (1) This paragraph applies if, in a case in which a notice of claim has been given, the relevant authority decides to take proceedings for the condemnation of the property by the court.

   (2) If the court is satisfied that the property is forfeitable property, it must condemn the property as forfeited.

   (3) If the court is not satisfied that the property is forfeitable property, the court must order the return of the property to the person appearing to the court to be entitled to it or, if there is more than one such person, to one of those persons.

Supplementary provision about forfeiture proceedings

9   Proceedings by virtue of this Schedule are civil proceedings and may be instituted—

          (a)   in the High Court, or

          (b)   in any magistrates' court in England or Wales.

10   (1)   In proceedings by virtue of this Schedule, the claimant or the claimant's solicitor must make an oath that, at the time of the seizure, the property was, or was to the best of that person's knowledge and belief, the property of the claimant.

    (2)   In proceedings by virtue of this Schedule instituted in the High Court—

          (a)   the court may require the claimant to give such security for the costs of the proceedings as may be determined by the court, and

          (b)   the claimant must comply with such a requirement.

    (3)   If a requirement of this paragraph is not complied with, the court must give judgment for the relevant authority.

11   (1)   In the case of proceedings by virtue of this Schedule instituted in a magistrates' court in England or Wales, either party may appeal against the decision of that court to the Crown Court.

    (2)   This paragraph does not affect any right to require the statement of a case for the opinion of the High Court.

12   Where an appeal has been made (whether by case stated or otherwise) against the decision of the court in proceedings by virtue of this Schedule in relation to property, the property is to be left with the relevant authority pending the final determination of the matter.

Effect of forfeiture

13   Where property is treated or condemned as forfeited under this Schedule, the forfeiture is to be treated as having taken effect as from the time of the seizure.

Disposal of property which is not returned

14   (1)   This paragraph applies where any property is required to be returned to a person under this Schedule.

    (2)   If the property is still in the relevant authority's possession after the end of the period of three months beginning with the day after the requirement to return it arose, the relevant authority may dispose of it in any manner it thinks fit.

    (3)   The relevant authority may exercise its power under this paragraph to dispose of property only if it is not practicable at the time when the power is exercised to dispose of the property by returning it immediately to the person to whom it is required to be returned.

Provisions as to proof

15   In proceedings under this Schedule, the fact, form and manner of the seizure of the property are to be taken, without further evidence and unless the contrary is shown, to have been as set forth in the process.

16   In any proceedings, the condemnation by a court of property as forfeited under this Schedule may be proved by the production of —

   (a)   the order or certificate of condemnation, or

   (b)   a certified copy of the order purporting to be signed by an officer of the court by which the order or certificate was made or granted.

Special provisions as to certain claimants

17   (1)   This paragraph applies where, at the time of the seizure of the property, it was —

   (a)   the property of a body corporate,

   (b)   the property of two or more partners, or

   (c)   the property of more than five persons.

   (2)   The oath required by paragraph 10, and any other thing required by this Schedule or by rules of court to be done by the owner of the property, may be sworn or done by —

   (a)   a person falling within sub-paragraph (3), or

   (b)   a person authorised to act on behalf of such a person.

   (3)   The persons are —

   (a)   where the owner is a body corporate, the secretary or some duly authorised officer of that body;

   (b)   where the owners are in partnership, any one or more of the owners;

   (c)   where there are more than five owners and they are not in partnership, any two or more of the owners acting on behalf of themselves and any of their co-owners who are not acting on their own behalf.

Power to destroy fish before condemnation, etc

18   (1)   The relevant authority may destroy any fish liable to be treated or condemned as forfeited under this Schedule, even if such fish have not yet been so treated or condemned.

   (2)   If in proceedings under this Schedule the court is not satisfied that any fish destroyed under this paragraph were forfeitable property, the relevant authority must, if requested to do so, pay to the claimant a sum of money equal to the market value of the fish at the time of seizure.

   (3)   A claimant who accepts any sum of money paid under sub-paragraph (2) is not entitled to maintain any action on account of the seizure, detention or destruction of the fish.

   (4)   For the purposes of sub-paragraph (2), the market value of any fish at the time of seizure is to be taken to be such amount as the relevant authority and the claimant may agree or, in default of agreement, as may be determined by a referee appointed by the court.

(5) The procedure on any reference to a referee under sub-paragraph (4) is to be such as may be determined by the referee.

(6) The referee's decision is final and conclusive.

Saving for owner's rights

19   Neither the imposition of a requirement by virtue of this Schedule to return property to a person nor the return of property to a person in accordance with such a requirement affects —

(a)   the rights in relation to that property of any other person, or

(b)   the right of any other person to enforce any rights against the person to whom it is returned.

Interpretation

20   In this Schedule —

"the court" is to be read in accordance with paragraph 9;

"forfeitable property" is to be read in accordance with paragraph 1(2).

SCHEDULE 19   Section 302

SCHEDULE 1A TO THE NATIONAL PARKS AND ACCESS TO THE COUNTRYSIDE ACT 1949

The following is the Schedule to be inserted as Schedule 1A to the National Parks and Access to the Countryside Act 1949 (c. 97) —

"SCHEDULE 1A

COASTAL ACCESS REPORTS

Introductory

1   In this Schedule —

(a)   "coastal access report" means a report submitted under section 51 pursuant to the coastal access duty;

(b)   references to a fair balance are references to a fair balance between —

(i)   the interests of the public in having rights of access over land, and

(ii)   the interests of any person with a relevant interest in the land,

(to which section 297(3) of the Marine and Coastal Access Act 2009 (general duties in connection with the coastal access duty) refers).

Advertising etc of coastal access reports

2   (1) Natural England must —

(a)   advertise a coastal access report, and

(b)   take such steps as are reasonable to give notice of the report to persons within sub-paragraph (2).

2740

Marine and Coastal Access Act 2009 (c. 23)
Schedule 19 — Schedule 1A to the National Parks and Access to the Countryside Act 1949

(2) Those persons are—

    (a)   persons with a relevant interest in affected land;

    (b)   each access authority for an area in which affected land is situated;

    (c)   each local access forum for an area in which affected land is situated;

    (d)   the Historic Buildings and Monuments Commission for England;

    (e)   the Environment Agency;

    (f)   such other persons as may be specified in regulations made by the Secretary of State.

(3) The Secretary of State may by regulations make provision about—

    (a)   the form and manner in which reports are to be advertised under sub-paragraph (1)(a);

    (b)   the form and manner in which notices are to be given under sub-paragraph (1)(b);

    (c)   the timing of any advertisement or the giving of any notice.

Objections by persons with relevant interest in affected land

3   (1)   Any person who has a relevant interest in affected land may make an objection to Natural England about a coastal access report.

    (2)   For the purposes of this Schedule an objection is not an admissible objection unless it—

        (a)   satisfies the conditions in sub-paragraphs (3) and (4), and

        (b)   is made in accordance with any requirements imposed by regulations under sub-paragraph (7)(b).

    (3)   The first condition is that the objection is made on the ground that the proposals in the report, in such respects as are specified in the objection, fail to strike a fair balance as a result of one or more of the following—

        (a)   the position of any part of the proposed route;

        (b)   the inclusion of proposals under subsection (2) of section 55B or the nature of any proposal under that subsection;

        (c)   the inclusion of, or failure to include, an alternative route under section 55C(2) or the position of any such alternative route or any part of such a route;

        (d)   the inclusion of, or failure to include, proposals under one or more of paragraphs (a) to (c) of section 55D(2) or the nature of any proposal made under such a paragraph;

        (e)   the inclusion of, or failure to include, a proposal under section 55D(5) or the terms of any such proposal;

        (f)   the exercise of a discretion conferred by section 301(2) or (3) of the Marine and Coastal Access Act 2009, or failure to exercise a discretion conferred by section 301(3) of that Act, in relation to a river.

    (4)   The second condition is that the objection specifies the reasons why the person making the objection is of the opinion that a fair balance is not struck as a result of the matter or matters within sub-paragraph (3)(a) to (f).

Marine and Coastal Access Act 2009 (c. 23)
Schedule 19 — Schedule 1A to the National Parks and Access to the Countryside Act 1949

2741

(5) An objection under this paragraph may propose modifications of the proposals in the report if the person making the objection considers—

    (a) that those modifications would remedy, or mitigate the effects of, the failure to strike a fair balance to which the objection relates, and

    (b) that the proposals as so modified would satisfy the requirements of sub-paragraph (6).

(6) Modified proposals satisfy the requirements of this sub-paragraph if what they propose—

    (a) is practicable,

    (b) takes account of the matters mentioned in section 297(2), and (where appropriate) section 301(4), of the Marine and Coastal Access Act 2009 (matters to which Natural England and the Secretary of State must have regard when discharging the coastal access duty), and

    (c) is in accordance with the scheme approved under section 298 of that Act (the scheme in accordance with which Natural England must act when discharging the coastal access duty) or, where that scheme has been revised, the revised scheme.

(7) The Secretary of State may by regulations make provision about—

    (a) the steps to be taken by Natural England to make persons with an interest in affected land aware of their entitlement to make objections under this paragraph;

    (b) the form and manner in which, and period within which, objections are to be made.

Referral of objections to the appointed person

4   (1) Natural England must send to the Secretary of State a copy of any objection received under paragraph 3 about a coastal access report.

    (2) The Secretary of State must refer any objection received under sub-paragraph (1) to a person appointed by the Secretary of State for the purposes of this Schedule ("the appointed person").

    (3) An appointment under sub-paragraph (2)—

        (a) must be in writing;

        (b) may relate to any particular objection specified in the appointment or to objections of a description so specified;

        (c) may provide for a payment or payments to be made to the appointed person.

    (4) An appointment under sub-paragraph (2) may, by notice in writing given to the appointed person, be revoked at any time by the Secretary of State in respect of any objection if the appointed person has not, before that time, given the Secretary of State a report containing a recommendation under paragraph 11 in relation to the objection.

2742

Marine and Coastal Access Act 2009 (c. 23)
Schedule 19 — Schedule 1A to the National Parks and Access to the Countryside Act 1949

(5) Where the appointment of the appointed person is revoked in respect of any objection, the Secretary of State must appoint another person under sub-paragraph (2) to deal with the objection afresh under this Schedule.

(6) Nothing in sub-paragraph (5) requires any person to be given an opportunity to make fresh representations or comments or to modify or withdraw any representations or comments already made.

Determination of admissibility of objections

5   Where an objection is referred under paragraph 4(2), the appointed person must—

(a) determine whether the objection is an admissible objection, and

(b) give notice of that determination, together with the reasons for it, to—

(i) the person who made the objection,

(ii) the Secretary of State, and

(iii) Natural England.

Admissible objections

6   (1) Where Natural England is notified under paragraph 5(b) that an objection is an admissible objection, it must send to the Secretary of State its comments on the objection.

(2) A notice under paragraph 5(b) that an objection is an admissible objection may require Natural England to include in its comments under sub-paragraph (1)—

(a) either—

(i) an outline of any relevant alternative modifications of the proposals in the coastal access report, or

(ii) if Natural England considers there are no such modifications, a statement to that effect;

(b) if an outline is included under paragraph (a)(i), an assessment of the effects of the relevant alternative modifications on the interests of the public in having rights of access over land and the interests of any person with a relevant interest in affected land;

(c) either—

(i) an outline of any relevant rejected proposals which were considered by Natural England in connection with the preparation of the coastal access report and of its reasons for rejecting them, or

(ii) if there are no such proposals, a statement to that effect;

(d) information of such other description as the appointed person may specify in the notice under paragraph 5(b), being information which the appointed person considers to be material for the purpose of making a determination under paragraph 10(2).

(3) In this paragraph, a reference to relevant alternative modifications of the proposals is to modifications of the proposals which Natural England considers —

    (a) might reasonably be regarded as relevant for the purpose of determining —

        (i) whether, in the respects identified in the objection, the proposals in the report strike a fair balance, or

        (ii) whether any modification of those proposals would produce proposals that strike a fair balance or mitigate the effects of any failure to strike a fair balance,

    (b) are materially different from any modifications included in the objection under paragraph 3(5), and

    (c) would, if made, result in proposals which satisfy the requirements of paragraph 3(6)(a) and (c).

(4) In this paragraph, a reference to relevant rejected proposals is to proposals which, if to be given effect to, would require modifications to be made of the proposals in the coastal access report which —

    (a) are materially different from —

        (i) any modifications included in the objection under paragraph 3(5), and

        (ii) any relevant alternative modifications outlined in Natural England's comments on the objection, and

    (b) would be relevant alternative modifications but for a failure to satisfy the requirement of paragraph 3(6)(a).

Representations about reports

7   (1) Representations about a coastal access report may be made by any person to Natural England.

    (2) The Secretary of State may by regulations make provision about —

    (a) the steps to be taken by Natural England to make persons aware of their entitlement to make representations under this paragraph;

    (b) the form and manner in which, and period within which, representations are to be made.

8   (1) Natural England must send to the Secretary of State —

    (a) a copy of any representations made by a person within paragraph 2(2)(b) to (f) about a coastal access report,

    (b) a summary of any other representations made about the report, and

    (c) Natural England's comments on representations within paragraph (a) or (b).

    (2) In this paragraph references to representations are to representations made under paragraph 7 in accordance with any requirements imposed by regulations under paragraph 7(2)(b).

2744

Marine and Coastal Access Act 2009 (c. 23)
Schedule 19 — Schedule 1A to the National Parks and Access to the Countryside Act 1949

Reference of objection to the appointed person

9   (1) This paragraph applies where the Secretary of State is notified under paragraph 5(b) that an objection made about a coastal access report is an admissible objection.

   (2) The Secretary of State must send to the appointed person the relevant documents in relation to the objection.

   (3) The relevant documents are—
      (a) a copy of the coastal access report to which the objection relates,
      (b) a copy of Natural England's comments on the objection received under paragraph 6,
      (c) a copy of any representations received under paragraph 8(1)(a) about the coastal access report, so far as those representations appear to the Secretary of State to be relevant to the objection,
      (d) if there are such representations, a copy of Natural England's comments on them received under paragraph 8(1)(c),
      (e) if a summary of representations about the coastal access report has been received under paragraph 8(1)(b), a copy of any part of the summary which appears to the Secretary of State to be relevant to the objection, and
      (f) if there is such a part, a copy of Natural England's comments on the representations to which the part relates received under paragraph 8(1)(c).

Consideration of objections by appointed person

10 (1) This paragraph applies where the appointed person—
      (a) has determined that an objection about a coastal access report is an admissible objection, and
      (b) has received, under paragraph 9, the relevant documents in relation to the objection.

   (2) The appointed person must determine whether the proposals set out in the report fail, in the respects specified in the objection, to strike a fair balance as a result of the matter or matters within paragraph 3(3)(a) to (f) specified in the objection.

   (3) If the appointed person is minded to determine that the proposals fail to strike a fair balance, the appointed person must comply with sub-paragraphs (4) and (5) before making such a determination.

   (4) The appointed person must publish a notice containing—
      (a) details of the objection and Natural England's comments on it under paragraph 6,
      (b) a statement that the appointed person is minded to determine that the proposals fail to strike a fair balance, and
      (c) an invitation to submit to the appointed person representations about—

(i)   the objection (including any modifications of the proposals proposed by the objection),

(ii)   any relevant alternative modifications contained in Natural England's comments on the objection under paragraph 6, and

(iii)   any observations which the appointed person has made in the notice regarding any such relevant alternative modifications or any modifications proposed by the objection.

(5) The appointed person must give a copy of that notice to —

(a)   Natural England;

(b)   any person with a relevant interest in —

(i)   affected land to which the objection relates, or

(ii)   land which is not affected land but would be such land if any of the modifications referred to in sub-paragraph (4)(c)(i) or (ii) were made to the proposals;

(c)   any person within paragraph 2(2)(b) to (f).

(6) The Secretary of State may by regulations make provision about—

(a)   the form and manner in which notices are to be published or given under this paragraph,

(b)   the timing of the publication or giving of notices under this paragraph, and

(c)   the form and manner in which, and period within which, representations are to be made in response to an invitation in a notice under this paragraph.

(7) The appointed person may require the Secretary of State, at the Secretary of State's expense —

(a)   to discharge the appointed person's duty to publish or give a notice under this paragraph;

(b)   to receive on behalf of the appointed person any representations made in response to an invitation in a notice under this paragraph and forward such representations to the appointed person.

Recommendations of the appointed person

11   (1) Where a determination is made in respect of an objection under paragraph 10(2), the appointed person must give the Secretary of State a report which —

(a)   sets out that determination, and

(b)   makes one or more recommendations in accordance with this paragraph.

(2) Sub-paragraph (3) applies if the appointed person concludes under paragraph 10(2) that the proposals do not fail, in the respects specified in the objection, to strike a fair balance as a result of any of the matters within paragraph 3(3)(a) to (f) specified in the objection.

2746

Marine and Coastal Access Act 2009 (c. 23)
Schedule 19 — Schedule 1A to the National Parks and Access to the Countryside Act 1949

(3) The appointed person must recommend that the Secretary of State makes a determination to that effect.

(4) Sub-paragraphs (5) and (7) apply if the appointed person concludes that the proposals fail, in the respects (or certain of the respects) specified in the objection, to strike a fair balance as a result of one or more of the matters within paragraph 3(3)(a) to (f) specified in the objection.

(5) The appointed person must determine whether there are any modifications of the proposals which would meet the coastal access requirements.

(6) For the purposes of this paragraph, modifications meet the coastal access requirements if they —

    (a) remedy the failure to strike a fair balance identified by the objection, and

    (b) produce proposals which satisfy the requirements of paragraph 3(6).

(7) The appointed person must —

    (a) recommend that the Secretary of State determines that the proposals fail, in one or more of the respects specified in the objection, to strike a fair balance but that there is no modification which would satisfy the coastal access requirements,

    (b) recommend that, if minded to approve the proposals, the Secretary of State approves the proposals with modifications of a kind described in the recommendation, being modifications which the appointed person considers would meet the coastal access requirements, or

    (c) recommend that, if minded to approve the proposals, the Secretary of State considers whether modifications of a kind described in the recommendation would meet the coastal access requirements.

(8) Where a report contains a recommendation under sub-paragraph (7)(a), the appointed person may include in the report —

    (a) a recommendation that, if minded to approve the proposals, the Secretary of State should approve the proposals with modifications of a kind described in the recommendation, being modifications which the appointed person considers would mitigate the effects of the failure to strike a fair balance, or

    (b) a recommendation that, if minded to approve the proposals, the Secretary of State should consider whether modifications of a kind described in the recommendation would mitigate the effects of the failure to strike a fair balance.

(9) Sub-paragraph (10) applies where, in a case to which sub-paragraph (4) applies, the appointed person also determines that the proposals do not fail, in the respects (or certain of the respects) specified in the objection, to strike a fair balance by reason of one or more of the matters within paragraph 3(3)(a) to (f) specified in the objection.

    (10) The appointed person must recommend that the Secretary of State makes a determination to that effect (in addition to any recommendation under sub-paragraph (7) or (8)).

    (11) A report under this paragraph must also set out the appointed person's reasons for any recommendation contained in the report.

Information and documents

12   (1) The appointed person may give Natural England a notice requiring it to provide the appointed person with information or documents —

      (a) which is or are in the possession of Natural England, and

      (b) which the appointed person reasonably requires for the purpose of exercising functions under this Schedule.

    (2) Natural England must send the Secretary of State a copy of any information or document provided by it in response to a notice under sub-paragraph (1).

    (3) The appointed person may give the Secretary of State a notice requiring the Secretary of State to provide the appointed person with —

      (a) a copy of any coastal access report specified in the notice which the appointed person reasonably requires for the purpose of exercising functions under this Schedule;

      (b) any information in the possession of the Secretary of State which the appointed person reasonably so requires.

Holding of local inquiries and other hearings by appointed person

13   (1) Where the appointed person considers it necessary or expedient to do so, the appointed person may hold a local inquiry or other hearing in connection with the consideration of an objection under this Schedule.

    (2) Subject to sub-paragraph (3), the costs of a local inquiry or other hearing held under this paragraph are to be defrayed by the Secretary of State.

    (3) Subsections (2) to (5) of section 250 of the Local Government Act 1972 (local inquiries: evidence and costs) apply to local inquiries or other hearings held under this Schedule by the appointed person as they apply to inquiries caused to be held under that section by a Minister, but as if —

      (a) in subsection (2) (evidence) the reference to the person appointed to hold the inquiry were a reference to the appointed person,

      (b) in subsection (4) (recovery of costs of holding the inquiry) —

         (i) references to the Minister causing the inquiry to be held were references to the appointed person, and

        (ii) references to a local authority were references to Natural England, and

(c)   in subsection (5) (orders as to the costs of the parties) the reference to the Minister causing the inquiry to be held were a reference to the appointed person.

Supplementary provision about procedure in connection with objections

14   (1)   Subject to the provisions of this Schedule, the Secretary of State may, by regulations, make provision about the consideration of objections by the appointed person.

      (2)   Such regulations may, in particular, include —

          (a)   provision enabling two or more objections, in the circumstances specified in the regulations, to be considered by the appointed person together;

          (b)   provision enabling the appointed person to conduct an inspection of any land;

          (c)   provision about the procedure for the conduct of local inquiries and other hearings.

Preliminary consultation

15   (1)   The Secretary of State may, by regulations, make provision about the procedure to be followed where, before determining whether or not to approve the proposals in a coastal access report (with or without modifications), the Secretary of State wishes —

          (a)   to identify or investigate possible modifications of the proposals to which it might be appropriate to give further consideration, and

          (b)   to consult persons for the purposes of identifying or investigating such modifications.

      (2)   Regulations under this paragraph may, in particular, apply any provision of this Schedule (with or without modifications).

Determinations under section 52

16   (1)   Before making a determination under section 52 in respect of a coastal access report, the Secretary of State must consider —

          (a)   any objection about the report which the appointed person has determined is an admissible objection,

          (b)   Natural England's comments under paragraph 6 on any such objections,

          (c)   any report under paragraph 11 in respect of any such objection,

          (d)   any representations made about the coastal access report, or summary of such representations, and any comments on those representations, received under paragraph 8, and

          (e)   any information or document a copy of which is sent to the Secretary of State under paragraph 12(2).

      (2)   The power under section 52 to approve proposals contained in a report submitted under section 51 pursuant to the coastal access duty includes a power to approve those proposals (with or

without modifications) so far as they relate to one or more parts of the route only, and reject the remaining proposals.

(3) Where a report required to be considered under sub-paragraph (1)(c) contains a statement of a finding of fact, the Secretary of State in making the determination is bound by that finding unless the Secretary of State is satisfied —

   (a) that the finding involves an assessment of the significance of a matter to any person with a relevant interest in land or to the public,

   (b) that there was insufficient evidence to make the finding,

   (c) that the finding was made by reference to irrelevant factors or without regard to relevant factors, or

   (d) that the finding was otherwise perverse or irrational.

(4) The Secretary of State may, by regulations, make provision about the procedure to be followed where the Secretary of State is minded to approve proposals with modifications other than modifications made in accordance with a recommendation under paragraph 11(7)(b) or (c) or (8)(a) or (b).

(5) For the purposes of sub-paragraph (4) a modification is to be regarded as made in accordance with a recommendation under paragraph 11(7)(b) or (c) or (8)(a) or (b) if it is not materially different from a modification which could be so made.

(6) Regulations under sub-paragraph (4) may, in particular, apply any provision of this Schedule (with or without modifications).

(7) Any requirement imposed by virtue of sub-paragraph (4) is in addition to the duty to consult imposed by section 52(1).

Notice of determinations under section 52

17 (1) Where the Secretary of State makes a determination under section 52 in respect of a coastal access report, the Secretary of State must, as soon as reasonably practicable, comply with this paragraph.

(2) The Secretary of State must —

   (a) take reasonable steps to give notice of the determination to persons with a relevant interest in affected land, or

   (b) if the Secretary of State considers it appropriate, publish a notice of the determination in such manner as the Secretary of State considers likely to bring it to the attention of those persons.

(3) The Secretary of State (in addition to complying with section 52(2)) must give notice of the determination to —

   (a) any body of a kind mentioned in section 52(2) in whose Park or area affected land is situated (but which is not required to be notified under section 52(2)),

   (b) any London borough council for an area in which affected land is situated,

   (c) any local access forum for an area in which affected land is situated,

          (d)   the Historic Buildings and Monuments Commission for England, and

          (e)   the Environment Agency.

    (4) Where the Secretary of State was required under paragraph 16(1)(a) to consider an objection when making the determination, a statement of the reasons for the determination (so far as relevant to the objection) must be included in—

          (a)   any notice given or published under sub-paragraph (2),

          (b)   any notification of the determination under section 52(2), and

          (c)   any notice given under sub-paragraph (3).

    (5) Where the Secretary of State was required under paragraph 16(1)(c) to consider a report and the Secretary of State in making the determination does not follow a recommendation in the report, the statement of reasons required by sub-paragraph (4) must also include the reasons for not following the recommendation.

Interpretation

18   In this Schedule—

      "admissible objection" is to be construed in accordance with paragraph 3(2);

      "the appointed person" has the meaning given by paragraph 4(2);

      "coastal access report" has the meaning given by paragraph 1(a);

      "fair balance" is to be construed in accordance with paragraph 1(b);

      "relevant alternative modifications" has the meaning given by paragraph 6(3);

      "the relevant documents", in relation to an objection, has the meaning given by paragraph 9(3)."

SCHEDULE 20   Section 304

ESTABLISHMENT AND MAINTENANCE OF THE ENGLISH COASTAL ROUTE ETC

Extension of Chapter 3 of Part 1 of the CROW Act

1   (1) Chapter 3 of Part 1 of the CROW Act (means of access) applies in relation to section 15 route land as it applies in relation to access land.

    (2) Functions conferred by that Chapter which are exercisable in relation to any land by the access authority in relation to the land (including those exercisable by virtue of sub-paragraph (1)) are also exercisable in relation to the land by Natural England for the purposes of the coastal access duty.

    (3) In this paragraph—

      "access land" has the same meaning as in Chapter 3 of Part 1 of the CROW Act;

Marine and Coastal Access Act 2009 (c. 23)
Schedule 20 — Establishment and maintenance of the English coastal route etc

2751

"section 15 route land" means land —
- (a) over which the English coastal route (or any part of it) passes, and
- (b) which, for the purposes of section 1(1) of the CROW Act, is treated by section 15(1) of that Act as being accessible to the public apart from that Act.

Agreements relating to establishment and maintenance of route

2 (1) Where, in respect of any land, it appears to Natural England that it is appropriate for works within sub-paragraph (3) to be carried out for the purposes of the coastal access duty, Natural England may enter into an agreement with the owner or occupier of the land as to the carrying out of the works.

(2) Where, in respect of any land, it appears to the access authority in relation to that land that it is appropriate for works within sub-paragraph (3) to be carried out for the purpose of assisting Natural England to discharge the coastal access duty, the access authority may enter into an agreement with the owner or occupier of the land as to the carrying out of the works.

(3) The works within this sub-paragraph are —
- (a) the clearance or maintenance of land for the purpose of facilitating the use of the English coastal route by the public for journeys on foot;
- (b) the removal, for that purpose, of any obstruction of the route;
- (c) the clearance or maintenance of land which is coastal margin for the purpose of facilitating the exercise by the public of any right to enter or remain on the land on a bicycle or on horseback which is conferred by section 2(1) of the CROW Act (by virtue of the removal or relaxation of any of the general restrictions in Schedule 2 to that Act);
- (d) the drainage or levelling of land, or the improvement of its surface, for the purpose mentioned in paragraph (a) or, if the land is coastal margin, the purpose mentioned in paragraph (c);
- (e) the construction, removal, repair or improvement of any wall, rail, fence or other barrier or any posts, or the planting of any hedge.

(4) An agreement under this paragraph may provide —
- (a) for the carrying out of works by the owner or occupier or by the contracting authority, and
- (b) for the making of payments by the contracting authority as a contribution towards, or for the purpose of meeting, costs incurred by the owner or occupier in carrying out any works for which the agreement provides.

(5) Sub-paragraph (6) applies if the owner or occupier of any land fails to carry out within the required period any works which the owner or occupier is required by an agreement under this paragraph to carry out.

(6) The contracting authority may take all necessary steps for carrying out the works, but it may do so only after giving at least 21 days' notice of its intention to do so to the owner or occupier required by the agreement to carry out the works.

(7) Where the contracting authority carries out any works by virtue of sub-paragraph (6), the authority may recover the relevant expenses from the

person by whom, under the agreement, the cost of carrying out the works (after deduction of the authority's contribution) would fall to be borne.

(8) In this paragraph —

"contracting authority" means —

    (a)   in relation to an agreement under sub-paragraph (1), Natural England, and

    (b)   in relation to an agreement under sub-paragraph (2), the access authority by which the agreement is made;

"relevant expenses", in relation to works carried out under sub-paragraph (6) by a contracting authority, means the amount of any expenses reasonably incurred by the authority in carrying out the works, reduced by its contribution under the agreement;

"the required period" means —

    (a)   the period specified in, or determined in accordance with, the agreement as that within which the works must be carried out, or

    (b)   if there is no such period, a reasonable period.

Establishment and maintenance of route in absence of agreement

3   (1)   This paragraph applies where —

    (a)   it appears to Natural England that, for the purposes of the coastal access duty, it is necessary for works within paragraph 2(3) to be carried out on any land, or

    (b)   it appears to the access authority in relation to any land that, for the purpose of Natural England discharging the coastal access duty, it is necessary for such works to be carried out on that land.

(2) In this paragraph —

"the relevant authority" means —

    (a)   in a case within sub-paragraph (1)(a), Natural England, and

    (b)   in a case within sub-paragraph (1)(b), the access authority in question;

"the required works" means the works within paragraph 2(3) which the relevant authority considers it necessary to carry out for the purposes mentioned in sub-paragraph (1)(a) or (b).

(3) If the relevant authority is satisfied that it is unable to conclude on reasonable terms an agreement under paragraph 2 with the owner or occupier of the land for the carrying out of the required works, it may give the owner or occupier a notice stating that, after the end of the specified period, it intends to take all necessary steps for carrying out the required works.

(4) The "specified period" means the period specified in the notice, being a period of not less than 21 days beginning with the day on which the notice is given.

(5) A notice under sub-paragraph (3) must contain particulars of the right of appeal conferred by paragraph 4.

(6) Where a notice under sub-paragraph (3) is given to any person as the owner or occupier, the relevant authority must give a copy of the notice to every other owner or occupier of the land.

(7) If, at the end of the period specified in the notice under sub-paragraph (3), any of the required works have not been carried out, the relevant authority may take all necessary steps for carrying out those works.

(8) The relevant authority exercising the power conferred by sub-paragraph (7) in respect of any land must have regard to the requirements of efficient management of the land in deciding how to carry out the required works.

Appeals relating to notices under paragraph 3

4   (1) Where a notice under paragraph 3(3) has been given to a person in respect of any land, that person or any other owner or occupier of the land may appeal against the notice to the Secretary of State.

(2) An appeal against a notice under paragraph 3(3) may be brought on any of the following grounds —
   (a) that the notice requires the carrying out of any works which it is not necessary to carry out for the purposes of the coastal access duty;
   (b) that any of the works have already been carried out;
   (c) that the period specified in the notice as the period after which steps are to be taken to carry out the works is too short.

(3) On an appeal under this paragraph, the Secretary of State may —
   (a) confirm the notice with or without modifications, or
   (b) cancel the notice.

(4) Sections 7 and 8 of, and Schedule 3 to, the CROW Act have effect in relation to an appeal under this paragraph as they have effect in relation to an appeal under section 6 of that Act.

(5) Regulations may make provision as to —
   (a) the period within which and manner in which appeals under this paragraph are to be brought,
   (b) the advertising of such appeals, and
   (c) the manner in which such appeals are to be considered.

(6) Where an appeal has been brought under this paragraph against a notice under paragraph 3(3) given by Natural England or an access authority, it may not exercise its powers under paragraph 3(7) pending the determination or withdrawal of the appeal.

Power for Natural England to fund works

5   Natural England may meet or contribute towards expenditure incurred or to be incurred by any person in carrying out —
   (a) works of a kind which could be the subject of an agreement under paragraph 2, and
   (b) works of a kind which could be the subject of an agreement under section 35 of the CROW Act entered into by Natural England by virtue of paragraph 1.

Erection and maintenance of notices and signs

6   (1) Natural England may erect and maintain notices or signs within sub-paragraph (2) on —

2754

Marine and Coastal Access Act 2009 (c. 23)
Schedule 20 — Establishment and maintenance of the English coastal route etc

(a) any land over which the English coastal route passes, and

(b) any other land which is within section 296(5)(a) (land which is accessible to the public by virtue of section 3A of the CROW Act).

(2) The notices or signs within this sub-paragraph are those which —

(a) identify, or provide information about, the English coastal route (or any part of it), or

(b) warn the public of the existence of obstacles or hazards along that route,

and any other notices or signs which relate to the English coastal route.

(3) Before erecting a notice or sign on any land under this paragraph, Natural England must, so far as reasonably practicable, consult the owner and (if different) the person in lawful occupation of the land.

(4) Natural England may meet or contribute towards expenditure incurred or to be incurred by any person in displaying notices or signs of a kind which may be erected under this paragraph.

(5) Natural England may, in relation to any land, delegate to the access authority in relation to the land any function conferred on Natural England by this paragraph.

(6) Nothing in this paragraph applies in relation to the English coastal route in so far as it passes along —

(a) a public right of way over which there are rights of way for mechanically propelled vehicles, or

(b) a footway comprised in a highway which also comprises a way within paragraph (a).

(7) For the purposes of sub-paragraph (6) —

"mechanically propelled vehicle" does not include a vehicle falling within paragraph (c) of section 189(1) of the Road Traffic Act 1988 (c. 52);

"footway" has the same meaning as in section 329 of the Highways Act 1980 (c. 66).

7   In section 19 of the CROW Act (notices indicating boundaries of access land etc), after subsection (4) insert —

"(5) In the case of access land that is coastal margin, the powers conferred on an access authority by this section are also exercisable by Natural England."

Removal of notices and signs

8   (1) Any notice or sign to which this paragraph applies may be removed by —

(a) Natural England, or

(b) where authorised to act on its behalf, the access authority in relation to the land on which the sign or notice is erected.

(2) This paragraph applies to —

(a) a notice or sign erected under paragraph 6, and

(b) a notice erected under section 19 of the CROW Act (notices indicating boundaries of access land, etc) in relation to land which is coastal margin.

Marine and Coastal Access Act 2009 (c. 23)
Schedule 20 — Establishment and maintenance of the English coastal route etc

2755

(3) Before removing a notice or sign on any land under sub-paragraph (1), a person must, so far as reasonably practicable, consult the owner of the land and (if different) the person in lawful occupation of the land.

(4) Natural England may meet or contribute towards expenditure incurred or to be incurred by any person in removing notices or signs of a kind which may be erected under paragraph 6 or (in relation to land which is coastal margin) under section 19 of the CROW Act.

Powers of entry

9   (1) A person who is authorised by Natural England may enter any land —

   (a) for the purpose of surveying that or any other land in connection with the preparation of a report under section 51 or 55 of the 1949 Act pursuant to the coastal access duty;

   (b) in connection with the consideration of any representations made to Natural England in respect of a report submitted under section 51 of that Act pursuant to that duty;

   (c) for the purpose of assisting Natural England to determine whether to exercise the power conferred by section 301(2) (including the power conferred by section 301(3)(b)) (decision to treat waters of river as part of the sea);

   (d) for the purpose of assisting Natural England to provide the Secretary of State with advice in connection with the exercise of the Secretary of State's power under section 300(2)(b) (power to specify islands).

(2) A person who is authorised by Natural England or the appropriate access authority may enter any land —

   (a) for the purpose of determining whether any works of the kind mentioned in paragraph 2(3) are required in respect of any land;

   (b) for the purpose of carrying out works under —

      (i) an agreement entered into pursuant to paragraph 2(4)(a), or

      (ii) an agreement entered into pursuant to section 35(2)(a) of the CROW Act for the purposes of the coastal access duty;

   (c) for the purposes of —

      (i) carrying out works under paragraph 2(6) or 3(7),

      (ii) carrying out works under section 36(1) or (5) of the CROW Act in connection with an agreement entered into for the purposes of the coastal access duty, or

      (iii) carrying out works under section 37(5) of that Act for the purposes of that duty;

   (d) for the purpose of ascertaining whether members of the public are being permitted to exercise the rights conferred on them in relation to section 15 route land by or under an enactment mentioned in section 15(1) of the CROW Act;

   (e) in connection with an appeal under paragraph 4;

   (f) for the purpose of erecting, maintaining or removing notices or signs under paragraph 6 or 8 or, in relation to land which is coastal margin, under section 19 of the CROW Act.

(3) Subsections (5) to (7), (9) and (10) of section 40 of the CROW Act (powers of entry for the purposes of Part 1 of that Act) apply in relation to a person acting in the exercise of a power conferred by this paragraph, and the rights conferred by this paragraph, as they apply in relation to a person acting in

the exercise of a power conferred by that section and the rights conferred by that section.

(4) Section 41 of that Act (compensation relating to powers under section 40) has effect as if the reference to section 40 of that Act included a reference to this paragraph.

(5) A person may not under this paragraph demand admission as of right to any occupied land, other than access land or land over which the English coastal route passes, unless —

    (a)   in a case where the power of entry is exercised for the purposes of carrying out works as mentioned in sub-paragraph (2)(b) or (c) —

        (i)   the works are to be carried out on the land and a notice has been given to the occupier of the land under paragraph 2(6) or 3(3) or under section 36(1) or (3) or 37(1) of the CROW Act in connection with the works, or

        (ii)   at least 7 days' notice of the intended entry has been given to the occupier;

    (b)   in any other case, at least 24 hours' notice of the intended entry has been given to the occupier or it is not reasonably practicable to give such notice.

(6) In this paragraph —

    "access land" has the same meaning as in Chapter 3 of Part 1 of the CROW Act;

    "appropriate access authority" means the access authority in relation to the land in respect of which the right of entry is being exercised;

    "section 15 route land" means land —

        (a)   over which the English coastal route (or any part of it) passes, and

        (b)   which, for the purposes of section 1(1) of the CROW Act, is treated by section 15(1) of that Act as being accessible to the public apart from that Act.

Interpretation of Schedule

10   (1) In this Schedule —

    "coastal margin" has the same meaning as in Part 1 of the CROW Act;

    "owner" has the same meaning as in that Part.

(2) For the purposes of this Schedule —

    (a)   an official alternative route, in relation to the English coastal route, is to be regarded as part of the English coastal route,

    (b)   a temporary route which has effect by virtue of section 55I of the 1949 Act is to be treated as part of the English coastal route, and

    (c)   where by virtue of section 3A(6)(a) of the CROW Act any land is not yet accessible under section 2(1) of that Act, the references in this Schedule to the English coastal route include any route which would form part of the English coastal route if that land were so accessible.

(3) In sub-paragraph (2)(a) "official alternative route" has the meaning given by section 55J of the 1949 Act.

SCHEDULE 21 — Section 315

AMENDMENTS OF THE HARBOURS ACT 1964

1   The Harbours Act 1964 (c. 40) is amended as follows.

Provision that may be made by harbour empowerment order

2   (1) Section 16 (power to make harbour empowerment orders) is amended as follows.

    (2) In subsection (6) after "any Act (including this Act)" insert "and for repealing any statutory provision of local application affecting the area in relation to which the powers are intended to be exercised".

Delegation of certain functions under the Act

3   (1) After section 42 (accounts and reports) insert —

"Delegation of certain functions

42A Power to make orders delegating functions

    (1) The relevant authority may by order provide for such of the delegable functions as are designated in the order to be exercisable by such person as is designated in the order.

    (2) An authority may make an order under subsection (1) only with the consent of the person designated in it ("the delegate").

    (3) The delegate —
        (a) must comply with the order, and
        (b) is to be taken to have all the powers necessary to do so.

    (4) For so long as an order under subsection (1) remains in force, the functions designated in the order —
        (a) are exercisable by the delegate acting on behalf of the authority, and
        (b) are not exercisable by the authority.
      This subsection is subject to subsections (5) and (6).

    (5) The delegate must obtain the consent of the relevant authority before exercising any function under —
        (a) section 15;
        (b) section 15A;
        (c) section 18.

    (6) Subsection (4)(b) does not apply to any function under —
        (a) section 15;
        (b) section 15A;
        (c) section 18.

    (7) If a function is, by virtue of an order under subsection (1), exercisable by a person, any reference in this Act to the relevant authority is to be read, so far as relating to that function or the exercise of it, as a reference to that person.

(8) An order under subsection (1) may make different provision for different cases, different areas or different persons.

(9) The delegable functions are functions under the following sections —

    (a) section 14 (making harbour revision orders, except as mentioned in paragraph (b) below);

    (b) section 15 (making harbour revision orders for limited purposes for securing harbour efficiency);

    (c) section 15A (making orders varying powers of appointment in the constitutions of harbour authorities);

    (d) section 16 (making harbour empowerment orders);

    (e) section 18 (confirming or making harbour reorganisation schemes);

    (f) section 60 (making orders amending Acts of local application).

(10) In this section "the relevant authority", in relation to any delegable function, means the authority by whom (apart from any order under subsection (1)) the function is exercisable.

42B Directions as to performance of delegated functions

(1) This section applies where any functions are exercisable by or in relation to a person by virtue of an order made under section 42A by a relevant authority.

(2) The authority may from time to time give directions to the person with respect to the performance of the functions.

(3) A person to whom directions are given under this section must comply with the directions.

(4) An authority which gives a direction under this section must publish the direction in a manner likely to bring the direction to the attention of persons likely to be affected by it.".

(2) In section 54 (orders and regulations) after subsection (2) insert —

    "(3) Subsection (4) applies to any statutory instrument containing —

        (a) an order made under section 42A by a relevant authority in relation to a delegable function, or

        (b) an order made by any person, by virtue of an order under that section, in the exercise of a delegable function under section 14, 15, 16 or 18.

    (4) A statutory instrument to which this subsection applies —

        (a) if the relevant authority in relation to the delegable function is the Secretary of State, is subject to annulment in pursuance of a resolution of either House of Parliament;

        (b) if the relevant authority in relation to the delegable function is the Welsh Ministers, is subject to annulment in pursuance of a resolution of the National Assembly for Wales.".

Consent of Welsh Ministers or Secretary of State required for making of certain harbour orders

4 After section 42B (inserted by paragraph 3(1)) insert—

"42C Consent of Welsh Ministers required for certain orders and schemes

(1) This section applies to any harbour revision order or harbour empowerment order which makes provision excluding, modifying or repealing—

(a) any provision of the Marine and Coastal Access Act 2009 in so far as it applies to Wales;

(b) any instrument made under that Act by the Welsh Ministers;

(c) any statutory provision of local application made by the Welsh Ministers.

(2) This section also applies to any harbour reorganisation scheme which makes provision repealing or amending any statutory provision of local application made by the Welsh Ministers.

(3) The Secretary of State must notify the Welsh Ministers of any intention to make an order or scheme to which this section applies.

(4) The order or scheme must not include any provision falling within subsection (1) or, as the case may be, (2) if, within the prescribed period beginning with the date of the notification under subsection (3), the Welsh Ministers refuse their consent to the inclusion of that provision in the order or scheme.

(5) In this section "prescribed period" means such period as is prescribed in an order made by the Secretary of State for the purposes of this section.

42D Consent of Secretary of State required for certain orders and schemes

(1) This section applies to any harbour revision order or harbour empowerment order which makes provision excluding, modifying or repealing—

(a) any provision of the Marine and Coastal Access Act 2009 in so far as it applies to England;

(b) any instrument made under that Act by the Secretary of State;

(c) any statutory provision of local application made by the Secretary of State.

(2) This section also applies to any harbour reorganisation scheme which makes provision repealing or amending any statutory provision of local application made by the Secretary of State.

(3) The Welsh Ministers must notify the Secretary of State of any intention to make an order or scheme to which this section applies.

(4) The order or scheme must not include any provision falling within subsection (1) or, as the case may be, (2) if, within the prescribed period beginning with the date of the notification under subsection (3), the Secretary of State refuses consent to the inclusion of that provision in the order or scheme.

(5) In this section "prescribed period" means such period as is prescribed in an order made by the Secretary of State for the purposes of this section.".

Procedure for dealing with applications for harbour orders

5 (1) In Schedule 3 (procedure for making harbour revision and empowerment orders), paragraph 18 (which provides for the holding of an inquiry or public hearing when an objection is made) is amended as follows.

(2) For sub-paragraph (1) substitute —

"(1) This paragraph applies if an objection to the application was made to the appropriate authority and has not been withdrawn.

(1A) This paragraph does not apply if —
   (a) the appropriate authority decides that the application is not to proceed further,
   (b) the appropriate authority considers that the objection is frivolous or trivial,
   (c) the objection does not specify the grounds on which it is made, or
   (d) the objection was not made within the period allowed for making it.

(1B) Before deciding the application under paragraph 19, the appropriate authority may —
   (a) cause an inquiry to be held, or
   (b) give to the person who made the objection an opportunity of appearing before, and being heard by, a person appointed by the appropriate authority.

(1C) If the objection —
   (a) was made by the Welsh Ministers to the Secretary of State, and
   (b) is not an objection regarding compulsory acquisition of a parcel of land,
   the Secretary of State must cause an inquiry to be held under sub-paragraph (1B)(a).

(1D) If, in a case where sub-paragraph (1C) does not apply, —
   (a) the objection was made by a person within sub-paragraph (1E), and
   (b) that person makes a request in writing to the appropriate authority that the objection be referred to an inquiry or dealt with in accordance with sub-paragraph (1B)(b),
   the appropriate authority must either cause an inquiry to be held under sub-paragraph (1B)(a) or cause the objection to be dealt with in accordance with sub-paragraph (1B)(b), as the appropriate authority may determine.

(1E) The persons within this sub-paragraph are —
   (a) in the case of an application to the Secretary of State, the Welsh Ministers;

   (b) any local authority for an area in which the harbour (or any part of it) is situated;

   (c) the relevant conservation body;

   (d) if the order will authorise the compulsory acquisition of land, any person who is entitled to be served with notice under paragraph 11.".

 (3) In sub-paragraph (2) —

   (a) for "sub-paragraph (1)(a)" substitute "sub-paragraph (1B)(b)",

   (b) for "Secretary of State" substitute "appropriate authority", and

   (c) for "he" substitute "the authority".

 (4) In sub-paragraph (3) —

   (a) for "Secretary of State" substitute "appropriate authority",

   (b) omit paragraph (a), and

   (c) in paragraph (b), for "he" substitute "the appropriate authority".

 (5) After sub-paragraph (3) insert —

   "(4) In this paragraph —

    "the appropriate authority" means —

     (a) in a case where the application was made to the Secretary of State, the Secretary of State;

     (b) in a case where the application was made to the Welsh Ministers, the Welsh Ministers;

    "local authority" means —

     (a) in England, a county council, a district council, a London borough council, the Common Council of the City of London, the Council of the Isles of Scilly, a parish council and a parish meeting of a parish not having a separate parish council, and

     (b) in Wales, a county council, a county borough council and a community council;

    "the relevant conservation body" means —

     (a) if the harbour (or any part of it) is situated in England, Natural England, and

     (b) if the harbour (or any part of it) is situated in Wales, the Countryside Council for Wales.".

Procedure where harbour revision orders are made otherwise than on application

6 (1) For paragraph 28 of Schedule 3 (inquiry to be held in most cases where an objection is made) substitute —

  "28 (1) This paragraph applies if an objection to the proposal was made to the proposing authority and has not been withdrawn.

   (2) This paragraph does not apply if —

    (a) the proposing authority decides that the proposal is not to proceed further,

    (b) the proposing authority considers that the objection is frivolous or trivial,

    (c) the objection does not specify the grounds on which it is made, or

      (d)   the objection was not made within the period allowed for making it.

  (3) Before deciding the application under paragraph 29, the proposing authority may—

      (a)   cause an inquiry to be held, or

      (b)   give to the person who made the objection an opportunity of appearing before, and being heard by, a person appointed by the proposing authority.

  (4) If the objection was made by the Welsh Ministers to the Secretary of State, the Secretary of State must cause an inquiry to be held under sub-paragraph (3)(a).

  (5) Where—

      (a)   the objection was made by a person within sub-paragraph (6), and

      (b)   that person makes a request in writing to the proposing authority that the objection be referred to an inquiry or dealt with in accordance with sub-paragraph (3)(b),

  the proposing authority must either cause an inquiry to be held under sub-paragraph (3)(a) or cause the objection to be dealt with in accordance with sub-paragraph (3)(b), as the proposing authority may determine.

  (6) The persons within this sub-paragraph are—

      (a)   any local authority for an area in which the harbour (or any part of it) is situated, and

      (b)   the relevant conservation body.

  (7) Where an objector is heard in accordance with sub-paragraph (3)(b), the proposing authority must allow such other persons as the proposing authority thinks appropriate to be heard on the same occasion.

  (8) In this paragraph—

      "local authority" has the same meaning as in paragraph 18;

      "the proposing authority" means—

      (a)   the Secretary of State, in a case where it is the Secretary of State who proposes to make a harbour revision order;

      (b)   the Welsh Ministers, in a case where it is the Welsh Ministers who propose to make a harbour revision order;

      "the relevant conservation body" has the same meaning as in paragraph 18.".

(2) In paragraph 29 of that Schedule (decision on harbour revision order proposed by Secretary of State), in sub-paragraph (1)(b), after "inquiry" insert "and of any person appointed for the purpose of hearing an objector".

Application of paragraphs 5 and 6

7   The amendments made by paragraphs 5 and 6 apply to objections made on or after the date on which those amendments come into force.

Marine and Coastal Access Act 2009 (c. 23)
Schedule 22 — Repeals
Part 1 — EEZ, UK marine area and Welsh zone

2763

SCHEDULE 22   Section 321

REPEALS

PART 1

EEZ, UK MARINE AREA AND WELSH ZONE

Short title and chapter	Extent of repeal
Fishery Limits Act 1976 (c. 86)	Section 1(3) and (4).
Government of Wales Act 2006 (c. 32)	In section 158(1), the word "and" preceding the definition of "Wales".

PART 2

MARINE LICENSING

Short title and chapter	Extent of repeal
Coast Protection Act 1949 (c. 74)	Part 2. Section 47(a), (b) and (d). Section 49(2A).
Telecommunications Act 1984 (c. 12)	In Schedule 2, in paragraph 11 — (a) sub-paragraphs (3) to (10); (b) in sub-paragraph (11), the definition of "remedial works".
Food and Environment Protection Act 1985 (c. 48)	In section 5 — (a) paragraph (b); (b) in paragraph (e), sub-paragraph (ii) and the "or" preceding that sub-paragraph. In section 6(1)(a), sub-paragraph (ii) and the "or" preceding it. Section 7A(5). In section 8(6), the words "evidence, and in Scotland". Section 9(5) to (7). Section 21(8). In section 24(1) — (a) the definitions of "adjacent to Scotland", "Gas Importation and Storage Zone", "United Kingdom waters" and "United Kingdom controlled waters"; (b) in the definition of "licensing authority", paragraph (a) and, in paragraph (b)(iii), the words from "and the functions" to the end. Section 24(2A). Sections 25(3) and 26.
Merchant Shipping Act 1988 (c. 12)	Section 36.
Environmental Protection Act 1990 (c. 43)	Section 146(2) to (5) and (7).

Short title and chapter	*Extent of repeal*
Government of Wales Act 2006 (c. 32)	In Schedule 3, paragraph 4(1)(a).
Planning Act 2008 (c. 29)	Sections 148 and 149. In Schedule 5, paragraphs 27 to 30.

The repeals in the Coast Protection Act 1949 (c. 74) and the Merchant Shipping Act 1988 (c. 12) extend to England and Wales only.

PART 3

NATURE CONSERVATION

Short title and chapter	*Extent of repeal*
Wildlife and Countryside Act 1981 (c. 69)	Sections 36 and 37. In section 67(2), "36". Schedule 12.
Territorial Sea Act 1987 (c. 49)	Section 3(2)(b). In Schedule 1, paragraph 6.
Water Act 1989 (c. 15)	In Schedule 25, paragraph 66(2).
Local Government (Wales) Act 1994 (c. 19)	In Schedule 16, paragraph 65(4) and (10).

PART 4

MANAGEMENT OF INSHORE FISHERIES

Short title and chapter	*Extent of repeal*
Coast Protection Act 1949 (c. 74)	In section 2— (a) in subsection (2)(b), "local fisheries committee,"; (b) in subsection (8)(a), "or local fisheries committee,". In section 45(1)(b), "local fisheries committee,". In section 49(1), the definition of "local fisheries committee". In Part 1 of the First Schedule, in paragraph 1(b), "local fisheries committee,".
Nuclear Installations Act 1965 (c. 57)	In section 3(3)(b), the words "or any local fisheries committee".
Sea Fisheries Regulation Act 1966 (c. 38)	The whole Act.
Sea Fisheries (Shellfish) Act 1967 (c. 83)	In Schedule 2, the entry for the Sea Fisheries Regulation Act 1966.

Marine and Coastal Access Act 2009 (c. 23)
Schedule 22 – Repeals
Part 4 – Management of inshore fisheries

2765

Short title and chapter	Extent of repeal
Sea Fish (Conservation) Act 1967 (c. 84)	In section 3(7), the words from "or in any byelaw" to "the Sea Fisheries Regulation Act 1966,". Section 13. In section 16— (a) paragraph (d) of subsection (1) (but not the "and" following that paragraph); (b) subsection (2). Section 17. In section 22(1), the definition of "local fisheries committee".
Prevention of Oil Pollution Act 1971 (c. 60)	Section 19(6).
Local Government Act 1972 (c. 70)	Section 101(9)(d).
Local Government Act 1974 (c. 7)	In section 31A(3), paragraph (b) (but not the "or" following that paragraph).
Fishery Limits Act 1976 (c. 86)	In Schedule 1, paragraph 1.
Fisheries Act 1981 (c. 29)	In Schedule 4, paragraph 10.
Wildlife and Countryside Act 1981 (c. 69)	In section 27(1), in paragraph (c) of the definition of "authorised person", the words "or a local fisheries committee constituted under the Sea Fisheries Regulation Act 1966".
Local Government Act 1985 (c. 51)	In Schedule 8, paragraph 19.
Salmon Act 1986 (c. 62)	Section 37.
Water Act 1989 (c. 15)	In Schedule 17— (a) paragraph 1(4)(a); (b) paragraph 5.

Local Government and Housing Act 1989 (c. 42)	In section 5—
	
	(a) subsection (4);
	
	(b) in subsection (5)—
	
	    (a) the words "and of any such committee as is mentioned in subsection (4) above";
	
	    (b) in paragraph (a), the words "or committee";
	
	(c) in subsection (8), the word "and" at the end of the definition of "chief finance officer".
	Section 13(4)(b).
	In Schedule 1, paragraph 2(1)(d).

Water Consolidation (Consequential Provisions) Act 1991 (c. 60)	In Schedule 1, paragraph 16.

2766

Marine and Coastal Access Act 2009 (c. 23)
Schedule 22 — Repeals
Part 4 — Management of inshore fisheries

Short title and chapter	Extent of repeal
Sea Fisheries (Wildlife Conservation) Act 1992 (c. 36)	In section 1 — (a) in subsection (1), the words "or any relevant body"; (b) in subsection (2), the definition of "relevant body".
Radioactive Substances Act 1993 (c. 12)	In section 47(1), in the definition of "relevant water body", the words "or a local fisheries committee". In Schedule 3, paragraph 3.
Local Government (Wales) Act 1994 (c. 19)	In Schedule 16, paragraph 26.
Environment Act 1995 (c. 25)	Section 102. In Schedule 15 — (a) paragraph 2(4)(a); (b) paragraph 5; (c) paragraph 24.
Freedom of Information Act 2000 (c. 36)	In Schedule 1, paragraph 35A.
Natural Environment and Rural Communities Act 2006 (c. 16)	In Schedule 11, paragraph 38.
Regulatory Enforcement and Sanctions Act 2008 (c. 13)	In Schedules 3, 6 and 7, the entry relating to the Sea Fisheries Regulation Act 1966 (c. 38). In Schedule 5, the entry relating to local fisheries committees.

The repeal of any enactment by Part 4 of this Schedule has the same extent as the enactment repealed.

PART 5

FISHERIES

(A) REPEALS RELATING TO CHAPTERS 1 AND 2 OF PART 7

Short title and chapter	Extent of repeal
Sea Fisheries (Shellfish) Act 1967 (c. 83)	Section 1(4). In section 4(7), ", is subsequently convicted of another such offence". In Schedule 1, paragraphs 4(1) and 5.
Sea Fish (Conservation) Act 1967 (c. 84)	In section 11(1) — (a) paragraph (b); (b) in paragraph (c), "1, 2," and ", 6(5) or (5A)(b)". In section 15(2C), paragraph (b) and the word "or" preceding it.
Sea Fisheries Act 1968 (c. 77)	Section 15(2).
Fisheries Act 1981 (c. 29)	Section 19(2)(c).

Short title and chapter	Extent of repeal
Fisheries Act 1981 (c. 29) — *cont.*	In section 22 — (a) subsection (2)(a); (b) subsection (3). Section 28.
Sea Fish (Conservation) Act 1992 (c. 60)	In section 5, paragraph (b).
Criminal Justice and Public Order Act 1994 (c. 33)	In Part 1 of Schedule 8, the entries relating to sections 3(3) and 7(4) of the Sea Fisheries (Shellfish) Act 1967.
Merchant Shipping Act 1995 (c. 21)	In Schedule 13, paragraph 38(a) and (b).
Sea Fisheries (Shellfish) (Amendment) Act 1997 (c. 3)	Section 1.

(B) Repeals relating to Chapter 3 of Part 7 (migratory and freshwater fish)

Short title and chapter	Extent of repeal
Theft Act 1968 (c. 60)	In Schedule 1, paragraph 2(2).
Salmon and Freshwater Fisheries Act 1975 (c. 51)	In section 1 — (a) in subsection (1), the words "Subject to subsection (4) below,"; (b) subsection (4). Section 3. In section 4 — (a) in subsection (1), the words "Subject to subsection (2) below"; (b) subsection (2). Sections 6 to 8. Sections 16 and 17. Sections 19 to 22. Sections 23 and 24. In section 25 — (a) in subsection (4), the words from "gaff" to "tailer or"; (b) subsections (5) and (6). In section 31(1) — (a) in paragraph (b), the words "in contravention of this Act"; (b) in paragraph (c)(i), the words "which has been caught in contravention of this Act". Section 32(1)(ii) and the preceding "or". In section 34 — (a) in the heading, the words "at night"; (b) the words from "between the end" to "following morning". Section 35(2). Schedule 1.

Short title and chapter	*Extent of repeal*
Salmon and Freshwater Fisheries Act 1975 (c. 51)—*cont.*	In Schedule 2— (a) in paragraph 11, the words from "together" to the end; (b) paragraph 12. In Schedule 4, in the table in paragraph 1(2), the entries relating to section 19(2), section 19(4), section 19(6), section 19(7) and section 21.
Fisheries Act 1981 (c. 29)	In Schedule 4— (a) paragraph 2; (b) paragraph 4; (c) in paragraph 6(c), the words "(not being a fixed engine)"; (d) in paragraph 6(d), the words "(not being fixed engines)"; (e) paragraph 28.
Salmon Act 1986 (c. 62)	In section 32— (a) in subsection (1), the words "by or for the benefit of another person"; (b) subsection (6)(a). Section 33(1) and (2).
Territorial Sea Act 1987 (c. 49)	In Schedule 1, paragraph 3.
Water Act 1989 (c. 15)	In Schedule 17, paragraph 7(3), (4), (9)(b) and (12).
Water Resources Act 1991 (c. 57)	In section 212— (a) in subsection (2)(a), the words "(not being a fixed engine)"; (b) in subsection (2)(b), the words "(not being fixed engines)"; (c) subsection (3). In Schedule 25— (a) in paragraph 6(2), the words "Subject to paragraph 7(1) below"; (b) in paragraph 6(2)(c), the words "(not being a fixed engine)"; (c) in paragraph 6(2)(d), the words "(not being fixed engines)"; (d) in paragraph 6(2)(g), the word "licensed"; (e) paragraph 6(3) and (4); (f) paragraph 7.
Environment Act 1995 (c. 25)	In Schedule 15, paragraphs 8, 9, 15 and 22.
Criminal Justice Act 2003 (c. 44)	In Schedule 25, paragraph 70. In Part 9 of Schedule 37, the entry relating to the Theft Act 1968 (c. 60).
Serious Crime Act 2007 (c. 27)	In Schedule 1, in paragraph 13(1), the words "for salmon, trout or freshwater fish".

(C) REPEALS RELATING TO CHAPTER 4 OF PART 7 (OBSOLETE ENACTMENTS)

Short title and chapter	Extent of repeal
White Herring Fisheries Act 1771 (c. 31)	The whole Act.
Seal Fishery Act 1875 (c. 18)	The whole Act.
Fisheries Act 1891 (c. 37)	Section 13.
North Sea Fisheries Act 1893 (c. 17)	The whole Act.
Behring Sea Award Act 1894 (c. 2)	The whole Act.
Seal Fisheries (North Pacific) Act 1895 (c. 21)	The whole Act.
Seal Fisheries (North Pacific) Act 1912 (c. 10)	The whole Act.
Port of London Act 1968 (c. xxxii)	Sections 86, 87 and 163. In section 167, paragraph (b). In section 168(2), the words from ", except for byelaws" to the end.
Customs and Excise Management Act 1979 (c. 2)	In paragraph 12 of Schedule 4, the entry relating to the Seal Fisheries (North Pacific) Act 1912.
Statute Law (Repeals) Act 1993 (c. 50)	In Schedule 2, paragraph 8.
Merchant Shipping Act 1995 (c. 21)	In Schedule 13, paragraphs 11 and 12.
Courts Act 2003 (c. 39)	In Schedule 8, paragraph 65.
Criminal Justice Act 2003 (c. 44)	In Schedule 25, paragraphs 12 and 13.

PART 6

ENFORCEMENT

Short title and chapter	Extent of repeal
Sea Fisheries Act 1968 (c. 77)	In section 7 — (a) in subsection (1)(d), the words "of the Secretary of State or"; (b) subsection (5)(a).

PART 7

COASTAL ACCESS

Short title and chapter	Extent of repeal
Countryside and Rights of Way Act 2000 (c. 37)	In section 1(1), the word "or" at the end of paragraph (d). In section 16(6), the word "and" at the end of paragraph (c).

Short title and chapter	*Extent of repeal*
Countryside and Rights of Way Act 2000 (c. 37) —*cont.*	In section 20(1), the word "and" at the end of paragraph (a).

PART 8

MISCELLANEOUS

Short title and chapter	*Extent of repeal*
Harbours Act 1964 (c. 40)	In Schedule 3, paragraph 18(3)(a).
Civil Contingencies Act 2004 (c. 36)	In Schedule 1, paragraph 11A.
Natural Environment and Rural Communities Act 2006 (c. 16)	In Schedule 11, paragraph 174.

Welfare Reform Act 2009

CHAPTER 24

CONTENTS

Contributory jobseeker's allowance and employment and support allowance

Disability living allowance

Abolition of adult dependency increases

External provider social loans and community care grants

Payments on account

Up-rating of benefits

Benefit sanctions for offenders

Pilot schemes

Miscellaneous

PART 2

DISABLED PEOPLE: RIGHT TO CONTROL PROVISION OF SERVICES

Introductory

Power to make regulations

Supplementary

PART 3

CHILD MAINTENANCE

PART 4

BIRTH REGISTRATION

PART 5

GENERAL

Welfare Reform Act 2009

2009 CHAPTER 24

An Act to amend the law relating to social security; to make provision enabling disabled people to be given greater control over the way in which certain public services are provided for them; to amend the law relating to child support; to make provision about the registration of births; and for connected purposes. [12th November 2009]

B E IT ENACTED by the Queen's most Excellent Majesty, by and with the advice and consent of the Lords Spiritual and Temporal, and Commons, in this present Parliament assembled, and by the authority of the same, as follows:—

PART 1

SOCIAL SECURITY

"Work for your benefit" schemes etc.

1 Schemes for assisting persons to obtain employment: "work for your benefit" schemes etc.

(1) The Jobseekers Act 1995 (c. 18) is amended as follows.

(2) After section 17 insert—

""Work for your benefit" schemes etc.

17A Schemes for assisting persons to obtain employment: "work for your benefit" schemes etc.

(1) Regulations may make provision for or in connection with imposing on claimants in prescribed circumstances a requirement to participate in schemes of any prescribed description that are designed to assist them to obtain employment.

(2) Regulations under this section may, in particular, require participants to undertake work, or work-related activity, during any prescribed period with a view to improving their prospects of obtaining employment.

(3) In subsection (2) "work-related activity", in relation to any person, means activity which makes it more likely that the person will obtain or remain in work or be able to do so.

(4) Regulations under this section may not require a person to participate in a scheme unless the person would (apart from the regulations) be required to meet the jobseeking conditions.

(5) Regulations under this section may, in particular, make provision —
   (a) for notifying participants of the requirement to participate in a scheme within subsection (1);
   (b) for securing that participants are not required to meet the jobseeking conditions or are not required to meet such of those conditions as are specified in the regulations;
   (c) for suspending any jobseeker's agreement to which a person is a party for any period during which the person is a participant;
   (d) for securing that the appropriate consequence follows if a participant has failed to comply with the regulations and it is not shown, within a prescribed period, that the participant had good cause for the failure;
   (e) prescribing matters which are, or are not, to be taken into account in determining whether a participant has good cause for any failure to comply with the regulations;
   (f) prescribing circumstances in which a participant is, or is not, to be regarded as having good cause for any failure to comply with the regulations.

(6) In the case of a jobseeker's allowance other than a joint-claim jobseeker's allowance, the appropriate consequence for the purposes of subsection (5)(d) is that the allowance is not payable for such period (of at least one week but not more than 26 weeks) as may be prescribed.

(7) In the case of a joint-claim jobseeker's allowance, the appropriate consequence for the purposes of subsection (5)(d) is that the participant is to be treated as subject to sanctions for the purposes of section 20A for such period (of at least one week but not more than 26 weeks) as may be prescribed.

(8) Regulations under this section may make provision for an income-based jobseeker's allowance to be payable in prescribed circumstances even though other provision made by the regulations would prevent payment of it.

This subsection does not apply in the case of a joint-claim jobseeker's allowance (corresponding provision for which is made by section 20B(4)).

(9) The provision that may be made by the regulations by virtue of subsection (8) includes, in particular, provision for the allowance to be —
   (a) payable only if prescribed requirements as to the provision of information are complied with;

     (b)   payable at a prescribed rate;

     (c)   payable for a prescribed period (which may differ from any period mentioned in subsection (6)).

(10)   In this section—

"claimant", in relation to a joint-claim couple claiming a joint-claim jobseeker's allowance, means either or both of the members of the couple;

"the jobseeking conditions" means the conditions set out in section 1(2)(a) to (c);

"participant", in relation to any time, means any person who is required at that time to participate in a scheme within subsection (1).

17B   Section 17A: supplemental

(1)   For the purposes of, or in connection with, any scheme within section 17A(1) the Secretary of State may—

    (a)   make arrangements (whether or not with other persons) for the provision of facilities;

    (b)   provide support (by whatever means) for arrangements made by other persons for the provision of facilities;

    (c)   make payments (by way of fees, grants, loans or otherwise) to persons undertaking the provision of facilities under arrangements within paragraph (a) or (b);

    (d)   make payments (by way of grants, loans or otherwise) to persons participating in the scheme;

    (e)   make payments in respect of incidental expenses.

(2)   For the purposes of, or in connection with, any scheme within section 17A(1)—

    (a)   the Scottish Ministers, and

    (b)   the Welsh Ministers,

may make payments (by way of fees, grants, loans or otherwise) to persons (including the Secretary of State) undertaking the provision of facilities under arrangements within subsection (1)(a) or (b) if the following condition is met.

(3)   The condition is that the Scottish Ministers or the Welsh Ministers consider that the facilities are capable of supporting the training in Scotland or Wales of persons for employment.

(4)   Unless the Scottish Ministers or Welsh Ministers otherwise specify, the payments may be used by the person to whom they are made for the provision of any of the facilities provided under the arrangements.

(5)   In subsections (1) to (4) "facilities" includes services, and any reference to the provision of facilities includes the making of payments to persons participating in the scheme.

(6)   The power of the Secretary of State to make an order under section 26 of the Employment Act 1988 (status of trainees etc) includes power to make, in relation to—

    (a)   persons participating in any scheme within section 17A(1), and

    (b)   payments received by them by virtue of subsection (1) above, provision corresponding to any provision which (by virtue of section 26(1) or (2) of that Act) may be made in relation to persons using such facilities, and to such payments received by them, as are mentioned in section 26(1) of that Act."

(3) In section 36 (regulations and orders), after subsection (4) insert—

"(4A) Without prejudice to the generality of the provisions of this section—
  (a) regulations under section 17A may make different provision for different areas;
  (b) regulations under section 17A may make provision which applies only in relation to an area or areas specified in the regulations."

(4) In paragraph 3 of Schedule 3 to the Social Security Act 1998 (c. 14) (decisions against which an appeal lies: payability of benefit), after paragraph (d) insert—
  "(da) regulations made under section 17A of the Jobseekers Act;".

(5) In section 8(2)(b)(i) of the Social Security Fraud Act 2001 (c. 11) (effect of offence on joint-claim jobseeker's allowance), after "is" insert "(or is treated as being)".

Revised system of working-age benefits

2 Work-related activity: income support claimants and partners of claimants

(1) The Social Security Administration Act 1992 (c. 5) is amended as follows.

(2) After section 2C insert—

"2D Work-related activity

(1) Regulations may make provision for or in connection with imposing on a person who—
  (a) is entitled to income support, and
  (b) is not a lone parent of a child under the age of 3,
a requirement to undertake work-related activity in accordance with regulations as a condition of continuing to be entitled to the full amount of income support payable apart from the regulations.

(2) Regulations may make provision for or in connection with imposing on a person ("P") who—
  (a) is under pensionable age, and
  (b) is a member of a couple the other member of which ("C") is entitled to a benefit to which subsection (3) applies at a higher rate referable to P,
a requirement to undertake work-related activity in accordance with regulations as a condition of the benefit continuing to be payable to C at that rate.

(3) The benefits to which this subsection applies are—
  (a) income support;
  (b) an income-based jobseeker's allowance other than a joint-claim jobseeker's allowance; and
  (c) an income-related employment and support allowance.

(4) Regulations under this section may, in particular, make provision—

    (a)   prescribing circumstances in which a person is to be subject to any requirement imposed by the regulations (a "relevant requirement");

    (b)   for notifying a person of a relevant requirement;

    (c)   prescribing the time or times at which a person who is subject to a relevant requirement is required to undertake work-related activity and the amount of work-related activity the person is required at any time to undertake;

    (d)   prescribing circumstances in which a person who is subject to a relevant requirement is, or is not, to be regarded as undertaking work-related activity;

    (e)   in a case where C is a member of more than one couple, for determining which of the members of the couples is to be subject to a relevant requirement or requiring each of them to be subject to a relevant requirement;

    (f)   for securing that the appropriate consequence follows if —

        (i)   a person who is subject to a relevant requirement has failed to comply with the requirement, and

        (ii)   it is not shown, within a prescribed period, that the person had good cause for that failure;

    (g)   prescribing the evidence which a person who is subject to a relevant requirement needs to provide in order to show compliance with the requirement;

    (h)   prescribing matters which are, or are not, to be taken into account in determining whether a person had good cause for any failure to comply with a relevant requirement;

    (i)   prescribing circumstances in which a person is, or is not, to be regarded as having good cause for any such failure.

(5)   For the purposes of subsection (4)(f) the appropriate consequence is that the amount of the benefit payable is to be reduced by the prescribed amount until the prescribed time.

(6)   Regulations under subsection (5) may, in relation to any such reduction, provide —

    (a)   for the amount of the reduction to be calculated in the first instance by reference to such amount as may be prescribed;

    (b)   for the amount as so calculated to be restricted, in prescribed circumstances, to the prescribed extent.

(7)   Regulations under this section may include provision that in such circumstances as the regulations may provide a person's obligation under the regulations to undertake work-related activity at a particular time is not to apply, or is to be treated as not having applied.

(8)   Regulations under this section must include provision for securing that lone parents are entitled (subject to meeting any prescribed conditions) to restrict the times at which they are required to undertake work-related activity.

(9)   For the purposes of this section and sections 2E and 2F —

    (a)   "couple" has the meaning given by section 137(1) of the Contributions and Benefits Act;

    (b)   "lone parent" means a person who—

> > (i)   is not a member of a couple, and
> >
> > (ii) is responsible for, and a member of the same household as, a child;
>
> (c) "prescribed" means specified in, or determined in accordance with, regulations;
>
> (d) "work-related activity", in relation to a person, means activity which makes it more likely that the person will obtain or remain in work or be able to do so;
>
> (e) any reference to a person attaining pensionable age is, in the case of a man born before 6 April 1955, a reference to the time when a woman born on the same day as the man would attain pensionable age;
>
> (f) any reference to a benefit payable to C at a higher rate referable to P is a reference to any case where the amount payable is more than it would be if C and P were not members of the same couple.

(10) For the purposes of this section regulations may make provision —

> (a) as to circumstances in which one person is to be treated as responsible or not responsible for another;
>
> (b) as to circumstances in which persons are to be treated as being or not being members of the same household.

(11) Information supplied in pursuance of regulations under this section is to be taken for all purposes to be information relating to social security.

2E   Action plans in connection with work-focused interviews

(1) The Secretary of State must in prescribed circumstances provide a document (referred to in this section as an "action plan") prepared for such purposes as may be prescribed to a person who is subject to a requirement imposed under section 2A or 2AA in relation to any of the following benefits.

(2) The benefits are —

> (a) income support;
>
> (b) an income-based jobseeker's allowance other than a joint-claim jobseeker's allowance; and
>
> (c) an income-related employment and support allowance.

(3) Regulations may make provision about —

> (a) the form of action plans;
>
> (b) the content of action plans;
>
> (c) the review and updating of action plans.

(4) Regulations under this section may, in particular, make provision for action plans which are provided to a person who is subject under section 2D to a requirement to undertake work-related activity to contain particulars of activity which, if undertaken, would enable the requirement to be met.

(5) Regulations may make provision for reconsideration of an action plan at the request of the person to whom it is provided and may, in particular, make provision about —

> (a) the circumstances in which reconsideration may be requested;

    (b)   the period within which any reconsideration must take place;

    (c)   the matters to which regard must be had when deciding on reconsideration whether the plan should be changed;

    (d)   notification of the decision on reconsideration;

    (e)   the giving of directions for the purpose of giving effect to the decision on reconsideration.

(6)   In preparing any action plan, the Secretary of State must have regard (so far as practicable) to its impact on the well-being of any person under the age of 16 who may be affected by it.

2F   Directions about work-related activity

(1)   In prescribed circumstances, the Secretary of State may by direction given to a person subject to a requirement imposed under section 2D provide that the activity specified in the direction is—

    (a)   to be the only activity which, in the person's case, is to be regarded as being work-related activity; or

    (b)   to be regarded, in the person's case, as not being work-related activity.

(2)   But a direction under subsection (1) may not specify medical or surgical treatment as the only activity which, in any person's case, is to be regarded as being work-related activity.

(3)   A direction under subsection (1) given to any person—

    (a)   must be reasonable, having regard to the person's circumstances;

    (b)   must be given to the person by being included in an action plan provided to the person under section 2E; and

    (c)   may be varied or revoked by a subsequent direction under subsection (1).

(4)   Where a direction under subsection (1) varies or revokes a previous direction, it may provide for the variation or revocation to have effect from a time before the giving of the direction.

2G   Contracting-out

(1)   The following functions of the Secretary of State may be exercised by, or by employees of, such person (if any) as the Secretary of State may authorise for the purpose, namely—

    (a)   conducting interviews under section 2A or 2AA;

    (b)   providing documents under section 2E;

    (c)   giving, varying or revoking directions under section 2F.

(2)   Regulations may provide for any of the following functions of the Secretary of State to be exercisable by, or by employees of, such person (if any) as the Secretary of State may authorise for the purpose—

    (a)   any function under regulations under any of sections 2A to 2F, except the making of an excluded decision (see subsection (3));

    (b)   the function under section 9(1) of the 1998 Act (revision of decisions) so far as relating to decisions (other than excluded decisions) that relate to any matter arising under regulations under any of sections 2A to 2F;

    (c)   the function under section 10(1) of the 1998 Act (superseding of decisions) so far as relating to decisions (other than excluded decisions) of the Secretary of State that relate to any matter arising under regulations under any of sections 2A to 2F;

    (d)   any function under Chapter 2 of Part 1 of the 1998 Act (social security decisions), except section 25(2) and (3) (decisions involving issues arising on appeal in other cases), which relates to the exercise of any of the functions within paragraphs (a) to (c).

(3)   Each of the following is an "excluded decision" for the purposes of subsection (2) —

    (a)   a decision about whether a person has failed to comply with a requirement imposed by regulations under section 2A, 2AA or 2D;

    (b)   a decision about whether a person had good cause for failure to comply with such a requirement;

    (c)   a decision about the reduction of a benefit in consequence of a failure to comply with such a requirement.

(4)   Regulations under subsection (2) may provide that a function to which that subsection applies may be exercised —

    (a)   either wholly or to such extent as the regulations may provide,

    (b)   either generally or in such cases as the regulations may provide, and

    (c)   either unconditionally or subject to the fulfilment of such conditions as the regulations may provide.

(5)   An authorisation given by virtue of any provision made by or under this section may authorise the exercise of the function concerned —

    (a)   either wholly or to such extent as may be specified in the authorisation,

    (b)   either generally or in such cases as may be so specified, and

    (c)   either unconditionally or subject to the fulfilment of such conditions as may be so specified;

but, in the case of an authorisation given by virtue of regulations under subsection (2), this subsection is subject to the regulations.

(6)   An authorisation given by virtue of any provision made by or under this section —

    (a)   may specify its duration,

    (b)   may be revoked at any time by the Secretary of State, and

    (c)   does not prevent the Secretary of State or any other person from exercising the function to which the authorisation relates.

(7)   Anything done or omitted to be done by or in relation to an authorised person (or an employee of that person) in, or in connection with, the exercise or purported exercise of the function concerned is to be treated for all purposes as done or omitted to be done by or in relation to the Secretary of State.

(8)   But subsection (7) does not apply —

    (a)   for the purposes of so much of any contract made between the authorised person and the Secretary of State as relates to the exercise of the function, or

(b) for the purposes of any criminal proceedings brought in respect of anything done by the authorised person (or an employee of that person).

(9) Any decision which an authorised person makes in exercise of the function concerned has effect as a decision of the Secretary of State under section 8 of the 1998 Act.

(10) Where —

(a) the authorisation of an authorised person is revoked at any time, and

(b) at the time of the revocation so much of any contract made between the authorised person and the Secretary of State as relates to the exercise of the function is subsisting,

the authorised person is entitled to treat the contract as repudiated by the Secretary of State (and not as frustrated by reason of the revocation).

(11) In this section —

(a) "the 1998 Act" means the Social Security Act 1998;

(b) "authorised person" means a person authorised to exercise any function by virtue of any provision made by or under this section;

(c) references to functions of the Secretary of State under any enactment (including one comprised in regulations) include functions which the Secretary of State has by virtue of the application of section 8(1)(c) of the 1998 Act in relation to the enactment.

2H Good cause for failure to comply with regulations

(1) This section applies to any regulations made under section 2A, 2AA or 2D that prescribe matters to be taken into account in determining whether a person has good cause for any failure to comply with the regulations.

(2) The provision made by the regulations prescribing those matters must include provision relating to —

(a) the person's physical or mental health or condition;

(b) the availability of childcare."

(3) In the italic heading before section 2A, insert "*and work-related activity*".

(4) In section 189(7A) (regulations which may make provision only in relation to specified areas), for "2C" substitute "2F".

(5) In section 72(3) of the Welfare Reform and Pensions Act 1999 (c. 30) (supply of information for certain purposes), for paragraphs (a) and (aa) substitute —

"(a) any of sections 2A to 2F and 7A of the Administration Act,".

3 Lone parents

(1) In section 124 of the Social Security Contributions and Benefits Act 1992 (c. 4) (conditions for income support), after subsection (1) insert —

"(1A) Regulations under paragraph (e) of subsection (1) must secure that a person who —

(a) is not a member of a couple, and

    (b)   is responsible for, and a member of the same household as, a child under the age of 7,

falls within a category of person prescribed under that paragraph.

  (1B)   Subsection (1A) does not apply if regulations under subsection (4)(c) of section 1A of the Jobseekers Act 1995 containing the provision mentioned in subsection (5) of that section are in force."

(2)   In section 2A of the Social Security Administration Act 1992 (c. 5) (work-focused interviews)—

   (a)   after subsection (2) insert—

    "(2A)   No requirement may be imposed by virtue of this section on a person who—

      (a)   is not a member of a couple, and

      (b)   is responsible for, and a member of the same household as, a child under the age of one.

    (2B)   For the purposes of subsection (2A)(b) regulations may make provision—

      (a)   as to circumstances in which one person is to be treated as responsible or not responsible for another;

      (b)   as to circumstances in which persons are to be treated as being or not being members of the same household.", and

   (b)   in subsection (8), after "In this section—" insert—

      ""couple" has the meaning given by section 137(1) of the Contributions and Benefits Act;".

(3)   In section 12 of the Welfare Reform Act 2007 (c. 5) (employment and support allowance: work-focused interviews), in subsection (1)(b), at the end insert "or a lone parent of a child under the age of one".

(4)   In section 13 of that Act (employment and support allowance: work-related activity)—

   (a)   in subsection (1), after "section 12(1)" insert ", and who is not a lone parent of a child under the age of 3,", and

   (b)   after subsection (6) insert—

    "(6A)   Regulations under this section shall include provision for securing that lone parents are entitled (subject to meeting any prescribed conditions) to restrict the times at which they are required to undertake work-related activity."

(5)   In section 24 of that Act (interpretation of Part 1), after subsection (3) insert—

    "(3A)   For the purposes of this Part, a person is a lone parent if the person—

      (a)   is not a member of a couple (within the meaning given by section 137(1) of the Contributions and Benefits Act), and

      (b)   is responsible for, and a member of the same household as, a person under the age of 16.

    (3B)   For the purposes of subsection (3A)(b) regulations may make provision—

      (a)   as to circumstances in which one person is to be treated as responsible or not responsible for another;

    (b)   as to circumstances in which persons are to be treated as being or not being members of the same household."

4   Entitlement to jobseeker's allowance without seeking employment etc.

    (1)   The Jobseekers Act 1995 (c. 18) is amended as follows.

    (2)   In section 1 (the jobseeker's allowance) —

        (a)   for subsections (2) to (2D) substitute—

            "(1A)   The circumstances in which a claimant is entitled to a jobseeker's allowance are set out in —

                (a)   section 1A (jobseeker's allowance other than joint-claim jobseeker's allowance), and

                (b)   section 1B (joint-claim jobseeker's allowance).", and

        (b)   in subsection (4), for the definition of "a joint-claim couple" substitute —

                ""a joint-claim couple" means a couple other than a couple of a prescribed description;".

    (3)   After section 1 insert —

"1A   Jobseeker's allowance other than joint-claim jobseeker's allowance

    (1)   A claimant is entitled to a jobseeker's allowance if the claimant meets —

        (a)   the basic conditions; and

        (b)   the conditions set out in section 2 (the contribution-based conditions).

    (2)   A claimant who —

        (a)   is not a member of a joint-claim couple, or

        (b)   is a member of a joint-claim couple the other member of which has limited capability for work,

    is entitled to a jobseeker's allowance if the claimant meets condition A or B.

    (3)   Condition A is that the claimant meets —

        (a)   the basic conditions; and

        (b)   the applicable conditions set out in section 3 (the income-based conditions).

    (4)   Condition B is that the claimant —

        (a)   is not otherwise entitled to a jobseeker's allowance;

        (b)   meets the basic conditions other than the jobseeking conditions;

        (c)   falls within a prescribed description of person; and

        (d)   meets the applicable conditions set out in section 3.

    (5)   Regulations under paragraph (c) of subsection (4) must secure that a person who —

        (a)   is not a member of a couple, and

        (b)   is responsible for, and a member of the same household as, a child under the age of 7,

    falls within a description of person prescribed under that paragraph.

(6) Subsection (5) does not apply if regulations under subsection (1)(e) of section 124 of the Benefits Act containing the provision mentioned in subsection (1A) of that section are in force.

(7) For the purposes of this Act a person meets the basic conditions if the person—

    (a) is available for employment;

    (b) has entered into a jobseeker's agreement which remains in force;

    (c) is actively seeking employment;

    (d) is not engaged in remunerative work;

    (e) does not have limited capability for work;

    (f) is not receiving relevant education;

    (g) is under pensionable age; and

    (h) is in Great Britain.

(8) Regulations may prescribe circumstances in which subsection (2) is to apply to a claimant who is a member of a joint-claim couple the other member of which does not have limited capability for work.

(9) Subsections (1) and (2) are subject to the provisions of this Act.

1B   Joint-claim jobseeker's allowance

(1) A joint-claim couple are entitled to a jobseeker's allowance if—

    (a) a claim for the allowance is made jointly by the couple;

    (b) each member of the couple meets the basic conditions; and

    (c) the conditions set out in section 3A are met in relation to the couple.

(2) Regulations may, in respect of cases where a person would (but for the regulations) be a member of two or more joint-claim couples, make provision for only one of those couples to be a joint-claim couple.

(3) The regulations may, in particular, make provision for the couple which is to be the joint-claim couple to be nominated—

    (a) by the persons who are members of the couple; or

    (b) in default of one of the couples being so nominated, by the Secretary of State.

(4) Subsection (1) is subject to the provisions of this Act."

(4) Schedule 1 contains—

    (a) amendments of the Jobseekers Act 1995 (c. 18) to provide for work-focused interviews, and action plans in consequence of work-focused interviews, for persons entitled to a jobseeker's allowance without being required to meet the jobseeking conditions,

    (b) amendments of that Act to provide for the imposition on such persons of requirements to undertake work-related activity, and

    (c) other amendments in consequence of, or otherwise in connection with, the amendments made by this section or the amendments mentioned in paragraphs (a) and (b).

5   Couples where at least one member capable of work

(1)   In section 124 of the Social Security Contributions and Benefits Act 1992 (c. 4) (conditions for income support) —

    (a)   in subsection (1), after paragraph (g) (but before the "and" at the end of it) insert —

        "(ga)   except in such circumstances as may be prescribed, if he is a member of a couple, the other member of the couple has limited capability for work;",

    (b)   after subsection (6) insert —

        "(6A)   The question whether a person has, or does not have, limited capability for work shall be determined for the purposes of this section in accordance with the provisions of Part 1 of the Welfare Reform Act 2007 (employment and support allowance).

        (6B)   References in that Part to the purposes of that Part shall be construed, where the provisions of that Part have effect for the purposes of this section, as references to the purposes of this section.", and

    (c)   in subsection (7), for "Part 1 of the Welfare Reform Act 2007 (employment and support allowance)" substitute "that Part".

(2)   In paragraph 6 of Schedule 1 to the Welfare Reform Act 2007 (c. 5) (conditions for income-related employment and support allowance) —

    (a)   in sub-paragraph (1), after paragraph (d) insert —

        "(da)   is not a member of a couple the other member of which does not have limited capability for work;", and

    (b)   after sub-paragraph (2) insert —

        "(2A)   Regulations may prescribe circumstances in which sub-paragraph (1)(da) does not apply."

6   Statutory sick pay and employment and support allowance

In section 20 of the Welfare Reform Act 2007 (relationship of employment and support allowance with statutory sick pay and other statutory payments), for subsection (1) substitute —

    "(1)   A person —

        (a)   is not entitled to a contributory allowance in respect of a day, and

        (b)   except as regulations may provide, is not entitled to an income-related allowance in respect of a day,

if, for the purposes of statutory sick pay, that day is a day of incapacity for work in relation to a contract of service and falls within a period of entitlement (whether or not it is a qualifying day)."

7   Transitional provision relating to sections 4 to 6

(1)   The Secretary of State may by regulations make such provision as the Secretary of State considers necessary or expedient for the purposes of, or in connection with, the transition of persons to —

    (a)   income-based jobseeker's allowance, or

      (b)   income-related employment and support allowance,

by virtue of any provision of sections 4 to 6.

(2)   Regulations under this section may, in particular, make provision—

     (a)   for the termination or cancellation of awards of income support or income-related employment and support allowance;

     (b)   for a person whose award of income support or income-related employment and support allowance has been terminated or cancelled under regulations made by virtue of paragraph (a) to be treated as having been awarded a transitional allowance;

     (c)   for any such award of a transitional allowance to be—

        (i)   of such a kind,

        (ii)   for such period,

        (iii)   of such an amount, and

        (iv)   subject to such conditions,

as may be determined in accordance with the regulations;

     (d)   for a person's continuing entitlement to a transitional allowance to be determined by reference to such provision as may be made by the regulations;

     (e)   for the termination of an award of a transitional allowance;

     (f)   for the review of an award of a transitional allowance;

     (g)   that—

        (i)   days which were days of entitlement to income support or income-related employment and support allowance, and

        (ii)   such other days as may be specified in or determined in accordance with the regulations,

are to be treated as having been days during which a person was, or would have been, entitled to an income-based jobseeker's allowance or income-related employment and support allowance.

(3)   Subsections (3) to (5) of section 175 of the Social Security Contributions and Benefits Act 1992 (c. 4) (supplementary provisions in relation to powers to make subordinate legislation under that Act) apply in relation to the power to make regulations under this section as they apply to any power to make regulations under that Act.

(4)   The power to make regulations under this section is exercisable by statutory instrument.

(5)   A statutory instrument containing regulations under this section is subject to annulment in pursuance of a resolution of either House of Parliament.

(6)   In this section—

     "income-based jobseeker's allowance" has the same meaning as in the Jobseekers Act 1995 (c. 18);

     "income-related employment and support allowance" means an income-related allowance under Part 1 of the Welfare Reform Act 2007 (c. 5) (employment and support allowance);

     "transitional allowance" means an income-based jobseeker's allowance or income-related employment and support allowance.

8   **Parliamentary procedure: regulations imposing work-related activity requirements on lone parents of children under 7**

(1)   This section applies to regulations made under any relevant provision which impose a requirement on any lone parent of a child under the age of 7 to undertake work-related activity (within the meaning of the regulations).

(2)   In subsection (1) "relevant provision" means —
     (a)   section 2D(1) of the Social Security Administration Act 1992 (c. 5),
     (b)   section 18B of the Jobseekers Act 1995 (c. 18), or
     (c)   section 13 of the Welfare Reform Act 2007 (c. 5).

(3)   A statutory instrument containing regulations to which this section applies (whether alone or with other provision) may not be made at any time during the period of 5 years beginning with the day on which this Act is passed unless a draft of the statutory instrument has been laid before, and approved by a resolution of, each House of Parliament.

(4)   If subsection (3) applies to any regulations, any provision of an Act under which a statutory instrument containing the regulations would be subject to annulment in pursuance of a resolution of either House of Parliament does not apply.

Abolition of income support

9   **Abolition of income support**

(1)   This section applies if, whether as a result of —
     (a)   provision made by any regulations under section 1A(4)(c) or (8) of the Jobseekers Act 1995 (as inserted by section 4 above), or
     (b)   provision made by or under any other enactment, or otherwise,
     the Secretary of State considers that it is no longer appropriate for any category of person to be prescribed under section 124(1)(e) of the Social Security Contributions and Benefits Act 1992 (c. 4) (conditions for income support).

(2)   The Secretary of State may by order provide for section 124 of the Social Security Contributions and Benefits Act 1992 (which establishes the entitlement to income support) to cease to have effect.

(3)   If an order is made under subsection (2) —
     (a)   the amendments made by Schedule 2, and
     (b)   the repeals in Part 1 of Schedule 7,
     have effect in accordance with provision made by the order.

(4)   The Secretary of State may by order make such transitional or consequential provision or savings as the Secretary of State considers necessary or expedient for the purposes of or in connection with the abolition of income support (including provision of the kind mentioned in section 7(2)).

(5)   The consequential provision that may be made by an order under subsection (4) includes, in particular, provision amending, repealing or revoking —
     (a)   any provision of any Act (whenever passed), or
     (b)   any provision of any instrument made under any Act (whenever made).

(6)   In subsection (5) "Act" means —

    (a)   an Act of Parliament,

    (b)   an Act of the Scottish Parliament, or

    (c)   a Measure or Act of the National Assembly for Wales.

(7)   Subsections (3) to (5) of section 175 of the Social Security Contributions and Benefits Act 1992 (c. 4) (supplementary provisions in relation to powers to make subordinate legislation under that Act) apply in relation to any power to make an order under this section as they apply to any power to make orders under that Act.

(8)   Any power to make an order under this section is exercisable by statutory instrument.

(9)   An order under subsection (2) may not be made unless a draft of the statutory instrument containing the order (whether alone or with other provision) has been laid before, and approved by a resolution of, each House of Parliament.

(10)   A statutory instrument containing an order under subsection (4) is (unless a draft of it has been approved by a resolution of each House of Parliament) subject to annulment in pursuance of a resolution of either House of Parliament.

Work-related activity for claimants of employment and support allowance

10   Power to direct claimant to undertake specific work-related activity

In section 15 of the Welfare Reform Act 2007 (c. 5) (directions about work-related activity), for subsections (1) and (2) substitute—

    "(1)   In prescribed circumstances, the Secretary of State may by direction given to a person subject to a requirement imposed under section 13(1) provide that the activity specified in the direction is—

        (a)   to be the only activity which, in the person's case, is to be regarded as being work-related activity; or

        (b)   to be regarded, in the person's case, as not being work-related activity.

    (1A) But a direction under subsection (1) may not specify medical or surgical treatment as the only activity which, in any person's case, is to be regarded as being work-related activity.

    (2)   A direction under subsection (1) given to any person—

        (a)   must be reasonable, having regard to the person's circumstances;

        (b)   must be given to the person by being included in an action plan provided to the person under section 14; and

        (c)   may be varied or revoked by a subsequent direction under subsection (1)."

Jobseeker's allowance and employment and support allowance: drugs

11   Claimants dependent on drugs etc.

(1)   Part 1 of Schedule 3 makes provision for or in connection with imposing requirements on claimants for a jobseeker's allowance in cases where—

> (a) they are dependent on, or have a propensity to misuse, any drug, and
>
> (b) any such dependency or propensity is a factor affecting their prospects of obtaining or remaining in work.

(2) Part 1 of that Schedule also contains a power for the provisions concerned to apply in relation to alcohol.

(3) Part 2 of that Schedule makes similar provision in relation to claimants for an employment and support allowance.

Contributory jobseeker's allowance and employment and support allowance

12 Conditions for contributory jobseeker's allowance

(1) Section 2 of the Jobseekers Act 1995 (c. 18) (jobseeker's allowance: the contribution-based conditions) is amended as follows.

(2) In subsection (2), for paragraph (b) substitute –

> "(b) the claimant's relevant earnings for the base year upon which primary Class 1 contributions have been paid or treated as paid are not less than the base year's lower earnings limit multiplied by 26."

(3) After that subsection insert –

> "(2A) Regulations may make provision for the purposes of subsection (2)(b) for determining the claimant's relevant earnings for the base year.
>
> (2B) Regulations under subsection (2A) may, in particular, make provision –
>
> > (a) for making that determination by reference to the amount of a person's earnings for periods comprised in the base year;
> >
> > (b) for determining the amount of a person's earnings for any such period by –
> >
> > > (i) first determining the amount of the earnings for the period in accordance with regulations made for the purposes of section 3(2) of the Benefits Act, and
> > >
> > > (ii) then disregarding so much of the amount found in accordance with sub-paragraph (i) as exceeded the base year's lower earnings limit (or the prescribed equivalent)."

(4) In subsection (3A), for "subsections (2)(b) and (3)" substitute "subsection (3)".

(5) After that subsection insert –

> "(3B) Regulations may –
>
> > (a) provide for the first set of conditions to be taken to be satisfied in the case of persons –
> >
> > > (i) who have been entitled to any prescribed description of benefit during any prescribed period or at any prescribed time, or
> > >
> > > (ii) who satisfy other prescribed conditions;
> >
> > (b) with a view to securing any relaxation of the requirements of the first set of conditions in relation to persons who have been entitled as mentioned in paragraph (a)(i), provide for that set of

conditions to apply in relation to them subject to prescribed modifications.

(3C) In subsection (3B) —

"the first set of conditions" means the condition set out in subsection (1)(a) and the additional conditions set out in subsection (2);

"benefit" means —

 (a) any benefit within the meaning of section 122(1) of the Benefits Act,

 (b) any benefit under Parts 7 to 12 of the Benefits Act,

 (c) credits under regulations under section 22(5) of the Benefits Act,

 (d) a contribution-based jobseeker's allowance, and

 (e) working tax credit."

(6) In paragraph 45 of Schedule 1 to the National Insurance Contributions Act 2002 (c. 19) (which amended section 2(2)(b) of the Jobseekers Act 1995 (c. 18)), for "section 2(2)(b) and (3)" substitute "section 2(3)".

13 Conditions for contributory employment and support allowance

(1) Paragraph 1 of Schedule 1 to the Welfare Reform Act 2007 (c. 5) (employment and support allowance: conditions relating to national insurance) is amended as follows.

(2) In sub-paragraph (1)(a) (Class 1 or Class 2 contributions to have been paid in respect of one of last three complete tax years), for "three" substitute "two".

(3) In sub-paragraph (1), for paragraph (c) substitute —

"(c) the claimant's earnings determined in accordance with sub-paragraph (2) must be not less than the base tax year's lower earnings limit multiplied by 26."

(4) For sub-paragraphs (2) and (3) substitute —

"(2) The earnings referred to in sub-paragraph (1)(c) are the aggregate of —

 (a) the claimant's relevant earnings for the base tax year upon which primary Class 1 contributions have been paid or treated as paid, and

 (b) the claimant's earnings factors derived from Class 2 contributions.

(3) Regulations may make provision for the purposes of sub-paragraph (2)(a) for determining the claimant's relevant earnings for the base tax year.

(3A) Regulations under sub-paragraph (3) may, in particular, make provision —

 (a) for making that determination by reference to the amount of a person's earnings for periods comprised in the base tax year;

 (b) for determining the amount of a person's earnings for any such period by —

       (i)   first determining the amount of the earnings for the period in accordance with regulations made for the purposes of section 3(2) of the Contributions and Benefits Act, and

       (ii)   then disregarding so much of the amount found in accordance with sub-paragraph (i) as exceeded the base tax year's lower earnings limit (or the prescribed equivalent)."

(5)   In sub-paragraph (4) —

   (a)   in paragraph (a), for "persons who" substitute "persons —

       (i)   who",

   (b)   in that paragraph, after "prescribed time" insert ", or

       (ii)   who satisfy other prescribed conditions", and

   (c)   in paragraph (b), for "so entitled" substitute "entitled as mentioned in paragraph (a)(i)".

Disability living allowance

14 Mobility component

(1)   Section 73 of the Social Security Contributions and Benefits Act 1992 (c. 4) (mobility component of disability living allowance) is amended as follows.

(2)   In subsection (1), for paragraph (b) (together with the "or" at the end of it) substitute —

   "(ab)   he falls within subsection (1AB) below; or

   (b)   he does not fall within that subsection but does fall within subsection (2) below; or".

(3)   In subsection (1A)(a), after "paragraph (a)," insert "(ab),".

(4)   After subsection (1A) insert —

   "(1AB)   A person falls within this subsection if —

   (a)   he has such severe visual impairment as may be prescribed; and

   (b)   he satisfies such other conditions as may be prescribed."

(5)   In subsection (11)(a), after "subsection (1)(a)," insert "(ab),".

Abolition of adult dependency increases

15 Maternity allowance and carer's allowance

(1)   The following provisions of the Social Security Contributions and Benefits Act 1992 (c. 4) ("the Benefits Act") are omitted on 6 April 2010 —

   (a)   section 82 (maternity allowance: increase for adult dependants); and

   (b)   section 90 (carer's allowance: increase for adult dependants).

(2)   Nothing in subsection (1) or Part 2 of Schedule 7 applies in relation to —

   (a)   the amount of a maternity allowance payable for a maternity allowance period (within the meaning of section 35(2) of the Benefits Act) which begins before 6 April 2010 but ends on or after that date, or

    (b)   the amount of a carer's allowance payable to a qualifying person at any time on or after 6 April 2010 but before the appropriate date.

(3)   In subsection (2)(b) —

    "a qualifying person" means a person who —

        (a)   has, before 6 April 2010, made a claim for an increase in a carer's allowance under section 90 of the Benefits Act; and

        (b)   immediately before that date is either entitled to the increase claimed or a beneficiary to whom section 92 of the Benefits Act applies in respect of that increase (continuation of awards where fluctuating earnings);

    "the appropriate date" means whichever is the earlier of —

        (a)   6 April 2020; and

        (b)   the date when the qualifying person ceases to be either entitled to that increase or a beneficiary to whom section 92 of the Benefits Act applies in respect of that increase.

External provider social loans and community care grants

16   External provider social loans

(1)   After Part 8 of the Social Security Contributions and Benefits Act 1992 (c. 4) insert—

"PART 8ZA

EXTERNAL PROVIDER SOCIAL LOANS

140ZA   Arrangements for external provider social loans

   (1)   The Secretary of State may with the consent of the Treasury make such arrangements as the Secretary of State thinks fit with any person for the purpose of securing the making by that person ("the lender") of loans to eligible persons.

   (2)   In subsection (1) "eligible person" means an individual who —

       (a)   is in receipt of a prescribed benefit, or

       (b)   has needs of a prescribed description.

   (3)   Arrangements under this section may relate to particular areas in Great Britain or to the whole of Great Britain.

   (4)   Arrangements under this section may provide for the making of payments by the Secretary of State to the lender —

       (a)   in respect of sums required for making loans, and

       (b)   in respect of other expenses of the lender.

   (5)   Arrangements under this section may in particular —

       (a)   specify categories of eligible person to whom a loan may not be made,

       (b)   make provision as to the criteria to be applied by the lender in determining whether to make a particular loan;

       (c)   specify circumstances in which a loan may or may not be made;

(d)   make provision as to the manner in which the terms and conditions relating to repayment of the loan are to be determined by the lender;

(e)   make provision as to the keeping of accounts by the lender;

(f)   require the provision of information by the lender to the Secretary of State;

(g)   require the provision to prospective borrowers of information or guidance about budgeting.

(6)   Arrangements under this section may also—

    (a)   make provision as to the duration of the arrangements and as to the circumstances in which they may be terminated;

    (b)   provide for the making of payments by the lender to the Secretary of State if the arrangements cease to be in force.

(7)   Any payments by virtue of subsection (4)(a) are to be made out of the social fund.

(8)   Any sums received by virtue of subsection (6)(b) are to be paid into the social fund.

(9)   In this Part a loan made by virtue of arrangements under this section is referred to as an "external provider social loan".

140ZB   Transfer of loans

(1)   Arrangements under section 140ZA may provide—

    (a)   for the right to repayment of a loan made under section 138(1)(b) before the arrangements come into force to be transferred to the person with whom the arrangements are made, and

    (b)   for the right to repayment of an external provider social loan to be transferred to the Secretary of State on the arrangements ceasing to be in force.

(2)   Regulations may make provision modifying any provision of this Act, the Administration Act or the Social Security Act 1998 in its application to loans in relation to which provision made by virtue of subsection (1)(a) or (b) has effect.

140ZC   Annual report on operation of arrangements

(1)   The Secretary of State shall prepare an annual report on the operation of arrangements under section 140ZA.

(2)   A copy of every such report shall be laid before each House of Parliament."

(2)   After section 78 of the Social Security Administration Act 1992 (c. 5) insert—

"Repayments of external provider social loans

78A   Repayments of external provider social loans

(1)   Regulations may provide for the collection by the Secretary of State of repayments of a qualifying loan—

    (a)   by deduction in accordance with the regulations from prescribed benefits payable to—

            (i)   the borrower, or

            (ii) where the borrower is a member of a couple, the other member of the couple, or

   (b)   in any other way.

(2)   In subsection (1) "qualifying loan" means —

   (a)   an external provider social loan, as defined by subsection (9) of section 140ZA of the Contributions and Benefits Act, or

   (b)   a loan made by virtue of arrangements made under any provision having effect in Northern Ireland and corresponding to that section.

(3)   The Secretary of State must pay any amounts collected to the person to whom the loan is repayable, except to the extent that the regulations otherwise provide.

(4)   In this section "couple" has the meaning given by section 137(1) of the Contributions and Benefits Act."

17   Power to restrict availability of social fund loans

In section 138 of the Social Security Contributions and Benefits Act 1992 (payments out of the social fund) after subsection (2) insert —

"(2A)   Regulations may restrict the making of payments by way of crisis loan or budgeting loan to persons living in areas in which external provider social loans (as defined by section 140ZA(9)) are to any extent available."

18   Supply of information to or by lenders making external provider social loans

After section 122F of the Social Security Administration Act 1992 (c. 5) insert —

"Lenders making external provider social loans

122G Supply of information in connection with external provider social loans

(1)   Regulations may make provision —

   (a)   authorising the Secretary of State, or a person providing services to the Secretary of State, to supply to relevant persons information relating to social security, and

   (b)   authorising or requiring relevant persons to supply to the Secretary of State, or a person providing services to the Secretary of State, information relating to the operation of arrangements under section 140ZA of the Contributions and Benefits Act (external provider social loans).

(2)   In this section "relevant person" means —

   (a)   a person with whom arrangements have been made under section 140ZA of the Contributions and Benefits Act, or

   (b)   a person providing services to such a person.

(3)   Regulations under this section must specify the purposes for which information may be supplied by virtue of subsection (1)(a), which must be purposes connected with external provider social loans.

(4)   Regulations may make provision as to the use or disclosure of information supplied under the regulations (including provision creating criminal offences).

(5)   In this section "external provider social loan" has the meaning given by section 140ZA(9) of the Contributions and Benefits Act."

19   Community care grants relating to specified goods or services

(1)   The Social Security Contributions and Benefits Act 1992 (c. 4) is amended as follows.

(2)   In section 138 (payments out of social fund), before subsection (3) insert—

"(2B)   If or to the extent that directions issued under subsection (2) of section 140 by virtue of subsection (4)(ca) of that section require the award of a community care grant to be expressed as the award of a payment for goods or services specified in the award, the power to make a payment out of the social fund under subsection (1)(b) shall be exercised by making a payment to a third party specified in the award, with a view to the third party providing, or arranging for the provision of, the specified goods or services for the applicant."

(3)   In subsection (3) of that section, for "The power" substitute "If or to the extent that subsection (2B) does not apply, the power".

(4)   In section 139 (awards by social fund officers), in subsection (1), after "how much it is to be" insert "or, where section 138(2B) applies, what goods or services are to be specified".

(5)   For subsection (5) of that section substitute—

"(5)   Payment of an award shall be made to the applicant unless—
    (a)   section 138(2B) applies, or
    (b)   the appropriate officer determines otherwise."

(6)   In section 140 (principles of determination), in subsection (4), after paragraph (c) insert—

"(ca)   that, except in circumstances specified in the direction, an appropriate officer shall express an award of a community care grant as the award of a payment for goods or services that are—
    (i)   determined by the appropriate officer in accordance with the direction,
    (ii)   specified in the award, and
    (iii)   to be provided by, or under arrangements made by, a specified person with whom arrangements have been made by the Secretary of State."

(7)   After that subsection insert—

"(4A)   The reference in subsection (1) to the amount or value to be awarded is, in a case where directions under subsection (4)(ca) apply, to be read as a reference to the goods or services to be specified in the award."

20   Community care grants: reviews and information

(1)   In section 38 of the Social Security Act 1998 (c. 14) (reviews of determinations) in subsection (1) –

    (a)   in paragraph (a), after "social fund determination" insert "other than an excluded determination", and

    (b)   in paragraph (b), for "such a determination" substitute "a social fund determination".

(2)   After that subsection insert –

    "(1A)   For the purposes of subsection (1)(a) an "excluded determination" is any determination to award a community care grant where the award is expressed as the award of a payment for goods or services specified in the award, other than such a determination made in prescribed circumstances."

(3)   After section 122G of the Social Security Administration Act 1992 (c. 5) insert –

"Persons supplying goods and services to recipients of community care grants

122H   Supply of information in connection with community care grants

(1)   In this section "relevant supplier" means –

    (a)   a person with whom the Secretary of State has made arrangements of the kind mentioned in section 140(4)(ca)(iii) of the Contributions and Benefits Act (arrangements for supply of goods or services in connection with community care grants), or

    (b)   a person providing services to such a person.

(2)   Regulations may make provision authorising the Secretary of State, or a person providing services to the Secretary of State, to supply to relevant suppliers information relating to community care grants.

(3)   Regulations may make provision authorising or requiring relevant suppliers to supply to the Secretary of State or a person providing services to the Secretary of State, information relating to the operation of the arrangements.

(4)   Regulations under this section must specify the purposes for which information may be supplied by virtue of subsection (2) or (3), which must be purposes connected with community care grants.

(5)   Regulations may make provision as to the use or disclosure of information supplied under the regulations (including provision creating criminal offences).

(6)   In this section "community care grant" has the same meaning as in Part 8 of the Contributions and Benefits Act."

21   Regulations relating to information: parliamentary control

In section 190 of the Social Security Administration Act 1992 (parliamentary control of orders and regulations), in subsection (1), before the "or" at the end of paragraph (ab) insert –

    "(ac)   regulations under section 122G(4) or 122H(5) which create an offence or increase the penalty for an offence;".

Payments on account

22   Payments on account

(1)   The Social Security Administration Act 1992 (c. 5) is amended as follows.

(2)   In section 5 (regulations about claims for and payments of benefit) —

    (a)   in subsection (1), omit paragraph (r) (which relates to payments on account), and

    (b)   after that subsection insert —

      "(1A)   Regulations may provide for the making of a payment on account of housing benefit —

        (a)   where no claim has been made and it is impracticable for one to be made immediately;

        (b)   where a claim has been made and it is impracticable for the claim to be immediately determined;

        (c)   where an award has been made but it is impracticable to pay the full amount of the benefit immediately.

      (1B)   Regulations may provide for the making of a payment on account of any other benefit to which this section applies —

        (a)   where a person by or in respect of whom a claim has been or might be made (including a person in respect of whom an award has been made) would be in need if no payment on account were made;

        (b)   where an award has been made but it is impracticable to pay the full amount of the benefit immediately.

      (1C)   Regulations may make provision about the manner in which payments on account of a benefit to which this section applies are to be set against subsequent payments of benefit (other than payments on account)."

(3)   In section 7 (which relates to the relationship between benefits), in subsection (2)(a), for "section 5(1)(r)" substitute "section 5(1A) or (1B)".

(4)   In section 16 (emergency payments by local authorities and other bodies), in subsection (1), for "subsection (1)(r)" substitute "subsection (1B)".

(5)   In section 71 (overpayments — general), for subsection (7) substitute —

    "(7)   Circumstances may be prescribed in which a payment on account by virtue of section 5(1B) may be recovered to the extent that it is not set against subsequent payments of the benefit to which it relates."

Up-rating of benefits

23   Power to up-rate benefits following review in tax year 2009-10

In relation to the review under subsection (1) of section 150 of the Social Security Administration Act 1992 (annual up-rating of benefits) in the tax year ending with 5 April 2010, the other provisions of that section are to have effect as if —

(a) after subsection (2) there were inserted —

"(2A) Where it appears to the Secretary of State that the general level of prices is no greater at the end of the period under review than it was at the beginning of that period, the Secretary of State may, if the Secretary of State considers it appropriate having regard to the national economic situation and any other matters which the Secretary of State considers relevant, lay before Parliament the draft of an up-rating order —

   (a) which increases by such a percentage or percentages as the Secretary of State thinks fit any of the sums mentioned in subsection (1); and

   (b) stating the amount of any sums which are mentioned in subsection (1) but which the order does not increase.",

(b) in subsection (5), after "(2)" there were inserted "or (2A)", and

(c) in subsection (6) —

   (i) after "(2)" there were inserted "or (2A)", and

   (ii) after "requires" there were inserted "or authorises".

Benefit sanctions for offenders

24 Loss of benefit provisions

(1) Before section 7 of the Social Security Fraud Act 2001 (c. 11) (but after the italic heading immediately before that section) insert —

"6A Meaning of "disqualifying benefit" and "sanctionable benefit" for purposes of sections 6B and 7

(1) In this section and sections 6B and 7 —

"disqualifying benefit" means (subject to any regulations under section 10(1)) —

   (a) any benefit under the Jobseekers Act 1995 or the Jobseekers (Northern Ireland) Order 1995;

   (b) any benefit under the State Pension Credit Act 2002 or the State Pension Credit Act (Northern Ireland) 2002;

   (c) any benefit under Part 1 of the Welfare Reform Act 2007 or Part 1 of the Welfare Reform Act (Northern Ireland) 2007 (employment and support allowance);

   (d) any benefit under the Social Security Contributions and Benefit Act 1992 or the Social Security Contributions and Benefits (Northern Ireland) Act 1992 other than —

      (i) maternity allowance;

      (ii) statutory sick pay and statutory maternity pay;

   (e) any war pension;

"sanctionable benefit" means (subject to subsection (2) and to any regulations under section 10(1)) any disqualifying benefit other than —

   (a) joint-claim jobseeker's allowance;

   (b) any retirement pension;

   (c) graduated retirement benefit;

   (d) disability living allowance;

        (e)   attendance allowance;

        (f)   child benefit;

        (g)   guardian's allowance;

        (h)   a payment out of the social fund in accordance with Part 8 of the Social Security Contributions and Benefits Act 1992;

        (i)   a payment under Part 10 of that Act (Christmas bonuses).

(2)   In their application to Northern Ireland sections 6B and 7 shall have effect as if references to a sanctionable benefit were references only to a war pension.

6B   Loss of benefit in case of conviction, penalty or caution for benefit offence

(1)   Subsection (4) applies where a person ("the offender") —

        (a)   is convicted of one or more benefit offences in any proceedings,

        (b)   after being given a notice under subsection (2) of the appropriate penalty provision by an appropriate authority, agrees in the manner specified by the appropriate authority to pay a penalty under the appropriate penalty provision to the appropriate authority by reference to an overpayment, in a case where the offence mentioned in subsection (1)(b) of the appropriate penalty provision is a benefit offence, or

        (c)   is cautioned in respect of one or more benefit offences.

(2)   In subsection (1)(b) —

        (a)   "the appropriate penalty provision" means section 115A of the Administration Act (penalty as alternative to prosecution) or section 109A of the Social Security Administration (Northern Ireland) 1992 (the corresponding provision for Northern Ireland);

        (b)   "appropriate authority" means —

            (i)   in relation to section 115A of the Administration Act, the Secretary of State or an authority which administers housing benefit or council tax benefit, and

            (ii)   in relation to section 109A of the Social Security Administration (Northern Ireland) Act 1992, the Department (within the meaning of that Act) or the Northern Ireland Housing Executive.

(3)   Subsection (4) does not apply by virtue of subsection (1)(a) if, because the proceedings in which the offender was convicted constitute the later set of proceedings for the purposes of section 7, the restriction in subsection (2) of that section applies in the offender's case.

(4)   If this subsection applies and the offender is a person with respect to whom the conditions for an entitlement to a sanctionable benefit are or become satisfied at any time within the disqualification period, then, even though those conditions are satisfied, the following restrictions shall apply in relation to the payment of that benefit in the offender's case.

(5) Subject to subsections (6) to (10), the sanctionable benefit shall not be payable in the offender's case for any period comprised in the disqualification period.

(6) Where the sanctionable benefit is income support, the benefit shall be payable in the offender's case for any period comprised in the disqualification period as if the applicable amount used for the determination under section 124(4) of the Social Security Contributions and Benefits Act 1992 of the amount of the offender's entitlement for that period were reduced in such manner as may be prescribed.

(7) The Secretary of State may by regulations provide that, where the sanctionable benefit is jobseeker's allowance, any income-based jobseeker's allowance shall be payable, during the whole or a part of any period comprised in the disqualification period, as if one or more of the following applied —

    (a) the rate of the allowance were such reduced rate as may be prescribed;

    (b) the allowance were payable only if there is compliance by the offender with such obligations with respect to the provision of information as may be imposed by the regulations;

    (c) the allowance were payable only if the circumstances are otherwise such as may be prescribed.

(8) The Secretary of State may by regulations provide that, where the sanctionable benefit is state pension credit, the benefit shall be payable in the offender's case for any period comprised in the disqualification period as if the rate of the benefit were reduced in such manner as may be prescribed.

(9) The Secretary of State may by regulations provide that, where the sanctionable benefit is employment and support allowance, any income-related allowance shall be payable, during the whole or a part of any period comprised in the disqualification period, as if one or more of the following applied —

    (a) the rate of the allowance were such reduced rate as may be prescribed;

    (b) the allowance were payable only if there is compliance by the offender with such obligations with respect to the provision of information as may be imposed by the regulations;

    (c) the allowance were payable only if the circumstances are otherwise such as may be prescribed.

(10) The Secretary of State may by regulations provide that, where the sanctionable benefit is housing benefit or council tax benefit, the benefit shall be payable, during the whole or a part of any period comprised in the disqualification period, as if one or more of the following applied —

    (a) the rate of the benefit were reduced in such manner as may be prescribed;

    (b) the benefit were payable only if the circumstances are such as may be prescribed.

(11) For the purposes of this section the disqualification period, in relation to any disqualifying event, means the period of four weeks beginning with such date, falling after the date of the disqualifying event, as may

be determined by or in accordance with regulations made by the Secretary of State.

(12)   This section has effect subject to section 6C.

(13)   In this section and section 6C –

"benefit offence" means –

    (a)   any post-commencement offence in connection with a claim for a disqualifying benefit;

    (b)   any post-commencement offence in connection with the receipt or payment of any amount by way of such a benefit;

    (c)   any post-commencement offence committed for the purpose of facilitating the commission (whether or not by the same person) of a benefit offence;

    (d)   any post-commencement offence consisting in an attempt or conspiracy to commit a benefit offence;

"disqualifying event" means the conviction falling within subsection (1)(a), the agreement falling within subsection (1)(b) or the caution falling within subsection (1)(c);

"post-commencement offence" means any criminal offence committed after the commencement of this section.

6C   Section 6B: supplementary provisions

(1)   Where –

    (a)   the conviction of any person of any offence is taken into account for the purposes of the application of section 6B in relation to that person, and

    (b)   that conviction is subsequently quashed,

all such payments and other adjustments shall be made as would be necessary if no restriction had been imposed by or under section 6B that could not have been imposed if the conviction had not taken place.

(2)   Where, after the agreement of any person ("P") to pay a penalty under the appropriate penalty provision is taken into account for the purposes of the application of section 6B in relation to that person –

    (a)   P's agreement to pay the penalty is withdrawn under subsection (5) of the appropriate penalty provision, or

    (b)   it is decided on an appeal or in accordance with regulations under the Social Security Act 1998 or the Social Security (Northern Ireland) Order 1998 that the overpayment to which the agreement relates is not recoverable or due,

all such payments and other adjustments shall be made as would be necessary if no restriction had been imposed by or under section 6B that could not have been imposed if P had not agreed to pay the penalty.

(3)   Where, after the agreement ("the old agreement") of any person ("P") to pay a penalty under the appropriate penalty provision is taken into account for the purposes of the application of section 6B in relation to P, the amount of the overpayment to which the penalty relates is revised on an appeal or in accordance with regulations under the Social Security Act 1998 or the Social Security (Northern Ireland) Order 1998 –

(a) section 6B shall cease to apply by virtue of the old agreement, and

(b) subsection (4) shall apply.

(4) Where this subsection applies —

   (a) if there is a new disqualifying event consisting of —

      (i) P's agreement to pay a penalty under the appropriate penalty provision in relation to the revised overpayment, or

      (ii) P being cautioned in relation to the offence to which the old agreement relates,

   the disqualification period relating to the new disqualifying event shall be reduced by the number of days in so much of the disqualification period relating to the old agreement as had expired when section 6B ceased to apply by virtue of the old agreement, and

   (b) in any other case, all such payments and other adjustments shall be made as would be necessary if no restriction had been imposed by or under section 6B that could not have been imposed if P had not agreed to pay the penalty.

(5) For the purposes of section 6B —

   (a) the date of a person's conviction in any proceedings of a benefit offence shall be taken to be the date on which the person was found guilty of that offence in those proceedings (whenever the person was sentenced) or in the case mentioned in paragraph (b)(ii) the date of the order for absolute discharge; and

   (b) references to a conviction include references to —

      (i) a conviction in relation to which the court makes an order for absolute or conditional discharge or a court in Scotland makes a probation order,

      (ii) an order for absolute discharge made by a court of summary jurisdiction in Scotland under section 246(3) of the Criminal Procedure (Scotland) Act 1995 without proceeding to a conviction, and

      (iii) a conviction in Northern Ireland.

(6) In this section "the appropriate penalty provision" has the meaning given by section 6B(2)(a)."

(2) In Schedule 4 —

   (a) Part 1 contains further amendments of the Social Security Fraud Act 2001 (c. 11), and

   (b) Part 2 contains related amendments of other Acts.

25 Jobseeker's allowance: sanctions for violent conduct etc. in connection with claim

(1) The Jobseekers Act 1995 (c. 18) is amended as follows.

(2)   After section 20B insert—

"Violent conduct etc. in connection with claim

20C   Sanctions for violent conduct etc. in connection with claim

(1)   This section applies if—
   (a)   a person ("the offender") is convicted of, or in England and Wales is cautioned in respect of, an offence involving violence or harassment,
   (b)   the conduct constituting the offence was done to, or in relation to, a person who was in the course of exercising functions under this Act on any premises,
   (c)   the conduct occurred while the offender was on those premises for the purposes of a claim to a jobseeker's allowance, and
   (d)   the offender is a person, or a member of a joint-claim couple, with respect to whom the conditions for entitlement to a jobseeker's allowance are or become satisfied.

(2)   In the case of a jobseeker's allowance other than a joint-claim jobseeker's allowance—
   (a)   the allowance is not to be payable in respect of the offender for the period of one week beginning with such date as may be prescribed (even though the conditions for entitlement are satisfied); and
   (b)   on the first occasion (if any) on which another sanctions provision applies in the case of the offender, the sanctions period is to be extended in that case by a period of five weeks.

(3)   For the purposes of subsection (2)(b)—
   (a)   the reference to another sanctions provision is to any provision made by or under this Act (other than subsection (2)) which provides for a jobseeker's allowance not to be payable for a period; and
   (b)   the reference to the sanctions period is to the period for which the allowance would (but for subsection (2)(b)) not be payable by virtue of that provision.

(4)   In the case of a joint-claim jobseeker's allowance—
   (a)   the offender is to be treated as subject to sanctions for the purposes of section 20A for the period of one week beginning with such date as may be prescribed (even though the conditions for entitlement are satisfied); and
   (b)   on the first occasion (if any) on which another sanctions provision applies in the case of the offender, the sanctions period is to be extended in that case by a period of five weeks.

(5)   For the purposes of subsection (4)(b)—
   (a)   the reference to another sanctions provision is to any provision made by or under this Act (other than subsection (4)) which provides for a member of a joint-claim couple to be (or be treated as being) subject to sanctions for the purposes of section 20A for a period; and
   (b)   the reference to the sanctions period is to the period for which the member of the couple would (but for subsection (4)(b)) be

(or be treated as being) subject to sanctions for those purposes by virtue of that provision.

(6) Regulations may make provision for subsections (2) and (4) not to apply at any time after the end of a prescribed period or otherwise in prescribed circumstances.

(7) Regulations may make provision for an income-based jobseeker's allowance to be payable in prescribed circumstances even though the preceding provisions of this section prevent payment of it.

This subsection does not apply in the case of a joint-claim jobseeker's allowance (corresponding provision for which is made by section 20B(4)).

(8) The provision that may be made by regulations by virtue of subsection (7) includes, in particular, provision for the allowance to be—

    (a) payable only if prescribed requirements as to the provision of information are complied with;

    (b) payable at a prescribed rate;

    (c) payable for only part of a week.

(9) If—

    (a) a jobseeker's allowance was not payable, or was payable at a reduced rate, as a result of the application of this section in a case where a person was convicted of an offence involving violence or harassment, and

    (b) the person's conviction is subsequently quashed,

all such payments and other adjustments are to be made as would be necessary if the person had never been convicted of the offence.

20D Section 20C: supplementary

(1) For the purposes of section 20C in its application in relation to England and Wales each of the following is an offence involving violence or harassment—

    (a) common assault or battery;

    (b) an offence under section 16, 18, 20 or 47 of the Offences against the Person Act 1861;

    (c) an offence under section 3, 4, 4A or 5 of the Public Order Act 1986;

    (d) an offence under section 2 or 4 of the Protection from Harassment Act 1997;

    (e) an offence under section 29, 31 or 32 of the Crime and Disorder Act 1998;

    (f) an ancillary offence in relation to an offence within any of paragraphs (a) to (e).

(2) In subsection (1)(f) "ancillary offence", in relation to an offence, means any of the following—

    (a) aiding, abetting, counselling or procuring the commission of the offence;

    (b) an offence under Part 2 of the Serious Crime Act 2007 (encouraging or assisting crime) in relation to the offence;

    (c) attempting or conspiring to commit the offence.

(3) For the purposes of section 20C in its application in relation to Scotland each of the following is an offence involving violence or harassment—

(a) assault;

(b) a breach of the peace;

(c) an offence under section 50A of the Criminal Law (Consolidation) Scotland Act 1995;

(d) an ancillary offence in relation to an offence within any of paragraphs (a) to (c).

(4) In subsection (3)(d) "ancillary offence", in relation to an offence, means any of the following—

(a) being art and part in the commission of the offence or counselling or procuring its commission;

(b) inciting a person to commit the offence;

(c) attempting or conspiring to commit the offence.

(5) For the purposes of section 20C references to a conviction include references to a conviction in relation to which the court makes an order for conditional discharge or a court in Scotland makes a probation order.

(6) For the purposes of section 20C "cautioned" means—

(a) cautioned after the person concerned has admitted the offence, or

(b) reprimanded or warned within the meaning given by section 65 of the Crime and Disorder Act 1998.

(7) Regulations may make provision for or in connection with requiring such persons as may be prescribed to notify the Secretary of State about prescribed matters for the purposes of section 20C.

(8) Regulations may amend subsections (1) to (4) by adding or removing an offence."

(3) In section 37(1)(c) (regulations subject to the affirmative resolution procedure), after "7," insert "20D(8),".

(4) In paragraph 3(d) of Schedule 3 to the Social Security Act 1998 (c. 14) (decisions against which an appeal lies: payability of benefit), before "of the Jobseekers Act" insert "or 20C".

26 Repeal of sections 62 to 66 of the Child Support, Pensions and Social Security Act 2000

In the Child Support, Pensions and Social Security Act 2000 (c. 19), omit sections 62 to 66 (loss of benefit for breach of community order).

Pilot schemes

27 State pension credit: pilot schemes

(1) The State Pension Credit Act 2002 (c. 16) is amended as follows.

(2) Before section 19 (but after the italic heading immediately before that section)

insert—

"18A Pilot schemes

(1) Any regulations to which this subsection applies may be made so as to have effect for a specified period not exceeding 12 months.

(2) Subject to subsection (3), subsection (1) applies to—
  (a) regulations made under this Act, and
  (b) regulations made under section 1 or 5 of the Administration Act.

(3) Subsection (1) only applies to regulations if they are made with a view to ascertaining whether their provisions will—
  (a) make it more likely that persons who are entitled to claim state pension credit will do so;
  (b) make it more likely that persons who are entitled to claim state pension credit will receive it.

(4) Regulations which, by virtue of subsection (1), are to have effect for a limited period are referred to in this section as a "pilot scheme".

(5) A pilot scheme may, in particular—
  (a) provide for a relevant provision not to apply, or to apply with modifications, for the purposes of the pilot scheme, and
  (b) make different provision for different cases or circumstances.

(6) For the purposes of subsection (5)(a), a "relevant provision" is—
  (a) any provision of this Act, and
  (b) section 1 of the Administration Act.

(7) A pilot scheme may provide that no account is to be taken of any payment made under the pilot scheme in considering a person's—
  (a) liability to tax,
  (b) entitlement to benefit under an enactment relating to social security (irrespective of the name or nature of the benefit), or
  (c) entitlement to a tax credit.

(8) A pilot scheme may provide that its provisions are to apply only in relation to—
  (a) one or more specified areas or localities;
  (b) one or more specified classes of person;
  (c) persons selected—
      (i) by reference to prescribed criteria, or
      (ii) on a sampling basis.

(9) A pilot scheme may make consequential or transitional provision with respect to the cessation of the scheme on the expiry of the specified period.

(10) A pilot scheme may be replaced by a further pilot scheme making the same or similar provision.

(11) The power of the Secretary of State to make regulations which, by virtue of this section, are to have effect for a limited period is exercisable only with the consent of the Treasury."

(3)   In section 19 (regulations and orders) after subsection (2) insert—

"(2A)   A statutory instrument containing regulations which, by virtue of section 18A, are to have effect for a limited period shall not be made unless a draft of the instrument has been laid before, and approved by a resolution of, each House of Parliament."

28   Period for which pilot schemes have effect etc.

(1)   In section 29 of the Jobseekers Act 1995 (c. 18) (pilot schemes)—
   (a)   in subsection (1), for "12 months" substitute "36 months", and
   (b)   in subsection (8), for the words from "facilitate" to the end substitute "make it more likely that persons will obtain or remain in work or be able to do so".

(2)   In section 19(1) of the Welfare Reform Act 2007 (c. 5) (pilot schemes), for "24 months" substitute "36 months".

Miscellaneous

29   Exemption from jobseeking conditions for victims of domestic violence

(1)   In Schedule 1 to the Jobseekers Act 1995 (supplementary provisions), after paragraph 8A insert—

"8B (1)   This paragraph applies if domestic violence has been inflicted on or threatened against a person ("V") in prescribed circumstances.

   (2)   The Secretary of State must exercise the powers to make regulations under sections 6(4) and 7(4) so as to secure that, for an exempt period, V is treated as—
      (a)   being available for employment; and
      (b)   actively seeking employment.

   (3)   If V has not entered into a jobseeker's agreement before the exempt period begins, the Secretary of State must also exercise the power to make regulations under section 9(10) so as to secure that V is treated as having entered into a jobseeker's agreement which is in force for the exempt period.

   (4)   In this paragraph—
         "domestic violence" has such meaning as may be prescribed;
         "exempt period" means a period of 13 weeks beginning no later than a prescribed period after the date (or last date) on which the domestic violence was inflicted or threatened.

   (5)   Regulations may make provision for the purposes of this paragraph prescribing circumstances in which domestic violence is, or is not, to be regarded as being inflicted on or threatened against a person."

(2)   In section 37(1)(c) of that Act (regulations subject to the affirmative resolution procedure), after "or paragraph" insert "8B or".

30   Good cause for failure to comply with regulations etc.

(1)   In Schedule 1 to the Jobseekers Act 1995 (supplementary provisions), after

paragraph 14A insert—

"Good or just cause for acts or omissions

14B (1) This paragraph applies to any regulations made under this Act that prescribe matters to be taken into account in determining whether a person has good cause or just cause for any act or omission (including any failure to comply with the regulations).

   (2) The provision made by the regulations prescribing those matters must include provision relating to—
      (a) the person's physical or mental health or condition;
      (b) the availability of childcare."

(2) In Schedule 2 to the Welfare Reform Act 2007 (c. 5) (employment and support allowance: supplementary provisions), after paragraph 10 insert—

"Good cause for failure to comply with certain regulations

10A (1) This paragraph applies to any regulations made under section 11, 12 or 13 that prescribe matters to be taken into account in determining whether a person has good cause for any failure to comply with the regulations.

   (2) The provision made by the regulations prescribing those matters must include provision relating to—
      (a) the person's physical or mental health or condition;
      (b) the availability of childcare."

31 Jobseekers' agreements and action plans: well-being of children

(1) In section 9 of the Jobseekers Act 1995 (c. 18) (the jobseeker's agreement), after subsection (4) insert—

   "(4A) In preparing a jobseeker's agreement for a claimant, the officer must have regard (so far as practicable) to its impact on the well-being of any child who may be affected by it."

(2) In section 14 of the Welfare Reform Act 2007 (employment and support allowance: action plans in connection with work-focused interviews), at the end insert—

   "(5) In preparing any action plan, the Secretary of State must have regard (so far as practicable) to its impact on the well-being of any person under the age of 16 who may be affected by it."

32 Contracting out functions under Jobseekers Act 1995

(1) The Jobseekers Act 1995 is amended as follows.

(2) Before section 21 (but after the italic heading immediately before that section)

insert —

"20E Contracting out

(1) The following functions of the Secretary of State may be exercised by, or by employees of, such person (if any) as the Secretary of State may authorise for the purpose, namely —

   (a)   conducting interviews under section 11A;

   (b)   providing documents under section 11C;

   (c)   giving, varying or revoking directions under section 18B(5);

   (d)   asking questions under paragraph 1 of Schedule A1;

   (e)   making decisions under paragraph 2 or 3 of that Schedule;

   (f)   exercising any functions in relation to rehabilitation plans under paragraph 5 or 6 of that Schedule.

(2) The following functions of officers of the Secretary of State may be exercised by, or by employees of, such person (if any) as the Secretary of State may authorise for the purpose, namely —

   (a)   specifying places and times, and being contacted, under section 8;

   (b)   entering into or varying any jobseeker's agreement under section 9 or 10 and referring any proposed agreement or variation to the Secretary of State under section 9 or 10;

   (c)   giving notifications under section 16 or 18A;

   (d)   giving, varying or revoking directions under section 18A.

(3) Regulations may provide for any of the following functions of the Secretary of State to be exercisable by, or by employees of, such person (if any) as the Secretary of State may authorise for the purpose —

   (a)   any function under regulations under section 8, 11A, 11C, 17A or 18B or Schedule A1, except the making of an excluded decision (see subsection (4));

   (b)   the function under section 9(1) of the 1998 Act (revision of decisions) so far as relating to decisions (other than excluded decisions) that relate to any matter arising under any such regulations;

   (c)   the function under section 10(1) of the 1998 Act (superseding of decisions) so far as relating to decisions (other than excluded decisions) of the Secretary of State that relate to any matter arising under any such regulations;

   (d)   any function under Chapter 2 of Part 1 of the 1998 Act (social security decisions), except section 25(2) and (3) (decisions involving issues arising on appeal in other cases), which relates to the exercise of any of the functions within paragraphs (a) to (c).

(4) Each of the following is an "excluded decision" for the purposes of subsection (3) —

   (a)   a decision about whether a person has failed to comply with a requirement imposed by regulations under section 8, 11A or 17A or Schedule A1;

   (b)   a decision about whether a person had good cause for failure to comply with such a requirement;

      (c)   a decision about not paying or reducing a jobseeker's allowance in consequence of a failure to comply with such a requirement.

(5)   Regulations under subsection (3) may provide that a function to which that subsection applies may be exercised –

      (a)   either wholly or to such extent as the regulations may provide,

      (b)   either generally or in such cases as the regulations may provide, and

      (c)   either unconditionally or subject to the fulfilment of such conditions as the regulations may provide.

(6)   An authorisation given by virtue of any provision made by or under this section may authorise the exercise of the function concerned –

      (a)   either wholly or to such extent as may be specified in the authorisation,

      (b)   either generally or in such cases as may be so specified, and

      (c)   either unconditionally or subject to the fulfilment of such conditions as may be so specified;

but, in the case of an authorisation given by virtue of regulations under subsection (3), this subsection is subject to the regulations.

(7)   An authorisation given by virtue of any provision made by or under this section –

      (a)   may specify its duration,

      (b)   may be revoked at any time by the Secretary of State, and

      (c)   does not prevent the Secretary of State or any other person from exercising the function to which the authorisation relates.

(8)   Anything done or omitted to be done by or in relation to an authorised person (or an employee of that person) in, or in connection with, the exercise or purported exercise of the function concerned is to be treated for all purposes as done or omitted to be done by or in relation to the Secretary of State or (as the case may be) an officer of the Secretary of State.

(9)   But subsection (8) does not apply –

      (a)   for the purposes of so much of any contract made between the authorised person and the Secretary of State as relates to the exercise of the function, or

      (b)   for the purposes of any criminal proceedings brought in respect of anything done by the authorised person (or an employee of that person).

(10)   Any decision which an authorised person makes in exercise of a function of the Secretary of State has effect as a decision of the Secretary of State under section 8 of the 1998 Act.

(11)   Where –

      (a)   the authorisation of an authorised person is revoked at any time, and

      (b)   at the time of the revocation so much of any contract made between the authorised person and the Secretary of State as relates to the exercise of the function is subsisting,

the authorised person is entitled to treat the contract as repudiated by the Secretary of State (and not as frustrated by reason of the revocation).

(12) In this section –
    (a) "the 1998 Act" means the Social Security Act 1998;
    (b) "authorised person" means a person authorised to exercise any function by virtue of any provision made by or under this section;
    (c) references to functions of the Secretary of State under any enactment (including one comprised in regulations) include functions which the Secretary of State has by virtue of the application of section 8(1)(c) of the 1998 Act in relation to the enactment."

(3) In each of the following provisions for "employment officer" substitute "officer of the Secretary of State" –
    (a) section 8(1)(a),
    (b) section 9(1), (5), (6) and (7)(b),
    (c) section 10(1), (4), (5) and (6)(b)(ii),
    (d) section 16(3)(b)(ii),
    (e) section 19(5)(b)(ii), (6)(c) and (10)(b) (as the section has effect before its substitution by paragraph 6 of Schedule 1 to this Act), and
    (f) section 20A(2)(b)(ii) and (f) (as the section has effect before its substitution by paragraph 7 of that Schedule).

(4) In section 8(1A)(a), for "the Secretary of State" substitute "an officer of the Secretary of State".

(5) In relation to any time before paragraph 4 of Schedule 1 to this Act is fully in force, section 20E(2)(c) and (d) of the Jobseekers Act 1995 (c. 18) have effect as if they included references to the giving of notifications or directions under section 19 or 20A of that Act.

33 Attendance in connection with jobseeker's allowance: sanctions

(1) Section 8 of the Jobseekers Act 1995 (attendance, information and evidence) is amended as follows.

(2) In subsection (2), for paragraphs (a) to (c) (together with the "and" at the end of paragraph (c)) substitute –
    "(a) prescribe circumstances in which a jobseeker's allowance is not to be payable for a prescribed period (of at least one week but not more than two weeks) in the case of –
        (i) a claimant (other than a joint-claim couple claiming a joint-claim jobseeker's allowance) who fails to comply with any regulations made under that subsection, or
        (ii) a joint-claim couple claiming a joint-claim jobseeker's allowance a member of which fails to comply with any such regulations;
    (b) provide for the consequence set out in paragraph (a) not to follow if, within a prescribed period of a person's ("P") failure to comply with any such regulations ("the relevant period"), P or, if P is a member of a joint-claim couple, either member of the couple –
        (i) makes prescribed contact with an officer of the Secretary of State, and
        (ii) shows that P had good cause for the failure;

     (c)   provide for entitlement to a jobseeker's allowance to cease at such time as may be determined in accordance with any such regulations if P or, as the case may be, a member of the couple does not make prescribed contact with an officer of the Secretary of State in the relevant period;

    (ca) prescribe circumstances in which a jobseeker's allowance is to be payable in respect of a claimant even though provision made by any such regulations by virtue of paragraph (a) prevents payment of a jobseeker's allowance in respect of the claimant; and".

(3)   After that subsection insert—

"(2A) The provision that may be made by any such regulations by virtue of subsection (2)(ca) includes, in particular, provision for a jobseeker's allowance payable by virtue of that paragraph to be—

    (a)   payable only if prescribed requirements as to the provision of information are complied with;

    (b)   payable at a prescribed rate;

    (c)   payable for a prescribed period (which may differ from the period mentioned in subsection (2)(a))."

(4)   In paragraph 3(da) of Schedule 3 to the Social Security Act 1998 (c. 14) (decisions against which an appeal lies: payability of benefit), which is inserted by section 1 of this Act, after "section" insert "8 or".

34 Social security information and employment or training information

(1)   In section 2A of the Social Security Administration Act 1992 (c. 5) (claim or full entitlement to certain benefits conditional on work-focused interview), after subsection (7) insert—

"(7A) Information supplied in pursuance of regulations under this section shall be taken for all purposes to be information relating to social security."

(2)   In section 2AA of that Act (full entitlement to certain benefits conditional on work-focused interview for partner), after subsection (6) insert—

"(6A) Information supplied in pursuance of regulations under this section shall be taken for all purposes to be information relating to social security."

(3)   In Schedule 1 to the Jobseekers Act 1995 (c. 18) (supplementary provisions relating to jobseeker's allowance), at the end insert—

"Treatment of information supplied as information relating to social security

    19   Information supplied in pursuance of any provision made by or under this Act shall be taken for all purposes to be information relating to social security."

(4)   In section 72 of the Welfare Reform and Pensions Act 1999 (c. 30) (supply of information for certain purposes)—

    (a)   in subsection (1)(a) and (b), after "social security information" insert ", or information relating to employment or training,", and

   (b)   in subsection (7), for "purposes connected with employment or training includes purposes connected with" substitute "information relating to, or purposes connected with, employment or training includes information relating to, or purposes connected with,".

35   Persons under pensionable age to take part in work-focused interviews etc.

(1)   The Social Security Administration Act 1992 (c. 5) is amended as follows.

(2)   In section 2A (claim or full entitlement to certain benefits conditional on work-focused interview) —
   (a)   in subsection (1)(a), for sub-paragraph (ii) substitute —
>   "(ii)   has not attained pensionable age at the time of making the claim (but see subsection (1A)),",
   (b)   in subsection (1)(b)(i), for "is under that age and" substitute "has not attained pensionable age and is", and
   (c)   after subsection (1) insert —

>   "(1A)   For the purposes of subsection (1) a man born before 6 April 1955 is treated as attaining pensionable age when a woman born on the same day as the man would attain pensionable age."

(3)   In section 2AA (full entitlement to certain benefits conditional on work-focused interview for partner) —
   (a)   in subsection (1)(a), for sub-paragraphs (i) and (ii) substitute —
>   "(i)   has not attained pensionable age (but see subsection (1A)), and
>   (ii)   has a partner who has also not attained pensionable age,", and
   (b)   after subsection (1) insert —

>   "(1A)   For the purposes of subsection (1) a man born before 6 April 1955 is treated as attaining pensionable age when a woman born on the same day as the man would attain pensionable age."

(4)   In sections 2A(1)(a) and 2AA(1), for "a work-focused interview" substitute "one or more work-focused interviews", and in section 2A(1)(b), for "such an interview" substitute "one or more work-focused interviews".

36   Power to rename council tax benefit

(1)   The Secretary of State shall by order provide for the benefit referred to in section 123(1)(e) of the Social Security Contributions and Benefits Act 1992 (council tax benefit) to be known instead, either generally or in cases prescribed by the order, as council tax rebate.

(2)   An order under this section may —
   (a)   amend references to council tax benefit in any Act (whenever passed) or in any instrument made under any Act (whenever made);
   (b)   make provision about the interpretation of references to council tax benefit in other documents;
   (c)   make different provision for different areas.

(3)   In subsection (2)(a) "Act" means —
   (a)   an Act of Parliament,

    (b)   an Act of the Scottish Parliament, or

    (c)   a Measure or Act of the National Assembly for Wales.

(4)   The power to make an order under this section is exercisable by statutory instrument.

(5)   Subsections (3) to (5) of section 175 of the Social Security Contributions and Benefits Act 1992 (general provisions as to regulations and orders) apply in relation to the power conferred by this section as they apply in relation to a power conferred by that Act to make an order.

(6)   The first order under this section may not be made unless a draft of the statutory instrument containing the order has been laid before, and approved by a resolution of, each House of Parliament.

(7)   A statutory instrument containing an order under this section to which subsection (6) does not apply is subject to annulment in pursuance of a resolution of either House of Parliament.

37   Minor amendments

(1)   Sections 80 and 81 of the Benefits Act (which continue to have effect in certain cases despite their repeal by the Tax Credits Act 2002 (c. 21)) are to have effect as if the references in those sections to a child or children included references to a qualifying young person or persons.

(2)   "Qualifying young person" has the same meaning as in Part 9 of the Benefits Act.

(3)   In section 150(2) of the Benefits Act (interpretation of Part 10: Christmas bonus), in the definition of "qualifying employment and support allowance", for "an employment and support allowance" substitute "a contributory allowance".

(4)   Despite the provision made by the Welfare Reform Act 2007 (Commencement No. 6 and Consequential Provisions) Order 2008 (S.I. 2008/ 787), paragraph 9(7) and (8) of Schedule 3 to the Welfare Reform Act 2007 (c. 5) (which amend sections 88 and 89 of the Benefits Act) are deemed not to be in force by virtue of the provision made by that order at any time after the passing of this Act.

(5)   In this section "the Benefits Act" means the Social Security Contributions and Benefits Act 1992 (c. 4).

PART 2

DISABLED PEOPLE: RIGHT TO CONTROL PROVISION OF SERVICES

Introductory

38   Purpose of Part 2

The purpose of this Part is to enable disabled people aged 18 or over to exercise greater choice in relation to, and greater control over, the way in which relevant services (as defined by section 39) are provided to or for them, in cases where the provision of the relevant services is a function of a relevant authority (as defined by section 40).

39   Relevant services

(1)   In this Part "relevant services" means services –

    (a)   which are provided to or for the benefit of a disabled person ("P") (whether or not in connection with P's disability), and

    (b)   which relate to one or more of the following matters.

(2)   Those matters are –

    (a)   the provision of further education for P;

    (b)   facilitating the undertaking by P of further education or higher education;

    (c)   the provision of training for P;

    (d)   securing employment for P;

    (e)   facilitating P's continued employment;

    (f)   enabling P to live independently or more independently in P's home;

    (g)   the provision of residential accommodation for P;

    (h)   enabling P to overcome barriers to participation in society.

(3)   Relevant services also include the provision by or on behalf of a relevant authority to or for the benefit of a disabled person of grants or loans relating to one or more of the matters mentioned in subsection (2).

(4)   Relevant services do not include excluded services (provision as to direct payments relating to excluded services being made by other legislation).

(5)   Subsection (4) is subject to section 44(4) (which relates to pilot schemes) and to section 48 (which gives power to repeal the exclusion of community care services).

(6)   In relation to England and Wales, the following are excluded services –

    (a)   community care services,

    (b)   services provided under the Carers and Disabled Children Act 2000 (c. 16), and

    (c)   services provided under section 17 of the Children Act 1989 (c. 41) (provision of services for children in need, their families and others).

(7)   In relation to Scotland, the following are excluded services –

    (a)   community care services, and

    (b)   services provided under section 22(1) of the Children (Scotland) Act 1995 (c. 36) (promotion of welfare of children in need).

(8)   In this section "further education" and "higher education" –

    (a)   in relation to England and Wales, have the same meaning as in the Education Act 1996 (c. 56);

    (b)   in relation to Scotland, have the same meaning as in the Further and Higher Education (Scotland) Act 1992 (c. 37).

40   Relevant authority

(1)   In this Part "relevant authority" means –

    (a)   a Minister of the Crown or government department;

    (b)   the Scottish Ministers;

    (c)   the Welsh Ministers;

    (d)   a local authority;

      (e)   a person or body whose functions are exercised on behalf of the Crown;

      (f)   any other body which meets conditions A and B below.

(2)   Condition A is that the body is established by virtue of Her Majesty's prerogative or by an enactment or is established in any other way by a Minister of the Crown acting as such or by a government department.

(3)   Condition B is that the body's revenues derive wholly or mainly from public funds.

(4)   In subsection (1)(d) "local authority" means—

      (a)   a local authority within the meaning of the Local Government Act 1972 (c. 70),

      (b)   a council constituted under section 2 of the Local Government etc. (Scotland) Act 1994 (c. 39),

      (c)   the Greater London Authority,

      (d)   the Common Council of the City of London in its capacity as a local authority, or

      (e)   the Council of the Isles of Scilly.

(5)   In subsection (2) "Minister of the Crown" includes the Scottish Ministers and the Welsh Ministers.

Power to make regulations

41   Power to make provision enabling exercise of greater choice and control

(1)   The appropriate authority (as defined by section 45) may by regulations made by statutory instrument make any provision that would in the opinion of the authority making the regulations serve the purpose of this Part.

(2)   Regulations under this section may, in particular, make provision for and in connection with requiring a relevant authority to take the following steps in relation to a disabled person ("P") for whom it is obliged, or has decided, to provide, or arrange the provision of, relevant services—

      (a)   to inform P of the right to control conferred by virtue of the regulations, of the value of the relevant services to which P is entitled and of the choices available to P by virtue of the regulations;

      (b)   to work with P to determine the outcomes to be achieved by the provision of the relevant services;

      (c)   to work with P to prepare a plan (a "support plan") setting out how those outcomes will be achieved;

      (d)   to work with P to review and revise the support plan in prescribed circumstances;

      (e)   if P so requests, to make payments to P in respect of P securing the provision of an equivalent service;

      (f)   to the extent that P chooses to receive relevant services provided or arranged by the relevant authority, to provide, or arrange for them to be provided, in accordance with P's support plan as far as it is reasonably practicable to do so.

(3)   Regulations under this section may also—

      (a)   specify who is or is not to be treated as a disabled person for any purpose of the regulations;

     (b)   make provision about the circumstances in which a relevant authority is to be taken to have decided to provide a relevant service to a person;

     (c)   make provision as to matters to which a relevant authority must, or may, have regard when making a decision for the purposes of a provision of the regulations;

     (d)   make provision as to steps which a relevant authority must, or may, take before, or after, the relevant authority makes a decision for the purposes of a provision of the regulations (including provision requiring the relevant authority to review its decision).

(4)   Regulations under this section may enable or require the disclosure of information by one relevant authority to another for prescribed purposes of the regulations.

(5)   Regulations under this section may, for the purpose of this Part—

     (a)   vary the conditions attached to any power of a relevant authority to provide financial assistance to disabled people;

     (b)   vary the conditions attached to any power of a relevant authority to provide financial assistance to another relevant authority in connection with the provision of relevant services to disabled people by the other authority.

(6)   Regulations under this section may require a relevant authority exercising any function under the regulations to have regard to any guidance given from time to time by the appropriate authority.

42   Provision that may be made about direct payments

(1)   In this section "direct payments regulations" means regulations under section 41 making provision by virtue of subsection (2)(e) of that section and "direct payments" means payments made by a relevant authority under the regulations.

(2)   Direct payments regulations relating to a relevant service ("the qualifying service") of a relevant authority ("the providing authority") may in particular—

     (a)   specify circumstances in which the providing authority is or is not required to comply with a request for direct payments to be made under the regulations, whether those circumstances relate to the disabled person or to the qualifying service;

     (b)   make provision about the manner in which a request for direct payments is to be made;

     (c)   make provision enabling a disabled person to require a providing authority to assess the amount of the payments to which the person would be entitled if the person were to request the authority to make them;

     (d)   enable a disabled person to require a providing authority to comply with a request to provide direct payments in place of the qualifying service (or its provision at certain times or in certain circumstances) while providing, or continuing to provide, other relevant services (or providing, or continuing to provide, the qualifying service at other times or in other circumstances);

     (e)   make provision displacing functions or obligations of the providing authority with respect to the provision of the qualifying service (whether arising under any enactment, under any trust or otherwise) to such extent and subject to such conditions as may be prescribed.

(3) Direct payments regulations must include provision excluding any duty of a providing authority to comply with a request for direct payments, or a class of such requests, if compliance with the request, or with requests falling within that class, would in all the circumstances impose an unreasonable financial burden on the providing authority.

(4) Direct payments regulations may —

   (a) make provision for and in connection with requiring or authorising the providing authority to make direct payments to the disabled person or such other person as the authority may determine ("the payee") in accordance with the regulations in respect of the person securing the provision of the equivalent service;

   (b) make provision as to the conditions falling to be complied with by the payee in relation to the direct payments;

   (c) prescribe circumstances in which the providing authority may or must terminate the making of direct payments;

   (d) prescribe circumstances in which the providing authority may require repayment (whether by the payee or otherwise) of the whole or any part of the direct payments;

   (e) make provision for any sum falling to be paid or repaid to the providing authority by virtue of any condition or other requirement imposed in pursuance of the regulations to be recoverable as a debt due to the authority;

   (f) prescribe circumstances in which any sum is to cease to be payable by virtue of paragraph (d);

   (g) make provision authorising direct payments to be made to a prescribed person on behalf of the disabled person.

(5) For the purposes of subsection (4)(b), the conditions that are to be taken to be conditions in relation to direct payments include, in particular, conditions relating to —

   (a) what is or is not to be regarded as an equivalent service,

   (b) the securing of the provision of the equivalent service,

   (c) the provider of the service,

   (d) the person to whom the payments are made in respect of the provision of the service, or

   (e) the provision of the service.

43 Exercise of rights on behalf of persons who lack capacity

(1) Regulations under section 41 may make provision for and in connection with enabling any request or consent for the purposes of the regulations (including any request or consent relating to payments by virtue of subsection (2)(e) of that section) to be made or given on behalf of a disabled person who falls within subsection (2) by a person of a prescribed description.

(2) A person falls within this subsection —

   (a) in relation to England and Wales, if the person lacks capacity, within the meaning of the Mental Capacity Act 2005 (c. 9), in relation to the decision concerned, and

(b)   in relation to Scotland, if the person is incapable, within the meaning of the Adults with Incapacity (Scotland) Act 2000 (asp 4), in relation to that decision.

44   Pilot schemes

(1)   Regulations to which this subsection applies may be made so as to have effect for a specified period not exceeding 36 months.

(2)   Subsection (1) applies to regulations under section 41 that are made with a view to ascertaining—

(a)   the extent to which their provisions contribute to achieving the purpose of this Part,

(b)   the extent of any beneficial effects on the lives of the disabled people affected, and

(c)   the extent of any financial burden imposed on the relevant authorities to which the regulations relate.

(3)   Regulations which, by virtue of subsection (1), are to have effect for a limited period are referred to in this section as a "pilot scheme".

(4)   Subsections (6)(a) and (7)(a) of section 39 do not restrict the power to make a pilot scheme; and accordingly a pilot scheme may relate to community care services.

(5)   A pilot scheme may provide that its provisions are to apply only in relation to—

(a)   one or more specified areas;

(b)   one or more specified classes of person;

(c)   persons selected—

(i)   by reference to prescribed criteria, or

(ii)   on a sampling basis.

(6)   A pilot scheme may make consequential or transitional provision with respect to the cessation of the scheme on the expiry of the specified period.

(7)   A pilot scheme may be replaced by a further pilot scheme making the same or similar provision.

(8)   The appropriate authority which made a pilot scheme must prepare and publish a report on the operation of the scheme.

Supplementary

45   The appropriate authority by which regulations under section 41 are made

(1)   Subsection (2) has effect to determine the appropriate authority by which regulations under section 41 may be made.

(2)   The Secretary of State is the appropriate authority, except that—

(a)   in relation to provision that would be within the legislative competence of the Scottish Parliament if it were included in an Act of that Parliament, the Scottish Ministers are the appropriate authority,

(b)   in relation to provision that would be within the legislative competence of the National Assembly for Wales if it were included in a Measure of the Assembly (or, if regulations are made after the Assembly Act provisions come into force, an Act of the Assembly), the Welsh Ministers are the appropriate authority,

(c) in relation to provision that does not fall within paragraph (b) and relates to relevant services in Wales with respect to which functions are exercisable—

    (i) by a Minister of the Crown, and

    (ii) by the Welsh Ministers, the First Minister or the Counsel General,

the Secretary of State or the Welsh Ministers are the appropriate authority, and

(d) in relation to provision that does not fall within paragraph (b) or (c) and relates to relevant services in Wales with respect to which functions are exercisable by the Welsh Ministers, the First Minister or the Counsel General, the Welsh Ministers are the appropriate authority.

(3) Any power of the Secretary of State to make regulations under section 41—

    (a) is exercisable only with the consent of the Treasury; and

    (b) does not include power to make provision—

        (i) removing or modifying any function of the Welsh Ministers, the First Minister or the Counsel General, or

        (ii) conferring or imposing any function on the Welsh Ministers, the First Minister or the Counsel General.

(4) Any power of the Welsh Ministers to make regulations under section 41 by virtue of subsection (2)(c) or (d) does not include power to make provision—

    (a) removing or modifying any function of a Minister of the Crown, or

    (b) conferring or imposing any function on a Minister of the Crown.

(5) In this section—

    "the Assembly Act provisions" has the meaning given by section 103(8) of the Government of Wales Act 2006 (c. 32);

    "the Counsel General" means the Counsel General to the Welsh Assembly Government;

    "the First Minister" means the First Minister for Wales;

    "Minister of the Crown" includes the Treasury.

46 Regulations under section 41: supplementary provisions

(1) Any power to make regulations under section 41 may be exercised—

    (a) in relation to all cases to which it extends,

    (b) in relation to those cases subject to specified exceptions, or

    (c) in relation to any specified cases or classes of case.

(2) Any such power may be exercised so as to make, as respects the cases in relation to which it is exercised—

    (a) the full provision to which the power extends or any less provision (whether by way of exception or otherwise);

    (b) the same provision for all cases in relation to which it is exercised, or different provision for different cases or different classes of case or different provision as respect the same case or class of case for different purposes;

     (c)   any such provision either unconditionally or subject to any specified condition.

(3)   Where any such power is expressed to be exercisable for alternative purposes, it may be exercised in relation to the same case for all or any of those purposes.

(4)   Any such power includes power —

     (a)   to make such incidental, supplementary, consequential or saving provision as the authority making the regulations considers to be necessary or expedient;

     (b)   to provide for a person to exercise a discretion in dealing with any matter;

     (c)   to amend or repeal an enactment whenever passed or made.

47   Consultation

(1)   Before laying before Parliament (or the Scottish Parliament or the National Assembly for Wales) a draft of a statutory instrument containing regulations under section 41, the appropriate authority must —

     (a)   publish draft regulations in such manner as it thinks fit, and

     (b)   invite representations to be made to it about the draft, during a specified period of not less than 12 weeks, by persons appearing to it to be affected by the proposals.

(2)   In this section "the appropriate authority" is to be read in accordance with section 45(2).

48   Power to repeal exclusion of community care services

(1)   An order under this subsection may repeal section 39(6)(a).

(2)   The power to make an order under subsection (1) is exercisable —

     (a)   in relation to England, by the Secretary of State with the consent of the Treasury, and

     (b)   in relation to Wales, by the Welsh Ministers.

(3)   The power of the Secretary of State to make an order under subsection (1) is exercisable only if —

     (a)   the Secretary of State has previously made a pilot scheme that relates to community care services, and has in accordance with section 44(8) published a report on the operation of the pilot scheme, or

     (b)   the Secretary of State has previously given directions under a relevant enactment with a view to enabling disabled people to exercise (either in England generally or in a specified area or areas) greater choice in relation to, and greater control over, the way in which community care services are provided to or for them.

(4)   In subsection (3) —

     (a)   "pilot scheme" has the meaning given by section 44(3);

     (b)   "relevant enactment" means —

          (i)   section 7A of the Local Authority Social Services Act 1970 (directions by Secretary of State as to exercise of social services functions), or

   (ii) section 47(4) of the National Health Service and Community Care Act 1990 (directions by Secretary of State in relation to assessment of needs for community care services).

(5) The Scottish Ministers may by order repeal section 39(7)(a).

(6) An order under subsection (1) or (5) may make any consequential modification of section 39(5) or 44(4).

(7) The power to make an order under subsection (1) or (5) is exercisable by statutory instrument.

49 Regulations and orders: control by Parliament or other legislature

(1) The Secretary of State may not make a statutory instrument containing regulations under section 41 or an order under section 48(1) unless a draft of the instrument has been laid before, and approved by a resolution of, each House of Parliament.

(2) The Scottish Ministers may not make a statutory instrument containing regulations under section 41 or an order under section 48(5) unless a draft of the instrument has been laid before, and approved by a resolution of, the Scottish Parliament.

(3) The Welsh Ministers may not make a statutory instrument containing regulations under section 41 or an order under section 48(1) unless a draft of the instrument has been laid before, and approved by a resolution of, the National Assembly for Wales.

50 Interpretation of Part 2

In this Part—

  "community care services" means—

   (a) in relation to England and Wales, community care services as defined by section 46(3) of the National Health Service and Community Care Act 1990 (c. 19);

   (b) in relation to Scotland, community care services as defined by section 5A of the Social Work (Scotland) Act 1968 (c. 49);

  "employment" includes self-employment;

  "enactment" means an enactment contained in, or in an instrument made under—

   (a) an Act of Parliament,

   (b) an Act of the Scottish Parliament, or

   (c) a Measure or Act of the National Assembly for Wales;

  "prescribed" means specified in, or determined in accordance with, regulations under section 41;

  "relevant authority" has the meaning given by section 40;

  "relevant services" has the meaning given by section 39.

PART 3

CHILD MAINTENANCE

51   Disqualification for holding etc. driving licence or travel authorisation

(1)   The Child Support Act 1991 (c. 48) is amended as follows.

(2)   In section 39B (disqualification for holding or obtaining travel authorisation) —

    (a)   in subsection (1), for "The Commission may apply to the court for an order under this section" substitute "The Commission may make an order under this section (referred to in this section and sections 39C to 39F as a "disqualification order")", and

    (b)   for subsections (3) to (13) substitute —

        "(3)   A disqualification order shall provide that the person against whom it is made is disqualified for holding or obtaining —

            (a)   a driving licence,

            (b)   a travel authorisation, or

            (c)   both a driving licence and a travel authorisation,

        while the order has effect.

        (4)   Before making a disqualification order against a person, the Commission shall consider whether the person needs the relevant document in order to earn a living.

        (5)   A disqualification order shall specify the amount in respect of which it is made.

        (6)   That amount shall be the aggregate of —

            (a)   the amount sought to be recovered as mentioned in subsection (1)(a), or so much of it as remains unpaid; and

            (b)   the amount which the person against whom the order is made is required to pay by the order under section 39DA(1).

        (7)   The Commission shall serve a copy of the disqualification order (together with a copy of the order under section 39DA(1)) on the person against whom it is made.

        (8)   In this section —

            "driving licence" means a licence to drive a motor vehicle granted under Part 3 of the Road Traffic Act 1988;

            "relevant document", in relation to a disqualification order made against a person, means the document (or documents) for the holding or obtaining of which the person is disqualified by the order;

            "travel authorisation" means —

                (a)   a United Kingdom passport (within the meaning of the Immigration Act 1971);

                (b)   an ID card issued under the Identity Cards Act 2006 that records that the person to whom it has been issued is a British citizen."

(3) In section 39C (period for which orders under section 39B are to have effect), for subsection (1) substitute—

"(1) A disqualification order shall specify the period for which it is to have effect.

(1A) That period shall not exceed 12 months (subject to any extension under section 39CA or 39CB).

(1B) That period shall begin to run with—
   (a) the first day after the end of the period within which an appeal may be brought against the order under section 39CB(1); or
   (b) if the running of the period is suspended at that time, the first day when its running is no longer suspended."

(4) After that section insert—

"39CA Surrender of relevant documents

(1) A person against whom a disqualification order is made who holds any relevant document shall surrender it in the prescribed manner to the prescribed person within the required period.

(2) For this purpose "the required period" means the period of 7 days beginning with the start of the period for which the order has effect or has effect again following a period of suspension.

(3) But, if immediately before the end of the required period the person has a good reason for not surrendering any relevant document, the person shall instead surrender it as soon as practicable after the end of that period.

(4) The Secretary of State may by regulations make provision prescribing circumstances in which a person is, or is not, to be regarded for the purposes of subsection (3) as having a good reason for not surrendering any relevant document.

(5) The requirements imposed by subsections (1) and (3) cease to have effect if the period for which the disqualification order has effect is suspended or ends.

(6) A person who fails to comply with a requirement imposed by subsection (1) or (3) commits an offence.

(7) A person guilty of an offence under subsection (6) shall be liable on summary conviction to a fine not exceeding level 3 on the standard scale.

(8) On sentencing a person for an offence under that subsection the court may by order extend the period for which the disqualification order is to have effect by such period as may be specified in the order under this subsection.

(9) But the power conferred by subsection (8) may not be exercised so as to provide for the disqualification order to have effect for a period exceeding 2 years in total.

(10) In this section "relevant document" has the same meaning as in section 39.

(11) Where this section applies in relation to a driving licence at any time before the commencement of Schedule 3 to the Road Safety Act 2006, any reference in this section to any relevant document includes the licence's counterpart (within the meaning of section 108(1) of the Road Traffic Act 1988).

39CB Appeals against disqualification orders

(1) A person against whom a disqualification order is made may appeal to the court against the order within a prescribed period (which must begin with the first day on which that person had actual notice of the order).

(2) Where an appeal is brought under subsection (1), the running of the period for which the order has effect shall be suspended until the time at which the appeal is determined, withdrawn or discontinued.

(3) If —
   (a) the person against whom a disqualification order is made does not bring an appeal within the period specified in subsection (1), and
   (b) prescribed conditions are satisfied,
   the court may grant leave for an appeal to be brought after the end of that period.

(4) On granting leave under subsection (3) the court may suspend the running of the period for which the order has effect until such time and on such conditions (if any) as it thinks just.

(5) On an appeal under this section the court —
   (a) shall reconsider the exercise by the Commission of its powers under section 39B; and
   (b) may by order affirm, vary or revoke the disqualification order.

(6) On an appeal under this section the court shall not question —
   (a) the liability order by reference to which the Commission acted as mentioned in section 39B(1)(a);
   (b) any liability order made against the same person after the disqualification order was made; or
   (c) the maintenance calculation by reference to which any liability order within paragraph (a) or (b) was made.

(7) The power under subsection (5) to vary a disqualification order includes power to extend the period for which it has effect; but that power may not be exercised so as to provide for it to have effect for a period exceeding 2 years in total.

(8) If, on appeal under this section, the court affirms or varies a disqualification order, the court shall substitute for the amount specified under section 39B(5) the aggregate of —
   (a) the amount sought to be recovered as mentioned in section 39B(1)(a), or so much of it as remains unpaid;
   (b) the amount which the person against whom the order was made is required to pay by the order under section 39DA(1), so far as remaining unpaid;

    (c)   the amount which that person is required to pay by the order under section 39DA(2); and

    (d)   if a liability order has been made against that person since the disqualification order was made, the amount in respect of which the liability order was made, so far as remaining unpaid.

(9)   On the affirmation or variation of the disqualification order by the court, any existing suspension of the running of the period for which the order is to have effect shall cease.

(10)   But the court may suspend the running of that period until such time and on such conditions (if any) as it thinks fit if—

    (a)   the person against whom the disqualification order was made agrees to pay the amount specified in the order; or

    (b)   the court is of the opinion that the suspension in question is justified by exceptional circumstances.

(11)   If, on an appeal under this section, the court revokes a disqualification order, the court shall also revoke the order made under section 39DA(1).

(12)   But subsection (11) does not apply if the court is of the opinion that, having regard to all the circumstances, it is reasonable to require the person against whom the disqualification order was made to pay the costs mentioned in section 39DA(1).

(13)   In this section "the court" means—

    (a)   in relation to England and Wales, a magistrates' court;

    (b)   in relation to Scotland, the sheriff."

(5)   After section 39D insert—

"39DA Recovery of Commission's costs

(1)   On making a disqualification order against any person the Commission shall also make an order requiring that person to pay an amount in respect of the costs incurred by the Commission in exercising its functions under section 39B.

(2)   If on an appeal under section 39CB the court affirms or varies a disqualification order made against any person, the court shall also make an order requiring that person to pay an amount in respect of the costs incurred by the Commission in connection with the appeal ("the Commission's appeal costs").

(3)   If—

    (a)   on an appeal under that section the court revokes a disqualification order made against any person, and

    (b)   the court is satisfied that, having regard to all the circumstances, it is reasonable to require that person to pay an amount in respect of the Commission's appeal costs,

the court shall also make an order requiring that person to pay an amount in respect of those costs.

(4)   Any amount payable by virtue of an order made under this section shall be—

    (a)   specified in the order; and

   (b)   determined in accordance with regulations made by the Secretary of State.

   (5)   The provisions of this Act with respect to —
      (a)   the collection of child support maintenance, and
      (b)   the enforcement of an obligation to pay child support maintenance,
   apply equally (with any necessary modifications) to amounts which a person is required to pay under this section."

(6)   Schedule 5 contains consequential amendments and other amendments related to the provision made by this section.

52   Report on operation of driving licence amendments

(1)   The Secretary of State must prepare a report on the operation during the review period of the amendments of the 1991 Act made by section 51 and Schedule 5 so far as those amendments relate to the disqualification of any person for holding or obtaining a driving licence.

(2)   "The review period" is the period of 24 months beginning with the day on which section 51 and Schedule 5 come into force in relation to the disqualification of any person for holding or obtaining a driving licence.

(3)   The Secretary of State must —
      (a)   prepare the report, and
      (b)   lay it before Parliament,
   within 6 months from the end of the review period.

(4)   The continued effect of the driving licence amendments depends on whether the Secretary of State makes an order under this subsection within the relevant period providing for those provisions to continue to have effect.

(5)   "The relevant period" means the period of 30 days beginning with the day on which the report is laid before Parliament; and, in reckoning this period, no account is to be taken of any time during which Parliament —
      (a)   is dissolved or prorogued, or
      (b)   is adjourned for more than 4 days.

(6)   If no order is made as mentioned in subsection (4), the Secretary of State must instead make an order under this subsection containing such amendments of the 1991 Act as the Secretary of State considers necessary to secure that the effect of the driving licence amendments is reversed.

(7)   The effect of the driving licence amendments is to be regarded as reversed if the 1991 Act is amended so that it has the same effect in relation to the disqualification of any person for holding or obtaining a driving licence as it would have had if this Act had not been passed.

(8)   An order under subsection (6) may contain consequential provision and transitional provision or savings.

(9)   The consequential provision that may be made by an order under subsection (6) includes, in particular, provision amending, repealing or revoking —
      (a)   any provision of any Act passed before the making of the order, or
      (b)   any provision of any instrument made under any Act before the making of the order.

(10) Any power to make an order under this section is exercisable by statutory instrument.

(11) An order under subsection (4) may not be made unless a draft of the statutory instrument containing the order has been laid before, and approved by a resolution of, each House of Parliament.

(12) A statutory instrument containing an order under subsection (6) is subject to annulment in pursuance of a resolution of either House of Parliament.

(13) In this section—

"the 1991 Act" means the Child Support Act 1991 (c. 48);

"driving licence" has the same meaning as in section 39B of the 1991 Act;

"the driving licence amendments" means the amendments of the 1991 Act made by section 51 and Schedule 5 so far as relating to the disqualification of any person for holding or obtaining a driving licence.

53 Report on operation of travel authorisation amendments

(1) The Secretary of State must prepare a report on the operation during the review period of the amendments of the 1991 Act made by section 51 and Schedule 5 so far as those amendments relate to the disqualification of any person for holding or obtaining a travel authorisation.

(2) "The review period" is the period of 24 months beginning with the day on which section 51 and Schedule 5 come into force in relation to the disqualification of any person for holding or obtaining a travel authorisation.

(3) The Secretary of State must—
   (a) prepare the report, and
   (b) lay it before Parliament,
   within 6 months from the end of the review period.

(4) The continued effect of the travel authorisation amendments depends on whether the Secretary of State makes an order under this subsection within the relevant period providing for those amendments to continue to have effect.

(5) "The relevant period" means the period of 30 days beginning with the day on which the report is laid before Parliament; and, in reckoning this period, no account is to be taken of any time during which Parliament—
   (a) is dissolved or prorogued, or
   (b) is adjourned for more than 4 days.

(6) If no order is made as mentioned in subsection (4), the Secretary of State must instead make an order under this subsection containing such amendments of the 1991 Act as the Secretary of State considers necessary to secure that the effect of the travel authorisation amendments is reversed.

(7) The effect of the travel authorisation amendments is to be regarded as reversed if the 1991 Act is amended so that it has the same effect in relation to the disqualification of any person for holding or obtaining a travel authorisation as it would have had if this Act had not been passed.

(8) An order under subsection (6) may contain consequential provision and transitional provision or savings.

(9) The consequential provision that may be made by an order under subsection (6) includes, in particular, provision amending, repealing or revoking —

    (a) any provision of any Act passed before the making of the order, or

    (b) any provision of any instrument made under any Act before the making of the order.

(10) Any power to make an order under this section is exercisable by statutory instrument.

(11) An order under subsection (4) may not be made unless a draft of the statutory instrument containing the order has been laid before, and approved by a resolution of, each House of Parliament.

(12) A statutory instrument containing an order under subsection (6) is subject to annulment in pursuance of a resolution of either House of Parliament.

(13) In this section —

    "the 1991 Act" means the Child Support Act 1991 (c. 48);

    "travel authorisation" has the same meaning as in section 39B of the 1991 Act;

    "the travel authorisation amendments" means the amendments of the 1991 Act made by section 51 and Schedule 5 so far as relating to the disqualification of any person for holding or obtaining a travel authorisation.

54 Payments of child support maintenance

(1) Section 29 of the Child Support Act 1991 (collection of child support maintenance) is amended as follows.

(2) In subsection (3) (provision which may be made by regulations for payment of child support maintenance), for paragraph (c) substitute —

    "(c) for determining, on the basis of prescribed assumptions, the total amount of the payments of child support maintenance payable in a reference period (including provision for adjustments to such an amount);

    (ca) requiring payments of child support maintenance to be made —

        (i) by reference to such an amount and a reference period; and

        (ii) at prescribed intervals falling in a reference period;".

(3) After that subsection insert —

    "(3A) In subsection (3)(c) and (ca) "a reference period" means —

        (a) a period of 52 weeks beginning with a prescribed date; or

        (b) in prescribed circumstances, a prescribed period."

55 Child support maintenance: offences relating to information

(1) Section 14A of the Child Support Act 1991 (offences relating to information) is amended as follows.

(2) For subsection (3A) substitute —

    "(3A) In the case of regulations under section 14 which require a person liable to make payments of child support maintenance to notify —

(a) a change of address, or

(b) any other change of circumstances,

a person who fails to comply with the requirement is guilty of an offence."

(3) After subsection (5) insert—

"(6) In England and Wales, an information relating to an offence under subsection (2) may be tried by a magistrates' court if it is laid within the period of 12 months beginning with the commission of the offence.

(7) In Scotland, summary proceedings for an offence under subsection (2) may be commenced within the period of 12 months beginning with the commission of the offence.

(8) Section 136(3) of the Criminal Procedure (Scotland) Act 1995 (c. 46) (date when proceedings deemed to be commenced) applies for the purposes of subsection (7) as it applies for the purposes of that section."

PART 4

BIRTH REGISTRATION

56 Registration of births

Schedule 6 contains—

(a) amendments of the Births and Deaths Registration Act 1953 (c. 20) relating to the registration of the births of children whose parents are neither married to each other nor civil partners of each other,

(b) amendments of that Act relating to the late registration of births, and

(c) related amendments of other legislation.

PART 5

GENERAL

57 Consequential amendments of subordinate legislation

(1) The Secretary of State may by regulations made by statutory instrument make such provision amending or revoking any instrument made under any other Act before the passing of this Act as appears to the Secretary of State to be appropriate in consequence of any provision of this Act, other than a provision contained in Part 2.

(2) Regulations under this section may include—

(a) transitional provisions or savings, and

(b) provision conferring a discretion on any person.

(3) A statutory instrument containing regulations under this section is subject to annulment in pursuance of a resolution of either House of Parliament.

58 Repeals and revocations

(1) Schedule 7 contains repeals and revocations.

(2) The following repeals and revocation in Part 2 of that Schedule (which are made in consequence of section 15(1)) have effect on 6 April 2010 –

    (a) the repeals in the Social Security Contributions and Benefits Act 1992 (c. 4) other than those of sections 88, 89, 91 and 92;

    (b) the repeal of paragraph 24 of Schedule 1 to the Jobseekers Act 1995 (c. 18);

    (c) the repeals in the Welfare Reform and Pensions Act 1999 (c. 30), the Tax Credits Act 2002 (c. 21), the Civil Partnership Act 2004 (c. 33) and the Child Benefit Act 2005 (c. 6); and

    (d) the revocation in the Regulatory Reform (Carer's Allowance) Order 2002 (S.I. 2002/ 1457).

(3) The repeal in that Part of paragraph 9 of Part 4 of Schedule 4 to the Social Security Contributions and Benefits Act 1992 is not to be taken as affecting the operation of article 3 of the Tax Credits Act 2002 (Commencement No. 3 and Transitional Provisions and Savings) Order 2003 (S.I. 2003/ 938) (savings in relation to the abolition of child dependency increases).

59 Financial provisions

(1) There is to be paid out of money provided by Parliament –

    (a) any expenditure incurred in consequence of this Act by a Minister of the Crown, a government department or the Registrar General for England and Wales, and

    (b) any increase attributable to this Act in the sums payable under any other Act out of money so provided.

(2) There is to be paid into the Consolidated Fund any increase attributable to this Act in the sums payable into that Fund under any other Act.

60 Extent

(1) The following provisions of this Act extend to England and Wales, Scotland and Northern Ireland –

    section 24 and Schedule 4 (loss of benefit provisions);

    section 36 (power to rename council tax benefit); and

    this section and sections 61 and 62.

(2) Section 56 and Schedule 6 (birth registration) extend to England and Wales only.

(3) Subject to subsection (4), the other provisions of this Act extend to England and Wales and Scotland only.

(4) Any amendment, repeal or revocation made by this Act has the same extent as the enactment to which it relates.

(5) Subsection (4) is subject to paragraph 20(2) of Schedule 6.

61 Commencement

(1) The following provisions of this Act come into force on the day on which this Act is passed –

    sections 1 and 2;

    section 8;

section 11;

section 23;

sections 27 and 28;

section 37;

section 57;

sections 59 and 60;

this section;

section 62; and

Schedule 3.

(2)   The following provisions of this Act come into force at the end of the period of 2 months beginning with the day on which this Act is passed—

section 15;

section 34;

Part 2;

section 58(2) and (3); and

Part 2 of Schedule 7 so far as relating to the repeals and revocation mentioned in section 58(2).

(3)   The other provisions of this Act come into force on such day as the Secretary of State may by order made by statutory instrument appoint.

(4)   An order under subsection (3) may—

   (a)   appoint different days for different purposes and in relation to different areas;

   (b)   make such provision as the Secretary of State considers necessary or expedient for transitory, transitional or saving purposes in connection with the coming into force of any provision falling within that subsection.

(5)   Before making an order under subsection (3) in relation to any provision of Part 1 of Schedule 6 (birth registration), the Secretary of State must consult the Registrar General for England and Wales.

62   Short title

This Act may be cited as the Welfare Reform Act 2009.

SCHEDULES

SCHEDULE 1

Section 4

AMENDMENTS CONNECTED TO SECTION 4

PART 1

AMENDMENTS OF JOBSEEKERS ACT 1995

Introduction

1   The Jobseekers Act 1995 (c. 18) is amended as follows.

Work-focused interviews etc.

2   In section 8(1) (attendance, information and evidence), after "other than a" insert "claimant whose claim is based on meeting condition B in section 1A or".

3   After section 11 insert—

"Work-focused interviews etc.

11A   Persons not required to meet the jobseeking conditions

(1)   Regulations may make provision for or in connection with imposing on a person—

    (a)   who makes a claim for a jobseeker's allowance (other than a joint-claim jobseeker's allowance), and

    (b)   to whom section 8(1) does not apply,

a requirement to take part in a work-focused interview as an additional condition which the person must meet before the person becomes entitled to the allowance.

(2)   Regulations may make provision for or in connection with imposing on a person—

    (a)   who is entitled to a jobseeker's allowance (other than a joint-claim jobseeker's allowance), and

    (b)   to whom section 8(1) does not apply,

a requirement to take part in one or more work-focused interviews as a condition of continuing to be entitled to the full amount of the allowance payable apart from the regulations.

(3)   No requirement may be imposed by virtue of this section on a person who—

    (a)   is not a member of a couple, and

2836

Welfare Reform Act 2009 (c. 24)
Schedule 1 – Amendments connected to section 4
Part 1 – Amendments of Jobseekers Act 1995

    (b)   is responsible for, and a member of the same household as, a child under the age of one.

(4)   In this section and sections 11B and 11C "work-focused interview", in relation to any person, means an interview conducted for such purposes connected with employment or training in the case of that person as may be prescribed.

(5)   The purposes which may be so prescribed include—

    (a)   purposes connected with a person's existing or future employment or training prospects or needs; and

    (b)   (in particular) assisting or encouraging a person to enhance the person's employment prospects.

11B   Provision which may be made by regulations under section 11A

(1)   Regulations under section 11A(1) or (2) may, in particular, make provision—

    (a)   prescribing circumstances in which a person is to be subject to a requirement to take part in one or more work-focused interviews (a "relevant requirement");

    (b)   for notifying a person of a relevant requirement;

    (c)   prescribing the work-focused interviews in which a person who is subject to a relevant requirement is required to take part;

    (d)   for determining, in relation to work-focused interviews under the regulations, when and how the interview is to be conducted and, if it is to be conducted face to face, where it is to take place;

    (e)   for notifying persons who are subject to a relevant requirement of what is determined in respect of the matters mentioned in paragraph (d);

    (f)   prescribing circumstances in which a person who is a party to a work-focused interview under the regulations is to be regarded as having, or not having, taken part in it;

    (g)   for securing that the appropriate consequence follows if a person who is subject to a relevant requirement—

        (i)   fails to take part in the work-focused interview, and

        (ii)   does not, within a prescribed period, show that the person had good cause for that failure;

    (h)   prescribing matters which are, or are not, to be taken into account in determining whether a person has good cause for any failure to comply with the regulations;

    (i)   prescribing circumstances in which a person is, or is not, to be regarded as having good cause for any such failure.

(2)   For the purposes of subsection (1)(g) "the appropriate consequence" means—

    (a)   in the case of regulations under section 11A(1), that the person is to be regarded as not having made a claim for the allowance or, if the allowance has already been awarded (because the case is within subsection (6)), the entitlement to it is to cease immediately;

(b)   in the case of regulations under section 11A(2), that the amount of the allowance is to be reduced by the prescribed amount until the prescribed time.

(3)   Regulations under section 11A(2) may, in relation to any such reduction, provide—

(a)   for the amount of the reduction to be calculated in the first instance by reference to such amount as may be prescribed;

(b)   for the amount as so calculated to be restricted, in prescribed circumstances, to the prescribed extent;

(c)   where the person is also entitled to one or more relevant benefits, for determining the extent, and the order, in which the jobseeker's allowance and the relevant benefits are to be reduced in order to give effect to the required reduction.

(4)   Regulations under section 11A(1) or (2) may provide that a relevant requirement that would otherwise apply to a person by virtue of the regulations—

(a)   is, in any prescribed circumstances, either not to apply or not to apply until such time as is prescribed;

(b)   is not to apply if the Secretary of State determines that a work-focused interview would not be of assistance to the person or would otherwise not be appropriate in the circumstances;

(c)   is not to apply until such time as the Secretary of State determines, if the Secretary of State determines that a work-focused interview would not be of assistance to the person, or would otherwise not be appropriate in the circumstances, until that time.

(5)   The regulations may make provision for treating a person in relation to whom a relevant requirement does not apply, or does not apply until a particular time, as having complied with the requirement to such extent and for such purposes as may be prescribed.

(6)   Where—

(a)   a person is subject to a relevant requirement as a result of regulations under section 11A(1), and

(b)   the interview is postponed by or under provision of the regulations made as a result of subsection (4)(a) or (c) above,

the time to which it is so postponed may be a time falling after an award of the allowance.

(7)   In this section "relevant benefit", in relation to any person, means any benefit in relation to which the person is required to take part in a work-focused interview by virtue of regulations made under section 2A of the Administration Act.

11C   Action plans in connection with work-focused interviews

(1)   The Secretary of State must in prescribed circumstances provide an action plan to a person subject to a requirement imposed under section 11A to take part in a work-focused interview.

(2)   In this section an "action plan" means a document prepared for such purposes as may be prescribed.

2838

*Welfare Reform Act 2009 (c. **24**)*
Schedule 1 — Amendments connected to section 4
Part 1 — Amendments of Jobseekers Act 1995

(3) Regulations may make provision about—
    (a) the form of action plans;
    (b) the content of action plans;
    (c) the review and updating of action plans.

(4) Regulations may make provision for reconsideration of an action plan at the request of the person to whom it is provided and may, in particular, make provision about—
    (a) the circumstances in which reconsideration may be requested;
    (b) the period within which any reconsideration must take place;
    (c) the matters to which regard must be had when deciding on reconsideration whether the plan should be changed;
    (d) notification of the decision on reconsideration;
    (e) the giving of directions for the purpose of giving effect to the decision on reconsideration.

(5) In preparing any action plan, the Secretary of State must have regard (so far as practicable) to its impact on the well-being of any child who may be affected by it."

Directions given by officers of the Secretary of State etc.

4   After section 18 insert—

"Claimants to comply with directions etc.

18A Requirements imposed on claimants by officers of the Secretary of State

(1) A claimant must carry out any direction given by an officer of the Secretary of State to the claimant with a view to achieving one or both of the following—
    (a) assisting the claimant to find employment;
    (b) improving the claimant's existing or future prospects of being or remaining employed.

(2) A direction under subsection (1)—
    (a) must be reasonable, having regard to the claimant's circumstances;
    (b) must be in writing; and
    (c) may be varied or revoked by a subsequent direction given under that subsection.

(3) If an officer of the Secretary of State notifies a claimant of a place on a training scheme which is vacant or about to become vacant, the claimant—
    (a) must apply for the place, and
    (b) if offered the place, must accept it and attend the scheme.

(4) If an officer of the Secretary of State notifies a claimant of a place on an employment programme which is vacant or about to become vacant, the claimant—
    (a) must apply for the place, and

      (b)   if offered the place, must accept it and attend the programme.

(5)   If an officer of the Secretary of State notifies a claimant of a situation in any employment which is vacant or about to become vacant, the claimant —

     (a)   must apply for the situation, and

     (b)   if offered the situation, must accept it.

(6)   In the case of a person whose claim to a jobseeker's allowance is based on meeting condition B in section 1A —

     (a)   a subsection (1)(a) direction may not be given except as mentioned in subsection (7); and

     (b)   subsections (4) and (5) do not apply (but see subsection (7)).

(7)   If a person whose claim to a jobseeker's allowance is based on meeting condition B in section 1A so agrees —

     (a)   a subsection (1)(a) direction may be given to the person; and

     (b)   a subsection (1)(b) direction may require the person to apply for a place on an employment programme and, if offered the place, accept it and attend the programme.

(8)   Regulations may, in the case of a person of a prescribed description whose claim to a jobseeker's allowance is based on meeting condition B in section 1A, provide —

     (a)   for a subsection (1)(b) direction not to be given or not to be given in prescribed circumstances;

     (b)   for subsection (3) not to apply or not to apply in prescribed circumstances.

(9)   For the purposes of this section —

     "employment programme" has such meaning as may be prescribed;

     "subsection (1)(a) direction" means a direction under subsection (1) given with a view to achieving the purpose mentioned in paragraph (a) of that subsection;

     "subsection (1)(b) direction" means a direction under subsection (1) given with a view to achieving the purpose mentioned in paragraph (b) of that subsection;

     "training scheme" has such meaning as may be prescribed.

(10)   For the purposes of the application of this section in the case of a joint-claim couple claiming a joint-claim jobseeker's allowance —

     (a)   a direction or notification under this section may be given to only one member of the couple, or

     (b)   separate directions or notifications under this section may be given to each member of the couple,

   and references in this section to a claimant are to be read accordingly.

(11)   Nothing in any provision of this section is to be read as prejudicing the generality of any other provision of this section or of section 18B.

(12)   For the sanctions for failure to comply with this section, see sections 19 and 20A (as read with sections 18C and 18D).

2840

Welfare Reform Act 2009 (c. 24)
Schedule 1 — Amendments connected to section 4
Part 1 — Amendments of Jobseekers Act 1995

18B   Work-related activity: section 1A(4) claimants

(1)   Regulations may make provision for or in connection with imposing on a person —

    (a)   whose claim to a jobseeker's allowance is based on meeting condition B in section 1A, and

    (b)   who is not a lone parent of a child under the age of 3,

a requirement to undertake work-related activity in accordance with regulations.

(2)   Regulations under this section may, in particular, make provision —

    (a)   prescribing circumstances in which a person is to be subject to any requirement imposed by the regulations (a "relevant requirement");

    (b)   for notifying a person of a relevant requirement;

    (c)   prescribing the time or times at which a person who is subject to a relevant requirement is required to undertake work-related activity and the amount of work-related activity the person is required at any time to undertake;

    (d)   prescribing circumstances in which a person who is subject to a relevant requirement is, or is not, to be regarded as undertaking work-related activity.

(3)   Regulations under this section may include provision that in such circumstances as the regulations may provide a person's obligation under the regulations to undertake work-related activity at a particular time is not to apply, or is to be treated as not having applied.

(4)   Regulations under this section must include provision for securing that lone parents are entitled (subject to meeting any prescribed conditions) to restrict the times at which they are required to undertake work-related activity.

(5)   In prescribed circumstances, the Secretary of State may by direction given to a person subject to a requirement imposed under subsection (1) provide that the activity specified in the direction is —

    (a)   to be the only activity which, in the person's case, is to be regarded as being work-related activity; or

    (b)   to be regarded, in the person's case, as not being work-related activity.

(6)   But a direction under subsection (5) may not specify medical or surgical treatment as the only activity which, in any person's case, is to be regarded as being work-related activity.

(7)   A direction under subsection (5) given to any person —

    (a)   must be reasonable, having regard to the person's circumstances;

    (b)   must be given to the person by being included in an action plan provided to the person under section 11C; and

    (c)   may be varied or revoked by a subsequent direction under that subsection.

(8) Where a direction under subsection (5) varies or revokes a previous direction, it may provide for the variation or revocation to have effect from a time before the giving of the direction.

(9) For the purposes of this section —
"lone parent" means a person who —
    (a) is not a member of a couple, and
    (b) is responsible for, and a member of the same household as, a child;
"work-related activity", in relation to a person, means activity which makes it more likely that the person will obtain or remain in work or be able to do so.

(10) Nothing in this section is to be read as prejudicing the generality of any provision of section 18A.

(11) For the sanctions for failure to comply with this section, see section 19 (as read with sections 18C and 18D)."

5   Before section 19 (but after the italic heading immediately before that section) insert —

"18C Definitions for purposes of sections 19 and 20A

(1) This section applies for the purposes of sections 19 and 20A.

(2) A person ("P") is in breach of a jobseeker's direction if P has, without good cause, refused or failed to carry out a direction given to P under section 18A(1).

(3) A person ("P") is in breach of a training scheme requirement if P —
    (a) has, without good cause, refused or failed to do as mentioned in section 18A(3);
    (b) has, without good cause, neglected to avail himself or herself of a reasonable opportunity of a place on a training scheme;
    (c) has, without good cause, given up a place on a training scheme;
    (d) has, without good cause, failed to attend a training scheme on which P has been given a place; or
    (e) has lost a place on a training scheme through misconduct.

(4) A person ("P") is in breach of an employment programme requirement if P —
    (a) has, without good cause, refused or failed to do as mentioned in section 18A(4);
    (b) has, without good cause, neglected to avail himself or herself of a reasonable opportunity of a place on an employment programme;
    (c) has, without good cause, given up a place on an employment programme;
    (d) has, without good cause, failed to attend an employment programme on which P has been given a place; or
    (e) has lost a place on an employment programme through misconduct.

(5) A person ("P") is in breach of an employment requirement if P —

2842

Welfare Reform Act 2009 (c. 24)
Schedule 1 — Amendments connected to section 4
Part 1 — Amendments of Jobseekers Act 1995

    (a)   has, without good cause, refused or failed to do as mentioned in section 18A(5);

    (b)   has lost employment as an employed earner through misconduct;

    (c)   has, without just cause, voluntarily left employment as an employed earner; or

    (d)   has, without good cause, neglected to avail himself or herself of a reasonable opportunity of employment.

(6)   A person ("P") is in breach of a work-related activity requirement if P has, without good cause, refused or failed to comply with a requirement imposed on P under section 18B.

(7)   In this section "employment programme" and "training scheme" have the same meaning as in section 18A.

18D   Section 18C: supplemental

(1)   A person is not to be regarded as breaching any requirement under section 18C merely because the person refuses to seek or accept employment in a situation which is vacant in consequence of a stoppage of work due to a trade dispute.

(2)   A person is not to be regarded as breaching a jobseeker's direction, a training scheme requirement or an employment programme requirement under section 18C if —

    (a)   a direction is in force under section 16 with respect to the person; and

    (b)   the person has acted in such a way as to risk —

        (i)   having that direction revoked under section 16(3)(b), or

        (ii) having the amount of jobseeker's allowance reduced by virtue of section 17 because the condition mentioned in section 17(3)(b) or (c) is satisfied.

(3)   In such circumstances as may be prescribed, a person who might otherwise be regarded as having left employment voluntarily is to be treated for the purposes of section 18C as not having left voluntarily.

(4)   The circumstances that may be prescribed include, in particular, where the person has been dismissed by reason of redundancy within the meaning of section 139(1) of the Employment Rights Act 1996 after volunteering or agreeing to be so dismissed.

(5)   Regulations must make provision for the purpose of enabling any person of a prescribed description to accept any employed earner's employment without breaching an employment requirement by virtue of section 18C(5)(c) or (d) should the person leave that employment voluntarily and without just cause at any time during a trial period.

(6)   "Trial period" has such meaning as may be prescribed.

(7)   Regulations may for the purposes of section 18C —

    (a)   prescribe matters which are, or are not, to be taken into account in determining whether a person has good cause or just cause for any act or omission;

Welfare Reform Act 2009 (c. 24)
Schedule 1 — Amendments connected to section 4
Part 1 — Amendments of Jobseekers Act 1995

2843

(b)   prescribe circumstances in which a person is, or is not, to be regarded as having good cause or just cause for any act or omission.

(8)   Subject to those regulations, in determining whether, for the purposes of section 18C, a person has, or does not have, good cause or just cause for any act or omission, any matter relating to the level of remuneration in the employment in question is to be disregarded.

(9)   Regulations may, in the case of a person of a prescribed description whose claim to a jobseeker's allowance is based on meeting condition B in section 1A, provide that section 18C(3)(b) to (e) —

   (a)   are not to apply, or

   (b)   are not to apply in prescribed circumstances.

(10)   Regulations may make provision for the purposes of section 18C(6) —

   (a)   prescribing the evidence which a person who is subject to a requirement imposed under section 18B needs to provide in order to show compliance with the requirement;

   (b)   prescribing matters which are, or are not, to be taken into account in determining whether a person has complied with such a requirement.

(11)   Regulations may make provision for determining, for the purposes of this section, the day on which a person's employment is to be regarded as starting."

6   For sections 19 and 20 substitute —

"19   Certain circumstances in which a jobseeker's allowance is not payable

(1)   This section applies in relation to a jobseeker's allowance other than a joint-claim jobseeker's allowance (as to which see section 20A).

(2)   In the case of a claimant whose claim to a jobseeker's allowance is not based on meeting condition B in section 1A, a jobseeker's allowance is not payable in respect of the claimant for the relevant period if the claimant is in breach of —

   (a)   a jobseeker's direction,

   (b)   a training scheme requirement,

   (c)   an employment programme requirement, or

   (d)   an employment requirement,

even though the claimant meets the conditions for entitlement to the allowance.

(3)   In the case of a claimant whose claim to a jobseeker's allowance is based on meeting condition B in section 1A, a jobseeker's allowance is not payable in respect of the claimant for the relevant period if the claimant is in breach of —

   (a)   a jobseeker's direction,

   (b)   a training scheme requirement, or

   (c)   a work-related activity requirement,

even though the claimant meets the conditions for entitlement to the allowance.

2844   *Welfare Reform Act 2009 (c. 24)*
Schedule 1 — Amendments connected to section 4
Part 1 — Amendments of Jobseekers Act 1995

(4)   In this section "the relevant period" means —

      (a)   in any case where the allowance is not payable because the claimant is in breach of an employment requirement, such period as may be determined by the Secretary of State; and

      (b)   in any other case, such period as may be prescribed.

(5)   The period which may be determined or prescribed under subsection (4) must be at least one week but not more than 26 weeks.

(6)   Regulations may prescribe —

      (a)   circumstances which the Secretary of State is to take into account, and

      (b)   circumstances which the Secretary of State is not to take into account,

in determining a period under subsection (4)(a).

20   Exemptions from section 19

(1)   In such circumstances as may be prescribed, an income-based jobseeker's allowance is payable in respect of a claimant even though section 19 prevents payment of a jobseeker's allowance to the claimant.

(2)   An income-based jobseeker's allowance is payable by virtue of subsection (1) only if the claimant has complied with such requirements as to the provision of information as may be prescribed for the purposes of this subsection.

(3)   Regulations under subsection (1) may, in particular, provide for an income-based jobseeker's allowance payable by virtue of that subsection to be —

      (a)   payable at a prescribed rate;

      (b)   payable for a prescribed period (which may differ from the period fixed under section 19(4))."

7   For sections 20A and 20B substitute —

"20A   Certain circumstances in which a joint-claim jobseeker's allowance is not payable

(1)   This section applies in relation to a joint-claim jobseeker's allowance.

(2)   A member of a joint-claim couple is subject to sanctions for the purposes of this section for the relevant period if the member is in breach of —

      (a)   a jobseeker's direction,

      (b)   a training scheme requirement,

      (c)   an employment programme requirement, or

      (d)   an employment requirement.

(3)   In this section "the relevant period" means —

      (a)   in any case where the member is subject to sanctions because the member is in breach of an employment requirement, such period as may be determined by the Secretary of State; and

      (b)   in any other case, such period as may be prescribed.

Welfare Reform Act 2009 (c. 24)
Schedule 1 — Amendments connected to section 4
Part 1 — Amendments of Jobseekers Act 1995

2845

(4) The period which may be determined or prescribed under subsection (3) must be at least one week but not more than 26 weeks.

(5) Even though the couple meet the conditions for entitlement to a joint-claim jobseeker's allowance —

    (a) the allowance is not payable for any period during which both members of the couple are subject to sanctions; and

    (b) the amount of the allowance payable in respect of the couple for any period during which only one member of the couple is subject to sanctions is reduced to an amount calculated by the prescribed method ("the reduced amount").

(6) The method prescribed for calculating the reduced amount may, in particular, involve —

    (a) deducting amounts from, or making percentage reductions of, the amount which would be the amount of the allowance if neither member of the couple were subject to sanctions;

    (b) disregarding portions of the applicable amount;

    (c) treating amounts as being income or capital of the couple.

(7) During any period for which the amount of a joint-claim jobseeker's allowance is the reduced amount, the allowance is payable to the member of the couple who is not subject to sanctions.

(8) Regulations may prescribe —

    (a) circumstances which the Secretary of State is to take into account, and

    (b) circumstances which the Secretary of State is not to take into account,

in determining a period under subsection (3)(a).

20B Exemptions from section 20A

(1) In such circumstances as may be prescribed, a joint-claim jobseeker's allowance is payable in respect of a joint-claim couple even though section 20A(5)(a) prevents payment of the allowance to the couple.

(2) A jobseeker's allowance is payable by virtue of subsection (1) only if the couple have complied with such requirements as to the provision of information as may be prescribed for the purposes of this subsection.

(3) Regulations under subsection (1) may, in particular, provide for a jobseeker's allowance payable by virtue of that subsection to be —

    (a) payable at a prescribed rate;

    (b) payable for a prescribed period (which may differ from the period during which both members of the couple are subject to sanctions for the purposes of section 20A)."

Other amendments

8   In section 1(4) (the jobseeker's allowance), for the definition of "a joint-claim jobseeker's allowance" substitute —

        ""a joint-claim jobseeker's allowance" means a jobseeker's allowance entitlement to which is based on section 1B."

2846

Welfare Reform Act 2009 (c. 24)
Schedule 1 — Amendments connected to section 4
Part 1 — Amendments of Jobseekers Act 1995

9   In section 2(1) (the contribution-based conditions), for "section 1(2)(d)" substitute "section 1A(1)(b)".

10   (1) Section 3 (the income-based conditions) is amended as follows.

     (2) In subsection (1), for "section 1(2A)(b)" substitute "section 1A(3)(b)".

     (3) After that subsection insert—

          "(1A)   The conditions referred to in section 1A(4)(d) are that the claimant—
                  (a)   satisfies the conditions set out in subsection (1)(a), (b), (c), (dd), (de) and (e) above;
                  (b)   is not a member of a couple the other member of which is entitled to an income-based jobseeker's allowance; and
                  (c)   is a person—
                        (i)   who has reached the age of 18; or
                        (ii)   who has reached the age of 16 but not the age of 18 and falls within a prescribed description of person."

11   In section 3A(1) (the conditions for claims by joint-claim couples), for "section 1(2B)(c)" substitute "section 1B(1)(c)".

12   In section 4(11A) (amount payable by way of a jobseeker's allowance), for "section 1(2C)" substitute "section 1A(8)".

13   In section 9 (the jobseeker's agreement)—
         (a)   in subsection (2), for "section 1" substitute "section 1A",
         (b)   in subsection (5), for "section 1(2)(a) and (c)" substitute "section 1A(7)(a) and (c)",
         (c)   in subsection (6)(a)—
               (i)   in sub-paragraph (i), for "section 1(2)(a)" substitute "section 1A(7)(a)", and
               (ii)   in sub-paragraph (ii), for "section 1(2)(c)" substitute "section 1A(7)(c)", and
         (d)   in subsection (10), for "section 1(2)(b)" substitute "section 1A(7)(b)".

14   In section 10 (variation of jobseeker's agreement)—
         (a)   in subsection (4), for "section 1(2)(a) and (c)" substitute "section 1A(7)(a) and (c)", and
         (b)   in subsection (5)(a)—
               (i)   in sub-paragraph (i), for "section 1(2)(a)" substitute "section 1A(7)(a)", and
               (ii)   in sub-paragraph (ii), for "section 1(2)(c)" substitute "section 1A(7)(c)".

15   (1) Section 14 (trade disputes) is amended as follows.

     (2) In subsection (1), at the beginning insert "Except in prescribed circumstances,".

     (3) In subsection (2), at the beginning insert "Except in prescribed circumstances,".

     (4) After subsection (2) insert—

          "(2A)   Subsections (1) and (2) do not apply to a person who is a member of a couple unless the other member of the couple is a person to whom

Welfare Reform Act 2009 (c. 24)
Schedule 1 – Amendments connected to section 4
Part 1 – Amendments of Jobseekers Act 1995

2847

either of those subsections apply (but see instead the provision made by section 15)."

16   (1)   Section 15 (effect on other claimants) is amended as follows.

     (2)   For subsection (1) substitute —

> "(1)   Except in prescribed circumstances, subsection (2) applies in relation to any person ("P") who—
>
> > (a)   is a member of a couple, and
> > (b)   claims an income-based jobseeker's allowance,
>
> in any case where, if subsection (2A) of section 14 were to be disregarded, either P or the other member of the couple (but not both) would be prevented by that section from being entitled to a jobseeker's allowance.
>
> (1A)   In this section any reference to the relevant person is to the member of the couple concerned who would be prevented by that section from being so entitled (whether or not that person is also the claimant)."

     (3)   In subsection (2)—

> (a)   in paragraph (a), for "A" substitute "the relevant person",
> (b)   in paragraph (b), for the words from "where" to "them" substitute "any portion of the applicable amount which is included in respect of the couple", and
> (c)   in paragraph (c), for "A" (in both places) substitute "the relevant person" and for "A's" substitute "that person's".

     (4)   In subsection (4), for "A" (in both places) substitute "the relevant person".

17   (1)   Section 15A (trade disputes: joint-claim couples) is amended as follows.

     (2)   After subsection (1), insert—

> "(1A)   Section 14 shall apply as if subsection (2A) of that section were omitted."

     (3)   In subsection (4), omit paragraph (b) (together with the "or" immediately before it).

     (4)   In subsection (5)—

> (a)   for paragraph (b) substitute—
>
> > "(b)   references to the relevant person are to the person mentioned in subsection (4)(a) above;", and
>
> (b)   omit paragraph (c) (but not the "and" at the end of it).

18   After section 15A insert—

"15B   Other provision relating to a person's return to work

> (1)   This section applies if a person ("P") returns to work with the same employer after a period during which—
>
> > (a)   P is, or would be, prevented by section 14 from being entitled to a jobseeker's allowance, or
> > (b)   section 15(2) applies in a case where (if subsection (2A) of section 14 were to be disregarded) P would be prevented by that section from being so entitled.

2848

Welfare Reform Act 2009 (c. 24)
Schedule 1 — Amendments connected to section 4
Part 1 — Amendments of Jobseekers Act 1995

(2) It does not matter whether or not the return to work is before the end of the stoppage of work in question.

(3) In the case of a claim for an income-based jobseeker's allowance other than a joint-claim jobseeker's allowance —

    (a) P is to be treated as not engaged in remunerative work until the end of the period of 15 days beginning with the day on which P returns to work, and

    (b) any sum paid by way of a jobseeker's allowance for that period of 15 days to P or, if P is a member of a couple, to the other member of the couple is recoverable in accordance with regulations from the person to whom it was paid or from any prescribed person or, where the person to whom it was paid is a member of a couple, from the other member of the couple.

(4) In the case of a claim for a joint-claim jobseeker's allowance —

    (a) P is to be treated as meeting the jobseeking conditions, and as not engaged in remunerative work, until the end of the period of 15 days beginning with the day on which P returns to work, and

    (b) any sum paid by way of a joint-claim jobseeker's allowance for that period of 15 days in respect of the couple is recoverable in accordance with regulations from each member of the couple or from any prescribed person."

19   In —

    (a) section 17A(8) (schemes for assisting persons to obtain employment: "work for your benefit" schemes etc.), which is inserted by section 1 of this Act,

    (b) section 20C(7) (sanctions for violent conduct in connection with claim), which is inserted by section 25 of this Act, and

    (c) paragraph 7(4) of Schedule A1 (claimants dependent on drugs etc.), which is inserted by Schedule 3 to this Act,

for "section 20B(4)" substitute "section 20B(1)".

20   In section 22(2) (members of the forces), for "section 19(6)(b)" substitute "section 18C(5)(c)".

21   In section 35(1) (interpretation) —

    (a) after the definition of "the applicable amount" insert —

        ""the basic conditions" means the conditions set out in section 1A(7);", and

    (b) after the definition of "jobseeker's agreement" insert —

        ""the jobseeking conditions" means the conditions set out in section 1A(7)(a) to (c);".

22   In section 36(4A)(b) (regulations and orders), which is inserted by section 1 of this Act, after "section" insert "11A, 11C, 18B or".

23   (1) Schedule 1 (supplementary provisions) is amended as follows.

    (2) In paragraph 2, at the end insert —

        "(3) Regulations may provide that the condition in section 1A(7)(e) (person not to have limited capability for work) is not to apply in prescribed circumstances to a person whose claim to a jobseeker's allowance is based on meeting condition B in section 1A."

(3) For paragraph 8 substitute —

"8 Regulations may prescribe circumstances in which a person may be entitled to an income-based jobseeker's allowance without being required to meet the jobseeking conditions in any case where the person would not otherwise be so entitled."

(4) In paragraph 8A(1), for "conditions referred to in section 1(2B)(b)" substitute "basic conditions".

(5) In paragraph 14 —
    (a) renumber the existing text as sub-paragraph (1), and
    (b) after that sub-paragraph (as renumbered) insert —

        "(2) Regulations may provide that the condition in section 1A(7)(f) (person not to be receiving relevant education) is not to apply in prescribed circumstances to a person whose claim to a jobseeker's allowance is based on meeting condition B in section 1A."

(6) After paragraph 14 insert —

"Pensionable age

14A Regulations may provide that in prescribed circumstances the condition in section 1A(7)(g) (person to be under pensionable age) is to have effect in relation to a person whose claim to a jobseeker's allowance is based on meeting condition B in section 1A as if for "pensionable age" there were substituted "the qualifying age for state pension credit (within the meaning of the State Pension Credit Act 2002)"."

PART 2

AMENDMENTS OF OTHER ACTS

Social Security Administration Act 1992 (c. 5)

24 In section 2A of the Social Security Administration Act 1992 (claim or full entitlement to certain benefits conditional on work-focused interview), at the end insert —

    "(9) For the purposes of this section —
        (a) the references in subsections (3)(a) and (5)(c) to a relevant benefit include references to a jobseeker's allowance in relation to which a person is required to take part in a work-focused interview by virtue of regulations made under section 11A of the Jobseekers Act 1995;
        (b) the reference in subsection (5)(c) to any reduction of the amount of benefit payable to any person under subsection (4)(b) includes a reference to any reduction of the amount of a jobseeker's allowance payable in respect of that person by virtue of those regulations."

2850

Welfare Reform Act 2009 (c. 24)
Schedule 1 — Amendments connected to section 4
Part 2 — Amendments of other Acts

Social Security Act 1998 (c. 14)

25   In paragraph 3(d) of Schedule 3 to the Social Security Act 1998 (decisions against which an appeal lies), after "section 19" insert "or 20A".

Welfare Reform Act 2007 (c. 5)

26   In section 1(6) of the Welfare Reform Act 2007 (employment and support allowance), in the definition of "joint-claim jobseeker's allowance", for "section 1(2B)" substitute "section 1B".

SCHEDULE 2   Section 9

ABOLITION OF INCOME SUPPORT: CONSEQUENTIAL AMENDMENTS

Magistrates' Courts Act 1980 (c. 43)

1   In sections 89(2A) and 90(3A) of the Magistrates' Courts Act 1980 (transfer of fine order), for "income support" substitute "jobseeker's allowance etc".

Criminal Justice Act 1991 (c. 53)

2   In section 24 of the Criminal Justice Act 1991 (recovery of fines etc. by deductions from income support), in the title, for "income support" substitute "jobseeker's allowance etc".

Social Security Administration Act 1992 (c. 5)

3   In section 74 of the Social Security Administration Act 1992 (income support and other payments), in the title, for "Income support" substitute "Income-based jobseeker's allowance".

Local Government Finance Act 1992 (c. 14)

4   In paragraph 12(1) of Schedule 4 to the Local Government Finance Act 1992 (enforcement: relationship between remedies) —

    (a)   in paragraph (b), for "income support" substitute "jobseeker's allowance payable to any person whose claim to the allowance is based on meeting condition B in section 1A of the Jobseekers Act 1995", and

    (b)   in paragraph (d), for "income support" substitute "jobseeker's allowance payable as mentioned in paragraph (b)".

Jobseekers Act 1995 (c. 18)

5   The Jobseekers Act 1995 is amended as follows.

6   In section 2(1) (the contribution-based conditions), at the end of paragraph (b) insert "and".

7   In section 3A(1)(c) (the conditions for claims by joint-claim couples), for "any such family" substitute "a family of which the couple are members".

Immigration and Asylum Act 1999 (c. 33)

8   In section 97(5) of the Immigration and Asylum Act 1999 (persons for whom support may be provided: supplemental), for paragraph (a) (together with the "or" at the end of it) substitute —

> "(a)   to such portion of the applicable amount in respect of an income-based jobseeker's allowance provided under section 4 of the Jobseekers Act 1995, or".

Social Security Fraud Act 2001 (c. 11)

9   The Social Security Fraud Act 2001 is amended as follows.

10   In section 6B(5) (loss of benefit in case of conviction, penalty or caution for benefit offence), which is inserted by section 24 of this Act, for "subsections (6)" substitute "subsections (7)".

11   In section 7(2) (loss of benefit for commission of benefit offences), for "subsections (3)" substitute "subsections (4)".

Courts Act 2003 (c. 39)

12   The Courts Act 2003 is amended as follows.

13   In paragraph 10(a) of Schedule 5 (applications for benefit deductions), for "income support" substitute "jobseeker's allowance".

14   In paragraph 2(1)(a)(v) of Schedule 6 (discharge of fines by unpaid work), for "income support" substitute "jobseeker's allowance".

Child Trust Funds Act 2004 (c. 6)

15   In section 9(8)(a) of the Child Trust Funds Act 2004 (supplementary contribution by HMRC), for "income support, or income-based jobseeker's allowance," substitute "income-based jobseeker's allowance".

Age-Related Payments Act 2004 (c. 10)

16   In section 2(3)(b) of the Age-Related Payments Act 2004 (entitlement: basic cases), at the end of sub-paragraph (i) insert "or".

Welfare Reform Act 2007 (c. 5)

17   In paragraph 11 of Schedule 4 to the Welfare Reform Act 2007 (transition relating to Part 1 of Act), after the definition of "incapacity benefit" insert —

> ""income support" means income support under section 124 of the Contributions and Benefits Act;".

2852

*Welfare Reform Act 2009 (c. **24**)*
Schedule 3 — Claimants dependent on drugs etc.
Part 1 — Jobseeker's allowance

SCHEDULE 3   Section 11

CLAIMANTS DEPENDENT ON DRUGS ETC.

PART 1

JOBSEEKER'S ALLOWANCE

Requirements imposed on claimants dependent on drugs etc.

1   After section 17B of the Jobseekers Act 1995 (c. 18) (which is inserted by section 1 of this Act) insert—

"Persons dependent on drugs etc.

17C   Persons dependent on drugs etc.

(1)   Schedule A1 makes provision for or in connection with imposing requirements on persons in cases where—
   (a)   they are dependent on, or have a propensity to misuse, any drug, and
   (b)   any such dependency or propensity is a factor affecting their prospects of obtaining or remaining in work.

(2)   That Schedule also contains a power for its provisions to apply in relation to alcohol."

2   Before Schedule 1 to the Jobseekers Act 1995 insert—

"SCHEDULE A1   Section 17C

PERSONS DEPENDENT ON DRUGS ETC.

Requirements imposed in relation to use of drugs

1   (1)   Regulations may make provision for or in connection with imposing on a claimant a requirement to attend at such time and place as may be determined in accordance with the regulations in order to answer questions within sub-paragraph (2).

(2)   A question is within this sub-paragraph if it is asked for the purpose of ascertaining—
   (a)   whether the person required to answer it may be dependent on, or have a propensity to misuse, any drug, and
   (b)   (if so) whether any such dependency or propensity may be a factor affecting that person's prospects of obtaining or remaining in work.

(3)   Regulations under this paragraph may, in particular, make provision prescribing the questions which a person may be required to answer under the regulations (which may include questions relating to any use of the drug in question or any treatment connected with its use).

Welfare Reform Act 2009 (c. 24)
Schedule 3 – Claimants dependent on drugs etc.
Part 1 – Jobseeker's allowance

2853

(4) Regulations under this paragraph may not impose a requirement on a person at any time unless the person is required to meet the jobseeking conditions at that time.

2 (1) Regulations may make provision for or in connection with imposing on a person who is subject to a requirement imposed under paragraph 1 a requirement to take part in —

  (a) a substance-related assessment, and

  (b) a subsequent interview (a "drugs interview") with an approved person to discuss any matters arising out of that assessment.

(2) For the purposes of this paragraph —

  a "substance-related assessment" means an assessment by an approved person carried out for the purpose of assessing —

    (a) whether a person is dependent on, or has a propensity to misuse, any drug, and

    (b) (if so) whether the person's dependency or propensity is such as requires and may be susceptible to treatment;

  an "approved person" means a person having the necessary qualifications or experience who is approved by the Secretary of State for the purposes of this paragraph.

(3) Regulations under this paragraph must include provision for the requirement mentioned in sub-paragraph (1) to be imposed on a person only if the Secretary of State has reasonable grounds for suspecting that —

  (a) the person may be dependent on, or have a propensity to misuse, any drug, and

  (b) any such dependency or propensity may be a factor affecting the person's prospects of obtaining or remaining in work.

(4) Regulations under this paragraph may, in particular, make provision —

  (a) for notifying a person of a requirement to take part in a substance-related assessment or a drugs interview;

  (b) for the determination, and notification, of the time and place of any substance-related assessment or drugs interview in which a person is required to take part.

(5) Regulations under this paragraph may, in particular, make provision for a requirement imposed on a person ("P") under this paragraph to cease to have effect if —

  (a) P agrees to provide a sample, in accordance with instructions given by an approved person, for the purpose of ascertaining whether there is or has been any drug in P's body, and

  (b) the sample provided indicates that no drug is or has been in P's body.

2854
Welfare Reform Act 2009 (c. 24)
Schedule 3 — Claimants dependent on drugs etc.
Part 1 — Jobseeker's allowance

(6) Regulations under this paragraph may not impose a requirement on a person at any time unless the person is required to meet the jobseeking conditions at that time.

3 (1) Regulations may make provision for or in connection with imposing on a person who —

    (a) is subject to a requirement imposed under paragraph 2, and

    (b) fails to comply with it without it being shown, within a prescribed period, that the person had good cause for the failure,

a requirement to take part in one or more relevant tests for the purpose of ascertaining whether there is or has been any drug in the person's body.

(2) Regulations under this paragraph must include provision for the requirement mentioned in sub-paragraph (1) to be imposed on a person only if the Secretary of State is satisfied that the proposed test or tests will, or will be likely to, assist in determining whether the person is dependent on, or has a propensity to misuse, any drug.

(3) Regulations under this paragraph must include provision for informing a person of the consequence of failing to comply with a requirement to take part in a relevant test.

(4) Regulations under this paragraph may, in particular, make provision —

    (a) for notifying a person of a requirement to take part in a relevant test;

    (b) for the determination, and notification, of the time and place of any relevant test in which a person is required to take part.

(5) Regulations under this paragraph may not impose a requirement on a person at any time unless the person is required to meet the jobseeking conditions at that time.

(6) For the purposes of this paragraph a person takes part in a relevant test if the person provides a permissible sample in accordance with instructions given by an approved person (within the meaning of paragraph 2).

(7) In sub-paragraph (6) "permissible sample", in relation to any drug, means —

    (a) a sample of urine, or

    (b) such sample (other than an intimate sample) as may be prescribed in relation to that drug.

(8) In sub-paragraph (7)(b) "intimate sample" means —

    (a) a sample of blood, semen or any other tissue fluid or pubic hair;

    (b) a dental impression;

    (c) a swab taken from any part of a person's genitals (including pubic hair) or from a person's body orifice other than the mouth.

Welfare Reform Act 2009 (c. 24) 2855
Schedule 3 — Claimants dependent on drugs etc.
Part 1 — Jobseeker's allowance

Paragraphs 1 to 3: supplementary

4   (1) A person must comply with a requirement imposed by regulations under any of paragraphs 1 to 3 even if doing so might constitute evidence that the person has committed an offence.

     (2) But in criminal proceedings in which a person is charged with an offence —

          (a) no evidence relating to any answer given, or anything else done, in pursuance of the regulations may be adduced by or on behalf of the prosecution, and

          (b) no question relating to those matters may be asked by or on behalf of the prosecution,

          unless evidence relating to those matters is adduced, or a question relating to those matters is asked, in the proceedings by or on behalf of the person.

     (3) Sub-paragraph (2) does not apply to —

          (a) an offence under section 112 of the Administration Act;

          (b) an offence under section 5 of the Perjury Act 1911 (false statements made otherwise than on oath in England and Wales); or

          (c) an offence under section 44(2) of the Criminal Law (Consolidation) (Scotland) Act 1995 (corresponding provision for Scotland).

Voluntary and mandatory rehabilitation plans

5   (1) Regulations may make provision for or in connection with —

          (a) securing that a person ("P") who at any time complies with a voluntary rehabilitation plan is not required to meet the jobseeking conditions at that time; and

          (b) suspending any jobseeker's agreement to which P is a party for any period during which P complies with a voluntary rehabilitation plan.

     (2) Regulations under this paragraph may include provision for the consequences set out in sub-paragraph (1)(a) and (b) to follow only if the Secretary of State is satisfied that —

          (a) P is dependent on, or has a propensity to misuse, any drug, and

          (b) P's dependency or propensity is a factor affecting P's prospects of obtaining or remaining in work.

     (3) For the purposes of this paragraph a "voluntary rehabilitation plan" is an agreement entered into by the Secretary of State and P under which P agrees to take one or more of the following steps.

     (4) The steps are —

          (a) submitting to treatment by or under the direction of a person having the necessary qualifications or experience,

          (b) taking part in specified interviews, and specified assessments, at specified places and times, and

          (c) taking such other steps (if any) as may be specified,

2856

Welfare Reform Act 2009 (c. 24)
Schedule 3 — Claimants dependent on drugs etc.
Part 1 — Jobseeker's allowance

with a view to the reduction or elimination of P's dependency on, or propensity to misuse, the drug in question.

(5) The treatment may be —

    (a) treatment as a resident in a specified institution or place, or

    (b) treatment as a non-resident at a specified institution or place, and at specified intervals.

(6) Regulations under this paragraph may, in particular, make provision —

    (a) as to the maximum period for which a person may benefit from the provision made by the regulations;

    (b) about the form of voluntary rehabilitation plans (including provision as to their signing);

    (c) about the review, variation and revocation of voluntary rehabilitation plans;

    (d) for securing that a person who agrees to comply with a voluntary rehabilitation plan provides information, and such evidence as may be prescribed, as to compliance with the plan.

(7) A jobseeker's allowance may also be known as a "treatment allowance" at any time when —

    (a) it is payable in respect of a person to whom this paragraph applies, or

    (b) it is payable in respect of a joint-claim couple both members of which are persons to whom this paragraph applies.

(8) In this paragraph "specified", in relation to a voluntary rehabilitation plan, means specified in or determined in accordance with the plan.

6 (1) Regulations may make provision for or in connection with imposing on a person a requirement to comply with a mandatory rehabilitation plan.

(2) Regulations under this paragraph must include provision for securing that a person is subject to the requirement mentioned in sub-paragraph (1) at any time only if —

    (a) the person has not at that time agreed to comply with a voluntary rehabilitation plan under paragraph 5, and

    (b) the Secretary of State is satisfied as mentioned in sub-paragraph (2) of that paragraph.

(3) For the purposes of this paragraph a "mandatory rehabilitation plan" is a document —

    (a) which is provided to the person by the Secretary of State, and

    (b) which contains one or more of the following requirements.

(4) The requirements are that the person —

    (a) must attend an educational programme at a specified place and at specified times,

Welfare Reform Act 2009 (c. 24)
Schedule 3 – Claimants dependent on drugs etc.
Part 1 – Jobseeker's allowance

2857

      (b)   must take part in specified interviews, and specified assessments, at specified places and times, and

      (c)   must take such other steps (if any) as may be specified,

with a view to the reduction or elimination of the person's dependency on, or propensity to misuse, the drug in question.

(5) Nothing may be specified in a mandatory rehabilitation plan which requires a person to submit to medical or surgical treatment.

(6) Regulations under this paragraph may, in particular, make provision—

      (a)   as to the involvement of a person in determining the particular requirements to be contained in a mandatory rehabilitation plan with which the person is to be required to comply;

      (b)   about the form of mandatory rehabilitation plans (including provision as to their signing);

      (c)   about the review, variation and revocation of mandatory rehabilitation plans;

      (d)   for securing that a person who is required to comply with a mandatory rehabilitation plan provides information, and such evidence as may be prescribed, as to compliance with the plan.

(7) Regulations under this paragraph may not impose a requirement on a person at any time unless the person would (apart from the regulations) be required to meet the jobseeking conditions at that time.

(8) In this paragraph "specified", in relation to a mandatory rehabilitation plan, means specified in or determined in accordance with the plan.

Sanctions

7   (1) Regulations under paragraph 1, 2, 3 or 6 may, in particular, make provision—

      (a)   for securing that the appropriate consequence follows if a person has failed to comply with any requirement imposed by any such regulations and it is not shown, within a prescribed period, that the person had good cause for the failure;

      (b)   prescribing matters which are, or are not, to be taken into account in determining whether a person has good cause for any failure to comply with any such requirement;

      (c)   prescribing circumstances in which a person is, or is not, to be regarded as having good cause for any failure to comply with any such requirement.

(2) In the case of a jobseeker's allowance other than a joint-claim jobseeker's allowance, the appropriate consequence for the purposes of sub-paragraph (1)(a) is that the allowance is not payable for such period (of at least one week but not more than 26 weeks) as may be prescribed.

2858

Welfare Reform Act 2009 (c. 24)
Schedule 3 — Claimants dependent on drugs etc.
Part 1 — Jobseeker's allowance

(3) In the case of a joint-claim jobseeker's allowance, the appropriate consequence for the purposes of sub-paragraph (1)(a) is that the person is to be treated as subject to sanctions for the purposes of section 20A for such period (of at least one week but not more than 26 weeks) as may be prescribed.

(4) Regulations under paragraph 1, 2, 3 or 6 may make provision for an income-based jobseeker's allowance to be payable in prescribed circumstances even though other provision made by the regulations prevents payment of it.

This sub-paragraph does not apply in the case of a joint-claim jobseeker's allowance (corresponding provision for which is made by section 20B(4)).

(5) The provision that may be made by the regulations by virtue of sub-paragraph (4) includes, in particular, provision for the allowance to be—

  (a) payable only if prescribed requirements as to the provision of information are complied with;

  (b) payable at a prescribed rate;

  (c) payable for a prescribed period (which may differ from any period mentioned in sub-paragraph (2)).

Information

8 (1) Regulations may make provision for or in connection with authorising the supply of information, other than excluded information, held by—

  (a) a police force,

  (b) the probation service, or

  (c) such other person as may be prescribed,

to a person within sub-paragraph (2) for use for the purposes of any provision of this Schedule.

(2) The persons within this sub-paragraph are—

  (a) the Secretary of State;

  (b) a person providing services to the Secretary of State;

  (c) an approved person (within the meaning of paragraph 2).

(3) Information supplied under the regulations may not be supplied by the recipient to any other person unless—

  (a) it could be supplied to that person under the regulations;

  (b) it is supplied for the purposes of any civil or criminal proceedings; or

  (c) it is required to be supplied under any enactment.

(4) In sub-paragraph (1) "excluded information" means any information relating to or acquired as a result of—

  (a) the provision of medical or surgical treatment or care, or

  (b) the provision of services by a social worker,

other than information as to whether a person is having (or has had) treatment in respect of the person's use of any drug.

(5) In sub-paragraph (1) "the probation service" means—

Welfare Reform Act 2009 (c. 24)
Schedule 3 — Claimants dependent on drugs etc.
Part 1 — Jobseeker's allowance

2859

(a) in England and Wales, a local probation board established under section 4 of the Criminal Justice and Court Services Act 2000 or a provider of probation services;

(b) in Scotland, a local authority within the meaning of the Social Work (Scotland) Act 1968.

Interpretation

9 In this Schedule—

"drug" means such controlled drug (as defined by section 2 of the Misuse of Drugs Act 1971) as may be prescribed;

"the jobseeking conditions" means the conditions set out in section 1(2)(a) to (c).

Power to extend provisions to alcohol

10 (1) If regulations so provide and subject as follows, the preceding paragraphs of this Schedule are to apply in relation to alcohol as they apply in relation to drugs.

(2) Regulations under this paragraph may provide for a different definition of a "relevant test" to apply in relation to alcohol for the purposes of paragraph 3."

Consequential amendments

3 (1) The Jobseekers Act 1995 (c. 18) is amended as follows.

(2) In section 36(4A)(a) and (b) (regulations and orders), which is inserted by section 1 of this Act, after "17A" insert "or Schedule A1".

(3) In section 37(1)(c) (regulations subject to the affirmative resolution procedure), after "section 35(1)" insert ", any paragraph of Schedule A1".

(4) In paragraph 19 of Schedule 1 (treatment of information), as inserted by section 34(3) of this Act, after "this Act" insert "(other than paragraph 8 of Schedule A1)".

4 In paragraph 3(da) of Schedule 3 to the Social Security Act 1998 (c. 14) (decisions against which an appeal lies), which is inserted by section 1 of this Act, after "17A of" insert ", or Schedule A1 to,".

Report on initial operation of drugs provisions

5 (1) The Secretary of State must prepare a report on the operation of the first set of regulations made under paragraphs 1, 2, 3, 5 and 6 of Schedule A1 to the Jobseekers Act 1995 during the review period.

(2) "The review period" is the period of 24 months beginning with the day on which those regulations come into force.

(3) The Secretary of State must—
(a) prepare the report, and
(b) lay it before Parliament,
within 6 months from the end of the review period.

2860

Welfare Reform Act 2009 (c. 24)
Schedule 3 – Claimants dependent on drugs etc.
Part 1 – Jobseeker's allowance

(4) The continued effect of the drugs provisions depends on whether the Secretary of State makes an order under this sub-paragraph within the relevant period providing for those provisions to continue to have effect.

(5) "The relevant period" means the period of 30 days beginning with the day on which the report is laid before Parliament; and, in reckoning this period, no account is to be taken of any time during which Parliament—

   (a) is dissolved or prorogued, or

   (b) is adjourned for more than 4 days.

(6) If no order is made as mentioned in sub-paragraph (4), the Secretary of State must instead make an order under this sub-paragraph providing for the repeal of the drugs provisions on a date specified in the order.

(7) An order under sub-paragraph (6) may contain transitional provision or savings.

(8) Any power to make an order under this paragraph is exercisable by statutory instrument.

(9) An order under sub-paragraph (4) may not be made unless a draft of the statutory instrument containing the order has been laid before, and approved by a resolution of, each House of Parliament.

(10) A statutory instrument containing an order under sub-paragraph (6) is subject to annulment in pursuance of a resolution of either House of Parliament.

(11) In this paragraph "the drugs provisions" means—

   (a) section 17C of, and Schedule A1 to, the Jobseekers Act 1995 (c. 18),

   (b) the words inserted into that Act, and the Social Security Act 1998 (c. 14), by paragraphs 3 and 4 of this Schedule, and

   (c) paragraphs 1 to 4 of this Schedule.

(12) This paragraph applies whether or not the regulations mentioned in sub-paragraph (1) are, by virtue of section 29 of the Jobseekers Act 1995 (pilot schemes), made so as to have effect for a limited period.

PART 2

EMPLOYMENT AND SUPPORT ALLOWANCE

Requirements imposed on persons dependent on drugs etc.

6   After section 15 of the Welfare Reform Act 2007 (c. 5) insert—

"Persons dependent on drugs etc.

15A Persons dependent on drugs etc.

   (1) Schedule 1A makes provision for or in connection with imposing requirements on persons in cases where—

      (a) they are dependent on, or have a propensity to misuse, any drug, and

      (b) any such dependency or propensity is a factor affecting their prospects of obtaining or remaining in work.

Welfare Reform Act 2009 (c. 24)
Schedule 3 — Claimants dependent on drugs etc.
Part 2 — Employment and support allowance

2861

(2) That Schedule also contains a power for its provisions to apply in relation to alcohol."

7   After Schedule 1 to the Welfare Reform Act 2007 (c. 5) insert—

"SCHEDULE 1A   Section 15A

PERSONS DEPENDENT ON DRUGS ETC.

Requirements imposed in relation to use of drugs

1   (1) Regulations may make provision for or in connection with imposing on a person who is—

   (a) entitled to an employment and support allowance, and
   (b) not a member of the support group,

a requirement to answer questions within sub-paragraph (2) as a condition of continuing to be entitled to the full amount payable to the person in respect of the allowance apart from the regulations.

   (2) A question is within this sub-paragraph if it is asked for the purpose of ascertaining—

   (a) whether the person may be dependent on, or have a propensity to misuse, any drug, and
   (b) (if so) whether any such dependency or propensity may be a factor affecting the person's prospects of obtaining or remaining in work.

   (3) Regulations under this paragraph may, in particular, make provision—

   (a) prescribing the questions which a person may be required to answer under the regulations (which may include questions relating to any use of the drug in question or any treatment connected with its use);
   (b) for notifying a person of any requirement to answer questions under the regulations;
   (c) for the determination, and notification, of the time and place at which a person is required to answer questions under the regulations.

   (4) Regulations under this paragraph must include provision for a requirement imposed on a person by the regulations to cease to have effect if the person becomes a member of the support group.

2   (1) Regulations may make provision for or in connection with imposing on a person who is subject to a requirement imposed under paragraph 1 a requirement to take part in—

   (a) a substance-related assessment, and
   (b) a subsequent interview (a "drugs interview") with an approved person to discuss any matters arising out of that assessment,

as a condition of continuing to be entitled to the full amount payable to the person in respect of an employment and support allowance apart from the regulations.

   (2) For the purposes of this paragraph—

2862　　　　　　　　　　　　　　　　　　　*Welfare Reform Act 2009 (c. 24)*
Schedule 3 — Claimants dependent on drugs etc.
Part 2 — Employment and support allowance

a "substance-related assessment" means an assessment by an approved person carried out for the purpose of assessing —

    (a)   whether a person is dependent on, or has a propensity to misuse, any drug, and

    (b)   (if so) whether the person's dependency or propensity is such as requires and may be susceptible to treatment;

an "approved person" means a person having the necessary qualifications or experience who is approved by the Secretary of State for the purposes of this paragraph.

(3) Regulations under this paragraph must include provision for the requirement mentioned in sub-paragraph (1) to be imposed on a person only if the Secretary of State has reasonable grounds for suspecting that —

    (a)   the person may be dependent on, or have a propensity to misuse, any drug, and

    (b)   any such dependency or propensity may be a factor affecting the person's prospects of obtaining or remaining in work.

(4) Regulations under this paragraph may, in particular, make provision —

    (a)   for notifying a person of a requirement to take part in a substance-related assessment or a drugs interview;

    (b)   for the determination, and notification, of the time and place of any substance-related assessment or drugs interview in which a person is required to take part.

(5) Regulations under this paragraph may, in particular, make provision for a requirement imposed on a person ("P") under this paragraph to cease to have effect if —

    (a)   P agrees to provide a sample, in accordance with instructions given by an approved person, for the purpose of ascertaining whether there is or has been any drug in P's body, and

    (b)   the sample provided indicates that no drug is or has been in P's body.

(6) Regulations under this paragraph must include provision for a requirement imposed on a person by the regulations to cease to have effect if the person becomes a member of the support group.

3   (1) Regulations may make provision for or in connection with imposing on a person who —

    (a)   is subject to a requirement imposed under paragraph 2, and

    (b)   fails to comply with it without showing, within a prescribed period, good cause for the failure,

a requirement to take part in one or more relevant tests as a condition of continuing to be entitled to the full amount payable to the person in respect of an employment and support allowance apart from the regulations.

Welfare Reform Act 2009 (c. 24)
Schedule 3 — *Claimants dependent on drugs etc.*
Part 2 — *Employment and support allowance*

2863

(2) Regulations under this paragraph must include provision for the requirement mentioned in sub-paragraph (1) to be imposed on a person only if the Secretary of State is satisfied that the proposed test or tests will, or will be likely to, assist in determining whether the person is dependent on, or has a propensity to misuse, any drug.

(3) Regulations under this paragraph must include provision for informing a person of the consequence of failing to comply with a requirement to take part in a relevant test.

(4) Regulations under this paragraph may, in particular, make provision —
   (a) for notifying a person of a requirement to take part in a relevant test;
   (b) for the determination, and notification, of the time and place of any relevant test in which a person is required to take part.

(5) Regulations under this paragraph must include provision for a requirement imposed on a person by the regulations to cease to have effect if the person becomes a member of the support group.

(6) For the purposes of this paragraph a person takes part in a relevant test if the person provides a permissible sample in accordance with instructions given by an approved person (within the meaning of paragraph 2) for the purpose of ascertaining whether there is or has been any drug in the person's body.

(7) In sub-paragraph (6) "permissible sample", in relation to any drug, means —
   (a) a sample of urine, or
   (b) such sample (other than an intimate sample) as may be prescribed in relation to that drug.

(8) In sub-paragraph (7)(b) "intimate sample" means —
   (a) a sample of blood, semen or any other tissue fluid or pubic hair;
   (b) a dental impression;
   (c) a swab taken from any part of a person's genitals (including pubic hair) or from a person's body orifice other than the mouth.

Paragraphs 1 to 3: supplementary

4   (1) A person must comply with a requirement imposed by regulations under any of paragraphs 1 to 3 even if doing so might constitute evidence that the person has committed an offence.

   (2) But in criminal proceedings in which a person is charged with an offence —
      (a) no evidence relating to any answer given, or anything else done, in pursuance of the regulations may be adduced by or on behalf of the prosecution, and
      (b) no question relating to those matters may be asked by or on behalf of the prosecution,

2864

Welfare Reform Act 2009 (c. 24)
Schedule 3 – Claimants dependent on drugs etc.
Part 2 – Employment and support allowance

unless evidence relating to those matters is adduced, or a question relating to those matters is asked, in the proceedings by or on behalf of the person.

(3) Sub-paragraph (2) does not apply to—

    (a) an offence under section 112 of the Administration Act;

    (b) an offence under section 5 of the Perjury Act 1911 (false statements made otherwise than on oath in England and Wales); or

    (c) an offence under section 44(2) of the Criminal Law (Consolidation) (Scotland) Act 1995 (corresponding provision for Scotland).

Voluntary and mandatory rehabilitation plans

5   (1) Regulations may make provision for or in connection with securing that a person ("P") who at any time complies with a voluntary rehabilitation plan is not required at that time—

    (a) to take part in a work-focused interview under section 12(1), or

    (b) to undertake work-related activity under section 13(1).

(2) Regulations under this paragraph may include provision for P not to be required to do the things mentioned in sub-paragraph (1)(a) or (b) only if the Secretary of State is satisfied that—

    (a) P is dependent on, or has a propensity to misuse, any drug, and

    (b) P's dependency or propensity is a factor affecting P's prospects of obtaining or remaining in work.

(3) For the purposes of this paragraph a "voluntary rehabilitation plan" is an agreement entered into by the Secretary of State and P under which P agrees to take one or more of the following steps.

(4) The steps are—

    (a) submitting to treatment by or under the direction of a person having the necessary qualifications or experience,

    (b) taking part in specified interviews, and specified assessments, at specified places and times, and

    (c) taking such other steps (if any) as may be specified,

with a view to the reduction or elimination of P's dependency on, or propensity to misuse, the drug in question.

(5) The treatment may be—

    (a) treatment as a resident in a specified institution or place, or

    (b) treatment as a non-resident at a specified institution or place, and at specified intervals.

(6) Regulations under this paragraph may, in particular, make provision—

    (a) as to the maximum period for which a person may benefit from the provision made by the regulations;

    (b) about the form of voluntary rehabilitation plans (including provision as to their signing);

Welfare Reform Act 2009 (c. 24)
Schedule 3 — Claimants dependent on drugs etc.
Part 2 — Employment and support allowance

2865

        (c)   about the review, variation and revocation of voluntary rehabilitation plans;

        (d)   for securing that a person who agrees to comply with a voluntary rehabilitation plan provides information, and such evidence as may be prescribed, as to compliance with the plan.

(7) An employment and support allowance may also be known as a "treatment allowance" at any time when it is payable to a person to whom this paragraph applies.

(8) In this paragraph "specified", in relation to a voluntary rehabilitation plan, means specified in or determined in accordance with the plan.

6   (1) Regulations may make provision for or in connection with imposing on a person a requirement to comply with a mandatory rehabilitation plan as a condition of continuing to be entitled to the full amount payable to the person in respect of an employment and support allowance apart from the regulations.

    (2) Regulations under this paragraph must include provision for securing that a person is subject to the requirement mentioned in sub-paragraph (1) at any time only if —

        (a)   the person has not at that time agreed to comply with a voluntary rehabilitation plan under paragraph 5, and

        (b)   the Secretary of State is satisfied as mentioned in sub-paragraph (2) of that paragraph.

    (3) For the purposes of this paragraph a "mandatory rehabilitation plan" is a document —

        (a)   which is provided to the person by the Secretary of State, and

        (b)   which contains one or more of the following requirements.

    (4) The requirements are that the person —

        (a)   must attend an educational programme at a specified place and at specified times,

        (b)   must take part in specified interviews, and specified assessments, at specified places and times, and

        (c)   must take such other steps (if any) as may be specified,

with a view to the reduction or elimination of the person's dependency on, or propensity to misuse, the drug in question.

    (5) Nothing may be specified in a mandatory rehabilitation plan which requires a person to submit to medical or surgical treatment.

    (6) Regulations under this paragraph may, in particular, make provision —

        (a)   as to the involvement of a person in determining the particular requirements to be contained in a mandatory rehabilitation plan with which the person is to be required to comply;

        (b)   about the form of mandatory rehabilitation plans (including provision as to their signing);

2866

Welfare Reform Act 2009 (c. 24)
Schedule 3 — Claimants dependent on drugs etc.
Part 2 — Employment and support allowance

   (c) about the review, variation and revocation of mandatory rehabilitation plans;

   (d) for securing that a person who is required to comply with a mandatory rehabilitation plan provides information, and such evidence as may be prescribed, as to compliance with the plan.

 (7) Regulations under this paragraph must include provision for a requirement imposed on a person under this paragraph to cease to have effect if the person becomes a member of the support group.

 (8) In this paragraph "specified", in relation to a mandatory rehabilitation plan, means specified in or determined in accordance with the plan.

Sanctions

7 (1) Regulations under paragraph 1, 2, 3 or 6 may, in particular, make provision—

   (a) for securing that the appropriate consequence follows if a person has failed to comply with any requirement imposed by any such regulations and the person does not show, within a prescribed period, good cause for the failure;

   (b) prescribing matters which are, or are not, to be taken into account in determining whether a person has good cause for any failure to comply with any such requirement;

   (c) prescribing circumstances in which a person is, or is not, to be regarded as having good cause for any failure to comply with any such requirement.

 (2) The appropriate consequence for the purposes of sub-paragraph (1)(a) is that the amount payable to the person in question in respect of an employment and support allowance is reduced in accordance with the regulations.

 (3) The provision that may be made by virtue of sub-paragraph (2) includes, in particular, provision for determining—

   (a) the amount by which an allowance is to be reduced,

   (b) when the reduction is to start, and

   (c) how long it is to continue,

and may include provision prescribing circumstances in which the amount of the reduction is to be nil.

Information

8 (1) Regulations may make provision for or in connection with authorising the supply of information, other than excluded information, held by—

   (a) a police force,

   (b) the probation service, or

   (c) such other person as may be prescribed,

to a person within sub-paragraph (2) for use for the purposes of any provision of this Schedule.

Welfare Reform Act 2009 (c. 24)
Schedule 3 — Claimants dependent on drugs etc.
Part 2 — Employment and support allowance

2867

(2) The persons within this sub-paragraph are—
    (a)   the Secretary of State;
    (b)   a person providing services to the Secretary of State;
    (c)   an approved person (within the meaning of paragraph 2).

(3) Information supplied under the regulations may not be supplied by the recipient to any other person unless—
    (a)   it could be supplied to that person under the regulations;
    (b)   it is supplied for the purposes of any civil or criminal proceedings; or
    (c)   it is required to be supplied under any enactment.

(4) In sub-paragraph (1) "excluded information" means any information relating to or acquired as a result of—
    (a)   the provision of medical or surgical treatment or care, or
    (b)   the provision of services by a social worker,
other than information as to whether a person is having (or has had) treatment in respect of the person's use of any drug.

(5) In sub-paragraph (1) "the probation service" means—
    (a)   in England and Wales, a local probation board established under section 4 of the Criminal Justice and Court Services Act 2000 or a provider of probation services;
    (b)   in Scotland, a local authority within the meaning of the Social Work (Scotland) Act 1968.

Interpretation

9   In this Schedule "drug" means such controlled drug (as defined by section 2 of the Misuse of Drugs Act 1971) as may be prescribed.

Power to extend provisions to alcohol

10   (1) If regulations so provide and subject as follows, the preceding paragraphs of this Schedule are to apply in relation to alcohol as they apply in relation to drugs.

(2) Regulations under this paragraph may provide for a different definition of a "relevant test" to apply in relation to alcohol for the purposes of paragraph 3."

Consequential amendments

8   (1) Part 1 of the Welfare Reform Act 2007 (c. 5) (employment and support allowance) is amended as follows.

(2) In section 16 (contracting out)—
    (a)   in subsection (1), at the end insert—
           "(d)   asking questions under paragraph 1 of Schedule 1A;
           (e)   making decisions under paragraph 2 or 3 of that Schedule;
           (f)   exercising any functions in relation to rehabilitation plans under paragraph 5 or 6 of that Schedule.",
    (b)   in subsection (2)(a), after "15" insert "or Schedule 1A", and

2868
Welfare Reform Act 2009 (c. 24)
Schedule 3 — Claimants dependent on drugs etc.
Part 2 — Employment and support allowance

    (c)   in subsection (3)(a), after "13" insert "or Schedule 1A".

(3) In section 25(6) (regulations), after "15" insert "or Schedule 1A".

(4) In section 26(1) (regulations subject to the affirmative resolution procedure), after paragraph (c) insert—

> "(d)   regulations under any paragraph of Schedule 1A."

(5) In Schedule 2 (employment and support allowance: supplementary provisions)—

    (a)   in paragraph 10A(1), which is inserted by section 30(2), after "13" insert "or Schedule 1A",

    (b)   in paragraph 12(c), after "13," insert—

> "(ca)   Schedule 1A,", and

    (c)   in paragraph 13, after "13" insert ", or under any paragraph of Schedule 1A other than paragraph 8,".

Report on the initial operation of drugs provisions

9   (1) The Secretary of State must prepare a report on the operation of the first set of regulations made under paragraphs 1, 2, 3, 5 and 6 of Schedule 1A to the Welfare Reform Act 2007 (c. 5) during the review period.

(2) "The review period" is the period of 24 months beginning with the day on which those regulations come into force.

(3) The Secretary of State must—

    (a)   prepare the report, and

    (b)   lay it before Parliament,

within 6 months from the end of the review period.

(4) The continued effect of the drugs provisions depends on whether the Secretary of State makes an order under this sub-paragraph within the relevant period providing for those provisions to continue to have effect.

(5) "The relevant period" means the period of 30 days beginning with the day on which the report is laid before Parliament; and, in reckoning this period, no account is to be taken of any time during which Parliament—

    (a)   is dissolved or prorogued, or

    (b)   is adjourned for more than 4 days.

(6) If no order is made as mentioned in sub-paragraph (4), the Secretary of State must instead make an order under this sub-paragraph providing for the repeal of the drugs provisions on a date specified in the order.

(7) An order under sub-paragraph (6) may contain transitional provision or savings.

(8) Any power to make an order under this paragraph is exercisable by statutory instrument.

(9) An order under sub-paragraph (4) may not be made unless a draft of the statutory instrument containing the order has been laid before, and approved by a resolution of, each House of Parliament.

Welfare Reform Act 2009 (c. 24)
Schedule 3 – Claimants dependent on drugs etc.
Part 2 – Employment and support allowance

2869

(10) A statutory instrument containing an order under sub-paragraph (6) is subject to annulment in pursuance of a resolution of either House of Parliament.

(11) In this paragraph "the drugs provisions" means —

    (a) section 15A of, and Schedule 1A to, the Welfare Reform Act 2007 (c. 5),

    (b) the words inserted into that Act by paragraph 8 of this Schedule, and

    (c) paragraphs 6 to 8 of this Schedule.

(12) This paragraph applies whether or not the regulations mentioned in sub-paragraph (1) are, by virtue of section 19 of the Welfare Reform Act 2007 (pilot schemes), made so as to have effect for a limited period.

SCHEDULE 4 Section 24

LOSS OF BENEFIT PROVISIONS: FURTHER AMENDMENTS

PART 1

FURTHER AMENDMENTS OF SOCIAL SECURITY FRAUD ACT 2001

1   In this Part of this Schedule "the 2001 Act" means the Social Security Fraud Act 2001 (c. 11).

2   (1) Section 7 of the 2001 Act (loss of benefit for commission of benefit offences) is amended as follows.

     (2) In subsection (8) —

        (a) after the definition of "benefit offence" insert —

             " "post-commencement offence" means an offence committed on or after 1 April 2002 (the day on which this section came into force).", and

        (b) omit the definitions of "disqualifying benefit" and "sanctionable benefit".

     (3) In subsection (9) —

        (a) in paragraph (a), after "sentenced)" insert "or in the case mentioned in paragraph (b)(ii) the date of the order for absolute discharge", and

        (b) for paragraph (b) substitute —

             "(b) references to a conviction include references to —

                (i) a conviction in relation to which the court makes an order for absolute or conditional discharge or a court in Scotland makes a probation order,

                (ii) an order for absolute discharge made by a court of summary jurisdiction in Scotland under section 246(3) of the Criminal Procedure (Scotland) Act 1995 without proceeding to a conviction, and

               (iii) a conviction in Northern Ireland.".

     (4) Omit subsection (11).

2870

Welfare Reform Act 2009 (c. 24)
Schedule 4 — *Loss of benefit provisions: further amendments*
Part 1 — *Further amendments of Social Security Fraud Act 2001*

(5) In the heading, for "commission of benefit offences" substitute "second or subsequent conviction of benefit offence".

3   (1) Section 8 of the 2001 Act (effect of offence on joint-claim jobseeker's allowance) is amended as follows.

(2) In subsection (1)(b), for "the restriction in subsection (2) of section 7" substitute "an offence-related restriction".

(3) After subsection (1) insert—

"(1A)   In this section—

(a) "an offence-related restriction" means the restriction in subsection (5) of section 6B or the restriction in subsection (2) of section 7, and

(b) in relation to an offence-related restriction, any reference to the relevant period is a reference to a period which is the disqualification period for the purposes of section 6B or section 7, as the case requires."

(4) In subsection (2)—

(a) for "the disqualification period" substitute "the relevant period",

(b) in paragraph (a), for "the restriction in subsection (2) of section 7" substitute "an offence-related restriction", and

(c) in paragraph (b), for "that restriction" substitute "an offence-related restriction".

(5) In subsection (3)—

(a) for "the disqualification period" substitute "the relevant period", and

(b) in paragraph (b), for "convictions section 7" substitute "conduct section 6B or 7".

(6) In subsection (4), for "the disqualification period" substitute "the relevant period".

(7) After subsection (6) insert—

"(7)   Where, after the agreement of any member of a couple ("M") to pay a penalty under the appropriate penalty provision is taken into account for the purposes of any restriction imposed by virtue of any regulations under this section—

(a) M's agreement to pay the penalty is withdrawn under subsection (5) of the appropriate penalty provision, or

(b) it is decided on an appeal or in accordance with regulations under the Social Security Act 1998 or the Social Security (Northern Ireland) Order 1998 that the overpayment to which the agreement relates is not recoverable or due,

all such payments and other adjustments shall be made as would be necessary if no restriction had been imposed by or under this section that could not have been imposed had M not agreed to pay the penalty.

(8)   Where, after the agreement ("the old agreement") of any member of a couple ("M") to pay a penalty under the appropriate penalty provision is taken into account for the purposes of any restriction imposed by virtue of any regulations under this section, the amount of the overpayment to which the penalty relates is revised on an

Welfare Reform Act 2009 (c. 24)
Schedule 4 — Loss of benefit provisions: further amendments
Part 1 — Further amendments of Social Security Fraud Act 2001

2871

appeal or in accordance with regulations under the Social Security Act 1998 or the Social Security (Northern Ireland) Order 1998 —

    (a)   if there is a new disqualifying event for the purposes of section 6B consisting of M's agreement to pay a penalty under the appropriate penalty provision in relation to the revised overpayment or M being cautioned in relation to the offence to which the old agreement relates, the new disqualification period for the purposes of section 6B falls to be determined in accordance with section 6C(4)(a), and

    (b)   in any other case, all such payments and other adjustments shall be made as would be necessary if no restriction had been imposed by or under this section that could not have been imposed had M not agreed to pay the penalty.

    (9)   In this section "the appropriate penalty provision" has the meaning given by section 6B(2)(a)."

4   (1)   Section 9 of the 2001 Act (effect of offence on benefits for members of offender's family) is amended as follows.

    (2)   In subsection (2)(b), for "section 7" substitute "section 6B or 7".

    (3)   After subsection (6) insert —

    "(7)   Where, after the agreement of any member of a person's family ("M") to pay a penalty under the appropriate penalty provision is taken into account for the purposes of any restriction imposed by virtue of any regulations under this section —

    (a)   M's agreement to pay the penalty is withdrawn under subsection (5) of the appropriate penalty provision, or

    (b)   it is decided on an appeal or in accordance with regulations under the Social Security Act 1998 or the Social Security (Northern Ireland) Order 1998 that the overpayment to which the agreement relates is not recoverable or due,

all such payments and other adjustments shall be made as would be necessary if no restriction had been imposed that could not have been imposed had M not agreed to pay the penalty.

    (8)   Where, after the agreement ("the old agreement") of any member of a person's family ("M") to pay a penalty under the appropriate penalty provision is taken into account for the purposes of any restriction imposed by virtue of any regulations under this section, the amount of the overpayment to which the penalty relates is revised on an appeal or in accordance with regulations under the Social Security Act 1998 or the Social Security (Northern Ireland) Order 1998 —

    (a)   if there is a new disqualifying event for the purposes of section 6B consisting of M's agreement to pay a penalty under the appropriate penalty provision in relation to the revised overpayment or M being cautioned in relation to the offence to which the old agreement relates, the new disqualification period for the purposes of section 6B falls to be determined in accordance with section 6C(4)(a), and

    (b)   in any other case, all such payments and other adjustments shall be made as would be necessary if no restriction had

2872

Welfare Reform Act 2009 (c. 24)
Schedule 4 — Loss of benefit provisions: further amendments
Part 1 — Further amendments of Social Security Fraud Act 2001

been imposed by or under this section that could not have been imposed had M not agreed to pay the penalty.

(9) In this section "the appropriate penalty provision" has the meaning given by section 6B(2)(a)."

5 (1) Section 10 of the 2001 Act (power to supplement and mitigate loss of benefit provisions) is amended as follows.

(2) In subsection (1), for "sections 7 to 9" substitute "sections 6A to 9".

(3) In subsection (2), after "section" insert "6B,".

6 (1) Section 11 of the 2001 Act (loss of benefit regulations) is amended as follows.

(2) In subsections (1) and (2), for "sections 7 to 10" substitute "sections 6B to 10".

(3) In subsection (3) —

(a) in paragraph (a), after "section" insert "6B or",
(b) in paragraph (b), after "section" insert "6B(6),", and
(c) in paragraph (c), after "section" insert "6B(7), (8), (9) or (10),".

(4) In subsections (4) and (5), for "sections 7 to 10" substitute "sections 6B to 10".

7 (1) Section 13 of the 2001 Act (interpretation of sections 7 to 12) is amended as follows.

(2) For the words "sections 7 to 12", both in the section and in the heading to the section, substitute "sections 6A to 12".

(3) After the definition of "benefit" insert—

" "cautioned", in relation to any person and any offence, means cautioned after the person concerned has admitted the offence; and "caution" is to be interpreted accordingly;".

(4) Omit the definitions of "disqualification period" and "post-commencement offence".

(5) In the definition of "sanctionable benefit", for "section 7(8)" substitute "section 6A(1)".

8 In section 21(2) of the of the 2001 Act (extent), after "sections 5(2)," insert "6A, 6B and 6C".

PART 2

RELATED AMENDMENTS OF OTHER ACTS

Social Security Administration Act 1992 (c. 5)

9 In section 170 of the Social Security Administration Act 1992 (functions of Social Security Advisory Committee in relation to the relevant enactments and the relevant Northern Ireland enactments), in subsection (5) —

(a) in the definition of the "relevant enactments", in paragraph (ag), for "sections 7 to 11" substitute "sections 6A to 11", and
(b) in the definition of "the relevant Northern Ireland enactments", in paragraph (ag), for "sections 7 to 11" substitute "sections 6A to 11".

Welfare Reform Act 2009 (c. 24)
Schedule 4 – Loss of benefit provisions: further amendments
Part 2 – Related amendments of other Acts

2873

Social Security Act 1998 (c. 14)

10 In paragraph 3 of Schedule 3 to the Social Security Act 1998 (decisions against which an appeal lies), in paragraph (f), after "section" insert "6B,".

SCHEDULE 5   Section 51

SECTION 51: CONSEQUENTIAL AMENDMENTS ETC.

Child Support Act 1991 (c. 48)

1 The Child Support Act 1991 is amended as follows.

2 In section 39B (disqualification for holding or obtaining travel authorisation), in the title, after "**obtaining**" insert "**driving licence or**".

3 (1) Section 39C (period for which orders under section 39B are to have effect) is amended as follows.

   (2) In subsection (2) –
       (a) for "an order under section 39B, the court" substitute "a disqualification order, the Commission", and
       (b) for "as the court" substitute "as the Commission".

   (3) In subsection (3) –
       (a) for "such an order the court" substitute "a disqualification order, the Commission", and
       (b) for "as the court" substitute "as the Commission".

   (4) In subsection (4) –
       (a) for "court" (in both places) substitute "Commission", and
       (b) in paragraph (a), for "the order under section 39B" substitute "the disqualification order".

   (5) In subsection (5) –
       (a) for "application under section 39B" substitute "disqualification order", and
       (b) for "an order under that section" substitute "a previous disqualification order".

   (6) In the title, for "**orders under section 39B**" substitute "**disqualification orders**".

4 In section 39D (power to order search), for subsections (1) and (2) substitute –

   "(1) On an appeal under section 39CB the court may order the person against whom the disqualification order was made to be searched.

   (2) Any money found on such a search shall, unless the court otherwise directs, be applied towards payment of any amount that would otherwise, on the affirmation or variation of the order, be substituted under section 39CB(8) for the amount specified under section 39B(5); and the balance (if any) shall be returned to the person searched."

5   (1) Section 39E (variation and revocation of orders following payment) is amended as follows.

      (2) In subsection (1) –

          (a) for "an order under section 39B" substitute "a disqualification order",

          (b) for "court" substitute "Commission",

          (c) omit "the Commission or", and

          (d) in paragraphs (a) and (b), for "the order under section 39B" substitute "the disqualification order".

      (3) After that subsection insert –

        "(1A) The power conferred by subsection (1) shall be exercisable by the court instead of by the Commission at any time when an appeal brought under section 39CB against the order has not been determined, withdrawn or discontinued."

      (4) In subsection (2) –

          (a) for "an order under section 39B" substitute "a disqualification order",

          (b) for "court" substitute "Commission",

          (c) omit "the Commission or", and

          (d) for "the order under section 39B" substitute "the disqualification order".

      (5) Omit subsections (3) to (5).

6   For section 39F substitute –

"39F   Power to make supplementary provision

      (1) The Secretary of State may by regulations make provision with respect to –

          (a) disqualification orders;

          (b) appeals against disqualification orders; and

          (c) orders under section 39DA.

      (2) The regulations may, in particular, make provision –

          (a) as to the form and content of a disqualification order;

          (b) as to the surrender of documents under section 39CA and their return when the period for which a disqualification order has effect is suspended or has ended;

          (c) that a statement in writing to the effect that wages of any amount have been paid to a person during any period, purporting to be signed by or on behalf of the person's employer, shall be evidence (or, in Scotland, sufficient evidence) of the facts stated for the purposes of an appeal under section 39CB;

          (d) permitting or requiring the court to dismiss an appeal brought under that section where the person who brought it fails to appear at the hearing;

          (e) requiring the court to send notice to the Commission of any order made on an appeal under that section;

          (f) as to the exercise by the Commission and the court of the power conferred by section 39E(1);

(g) as to the revival of a disqualification order in such circumstances as may be prescribed;

(h) for sections 39C to 39E to have effect with prescribed modifications in cases where a person against whom a disqualification order has effect is outside the United Kingdom."

7   Omit section 39G (application of sections 39B and 39F to Scotland).

8   Omit section 40B (disqualification for holding or obtaining driving licence).

9   In section 52(2A)(b) (regulations and orders: affirmative resolution procedure), after "under section" insert "39CA(4), 39CB(3)(b),".

Child Maintenance and Other Payments Act 2008 (c. 6)

10   In section 59(5) and (6) of the Child Maintenance and Other Payments Act 2008 (transition), after "39B," insert "39CB,".

SCHEDULE 6

Section 56

REGISTRATION OF BIRTHS

PART 1

AMENDMENTS OF BIRTHS AND DEATHS REGISTRATION ACT 1953

1   In this Schedule "the 1953 Act" means the Births and Deaths Registration Act 1953 (c. 20).

2   (1) Section 1 of the 1953 Act (particulars of births required to be registered) is amended as follows.

(2) In subsection (2), for paragraph (a) substitute —
"(a)   the mother of the child;
(aa)   the father of the child where —
(i)   the child is one whose father and mother were married to each other at the time of the child's birth, or
(ii)   the father is a qualified informant by virtue of subsection (2)(a) of section 10 (registration of father where parents not married or of second female parent where parents not civil partners) or by virtue of regulations under subsection (6)(b) of section 2E (scientific tests);".

(3) For subsection (3) substitute —

"(3)   In subsection (2)(aa) —
(a)   the first reference to the father is, in the case of a child who has a parent by virtue of section 42 or 43 of the Human Fertilisation and Embryology Act 2008, to be read as a reference to the woman who is a parent by virtue of that section;

2876

Welfare Reform Act 2009 (c. 24)
Schedule 6 — Registration of births
Part 1 — Amendments of Births and Deaths Registration Act 1953

(b) the reference in sub-paragraph (ii) to the father being a qualified informant by virtue of section 10(2)(a) is, in the case of a child who has a parent by virtue of section 43 of that Act, to be read as a reference to that parent being a qualified informant by virtue of section 10(2Å)(a)."

(4) After subsection (3) insert—

"(4) In this Part, references to a child whose father and mother were, or were not, married to each other at the time of the child's birth are to be read in accordance with section 1 of the Family Law Reform Act 1987 (which extends the cases in which a person is treated as being a person whose father and mother were married to each other at the time of the person's birth)."

3 (1) Section 2 of the 1953 Act (information concerning birth to be given to registrar within 42 days) is amended as follows.

(2) In subsection (1), after "every birth" insert "of a child whose father and mother were married to each other at the time of the child's birth".

(3) In subsection (2), for "subsection (1)" substitute "subsection (1)(a) and (b)".

(4) In the title, for the words from "to be given" onwards substitute "of child whose parents are married".

4 After section 2 of the 1953 Act insert—

"2A Information concerning birth of child whose parents are not married

(1) In the case of every birth of a child whose father and mother were not married to each other at the time of the birth, it shall be the duty—
   (a) of the mother of the child, and
   (b) in the case of the death or inability of the mother, of each qualified informant falling within section 1(2)(b) to (e),
to give to the registrar, before the expiration of a period of 42 days from the date of the birth, information of the particulars required to be registered concerning the birth, together with any other information required by section 2B(1), and in the presence of the registrar to sign the register.

(2) The giving of information and the signing of the register by any one qualified informant shall act as a discharge of any duty under this section of every other qualified informant, but this does not affect—
   (a) any duty of the father by virtue of regulations under section 2C (confirmation of parentage information given by mother), or
   (b) any duty by virtue of regulations under section 2E (scientific tests).

(3) This section ceases to apply if, before the end of the period mentioned in subsection (1) and before the birth has been registered, an inquest is held at which the child is found to have been still-born.

(4) In the case of a child who has a parent by virtue of section 43 of the Human Fertilisation and Embryology Act 2008, the reference in subsection (2)(a) to the father is to be read as a reference to the woman who is a parent by virtue of that section.

Welfare Reform Act 2009 (c. 24)
Schedule 6 — Registration of births
Part 1 — Amendments of Births and Deaths Registration Act 1953

2877

2B Duties of unmarried mother when acting alone

(1) Where no request for the entry of a person's name as the father of the child is made by virtue of any of paragraphs (a) to (g) of section 10(1) (registration of father where parents are not married) or by virtue of regulations under section 2E (scientific tests), the information to be given under section 2A(1) by the mother includes such information relating to the father as may be prescribed for the purposes of this subsection by regulations made by the Minister, which may include information that is not intended to be entered on the register.

(2) The Registrar General may by regulations authorise or require the information relating to the father to be provided in a prescribed form or manner.

(3) Subsection (1) does not require the mother to provide information relating to the father if she makes in the presence of the registrar a declaration in the prescribed form stating that one or more of the following conditions is met.

(4) Those conditions are —
   (a) that by virtue of section 41 of the Human Fertilisation and Embryology Act 2008 the child has no father,
   (b) that the father has died,
   (c) that the mother does not know the father's identity,
   (d) that the mother does not know the father's whereabouts,
   (e) that the father lacks capacity (within the meaning of the Mental Capacity Act 2005) in relation to decisions under this Part,
   (f) that the mother has reason to fear for her safety or that of the child if the father is contacted in relation to the registration of the birth, and
   (g) any other conditions prescribed by regulations made by the Minister.

(5) Subsection (1) does not apply —
   (a) in the case of a still-birth,
   (b) if the child has died, or
   (c) if the mother acknowledges in accordance with regulations made by virtue of subsection (2)(b) of section 2D (declaration before registration by person claiming to be other parent) that a person who has previously given notice by virtue of subsection (2)(a) of that section is the other parent of the child.

(6) The Minister may by regulations provide that, except in such cases as the regulations may prescribe, where the mother is required by subsection (1) to give information relating to the father —
   (a) the mother's duty under section 2A to sign the register is to have effect as a duty to sign a declaration in such form as may be so prescribed,
   (b) the registrar is not to register the birth of the child until such time as may be determined in accordance with the regulations, and

2878

Welfare Reform Act 2009 (c. 24)
Schedule 6 — Registration of births
Part 1 — Amendments of Births and Deaths Registration Act 1953

(c)   the entry in the register is to be taken for the purposes of this Act to have been signed by the person who signed the declaration.

(7)   No information relating to the father is to be entered in the register merely because it is given by the mother by virtue of subsection (1).

(8)   In the case of a child who has a parent by virtue of section 43 of the Human Fertilisation and Embryology Act 2008 —

    (a)   references in this section to the father are to be read as references to the woman who is a parent by virtue of that section,

    (b)   the reference in subsection (1) to paragraphs (a) to (g) of section 10(1) is to be read as a reference to paragraphs (a) to (f) of section 10(1B), and

    (c)   paragraphs (a) and (c) of subsection (4) do not apply.

2C   Confirmation of parentage information given by mother

(1)   The Minister may by regulations provide for a procedure under which a person may be registered as the father of a child in a case where information relating to that person is given by virtue of section 2B(1) by the mother of the child and is subsequently confirmed by that person.

(2)   Regulations under this section may in particular —

    (a)   enable or require the registrar by notice to require the person in relation to whom information has been given by virtue of section 2B(1) by the mother ("the alleged father") to state whether or not he acknowledges that he is the father of the child,

    (b)   where the alleged father acknowledges that he is the father of the child, require the alleged father to give prescribed information to the registrar,

    (c)   where the alleged father gives that information to the registrar, require the registrar to enter the alleged father's name in the register as the father of the child or, where the birth has already been registered, to re-register the birth so as to show the alleged father as the father, and

    (d)   provide that in prescribed cases where the alleged father is not required by the regulations to sign the register, the entry in the register is to be taken for the purposes of this Act to have been signed by the alleged father.

(3)   In the case of a child who has a parent by virtue of section 43 of the Human Fertilisation and Embryology Act 2008, references in subsection (1) or (2) to the father are to be read as references to the woman who is a parent by virtue of that section (and references to the alleged father have a corresponding meaning).

(4)   Regulations under this section may —

    (a)   require anything to be done in a prescribed form or manner or in the presence of the registrar,

    (b)   make provision as to the time within which anything is required or authorised to be done.

Welfare Reform Act 2009 (c. 24)
Schedule 6 — Registration of births
Part 1 — Amendments of Births and Deaths Registration Act 1953

2879

(5) In this section "prescribed" means prescribed by regulations made under this section by the Minister.

2D   Declaration before registration by person claiming to be other parent

(1) The Minister may by regulations provide for a procedure under which a person may be registered as the father of a child whose father and mother were not married to each other at the time of the child's birth, on the basis of information that is —

    (a) given by that person (in the absence of the mother) before the birth is registered, and

    (b) confirmed by the mother when she provides information of the particulars required to be registered concerning the birth.

(2) Regulations under this section may in particular —

    (a) enable a person who believes himself to be the father of a child to make a declaration to that effect to the registrar before the birth of the child is registered,

    (b) require the mother of the child, on giving information concerning the birth of the child or in such other circumstances as may be prescribed, to state whether or not she acknowledges that the person is the father of the child,

    (c) where the mother acknowledges that the person is the father of the child, require the registrar to enter the person's name in the register as the father of the child, and

    (d) provide that in prescribed cases where the person is not required by the regulations to sign the register, the entry in the register is to be taken for the purposes of this Act to have been signed by the person.

(3) In the case of a child who has a parent by virtue of section 43 of the Human Fertilisation and Embryology Act 2008, references in subsections (1) and (2) to the father (except in the reference in subsection (1) to a child whose father and mother were not married to each other at the time of the child's birth) are to be read as references to the woman who is a parent by virtue of that section.

(4) Regulations under this section may —

    (a) require anything to be done in a prescribed form or manner or in the presence of the registrar,

    (b) make provision as to the time within which anything is required or authorised to be done.

(5) This section does not apply —

    (a) in relation to a still-birth, or

    (b) if the child has died.

(6) In this section "prescribed" means prescribed by regulations made under this section by the Minister.

2E   Use of scientific tests with consent of parties

(1) The Minister may by regulations make provision enabling a report of a qualifying scientific test to be used in connection with the registration or re-registration under this Act of the birth of a child in cases where —

2880

Welfare Reform Act 2009 (c. 24)
Schedule 6 — Registration of births
Part 1 — Amendments of Births and Deaths Registration Act 1953

       (a)   the birth has not been registered under this Act, or

       (b)   the birth has been registered but no person has been registered as the father of the child (or as a parent of the child by virtue of section 42, 43 or 46(1) or (2) of the Human Fertilisation and Embryology Act 2008).

(2)   A qualifying scientific test is a scientific test that complies with prescribed requirements and is carried out by a person who is accredited by the Minister for the purposes of this section in accordance with the regulations.

(3)   The regulations may not require any person to participate in a qualifying scientific test.

(4)   The regulations may not enable or require a report of a qualifying scientific test to be used as mentioned in subsection (1) unless, before the test is carried out, the mother and the man to whom the test relates—

       (a)   consent to the carrying out of the test, and

       (b)   agree in the prescribed manner that if the report of the test is positive the man's name will be entered in the register as the father of the child.

(5)   For the purposes of this section, the report of a qualifying scientific test is positive if the report states that the result of the test indicates to a prescribed degree of certainty that the man concerned is the father of the child.

(6)   Regulations under this section may—

       (a)   enable or require the mother or the man, if the report of the qualifying scientific test is positive, to apply for the registration (or re-registration) of the birth so as to show the man as the father,

       (b)   provide that where the regulations enable or require the man to apply for registration, the man is to be treated for the purposes of this Part as a qualified informant concerning the birth of the child,

       (c)   impose obligations on the registrar in relation to the registration (or re-registration) of the birth,

       (d)   require anything to be done in a prescribed form or manner or in the presence of the registrar,

       (e)   make provision as to the time within which anything is required or authorised to be done.

(7)   The regulations may not require the registrar to enter a man's name in the register as the father of a child if it appears to the registrar that by virtue of any provision of sections 35 to 47 of the Human Fertilisation and Embryology Act 2008 the man is not the father of the child.

(8)   This section does not apply in relation to a still-birth.

(9)   In this section "prescribed" means prescribed by regulations made under this section by the Minister."

Welfare Reform Act 2009 (c. 24)   2881
Schedule 6 – Registration of births
Part 1 – Amendments of Births and Deaths Registration Act 1953

5   In section 4 of the 1953 Act (registrar's power to require information concerning birth), in paragraph (a), for "three months" substitute "12 months".

6   In section 5 of the 1953 Act (registration of births free of charge) for "three months" substitute "12 months".

7   Omit section 6 of the 1953 Act (which makes special provision about registration between 3 and 12 months from the date of birth).

8   In section 7 of the 1953 Act (registration after twelve months from date of birth) omit subsection (3) (which excludes still-births).

9   In section 8 of the 1953 Act (penalty for improper registration after 3 months from date of birth) –

         (a)   for "the two last foregoing sections" substitute "section 7", and

         (b)   for "three months" (both in the section and in the title) substitute "12 months".

10   (1)   Section 9 of the 1953 Act (giving of information to a person other than the registrar) is amended as follows.

      (2)   After subsection (3) insert –

         "(3A)   Anything that section 2B (duties of unmarried mother when acting alone) requires to be done in the presence of, or in relation to, the registrar may, in prescribed cases, be done in the presence of, or in relation to, such officer as may be prescribed."

      (3)   After subsection (5) insert –

         "(6)   Regulations under section 2C, 2D, 2E, 10B or 10C may enable anything that would otherwise be required or authorised to be done under the regulations in the presence of, or in relation to, the registrar to be done instead in the presence of, or in relation to, such officer as may be prescribed by the regulations."

11   (1)   Section 10 of the 1953 Act (registration of father where parents not married or of second female parent where parents not civil partners) is amended as follows.

      (2)   In subsection (1) –

         (a)   for the words from the beginning to "the registrar" substitute "In the case of a child whose father and mother were not married to each other at the time of the child's birth, no person shall as father of the child be required to give information concerning the birth of the child except by virtue of regulations under section 2C or 2E, and the registrar",

         (b)   in paragraph (b) for sub-paragraph (ii) substitute –

                 "(ii)   a declaration in the prescribed form which is made by that person, states himself to be the father of the child, and is countersigned by a prescribed person; or",

         (c)   in paragraph (c) for sub-paragraph (ii) substitute –

                 "(ii)   a declaration in the prescribed form which is made by the mother, states that that person is the father of the child, and is countersigned by a prescribed person; or", and

2882

Welfare Reform Act 2009 (c. 24)
Schedule 6 — Registration of births
Part 1 — Amendments of Births and Deaths Registration Act 1953

  (d) at the end of paragraph (g) insert "or

     (h) in accordance with regulations made under section 2C (confirmation of parentage information given by mother), section 2D (declaration before registration by person claiming to be other parent) or section 2E (scientific tests)".

(3) In subsection (1B) —

  (a) for the words from the beginning to "that section" substitute "In the case of a child to whom section 1(3) of the Family Law Reform Act 1987 does not apply, no woman shall as parent of the child by virtue of section 43 of the Human Fertilisation and Embryology Act 2008 be required to give information concerning the birth of the child except by virtue of regulations under section 2C, and the registrar shall not enter the name of any woman as a parent of the child by virtue of that section",

  (b) in paragraph (b) for sub-paragraph (ii) substitute —

     "(ii) a declaration in the prescribed form which is made by the woman concerned, states herself to be a parent of the child by virtue of section 43 of that Act, and is countersigned by a prescribed person; or",

  (c) in paragraph (c) for sub-paragraph (ii) substitute —

     "(ii) a declaration in the prescribed form which is made by the mother, states that the woman concerned is a parent of the child by virtue of section 43 of that Act, and is countersigned by a prescribed person; or", and

  (d) at the end of paragraph (f) insert "or

     (g) in accordance with regulations made under section 2C (confirmation of parentage information given by mother) or section 2D (declaration before registration by person claiming to be other parent)".

(4) After subsection (1B) insert —

  "(1C) Subsections (1) and (1B) have effect subject to section 10ZA."

(5) In subsections (2)(b) and (2A)(b), for "section 2" substitute "section 2A".

(6) Omit subsection (3).

12 (1) Section 10A of the 1953 Act (Re-registration where parents neither married nor civil partners) is amended as follows.

(2) In subsection (1) —

  (a) in paragraph (b) for sub-paragraph (ii) substitute —

     "(ii) a declaration in the prescribed form which is made by that person, states himself to be the father of the child, and is countersigned by a prescribed person; or",

  (b) in paragraph (c) for sub-paragraph (ii) substitute —

     "(ii) a declaration in the prescribed form which is made by the mother, states that that person is

Welfare Reform Act 2009 (c. 24)
Schedule 6 – Registration of births
Part 1 – Amendments of Births and Deaths Registration Act 1953

2883

the father of the child, and is countersigned by a prescribed person; or".

(3) In subsection (1B) —

    (a) in paragraph (b) for sub-paragraph (ii) substitute —

        "(ii) a declaration in the prescribed form which is made by the woman concerned, states herself to be a parent of the child by virtue of section 43 of that Act, and is countersigned by a prescribed person; or",

    (b) in paragraph (c) for sub-paragraph (ii) substitute —

        "(ii) a declaration in the prescribed form which is made by the mother, states that the woman concerned is a parent of the child by virtue of section 43 of that Act, and is countersigned by a prescribed person; or".

(4) In subsection (2), omit paragraph (d) (requirement for signature by superintendent registrar where re-registration takes place more than 3 months after the birth) and the word "and" immediately before it.

13   After section 10A of the 1953 Act insert —

"10B Re-registration after sole registration: information provided by other parent and confirmed by mother

(1) The Minister may by regulations make provision for the re-registration of a birth to show a person as the father of a relevant child, on the basis of information given by that person after the birth is registered and confirmed by the mother.

(2) In this section a "relevant child" means a child —

    (a) whose father and mother were not married to each other at the time of the child's birth, and

    (b) whose birth has been registered before or after the commencement of this section without any person being registered as the father of the child (or as a parent of the child by virtue of section 42, 43 or 46(1) or (2) of the Human Fertilisation and Embryology Act 2008).

(3) Regulations under subsection (1) may —

    (a) enable a person who believes himself to be the father of a relevant child to make a declaration to that effect to the registrar,

    (b) enable or require the registrar by notice to require the mother to state whether or not she acknowledges that the person is the father of the child, and

    (c) where the mother acknowledges that the person is the father, require the registrar to re-register the birth so as to show the person as the father.

(4) In the case of a child who has a parent by virtue of section 43 of the Human Fertilisation and Embryology Act 2008, references in subsections (1) and (3) to the father are to be read as references to the woman who is a parent by virtue of that section.

(5) Regulations under this section may —

2884

Welfare Reform Act 2009 (c. 24)
Schedule 6 — Registration of births
Part 1 — Amendments of Births and Deaths Registration Act 1953

    (a)   require anything to be done in a prescribed form or manner or in the presence of the registrar,

    (b)   make provision as to the time within which anything is required or authorised to be done.

(6)   Regulations under this section may not provide for any birth to be re-registered except with the authority of the Registrar General.

(7)   In this section "prescribed" means prescribed by regulations made under this section by the Minister.

10C   Re-registration after sole registration: information provided by mother and confirmed by other parent

(1)   The Minister may by regulations make provision for the re-registration of a birth to show a person as the father of a relevant child, on the basis of information given by the mother after the birth is registered and confirmed by that person.

(2)   In this section a "relevant child" means a child —

    (a)   whose father and mother were not married to each other at the time of the child's birth, and

    (b)   whose birth has been registered before or after the commencement of this section without any person being registered as the father of the child (or as a parent of the child by virtue of section 42, 43 or 46(1) or (2) of the Human Fertilisation and Embryology Act 2008).

(3)   Regulations under subsection (1) may —

    (a)   enable the mother of a relevant child to make a declaration to the registrar stating that a specified person ("the alleged father") is the father of the child,

    (b)   enable or require the registrar by notice to require the alleged father to state whether or not he acknowledges that he is the father of the child,

    (c)   where the alleged father acknowledges that he is the father of the child, require the alleged father to give prescribed information to the registrar, and

    (d)   where the alleged father gives that information to the registrar, require the registrar to re-register the birth so as to show the alleged father as the father.

(4)   In the case of a child who has a parent by virtue of section 43 of the Human Fertilisation and Embryology Act 2008, references in subsections (1) and (3) to the father are to be read as references to the woman who is a parent by virtue of that section (and references to the alleged father have a corresponding meaning).

(5)   Regulations under this section may —

    (a)   require anything to be done in a prescribed form or manner or in the presence of the registrar,

    (b)   make provision as to the time within which anything is required or authorised to be done.

(6)   Regulations under this section may not provide for any birth to be re-registered except with the authority of the Registrar General.

Welfare Reform Act 2009 (c. 24)
Schedule 6 – Registration of births
Part 1 – Amendments of Births and Deaths Registration Act 1953

2885

(7) In this section "prescribed" means prescribed by regulations made under this section by the Minister."

14 In section 34 of the 1953 Act (entry in register as evidence of birth or death), in subsection (3), for paragraph (a) substitute—

"(a) if it appears that not more than 12 months have so intervened—

(i) the original entry was made after the commencement of paragraph 7 of Schedule 6 to the Welfare Reform Act 2009, or

(ii) the entry purports either to be signed by the superintendent registrar as well as by the registrar or to have been made with the authority of the Registrar General;".

15 In section 36 of the 1953 Act (penalties for failure to give information) after paragraph (a) insert—

"(aa) if, being required by regulations under section 2C, 2D, 2E, 10B or 10C to do anything within a particular time, he refuses or fails without reasonable excuse to do so;".

16 In section 39 of the 1953 Act (regulations), in paragraph (a), for "this Act" substitute "any provision of this Act other than sections 2B(1), (4) and (6), 2C, 2D, 2E, 10B and 10C".

17 After section 39 of the 1953 Act insert—

"**39A Regulations made by the Minister: further provisions**

(1) Regulations made by the Minister under the relevant provisions may—

(a) make different provision for different cases or areas,

(b) provide for exemptions from any of the provisions of the regulations, and

(c) contain such incidental, supplemental and transitional provision as the Minister considers appropriate.

(2) Before making regulations under the relevant provisions, the Minister must consult the Registrar General.

(3) Any power of the Minister to make regulations under the relevant provisions is exercisable by statutory instrument.

(4) A statutory instrument containing regulations made by the Minister under the relevant provisions is subject to annulment in pursuance of a resolution of either House of Parliament.

(5) In this section "the relevant provisions" means sections 2B(1), (4) and (6), 2C, 2D, 2E, 10B and 10C."

18 In section 41 of the 1953 Act (interpretation), in the definition of "prescribed", after " "prescribed"", insert "(except in sections 2B(1), (4) and (6), 2C, 2D, 2E, 10B and 10C)".

PART 2

OTHER AMENDMENTS

Perjury Act 1911 (c. 6)

19   In section 4 of the Perjury Act 1911 (false statements, etc, as to births or deaths) after subsection (1) insert—

"(1A)   For the purposes of subsection (1)(a), information which a person is required to provide to a registrar of births or deaths for the purposes of subsection (1) of section 2B of the Births and Deaths Registration Act 1953 (duties of unmarried mother when acting alone) is to be taken to be information concerning a birth."

Population (Statistics) Act 1938 (c. 12)

20   (1) In the Schedule to the Population (Statistics) Act 1938 (particulars which may be required on registration of a birth), in paragraph 1—

(a)   for paragraph (a) substitute—

"(a)   in all cases—

(i)   the age of the mother;

(ii)   the number of previous children of the mother, and how many of them were born alive or were still-born;".

(b)   for paragraph (c) substitute—

"(c)   where the birth is of a child whose father and mother were married to each other at the time of the child's birth (or is by reason of any marriage of the child's parents treated by section 1(2) of the Family Law Reform Act 1987 as such a child for the purposes of that Act)—

(i)   the date of the marriage, and

(ii)   whether the mother had been married, or had formed a civil partnership, before her marriage to the child's father;

(d)   where the birth is of a child to whom section 1(3) of that Act applies by reason of any civil partnership between the child's parents—

(i)   the date of the formation of the civil partnership, and

(ii)   whether the mother had been married, or had formed a civil partnership, before she formed the civil partnership with the child's other parent;

(e)   where the birth does not fall within paragraph (c) or (d), whether at any time before the birth the mother had been married or had formed a civil partnership."

(2) This paragraph does not extend to Scotland.

Children Act 1989 (c. 41)

21   (1) Section 4 of the Children Act 1989 (acquisition of parental responsibility by father) is amended as follows.

     (2) At the beginning of subsection (1)(a) insert "except where subsection (1C) applies,".

     (3) In subsection (1A), after paragraph (a) insert—
> "(aa)   regulations under section 2C, 2D, 2E, 10B or 10C of the Births and Deaths Registration Act 1953;".

     (4) After subsection (1B) insert—

> "(1C)   The father of a child does not acquire parental responsibility by virtue of subsection (1)(a) if, before he became registered as the child's father under the enactment in question—
>
> > (a)   the court considered an application by him for an order under subsection (1)(c) in relation to the child but did not make such an order, or
> >
> > (b)   in a case where he had previously acquired parental responsibility for the child, the court ordered that he was to cease to have that responsibility."

22   (1) Section 4ZA of the Children Act 1989 (acquisition of parental responsibility by second female parent) is amended as follows.

     (2) At the beginning of subsection (1)(a) insert "except where subsection (3A) applies,".

     (3) In subsection (2), after paragraph (a) insert—
> "(aa)   regulations under section 2C, 2D, 10B or 10C of the Births and Deaths Registration Act 1953;".

     (4) After subsection (3) insert—

> "(3A)   A person who is a parent of a child by virtue of section 43 of the Human Fertilisation and Embryology Act 2008 does not acquire parental responsibility by virtue of subsection (1)(a) if, before she became registered as a parent of the child under the enactment in question—
>
> > (a)   the court considered an application by her for an order under subsection (1)(c) in relation to the child but did not make such an order, or
> >
> > (b)   in a case where she had previously acquired parental responsibility for the child, the court ordered that she was to cease to have that responsibility."

Child Support Act 1991 (c. 48)

23   In section 26 of the Child Support Act 1991 (disputes about parentage), in subsection (2), in Case A2, in paragraph (b), after "10 or 10A of" insert ", or regulations made under section 2C, 2D, 2E, 10B or 10C of,".

Child Support (Northern Ireland) Order 1991 (S.I. 1991/2628 (N.I. 23))

24   In Article 27 of the Child Support (Northern Ireland) Order 1991 (disputes about parentage), in paragraph (2), in Case A2, in paragraph (b), after "10 or 10A of" insert ", or regulations made under section 2C, 2D, 2E, 10B or 10C of,".

Children (Scotland) Act 1995 (c. 36)

25   In section 3 of the Children (Scotland) Act 1995 (provisions relating both to parental responsibilities and parental rights), in subsection (3A), after paragraph (b) insert—
        "(ba)   regulations under section 2C, 2D, 10B or 10C of the Births and Deaths Registration Act 1953;".

Children (Northern Ireland) Order 1995 (S.I. 1995/755 (N.I. 2))

26   (1)   Article 7 of the Children (Northern Ireland) Order 1995 (acquisition of parental responsibility) is amended as follows.

      (2)   In paragraph (2A) for the "or" at the end of paragraph (b) substitute—
            "(ba)   regulations under section 2C, 2D, 2E, 10B or 10C of the Births and Deaths Registration Act 1953; or".

      (3)   In paragraph (2B), for the "or" at the end of paragraph (b) substitute—
            "(ba)   regulations under section 2C, 2D, 10B or 10C of the Births and Deaths Registration Act 1953; or".

SCHEDULE 7

Section 58

REPEALS AND REVOCATIONS

PART 1

ABOLITION OF INCOME SUPPORT

Reference	Extent of repeal or revocation
Maintenance Orders Act 1950 (c. 37)	In section 4— (a) subsection (1)(d), and (b) in subsection (2), the words "or the said section 106". In section 9— (a) subsection (1)(d), and (b) in subsection (2), the words "or the said section 106".
Transport Act 1982 (c. 49)	In section 70(2)(b), the words "income support,".
Social Security Act 1986 (c. 50)	In Schedule 10, paragraphs 35 and 36.
Children Act 1989 (c. 41)	In section 17(9), the words "of income support under Part VII of the Social Security Contributions and Benefits Act 1992,".

Welfare Reform Act 2009 (c. 24)
Schedule 7 – Repeals and revocations
Part 1 – Abolition of income support

2889

Reference	Extent of repeal or revocation
Children Act 1989 (c. 41) – *cont.*	In section 17A(5)(b), the words "of income support under Part 7 of the Social Security Contributions and Benefits Act 1992 (c. 4),". In section 29(3) and (3A), the words "of income support under Part VII of the Social Security Contributions and Benefits Act 1992,". In Schedule 2, in paragraph 21(4), the words "of income support under Part VII of the Social Security Contributions and Benefits Act 1992,".
Child Support Act 1991 (c. 48)	In section 54(1), the definition of "income support". In Schedule 1 (as it has effect apart from the Child Support, Pensions and Social Security Act 2000 (c. 6)), in paragraph 5(4), the words "income support,".
Criminal Justice Act 1991 (c. 53)	In section 24 – (a) in subsections (1) and (2)(d), the words "income support,", and (b) in subsection (4), the definition of "income support".
Social Security Contributions and Benefits Act 1992 (c. 4)	Section 123(1)(a) and (2). Section 124. Sections 126 and 127.
Social Security Administration Act 1992 (c. 5)	Section 2A(2)(a). Section 2AA(2)(a). Section 2D(1), (3)(a), (8), (9)(b) and (10). Section 2E(2)(a). Section 5(2)(b). In section 15A – (a) in subsection (1), the words "income support," in each place, and (b) in subsection (4), in the definition of "qualifying associate", the words "income support," and, in the definition of "relevant benefits", paragraph (b). Section 71(11)(b). In section 74 – (a) in subsections (1)(b), (2)(b) and (3)(b)(i) and (ii), the words "income support,", (b) in subsection (3)(c), the words "the income support or", and (c) in subsection (3), in the words following paragraph (c), the words "income support" and the words "the income support or". In section 74A(7), the words "income support,". In section 78(6)(d), the words "income support or". In section 105(1)(b), the words "income support,". Section 106.

2890

Welfare Reform Act 2009 (c. 24)
Schedule 7 – Repeals and revocations
Part 1 – Abolition of income support

Reference	*Extent of repeal or revocation*
Social Security Administration Act 1992 (c. 5) – *cont.*	Section 108. In section 109(1), the words "income support or" in both places. Section 124(2)(b). In section 126(1), the words "income support,". Sections 159 and 160. Section 163(2)(d)(i). Section 179(5)(a). In section 191, in the definition of "income-related benefit", paragraph (a).
Social Security (Consequential Provisions) Act 1992 (c. 6)	In Schedule 2, paragraphs 3(1)(a) and (b) and (2) and 108.
Local Government Finance Act 1992 (c. 14)	In Schedule 4, in paragraph 6(1) and (2)(b), the words "income support,". In Schedule 8, in paragraph 6(1) and (2)(b), the words "income support,".

Jobseekers Act 1995 (c. 18)	Section 1A(6).
	In section 2(1), paragraph (d) (together with the "and" immediately before it).
	In section 3 –
	  (a) in subsection (1)(b), the words "income support,",
	  (b) subsection (1)(c), and
	  (c) in subsection (1A)(a), the word "(c),".
	Section 3A(1)(b).
	In section 16(1)(a)(ii), the words "or to income support".
	In section 26 –
	  (a) in subsection (1), the words "or to income support",
	  (b) in subsection (3), the words "or (as the case may be) income support",
	  (c) in subsection (4)(d), the words "and periods of entitlement to income support",
	  (d) in subsection (4)(e), the words "wholly by way of income support or", and
	  (e) in subsection (4)(l), the words "or to income support".
	In section 28(1), the words "or income support".
	Section 31.
	In Schedule 2, paragraphs 30 to 32.

Employment Tribunals Act 1996 (c. 17)	In section 16(3)(a), (b) and (c) and (5)(e), the words ", income support". In section 17(1), the words ", income support" in both places and the words "or V".
Education Act 1996 (c. 56)	Section 457(4)(b)(i). Section 512ZB(4)(a)(i) and (b)(i).
Social Security Act 1998 (c. 14)	Section 8(3)(c). In section 34(3), the words "or to income support".

Welfare Reform Act 2009 (c. 24)
Schedule 7 – Repeals and revocations
Part 1 – Abolition of income support

2891

Reference	*Extent of repeal or revocation*
Social Security Act 1998 (c. 14) – *cont.*	In Schedule 2 – (a) paragraph 6(b)(i), and (b) in paragraph 7, the words "income support or" and the words "160(2) or". In Schedule 7, paragraphs 95 and 97.
Access to Justice Act 1999 (c. 22)	In Schedule 4, paragraph 48.
Welfare Reform and Pensions Act 1999 (c. 30)	In Schedule 7, paragraph 14. In Schedule 8, paragraphs 27 and 28.
Immigration and Asylum Act 1999 (c. 33)	Section 115(1)(e).
Children (Leaving Care) Act 2000 (c. 35)	In section 6(1), the words "income support or".
Social Security Fraud Act 2001 (c. 11)	Section 6B(6). Section 7(3). Section 9(1)(a) and (3). Section 11(3)(b).
Civil Jurisdiction and Judgments Order 2001 (S.I. 2001/3929)	In Schedule 3, paragraph 24.
State Pension Credit Act 2002 (c. 16)	In Schedule 2, paragraph 2.
Tax Credits Act 2002 (c. 21)	In Schedule 3, paragraphs 16(2)(a), 18(a) and 20(a).
Secretaries of State for Education and Skills and for Work and Pensions Order 2002 (S.I. 2002/1397)	In Schedule 1, paragraph 7.
Income Tax (Earnings and Pensions) Act 2003 (c. 1)	In Schedule 6, paragraph 179.
Age-Related Payments Act 2004 (c. 10)	In section 2(3)(b), sub-paragraph (iii) (together with the "or" immediately before it). In section 8(1), the definition of "income support".
Civil Partnership Act 2004 (c. 33)	In Schedule 24, paragraphs 42 to 44 and 123.
Welfare Reform Act 2007 (c. 5)	In section 1(3), paragraph (e) (but not the "and" at the end of it). In section 24(1), the definition of "income support". In Schedule 1, in paragraph 6(1)(d), the words ", income support". In Schedule 3, paragraph 9(9) and (10).
Pensions Act 2007 (c. 22)	In Schedule 1, paragraph 25.
Civil Jurisdiction and Judgments Regulations 2007 (S.I. 2007/1655)	In the Schedule, paragraph 16.

2892

Welfare Reform Act 2009 (c. 24)
Schedule 7 — Repeals and revocations
Part 1 — Abolition of income support

Reference	Extent of repeal or revocation
Child Maintenance and Other Payments Act 2008 (c. 6)	In Schedule 7, paragraph 2(2).
Saving Gateway Accounts Act 2009 (c. 8)	Section 3(2)(a).
This Act.	Section 3(1). Section 5(1). In Schedule 4, paragraph 9(3)(b).

The repeals and revocations made by this Part of this Schedule have effect in accordance with provision made by an order under section 9.

PART 2

ABOLITION OF ADULT DEPENDENCY INCREASES

Reference	Extent of repeal or revocation
Social Security Contributions and Benefits Act 1992 (c. 4)	In section 20(1)(d), the words "(with increase for adult dependants)". In section 63(c), the words "(with increase for adult dependants)". Section 82. Sections 88 to 92. In section 114(4), the word "82". In Part 4 of Schedule 4, paragraphs 3 and 9.
Social Security (Incapacity for Work) Act 1994 (c. 18)	In Schedule 1, paragraphs 25 to 27.
Jobseekers Act 1995 (c. 18)	In Schedule 2, paragraphs 24 and 27.
Welfare Reform and Pensions Act 1999 (c. 30)	In Schedule 8, paragraph 26.
Tax Credits Act 2002 (c. 21)	In Schedule 3, paragraph 34.
Regulatory Reform (Carer's Allowance) Order 2002 (S.I. 2002/1457)	In the Schedule, paragraph 2(d).
Civil Partnership Act 2004 (c. 33)	In Schedule 24, paragraph 35.
Child Benefit Act 2005 (c. 6)	In Schedule 1, paragraph 5.
Pensions Act 2004 (PPF Payments and FAS Payments) (Consequential Provisions) Order 2006 (S.I. 2006/343)	In the Schedule, paragraph 1(2).
Welfare Reform Act 2007 (c. 5)	In Schedule 3, paragraph 9(7) and (8).
Pensions Act 2007 (c. 22)	In Schedule 1, paragraphs 14 and 15.

Welfare Reform Act 2009 (c. 24)
Schedule 7 — Repeals and revocations
Part 3 — Social security: other repeals and revocations

2893

PART 3

SOCIAL SECURITY: OTHER REPEALS AND REVOCATIONS

Reference	*Extent of repeal or revocation*

Social Security Administration Act 1992 (c. 5)	In section 2A(8), in the definition of "the designated authority", paragraph (b).
	In section 2AA(7), in the definition of "designated authority", paragraph (b).
	Section 2B.
	Section 5(1)(r).
	In section 170(5) —
	  (a) in paragraph (ae) of the definition of "the relevant enactments", the word "60,",
	  (b) in paragraph (af) of the definition of "the relevant enactments", the words ", sections 62 to 65",
	  (c) in paragraph (ae) of the definition of "the relevant Northern Ireland enactments", the word "60,", and
	  (d) in paragraph (af) of the definition of "the relevant Northern Ireland enactments", the words "62 to 65,".

Jobseekers Act 1995 (c. 18)	Section 8(3).
	Section 9(13).
	In section 15A —
	  (a) in subsection (4), paragraph (b) (together with the "or" immediately before it), and
	  (b) in subsection (5), paragraph (c) (but not the "and" at the end of it).
	In section 16(4), the definition of "employment officer".
	In section 17A(10), the definition of "the jobseeking conditions".
	Section 19(10)(a).
	In section 36(1), the words ", other than an order under section 8(3), 9(13), 16(4) or 19(10)(a),".
	In Schedule A1, in paragraph 9, the definition of "the jobseeking conditions".

Employment Rights Act 1996 (c. 18)	In Schedule 1, in paragraph 67(2), paragraph (b) (together with the "and" immediately before it).
Social Security Act 1998 (c. 14)	In Schedule 2, paragraph 5A (together with the italic heading immediately before it). In Schedule 3, paragraph 3(e). In Schedule 7, paragraphs 141, 142 and 145.
Welfare Reform and Pensions Act 1999 (c. 30)	Section 60. Section 72(3)(b). In section 83(8) and (9), the words "60 or". In Schedule 7, paragraphs 2(2), (3) and (4)(b), 3, 4(1), 7(5) to (7), 12 and 13. In Schedule 8, paragraph 29(3), (5) and (6).

2894

Welfare Reform Act 2009 (c. 24)
Schedule 7 — Repeals and revocations
Part 3 — Social security: other repeals and revocations

Reference	Extent of repeal or revocation
Welfare Reform and Pensions Act 1999 (c. 30) — *cont.*	In Schedule 12, paragraph 87.
Child Support, Pensions and Social Security Act 2000 (c. 19)	Sections 62 to 66.
Criminal Justice and Court Services Act 2000 (c. 43)	In Schedule 7, paragraphs 205 to 207.
Scotland Act 1998 (Transfer of Functions to the Scottish Ministers etc.) Order 2000 (S.I. 2000/1563)	Article 4.
Social Security Fraud Act 2001 (c. 11)	In section 7— (a) in subsection (8), the definitions of "disqualifying benefit" and "sanctionable benefit", and (b) subsection (11). In section 8(2)(b), sub-paragraph (ii) and the word "or" before it. Section 12(1). In section 13, the definitions of "disqualification period" and "post-commencement offence".
State Pension Credit Act 2002 (c. 16)	In Schedule 2, paragraph 45(3).
Employment Act 2002 (c. 22)	In Schedule 7, paragraphs 9, 51 and 55.
Criminal Justice Act 2003 (c. 44)	In Schedule 32, paragraphs 130 to 132.
Civil Partnership Act 2004 (c. 33)	In Schedule 24, paragraphs 118, 120 and 121.
Welfare Reform Act 2007 (c. 5)	In Schedule 3, paragraphs 12(2), 20 and 23(3).
Criminal Justice and Immigration Act 2008 (c. 4)	In Schedule 4, paragraphs 65 to 67.
Transfer of Tribunal Functions Order 2008 (S.I. 2008/2833)	In Schedule 3, paragraph 102.

PART 4

CHILD MAINTENANCE

Reference	Extent of repeal
Road Traffic Act 1988 (c. 52)	In section 164(5), the words ", section 40B of the Child Support Act 1991".
Road Traffic Offenders Act 1988 (c. 53)	In section 27(3), the words from ", or if the holder" to "Child Support Act 1991, then,".
Child Support Act 1991 (c. 48)	In section 39E— (a) in subsections (1) and (2), the words "the Commission or", and (b) subsections (3) to (5). Section 39G.

Reference	Extent of repeal
Child Support Act 1991 (c. 48) – *cont.*	Section 40B.
Child Support, Pensions and Social Security Act 2000 (c. 19)	Section 16(3) to (5).
Road Safety Act 2006 (c. 49)	In Schedule 2, paragraph 33. In Schedule 3, paragraph 65(3)(b).
Child Maintenance and Other Payments Act 2008 (c. 6)	Section 30. In section 59(5) and (6), the word ", 40B". In Schedule 3, paragraph 42. In Schedule 7, paragraph 1(15) to (18).

PART 5

BIRTH REGISTRATION

Reference	Extent of repeal
Births and Deaths Registration Act 1953 (c. 20)	Section 6. Section 7(3). Section 10(3). In section 10A(2), paragraph (d) (together with the "and" immediately before it).

2896